Library of
Davidson College

THE

GRENVILLE PAPERS.

VOL. IV.

THE
GRENVILLE PAPERS:

BEING

THE CORRESPONDENCE

OF

RICHARD GRENVILLE EARL TEMPLE, K.G.,

AND

THE RIGHT HON: GEORGE GRENVILLE,

THEIR FRIENDS AND CONTEMPORARIES.

EDITED, WITH NOTES,
By WILLIAM JAMES SMITH

IN FOUR VOLUMES.—VOL. IV.

AMS PRESS
NEW YORK

Reprinted from the edition of 1953, London
First AMS EDITION published 1970
Manufactured in the United States of America

International Standard Book Number:
  complete set: 0-404-06150-8
  volume 4: 0-404-06154-0

Library of Congress Catalog Card Number: 72-119154

AMS PRESS, INC.
New York, N.Y. 10003

CONTENTS

OF

THE FOURTH VOLUME.

1767.

Page

Mr. Wilkes to Earl Temple. *February* 1.—His application to the Duke of Grafton. Determines to proceed for a reversal of his outlawry. Statement of his private affairs. Conduct of Humphrey Cotes. 1

The Earl of Suffolk to Mr. Grenville. *February* 28.—Grief for the recent death of Lady Suffolk. The Duke of Bedford's motion in the House of Lords upon the subject of America. Conduct without concert 4

Mr. Rigby to Mr. Grenville. *March* 7.—Affairs of the East India Company 6

Earl Temple to Mr. Grenville. *March* 18.—Close junction between Lords Bute and Chatham. [Lord Lyttelton's project for the formation of a Ministry by a coalition of the Grenvilles with the Rockinghams and Bedfords. *Note.*] . . . 7

Countess Temple to Earl Temple. *April* 18.—Death of the Duchess of Argyll. Lady Dalkeith. Lady George Sackville. Colonel Cuninghame. Lord Barrymore's marriage. Eastbury. 8

Mr. Whately to Mr. Grenville. *April* 21.—Political speculations. Rockinghams and Bedfords. Will of the Duchess of Argyll . 10

Mr. Grenville to Earl Powis. *May* 7.—Business in the House of Lords. [Letters from the Marquess of Rockingham on American affairs. Lord Clive's Parliamentary influence. *Notes*] 11

Mr. Wilkes to Earl Temple. *May* 11.—His embarrassments in consequence of the bankruptcy of Humphrey Cotes. If he dared to solicit any favours, Lord Temple should find they were not misapplied. His affection for his daughter. Extravagance during his exile. Resolution of future economy, &c. 15

CONTENTS. 1767.

	Page
The Duke of Bedford to Mr. Grenville. *May* 29.—The Duke of Newcastle and Lord Mansfield. The East India Bill	18
Mr. Grenville to the Duke of Bedford. *May* 29.—Lord Mansfield and the Bill for regulating the East India Company's dividends. Death of Mr. Keck, M.P. for Woodstock	19
The Dean of Exeter [Dr. Milles] to Mr. Grenville. *June* 11.— Offers the Deanery House at Exeter for the accommodation of himself and Mrs. Grenville during their tour in the West	20
Mr. William Gerard Hamilton to Earl Temple. *June* 27.—The King's letter to Lord Chatham. The Duke of Grafton desirous of resigning	23
Mr. Augustus Hervey to Mr. Grenville. *June* 30.—Resignation of his Irish Secretaryship. Description of a Court life	24
Mr. William Gerard Hamilton to Earl Temple. *July* 3.—State of political parties. Resignation of General Conway. Lord Egmont and Lord Chatham. The Marquess of Rockingham and the Duke of Grafton	26
Mr. Augustus Hervey to Mr. Grenville. *July* 4.—Interview with the King upon the resignation of his Irish Secretaryship. Conversation with Lord Bristol	29
Mr. William Gerard Hamilton to Earl Temple. *July* 6.—Lord Chatham's illness. Lord Northington's advice. Lord Shelburne's conference with the King. Lord Bute's intentions of going abroad. Dr. Addington. Lord Chatham's answer to the King's letter	31
Mr. Whately to Mr. Grenville. *July* 6.—The Duke of Grafton's determination to resign. The King's letter to Lord Chatham. Mr. Stuart Mackenzie's conversation with Wedderburn and Sir Fletcher Norton. Lord Gower and the Bedford party	33
Mr. William Gerard Hamilton to Earl Temple. *July* 8.—Offers to Lord Rockingham. Lord Chatham's illness	36
Mr. Whately to Earl Temple. *July* 8.—Supposed negotiation with Lord Rockingham by means of General Conway	39
Mr. William Gerard Hamilton to Earl Temple. *July* 10.— Charles Townshend's expectations. Lord Bristol's newly-appointed Secretary. Lord Rockingham and the Bedford party. Charles Townshend with the King	41
Mr. Grenville to Mr. Whately. *July* 12.—Lord Rockingham's visit to Woburn. Mr. Rigby at Wotton and Stowe	43
Mr. William Gerard Hamilton to Earl Temple. *July* 13.—The object of the negotiation with Lord Rockingham is to divide the Bedford and Grenville parties. Lord Holland's opinion of the terms offered to Lord Rockingham. Lord Chatham's health. Lord Bristol	45

	Page
Mr. Grenville to the Earl of Suffolk. *July* 14.—Particulars of the negotiation with Lord Rockingham and the Duke of Bedford	48
Earl Temple to Mr. Grenville. *July* 15	52
Mr. Grenville to Earl Temple. *July* 16.—Lord Rockingham overrated the powers supposed to be given to him . . .	53
Mr. Charles Lloyd to Earl Temple. *July* 16.—William Burke's account of Lord Rockingham's conduct. Duke of Grafton. Lord Bute. Lord Clive's audience of the King, on his return from India	54
Mr. Augustus Hervey to Mr. Grenville. *July* 16.—Lord Rockingham's refusal. Lord Bute. Lord Bristol. Lord Egmont. Lord Chatham	55
Earl Temple to Mr. Grenville. *July* 17	57
Mr. Rigby to Earl Temple and Mr. Grenville. *July* 18.—Enclosing letters by desire of the Duke of Bedford. [Lord Weymouth's letter to Rigby on the state of affairs. *Note.*] . .	57
Mr. Grenville to Earl Temple. *July* 18.—The Duke of Grafton's "jockey tricks" to divide parties	59
Earl Temple to Mr. Rigby. *July* 18	60
Mr. Rigby to Earl Temple and Mr. Grenville. *July* 19.—The Duke of Bedford's assurances that every circumstance of the late transactions has been communicated to Stowe and Wotton	61
Earl Temple to Mr. Rigby. *July* 19	61
Mr. William Gerard Hamilton to Earl Temple. *July* 20.—Lord Rockingham in negotiation with the Dukes of Grafton and Bedford. Lord Camden's conduct towards Lord Chatham . .	62
Mr. Whately to Earl Temple. *July* 20.—On the recent negotiation. Sir Fletcher Norton. Dingley's report of Lord Chatham's health	64
Mr. Whately to Mr. Grenville. *July* 20.—Wedderburn's account of a conversation with Lord Rockingham	66
Mr. Augustus Hervey to Mr. Grenville. *July* 21.—Account of a conversation with Colonel Fitzroy, relative to the Duke of Grafton's conduct in the late transactions. Mentions a communication to the newspapers	67
Mr. Whately to Lord George Sackville. *July* 21.—Communicates all the particulars of the late negotiations, by desire of Mr. Grenville. [Lord George Sackville's reply to Mr. Whately. *Note.*]	71
Mr. Rigby to Mr. Grenville. *July* 21.—Particulars of the meeting of the several leaders of parties at Bedford House. Causes of the failure of this negotiation. Account of the conference published in the *Political Register* attributed by Lord Rockingham to Lord Temple. *Note.*]	80

Page

Mr. William Gerard Hamilton to Earl Temple. *July* 22.—Opinion of the late negotiation. The Duke of Grafton's account of the conditions offered to Lord Rockingham. Lord Holland. Lord Northington. The Dukes of Newcastle and Bedford. Lord Rockingham and General Conway 86

Mr. William Gerard Hamilton to Earl Temple. *July* 22.—The Duke of Grafton, and the terms upon which he treated with Lord Rockingham. Lord Bute, Sir James Lowther, and Sir Fletcher Norton. Lord Townshend. Mr. Charles Townshend. Lord Holland 90

Mr. Whately to Mr. Grenville. *July* 22.—On the late negotiation, and the causes of its failure. Lord Clive's reception at Court 94

Mr. Grenville to Mr. Rigby. *July* 22.—Thanks for his letters, and remarks upon the late transactions 95

Mr. William Gerard Hamilton to Earl Temple. *July* 24.—General Conway endeavouring to reconcile Lord Rockingham and the Duke of Grafton. Lord Northington. Plans of the Court party 97

Mr. William Gerard Hamilton to Earl Temple. *July* 24.—Sir Fletcher Norton and Lord Bute.—Lord Granby's dissatisfaction at the conduct of the Duke of Grafton. Plan to detach the Bedford party from the Grenvilles. Mr. Charles Townshend. Lord North 99

Mr. Whately to Mr. Grenville. *July* 25.—Lord Rockingham's interview with the King. General Conway. Mr. Rigby. Mr. Charles Townshend. Lord Mansfield 102

Mr. Charles Lloyd to Earl Temple. *July* 25.—Lord Rockingham and General Conway. Dinner at the Thatched House. Lord Chatham. Sir James Gray. Lord Northington . . . 106

Mr. William Gerard Hamilton to Earl Temple. *July* 27.—Lord Rockingham's interview with the King. Lord Bristol's determination not to go to Ireland. Death of the Irish Lord Chancellor Bowes. Mr. Hutchinson's character. Sir Fletcher Norton and Lord Bute. Report of union between the Duke of Bedford and Lord Rockingham 108

Lord Lyttelton to Earl Temple. *July* 27.—On the late negotiations 113

Mr. William Gerard Hamilton to Earl Temple. *July* 29.—Lord Camden and Sir Fletcher Norton. Wedderburn's interview with Lord Bute. The Duke of Grafton and General Conway. Legacy to Lord Chatham 115

Mr. Whately to Mr. Grenville. *July* 29.—The Duke of Grafton, General Conway, and Lord Rockingham. Lord Mansfield.

CONTENTS.

Page

Wedderburn's conversation with Lord Bute. State of Lord Chatham's health 118
Lord George Sackville to Mr. Grenville. *July* 30 . . . 124
Mr. Grenville to Mr. Whately. *July* 30 125
The Earl of Mansfield to Mr. Grenville. *July* 31.—His opinion of the late negotiations founded upon the information of the Duke of Bedford, Lord Rockingham, and the Duke of Newcastle. Approves of Mr. Grenville's conduct, as communicated to him by Whately 126
Earl Temple to Mr. Grenville. *July* 31.—Sends a confidential letter from Mr. W. Gerard Hamilton 129
Mr. Augustus Hervey to Mr. Grenville. *July* 31.—The Duke of Grafton and Mr. Conway intend to remain in office. Charles Townshend much dissatisfied. Lord Egmont, Lord Townshend. Colonel Barré. Sir Thomas Sewell. Horace Walpole. Lord Hertford's favour with the King. Mr. Stanley. Marquess of Granby. A letter in the *Gazetteer* 130
Mr. Wedderburn to Mr. Grenville. *July* 31.—Interview with Lord Bute. Lord Clive. East India affairs 134
Mr. William Gerard Hamilton to Earl Temple. *August* 1.—Lord Bristol and Lord Mulgrave. De Grey. Hutchinson. Lord Verney 136
Mr. Whately to Mr. Grenville. *August* 1.—Account of a long conversation with Lord Mansfield upon the subject of Mr. Grenville's part in the late political transactions. Lord Clive and Mr. Wedderburn 138
Mr. Grenville to Colonel Hotham. *August* 2.—Death of Lady Suffolk 147
Earl Temple to Mr. Grenville. *August* 3.—Mr. Grenville to the Earl of Mansfield. *August* 5.—Expresses his conviction that the factious confusion of the present times can only be cured by a serious conviction and right measures, instead of annual struggles for places and pensions 148
Mr. Whately to Mr. Grenville. *August* 20.—Conversation with Lord Mansfield on the state of public affairs. Lord Chatham's health. Horace Walpole. Lord Northington . . . 150
Mr. Whately to Mr. Grenville. *August* 24.—Lord Mansfield's political opinions. The Queen, the Duke of Grafton, and the Vice-Admiralty of Scotland. Lord Chatham. Charles Townshend's last illness 155
Mr. William Gerard Hamilton to Earl Temple. *September.*— Lord Camden and Lord Chatham on their way to Bath. Charles Townshend's death. Indecision of General Conway. Lord Townshend 159

	Page
Mr. Wedderburn to Mr. Whately. *September.*—Lord Bute and the Duke of Grafton. Lord Rockingham and American Affairs. Sir Laurence Dundas	160
Mr. Charles Lloyd to Earl Temple. *September* 10.—Lord North and the Exchequer Seal. Lord Bute's illness. Lord Mansfield with the King	162
Mr. Whately to Mr. Grenville. *September* 11.—The Duke of Grafton, Lord North, and Lord Mansfield have audience of the King. Lord Chatham. Lord Bute. Lord Barrington	163
Captain Samuel Hood to Mr. Grenville. *September* 22.—Description of the Province of Nova Scotia	164
The Rev. Dr. Markham to Mr. Grenville. *September* 30.—On his being offered the Deanery of Christ Church	166
Mr. William Gerard Hamilton to Earl Temple. *October* 2.—Lord North, Chancellor of the Exchequer. Lord Chatham's refusal to put the Privy Seal in commission	167
Mr. Whately to Mr. Grenville. *October* 3.—Circumstances attending the Duke of York's death	168
Mr. Whately to Mr Grenville. *October* 5.—Council upon the affairs of Ireland. Lord Townshend	169
Mr. Whately to Mr. Grenville. *October* 8.—Another Council upon the affairs of Ireland. [The *Grand Council*, by the Author of Junius. *Note.*]	170
Mr. Augustus Hervey to Mr. Grenville. *October* 17	175
Mr. Grenville to Mr. Whately. *October* 20.—Lord Townshend and the Government of Ireland. The Duke of Bedford. Mr. D'Oyly.	176
Earl Temple to Mr. Grenville. *October* 23.—His willingness to coalesce with the Bedfords	178
Mr. Grenville to Mr. Wallace. *October* 25.—Respecting the adjustment of his accounts when Treasurer of the Navy	179
Mr. Augustus Hervey to Mr. Grenville. *November* 3.—Election politics at Bath. Mr. James Grenville. Lord Camden	180
Mr. Augustus Hervey to Mr. Grenville. *November* 5.—Lord Chatham, and the repurchase of Hayes. Lord Clare. Alderman Beckford	181
Mr. Whately to Mr. Grenville. *November* 5.—General Irwin's conversation with the King. The nature of Lord Chatham's illness. Admiral Keppel. Sir Charles Bunbury and the Duke of Grafton	183
Mr. Grenville to Mr. Wallace. *November* 14.—On the subject of the Pay Office accounts	187

Mr. Wilkes to Earl Temple. *November* 16.—Excuses some part of his conduct of which Lord Temple disapproves. The publi-

CONTENTS.

	Page
cation of his letter to Lord Temple describing his duel with Lord Talbot	188
Mr. Mackintosh to Mr. Grenville. *November* 16.—Election matters in Scotland	190
Earl Temple to Mr. Grenville. *November* 26.—[Lord Lyttelton's account of conversations with the Duke of Bedford and Lord Mansfield. *Note.*]	192
Mr. Whately to Mr. Grenville. *December* 9.—Proceedings in the House of Commons. Army in Ireland. East India Dividends. Land Tax	193
Mr. Whately to Mr. Grenville. *December* 14.—Ministerial negotiation with the Bedford party, for a separation from the Grenvilles	194
Mr. Whately to Mr. Grenville. *December* 25.—The Dukes of Bedford and Grafton. Mr. Rigby and General Conway. Lord Gower. Lord Chatham and Lord Shelburne. Preponderating influence of the Bedfords	197
Lord Clive to Mr. Grenville. *December* 28.—His health requires him to go to the South of France	200
Mr. Grenville to Mr. Whately. *December* 29.—*A Word at Parting* in the *Political Register*, attributed by the Bedfords to Lord Temple. [The authorship of the *Word at Parting*. *Note.*]	201
Lord Trevor to Mr. Grenville. *December* 29.—Rigby and Conway. The Duke of Newcastle. The Speaker Onslow.	205
Mr. Grenville to Lord Trevor. *December* 31.—American affairs, &c.	206
Mr. Grenville's Diary of Memorable Transactions: *continued from* vol. iii. p. 397	208

1768.

Mr. Whately to Mr. Grenville. *January* 1.—Lord Temple's disavowal of the *Word at Parting*. The Duke of Grafton's arrangement with the Bedfords. Sir Laurence Dundas. Rigby and General Conway. Lord Chatham. Lord Camden. Mr. Wedderburn. Lord Mansfield. [The Letter from Junius to Lord Chatham compared with those of Whately and Lord Lyttelton to Mr. Grenville and Lord Temple. *Note.*]	240
Lord Lyttelton to Earl Temple. *January* 1.—Conversations with the Duke of Bedford, Edmund Burke, and Lord Hardwicke. General state of political parties. Lord Chatham. Dr. Addington. The Bedfords and the Duke of Grafton	249
C. [the Author of Junius] to Mr. Grenville. *February* 6.—Expresses attachment to Mr. Grenville, and that hereafter he may claim the honour of being known to him. Encloses a paper on	

CONTENTS. 1768.

Page

the subject of the Budget, the Auction duty, and financial matters. [Remarks upon the Authorship of Junius. *Note.*] . 254

Mr. Wilkes to Earl Temple. *February* 13.—Asks advice as to the part he is to take with respect to the next Parliament, and on his conduct in the present situation of public affairs . . 262

Mr. Wedderburn to Mr. Grenville. *April* 3.—The elections in Yorkshire. Opinion of Wilkes and his supporters . . 263

Mr. Grenville to Mr. Whately. *April* 13.—The Assembly of New York. The East India Company. Mr. Wilkes's reception at Bath 266

Mr. Whately to Mr. Grenville. *April* 18.—The King's indignation at the insolence of the Mob. Lord Mansfield's audience in the Closet. Sir Fletcher Norton's difficulties in the prosecution of Wilkes 267

Mr. Whately to Mr. Grenville. *April* 22.—Augustus Hervey, and his suit for a divorce. Lord Mansfield's audience in the Closet. The King's complaint of the conduct of the Duke of Grafton with respect to a pardon for Wilkes. The Bedfords and Grenvilles. The Duke of Grafton and Nancy Parsons at the Opera. Lord Camden and Wilkes. [Junius and Nancy Parsons. *Note.*] 271

Earl Temple to Mr. Wilkes. *April* 28.—Offers to visit him in the King's Bench prison 279

The Countess of Chatham to Earl Temple. *April* 28 . 280

Earl Temple to the Countess of Chatham. *April* 28.—[The secret correspondence of Junius, compared with that between Lord Temple and his sister. *Note.*] 281

The Countess of Chatham to Earl Temple. *May* 1 . . 282

The Earl of Suffolk to Mr. Grenville. *May* 2.—Relates the subject of a conversation with Lord Mansfield. Lord Temple and Wilkes. Motion for an Address to the King to confer some mark of distinction upon the Lord Mayor . . . 283

Mr. Whately to Mr. Grenville. *May* 3.—Wilkes's writ of error. Lord Mansfield. Business at the meeting of the new Parliament 286

Mr. Whately to Mr. Grenville. *May* 7.—The meeting of Parliament 288

The Countess of Chatham to Earl Temple. *May* 8 . . 289

Earl Temple to the Countess of Chatham. *May* 8 . . 290

Mr. Whately to Mr. Grenville. *May* 9.—Proceedings in the Court of King's Bench on Wilkes's business. Wedderburn and Rigby. Lord Shelburne. Lord North. The Duke of Grafton. Lord Temple at the Opera 290

Mr. Whately to Mr. Grenville. *May* 21.—Political speculations.

	Page
Corsican affairs. Bill for securing the independence of the Irish Judges	294
Mr. Knox to Mr. Grenville. *May* 24.—Conversation with Lord Hillsborough on American affairs. Assembly of Massachusetts Bay. Lord Barrington and the Militia Bill. Nancy Parsons, the Duke of Grafton, and Lord Hertford	297
Mr. Whately to Mr. Grenville. *June* 4.—Speculation on the tactics of the various political parties. Lord Chesterfield. Lord Holland. Gerard Hamilton. The Duke of Bedford. The Duke of Grafton and Lord North. Adjutant-General Harvey and the state of the Army	299
Commodore Hood to Mr. Grenville. *July* 11.—State of affairs at Boston	306
Mr. Whately to Mr. Grenville. *July* 12.—The Duke of Grafton and Lord Shelburne on the appointment of Mr. Lynch to Turin. Lord Chatham and Mr. Taylor the architect. Wedderburn's conversation with Burke	308
Mr. Pownall to Mr. Grenville. *July* 14.—Publication of his pamphlet on the Administration of the Colonies	312
Mr. William Gerard Hamilton to Earl Temple. *July* 14.—Proposed dismissal of Lord Shelburne. The Duke of Bedford Chancellor of the University of Dublin. Difficulties of the Duke of Grafton	314
Mr. Grenville to Mr. Pownall. *July* 17.—American affairs. A scheme for the representation of the colonies in the House of Commons, entitled to serious and favourable consideration .	316
Mr. Knox to Mr. Grenville. *July* 23.—Proceedings at Boston, &c.	319
Mr. Whately to Mr. Grenville. *July* 26.—Alarm about America. Ministerial confusion	321
Countess Temple to Lady Brown. *July.*—A visit to Hagley. Masque of fairies. Verses by Lord Lyttelton addressed to Lady Temple	322
Mr. Whately to Mr. Grenville. *August* 4.—Lord Hillsborough and the dismission of Sir Jeffry Amherst. Appointment of Lord Botetourt to the government of Virginia. [The information in Whately's Letters compared with that given by the Author of Junius in his letters under various signatures. *Note.*]	326
Commodore Hood to Mr. Grenville. *August* 8.—Account of proceedings at Boston, &c.	332
Mr. Knox to Mr. Grenville. *August* 9.—American affairs. Lord Camden's speech on taxation and representation. The Duke of Grafton and the Bedfords. Lord Shelburne . . .	335
Mr. Whately to Mr. Grenville. *August* 10.—Alluding to some	

articles in the newspapers. Causes of the dismission of Sir Jeffry Amherst. Lord Bute's embarkation at Dover . . 337

Mr. Augustus Hervey to Mr. Grenville. *August* 13.—Lord Hillsborough, Sir Jeffry Amherst and Lord Botetourt. Account of the King of Denmark. Duke and Duchess of Bedford at Court. Lord Chatham. The King of Denmark's visit. The Divorce suit 340

Mr. Knox to Mr. Grenville. *August* 20.—Lord Hillsborough's Letter to Sir Jeffry Amherst 344

Mr. Whately to Mr. Grenville. *August* 24.—The Duke of Grafton and Nancy Parsons at Ranelagh. Lord Hillsborough and Sir Jeffry Amherst. State of affairs in America . . 347

C. [The Author of Junius] to Mr. Grenville. *September* 3.—Acknowledges himself to be the writer of some letters signed Lucius, one or two upon the New Commission of Trade, and a multitude of others 354

Mr. Augustus Hervey to Mr. Grenville. *September* 5.—Account of the death of his mother Mary Lepel Lady Hervey . . 356

Mr. Knox to Mr. Grenville. *September* 8.—The *State of the Nation*. Accounts from America. Lord Shelburne. Lord Barrington. Lord Hillsborough 359

The Princess Amelia to Countess Temple. *September* 6 . . 360

Commodore Hood to Earl Temple. *September* 14.—Proceedings at Boston 361

Earl Temple to Mr. Grenville. *September* 14.—The King of Denmark coming to Stowe 363

Mr. Knox to Mr. Grenville. *September* 15.—American affairs. Lord Shelburne. Lord Hillsborough 363

Mr. Grenville to Mr. Whately. *September* 18.—Account of the King of Denmark's visit to Stowe. American affairs . . 364

Mr. Knox to Mr. Grenville. *September* 27.—On the subject of America. Lord Chatham. Sir William Draper . . . 366

Mr. Knox to Mr. Grenville. *October* 4.—Sends his pamphlet on the *State of the Nation* 368

Mr. Whately to Mr. Grenville. *October* 11.—On American affairs. Lord Shelburne. Lord Rochford. Lord Egmont. The King of Denmark's levée. The Duke of Northumberland's entertainment at Sion. George Selwyn's *bon mot* . . 369

Commodore Hood to Mr. Grenville. *October* 15.—Governor Bernard and the state of affairs in America 373

Anonymous [the Author of Junius] to Mr. Grenville. *October* 20.—Encloses a letter under the signature of "Atticus." Acknowledges himself the author of the *Grand Council*, &c. . . 379

Mr. Charles Lloyd to Mr. Grenville. *October* 20.—Resignation

of Lord Shelburne. Lord Camden. The Duke of Grafton.
Lord Weymouth. Wilkes the author of a paper entitled a
Dreamer of Dreams 382
Mr. Augustus Hervey to Mr. Grenville. *October* 21.—Lord
Chatham's resignation. Ministerial arrangements. Death of
Colonel Brudenell. Lord Northington in the King's Closet. A
Letter to the Duke of Grafton in the *Political Register* . . 383
Mr. Cadwallader Colden to Mr. Grenville. *October* 22.—Vindication of his conduct as Governor of New York. Compensation
to Major James. The Stamp Act. Lord Hillsborough, &c. . 385
Mr. Whately to Mr. Grenville. *October* 27.— News from America.
Resignations of Lord Chatham and Lord Shelburne. The *State
of the Nation.* The Letters of Atticus 389
Mr. Whately to Mr. Grenville. *October* 28.—Rebellion at Boston. Mr. Wedderburn, Lord Rockingham, Mr. Burke, and the
State of the Nation. Memorial from the King of Sardinia.
Lord Mansfield, and Chief Justice Wilmot. Wilkes's birthday 391
Mr. Augustus Hervey to Mr. Grenville. *October* 31.—Offer of
the Privy Seal to Lord Bristol 393
Mr. Knox to Mr. Grenville. *November* 1.—The *State of the
Nation* attributed to Mr. Grenville. American affairs . . 394
Mr. John Temple to Mr. Grenville. *November* 7.— His conduct
as Commissioner of Customs at Boston 396
Mr. Grenville to the Earl of Suffolk. *November* 25.—Reconciliation of Lord Temple and Lord Chatham . . . 398
The Earl of Suffolk to Mr. Grenville. *November* 30 . . 399
Mr. Knox to Mr. Grenville. *December* 15.—Lord Hillsborough
and the Agents for the Colonies 400
Mr. Grenville's Diary of Memorable Transactions: *continued
from page* 240 402

1769.

Mr. Whately to Mr. Grenville. *January* 3.—Dissolution of Assemblies in America. Wilkes elected an Alderman of London.
The Bedfords and the Duke of Grafton 408
Lord Trevor to Mr. Grenville. *February* 23.—Enclosing letters
of M. de Montcalm on the subject of American Independence . 409
Mr. Grenville to Lord Trevor. *February* 24 410
Mr. Dowdeswell to Mr. Grenville. *February* 28.—Parliamentary
arrangements 411
The Earl of Buckinghamshire to Mr. Grenville. *March* 20.—
Courts of Berlin and St. Petersburgh. Duchess of Kingston.
Fire in Covent Garden 412
The Countess Temple to Earl Temple. *March* 21.— The

CONTENTS.

1769.

Page

Princess Amelia and Lord Temple's portrait. The Duchess of Kingston at the Drawing-room. Augustus Hervey. Lord Bristol 114
The Duke of Chandos to Mr. Grenville. *March* 23.—Procession of the Merchants with the City Address. Riot at St. James's. The Dukes of Kingston and Northumberland. Conduct of Lord Talbot 415
Mr. Whately to Mr. Grenville. *March* 25.—The mob at St. James's. Calm behaviour of the King. The Duke of Grafton. Lord Chatham. The Bedfords 417
Mr. Whately to Mr. Grenville. *March* 30.—The City Address. Proposed alteration in the Riot Act 418
Commodore Hood to Mr. Grenville. *April* 15.—American affairs 420
Lord Clive to Mr. Grenville. *May* 10.—Enclosing copies of his correspondence with Mr. Wedderburn upon offering him a seat in Parliament 422
Lord Lyttelton to Mr. Grenville. *June* 3 423
Mr. Grenville to Lord Lyttelton. *June* 8.—Mrs. Montagu. Mr. Glover's poem of Leonidas 424
Lord Lyttelton to Mr. Grenville. *June* 12.—Enclosing a letter from Mrs. Montagu. Mr. Grenville's speech on the expulsion of Wilkes 425
The Earl of Chatham to Earl Temple. *July* 7.—Reception by the King at the Levée, and in the Closet . . . 426
The Earl of Chatham to Earl Temple. *July* 18.—On his intended visit to Stowe 428
Lord Lyttelton to Mr. Grenville. *July* 25.—Lord Chatham's apparition at St. James's 429
Mr. Whately to Mr. Grenville. *August* 3.—Lord Chatham's conference with the King. The Duke of Bedford's reception in Devonshire. Lord Bute. [County Petitions. Paragraphs in the newspapers written by Lord Temple. *Note.*] . . 431
Mr. Whately to Mr. Grenville. *August* 5.—American news. Paragraph in the *Gazetteer* relating to Lord Bute . . 435
Lord Lyttelton to Earl Temple. *August* 13 . . . 436
The Earl of Suffolk to Mr. Grenville. *August* 19 . . 437
Mr. Edmund Burke to Mr. Whately. *August* 21.—On the proposed county meeting at Aylesbury 438
Commodore Hood to Earl Temple. *September* 2.—State of public feeling in America 439
Mr. Whately to Mr. Grenville. *September* 7.—Visit to Burke. Conversation respecting the proposed meeting at Aylesbury, and the general state of political parties. Dr. Musgrave's Letter. M. D'Eon. Election of a Mayor at Bedford. Russian fleet 440

	Page
Mr. Whately to Mr. Grenville. *September* 14.—Dr. Musgrave. M. D'Eon. County Petitions, &c.	452
Mr. Knox to Mr. Grenville. *September* 19.—Buckinghamshire Petition. American affairs. [Paragraphs in the newspapers written by Lord Temple. *Note.*]	453
The Earl of Buckinghamshire to Mr. Grenville. *September* 21 .	457
Mr. Whately to Mr. Grenville. *September* 22 —French and Russian politics. Duke of Grafton's visit to Stowe. Governor Sir Francis Bernard. Lord Hillsborough's circular letter	457
Mr. Whately to Earl Temple. *September* 22.—The Aylesbury Meeting. Duke of Grafton at Stowe. Apprehensions of war. Continental politics	460
The Countess of Chatham to Earl Temple. *September* 25 .	462
Mr. Whately to Mr. Grenville. *September* 26.—Dr. Musgrave's letter to Lord Bristol. Wedderburn and Burke at Lord Rockingham's	463
Mr. Whately to Mr. Grenville. *October* 7.—Petitions from Yorkshire and from the City of London. Sir Fletcher Norton	465
Mr. Weston to Mr. Grenville. *October* 13.—Denies that he is the author of a pamphlet recently attributed to him . .	468
Mr. Knox to Mr. Grenville. *October* 18.—Publication by Almon of Mr. Grenville's Speech on the expulsion of Wilkes. Sir Francis Bernard. Sir William Draper. Sir Henry Moore	468
Mr. Grenville to Mr. Knox. *October* 22 . . .	471
Mr. Grenville to Earl Temple. *October* 22.—Electors of the borough of Buckingham Duke of Grafton. Colonel Burgoyne. Preston election	473
Mr. Knox to Mr. Grenville. *October* 24	475
Mr. Weston to Mr. Grenville. *October* 27 . . .	476
The Earl of Chatham to Earl Temple. *November* 8.—Lord Camden's disapprobation of the proceedings with regard to the Middlesex election. Lord Camden's opinion on the right of petitioning. Duke of Grafton. Lord Granby . .	477
Mr. Knox to Mr. Grenville. *November* 10.—Opinions with respect to Mr. Grenville's speech on Wilkes's expulsion. Lord Hillsborough and Colonial affairs	479
Mr. Whately to Mr. Grenville. *November* 14.—Lord Temple and Lord Chatham. Wilkes's trial. The Courts of France and Spain	481
Mr. Cavendish to Mr. Whately. *November* 20 . . .	482
Mr. Harris to Mr. Grenville. *November* 23.—Notes of a debate on the Middlesex election	483
Mr. Charles Lloyd to Mr. Grenville. *December* 1.—Pension to Mr. Thynne. Junius's story relating to Mr. Hine and Colonel Burgoyne	484

	Page
Mr. Whately to Mr. Grenville. *December* 3.—French and American politics	485
Mr. Whately to Mr. Grenville. *December* 8.—On the death of Mrs. Grenville	487
Lord Chetwynd to Mr. Grenville. *December* 11	487
Mr. Augustus Hervey to Mr. Grenville. *December* 14.—Account of an attempt to assassinate the King of Portugal	488
Lord Vere to Earl Temple. *December* 19.—Death of Lady Betty Germain. Account of her will. [Lord Temple and the letter of Junius to the King. *Note.*]	490
Mr. Whately to Mr. Grenville. *December* 19, 20.—Lord Camden and the Duke of Grafton. Lord Chatham. Wilkes suspected to be Junius. The affair of Hine's patent	493
The Countess of Chatham to Mr. Grenville. *December* 26.—On the death of Mrs. Grenville. [Letter from Mrs. Montagu to Lord Lyttelton. *Note.*]	496
Mr. Whately to Mr. Grenville. *December* 27.—Reports about the Authorship of Junius	500

1770.

Mr. Whately to Mr. Grenville. *January* 11	502
Mr. Whately to Mr. Grenville. *January* 12.—Debate in the House of Commons, upon words used by Sir George Savile	503
Mr. Thomas Coleman [to Mr. Grenville?]. *March* 4.—The Falkland Islands. Description of the British settlement at Port Egmont	505
Mr. Charles Lloyd to Mr. Grenville. *March* 15.—Debate in the House of Lords upon the Civil List. The Duke of Grafton and Lord Chatham. Lord Marchmont. Lord Temple. The King's Answer to the City Remonstrance. [Letter from Sir George Savile to Dr. Moffatt on American affairs. *Note.*]	508
Mr. Whately to Mr. Grenville. *April* 10.—Debate in the House of Lords on Mr. Grenville's Bill for regulating Elections. The Tea Duty	515
Mr. Whately to Mr. Grenville *June* 3.—Departure of the Princess Dowager of Wales for Germany. The Lord Mayor Beckford, and his speech to the King. Ponds in St. James's Park	517
Mr. Whately to Mr. Grenville. *June* 10.—Affair of Falkland Islands. Lord Rockingham's visit to Lord Chatham	518
Mr. Charles Lloyd to Mr. Grenville. *June* 14.—Woodfall's trial for the publication of Junius's Letter to the King	519
Mr. Whately to Mr. Grenville. *June* 23.—Lord Chatham and the Pynsent cause. City arrangements on the death of the Lord Mayor Beckford. Death of Philip Carteret Webb	519

1770—1774. CONTENTS. xvii

Page

Mr. Charles Lloyd to Mr. Grenville. *July* 3.—Resignation of Mr. Bradshaw. The Duke of Cumberland and Lady Grosvenor . 521
The Princess Amelia to Countess Temple. *July* 10.—Visit to Stowe. Lady Henrietta Vernon. Lady Grosvenor . . 523
Mr. Augustus Hervey to Mr. Grenville. *August* 4.—The state of the Navy. Political gossip 524
Mr. Charles Lloyd to Mr. Grenville. *August* 8.—Description of a College in Wales, founded by Lady Huntingdon . . . 526
Lord Lyttelton to Mr. Grenville. *October* 8.—Account of Sir Richard Lyttelton's Will 527

1771.

Verses addressed to Countess Temple, by William Wyndham Grenville, afterwards Lord Grenville. *January* 2 . . . 528
The Earl of Suffolk to Earl Temple. *January* 22.—Announces his having kissed the King's hand for the office of Lord Privy Seal 529
Earl Temple to the Earl of Suffolk. *January* 24 . . . 530
The Countess of Chatham to Earl Temple. *March* 4 . . 531
The Earl of Chatham to Earl Temple. *April* 17.—Proposes a Petition for the dissolution of Parliament. Opinion with regard to Parliamentary Reform 534
The Princess Amelia to Countess Temple. *September* 2.—Intended visit to Stowe 535
Mr. Dayrell to Earl Temple. *September* 27 [?]—On the ensuing election for Lord Mayor. Wilkes and Bull the Sheriffs . 535
The Earl of Chatham to Earl Temple. *June* 9 . . . 537
Earl Temple to Messrs. Coutts. *June* 24 538
Mr. Glover to Earl Temple. *July* 12.—Panic in the money market. Bankruptcy of Fordyce and Co. Measures taken by himself and the Bank Directors 539
The Earl of Chatham to Earl Temple. *August* 30 . . . 541
Earl Temple to the Earl of Chatham. *September* 8 . . . 545

1773.

Lord Vere to Countess Temple. *July* 31 547
Mr. Horace Walpole to Countess Temple. *December* 20.—Relating to the purchase of some miniatures 548

1774.

Mr. George Grenville to Earl Temple. *March* 26.—Naples. Account of excavations at Pompeii 550
Mr. George Grenville to Earl Temple. *April* 16.—Rome. Illu-

VOL. IV. b

	Page
mination of St. Peter's. The Duke of Cumberland. The Russian Ambassador	555
Mr. George Grenville to Earl Temple. *May* 4.—Concerning his Election for the borough of Buckingham	559
Mr. George Grenville to Earl Temple. *July* 9.—Society at Vienna	563
Mr. Glover to Earl Temple. *July* 11.—Bankruptcy of Mackintosh	564

1775.

The Countess Temple to Earl Temple. *January* 12 . . 566

1776.

Earl Temple to the Bailiff and Burgesses of the Borough of Buckingham. *September.*—On the subject of rebuilding the Church at Buckingham 567

1777.

The Princess Amelia to Earl Temple. *April* 21.—On the death of Lady Temple	570
Earl Temple to the Princess Amelia. *April* —	570
Earl Temple to Mr. George Grenville. *September* —	571
The Earl of Chatham to Earl Temple. *September* 24	573
The Countess of Chatham to Earl Temple. *October* 17.—[Lord Temple's last letter to Almon, in August, 1779. *Note.*]	574

THE
GRENVILLE PAPERS.

MR. WILKES TO EARL TEMPLE.

Paris, Rue des Saints Pères, February 1, 1767.

My Lord,—When I had the happiness of being at London in November, I took the liberty of transmitting to your Lordship a copy of my letter to the Duke of Grafton[1]. I returned to England at that time because Colonel Fitzroy[2] told me that his brother was my real friend, extremely desirous to serve me, and that many interesting particulars respecting me could not be communicated by letter.

On my arrival, I desired Mr. Fitzherbert[3] to submit to his Grace the mode of application to the King for a pardon. The answer was a warm profession of service, and advice to write to Lord Chatham. Mr. Fitzherbert immediately saw the difficulty for me of such a step, and I afterwards convinced him that it was irreconcileable to every sentiment of honour, both public or private.

I then wrote to the Duke of Grafton the letter of which I had the honour of transmitting a copy to your Lordship. The answer to that was verbal likewise, " I do nothing without Lord Chatham, Mr. W. must write

---

[1] The *first* letter to the Duke of Grafton, dated March 1, 1766. It is printed in *Almon's Memoirs and Correspondence of Wilkes*, iii. 178.

[2] Afterwards Lord Southampton.

[3] Of Tissington; M.P. for Derby.

to Lord Chatham." The same evening I ordered a post-chaise and returned to Paris.

The last post I wrote a letter to Mr. Dunning, in which I desired him to settle with Mr. Sergeant Glynn a motion for the reversal of my outlawry. I thought, however, my Lord, that I owed it to the regard Mr. Dunning has ever shewn me to open my whole plan to him, and therefore explicitly to declare to him alone, that if Lord Mansfield insisted on special bail, as he might do by 4 and 5 of William and Mary, c. 18, s. 4, I would never give it, but if the outlawry could be reversed, without that circumstance, I would then proceed with all vigour against Lord Halifax, and if he advised it, I should not be averse to a personal appearance.

Your Lordship knows that through this whole affair I would never give bail, by which I preserve to myself the right of my own conduct. I chose the present term, and so late, because in case of Lord Mansfield's demanding special bail, the term would be at an end, before my answer from hence could arrive, and the following term does not begin 'till the 6th of May. When I saw Mr. Dunning here in September or October, I forget which, he seemed clearly of opinion, that I might easily reverse the outlawry, and obtain a verdict against Lord Halifax, before I could in any case be sued to a second outlawry.

I beg your Lordship's pardon for so tedious a detail. I was desirous that the whole of my conduct should be understood, where I am most ambitious it should be approved.

As to other more private affairs, I cannot explain myself so well as in the words of Cicero, ego tam misero tempore nihil novi consilii cepissem, nisi in reditu meo nihilo meliores res domesticas, quàm rempublicam offendissem.

Just before my outlawry, I signed full powers to Mr. Cotes for the management of my private affairs. It was in November, 1764. I have never received but 20 guineas since that time from him, nor can I get any account of what has been received or paid since I first left Great George Street. I have often importuned him by letter, but I have had no answer of any kind since my last return here, nor indeed a line on any subject, although I have wrote frequently. I drew from Rome on Mr. Cotes a bill for 50*l.*, which he suffered to be protested, and has never paid. When I came to England in May last, Mr. Cotes told me that he had many pardons to ask me for having applied the money he had received for me to his own account, that he must otherwise have directly become a bankrupt, but that he would soon replace it, and account with me for what he had received on my account[1]. He then gave me 20 guineas, which I even wanted as pocket money. He proposed to marry his daughter, then to get together what he could, and to retire to Amiens, or Arras, and offered to divide with me what he had, if I would come and live there with him. I not only refused, but remonstrated strongly against such a plan. I think I am cruelly used, that

---

[1] I might with truth have added to my former designation of Humphrey Cotes, that he was an accomplished swindler, for not only had he appropriated to himself the proceeds of certain sales which he had made of Wilkes's personal effects, but it appears that he had also received the sum of 1000*l.*, being the damages awarded by the verdict of the jury in the trial against Wood, the Under Secretary of State. Cotes became a bankrupt a few months after this time; it is most probable that Wilkes was a considerable loser by his defalcation, and equally so that Cotes had imposed upon the well-known generosity of Lord Temple.

not even a sketch of my private affairs is yet sent to me.

My only apology for this to your Lordship is, the very generous concern you have always shewn in my affairs, and the humani nihil à te alienum scio.

I hope to prove myself not totally unworthy of a protection which has done me so much honour, and I will contrive to let more than this age know my gratitude. I am, with the highest respect, my Lord, your Lordship's most obliged and devoted humble Servant,

JOHN WILKES.

Miss Wilkes joins with me in every compliment of respect to Lady Temple.

THE EARL OF SUFFOLK TO MR. GRENVILLE.

Elford, February 28, 1767.

DEAR SIR,—After all I have heard of the strange situation of matters in the political world, I cannot refrain from breaking in upon your better occupations, partly to shew myself not inattentive to the injunctions of your friendship, which bid me collect myself, rouse, divert the attention, and struggle with unavailing grief; partly too to repeat my zeal upon a subject in which of all others I think the interest of this country most concerned, the restoration of order and government in America.

I don't pretend at an hundred and twenty miles from London to pronounce on the Duke of Bedford's motive for timing this business as he did; my accounts say it was without any previous concert. Be that as it will, I think it was introduced at a moment well enough suited to business, and likely enough to turn its operations as we wish. Whatever acquiescence the Ministry have shewn to his Grace's motion, or whatever was his principle in making it (I am sure I think it was a sincere and honourable one; indeed, from the part he has taken, and the manner he has always expressed himself on these affairs, it cannot be otherwise), it must be followed up, by somebody or other.

It is therefore well worthy our consideration (I speak at a distance, and upon a supposition that concert and communication, which, by the bye, are things that I love, are out of the case) how to regulate our conduct so as to take with us our former opponents, without departing a jot from our principle, and object, to shew our firmness and temper, neither (to) propositions of efficacy, let them come from whatever quarter they may, nor (be) backward in producing them ourselves. The business is at present in the Duke of Bedford's hands. Perhaps it will be very difficult to have our ideas fully answered without concert, communication, and more co-operation than has existed between us of late; and it will be a nice affair to take the lead in it without disgusting and offending more than we could wish; unless the Duke of Bedford can be supposed to mean no more than moving the business for the consideration of the House, to be taken up afterwards by anybody, contenting himself merely with starting it, and thinking he has thereby done his duty, and is not bound to do anything further. But this is what I can hardly think a man in earnest, especially of his Grace's honour, ability, and experience, capable of [1].

[1] The Duke of Bedford had moved in the House of Lords, for all the correspondence of the several Governors in America, with the view of ascertaining the extent of American non-compliance, and of bringing the subject of America generally under the consideration of Government.

Forgive the freedom I take in submitting my thoughts to your consideration. It is indeed giving you an unnecessary trouble, for if they are just, they will have struck you already, and if they are otherwise, I am sure it is the height of folly and arrogance to lay them before you. All I mean is, that as our point is fixed, so should be our rule of action, the manner by which in this ticklish state of things we should endeavour to attain to it. You see I have all along concluded that my informations are true of conduct without concert.

As to myself, I do not want inclination to business, it was always agreeable to me, I believe it is now become necessary. But, trust me, I want ability to engage in it. My strength and spirits are gone, and I scarce ever am without some degree of slow fever, which air and exercise, and other applications, have not as yet been able to get the better of. However, such as I am, you shall see me in a very few days, and (thus much I will answer for) shall find me the same public friend from principle (pardon the word, it is almost obsolete), and the same private friend from gratitude and affection, which you have ever found me. I am, &c., SUFFOLK.

MR. RIGBY TO MR. GRENVILLE.

Saturday morning, (March 7, 1767.)

DEAR SIR,—I write this letter to leave at your door in case I have not the pleasure of finding you at home to communicate a thought come into my head this morning. The printing the East India papers I think a very wrong measure; I wish we had made a stand against it last night. I am told the Directors of that Company are much offended at it. You know those gentlemen and their sentiments much better than I do, but if you are of my mind, why may not a petition be obtained from the Directors against Monday, to be presented to the House, praying that the state of their affairs may not be exposed to all foreign powers, &c., &c.

If a precedent should in these times be thought necessary for Parliament to change its sentiments in so long a space of time as two days, last year furnishes one about the refusal to print the American papers, as you well remember[1]. I am, dear Sir, &c., &c.,

RICHARD RIGBY.

EARL TEMPLE TO MR. GRENVILLE.

Wednesday, March 18, 1767.

I hear there is great reason to believe Sir Fletcher Norton will be Attorney-General.

The privilege business, I suppose you know, has turned out ill. The particulars and what I did, I will explain to you. Your most affectionate, T.

Close junction betwixt Lord Bute and Chatham, at least for the present[2].

[1] Rigby's idea seems to have been adopted by the Opposition, and " accordingly," says Walpole, " on the 9th, Jones, an East India Director, a tool of Lord Sandwich, presented a petition from the Company, by surprise, against printing their papers, pleading that it would disclose their secrets to their enemies. . . . . . . Mr. Grenville quoted the precedent of reversing the order for printing the American papers and others, and the danger of informing France and the Mogul of the state of the Company's transactions." After a debate which lasted till nine at night, the Ministers disappointed the intended surprisal, and maintained their order for printing the papers.

[2] There appears to have been an expectation about this time that Lord Chatham would shortly resign. A few days afterwards Walpole writes :—" Conway came to me and said, the Duke of Grafton had told

COUNTESS TEMPLE TO EARL TEMPLE.

April 10, (1767.)

My dearest Lord,—If you have the same weather in the country that we have in town, I think you had him things could not go on as they were; that Lord Chatham must either come forth or quit, and he thought he would do the latter." Upon this supposition the following memorandum was sent by Lord Lyttelton to Mr. Grenville, on the 23rd March, 1767.

"PROJECT OF A MINISTRY to be formed if Lord Chatham should go out, by a coalition of the Grenvillians with the Rockinghams and Bedfords.

First Commissioner of the Treasury	G. Grenville.
Lord Chancellor	Charles Yorke.
President of the Council	Lord Winchilsea.
Lord Privy Seal	Duke of Newcastle or Lord Rockingham.
Secretary of State (South Department)	Charles Townshend.
Secretary of State (North Department)	Lord Sandwich or Lord Gower.
Lord Chamberlain	Earl of Hertford.
Master of the Horse	Lord Weymouth or Duke of Marlborough.
Lord Lieutenant of Ireland	Lord Halifax.
First Commissioner of the Admiralty	Lord Hyde.
First Commissioner of Trade	Lord Suffolk.
Cabinet Councillors Extraordinary	Lord Temple. Lord Mansfield. Lord Lyttelton.

"Military promotions for Mr. Conway.

"Q. Whether a more consistent Ministry might not be formed by leaving out all of the Rockingham party, except Charles Yorke, and filling the vacancy with *King's friends*, if Charles Townshend would take part in one of these?

"I have mentioned only the principal Cabinet officers, supposing that sufficient arrangements may be found for their most necessary followers in both Houses of Parliament. If all of the Rockingham party but the Yorkes were left out, an opposition from *them*, in conjunction with the discarded friends of Lord Chatham, must be expected; but they would draw ill together.

"If Lord Temple should go to the head of the Treasury, George Grenville would support him out of place, so that would make no change in the rest of the list.

"Q. Whom would he take for his Chancellor of the Exchequer?"

better come back: yesterday it snowed and hailed by fits all the morning. The Duchess of Argyll[1] is at last dead; she was pretty near 85. Lady Dalkeith gets about 3000*l.* a year, and what she can leave is equally divided amongst her daughters. I was with Lady George[2] last night, where I met with Cunningham[3], who told me he had seen Lord Chatham in his chariot, with a servant sitting by him; he looked very grave and sadly. Whatever was become of Lady Chatham, this looks as if they would not let him go out by himself, for he certainly does not like the company of servants. Lord Barrymore[4] was married last Thursday night; his legs shook all the while the ceremony was performing: the state of his body is so very bad, it is not thought he can live long. I had a letter from Mrs. H. Grenville, who says they are at Eastbury[5], and the child is much better. I am your most affectionate, A. TEMPLE.

[1] Jane Warburton, widow of John, second Duke of Argyll: she died on the 16th of April. Her daughter, Lady Dalkeith, was now the wife of Charles Townshend. She was created Baroness Greenwich, and died in 1794, when that Barony became extinct. Lady Strafford, Lady Betty Mackenzie, and Lady Mary Coke, were also daughters of the Duchess of Argyll.

[2] Lady George Sackville: she was the daughter of a Mr. Sambrooke, brother to Sir Jeremy Sambrooke, a Hertfordshire baronet.

[3] Colonel James Cuninghame: he was Adjutant-General in Ireland. See *Junius*, vol. ii. p. 156.

[4] Richard Barry, sixth Earl of Barrymore. He was married on the 16th instant to Lady Emilia Stanhope, third daughter of William, Earl of Harrington, and younger sister of the beautiful Lady Fortrose. Lord Barrymore died in August, 1773.

[5] In Dorsetshire, formerly the residence of Bubb Dodington, Lord Melcombe, after whose death it came by inheritance to Lord Temple, who at this time had lent it to his brother, Henry Grenville. The house was subsequently pulled down by Lord Temple, and some of the costly materials used in the improvements at Stowe, particularly some beautiful white marble chimney-pieces of Italian workmanship, and one or two of them were taken to Lord Temple's house in Pall Mall, where

MR. WHATELY TO MR. GRENVILLE.

April 21, 1767.

Dear Sir,—Nothing has happened since you left London which can be called news. I must, therefore, in the stead of it, send you speculations, of which we have plenty. The last division[1] furnishes great variety, for it is said to be equally decisive for and against the question upon the right. Lord Chatham will be unpardonable if he does not push it now that he has so declared a majority, say some people at this end of the town: he can never carry it, say some in the city, against an opposition who could number 157 upon so unfavourable a proposition as that on which they divided, and whilst some of the conquerors exult in their numbers, many of the vanquished hope that their defeat will bring different parties nearer together. Some large detachments of the Rockinghams, I hear, go still further; and by the language they hold of the propriety and possibility of a junction with Mr. Grenville, are understood to intimate their inclination, at all events, to accomplish it. This is now said more freely than before, and all the while the utter impossibility of Lord Chatham's continuing in his present situation is admitted from every quarter; and from *one quarter* I hear a new tone upon the respectable character of the Duke of Bedford, who was not used to be so highly spoken of there.

The death of the Duchess of Argyll is considered as

they still remain. The marble pavement of the saloon at Stowe was also brought from Eastbury.

[1] Upon Beckford's motion that the East India Committee should be adjourned 'till the 1st of May. It was opposed by Sir William Meredith, who desired an opportunity to put an end to it altogether. The motion was carried by 213 against 157.

a political event by many people; to me it seems to go no further than to remove one reason for Lady Dalkeith's attachment, as she has, partly by settlement and partly by will, succeeded to an income of 4000*l.* per annum for life. The estate at Adderbury, and the house in Bruton Street, go after her to the Duke of Buccleuch; but the villa at Ham, with some adjoining tenements, the furniture of all the three houses, and 11,000*l.* in money, which are altogether valued at 40,000*l.*, are in her own disposal. The Duchess has left 11,000*l.* to each of her daughters, her books to Lady Mary Coke, a ring to Lord Bute, and some other legacies not considerable.

MR. GRENVILLE TO EARL POWIS.

Bolton Street, May 7, 1767.

MY DEAR LORD,—I am very sorry to hear by your letter that you have found yourself under a necessity of going to Bath on account of your health. I sincerely wish that your journey thither may be attended with all possible success, and would upon no occasion interrupt the benefit you hope to receive by the waters, by calling you up to our London politicks, which you would find pretty much in the same state of uncertainty and indetermination in which you left them. There was a division yesterday in the House of Lords upon a motion made by Lord Gower, to lay before the House all the proceedings which had passed relative to the Bill of Massachusetts Bay for making compensation to the sufferers and pardoning the offenders, which you must remember was the subject of the former question[1]. It

[1] The following letters were transcribed by Mr. George Chalmers from copies in the handwriting of Mr. Harrison. "The letter to the

was said by the Court that the business would not be finished till Saturday next, and therefore they refused

Speaker," adds Mr. Chalmers, " was never published, on account of the sentiments about Dependency. It was printed in America by Lord Rockingham's friends."

Harrison was at this time a Commissioner of Customs at Boston: he had been Private Secretary to Lord Rockingham. Mr Astle has added in a note, that this letter to Mr. Harrison, " evinces, in opposition to Mr. Burke's assertions in Parliament, that the Marquess was dissatisfied with the conduct of the Americans, and it contains some sentiments worthy of observation."

THE MARQUESS OF ROCKINGHAM TO MR. HARRISON.

Grosvenor Square, May 11, 1767.

DEAR HARRISON,—I have been very uneasy at not hearing from you, having only received a short letter from you on your first arrival at Boston, and having since heard that you have been much out of order. I hope this will find you perfectly recovered, and shall be glad soon to receive an account of it from yourself.

It will appear a strange remissness in me not to have answered earlier the letter, &c., from the House of Representatives of Massachusetts Bay: in fact your indisposition has been partly the occasion. In December I had wrote my answer, and had taken charge of Lord Dartmouth's, meaning to send them by Governor Wentworth, but something prevented it, and I then proposed sending them to you, but upon hearing of your indisposition I delayed, put them into a drawer, and in fact did not recollect the matter 'till lately.

I now enclose my letter and Lord Dartmouth's to the Speaker, and desire you will deliver them, and apologize. I have sent you a copy of my letter. I cannot say that I am much satisfied with the behaviour of the Assembly in regard to tacking of their Indemnity Bill to the Compensation Bill. The power of pardoning crimes of the nature of which the Assembly has done, is not only much beyond the limits of their Constitution, but in fact would be dangerous for themselves; and the factions which have played off this engine here against Government, may make use of it to screen riots and violence against their own neighbours.

The bearer of this letter is brother to Mr. Perry Wentworth, who means to reside in North America, and is now going to Governor Wentworth's. I shall be glad if you will show him civility.

Sir George Savile is in tolerable health, bnt not in good spirits, being

to lay them before the House, at least till they could lay the whole together. The numbers were, of the Lords present, 52 against the motion, and 42 for it. I imagine some other questions concerning that Bill and other American business will be to come on in the House of Lords, but no day is fixed for any of them,

agitated much with the state of Mrs. Hewit's health, who is in a very bad way.

Politics are in the very zenith of confusion here: what may happen is difficult to foretell, but something must, as the state of this Administration is on various accounts exceedingly precarious.

Mr. Dowdeswell and Mr. Burke send their compliments to you, and are well. Our system of acting is, to be consistent. I don't think we have impaired the credit we were in when you last saw us, and I don't think we shall, because we are firm to all our political declarations, and don't mean to barter character for any temporary considerations.

I am, dear Harrison, with all good wishes to you and yours,
ROCKINGHAM.

THE MARQUESS OF ROCKINGHAM TO THE SPEAKER OF THE ASSEMBLY OF MASSACHUSETTS BAY.

London, May 11, 1767.

SIR,—The honour conferred upon me by the vote of the House of Representatives of Massachusetts Bay on account of the part I had taken for securing and cultivating the union of this country with its Colonies has given me the greatest satisfaction, and demands from me the most grateful acknowledgments. I shall always hope to maintain the continuance of their good opinion, by acting consistently upon the principles which I have fixed in my own judgment; and howsoever times may vary, and warm and ill-founded ideas and doctrines may arise on either side the Atlantic, I shall always consider, that this country, as the parent, ought to be tender and just; and that the Colonies, as the children, ought to be dutiful.

A system of arbitrary rule over the Colonies I would not adopt on this side; neither would I do otherwise than strenuously resist when attempts were made to throw off that dependency to which the Colonies ought to submit, not only for the advantage of this country, but for their own real happiness and safety.

I must beg the favour of you to communicate my answer to the House of Representatives, and so believe me to be, Sir, with great regard, &c., &c., ROCKINGHAM.

and I know not how to call you to town upon an uncertainty when your time is so well employed at Bath in the recovery of your health, though I am extremely sensible of your attention to me in your obliging offer to come whenever I think your attendance necessary[1].
I am, &c., &c., GEORGE GRENVILLE.

---

[1] The friendship of Lord Powis towards Mr. Grenville appears also in the following paper, in the handwriting of Lord Powis, which, if it had not been overlooked, I should have inserted after Lord Clive's letter, at vol. ii. p. 161.

"MINUTES BY LORD POWIS, in consequence of what passed on the 15th and 16th of November (1763), in conversation with Lord Clive.

"That Lord Clive called on Lord Powis about ten at night, and said he had *taken his part*, and voted with the majority [a]. That, as the majority was considerable, and wanted then no further assistance from him, he came away.

"That he wishes to put a stop to the contest at Bishop's-Castle, and if the Ministry have already interposed, and will engage Mr. Waring to desist, that he will defray the expense he has been at, as far as 1000*l.*, and when Mr. George Clive shall be elected, will (together with him and all his friends in Parliament) support the measures of the Government.

"That under these circumstances, as opportunities will offer for his giving the strongest proof of his attachment to His Majesty's service, he desires the favour of being advanced to a Peerage of England (at a convenient time), when the like favour shall be granted to others.

"That if these propositions be complied with, Lord Powis, in Lord Clive's absence (if occasion shall require), is to let Mr. Walsh and others know, it is Lord Clive's request 'that they will assist, and concur with the Ministry in Parliament.'"

Horace Walpole relates, about the same time, that "it occasioned much diversion that his (Lord Clive's) father, an old unfashioned man, who did not understand how decently corruption was practised, and how ridiculous it is to talk of what few are ashamed of doing, being asked by the King in the drawing-room, where his son Lord Clive was, replied, with all the honesty of bargain and sale, 'He is coming to town, Sir, and then your Majesty will have another vote.'"—*Memoirs of George III.*, vol. i. p. 334.

[a] In the affair of Wilkes.

MR. WILKES TO EARL TEMPLE.

Paris, Rue des Saints Pères, May 11, 1767.

MY LORD,—My brother has given me the greatest pleasure by some of his late letters, in which I find that I live still in your Lordship's kind remembrance and regard. Many years have now passed since I began to look upon the favour of Lord Temple as the most desirable thing in life, and I believe my conduct has left no doubt of the sincerity or the warmth of that attachment, which my heart will preserve 'till the last moment.

I took the liberty of sending to your Lordship the first copy I had from the press of my last letter to the Duke of Grafton[1], and I sent it by the post, as it bore my name, and two or three lines of the sentiments I shall ever entertain of the most superior character I have ever had the happiness of knowing.

I am sorry, my Lord, to touch again on any private affairs respecting an old friend, for whom I feel the utmost tenderness from his unhappy situation. Mr. Cotes has left me in the most cruel embarras, and has not served himself. I had an entire confidence in his conduct of my affairs, and from the state he sent me in 1764, a copy of which my brother has, I imagined he

---

[1] The second letter addressed by Wilkes to the Duke of Grafton, dated from Paris, December 12, 1766. It is a very spirited and clever composition. After mentioning his former intimacy with Lord Chatham, and attacking him with much bitterness, he gives a very dramatic account of his interview with Lords Halifax and Egremont, and his examination at the Secretary of State's Office, in 1763, before he was taken to the Tower on the charge of being the author of the *North Briton*. This letter will be found reprinted in *Almon's Memoirs of Wilkes*, vol. iii. p. 184.

was bringing everything into order. I gave him full powers, and he flattered me that he was paying several things for me. He sold my books for 427*l*., though, by his own stating since in his ledger, he was then my debtor considerably. His account is so obscure that I cannot make it out. The little tour to Boulogne only, he charges me 31*l*. 10*s*. Many particulars are not set down. As an outlaw I am incapable of doing any act, but I hear that Mr. Life intends to petition the Chancellor, that I may be admitted one of Mr. Cotes's creditors[1]. Mr. Life is a solicitor of character in Basinghall Street, who by Mr. Cotes's and my orders drew the deed of the powers I executed at Boulogne. He imagines at present that the balance in my favour amounts to 1300*l*. Mr. Cotes's own ledger states it at 487*l*. 14*s*. 6*d*.

I had always in my mind the state of my affairs, and I earnestly entreated Mr. Cotes to lay before me what his transactions had been. I begged to know the full state of the pecuniary obligations I had to your generosity, both on a public and private account, for hope, which has hitherto from time to time gilded my too gay prospects, was apt to whisper me that the hour would come, I might at length discharge such kind of debts, though those of gratitude I never could. Mr. Cotes only told me that I knew what I had received from your Lordship before I left England; and that as to what had happened since, it was only what your Lordship had supplied Mr. Phillips with from time to time,

---

[1] In one of his letters to Almon, Wilkes very delicately alludes to the circumstance of Humphrey Cotes having been recently Gazetted as a bankrupt: "I grieve exceedingly, both on a public and private account, for an article I have seen in the papers respecting Mr. Cotes."

and he desired me not to write to Phillips, as he was very suspicious of his character [1].

I believe I mentioned in a former letter that, for some time before I went to Italy in the end of 1764, I had not received any supply from Mr. Cotes, nor have I since, except 20 guineas when I was at London in May. I believe no man was ever left in a more cruel situation, and not in a capacity of doing himself justice.

I look forwards, however, with a gleam of hope, not I own from the public, which is too corrupt, too selfish, too unfeeling, but from some private advantages I still enjoy: the goodness of Lord Temple, and the affection of Miss Wilkes, who is all I can wish or desire. She is on the best terms with her mother's family, with whom she constantly corresponds. They all doat upon her, but I do not choose she should, on the verge of seventeen, be with them, because I would not have them choose a husband for her, instead of her father. Mr. Jacomb, the attorney of the old folks, told Miss Wilkes that, as an outlaw, I had no right in her, the whole right was in the mother; but nature told her the contrary. I therefore found it too dangerous to let my daughter remain with them, and I preferred the encountering with greater difficulties here. Time has cured me of a thousand follies, which too gay a nature had sowed my youth with. The golden fruit I hope comes on, and I wish to dedicate it to your Lordship. I am in part the political work of your hands. It had been better if the branch had been more pruned and lopt. It was too luxuriant, but it did not merit even of the others to be cut off.

[1] Phillips was an Attorney employed by Wilkes. He lived in Cecil Street, Strand.

My exile has been too noble, but I have bought experience, and dearly too. I am now turned to economy in earnest, and your Lordship should find, if I dare to solicit any favours, that they were not misapplied. I will not add more to so generous, so noble a nature as Lord Temple's, but I hope every six months will mend the finances of a man so long, so cruelly embarrassed.

As to the public, I will only add, that whenever His Majesty shall please so far to gratify the wishes of his people, as to give real power and confidence to the nobleman who the most merits both, (to him) I shall entirely submit my conduct, neither by my presence nor in any way causing the least difficulty with respect to me, but in every point demonstrating how much I am, my Lord, your Lordship's most devoted humble Servant,

JOHN WILKES.

THE DUKE OF BEDFORD TO MR. GRENVILLE.

May 29, 1767.

DEAR SIR,—As I was just sitting down to dinner, I received a letter from the Duke of Newcastle to let me know that he had quite misunderstood Lord Mansfield about the Bill which has passed the House of Commons, relating to the East India Company, and that he was unwilling to declare any opinion upon it before it came into our House. He, therefore, wishes that the information he gave me might not be mentioned to his Lordship, who, I think, by the Duke's letter, had pretty well scolded him for what he had said yesterday to me. I give you this hint, that in your conversation with him to-morrow the Duke of Newcastle nor myself be mentioned in it, for fear of giving him umbrage. I am, &c., &c., BEDFORD.

MR. GRENVILLE TO THE DUKE OF BEDFORD.

Bolton Street, May 29, 1767, 12 o'clock at night.

MY DEAR LORD,—I have had a long conversation with Lord Mansfield, who has but this moment left me. I found him quite unapprized of the contents of the Bill for regulating the East India Company's dividends; but after much talk upon the subject of it, he seemed to be perfectly satisfied that the right way would be to restrain the East India Company's dividends to $12\frac{1}{2}$ per cent. during the two years of our intended agreement with that Company, instead of the present Bill to restrain them to 10 per cent. 'till the next session of Parliament. This has always been my idea, and has not only been agreeable to the sentiments of the proprietors from the beginning of this Bill, but I understand is what they were ready to have adopted in their general Court to-day. We both agreed in thinking that if an offer to that effect were made in the Company's petition to the House of Lords, it would put the question upon the strongest ground.

As Lord Mansfield's opinion appeared to tally so much with my own upon the merits and substance of the Bill itself, we did not at all enter into the political or party consideration of it; and if your Grace shall see him, I should think it advisable to decline that topic entirely, as I believe there will be no sort of occasion for it; and I am convinced it was that which hurt him in the conversation with the Duke of Newcastle, of which I did not take the least notice, agreeably to the hint in your letter, nor of anything that passed between your Grace and me, except that I had the honour of waiting upon you last night.

I have this moment heard from my wife, who comes from Lady Charlotte Edwin, that Mr. Keck[1] was seized with an apoplexy to-day on the course at Epsom, and that he is since dead, which I think it right to give you this early notice of, that if you judge it proper you may apprize the Duke of Marlborough of it, with respect to the borough of Woodstock.

I understood from Lord Mansfield that he proposes to go out of town to-morrow, so that if you wish to see him it will be necessary to send to him early. I am, my dear Lord, &c., &c., GEORGE GRENVILLE.

THE DEAN OF EXETER[2] TO MR. GRENVILLE.

Sunning Hill, June 11, 1767.

SIR,—I have the honour of your letter from Wotton, and shall be very happy if the accommodations of the Deanery can contribute to yours or Mrs. Grenville's convenience in your tour. I have sent orders to have the rooms and beds very well aired, and the person who keeps the house to be ready for your arrival on the 19th or 20th. If Mrs. Grenville and you can be contented with plain roast and boiled butcher's meat and chicken, and some excellent sea fish, which our market produces in plenty, you need not be at the trouble of eating your

[1] Anthony Keck, of Great Tew, in Oxfordshire, M.P. for Woodstock.

[2] Dr. Jeremiah Milles; he succeeded the Bishop of Carlisle as President of the Society of Antiquaries in 1768. He is now chiefly remembered for his controversies with Horace Walpole on the subject of Richard the Third, and his vindication of the authenticity of Rowley's Poems. Mason has contributed to immortalize the Dean, by his wit in the "Archæological Epistle:" Dr. Milles died in February, 1784.

meals in any other place. My servant has sufficient skill for those things, and I hope my cellar will not be found deficient, at least I can promise Mrs. Grenville some excellent Madeira, which, I presume, may be the wine she drinks. If at your arrival you should want the assistance of any gentleman to wait on you and show you the city, Mr. Limbrey, the Collector of the Customs, and a particular friend to the Bishop of Carlisle and me, will think it an honour to attend you; but I would not commission him to that post lest ceremony of that kind might be disagreeable to Mrs. Grenville.

I must not omit a circumstance which does honour to the Deanery, and I suppose may give pleasure to you. King William took up his abode there after he landed at Torbay, and slept (though probably not so sweetly as you will) in the room prepared for your reception, but not in the same bed, for that which now stands there is a piece of work curious in its kind. The knotting of the bed was made by Bishop Pococke's mother, when she was very far advanced in years, and it was put together by her daughter. You will pardon me for being particular about what you may never see, but if Mrs. Grenville does see it, I imagine she would like to know its history.

As you seem to doubt, and very justly, whether you can reach Exeter in one day from Eastbury, I must acquaint you with the stages and character of the inns. From Blandford to Dorchester, 16 miles, the King's Arms the only inn there, moderate accommodation. To Bridport, 15 miles, the Bull Inn, a very indifferent one. To Axminster, 12 miles, a very hilly way, but a fine turnpike road. The Green Dragon, though not a good inn, is, I think, the best that you can stop or lie at if you cannot reach Exeter in a day. To Honiton, 9 miles, Golden Lion, a bad inn. To Exeter, 16 miles; there are three inns there, the Oxford Inn, London Inn, and New Inn. The first is rather the best, it is without the East Gate; but the New Inn will be more convenient, because your servants will be nearer to the Deanery.

If the weather or Mrs. Grenville's health should induce you to make any excursions from Exeter, there is a pleasant drive of ten miles to the sea-side at Exmouth, where there is a great curiosity if it be but in bloom,— a very fine magnolia tree, which blows every year several hundreds of fine flowers, and is almost singular in its kind

The view from the top of the Castle at Exeter is well worth seeing. There are, also, two pleasant walks in the suburbs, one called Northern-hay, the other Southern-hay. From the hill called Halldown, six miles west of Exeter, and in the Plymouth road, there is a most extensive and glorious prospect, and at the point of that hill, near the Obelisk, is Lord Lisburne's, a place famous for the very large plantation of firs with which Mr. Ball, he former possessor, clothed the barren side of that hill, and there is a terrace winding through it which commands a most beautiful view of Exmouth, the mouth of the river, and the adjoining country, which is very rich.

As I presume you will continue your journey to Plymouth, I should tell you that at Ashburton, half-way between the two places, 20 miles, there is a good inn, called the New Inn. I cannot commend the houses at

Plymouth, they are like those in other seaports, neither very neat nor quiet. Prince George's Head is esteemed the best.

I have nothing more to add, but to wish you a pleasant tour, and to Mrs. Grenville an enjoyment of good health, &c. I am, with great truth and respect, &c.,

JER. MILLES.

MR. WILLIAM GERARD HAMILTON TO EARL TEMPLE.

Saturday, 2 o'clock, (June 27, 1767.)

MY DEAR LORD,—My friend[1] has this moment informed me that the King has wrote to Lord Chatham, pressing him to give his advice as to the manner in which a new Administration should be formed[2], the Duke of Grafton persisting in his resolution not to continue. The King has, at the same time, acquainted Lord Chatham with his resolution to make an immediate alteration in his Government, without his Lordship's advice, provided he still continues to decline giving him any assistance, and my friend is of opinion that next week will produce the alteration talked of.

He lamented your Lordship's absence from town, and spoke, I thought, with much more reserve than usual. Yours, my dear Lord, in the utmost hurry, but in all situations most faithfully and affectionately,

---

[1] I believe it may be taken as an invariable rule, that the *friend* mentioned by Mr. Hamilton in his correspondence with Lord Temple, means Sir Fletcher Norton.

[2] See *Chatham Correspondence*, vol. iii. p. 275.

MR. AUGUSTUS HERVEY TO MR. GRENVILLE.

Park Place, June 30, 1767.

MY DEAR SIR,—As I returned here yesterday from two days' excursion to my own little retreat, I found the pleasure of your letter from Boconnock, but am sorry I must return you the memorial with only a desire of complying with what I have wrote on the back of it, as that is what Lord Bristol desired might be done, as those cases are now returned into the Lord Justice's hands to transmit hither; I sent it by Sir Robert Wilmot, with your request, as the most likely to be obtained, and had that answer back. I was glad, my dear Sir, that I could mark the last action and request of mine in that office with being joined to your name, as I am now to tell you I have this moment wrote (in the civilest manner) to desire to resign my employment[1], my brother's conduct and coolness to me making it impossible for me to keep it, as I would have done to have dropped with his change, if there is to be any, which is yet as doubtful as the first moment it was talked of, though I find it insinuated everywhere (and in the Closet too), that it is my constant attachment to you and your brother. Strange, that the same degree of constancy in one person's attachment is not to be reckoned a virtue as well as in another's! Stranger still, that what I stipulated at first should be imputed to me as crime now! at least, this is the only thing I have yet heard laid to me. I shall know more, I suppose, when I go in to His Majesty, which I think myself obliged to do from all this very disagreeable situation,

---

[1] As Secretary to the Lord Lieutenant of Ireland, which latter office Lord Bristol soon after resigned.

and which I should have imagined to have been a train laid for me had I not been too insignificant.

I am glad to hear Mrs. Grenville has continued so well; I have got this violent cold that is going about, but hope in the course of the summer to be able to pay my respects at Wotton and Stowe, as I shall be a private gentleman at my own disposal, except in my waiting week. You are very much in the right for having turned your back on politics; they are not at present worth any one's attention, much less yours; everything in the most confused state, and nothing settled; many things talked of, nothing to be credited; London the dullest of all dwellings, and if one did not meet with as little truth as company, one might forget one was in a Court, but the few people that are there act their parts so well, that in all the solitude of privacy one finds oneself at the same time in all the danger of eminence, and beset with all the inconveniences of a public life, without the advantages of the social part of it; there are constant avocations without any employments, and a great deal of idleness without any leisure; many words pronounced and nothing said, many people smiling and nobody pleased, many disappointments and little success, little grandeur and less happiness. Sunday, Lord Chamberlain was obliged to carry the sword, judge how few are in town; yesterday all ended in the Upper House, after a debate 'till six, without a division. I am, &c., &c., A. HERVEY.

MR. WILLIAM GERARD HAMILTON TO EARL TEMPLE.

Friday night, (July 3, 1767.)

MY DEAR LORD,—The Parliament closed yesterday without any alteration being made; contrary to the general expectation, but agreeable to what I always apprehended would be the case.

Diffident as one is of all intelligence which is circulated in times of expectation like the present, I think I can inform your Lordship with tolerable exactness of the situation which things stand in at this moment; and I have reasons for speaking with more than usual confidence upon the present occasion.

Though Mr. Conway's intention of resigning has been made public only within these few days, it was communicated by him to the King more than a month ago [1]; since which time every endeavour has been employed, both by the Court and by the Duke of Grafton, and by letters wrote with the King's own hand [2], to prevail on Lord Chatham to explain himself as to his wishes about retiring from his employment, or continuing in it; about the manner in which he would advise Mr. Conway's place should be supplied, and as to a variety of other particulars relative to the carrying on of Government, and to the strengthening the present Administration, or

[1] This intelligence is corroborated by the King's letter to Lord Chatham, dated May 30, in which His Majesty mentions "the resolution of Lieutenant-General Conway to retire, though without any view of entering into faction." See *Chatham Correspondence*, vol. iii. p. 260.

[2] The letters which passed between the King and Lord Chatham upon this occasion, are dated from the 30th May to the 25th of June inclusive, and no letter from the King of a later date is given in the *Chatham Correspondence* during the present year.

the change of it. To all which questions no other answer has been obtained, than that the state of his health was such as made him utterly incapable of giving any advice; and recommending it to them to proceed in any manner they thought proper; not doubting but the steps they took would be such as must merit everybody's approbation, but by no means pledging himself to approve.

This enigmatical conduct has dissatisfied and alarmed the Court exceedingly, and they are determined to persevere for some time longer in their attempts to procure from Lord Chatham some more precise and positive declaration.

The Duke of Grafton, however, has acquainted Lord Camden, Lord Northington, and the King himself, that he will not continue at the head of the Treasury, and be himself responsible for the conduct of Government under its present circumstances. That he took the situation which he now holds merely for the sake of acting under Lord Chatham, and not with a view of being Minister himself; and that unless Lord Chatham is both able and willing to stand forward, his determination is to retire. The Court, I am persuaded, will leave no expedient untried to accomplish one of these two points: to prevail on Lord Chatham to speak out explicitly; but if he perseveres in the ambiguous and unsatisfactory language he has held for some time past, to persuade the Duke of Grafton to continue on his own bottom, with every promise, and, as long as it suits the purpose of the Court, with every proof of their support. Your Lordship, I believe, may be assured that the present situation of the Ministry, and the present purpose of the Court, is pretty nearly what I state it to be.

In the meantime, however, Lord Egmont declares

he has refused the Seals, and his declaration is universally believed. His refusal, he says, proceeded from the same principle as his resignation. While Lord Chatham has any part in the Administration he will have no part in it; but when that difficulty is removed, he shall be happy to accept of any situation the Court prefer for him.

If the present system can be patched up, Shelburne is not to be absolutely removed, but to take the Northern Department, and the Southern is to be given to Mr. Townshend, who, it is said, has offered to accept of any situation with the Duke of Grafton; but no one, I think, seems disposed (however they may be at last necessitated to it) voluntarily to repose the least degree of confidence in him.

The friends of Lord Chatham, and particularly Lord Camden, are extremely apprehensive that there is some secret understanding between your Lordship and Lord Rockingham; and the fears of the Court are still more extensive, for in addition to that apprehension they entertain another, which is, that you likewise have some negotiation with Lord Chatham, and they think that you are spreading a net with which they are to be surrounded, and out of which they will find it difficult to escape.

This, my dear Lord, is the present distracted situation in which you have left them, and out of which, if they were wise, they would have recourse to you to relieve them.

The opinion of Lord Northington (who has not resigned, as it is reported) was that you would be sent to. But the prevailing idea is otherwise. Lord Rockingham and his people are hard at work, that they may be the persons applied to, and their language as to the Duke of Grafton is wonderfully changed. They speak of him in terms of very high commendation, and say that his single fault is being too great an enthusiast for Lord Chatham. Lord Bute is expected in town in about a fortnight, before which time no one seems to think any material alteration is likely to be made. Yours, my dear Lord, &c., — — —

MR. AUGUSTUS HERVEY TO MR. GRENVILLE.

Park Place, July 4, 1767.

MY DEAR SIR,—I think it right (although I wrote to you so lately) to tell you that I resigned the Secretary's place the 1st, that is, I have wrote to do so, but find that my successor must be named first; and as I was quite ignorant, but from reports, of the cause of my brother's coolness, I wrote to him (being told he did not wish to see me at his house) to know the reason. The enclosed paper is word for word the copy of the three letters that passed between us, which I showed the King on Thursday, in an audience I asked of him: wherein I found it necessary to do you, my dear Sir, that justice I owed your friendship and your honour, in the advice you had ever given me with regard to my brother; there was no other occasion for it. The King was as much surprised at my brother's *reasons* as I was, as the world is, and as, I believe, you will be. However, yesterday, at the Levée, I went up to him, and insisted on some eclaircissement, when all he had to say was, that he was told by people that he met Lord Temple and yourself several times at my house to transact business. I asked if that was a crime in me, if it had been so. I asked him if I had not always told him that my opinion and friendship was fixed with you, and that nothing should break it on either; and whether he thought Lord Temple or you capable, if I was, of being carrying anything on to his disadvantage; or that I might not have visitors exclusive of political ones. All he could say to me was, that he did not think I would have continued such an intimacy on. I laughed at all this, and told him I pitied him for letting such wretches break into such an attachment as I had showed to him; that I thought myself used worse than ever man was; that I had showed these letters to the King, and had there defied him to lay anything to my charge of any kind; that he had obliged me to throw myself on the King a second time; and that I desired he would never think more of me, but as a brother.

In short, my dear Sir, I ask pardon for troubling you with all this, but as you and your brother are the innocent principals, from your friendship to me, I could not help it. The King said your advice to me was like a man of honour and a friend: he made me very easy on every account; I was an hour, very near, with him, in which I did not fail to lay open all the treatment I had met with before this. I am very happy to find myself justified everywhere for giving up, and my brother as much condemned, for these letters are no secret; I have shown à droite et à gauche, and I have a right to do so, when it has been long insinuated that I was very ungrateful, and not only wanted to throw my brother in Lord Temple's and your hands, but flew in his face because I could not compass it, when I believe you know none of us would have given ourselves the trouble of undertaking anything so very little essential. I am, &c., &c., A. HERVEY.

MR. WILLIAM GERARD HAMILTON TO EARL TEMPLE.

Monday, (July 6, 1767.)

MY DEAR LORD,—The Duke of Grafton has declared he will not resign if Mr. Conway can be prevailed upon to continue, and the Court are using their utmost endeavours to succeed in that point. Contrary to all expectation, Lord Bute came to town on Saturday, and Lord Townshend's opinion is (who was with him an hour) that no alteration would be made these three weeks.

There was no Drawing-room yesterday[1]. The king continued at Richmond, and, as it is reported, not well: Mr. Conway, however, was with him there a considerable time. The object of that interview was certainly to prevail on Mr. Conway not to resign: the result of it I have not yet been able to learn; nor do I yet know whether Lord Chatham has returned any and what answer to the King's letter, which was wrote so long ago as last Wednesday[2]. The best intelligence I can get is,

[1] In the *Public Advertiser* of Wednesday, July 8th, I find the following: "Sunday the Earl of Bute was for a considerable time at Richmond, and it is remarked that there was no Court at St. James's on that day as usual." And again, in another paragraph, "The same morning there was a Cabinet Council held in South Audley Street, after which the Thane set out for a certain place near Q." (Kew.)

[2] July the 1st: the letter here alluded to does not appear in the *Chatham Correspondence*, but it is no doubt that which all the writers of the time, as well as some subsequent historians, mention as having elicited only a *verbal* reply. No letter from the King of a later date than Thursday the 25th of June having been found by the editors of the *Chatham Correspondence*, they were induced to believe, that in publishing the written reply to that communication, they were enabled to correct what appeared to them to be a mis-statement. Mr. Adolphus, however, one of the latest historians upon the subject, still asserts, even with the *Chatham Correspondence* before him, that " his Lordship by a *verbal* answer excused himself from interfering in any new arrangement, as his health was too much impaired for exertion." Horace

that Lord Chatham was exceedingly affected by what the King said to him, and much worse in consequence of it.

There is not a doubt, I believe, but that Lord Gower has had offers made to him, and refused them. It is generally understood that Lord Northington, before he left town, advised the King to have immediate recourse to your Lordship. Shelburne had last week two long conferences in the Closet, and everything which I either hear or observe, tends to confirm me in what I wrote to you last week, that the Court will at all events avoid making any change to which they are not drove by the most unavoidable necessity.

Your Lordship will probably have heard of the disagreement between Augustus Hervey and Lord Bristol, and of his having resigned the Secretaryship: his opinion is that young Jemmy Grenville will be his successor.

That Lord Bute has notions of going abroad, is a thing circulated by those who have the best opportunities of knowing whether there is truth in such a report, and unless there was some foundation for it, the having such an idea prevail seems to answer, to those who spread it, no one desirable purpose.

Since I wrote thus far, I have seen a person, who has

Walpole, writing upon the events of this period, says that Lord Chatham "would neither resign nor come forth, yet was continually sending Dr. Addington privately to the King to assure His Majesty he should be able to appear in a month or two." Dr. Addington was therefore very probably the medium of the verbal communication in reply to the King's letter of Wednesday the 1st of July, as it will be seen in a subsequent part of the present letter that he was in close attendance upon Lord Chatham on that day. It would seem, however, from the authority of Mr. Gerard Hamilton's letters, that the answer, if it had been given, had not been suffered to transpire for at least a week afterwards.

been for some time a patient of Dr. Addington's, and who tells me that Dr. Addington sent on Thursday an excuse for not attending him: his apology was that Lord Chatham had been seized with the influenza, had been blooded, was much out of order, and had desired that he would sit up with him all night.

This afternoon I hear that Lord Chatham's answer to the King was extremely equivocal[1], and that the impression it conveyed was, that he did not despair absolutely of being again able to serve His Majesty, but I think it will be in my power by the coach on Thursday to inform your Lordship more authentically upon that subject. Yours, &c., &c., — — —

MR. WHATELY TO MR. GRENVILLE.

Monday, July 6, 1767.

DEAR SIR,—For once I write, even in these fluctuating times, with some degree of confidence that my intelligence is true. That everything is afloat, and the dissolution of the present system approaching, seems to be certain; the steps by which things have been brought into this situation are these. Last Friday seven-night Lord Northington was in the Closet, and declared his opinion that it was impossible to go on, that he could not bear it, and said that if his place could facilitate any arrangement he would willingly quit it: out of the Closet, I believe, he was positive that he would do no more business; and on Wednesday last (July 1st) he

[1] This report appears to have been premature, as Mr. Hamilton's letter of the Wednesday following states that no answer had then been received.

set out for the Grange, expecting, however (as I since hear), to be sent for back, in order to assist in forming a new system.

On the same Wednesday that he set out, the Duke of Grafton notified his determination to the King to go on no longer in this way; the reasons for which are supposed to be that, finding himself deserted by Conway and Northington, not trusting to Shelburne or Townshend, and convinced that Chatham would do no business, he was sensible that his own situation was become too responsible and dangerous.

Whether these were or were not his reasons, he made the declaration, and, as I understand, suggested the necessity of calling upon Lord Chatham for an explanation of his sentiments upon so difficult a crisis.

On Thursday [1], the King wrote to Lord Chatham, stating the difficulties of Government, asking for his advice, and intimating that if it were not explicitly given his Lordship could not take it amiss if another system were formed without his concurrence; these are said to be the contents of the letter. I doubt the information, because it is so particular; but it is true that a letter was written.

No answer has, I believe, been yet received, and I have reason to think that Lord Chatham is really not in a condition to give any, for all last week he was extremely ill, I believe dangerously, and yesterday was so bad that Lady Chatham would not suffer Dr. Addington to leave him during the whole day, though he was engaged to a consultation.

[1] Mr. Gerard Hamilton says *Wednesday*, but perhaps the letter may not have been sent until the following day: the difference is unimportant: both authorities agree that the King did write to Lord Chatham about that time.

This step of the Duke of Grafton was taken, I am persuaded, without any concert with anybody. It is evident that Lord Bute's friends knew nothing of it, from several symptoms, one of which is, that but a day or two before, Mr. Mackenzie took an opportunity to enter into a conversation with Sir Fletcher Norton on his and Wedderburn's situation, lamenting that they were excluded from any share in an Administration so well established, and insinuating his inclination to negotiate for them; to which Sir Fletcher answered, that neither he nor Wedderburn were uneasy at their situation, and did not desire others to give themselves any trouble about them. Since that Mr. Mackenzie is gone out of town, apparently ignorant of the transaction; and some of Lord Bute's friends, by their language, appeared not to know it some time after I was acquainted with it. To this hour it is not very generally talked of, but all I have told you positively I take to be indisputably true.

The Duke of Grafton was with the King on Saturday, at Richmond, and yesterday General Conway and some of the other Ministers went there, but only upon ordinary business; His Majesty having the influenza to a great degree, did not come to town. The speculations you may be sure are very various, and speculations soon become assertions, so that it is already said that the Rockinghams, and the Bedfords, and the Grenvilles, will be or are sent to, each man believing as he wishes. There is no foundation yet, I believe, to say which way the current will turn. It is said that a negotiation has been attempted with the Rockinghams, for which I can find no other ground than that Conway is very anxious to bring it about, and has been lately with the Marquess. It is said with still more confidence that an attempt has been made upon the Bedfords, through the means of Lord Gower, the particulars of which I think I know precisely, and they are these. His Grace took an opportunity of breaking the subject to his Lordship at White's, by expressing his wishes that his Lordship's friends had a share in Government, and held a distant language upon it, which Lord Gower purposely understood as referring to *all* his connections, and therefore listened to, 'till the Duke began to contract his general discourse into particular expressions of regard for the Duke of Bedford; upon which Lord Gower threw out that his connections extended also to Mr. Grenville and Lord Temple; to which his Grace answered that he wished to see Lord Temple in the King's Government, and the terms he used induced Lord Gower to think he meant at the head of that Government; but the next day he either called upon him or sent for him, and explained his meaning to be only that he should be glad to see Lord Temple in a great office, but did not point at his forming an Administration. In the course of the conversation he observed that if such an union as he wished could take place, they might do what they pleased with Charles Townshend; and Lord Gower, I understand, was very explicit in letting him see that he had no room to expect any defection of the Bedfords from their connections with you.

MR. WILLIAM GERARD HAMILTON TO EARL TEMPLE.

Wednesday, (July 8, 1767.)

MY DEAR LORD,—I saw my friend late last night, at which time no answer whatever had been returned by

Lord Chatham to the King's letter. The Court, I understand, in order to put him as much in the wrong as possible, are determined to wait a day or two longer, and then to consider his silence as equivalent to a refusal.

Lord Bute continues still in town, and will remain here, as my friend informs me, 'till everything is settled. Offers have been made to Lord Rockingham, not to be himself at the head of the Treasury, but to support the Duke of Grafton there. Lord Rockingham's answer was, that he would take any office the Court thought fit for him, or be extremely well satisfied without any situation at all, but that his three conditions were, from neither of which he could possibly depart, that Mr. Yorke should be Chancellor, Lord Albemarle at the head of the army, and the Duke of Richmond Secretary of State. These terms have been refused, and that negotiation for the present is at an end. Lord Rockingham's engagements are, I understand, so very positive both to Mr. Yorke and Lord Albemarle, that he cannot himself accept of any situation 'till their expectations are gratified; and the laying aside Lord Camden and Lord Granby must, I should think, while the Duke of Grafton continues, be two very impracticable preliminaries[1].

Your Lordship will observe that hitherto all the negotiations of the Court have been with a view to support the present Administration, and not to supply the place of it, and Lord Rockingham was applied to, not to be the successor, but the auxiliary of the Duke of Grafton.

[1] Besides the offence to Conway, in proposing to place Lord Albemarle, a younger general, at the head of the army.

Whenever things are drove to that extremity, which they probably will be in the course of this week, that a total change shall become necessary, my friend tells me he has hopes (and he assures me likewise he has the strongest wishes) that your Lordship may be applied to in preference to any one, and the favourable light in which he says he knows you stand both with the King and with those[1] who are supposed to influence him, is the foundation of his opinion: though at the same time I was informed by him that both Lord Holland and Mr. Conway are endeavouring earnestly to procure the offer for Lord Rockingham and his friends.

This is, as nearly as I can collect, the situation of affairs at the moment I am writing, with one additional circumstance, which is, that the Duke of Grafton has declared he would go on himself without Lord Chatham, provided he could gain over *three* people.

My friend, I know, is one of the three, but who are the other two I can only conjecture.

Wednesday night, 11 o'clock.

I have seen my friend again this evening: he informs me that the Duke of Grafton goes out of town to-morrow, and returns on Saturday or Sunday, 'till which time the Court are determined to wait for Lord Chatham's answer, and if none is received from him by that time, their resolution is to proceed immediately to form a new Administration: the plan of propping the old one being now, I believe, laid aside. It is agreed on all hands that Lord Chatham is worse than ever. For

---

[1] Lord Northington was said, at this early stage of the Ministerial crisis, to have recommended the King to have recourse to the Grenvilles, and the report is corroborated by Horace Walpole, in his *Memoirs of George III.*

these last ten days he has not been out of the house, and for these two days he has not been out of his bed.

My friend seems still of opinion that your Lordship will be sent to, but at the same time declares that no man living can pretend to conjecture what resolution such a Court, with such advisers, will come to.

If there is an intention of having recourse to your Lordship, I am promised the earliest information of it. I will come immediately to Stowe, and give you an exact account (which I have the best reason to think I can obtain) of all the transactions since your absence, some circumstances leading me rather to doubt the truth of what is circulated by the friends of Lord Rockingham.

Though I apprehend I shall have very little to inform your Lordship of by the coach on Saturday, I will nevertheless have the pleasure of writing to you. In the mean time you will believe me, my dear Lord, &c., &c.

MR. WHATELY TO EARL TEMPLE [1].

July 8, 1767.

MY LORD,—I informed you in my last that a conversation had been held with Lord Gower, the tendency of which was to sound how far his friends might be in-

---

[1] In a letter to Mr. Grenville on the previous day, Whately said:— "I have informed Lord Temple of the news of the time, but if you should go over to Stowe, or he come to Wotton, I will beg the favour of you to let me know, that I may not continue to trouble him with letters, when you will be able to acquaint him with all the intelligence I can convey to you." I shall hereafter have occasion to notice the mutual communication of their correspondent's information, between Lord Temple and Mr. Grenville, particularly on subjects connected with the writings of Junius.

duced to leave the other parts of the Opposition. His Lordship is now gone to Trentham, and thus ends that negotiation. Another of much the same kind has been opened with Lord Rockingham, by the means of General Conway, but it was pushed so far as to get the Marquess to name his propositions, which were, that the Duke of Richmond should be Secretary of State, Lord Albemarle at the head of the army instead of Lord Granby, and Mr. Yorke Chancellor; if these were complied with, he desired no situation for himself; but still he said that neither this nor any arrangement would he accede to, in which your Lordship, Mr. Grenville, and the Duke of Bedford did not concur. I do not vouch for the truth of this, but I have it from men of so good authority that I cannot help believing it, and if it should be true, it is evident that he intended to leave the Treasury open. These propositions it is said have been rejected, but the story at Court to-day is, that some kind of negotiation is still open with him, and I know that to-day one who has easy access to him declared it was his Lordship's determination not to accede to any patch-work, or to any arrangement which did not comprehend all parts of the present Opposition.

I do not understand that this supposed negotiation is in consequence of any direct message, but soundings, conversations, reports of conversations, &c., and the whole must be received with some degree of caution, though I think it is so well authenticated in the manner I have related it to your Lordship, as to deserve a greater share of credit than I usually give to such kind of accounts. I have the honour to be, &c.,

THOMAS WHATELY.

MR. WILLIAM GERARD HAMILTON TO EARL TEMPLE.

Friday, July 10, 1767.

MY DEAR LORD,—Agreeable to what I apprehended, things remain precisely in the same situation as when I had last the honour of writing to you. The Duke of Grafton left town yesterday, declaring, as I understand, that if the King insisted upon it, he would still continue at the head of the Treasury, though it was both against his inclination and his opinion. But I am informed that this is a request which the King does not intend to make to him. In case there should be a change of Administration, the Duke of Grafton will then accept of any employment that is not an employment of business.

Mr. Conway went on Wednesday to Mr. Townshend's at Richmond, to desire he would be at Court on Thursday, but real or affected illness prevented him. Mr. Townshend, however, I hear, is confident that all these negotiations will terminate in his being at the head of the Treasury: an idea which I know Lord Mansfield ridicules, as being agreeable neither to you, to Lord Rockingham, nor even to Lord Bute. Mr. Conway is said to have objected strongly to the removing Lord Granby, upon any arrangement, from the head of the army.

Lord Bristol has not appointed your nephew his Secretary, but a Mr. Jones, who married a sister of Lord Tyrone's, and whom your Lordship may possibly have seen with the ladies in Upper Brook Street. A young man of the lowest birth, and remarkably illiterate, even in a country where being illiterate is not apt to be remarked; but to atone for these defects he has a very handsome face and rather an elegant person. This appointment is at present the reigning topic of conversation, and the source of much entertainment to the male, and of much resentment to the female world.

Lord Granby is at present enough out of order to be attended by Dr. Addington, who assured him, no longer ago than yesterday, that though Lord Chatham had been and was still exceedingly ill, yet he did not entertain a doubt of his entire and perfect recovery.

Negotiations are still going on with the Rockingham party, and they are in the course of every treaty threatened that, unless they become more moderate in their terms, your Lordship and Mr. Grenville will be applied to. What will be the effect of that terror I am a little at a loss to conjecture.

I avoid for the present troubling you with anything more, because since I have wrote thus far I have seen my friend, who has informed me that Rigby is gone to Wotton and to Stowe[1], from whom your Lordship will hear, not only of the offers made, and the preference given to Lord Rockingham, but of the express exclusion to the friends of your Lordship and Mr. Grenville.

Whatever little political disappointment I may feel upon this occasion, I assure you, my dear Lord, with the utmost sincerity and affection, it is more than balanced by the fresh opportunity with which it furnishes me of repeating to you in the strongest terms my esteem and attachment, which, as they were not founded in interest, no interest can change, and from which no prospect of

[1] From whence he returned to Woburn to meet Lord Rockingham and Admiral Keppel. See the Private Journal of the Duke of Bedford, in *Bedford Correspondence*, vol. iii. p. 365.

honour and advantage can ever divert me. Adieu, my dear Lord, and do me the justice to believe me yours, most faithfully and unalterably, — — —

I have this moment received your Lordship's letter of the 9th. Mr. Townshend came to-day by the King's express desire, though much out of order, to the Levée. He was in the Closet a long time; what passed I have not yet been able to collect.

MR. GRENVILLE TO MR. WHATELY.

Stowe, July 12, 1767.

DEAR WHATELY,—I came hither from Wotton last night, and return thither to-morrow morning. I found your two packets on my arrival on Friday night at Wotton, and Mr. Lloyd gave me a third from you dated yesterday. Mr. Rigby, whom I found at Wotton on Friday, went to Woburn yesterday, and came over hither this morning, and is now returned again to Woburn. Lord Rockingham came there yesterday to dinner, and intends to stay 'till this evening or to-morrow morning, when he goes back to London. Lord Temple and I have had a long conversation with Mr. Rigby, which concluded as amicably as is possible, and I have every reason to believe that my friends at Woburn are in the kindest and fairest dispositions towards me. My opinions upon all public business are the same as you have long known them. As to measures, what I have seen confirms me in them. As to arrangements with regard to persons and places, I wish to see one made which is likely to have credit, ability and permanency, and in which my friends may find an honourable place, but for my own part, I would upon no account be obtruded by any one upon the King, nor shall my pretensions be a bar to any establishment which shall be for the public advantage. An enlarged and united system is the only one which can be so, and if disorder of every kind, both at home and in our colonies, has been the consequence of instability and disunion, the properest means to assert the sovereignty of the kingdom is an Administration built on a strong basis. This is my sense and language at this time, and I believe that of the wisest and honestest men in this country. I am glad to find it universally adopted among all those whom I have seen or heard from, and this, I am told, is the language and determination of Lord Rockingham. I do not find that any specific proposition has yet been made. With regard to myself, I have insisted with Mr. Rigby that my name shall not be mentioned for any office whatsoever, but I sincerely wish that my friends may be properly placed, and if that can be done consistently with those principles we have adopted, and without breaking us to pieces, it will on all accounts be the happiest event that can befall me, and the most beneficial to the public. My being in office would only give jealousy to many, and throw difficulties in the way even if things are well intended, without my having the real means to enforce anything, whereas my friends taking post in Government would probably be some restraint to what is wrong, and a support to what is right. I am sure if I can meliorate the situation of my friends instead of sacrificing their just pretensions, myself to go into a great office, the change will be happy, both for my own ease, honour, and the public welfare. I am, &c., &c.,

GEORGE GRENVILLE.

MR. WILLIAM GERARD HAMILTON TO EARL TEMPLE.

Monday, (July 13, 1767.)

My dear Lord,—Though you have probably had a much more authentic account of all the late transactions with the Court than I can presume to give you, I shall nevertheless continue to communicate to you the intelligence I receive from my friend, and from others whose information I think deserves to be credited. In the first negotiation with Lord Gower, the Duke of Grafton intimated that the Court would have no objection to your Lordship's being at the head of the Treasury, but Lord Gower reminding his Grace of what he had said on this subject in a second interview, the Duke of Grafton evaded it by asserting that he spoke only what was his own belief, and not by any authority from the Court [1]. I mention this circumstance for the sake of explaining to your Lordship what the Duke of Grafton had in view by this piece of disingenuity. It had of late been much circulated, and by the Court it was much believed, that neither Mr. Grenville, nor the Duke of Bedford and his friends, would acquiesce in your Lordship's being placed at the head of the Treasury. The Duke of Grafton's object was to discover the truth or falsity of this idea, in hopes of creating a future disagreement between your Lordship and Mr. Grenville. But finding they were not likely to succeed in that plan of making a division, they are now endeavouring to divide Mr. Grenville and the Duke of Bedford, and this, I am persuaded, under whatever appearances it may be disguised, is the

---

[1] See Mr. Whately's report of the conversation between the Duke of Grafton and Lord Gower, *ante*, page 36.

great object of the Court, and of Lord Rockingham, in the present negotiation.

There is likely to arise a very great difference of opinion as to the powers which were given to Lord Rockingham to form a new Administration. His friends say that the proposition was an unlimited one in every respect, except that your Lordship and Mr. Grenville were excluded. This the Duke of Grafton denies absolutely. He owns that Lord Rockingham had an offer of the Treasury, but declares that offer was circumscribed by many conditions, such as that Lord Granby was to continue at the head of the army, and Lord Camden to remain Chancellor, with many other particulars; and this last account is much the most probable, as these were the very terms insisted on by the Court, in the negotiation with Lord Gower.

To Mr. Rigby, I understand, Lord Rockingham stated that he had the power of forming any Administration he thought proper, with the single exception of your Lordship and Mr. Grenville; but a variety of circumstances concur to make me believe (besides the assertions of the Duke of Grafton) that his Lordship overrated exceedingly, and departed a good deal from the truth, in the account he gave at Woburn of the Commission which was sent him by the Court.

In the first place I know that Lord Holland has always declared that the terms offered to Lord Rockingham were so confined that he neither could or would accept of them: and I apprehend his Lordship has very good opportunity of being acquainted with the nature of the transactions which have lately passed. I know likewise that Lord Rockingham himself has said to a person who lives with him in the greatest confidence, that the offers made him were rather an offence than a compliment, and that he could not accept them without being disgraced.

Upon this state of the case, which I am persuaded is the true one, I am at a loss to find what merit his Lordship's refusal can create with the Duke of Bedford and his friends, supposing he should refuse.

To say that he did it upon their account is a pretence and an imposition, by which I should think it was scarce possible they could be duped, and yet this notion prevails here, and very universally.

The report that Lord Chatham is recovering very fast gains ground, and gains credit. Lord Holland is of opinion, that upon Lord Rockingham's declining, Mr. Townshend will be promoted, and the present Administration be continued, with the addition of such recruits as can be collected.

In the midst of all this confusion, Lord Bristol is hastening as fast as possible to Ireland, lest a new arrangement should take place, and prevent him. It has been already hinted to your Lordship that Lord Bristol's success in Ireland would depend upon whether you chose to interest yourself or not upon that occasion. But if this should be an object of your attention, some measures must be taken, and I must have soon the honour of conversing with you.

I have this moment received your Lordship's letter of the 12th.

As I write not by the post, but by the coach, and my letter may escape unopened, I must beg leave to trouble you with my opinion (and at Stowe I shall take the liberty of troubling you with my reasons for it), that if any positive engagement has been entered into with Lord

Rockingham and his friends, by your Lordship and Mr. Grenville, it is a compact, upon whatever conditions it may be made, against which, as a politician, I beg leave to enter my protest; though as an individual, from my deference to your Lordship's judgment, I shall very readily accede to it.

I do not propose leaving town 'till Saturday, and shall therefore have the honour of writing to you again. Yours, my dear Lord, &c., &c.

MR. GRENVILLE TO THE EARL OF SUFFOLK.

Wotton, July 14, 1767.

My dear Lord,—You will have heard, before this can reach you, of the negotiation which has been opened with Lord Rockingham, by a message from the King through the Duke of Grafton, which was delivered at a meeting which they had at General Conway's house, on Tuesday last, the 7th of this month. The message was, that the King wished that Lord Rockingham and his friends might form his Administration, and that he intended his Lordship should resume the office of First Lord of the Treasury. Lord Rockingham having asked whether he was at liberty to communicate this to others besides his own friends, was answered, that the question had been foreseen, and that he might communicate it; but it seemed intended that this was meant to the Duke of Bedford and his friends only. After this conference, the Duke of Grafton went the next day to Newmarket, and was to stay there till yesterday, when Lord Rockingham was to make his proposals, and in the mean time he has neither seen nor heard from the King. The account of this conference was given by Lord Rockingham, in a letter to Lord Albemarle, who, with Lord Gower and Mr. Rigby, were at Woburn with the Duke of Bedford. The letter was writ the same night, and received on Wednesday morning. It was immediately shown, by Lord Rockingham's desire, to the Duke of Bedford, and concluded with a proposition from Lord Rockingham, to come down to Woburn, if the Duke of Bedford and his friends were disposed to act with them in Administration. The answer given was, that the Duke of Bedford and Mr. Grenville were one, and that he would not proceed without consulting me. The intended visit was, therefore, postponed 'till that was done, and Mr. Rigby proposed to go to London to know whether I was returned from the West, and to give Lord Rockingham the meeting, which he did accordingly that evening, and repeated to him their resolution not to do anything without me, and that they were determined not to be separated. In consequence of this, Mr. Rigby came hither on Friday, the 10th of this month, the day of my return home from the West, and from him I learnt the first intelligence of this negotiation. He assured me, in the strongest terms, of the Duke of Bedford's regard, and union with me both in system and in principles, and his own determination to cultivate it to the utmost. He said he had told Lord Rockingham, that neither the Duke of Bedford himself, nor he, as an individual, would ever depart from the ground we had taken, to assert and establish the entire sovereignty of Great Britain over our Colonies. That he was told in answer, that he, Lord Rockingham, declared for a wide and comprehensive system; but I do not know that anything either with regard to measures or men has been talked of in detail, nor is it certain to what degree Lord Rockingham is authorized. In this situation, after acknowledging the sense which I had of the behaviour of the Duke of Bedford and his friends towards me, my answer was, that as to measures my opinions were well known, especially with regard to the capital one of asserting and establishing the sovereignty of Great Britain over America, in which I was happy to find that the Duke of Bedford and his friends so perfectly agreed with me; that as to arrangement of offices, as no message was sent to me I had no answer to give, nor, if there had, would I have given any answer without Lord Temple; that I entirely approved of a wide and comprehensive plan for an Administration, as the ability, strength, and authority which might thereby be given to it, would be the likeliest means to give it permanency, without which no system for the public good could be pursued; that upon these principles I should be extremely glad to see my friends honourably placed in the King's Government, and would cheerfully support an Administration formed upon them, but that I would do it out of office, and I insisted that my name should not be mentioned for any whatsoever. Mr. Rigby went to Woburn, on Saturday the 11th, to meet Lord Rockingham, and I went the same day to Stowe. On Sunday morning Mr. Rigby came over to us from Woburn, and told me that the Duke of Bedford and Lord Gower were extremely satisfied with my answer, to which Lord Temple agreed in every particular, and we both assured Mr. Rigby, that no factious or interested views of ours should stand in the way of any public settlement, which, if possible, we sincerely wished to see made upon those principles in which Mr. Rigby assured us that we all concurred. His language in both visits was as open and as amicable as could be. Upon the whole, my dear Lord, I really wish that my friends could be honourably placed in the King's Government upon principles which I neither can depart from myself or advise others to. They might by that means be enabled to do some good, and I should be happy indeed, if by waving any pretensions of mine I could contribute to that great purpose instead of getting an office for myself, which would only give jealousy and umbrage, and could in the present moment be attended with no public benefit. I hope you will approve of what Lord Temple and I have said and done upon this occasion, and I trust that you will believe me when I earnestly beg of you to take no resolution contrary to it, out of your regard and kindness to me. Every motive as a public man makes me wish to see you honourably placed in Government, if that can be done, and you know me too well to think I would wish, much less propose it otherwise. What prospect there is that this negotiation will end as it ought to do, you will be able to judge as well as I can, from the account I have given you of all I know. The offer will only serve to weaken and incense if nothing is really intended, and instead of dividing will only unite. On the other hand, the conveying it through the Duke of Grafton and General Conway, and letting it rest there for six or seven days without Lord Rockingham's seeing the King, or hearing anything more of it, does not, according to the usual course of things, seem to promise much success, especially if it is true that on Friday last, during this interval, the King sent for Mr. Charles Townshend and had a conversation of an hour and a half with him, which Lord Rockingham knows nothing of. I have troubled you with this long letter that you may be fully apprised of all that has passed, and of my sentiments upon it, as far as I can form any in the present uncertain state; always wishing for your approbation and the continuance of that friendship from you with which I am, my dear Lord, &c., &c.,

GEORGE GRENVILLE.

P.S. As some of the particulars of this letter are not fit for the post, I have desired Mr. Lloyd to carry it to town, and to inquire at your house for some safer and less public conveyance.

EARL TEMPLE TO MR. GRENVILLE.

Stowe, Wednesday night, July 15, 1767.

MY DEAR BROTHER,—The enclosed to yourself came in a letter of Hervey's to the Lord of Eastbury, and I transmit it to you.

I send you, likewise, the only letters or intelligence I have received since we parted. My Arlington Street correspondent [1] is, I fancy, not far off the mark.

All Stowe salutes kindly all Wotton, and I am, &c.,

TEMPLE.

---

[1] Mr. William Gerard Hamilton was long a resident in Arlington Street, as was also Horace Walpole, who, in describing to Lady Ossory the effects of a storm on New Year's Day, 1779, mentions that " one of the Gothic towers at Lady Pomfret's house (now Single Speech Hamilton's), in my street, fell through the roof, and not a thought of it remains."

MR. GRENVILLE TO EARL TEMPLE.

Wotton, July 16, 1767.

MY DEAR BROTHER,—The intelligence you have transmitted to me from your London correspondents agrees exactly with my own opinion as to the sincerity of this transaction.

I have been convinced from the beginning that Lord Rockingham over-rated the powers supposed to be given to him by the message, and that the Duke of Grafton acted exactly the same part with Lord Gower and Lord Rockingham, with the same view of disuniting and getting some individuals.

The other speculations in your letters I am more doubtful of. For my own part, I have received no accounts whatever of what is going on since I saw you.

If it is true that Lord Rockingham stated to Mr. Rigby that his powers were unlimited, "with the single exception of your Lordship and myself," we might have saved ourselves the trouble of insisting that we should not be named for any office, as that was done to our hands; but though this may seem ridiculous, our answers could only be according to what was stated to us.

We shall soon hear further; in the mean time, the ground which we have left it upon is solid, and in all respects the properest for us to stand upon. I send you back your letters with many thanks, and I am, &c., &c.,

GEORGE GRENVILLE.

MR. CHARLES LLOYD TO EARL TEMPLE.

Thursday, July 16, 1767.

My Lord,—I was despairing of being able to give your Lordship any account beyond the level of common discourse, when I met Mr. Burke[1] (General Conway's late Under Secretary), who informed me that Lord Rockingham met the Duke of Grafton yesterday, and after complaining to his Grace of the reports prevailing in town that he had exceeded his commission, justified himself, before General Conway, from that charge. The conversation was very long. In the course of it Lord Rockingham observed that he was responsible to a large body of people for his conduct, and that his determination was to act in concert with the Duke of Bedford and his friends. Upon your Lordship's name and Mr. Grenville's being mentioned, and objected to, as I understand, by the Duke of Grafton, Lord Rockingham added that your conduct upon this occasion required him to consult you, and that he should not act, therefore, without such concert. Lord Rockingham was then asked whether he would make a part of the present Administration, to which he gave an absolute negative. "I am, then, to tell the King that the whole is off." Most certainly, replied Lord Rockingham.

My Gazette was rather confused in his delivery. I could not find out that any expostulations had passed between the Duke of Grafton and Lord Rockingham as to the varied question which your Lordship observes *took place yesterday*, only whether Lord Rockingham would make *a part of the present Administration.*

[1] William Burke.

The Duke of Grafton, in some part of the conversation, paused and hesitated, as if he meant to take it *ad referendum*, but the conclusion was the idea of telling the King that it was absolutely off.

Lord Bute was in town yesterday. The King stayed in town 'till five o'clock, and to-day 'till four, but to-day it was owing to his giving audience to Lord Clive [1], who has brought a diamond equal, it is said, to the Pitt diamond.

I will not trouble you with any observations, but just mention that the best description of the public situation has perhaps been given by a blundering Irish woman, a Mrs. Oliver, of Twickenham, whose house having been robbed, and the thief being taken and condemned, is become to her an object of compassion, and accordingly she has applied to Lord Hertford, who told her he did not know how things were, and he could not ask. She then went to Mr. Conway, who said he was *out;* and lastly to Lord Shelburne, who told her he was not *in;* and so the man will be hanged. I am, &c., &c.,

.LLOYD.

MR. AUGUSTUS HERVEY TO MR. GRENVILLE.

Park Place, July 16, 1767.

DEAR SIR,—I thank you for your obliging letter, which I received on my return to town, where I have been three days in all this confused scene, and which still continues. I should have wrote to you Tuesday evening, but concluded you had more authentic and more minute accounts of what was going on than I could possibly procure for you, at least than I could

[1] Lord Clive had just returned from India.

depend upon, for the accounts are various, and very much depending as every individual wishes. I was at Court this morning, when there was not at the Drawing-room any one person but who were of the family, and, properly speaking, in waiting, except four Foreign Ministers: but when the King was retired, the Duke of Grafton and Mr. Conway came, the first of which was in with the King about two hours, and, whilst there, received the final answer in a letter from Lord Rockingham[1], which I have been told from authority (that I could every way depend on) that it was a more peremptory refusal than ever. Lord Bute is in town still, and his people's language is now that the King is determined not to be a prisoner, but their looks do not look as if they thought they could long rely on those noble resolutions. The other Lord B—— (Bristol) now says he will by no means go to Ireland, unless absolutely commanded, and, by what I find, every person has refused Mr. Conway's Seals. Lord Egmont will not stir whilst Lord Chatham holds the Privy Seal, but, as I am told, is ready to take any step the King pleases if *he* is removed. I hear *you* are all cemented together, and 'tis therefore supposed you must at length succeed in oversetting; pour le reste après: no one can answer;

---

[1] Lord Rockingham, in a letter to the Duke of Bedford of this date, writes: "I have since had a note from his Grace to say that my letter did not get to him 'till after he came out of the King's Closet; and that so he could not send me an answer till he had seen the King to-morrow: by this means a little more time is gained for commenting upon my letter, and perhaps for consideration what steps now to take. I believe it is still doubtful what shall be done."—*Bedford Correspondence*, vol. iii. p. 369. Lord Rockingham seems to insinuate, what Mr. Hervey asserts, that the Duke of Grafton received his letter *in the King's presence*, and Mr. Hervey being in waiting, as one of the King's household, was probably well informed.

you know my wishes, my attachment, and my determinations. My dear Sir, I shall say no more, but, independent of myself, I do assure you without flattery, that I think 'till you can determine to take all our melancholy affairs under your direction, we can have no prospect of success. Whenever you can do so, I trust you will, and as much as I honour and love you, I do not wish to see you there, 'till it is entirely settled between yourself and the King. I am, &c.,   A. HERVEY.

EARL TEMPLE TO MR. GRENVILLE.

Stowe, July 17, 1767, past 3.

MY DEAR BROTHER,—I have nothing new to add to what I say in my letter to Mr. Rigby[1]; however insidious the Court has been at the outset, I think Lord Rockingham is up with them, and I take it for granted nothing will come of this business, though I cannot see what will be to take place. Your most affectionate,

TEMPLE.

MR. RIGBY TO EARL TEMPLE AND MR. GRENVILLE.

Woburn Abbey, 12 o'clock, Saturday, July 18, 1767.

MR. RIGBY has the honour to send the enclosed letters[2] to Stowe, and to Wotton, and at the Duke of

---

[1] See *Bedford Correspondence*, vol. iii. p. 379.

[2] The letters which passed upon this occasion between the Duke of Bedford, Lord Rockingham, and the Duke of Grafton are printed in the *Bedford Correspondence*, and therefore it is unnecessary to repeat

Bedford's request to add, that his Grace, who goes to London to-morrow, would be very desirous of hearing them here. The following, however, from Lord Weymouth to Rigby, has not, I believe, been printed.

Lord Weymouth to Mr. Rigby.

White's, Wednesday, 9 o'clock, (July 15, 1767.)

Dear Rigby,—I can't help writing, though I have very little information to send you. I have just seen the Marquess, who did not see the Duke of Grafton 'till this morning. He told him what was agreed at Woburn, and said that he now hoped to be able to form a Ministry upon a comprehensive plan; but as this differed a little from the first proposal from his Grace, he could not properly desire an audience till he knew whether His Majesty was disposed to receive a plan on this comprehensive idea. The Duke of Grafton staggered a little at the word *comprehensive*, desired to know what it meant, and said that every person who at present held an office might be removed by it. Lord Rockingham said that might or might not be, but that he could not think of putting places to men, or of saying who should be removed, 'till he had the honour of seeing His Majesty. The Duke of Grafton told him that it would have been better, if he could have formed an Administration with his and the Duke of Bedford's friends, and that it would have been less alarming to the Court. Lord Rockingham told him that it was impossible, and that we were determined to abide by our present resolution. He told his Grace of the report of the town, that he had exceeded his powers. The Duke confessed that he had not, and said he hoped they would not believe any idle reports of each other which might be propagated. Lord Rockingham expects to hear to-morrow more of this, and to know whether he is to see the King or not, but said that he did not think it worth while to send this account to the Duke of Bedford. I told him that I should, and as he thinks it not impossible that he may see Conway to-night, who is at this moment with the Duke of Grafton, he will immediately let me know, if he should hear anything more from him, that I may send it in the morning with this letter. The Duke of Grafton has seen the King this morning since his conversation with Lord Rockingham.

It is impossible, I think, to comment upon this, as it contains very little more than we knew before. I am, &c., Weymouth.

I have just heard for certain that the Thane[a] is come to town, and it is said that Lord B. (Bristol) has declared to the King that he will not go to Ireland.

[a] Lord Bute.

the sentiments of Lord Temple and Mr. Grenville upon the present crisis, in any manner they choose to convey them.

MR. GRENVILLE TO EARL TEMPLE.

Wotton, July 18, 1767.

MY DEAR BROTHER,—I send you enclosed the answers which I have given to Mr. Rigby's two notes, which I hope you will approve, and that you will think it right, in a matter of this delicate nature, to put into writing the answer which we both gave to him verbally at Stowe, especially as Lord Rockingham and the Duke of Bedford both refer to a plan agreed upon at Woburn, the particulars of which it is impossible that we should be yet thoroughly acquainted with.

I observe that the Duke of Grafton says repeatedly to Lord Rockingham that there would be great facility in the Court, if the negotiation were confined to his, Lord Rockingham's, and the Duke of Bedford's friends. What then are the articles of difficulty? You and I have insisted upon not being named for any office, nor have any of our friends been yet specifically mentioned either by us or to us. This, therefore, seems to me only a continuance of his Grace's jockey tricks, to endeavour to divide us, by persuading the Duke of Bedford's and Lord Rockingham's friends that they are sacrificed for us, which is the very reverse of the truth, and no notice is taken that we have insisted only upon measures, and that we have expressly declined being named for any office. This makes it necessary to be cautious, lest our true ground should be mistaken.

I have the pleasure to tell you that all our friends

whom I have heard from approve our conduct and answer, in the strongest terms.

Lord Suffolk came here from Wiltshire yesterday to dinner, and goes away this morning. Mr. Whately came in the evening from London, and brings me the same account of warm approbation from such of our friends as are in town. He talks of returning thither in a day or two, unless his longer stay would give him the pleasure of seeing you here, which we flatter ourselves will be the case, as I understood you proposed coming with our Eastbury guests about this time. I sincerely wish you would, as it is certainly better that we should be together when the denouement of this farce appears, which I think is not far off. Lord Suffolk, Mr. Whately, and all the inhabitants of Wotton, salute the inhabitants of Stowe most kindly. I am, my dear Brother, &c.,

GEORGE GRENVILLE.

I have heard from Mr. Augustus Hervey, that Lord Bristol has declared that he will not go to Ireland, and from other hands, that he has been with the King to resign, as Lord Chatham's authority is not to continue.

EARL TEMPLE TO MR. RIGBY.

Stowe, past 3, July 18, 1767.

LORD TEMPLE returns thanks to Mr. Rigby for all the obliging trouble he has taken, and sends back the Duke of Bedford's servant, without forwarding the papers by him to Wotton, as Lord Temple intends going over there himself this evening, and concerting with Mr. Grenville what may be the next proper step for them to take.

He will forthwith, through Mr. Rigby, apprize his Grace of the result, without any observation at present.

MR. RIGBY TO EARL TEMPLE AND MR. GRENVILLE.

Woburn Abbey, Sunday morning, July 19, 1767.

Mr. Rigby presents his best compliments to Lord Temple and Mr. Grenville, and having read their letter of last night to the Duke of Bedford, is desired by his Grace to assure them, that every circumstance of the present transaction, which has come to him, has been communicated to Stowe and Wotton, except a note received from Lord Rockingham this morning[1], containing nothing but expressions of his great satisfaction that the Duke of Bedford is going to London.

His Grace will inform Lord Temple and Mr. Grenville of what passes between Lord Rockingham and the King, and sincerely wishes their friends may be induced to accept of an honourable and becoming share in the arrangement, if one can be properly and happily effected.

EARL TEMPLE TO MR. RIGBY.

Stowe, July 19, 1767.

Lord Temple eagerly embraces the very first opportunit of assuring Mr. Rigby, and through him the Duke of Bedford, that there was not meant to be expressed, in the joint note of Mr. Grenville and Lord Temple, the smallest idea that there had not been a full communication to them on the part of his Grace of every circumstance of the present transaction.

[1] See *Bedford Correspondence*, vol. iii. p. 381.

On the contrary, many kind thanks are returned, and Lord Temple, being perfectly satisfied with what has hitherto passed, makes no doubt but the same sense and spirit will continue the same conduct to the end, or to good effect one way or other. As his Grace means to take the trouble of apprizing the Brothers of what passes between Lord Rockingham and the King, Lord Temple, to save trouble, apprizes Mr. Rigby that he dines at Wotton next Wednesday, and shall continue there two or three days.

MR. WILLIAM GERARD HAMILTON TO EARL TEMPLE.

Monday, (July 20, 1767.)

MY DEAR LORD,—The Duke of Bedford came to town last night, for the purpose, as I presume your Lordship knows, of adjusting with Lord Rockingham the intended plan for a comprehensive Administration, which is to be laid before the King upon Wednesday next, and which most people think, though I profess myself not to be one of that number, will at last be acquiesced in by the Court. The strongest reason, and in my opinion the only one, to justify the prevailing idea that Lord Rockingham's plan will be adopted, is this, which has been often dropped since the late coalition by the friends of the Duke of Grafton, and sometimes by the Duke of Grafton himself; that if no preliminary disagreement should arise about men or measures, and the Court should in that respect be disappointed, yet that a union of such contradictory opinions, and such rival interests, that such a concordia discors is never to be feared, because it is at any moment to be dissolved.

Lord Rockingham declares, politickly at least, if not sincerely, that it will be in vain for the Court to think of creating any differences by nominating your Lordship or Mr. Grenville to be at the head of the Treasury; for much as he prefers that situation to any other, he will accept of almost any employment rather than that the plan of reconciliation which he has so much at heart, and which he will study to perpetuate, should be disappointed. By what I can collect, rather than by what is expressly said, the offers to the Duke of Bedford's friends will be lavish and without bounds, for reasons which are extremely obvious, and which tally with what has been the governing principle in the whole transaction.

To the friends of your Lordship and Mr. Grenville, the plan professed is to be extremely liberal, and it certainly is likewise extremely sensible: for Lord Rockingham is well aware that your acquiescence in his being put at the head of the Treasury is of such importance, that it is scarce possible it should be bought too dear.

According, however, to my judgment, all this, my dear Lord, is idle speculation. I cannot as yet prevail on myself to think (though I find I am almost single in my opinion) that the Court will submit to the terms, be they what they may, which shall be prescribed by Lord Rockingham, and that they will not turn themselves to defeat, by some expedient or other, what they consider as a plan for their enslavement.

My wishes may possibly give a bias to my opinion, but it still appears to me highly probable, that the treaty with the Court being put an end to, it will all terminate, where I am even yet far from being satisfied the Court did not mean it should begin, in an application to your Lordship. Yours, my dear Lord, &c., &c.,

— — —

The idea of continuing Lord Camden as a friend of Lord Chatham's is extremely entertaining, if the accounts which I hear are true, and my authority is such that I have not a doubt of them; and they are, that in all places, the most violent man against Lord Chatham, and the harshest interpreter of his long sickness, and of his late conduct, in every particular, is Lord Camden [1].

MR. WHATELY TO EARL TEMPLE.

Parliament Street, July 20, 1767.

MY LORD,—Upon coming to town this morning I found few people here so well apprized as myself of the real situation of affairs, and none able to inform me authentically of any material event subsequent to the letter of Friday last. I have related the principal facts, and explained your Lordship's and Mr. Grenville's ideas, to such of our friends as I have seen, to Sir Fletcher Norton, Augustus Hervey, Gerard Hamilton, Dr. Hay, and Wedderburn [2], and have the satisfaction to inform

[1] This is exactly in accordance with the information sent by the author of Junius to Lord Chatham in January, 1768, and which I have noticed at that date.

[2] The following letter from Wedderburn was enclosed:—

Saturday, 3 o'clock, July 18, 1767.

DEAR WHATELY,—I have not seen the face of a politician since you left town, but I sent to one to-day for your satisfaction to ask what news, and received this answer:—"The negotiation proceeds so far you, that they all approve in the strongest manner of the parts you have taken, and the sentiments you express. None is more forward in his applause than Sir Fletcher Norton, who says that your conduct has been prudent, able, manly, and honest.

Speculations upon the event do not differ so much as to afford sufficient entertainment to one who loves speculation, for the opinion is very general that this negotiation will end in smoke; that opinion is formed upon the firm language held by the courtiers, that the King must not be forced; but still I think that the event cannot be guessed at, nor do I see any circumstances on which to form a judgment. I have not heard yet of Lord Rockingham's having seen the King; I suppose he may have seen him to-day, but I find his friends are aware of the caution necessary in the opening of his plan.

Rigby does not come to town 'till to-night, having company to dine with him in the country to-day.

that the general principle of Lord Rockingham's plan, a comprehension, is accepted, and the detail is to be prepared on that foundation."

The text you see is pretty large, but I am by no means qualified to comment upon it, nor can I form any guess how far the acceptance of a general principle so stated, to which no man in his senses could avow an objection, promises fair to secure the execution of it, when the detail comes to be explained. I am more anxious to know the sentiments of those you are with, than the daily transactions here, because I look upon the one as something fixed, the other as extremely precarious; from the one I could form some idea of my own conduct, from the other, I can neither draw any principle of conduct, nor even form a reasonable speculation of any sort. This I am certain is not my case alone, but that of many others who have no other curiosity upon the present whimsical occasion but to know Mr. Grenville's sentiments. I have been more fatigued since you saw me than I was that night, but I had some comfort in reflecting that such fatigues make a man very indifferent about news, and remove a great deal of anxious expectation, which is no small comfort at a time when in my apprehension there is very little good to be expected either for the public, or for those one loves and esteems most. Yours ever.

Lord Chatham is much better: he rides out, and returns from his ride in great spirits, his fever having entirely left him. Mr. Dingley [1] is quoted to me for this intelligence; I find it is believed that he has wrote to the King to desire leave to retire. I have the honour to be, &c., &c. THOMAS WHATELY.

MR. WHATELY TO MR. GRENVILLE.

July 20, 1767.

DEAR SIR,—Wedderburn having been repeatedly desired by Burke to call on Lord Rockingham, went to him last Sunday. The Marquis told him the whole transaction between him and the Duke of Grafton; said that though it was come to an audience he still did not believe it would succeed; mentioned his difficulties in forming an arrangement, which indeed were something diminished by the facilities given by his own friends with respect to their situations; expressed great jealousy of the Court's designing only to draw from him his plan; spoke with much spleen against the men who are ready to support all Administrations; held a general language of moderation towards denominations of men, as a language consistent with a comprehensive plan; was more violent against Lord Chatham than any other; mentioned Sir Fletcher Norton civilly, but coolly; and

---

[1] Lord Chatham occupied a house at North End, Hampstead, which belonged to Dingley—the "miserable Dingley" of Junius, who was set up as a candidate for Middlesex, in opposition to Wilkes, in March, 1769; but he did not get a single vote in his favour, and was besides so much injured both bodily and mentally that he died shortly afterwards. See a letter from Dingley to Lady Chatham, in the *Chatham Correspondence*, vol. iii. p. 352, *note*.

paid great compliments to Wedderburn, and intimated that in a coalition on an extended plan his pretensions would certainly be regarded. Wedderburn told him he was flattered with his good opinion, approved of a comprehensive plan, and turned the discourse upon it into expressions of his satisfaction that it was a plan in which Mr. Grenville concurred; Lord Rockingham said, very warmly, that Lord Temple and Mr. Grenville had behaved to him in the handsomest manner possible, and Wedderburn kept the conversation to that line in order to convey to his Lordship that his connections were there, informing him at the same time that Sir Fletcher Norton had no other. This conversation shows a little of Lord Rockingham's ideas, and therefore I send it you. You desired to have all the channels of intelligence opened that could be, and in the present moment opinions are as important as facts.

MR. AUGUSTUS HERVEY TO MR. GRENVILLE.

Park Place, July 21, 1767.

MY DEAR SIR,—Mr. Whately has just called on me, and tells me he has a conveyance for a letter which will be safe. He has given me but a quarter of an hour before he is to return for this, therefore I can only thank you for your attention in desiring him to shew me *what passed*, and which I shall take not the least notice of, but which I must confess I deserve for a very unalterable and most disinterested attachment to your public and private character.

I should have been with you now, but I know many

are going backwards and forwards to you, and though I
wish you to the full as well, and desire to be publicly
known for my attachment to you, yet I cannot persuade
myself to trouble you at this hurrying time with a visit,
unless anything should happen that I should wish to
relate to you. I will tell you that I find here all is very
variously described by the different people of different
sets: but yesterday I came to town to dine with Prince
Masserano; Fitzroy dined there also, and after dinner
sought me very assiduously, and got into the garden,
where he began with the present situation. I soon
found it was intended to let me know his brother would
by no means support Lord Rockingham's Administration if accepted, and that he took many opportunities in
his long conversation to tell me his brother the Duke of
Grafton's determination on that head, and his opinion of
you, and how much all this year in the House of Lords
he had avoided any personalities against Lord Temple
or you, and knew no man so fit to be at the head of our
House. This I found was meant me *to repeat*, I therefore could not help asking him, if this was the case, how
his brother could submit to carry such a message to
Lord Rockingham as the world says he did; viz. for
him, Lord Rockingham, to form a plan of Administration to lay before the King, whilst he, the Duke of
Grafton (who carried that message), was at the head of
the present Administration and looked upon as Minister.
He told me his brother would not be Minister, that the
King had before offered all to him, if he pleased; but
that though he would not be in that situation himself,
he had no objection to another being formed, nor would
be an obstruction to the King forming any that His
Majesty thought would carry on his business; though

(as Fitzroy repeated) he, the Duke of Grafton, would not support such a one as would place Lord Rockingham at the head. I stopped him here, and asked him why, in such a conference, and when such a *task* was *imposed* on him, his Grace did not make use of the same occasion, at least to say to the King what he thought of Lord Temple and Mr. Grenville, and recommend rather those whom he now seemed to think his brother would not have objected to. However, I did not push this, because I had no mind to break it off here, and I found *this rather puzzled*. He said his brother had shown his candour and his honesty throughout by sticking to his friend Lord Chatham as long as it was possible; that by that he had shewn, that those he professed to, that he was a man of honour and was to be relied on; that any one was sure of him to whom he professed to attach himself; but the close of every sentence was always, that *his brother* never but had a very good opinion of you, and no one more sensible of your abilities and integrity; that he could not think you would submit to act under Lord Rockingham, or that Lord Temple would. I said I really knew nothing of your intentions whatever, I had been in the country, and scarce knew as much as he had now told me, but that I knew you had several friends who, like myself, were determined only to act as we saw you should approve; that I, for one, made no secret of declaring that I wanted nothing but the Admiralty, which I thought I had a right to after those I had seen there, but that I never desired it 'till you came in, or supported the Administration; that he knew I might otherwise have been there at the opening of this present Administration. He talked to me a long time about the Duke of Grafton, thinking himself not very well used in this whole affair after all he had done, and told me, confidentially, which I desire may be a secret with you, that the Duke of Grafton was determined *to oppose* any Administration formed by Lord Rockingham, that was not on the comprehensive plan that he had formerly himself expressed.

Here we were interrupted by people coming into the garden, but I think this discourse of his, sought for, and who never before inclined to talk politics with me, was certainly intended for you to know; I therefore do tell it you from myself, as I desire always to let you know anything that I think you may draw any use to yourself from, and leave you the only judge as to the rest.

I find the Bute people more up than ever last night, and by what I should guess by that, should think they know *les fonds* et *les sous des cartes mieux que nous.* It is my opinion that the Rockinghams will still, if possible, close these people without the junto, notwithstanding all said. I find, from different discourses with some of their *under people*, that they are far from the same story. I myself think this not amiss, provided the Bedfords and you keep close, and that the King should now immediately throw himself into your hands; if not, I see the Butes will push the Duke of Grafton to make one out of what they have, and what they can of the divided Rockinghams. However, of all this you will have better intelligence than my poor collections; all I know is, that I love and wish you better than them all, and I hope the Gazetteer of a day or two hence, signed *a Briton*[1], will prove such a one *of this situation* as you will not dislike. I am, &c., &c. A. Hervey.

[1] Augustus Hervey was a frequent writer in the newspapers. His

MR. WHATELY TO LORD GEORGE SACKVILLE.

July 21, 1767.

My Lord,—I gave your Lordship some reason to expect from me an account of the present negotiations before I went to Wotton.

When I came there Mr. Grenville particularly desired that the whole might be communicated to you, and he has taken my word that your Lordship will excuse his not writing himself, as he has so much upon his hands, and I have the honour of your correspondence already. In one respect, perhaps, your Lordship will be no loser by the exchange, for I shall be more particular in my information than he, engaged as he is, possibly could be, because, on the presumption that others may have made as many mistakes in their intelligence as I have in mine, I will endeavour to rectify their errors, and atone for my own, by relating to you all that has passed from the beginning, *now* authentically, for 'till now your Lord-

---

communications are usually dated from " Somersetshire," and signed " A Briton," or " A. B." The letter alluded to above, appeared in the *Gazetteer* of Wednesday, July 22. It is principally devoted to abuse of Lord Chatham and praise of the Grenvilles. The following paragraph, with which the letter concludes, is a specimen of the latter.

" Happy for this country should the day be near when a Bedford, a Temple, or a Rockingham will join all their extensive influence to a Grenville's experienced abilities and integrity! Happy must it prove to this country when the greatest families will all unite to support a man at the head of an Administration, who, from every public and private situation, can have no interest but that of his Prince and his country's; whose children are born to inherit the amplest fortunes and titles already in him and his family; one whose character as a husband, father, friend, and master, prove him to be possessed of every social virtue, as much as he is known to be free from every private vice. May such a day be near which will ensure a permanent Administration, the King's happiness, and the kingdom's prosperity."

ship's conjectures have been to the full as certain as any information I have been able to give you.

Your Lordship, therefore, will permit me to carry you back to so distant a day as Tuesday, the 7th instant, when the negotiation, which had been for some time hovering, without any apparent authority, between General Conway and Lord Rockingham, assumed a new face, by the interposition of the Duke of Grafton, who, clad in all the ensigns of power, pronounced the destruction of it, by delivering to Lord Rockingham a message from the King, importing that His Majesty wished Lord Rockingham should return to the Treasury and form his Administration, in which arrangement the Duke offered to take a part, expressing, at the same time, a desire that some indulgence should be shown to the remains of Lord Chatham's friends, which expression he explained to relate particularly to the Chancellor (Lord Camden). His Lordship asked whether he was at liberty to consult any besides his own friends; in answer to which he was told that the question had been foreseen, and that he was at liberty; but that licence *seemed to be confined to the friends of the Duke of Bedford*, as the Marquis himself expressed it in the letter he wrote to Lord Albemarle, then at Woburn, in which he informed him of the particulars of the conversation, said that he had given no answer to the proposition concerning the Chancellor, and that it was needless to enter into it with Lord Albemarle, who knew his sentiments and determination on the subject, desired him to communicate his letter to the Duke of Bedford, and offered to wait upon his Grace at Woburn, if the Duke and his friends were inclined to act with him.

The Duke's answer was, that he could take no step

without previous concert with Lord Temple and Mr. Grenville. Mr. Rigby, therefore, came to town, saw Lord Rockingham, and told him the Duke of Bedford and Mr. Grenville were one, and were resolved never to be separated. He then proceeded to Wotton, and from thence to Stowe, again to Woburn, back again to Stowe, and on Sunday afternoon met Lord Rockingham at Woburn.

The substance of these conversations, both at Wotton and Stowe, were, on the part of Mr. Rigby, the strongest assurances of the firmest union between the Duke of Bedford and Mr. Grenville, both in system and principles generally, and particularly in the American measures, and a communication of Lord Rockingham's wish to form an extensive plan of Government, which should adopt such measures concerning America, as he did not doubt the Duke and his friends would approve of.

On the part of Lord Temple and Mr. Grenville, the answer was, their perseverance in their opinions concerning America; their resolution never to depart from them; their determination to take no office themselves in the new arrangement, and never to be obtruded on the King, but accompanied by a declaration that they concurred in the idea of a comprehensive plan as the only Administration likely to be permanent; as such, they would support it fairly out of office, if the measures adopted, and particularly the capital measure of asserting and establishing the sovereignty of Great Britain over its colonies, were such as they could approve of; and if an honourable share in Government were allotted to their friends, with whom in such case they would use their good offices to induce them to accept, intimating, however, that they should expect, by waiving their own pretensions, they should meliorate the condition of their friends. No particular arrangements were then, or have been since mentioned, and both Mr. Grenville and Lord Temple confine themselves to the extensive plan and the public measures. On these principles they would support a new Administration; but these must be the principles on which alone they can themselves, or they can apply to their friends, to support the intended arrangement.

Fraught with this concurrence, Lord Rockingham returned to town, and on Wednesday, the 15th instant, met the Duke of Grafton and General Conway, to whom he said that he could not proceed without knowing whether it was His Majesty's intention that he should prepare a comprehensive plan of Administration. Upon a suggestion from his Grace that this might extend to a dismission of *all* now in office, he declared that he did not mean to convey that idea; and he declined, though much pressed, to give an answer to the proposition of Lord Camden remaining Chancellor. At the same time, he desired that if the affair proceeded any further he might be permitted to lay his ideas before His Majesty himself.

Some questions were asked tending to insinuate that an Administration, formed of Lord Rockingham's and the Duke of Bedford's friends, might have met with great facility; but that on so very comprehensive a plan the idea might be too alarming to the Court.

It is, however, worthy of observation, that whatever may have been intended by such surmises, the accession of Lord Temple and Mr. Grenville, declining all office for themselves, cannot raise any personal jealousy, or occasion any real difficulties; nor is any one made a sacrifice for them, though, perhaps, the very reverse might be said with truth; but waiving these considerations, and to go on with my story: Lord Rockingham's answer produced a letter from the Duke of Grafton[1], informing him that the King wished him to specify the plan on which he and his friends would propose to come in, in order to extend and strengthen His Majesty's Administration. Lord Rockingham replied[2] that the principle on which he would proceed would be to consider the present Administration as at an end, notwithstanding the regard he had for some of those who composed it, and that if His Majesty thought fit for his service to form a new Ministry on an extensive plan, he desired to receive his commands from himself. Upon which a letter was written to him by the Duke of Grafton, acquainting him that the King's sentiments concurred with his Lordship's in regard to the forming of a comprehensive plan; that, being desirous to unite the hearts of all his subjects, he was ready to appoint such a one as should exclude no denomination of men attached to his person and Government; and that when his Lordship had prepared such a plan, His Majesty was willing that he should himself lay it before him.

On this encouragement Lord Rockingham desired the Duke of Bedford to come to town in order to assist in forming the arrangement, and to bring with him Lord Temple's and Mr. Grenville's ideas, particularly with respect to the situations they wished for their friends. They declined to give any list of the pretensions of their friends, but desired to know more of the

[1] *Bedford Correspondence*, vol. iii. p. 366.   [2] *Ibid.* p. 367.

proposed plan before they entered into particulars. They still abided by their original system of acceding only if they approved of the measures, and of applying to their friends to accept, as a favour done, not received.

The Duke of Bedford came to town as he was desired, and at a meeting last night between him and Lord Rockingham, the Dukes of Newcastle, Portland, and Richmond, the Lords Sandwich and Weymouth, Mr. Rigby and Mr. Dowdeswell, the conference was opened by Mr. Rigby's producing one of Mr. Grenville's letters, insisting (for in more than one, besides in the conversation, he had insisted) on the condition of asserting and establishing the sovereignty of Great Britain over its colonies. To *assert* and *establish* were objected to; the terms ought to have been to *maintain* and *support;* then it was an affront to suppose that any man meant to relinquish the sovereignty of the colonies; and lastly, no man had a right to demand of Lord Rockingham his plan of operations, though his plan on this head has been required from the beginning, the approbation of it being always made the condition sine quâ non of Mr. Grenville's and Lord Temple's concurrence, and its approximation to their ideas being the only reason they can allege to their friends for desiring them to accede to an Administration in which themselves declined to take any part.

The dispute upon this point was, however, postponed to future explanation, and the next step was to consider of an arrangement; but the first person named generally for a ministerial office by Lord Rockingham being General Conway, the Duke of Bedford excepted to him, and that he understood the military line was his choice, that he was a good officer, and that he wished him to have any regiment the King pleased to give him, but he could never think of him as a Minister, and the admitting him was contrary to the principles of a total change of Administration.

Another altercation hereupon arose, and at two in the morning, no further progress being made, and no explanation given of the American system, the company parted.

The Duke of Newcastle has been to-day with the Duke of Bedford to endeavour to bring the parties again together, but unless some precise specific idea upon the American measures be stated, I see little prospect of concurrence.

In the course of this business Lord Rockingham's profession has always been to subvert the present, and establish an entirely new system. The Duke of Bedford's favourite idea has been to prevent all future instabilities, by removing those he supposes to have been the causes of the frequent changes which have happened. Lord Temple's and Mr. Grenville's principle has been to concur in the support of any Ministry which has the appearance of permanency, provided they approve of the measures: they have not been actors in any part of the transaction; they only concur upon the public grounds, and wish to remove all difficulties which their personal situations could possibly occasion to any system of national utility. They go no further, are pledged to nothing, and have no knowledge of any designed arrangement, whether of favour or proscription.

I have endeavoured to give your Lordship the best state I can of the whole; if in any part, my account of it is unsatisfactory or obscure, you will oblige me by calling for an explanation; and I know too well the value of your Lordship's opinions, not to put in some sort of claim, which I think the length of my letter gives me, to your Lordship's sentiments upon the occasion. I have the honour to be, &c., &c.

THOMAS WHATELY.

22nd July.

I should be ashamed to add a postcript to this letter for any other purpose than to conclude this period of our political history, by informing your Lordship that at a second meeting desired by Lord Rockingham, and consisting only of his Lordship, the Dukes of Bedford and Newcastle, Messrs. Rigby and Dowdeswell, the same points were stated as at the former, but the subject of America was not pushed then very far, a suggestion being dropped on the part of Lord Rockingham, that the Duke of Bedford might arbitrate upon that matter between him and Mr. Grenville. He then named Mr. Conway to be Secretary of State, and consequently the Minister in the House of Commons. Your Lordship knows the manner in which the general idea of his being in a great civil office was received the night before.

This more particular nomination was still more strongly objected to, and the conference went to no further arrangements, the Marquess insisting as strongly on the necessity as the Duke urged the impossibility of this. They therefore parted with mutual declarations, that all which had passed during the whole transaction should be considered as if it had never been, and that both parties should be entirely free from all engagements to each other[1].

[1] The following is the reply from Lord George Sackville to Mr. Whately:—

Stoneland Lodge, July 23, 1767.

DEAR SIR,—I have read with great pleasure and satisfaction the clear and distinct account which you have sent me of the present interesting negotiation. I have not the least difficulty in understanding every part of your relation, and I must be very dull as well as unreasonable if I should wish for the smallest explanation.

I am greatly obliged to Mr. Grenville for his desiring you to give yourself so much trouble for my information; I was extremely anxious to know the part he had resolved to take, and though in general I was persuaded he would act with that judgment, temper, and spirit which became him, yet it was most acceptable to learn from you the particular grounds of his present conduct.

I had wrote thus far, and was proceeding to speculate upon these events, when your letter of the 22nd was brought to me, from which I conclude Lord Rockingham has been persuaded by those about him to attempt the forming of an Administration upon his own bottom, with the assistance of the *King's friends*, that he may avoid those explanations about America which were so explicitly required, and which he could not make without allowing his former conduct to have been highly blameable. I cannot, however, yet persuade myself but that, when he seriously begins his arrangement, difficulties of so many sorts will arise, as will show the attempt to be dangerous, if not ineffectual, and that he will be reduced to court the assistance of those whose demands at present appear inadmissible.

The pains which have been taken to exclude Mr. Grenville from any share in Administration do great honour to his abilities; for it is evident that those who advise the King live in dread of seeing that real strength and stability in Administration, which might withstand all private Court intrigues, and they believe such a system cannot be formed without Mr. Grenville's being at the head of the Treasury, and they will with great reason triumph in the success of their views, if Lord Rockingham should be induced to undertake the Government of this country upon so narrow a bottom as will put him under the necessity of suing for protection to those who have the principal weight in the Closet.

It is impossible Mr. Grenville could ever depart from his principles in regard to America, and were they once adopted, he would stand personally in a most respectable light in Parliament, and must have the real though not the nominal lead in the House of Commons; how long

MR. RIGBY TO MR. GRENVILLE.

St. James's Place, July 21, 1767.

DEAR SIR,—A very obliging note which I received from Lord Temple this morning, informing me that he is to be at Wotton to-morrow, will, I hope, plead my excuse to his Lordship for desiring this letter may be sufficient for his information, as well as for yours, of what has passed since I wrote to you on Sunday last, that the Duke of Bedford intended coming to town that day, in consequence of Lord Rockingham's request [1].

such a situation could have been maintained, I cannot judge, but the impropriety of his being out of office would strike the most ignorant; yet it was becoming his character not to permit himself to be forced upon His Majesty.

It is impossible Lord Rockingham could be serious in treating with the Duke of Bedford, &c., the moment Mr. Conway was produced as Secretary of State; for setting aside all his America demerit, what arrangement could be made of employments when his Lordship had appropriated the most important to himself, had destined Mr. Yorke for Chancellor, and had brought the Dukes of Richmond and Portland to the meeting, ready for other considerable departments; what would then have been left for the Duke of Bedford's friends; and when they had been sparingly served, where were the scraps for those who belonged to Mr. Grenville and Lord Temple? However, these speculations may be spared, and we must wait the result of Lord Rockingham's conference at St. James's.

I must beg the favour of you to present my respects to Mr. Grenville, and to assure him, if the approbation of so inconsiderable an individual as I am can give him the least satisfaction, that he has it upon this occasion in the strongest manner, and that for my own part I should have been ready, had this negotiation ended amicably, to have entered into, or remained out of employment, just as it would have been most agreeable to him. I hope in the course of next week to repeat my thanks personally to you for your great goodness and attention to me. I am, dear Sir, &c., &c.   GEO. SACKVILLE.

[1] Rigby's letter to Mr. Grenville, that from Whately to Lord George Sackville, written at the desire of Mr. Grenville, and Whately's letter of the 1st of August, relating his conversation with Lord Mansfield,

On Monday morning his Lordship paid the Duke of
Bedford a visit at Bedford House, which ended in a

contain a very full and comprehensive account of this negotiation from
its commencement to its termination. The parties were all too suspicious of each other to be in earnest, and therefore none of them ever
expected it would succeed. The immediate and apparent cause of, or
at least the pretext for its failure, must, I think, be certainly ascribed
to the objection of the Duke of Bedford to the appointment of General
Conway: this, it will be subsequently seen, was the opinion of Lord
Mansfield, who seems to have been trusted by all the parties, without
himself taking any part in the negotiation. The same view of it was
subsequently corroborated by the Duke of Richmond, who, in a letter
dated Oct. 4, to Lord Rockingham, says,—" Is it not a condition of
the union with Bedford House that Conway shall not be leader of the
House of Commons ? *Is not this the very same point you broke upon
before?*"[a] There may have been other and deeper reasons, for it seems
impossible that a scheme for the union of the Rockingham and Grenville parties, which should exclude the two principal Grenvilles, could
have been proposed with any other motive than to defeat an arrangement which it was pretended to facilitate. The subject of America was
also supposed to have presented a considerable difficulty, but it was
said that some arrangement might have been made by arbitration on
that point, which was in fact suggested by Lord Rockingham himself;
and at the second meeting Mr. Rigby admits " that a *more easy and
acquiescing temper prevailed* touching the words, *concerning the future
superintendency of this country over America*[b], *and that point was not
dwelt upon;*" but that the negotiation " ended *because we would not
consent to the proposition about Conway.*" On the other hand, Lord
Rockingham, in his letters to Dowdeswell, asserts that the Grenvilles
were the sole causes of the failure of the treaty, and that without
their interference he could have managed the union with the Duke of
Bedford, who, he says, " agreed more with us in system, than George
Grenville and Lord Temple would like to have known."

There also appeared shortly after, in Almon's *Political Register*,
what was called "*An impartial account of a late interesting conference,
with the several particulars previous and subsequent.*" It seems to be a
fair matter-of-fact statement in which I can find nothing *malicious,
indecent, false,* or *scandalous,* and therefore it is difficult to understand
why it should have given such extreme offence to Lord Rockingham, to
whom Almon had previously sent a sketch of what was intended to be

[a] *Lord Albemarle's Memoirs of Rockingham,* vol. ii. p. 61.
[b] See Lord Mansfield's opinion on this subject, *infra,* p. 143.

request that his Grace, with some of his friends, particularly naming Lord Weymouth and myself, would meet him and some of his own friends, at Newcastle House, that evening.

Accordingly, at nine o'clock we three, together with Lord Sandwich, met there the Dukes of Richmond, Portland, and Newcastle, Lord Rockingham, Admiral Keppel, and Mr. Dowdeswell.

The first matter agitated was the business of America, and great exception was taken by Lord Rockingham at some words in your letter to me on the 16th instant, a

published. In transmitting a copy of it to Mr. Dowdeswell, Lord Rockingham writes, "I then suppressed my indignation on the insidiousness and malice of the contents, because I thought that if the author or authors were apprized of any warmth, they might stifle the publication or lower the venom. In a former case I have known *the school* from whence this must come, take alarm and stop. My idea was, that all our friends, nay, and even the Duke of Bedford and his friends, would be offended with this indecent and injurious proceeding. It is now published somewhat different from the sketch, but equally malicious, indecent, false, and scandalous. One great use which I hope to make of this publication is, by shewing the Duke of Bedford that my ideas in regard to Lord Temple and that school have been now fully justified."[a] Lord Rockingham no doubt attributed it to *the school* of which he supposed Lord Temple the master, and it is not unlikely that the publication was at least approved by him, if not produced under his own immediate sanction and superintendence. Lord Albemarle, too, in a letter to Lord Rockingham, with reference to this publication, says:—"It is evidently the manufacture of Lord Temple or George Grenville. I am told it will be in the Political Register for next month; and if any of our friends know of it, I wish they would suppress their feelings till it has made its appearance in print, as I then think Lord Temple's retreat from it will be difficult. You will easily imagine that an account which I suppose to come from Lord Temple, or that school, is an insidious misrepresentation of what passed, perverting facts to bear a colour and carry a construction different from the truth."[b]

[a] *Cavendish Debates, Appendix,* p. 584.
[b] *Lord Albemarle's Memoirs of Rockingham,* vol. ii. p. 55.

copy of which the Duke of Bedford had shown to Lord Rockingham in the morning, and the original of which I read to the company; I mean those words by which you so properly desire that the sovereignty of this country should be *asserted* and *established* over America. His Lordship complained, with a great deal of heat, that those words cast a reflection upon his past conduct, which no man had a right to lay to his charge, as if he had ever been for sacrificing the interest of this country, and he would make no such declaration.

The Duke of Bedford replied with all the temper possible to his arguments, and was extremely desirous to soften the American business by every means that could be suggested to preserve the honour and opinions of both sides.

Dowdeswell desired to put in the words *maintain* and *support*, instead of *assert* and *establish* above mentioned, and we passed near four hours of our meeting upon this verbal dispute; which, however, was not finally resolved upon one way or the other. That is to say, it was not determined whether or no these words should be sent to Wotton to you, to know if such explanation of your American ideas would be satisfactory or not. This being rather postponed than determined either way, it was agreed to proceed to other matters, when Lord Rockingham dropping the words General Conway, as a person whose opinion would be necessary, the Duke of Bedford immediately desired to know if that gentleman was to be considered as part of the Administration, and receiving for answer from Lord Rockingham, that he thought his advice and assistance would be of great use to any Administration, the Duke of Bedford replied, that he loved to speak his mind out about men and things; that he differed very much from his Lordship in that idea; that he imagined Mr. Conway was to return to the military, where he wished him such preferment as the King might think proper to bestow upon him, but that, in a civil department of the Administration, he could give his consent to none where Mr. Conway was to make a part; that, from what had fallen from Lord Rockingham, he found also that the Duke of Grafton was to be part of the system, which had never been explained to him before, and concerning which he did not then think it necessary to say anything; but he thought he had some reason not to take it very kindly of Lord Rockingham, then, for the first time, to hear of Mr. Conway's name, after the negotiation had been carried on for a fortnight. The Duke of Richmond desired to explain Lord Rockingham's meaning, and said that it was not to be understood that it was Mr. Conway's own desire, but that it was Lord Rockingham's wish that Mr. Conway should be part of the new system. This did not seem to the Duke of Bedford and his friends to mend the matter a great deal, and about two o'clock in the morning thus we parted.

Lord Rockingham's expressions and behaviour were the reverse of what they were at Woburn, and of what is contained in his letters to the Duke of Bedford [1]. The whole appeared to be captious, as well what fell from Lord Rockingham, as from the Duke of Richmond, who affected to take a considerable lead.

The Duke of Bedford, who was the principal mouth of our friends, behaved with infinite ability and temper, though frequently very sufficiently provoked, for nothing

---

[1] See *Bedford Correspondence*, vol. iii.

is more tiresome than to throw away good sense and reason, in answer to ignorance and obstinacy.

I hear I am accused of showing too much partiality to you and your opinions, which I think does me infinite honour.

Wednesday morning, July 22, 1767.

HAVING wrote thus far yesterday morning, and ordered my servant to be ready to set out with my letter, I was interrupted by being informed that the Duke of Newcastle, and some other of their friends, were trying to bring about another meeting, and deprecated that the business might not end as above related. The Duke of Bedford, pressed by the Duke of Newcastle in person, and afterwards solicited by a letter from his Grace [1], wrote from Lord Rockingham's, consented to another meeting, and last night the Duke of Bedford, Duke of Newcastle, Lord Rockingham, Dowdeswell, and I met.

A more easy and acquiescing temper prevailed, touching the words concerning the future superintendency of this country over America, and that point was not dwelt upon. But when we came to the next object of our deliberation, which was Mr. Conway, Lord Rockingham declared that without Mr. Conway was Secretary of State, and Minister of the House of Commons, he would go no further. The Duke of Bedford and I expressed our astonishment, and declared we would never give our consent.

It is needless to trouble you with the panegyrics upon that gentleman from his Lordship, or with the very different sentiments the Duke of Bedford and I expressed about him, which I hope and trust he will be made acquainted with.

[1] This letter is not printed in the *Bedford Correspondence*.

Thus ended the negotiation, expressly because we would not consent to this proposition about Conway.

But, before we parted, I thought it incumbent upon me, both with regard to Lord Temple's frank and honest declarations that he had made, of giving support to the system, and for any future answer which he might be supposed to give, if sent for to Court, to have Lord Rockingham declare that the whole was at an end, and to be considered as if nothing whatsoever had ever passed between us, including Lord Temple and yourself, and him and his friends. And it is thoroughly understood and declared to be at this hour, as if not the smallest intercourse had ever been between us.

To write you all the nonsense I have heard from these people would take up a volume; I could not have conceived such inability, if I had not had such a trial of it. I should have been glad to have laughed it over with Lord Temple and you at Wotton, and would have done it, but I have engaged a good deal of company at my own house just at this time, where I shall go to-morrow or next day.

The Duke of Bedford goes to Trentham to-morrow. What remains to be done at Court, whether these people will go, or be suffered to go on, you know as much as I do. Believe me, dear Sir, your most affectionate and faithful humble Servant, RICHARD RIGBY.

MR. WILLIAM GERARD HAMILTON TO EARL TEMPLE.

Wednesday, (July 22, 1767.)

MY DEAR LORD,—I shall not trouble you with an account, which would probably be an imperfect one, of the late conferences at Newcastle House, as you will certainly have received before the arrival of this letter the most exact and authentic information of everything which passed at those interviews. I shall only relate a particular or two which may not perhaps be known to others as fully, and as satisfactorily, as they happen accidentally to be known to me, and which may tend to throw some degree of light on the late (I have ever thought them) very unaccountable transactions.

In the first place, my dear Lord, I must revert to what I mentioned very early, what I have often repeated to you, and the truth of which I should have apprehended ought to have been examined into, before any negotiation whatsoever had been begun; and that was, as to the precise terms of the message delivered by the Duke of Grafton, and the private conditions on which alone Lord Rockingham was invited to accept. If everything asserted by Lord Rockingham had not been taken for granted, if any endeavours had been used to come at the truth, which might very easily have been known, and what was said by the Duke of Grafton had been fairly stated to your Lordship, the Duke of Bedford, and Mr. Grenville, I am confident there is not one of you who would not have laughed at the idea of entering into a negotiation upon such slight grounds, and on so contracted a proposition; and the idea of a Coalition might have been formidable, instead of being, what it is now become, a subject of triumph to the Court, and of ridicule to the rest of the world.

The Duke of Grafton declares publicly that the disagreement which has happened is by no means an event which gives any particular satisfaction to the Administration, or to any part of the Court; that Lord Rockingham having no authority to do what he did, it never could have been approved of. He shows a message in writing, which is worded thus: "that Lord Rockingham is desired to come to Court, to assist the Chancellor and the rest of the Administration." He denies that Lord Chatham was ever mentioned as a person totally out of the question, and adds that no offer[1] was made to Lord Rockingham of the Treasury, but confesses that in conversation he declared how weary he himself was of that employment, and how willing he should be, *if the King approved of it*, to resign it to Lord Rockingham.

Lord Holland was well enough to be to-day at the Levée, and he was in the Closet for half an hour.

Lord Northington, I understand, has been sent for, and is come to town, which I consider as no unfavourable circumstance. Lord Rockingham was at Court to inform the King, as he says, that he had no plan to lay before him, upon which he could recommend it to His Majesty to form an Administration. He was asked by a friend of mine, upon coming out of the Closet, if he was to be first Lord of the Treasury. His answer was, "not this year, whatever might happen next."

[1] This statement is distinctly contradicted by Lord Rockingham in a letter to Lord Hardwicke, in which he gives an account of his audience with the King:—"His Majesty was very gracious, commended my correctness about Rigby's visit to George Grenville, and spoke with appearance of good humour—in short, a gracious audience. He made one remark, which was on the word *offer* of the Treasury, &c., but that I was right in understanding it was the intention. As soon as I came out I took the Duke of Grafton and General Conway aside, and told them what had passed on the word *offer*. The Duke of Grafton and Conway said, that was nothing, but from the beginning I had every right to represent that matter as understood. They then asked me what His Majesty had further said; they were much surprised at my answering, 'Nothing.'"—*Lord Albemarle's Memoirs of Lord Rockingham*, vol. ii. p. 54.

The Duke of Newcastle declares he has no idea, notwithstanding the differences which have happened, that Lord Rockingham will accept of anything, unless the Duke of Bedford is satisfied, and by his means, your Lordship and Mr. Grenville, and that the present disagreement can be reconciled. His Grace, I hear, manifested a very strong leaning to the Duke of Bedford during the whole of these conferences.

I saw Lord Granby to-day after Court. The Duke of Grafton had just then told him that no determination whatsoever was come to, but, from the turn of his conversation, I could perceive his opinion was, that no further offer would be made to Lord Rockingham. The whole, he said, depended on the Duke of Grafton's continuing or giving up; in the first case, the King would certainly go on, but that the Duke of Grafton wished to retire, and would do it immediately, if it was not for the importunity of friends, who were entreating him not to give them up; and it is obvious that the Duke of Grafton's only object is to make conditions for a few persons who are attached to him.

Though Lord Rockingham insisted in the last interview that Mr. Conway should be Secretary of State, Mr. Conway himself had only two days before pressed Mr. Townshend to accept it, and said he pressed it at Lord Rockingham's desire. Mr. Townshend declined saying whether he would take or refuse 'till he was acquainted with the whole arrangement.

Many people are of opinion that this condition in regard to Conway was forced on Lord Rockingham by the Cavendishes, and that he adhered to it, not so much out of choice as to avoid disunion amongst his own friends.

What shape this chaos will take, and in what all this distraction will terminate, it is impossible to say; I, as yet, see nothing to make me change my opinion, which I have long held, that it will end in a message to Stowe. Yours, my dear Lord, &c. — — —

MR. WILLIAM GERARD HAMILTON TO EARL TEMPLE.

Wednesday night, (July 22, 1767.)

MY DEAR LORD,—Agreeable to what I hinted at in a former, and explained more at large in my last letter, the Court and the Duke of Grafton both disavow publicly the having given to Lord Rockingham a commission of the extent pretended both by him and his friends.

The Duke of Grafton declares that the very term he made use of in his conversation with Lord Rockingham was, that there should be a *coalition* of parties between Lord Rockingham and his Grace; and moreover that it could not be understood, because it was particularly explained that if Lord Chatham recovered from his present indisposition, he was again to take the lead in the Administration, as much as he had done originally, when it was first formed. These are the declarations of the Duke of Grafton. The Court, on their part, assert that the King did expressly, and in terms, reserve to himself a right of approving, rejecting, or amending the propositions which should be made by Lord Rockingham.

When your Lordship has been informed of the many material and direct contradictions between the parties negotiating, I conclude you will be very little surprised at hearing that the terms delivered in to the Duke of

Grafton by Lord Rockingham were this morning absolutely rejected by the Court.

If there is any credit to be given to the most solemn asseverations, which in politics perhaps there is not, Lord Rockingham went to Wotton upon a very boyish, unauthorised errand, to which we minor politicians in town are astonished that you great politicians in the country could pay the least attention.

The offer of the Treasury (under any limitations) to Lord Rockingham, was so directly contrary to the strongest assurances given by Lord Bute to Sir James Lowther and my friend (*Sir Fletcher Norton*), that upon the first news of it Sir James went immediately to Luton, to upbraid his Lordship, and, if he avowed the measure, to break off instantly all connection with him; and my friend gave me his honour that he would do the same.

Lord Bute declared that he had not an idea so absurd a measure could be taken; that he was utterly ignorant of it, and would show how much he disapproved of it. He came to town late last night, and the whole thing was put an end to this morning.

Your Lordship, I believe, has never found me very easy of belief, nor childishly credulous as to any insinuations that may have been thrown out by the Court; but it is my firm, well-grounded persuasion, they meant your Lordship, and your Lordship only. And I am still further of opinion, that a great part of their present difficulty arises from an apprehension that the prior offer of the Treasury to Lord Rockingham may have so much exasperated you, that you will either not accept at all, or at least not without the removal of all who style themselves the King's friends, and the introduction of all those whom he thinks his enemies.

I wish sincerely that I, or what I should prefer, that some one more capable than I, had power to remove these impressions; but 'till I receive not only an authority, but express directions from you to that purpose, I shall certainly observe a most profound silence.

Lord Bristol, I understand, now says that he has laid aside the thoughts of going to Ireland; this, together with Mr. Conway's resignation (in which I hear he persisted), will reduce the Court to the necessity of an immediate change; and the language of those about the Duke of Grafton is that Lord Townshend will go to Ireland, and Charles have the Treasury, unless he can be satisfied by a Peerage for Lady Dalkeith, and being Secretary of State for the Southern Department.

The report circulated here by Lord Rockingham's people, on his return from Woburn, was that Mr. Grenville and your Lordship, upon the promotion of your friends, were perfectly satisfied that Lord Rockingham should be at the head of the Treasury, and should support a system, so formed, out of office.

Your Lordship may rely upon it, that in these active and interesting times the *Bee*[1] will be even more industrious than usual, and that he is never employed so perfectly to his own satisfaction as when he can contribute to your service, to your information, or even to your amusement; but in return he begs one favour, which is that whatever he communicates may be confined to your Lordship only, to the exclusion even of any other single individual.

Upon this confidence, I beg leave to hint (and I shall perhaps soon write, or rather speak to you more at large

---

[1] Probably a mere figurative expression to signify the industry with which he collected political gossip.

upon it), that my friend and Sir James, irritated by repeated violation of promises, and by a total neglect, are strongly disposed to enter into the most explicit engagements with your Lordship, and to disclaim every other connection.

Wednesday night, 11 o'clock.

I AM come this moment from my friend[1]; he tells me that Sir James has been with him from Lord Bute, who is in the utmost distress. Lord Rockingham's propositions are not absolutely rejected, but only taken under consideration. My friend thinks they will be accepted by the Court, or else that your Lordship will be sent for in eight-and-forty hours, as, in his opinion, the Court will not have resolution enough to form a new Administration or to prop the old one.

Sir James has been much pacified by Lord Bute, but my friend not at all. He has refused to go near him, though frequently sent to in the course of this evening.

The idea of giving the Treasury to Mr. Townshend is disclaimed.

Lord Holland is undoubtedly the adviser of these last measures. Lord Mansfield was with him upon Monday evening, and found him provoked beyond measure at Lord Rockingham's negotiations. The Court was never most certainly in such distress. I will send your Lordship a single line to-morrow night.

I found your letter of yesterday upon my return home this evening. I think I do know your Lordship, and it is because I know you that I am, and ever must be yours, &c., &c.

[1] It may be as well to repeat that "*my friend*," in Mr. Hamilton's letters, invariably means Sir Fletcher Norton.

MR. WHATELY TO MR. GRENVILLE.

July 22, 1767.

Dear Sir,—I take the opportunity of Mr. Hervey to convey a letter to you, though his relation and Mr. Rigby's letter preclude me from giving you any account of the whimsical dissolution of our Unions.

I do not find any great variations in the Rockingham state of the conversation, from that of Rigby, and the grounds they put it on are such as must be expected from them.

I think our friends seem inclined to rest it principally on the nomination of Conway to be the Minister in the House of Commons, in the office of Secretary of State, because of that, they say, there can be but one opinion in the world, of the American measure there are two: his nomination was made absolutely a *sine quâ non*, whereas the other was never specified, and encouragement was given to expect that it might be settled by negotiation; and then this material appointment was never mentioned before by Lord Rockingham, and was too material to be kept secret.

For my part, hitherto I have always mentioned both points as the causes of the difference, the one being discussed more the first night, and the other not fully opened 'till the second.

I have had a long conversation with Lord Clive, who seemed much pleased with the attention of the communication. He begs me to assure you of his firm attachment to you, which he will himself express in a visit he proposes to Wotton in his way to Bath, which he believes will be the middle of next week. He desired me to inform you that his reception at Court was most gracious;

that His Majesty told him he hoped his Lordship would endeavour to restore the affairs of the Company at home to the good order into which he had brought them abroad; and would not allow any other person than himself to bring him the presents from the Mogul. He estimates the revenues at 2,500,000*l.* per annum clear of all charges.

As for future events, I do not pretend to speculate upon them, and I am only sure that nobody can form any conclusion better than any other.

MR. GRENVILLE TO MR. RIGBY.

Wotton, July 22, 12 at night, (1767.)

DEAR SIR,—Your letter of yesterday and of this morning was delivered to me about half an hour ago, and I immediately communicated it to Lord Temple, who is here with me.

The part which the Duke of Bedford and you have taken in your two meetings at the Duke of Newcastle's, so exactly tallies with the conduct and declarations which you have adhered to from the very beginning of this negotiation, that Lord Temple and I, who have so strongly approved of the former, must give our warmest testimony to what has now passed, and express the highest sense of the dignity, temper, and firmness with which the Duke of Bedford and his friends have behaved during the whole course of it. We must and do sincerely wish, for the sake of the public, that your plan, which was to have given efficacy, authority, and permanency to Administration, had taken effect; but with these sentiments it was impossible. What is to follow this I cannot foresee, for if Lord Rockingham, supported by the Duke of Bedford and his friends, and by all who approved the principles on which his Grace acted, was scarcely sufficient to make the last Ministry agree that their Administration was at an end, he must, I think, reduce all his demands very considerably, if under the present circumstances he hopes to succeed in any. What is the opinion of Lord Rockingham's friends upon this extraordinary proposal of putting Mr. Conway into the first office of Government after himself? Do they think this the comprehensive plan? You do not tell us what the Duke of Newcastle said to it. Surely it was unnecessary to press the Duke of Bedford to a second meeting, if he knew this was to be the issue of it; but there would be no end to comments and questions upon this extraordinary occasion. I therefore hasten to a much clearer and more agreeable topic, which is to return to the Duke of Bedford and you Lord Temple's best thanks and mine for everything you have said and done in the course of this business with regard to us, which instead of dividing us, the purpose probably for which the plan of delusion was set on foot, has only served to cement our union if possible still more strongly, and add to that affectionate regard with which I am, &c., &c.,

GEORGE GRENVILLE.

P.S. I assure you that we have drunk the health of the Duke of Bedford[1] and his friends in a bumper in the Claremont style, with our earnest wishes to have had you here had it been possible.

---

[1] See *ante*, vol. iii. p. 393, Mr. Grenville's opinion of a negotiation, "*in which the poor Duke of Bedford is so much disgraced.*"

MR. WILLIAM GERARD HAMILTON TO EARL TEMPLE.

Friday morning, (July 24, 1767.)

MY DEAR LORD,—I give you the trouble of these few lines, for the sake of acknowledging the two letters which you did me the honour of writing to me, both dated from Wotton : one I received by the post, and the other by a private conveyance. Your Lordship will naturally imagine that very little could have occurred in the course of yesterday. As far as could be collected from appearances, Conway is endeavouring to reconcile Lord Rockingham and the Duke of Grafton, and some are of opinion, with a strong probability of success. It now turns out that the late negotiation took its rise neither from the King nor from the Duke of Grafton, but from Mr. Conway's representing in the Closet, that Lord Rockingham had of late, in several conversations, expressed himself as extremely desirous of contributing to the support of His Majesty's Government, which induced the King to send by the Duke of Grafton the message I mentioned to your Lordship in my last letter.

It is now, I understand, doubted whether the express which was sent to Lord Northington required his coming to town, or only that he should give his advice in writing.

My mind was so perfectly made up that the negotiation neither could nor ought to go on, that I was as little disappointed as I was concerned, when I heard of its being broke off.

A few days will certainly produce some Administration or other, no business having been done for this last fortnight by either of the Secretaries of State.

I am unwilling to leave the neighbourhood of town 'till something is adjusted, or as long as I can contribute, by continuing here, to your Lordship's information. I shall, however, for the future, trouble you less constantly with letters, and only when what has occurred shall be material enough to be communicated. All Lord Rockingham's people were at Court yesterday, in order to demonstrate (the contrary of which no one ever suspected) that they were not offended with the Court, and were far from being disinclined to enter into His Majesty's service.

With the world in general, the appearance of practicability in your Lordship may possibly do service; but I am apprehensive that another and less favourable construction is put by the Court upon what lately passed. They argue thus: That when a plan is laid to annihilate those who call themselves, and who are considered at St. James's, as the King's friends, Mr. Grenville and your Lordship will sacrifice yourselves for the accomplishment of that end; but upon a proposition from the Court you won't even negotiate, but insist upon an absolute, unconditional offer of the whole.

To exclude the Court, you will submit to divide with Lord Rockingham, but to exclude Lord Rockingham, you won't condescend to participate with the Court.

Upon the whole, my dear Lord, I have not a doubt but that those who influence the Court are at this moment disposed more favourably to you than to others, but that they are restrained by one general and one particular consideration.

The first is a fear that your view is to wait for a favourable opportunity of revenging yourself upon Lord Bute, and the last, that you will not consent to Lord Camden's continuance; a point which, unless I am much mistaken, will be strongly laboured. Yours, my dear Lord, &c., &c.

MR. WILLIAM GERARD HAMILTON TO EARL TEMPLE.

Friday, (July 24 ? 1767.)

MY DEAR LORD,—Whately's return from Wotton and from Stowe is expected this evening, and when my friend has learnt exactly the sentiments of your Lordship and Mr. Grenville, I am persuaded it is his intention to act conformable to them; and the late confusions have given him a weight with Lord Bute, which for this twelvemonth past I believe he has not had.

It is but justice to inform you that Lord Rockingham's people speak both of your Lordship's conduct and Mr. Grenville's in terms of strong commendation, and declare that they are sensible of your importance, and are determined not to acquiesce in anything that can be proposed unless you are both satisfied.

There is one reason which inclines me to do upon the present occasion what I am not disposed to do upon any, that is, to give credit to their declarations, and it is the strong aversion which they feel, and everywhere express, to the Duke of Grafton, and their eagerness to exclude him from all situations in Government.

Much industry having been employed to alarm the friends of Lord Bute, and to persuade them that their destruction was the very casus fœderis in this reconciliation of parties, Lord Rockingham has, I think prudently enough, studiously endeavoured to discourage any such idea, and Burke has been sent to Wedderburn upon that errand.

The Court assert confidently (but they gain no belief) that Conway will, if pressed to it, continue; and they add that Lord Rockingham's conduct in soliciting a reconciliation with your Lordship and Mr. Grenville, by means of the Duke of Bedford, has produced an entire disagreement between him and Mr. Conway. I profess I should think this not improbable, because I know that Lord Hertford and Mr. Walpole [1] were both astonished, and expressed themselves much exasperated upon the report that such an accommodation was likely to take place.

I perceive that Lord Granby and the rest of the Cabinet are dissatisfied with the Duke of Grafton's conduct in the management of the late negotiations, and I think that his weariness of business, and his eagerness to get to Newmarket with his mistress, made him leave more than he should have left in the hands of Conway.

I know how difficult it is to decide upon any measure that has been taken without an exact knowledge of the facts and circumstances upon which it was founded; but I think, nevertheless, that I can see distinctly it was scarce possible for your Lordship to do otherwise than you did in the late negotiation: yet in my view of things I consider the offer which has been made by the Court to Lord Rockingham, and his conduct in consequence of it, as very unfortunate, and as introductory of a new difficulty, where the embarrassments were already more than sufficient. Not because I suppose any positive engagement has been taken by your Lordship, but because I know you will consider an honorary engagement as equivalent to a positive one; and if Lord Rockingham has declined without your assistance, you will in return think yourself bound to decline without his, and will never suffer yourself to be outdone in a conflict of generosity.

---

[1] Horace Walpole was first cousin to Lord Hertford and General Conway, and had much influence with both. See *post*, p. 103, *note*.

Nothing, however, can alter my opinion as to the original object of this negotiation, and that the plan of accommodation was set on foot, and is continued, with a view of purchasing the Duke of Bedford and his friends, and with hopes that by time, attention, and opportunity, they may be gradually attached to Lord Rockingham, and drawn off from their connection with your Lordship and Mr. Grenville.

At the same time I am sensible how expedient it was to hold out such language as might not drive Lord Rockingham to accept the offers which had been made to him.

To-day, I understand, the Duke of Grafton has desired a fuller and more particular explanation of the proposal made by Lord Rockingham, which Lord Rockingham has declined delivering to the Duke of Grafton, but has expressed his readiness to lay it before His Majesty.

From this circumstance I am led to apprehend that the Court will not put an absolute negative on any plan 'till the arrangements are drawn out at length; entertaining very sanguine expectations that the contracting parties will stumble at the threshold, and that the King will be saved the odium of refusing what shall be proposed to him, by the previous disagreement of the parties amongst themselves.

This evening it is strongly reported that Mr. Townshend will at last accept of being Secretary of State, and that Lord North will be Chancellor of the Exchequer. For myself, I don't believe it. I shall have the honour of writing to you again by the coach on Tuesday. Yours, &c., &c.

Lord Bute went out of town early this morning.

MR. WHATELY TO MR. GRENVILLE.

July 25, 1767.

Dear Sir,—I saw Mr. Rigby this morning, and offered to convey any letters to you. He does not write, but desired me to tell you that Lord Rockingham having sent an offer to wait upon the Duke of Bedford, his Grace returned for answer that he was going towards Grosvenor Square, and would save his Lordship the trouble. This was I think on Thursday morning, and when the Duke called, Lord Rockingham told him, that as his Grace had been concerned in the transaction, he thought it right to communicate to him the conclusion of it, by informing him of the particulars which had passed in the Closet, where he told the King the steps he had taken, and concluded with stating the whole affair as at an end. When he mentioned the honour His Majesty had done him in thinking of putting him at the head of the Treasury, the King said he had authorized nobody to offer him that situation; and in the course of the conversation Lord Rockingham hoped that His Majesty would never suffer any *body of men in office* to act in general opposition to his Administration, though individuals might differ in particular measures, by which stroke he intimated to Rigby that he had done for himself. At coming out Lord Rockingham told the Duke of Grafton what the King had said concerning the Treasury; the Duke waived the subject, but by no means admitted that he had exceeded his authority. In a conversation with Rigby since, Lord Rockingham threw out that notwithstanding what had passed he should not despair of forming a stable Administration, if he were to set about it, without the assistance of Bedfords or Grenvilles: and being asked in the course of the conversation when his Lordship proposed to go out of town, he said in two or three days *if he could:* from which hints Rigby imagined that he had some hopes of coming in with his own friends only; and I just now hear from two different hands, one of them a very good one, that Conway has been attempting something of that kind, but that it is certainly over. I cannot find reason to believe that it has been anything more than a negotiation between Lord Rockingham and Mr. Conway, without the knowledge of the Closet, and whatever it may have been it is entirely at an end [1].

[1] This account is partially corroborated by Horace Walpole, in the *Memoirs of George III.*, pp. 86-90, where it appears that Lord Hertford and the Duke of Grafton, at the instigation of Walpole, had both advised the King to renew the offer of the Administration in form to Lord Rockingham. The King consented that the offer should again be made, but he would not yield to send himself to Lord Rockingham. Walpole continues—" The Duke, Mr. Conway, and I, consulted on the best method of delivering the message. Conway thought it was best to do it as I had advised, in a free, friendly way, exhorting the Marquis to let them all re-unite in their old system; and Conway added, 'If they refuse, your Grace and I must then do the best we can.' At night (July 23rd) the Duke, Conway, and Lord Rockingham met. The Duke, in the King's name, offered him the Treasury, in the amicable way agreed on. Lord Rockingham was all reserve, and would only say this was no message. The Duke, offended, and naturally cold and shy, would not repeat positively that it was; and thus the meeting broke off. * * * * * That Rockingham fluctuated between ambition and distrust was evident, for late that very night the Duke of Richmond came to Lord Hertford's door, and sent for me down to his chariot, when, though ashamed of the silly message imposed upon him, he made me this frantic and impertinent proposal from Lord Rockingham, which I was desired to deliver to Mr. Conway, that the latter would engage the King to allow the Marquis to try again to get the Bedfords —the Bedfords whom, two days before, Rockingham and all his party had absolutely broken with, and published as the most treacherous of men, and who had proscribed Conway himself. Should the Bedfords again refuse, the Marquis notified that he would then deign to accept the Administration. I neither wished his acceptance, nor chose to run

Charles Townshend sent to desire leave to wait on Mr. Rigby yesterday, and told him that he heard the Duke of Bedford had proscribed him. Rigby assured him that his name was never mentioned but once, and that was at the close of the whole affair, when he (Rigby) reminded Lord Rockingham that, by insisting upon Conway's having the lead, he had forgot there was such a man in the House as Mr. Townshend, &c., and told him that the arrangement had never gone so far as to bring up any discussion about his situation. Townshend was satisfied with Rigby's answer, launched out against Lord Rockingham, held up much to the Duke of Bedford and you, stated the present system as deplorable, said that he had stated it so to the King, yet believed it was resolved for the present to go on, but thought it impossible to stand the Sessions. His resentment against Lord Rockingham for neglecting him was sharp and real, and Rigby thinks he will not accept the Southern Department, if it should be offered to him, but understands that he will not at present resign. It is said, too, that the Duke of Grafton has given assurances that he will not distress the King's affairs, and will therefore continue 'till something can be done; and yet, unsettled as those affairs must be, he has gone out of town to stay 'till Tuesday. The report of Lord Northington's being sent for is still believed, but surely if it was true when I first heard it he should be come by this time. His language, as I hear from one who was at the Grange on Tuesday, was that the Rockinghams were fools for pushing so violently; that the King, by ——, must

any farther risks of it. Conway, to whom I communicated it, treated this senseless proposal as it deserved; and the Duke of Richmond did not attempt to defend it."

come to Grenville, and he hoped he would not be such a fool as to do too much at once; but still this gentleman thought that if his Lordship was sent for he would for the present press the Duke of Grafton to stay in office [1].

To my great surprise I hear, from more quarters than one, that the Duke of Grafton is inclined to the Bedfords and Grenvilles in preference now to the Rockinghams. I believe he is not pleased with the part which the Marquess has taken in this affair, and was not perhaps so well disposed towards him as was generally imagined. You have the satisfaction entire of knowing that your and Lord Temple's conduct is most universally approved by your friends, for the prudence and manliness of it; in the world abroad, for its moderation and public spirit; and at Court, for the respectfulness of it.

I heard yesterday that there were strong symptoms of an inclination in the King to call upon Lord Mansfield for his advice. It is rather, I own, unexpected, and yet the appearances are strong of a great leaning that way. Lord Mansfield, though four times sent for, declined to attend Lord Rockingham and the Duke of Newcastle to the meeting with the Duke of Bedford, and it has been observed that his language on the late occasion has corresponded exactly with yours: all this was said to me

---

[1] "At last," writes Horace Walpole, in a letter dated July 31, to Mr. Montague, "all is subsided; the Administration will go on pretty much as it was, with Mr. Conway for part of it. The fools and the rogues, or, if you like proper names, the Rockinghams and the Grenvilles, have bungled their own game, quarrelled, and thrown it away;" or, as Lord Northington is supposed to have characteristically expressed himself,—

"What that rogue loses, this rogue wins;
Both are birds of a feather;
Here's d—— the Outs, and d—— the Ins,
And d—— them all together."

in a way that plainly proved to me there was some design in mentioning it. He is a very good friend of yours who told it me, and I thought he wished first to know whether, if Lord Mansfield was consulted, he would advise the sending for you, upon which I enlarged upon the length of your intimacy, and the closeness of your connection; but I imagined he *principally* meant to insinuate that some attention to his Lordship would be peculiarly proper just now, and particularly that he should be apprized of all the circumstances of your conduct, and the motives for it, or, if you have not already written to him at all, perhaps you will see this as a reason for doing it, or, if you have written to him a short letter, you may make a fuller communication in the shape of copies of yours and Lord Temple's letters: no harm can be done; there can be no impropriety in it, and should this gentleman's apprehensions (which are not generally light and groundless) prove true, it may be of service that his Lordship should be perfectly master of all the circumstances; but if you do write to him, it must be done soon, or he will be set out upon the circuit.

I hear nothing material in the shape of a common report; those who generally judge best, incline to think that the present Administration will stand a little longer.

MR. CHARLES LLOYD TO EARL TEMPLE.

York Buildings (Salt Office), Saturday, July 25, 1767.

My Lord,—Indeed I did not mean to draw your Lordship into any correspondence. Your time is much better employed than in thinking of the political bubbles which are daily forming and breaking to the amusement and surprise of such idle people as myself. Even since Wednesday, I am well assured that Mr. Conway has been negotiating with Lord Rockingham to accede to the present system, but to no purpose. The King told Lord Rockingham in the Closet that he had never commissioned any one to offer his Lordship the Treasury. The Butes are in such high spirits, that they affect joking and laughing at the late storm which seemed to be impending: Jenkinson, I hear, calls the late conferences the meeting of the Barons at Runnymede. Ross Mackye[1] congratulates Royalty on being freed from its imprisonment. This may be a good Scotch jest, but translated into English runs heavily enough.

Lord Rockingham and his friends dined at the Thatched House on Thursday; the multitude was divided; most of them, especially the Newcastle part, were for strict and close connection with the Duke of Bedford. The only point they seem to unite in is, the doing justice to Lord Temple's conduct and Mr. Grenville's.

Many people will assert that Lord Chatham is re-

[1] John Ross Mackay was M.P. for Kirkcudbright. Wraxall, in his *Historical Memoirs,* says of him that he had been Private Secretary to Lord Bute, and afterwards, during seventeen years, Treasurer of the Ordnance. He relates some anecdotes concerning the amount of money said to have been expended in the purchase of votes from the Members of the House of Commons in support of the Peace of 1763, and that Mackay said that he had himself secured above 120 votes, and that 80,000*l.* had been set apart for the purpose. The authority of Wraxall in such matters is, however, not to be depended upon. He was never admitted to the confidence of official persons; and although in his relation of public occurrences he is very amusing and often correct, his private anecdotes must be considered, at the best, but apocryphal.

covering. If he should wake, and miss the crown on his pillow, he will surely address the Duke of Grafton in the pathos of Henry IV. :—

> " Is he so hasty, that he doth suppose
> My sleep my death?
> What! canst thou not forbear me half an hour?
> Then get thee gone, and dig my grave thyself."

Sir James Gray[1] sets out for Spain on Tuesday next: he told me to-day he does not expect to reach Madrid, and yet he is resolved to go. I have the honour to be, with great respect, &c., &c. CHARLES LLOYD.

Lord Northington has been sent for these two days, but Dr. Tarrant (perhaps to pay court to his patron) *swears* he will not come let who will send for him.

MR. WILLIAM GERARD HAMILTON TO EARL TEMPLE.

Monday, (July 27? 1767.)

MY DEAR LORD,—I am to acknowledge the honour of your letter, which I received by the hands of Mr. Hervey. No proposal can be more agreeable to me, than the proposal of coming to Stowe, and upon this day se'nnight I flatter myself I shall be able to wait upon you.

A general opinion seems to prevail, though on what it is grounded I am at a loss to conjecture, that no measure of any sort will for some time to come be taken by the Court, in regard to a new arrangement. But not-

---

[1] He was appointed Ambassador to the Court of Madrid, having been previously Envoy Extraordinary at Naples. He died suddenly after his return from Spain, in January, 1773.

withstanding this notion has been pretty generally conceived, I would recommend it to your Lordship not to set your heart too much upon your expedition to Mount Edgecumbe, as it seems to me not altogether improbable, that I may have this summer, as I had the last, the honour of attending you from Stowe to London.

Mr. Conway had three weeks ago acquainted the Foreign Ministers within his Department, that he should no longer receive any dispatches, or hold any conferences upon business; and in consequence of this declaration, he had for some time past neglected the one and the other, but on Friday he did both. Lord Rockingham has, I understand, confessed to Mr. Rigby, that his last interview in the Closet was a very cold one, and that the King explained to him that he had given no authority whatsoever to any one to make an offer of the Treasury, which was filled perfectly to his satisfaction by the Duke of Grafton, and from which his Grace, *while he thought proper to continue*, should never be removed.

Lord Bristol has to-day made a public declaration of his not intending to go to Ireland, and pretends that he has formed that resolution since he received an account of the Chancellor's death [1]. His Lordship went yesterday into the Closet, after the Drawing-room, and it was suspected he had in view the asking the Seals of Ireland for some one, before the Ministers, who don't return to town 'till Wednesday morning for the Levée, could be consulted: but I have strong reason to believe

---

[1] John Bowes had been Lord Chancellor of Ireland since the year 1757, and in 1758 had been created Baron Bowes of Clonlyon, County Meath. He was successively Solicitor and Attorney General in Ireland, and as he died without issue the title became extinct.

that His Majesty had been apprized of the Chancellor's death, and cautioned against too precipitate a determination upon that subject, and that his Lordship did by no means succeed in his request.

I should not, my dear Lord, have been without hopes, if things had been circumstanced exactly as I could wish, and your authority had been as decisive and unbounded as it ought to be, that upon this event, provided no material English purpose had interfered, you would have been kind enough to consider my friend Mr. Hutchinson. No man's qualifications are greater, and no one's pretensions can be superior. Ireland never bred a more able, nor any country a more honest man[1]. I have seen my friend since he had heard of this vacancy, and I think I can discover that he is turning it in his mind, to try if it can be made to answer his purpose. He told me, however, he was so circumstanced, that from the present people he should certainly take nothing, and in a conversation I lately had with him, I think he went so far as to say that the night before Mr. Grenville left town, he had told him he would never accept without his approbation.

What my friend wishes is, that Wilmot[2] could be

---

[1] Mr. Hamilton's honest friend had also the reputation of being one of the most insatiable and rapacious political jobbers of his time. It was of him that Lord North said:—" If you were to give him Great Britain and Ireland, he would ask for the Isle of Man for a potato-garden." He was at one and the same time reversionary Secretary of State, Major of the 4th Regiment of Horse, Provost of Trinity College, Dublin, &c., &c., and procured an Irish peerage for his wife by the title of Baroness Donoughmore. Hutchinson died at Dublin, in September, 1794.

[2] Lord Campbell, in his biography of Chief Justice Eardly Wilmot, has drawn a most amusing picture of his characteristic, but most unprofessional dread of the perils of promotion. Having been nominated a puisne judge of the Court of King's Bench without his knowledge or

bribed to take the Rolls, and that he might succeed Wilmot, provided Sewel would go to Ireland, which, by the way, he declared a month ago, in a conversation with my friend, he never would. If that should be the case, I don't perceive how any very considerable object can be obtained, by the disposal of that piece of preferment.

I must not, however, omit to inform your Lordship that my friend, in about ten days at farthest, proposes going to Wotton, and from thence paying a visit to Stowe, where I may very possibly meet him. He certainly has hopes of being able by that time to say something that will be very satisfactory, and perhaps likewise to consult your Lordship and Mr. Grenville, about the propriety of his acceptance, in case any Law-preferment should be vacated.

From every motive of opinion and of interest, I am sa-

---

consent, it was with the greatest reluctance that he submitted to the King's pleasure in accepting the appointment. In the judicial crisis which followed the death of Sir Dudley Ryder, Wilmot was again in danger of unsought promotion, until the Attorney-General, Murray, prevailed over the disinclination of the Duke of Newcastle, and was made Lord Chief Justice of England. When the Great Seal was put in commission upon the resignation of Lord Chancellor Hardwicke, Wilmot was made one of the Commissioners, and it was expected that he would shortly after become Lord Chancellor. He was frightened out of his wits by the apprehension of the Great Seal, that "much-coveted bauble" being offered to him, and he determined, at all events, to refuse the "pestiferous piece of metal." "I will not," he said, "give up the peace of my mind to any earthly consideration whatever. Bread and water are nectar and ambrosia when contrasted with the supremacy of a Court of Justice." He was subsequently doomed to another act of compulsion when he was appointed to the Chief Justiceship of the Common Pleas. He always steadily resisted the acceptance of the Great Seal, which was repeatedly pressed upon him both before and after the melancholy catastrophe of Mr. Charles Yorke, though he might have taken it with any peerage, pension, or reversion he would have named. He resigned his Chief Justiceship in 1776, and died at a great age in 1792.

tisfied he is endeavouring to allay the fears of Lord Bute, who is now and has been in town for some days past[1].

Lord Bristol's declarations that he will not go to Ireland must reduce the Court to the necessity of making an immediate change, at least in that department, and they will probably dispose of that employment in conformity to their general system.

It is not, I think, refining too much to suppose that the pains His Majesty took, in explaining to Lord Rockingham that there was no authority for making him an offer[2] of the Treasury, proceeds from an apprehension, that unless that impression was removed, a proposal hereafter to be made would be much less acceptable to any person who might be desired to hold that employment. There are who report, and who should know what they report, that the Duke of Bedford and Lord Rockingham, and their common friends, are likely to be again united: I don't wish it, and therefore I am determined not to believe it. Yours, my dear Lord, &c., &c.,

―――

[1] Burke writes to Lord Rockingham at this time, "Lord Bute is seldom a day out of town: I cannot find whether he confers directly and personally with the Ministry, but am told he does."

[2] See *ante*, p. 88, note. Mr. Grenville also, in a letter to Whately on the same day, says, "I had heard before that the Court absolutely denied that any offer had been made to Lord Rockingham of the office of First Lord of the Treasury, which I find has now been confirmed to him by the King himself. This I should think must be very disagreeable to Lord Rockingham, especially if it is true that the Duke of Grafton denies it likewise, which is not inconsistent with his general answer that he (the Duke of Grafton) had not exceeded his authority." As I have before stated, however, this story is completely *contradicted* by Lord Rockingham, in a letter to Lord Hardwicke, on the authority of the King himself.

LORD LYTTELTON TO EARL TEMPLE.

Bristol, July 27, 1767.

DEAR COUNTRY MOUSE[1],—As much a city mouse as you think me, I left London before your letter was writ, which I did not receive until last night on my arrival here, Mr. Lloyd instead of it having sent me one for Lord Buckingham.

However, though I have not been at Court for some time, I have been in the house of a great mouse, called Percy of the Vale[2], who may possibly be there before you, and is very willing to be there with any mice whatsoever, now the great cat[3] is gone; yet I think that Mouse Rockingham is not much in his favour, and that he had rather eat his bacon with you or your brother. I have more to tell you about him, which I shall reserve 'till I see you.

It does not surprise me that the late assembly of mice broke up *re infectâ*, their desires and connections being so different, that it is a much greater wonder they ever came together, than that they have separated. Such unnatural alliances are never lasting; but this trial has shown what can last, and will, in the end, be superior to every other connection.

In the meanwhile, if we remain country mice, there is no great harm done. Mouse Whately tells me that your conduct and your brother's on this occasion meets with the highest approbation even from those who have no prejudices in your favour. And great praise is due

---

[1] Lord Lyttelton seems to have been fresh from the study of Horace, as he evidently writes in allusion to the well-known illustration of the Town and Country Mouse.

[2] The Duke of Northumberland.   [3] Lord Chatham.

to Mouse Bedford; but yet I own to you, I don't quite comprehend his idea of your brother's taking the lead in the House of Commons, out of office, with the Marquess at the head of the Treasury; or (if that be not meant) why Conway might not be Secretary of State as well as any other, unless his Grace intended that office for Charles Townshend, which I have not heard that he did. But I repeat it again, our coalitions must be more homogeneous, to form anything solid. My ramble will be from hence to Piercefield, then to Ross, and lastly to our friend Velters Cornewall at Mochas Castle (Court?) near Hereford, where I shall stay from the 3rd to the 6th or 7th of August, and then to my wood at Hagley, where your brother will find me "*Prærupti nemoris patientem vivere dorso,*" unless you and he shall say to me, "*Vis tu homines urbemque feris præponere sylvis?*"[1] In which case I will obey you, and come out of my hole.

It seems as if the Court Mice must necessarily call for more help than they have among themselves at this time, and where can they call but on you? Perhaps you will not come when they do call, and indeed the Mouse of Stowe has no great temptation to remove to the Treasury Office, in the present state of the world, and after a predilection shown to another. Much, I think, will depend on the part that the Scotch Mouse[2] has really taken in this business. But these matters will be more properly talked of than written. If you are not sent for to town, why will you not come to Hagley for two or three days, with your brother, or before him? Your arch[3] is finished,

---

[1] *Horace*, lib. ii. Sat. 6.   [2] Lord Bute.

[3] The Corinthian Arch at the entrance of the Park at Stowe. It was said to have been designed by Mr. Thomas Pitt, afterwards Lord Camelford.

and you are there as much at home as at Stowe. Make Lord Aylesford's[1] your inn, and dine with me the next day. I will give you a cup of fine Malmsey *rich and healing, pray dip your whiskers and your tail in.* My love to the she Mouse, I flatter myself she will like to be of the party.

MR. WILLIAM GERARD HAMILTON TO EARL TEMPLE.

Wednesday, (July 29, 1767.)

MY DEAR LORD,—I am honoured by the receipt of your letter of the 25th. Lord Eglintoun's servant delivered it to me yesterday. I shall soon, I hope, have the pleasure of conversing with you upon the subject of it at large; but, in the mean time, I cannot help observing that it is of little importance what the Court may think of your Lordship's conduct, while the world in general consider it as both honourable and judicious; and while your friends (the part of the world every man must be most solicitous about) must look upon it as disinterested with regard to yourself, and affectionate with regard to them, in the last degree.

Lord Camden has been sounding my friend, if he would refuse the Rolls, provided the King should offer it to him, and Sewel should accept the Seals in Ireland. My friend prudently refused giving any answer to these hypothetical offers; but my persuasion is, though I may very possibly be mistaken, that he will refuse whatever they propose to him.

Lord Chief Justice Wilmot will, upon no inducement, quit the Common Pleas.

[1] Packington Hall, near Coleshill, Warwickshire.

Lord Camden's account of Lord Chatham is, that there are no hopes of him, and that he is now much worse than ever; but if the Duke of Grafton will continue, he says he shall be perfectly satisfied: that the Administration would then go on extremely well, and that he himself is the last man who will be for giving the thing up [1].

It is of very little importance what are the Duke of Grafton's sentiments, and still less what are his Lordship's, provided Lord Bute continues of the mind he seems to be in at present. His Lordship sent on Monday night for Wedderburn, and had with him a very long conversation. It began by upbraiding his conduct and my friend's for entering into a factious opposition to the King's Government, declaring, at the same time, that he did not so much disapprove the object they had in view, which he supposed was to make your Lordship and Mr. Grenville Ministers, as the means they had taken to bring it about; that the storming the Closet seemed to be the present plan; that, upon any other idea, it was both in your Lordship's power and Mr. Grenville's to have made yourselves Ministers at any time you had thought proper, and that, 'till you were, he was sensible there could be no Government that would be serviceable or reputable. Wedderburn of course said how disinclined you was to force yourself into Government, and recommended it to him to advise the King to

---

[1] Respecting Lord Camden the author of *Junius* thus writes to Lord Chatham on the 2nd of January following:—"The Chancellor, on whom you had particular reasons to rely, has played a sort of fast and loose game, and spoken of your Lordship with submission or indifference, according to the reports he heard of your health; nor has he altered his language until he found you were really returning to town."—*Chatham Correspondence*, vol. iii. p. 302. See also *ante*, p 64.

send for your Lordship and Mr. Grenville, whom he did not doubt would be found in every proposition as accommodating as could reasonably be expected. This, as near as I could collect, was the substance of their conversation. Lord Bute said he wished to see my friend, but that his behaviour, both to him and Mr. Mackenzie, gave him very little encouragement to think that he would come. My friend refused going to him upon such a general intimation, but said, upon an express message, he was at any time ready to wait upon him; and I have a belief, but not a certainty, that the express message has been sent.

Upon all this, my dear Lord, and upon a great deal more, I have but one observation to make, and it is this. The Court are apprehensive that you will make offers to Lord Rockingham and his friends, and they wish, if possible, to know your sentiments upon that subject. It is for your Lordship's consideration, how far it will be expedient to be communicative upon that point; but, in my own mind, I am convinced this is at present the single remora, and that the exclusion of their own people, and the admission of Lord Rockingham's, is the governing apprehension of the Court.

That the late negotiation has produced a disagreement between Mr. Conway and the Duke of Grafton is generally believed, and is highly probable. Mr. Conway's idea of becoming a part of the coalition, of dropping his Grace, and embarking again with Lord Rockingham, was insincere and interested beyond example, and in that light it is universally considered.

The friends of the Duke of Grafton complain exceedingly that your Lordship and Mr. Grenville, and the followers of the Duke of Bedford, have shown to Lord

Rockingham an attention which they have denied his Grace, by being willing to acquiesce that the one should be put at the head of the Treasury, and refusing to be satisfied if the other continued there.

The fashion of leaving legacies to Lord Chatham does not seem as yet to be quite over. It is reported that a person in the neighbourhood of Hayes has left him some land, which, while he lived there, he wanted to purchase, and which the man then refused to dispose of: the value is talked of as being about 2000*l*.

Lord Bristol is of opinion, that a very few days will bring to light the new system, be it what it may. I am rather concerned that your Lordship should set out upon your Cornish expedition sooner than you first intended, as the Court, however ripe they may be for their decision, may not be ripe to act in consequence of it before the 10th of next month.

I shall, however, at all events, have the happiness of kissing your hands at Stowe, and of assuring you, my dear Lord, how faithfully and affectionately, I am, &c., &c.

MR. WHATELY TO MR. GRENVILLE.

July 29, 1767.

DEAR SIR,—I went to wait on Lord Mansfield, with the letter to him, and not meeting with him, sent it, accompanied with a line from myself, offering to attend him at any time and to give him information of any particulars he might wish to know, which I told him you had in a letter to me desired me to do.

The inclosed note shows, I think, an inclination to receive that information, and a satisfaction in the offer.

I shall carry with me your letters, those between the Duke of Grafton and Lord Rockingham, and one of Lord Rockingham's to the Duke of Bedford, which is merely narrative. I mean, in short, to possess him of all the *facts* from papers, but to produce your *sentiments* only, not those of others, which kind of communication you are certainly at liberty to make to whom you please.

The account Mr. Rigby gave me of the answer made by the Duke of Grafton to Lord Rockingham, concerning the offer to him of the Treasury, was not very precise, but yet, as far as I could collect, it seemed to be far more particular than a mere general assertion that he had not exceeded his authority; it was, desiring not to enter into the subject, but insinuating that the *idea* was that Lord Rockingham should have the Treasury; and yet it is said for his Grace, on all hands, that he denies the *offer* was made him. It is a strange puzzle. You will see presently Lord Bute's solution of it, which I think comes nearer to a solution than any other. There has certainly been some sort of negotiation since; Burke's account of it to me yesterday was, that there had been two meetings; that the Duke of Grafton and General Conway had pressed Lord Rockingham to come in with his own friends; that he soon put an end to the idea, that he was gone out of town, and that perhaps he might never come into office; he would not, except in a manner that he liked.

The report of Lord Northington being sent for proves, as I apprehended, not to be true. Whether Lord Mansfield will be consulted I do not know, but there is good ground to surmise the probability of it. I shall, however, be particularly cautious not to let him suppose that I ever had any conversation with any one relative to him or his sentiments, and I shall govern myself in my communication to him, by the degree of frankness and of curiosity which I shall see in his Lordship. I heard once of his being with Lord Bute and Jenkinson for four hours; but I had some reasons then to doubt the truth of it, and I do not think it makes any great difference whether it be true or not.

Wedderburn was on Wednesday sent for by Lord Bute, who, you know, has not seen him for some months. The ostensible reason for desiring to see him now was, first, a trifling affair relative to Lady Erskine, and next, to speak to him about his election. Lord Bute told him, that he intended his second son for the Burghs which Wedderburn now represents, and asked him whether he was provided with a seat. Wedderburn's answer was, that he had several offers, and had no doubt of being able to provide a seat for himself. His Lordship told him he was very glad to know that; he had been very sorry that it was not in his power to bring him in again, for that he had the same regard for him as ever, though they had differed in politics *a little;* and yet, says he, "we have not differed fundamentally, for you are attached to Mr. Grenville, and I think of him just as I did four years ago. He is the only man in this kingdom fit to be at the Treasury; he alone can make a permanent Administration, and I wish the King may send for him; but that is the only way in which I wish him to come in. I oppose his being forced on the King, and you follow him on that idea, therein we differ."

Wedderburn answered that he believed Mr. Grenville never had had that idea, that his conversation had ever been the reverse, and that in the late negotiation he had particularly declared that he never would be obtruded on the King. He said upon that, that he had heard Mr. Grenville had behaved very handsomely upon the occasion, and pressed for an account of the transaction from Wedderburn, which he gave him fully. His observations, upon the whole, were that Mr. Grenville's behaviour throughout had been most perfectly proper; that the mistake about the offer of the Treasury had probably arisen from Lord Rockingham's confounding the King's message with the Duke of Grafton's personal declaration, that his situation should not stand in the way of any arrangement; that, indeed, the Duke of Grafton's letters carried on the idea of Lord Rockingham's forming an Administration; but that nothing better than mistakes could be expected from a business of this kind conducted by two boys; that it was ridiculous to suppose that Mr. Grenville would be drawn in to give a list of his friends; that he understood these affairs too well to be so caught, having been engaged in several negotiations, whereas this was Lord Rockingham's first exploit; and that he hoped Mr. Grenville's conduct on the occasion would remove those impressions against him upon the King's mind, which great pains had been taken to fix and strengthen. He then said that though nothing was too absurd for party prejudice to suggest, yet he trusted the world would not give him the credit of having advised the sending to Lord Rockingham, who, on every public and private account, was the last man he could think of. He denied, too, the having been concerned in suggesting the thought of sending for Mr. Pitt last year, said that some of his friends had indeed supported him, but that was from a principle of supporting the King's Government, and complained of the awkward and limited attention which had been shown to them. He then went through the several particulars of his conduct, blamed him for his behaviour to Lord Temple, yet wished his Lordship could have overlooked it, because now things would have been as they should be; wondered that he could break with the Bedfords, when their terms were so reasonable as two offices and three peerages, one of which last was hardly to be called a creation, and condemned his quarrelling with the Rockinghams for the sake of Mr. Shelley.

He spoke of the Bill for regulating the East India dividends as an idle interposition, and still more idle to persist in it, when they might have got off upon the arrival of the ship.

He mentioned Rigby's attack upon himself in the House, said it was unkind, for that he could not suppose they believed the foolish story of his having sent to Lord Holland. Wedderburn told him they certainly did believe it, and he fancied Lord Holland had given some grounds for it in his letter to Charles Townshend. He observed upon that, that they had better have *seen* the letter, and that the supposition was absurd, Lord Holland being past all business, and told Wedderburn that he had, a few days since, been in to the King to ask for a new coronet, which could only be to deck his hearse.

He spoke of the present system as at an end, called the late negotiation a total blow to the Administration, and wished again that the King might be advised to send for Mr. Grenville.

I have given you the detail of this conversation as well as I can recollect it, and as these are his Lordship's sentiments, they justify me in saying that it is matter of indifference whether Lord Mansfield has been with him or not; perhaps, too, you may think that the surmise that the King might consult Lord Mansfield, which I had from another quarter very wide of Lord Bute's channel, is not at all less, but rather more probable, from his Lordship's holding this language, for I think Lord Mansfield's would be the same in every particular.

The time, and the manner, and the continually recurring to you whenever the conversation wandered to other political topics, induced Wedderburn to believe that it was meant to be repeated, and he, therefore, desired me to transmit it to you. On the other hand, as he may be mistaken, and it is possible his Lordship might only intend to show his friendship for him, he begs you will be particularly cautious to keep the information he gives you entirely to yourself; and the necessity I may be under to show Wedderburn your letter in answer to this, explains my reason for desiring that General Græme's name may not be in it. I am fully convinced, from the whole tenor of Lord Bute's conduct upon all occasions lately, that he will not *appear* in any transaction; but there is certainly no harm in these being the sentiments of one who, without doubt, has opportunities to convey them, whatever influence they may have when they are so conveyed.

The same are also carried through another channel, so that I think a just representation of your conduct, and of the principles of it, is sufficiently taken care of.

Since writing the above, I find that Sir James Lowther has been holding the same language to Sir Fletcher Norton as Lord Bute did to Wedderburn. I hear authentically that Lord Chatham's state of health is this:—He sits most part of the day leaning his head down upon his hands, which are rested on the table. Lady Chatham does not continue generally in the room; if he wants anything, he knocks with his stick; he says little even to her if she comes in; and is so averse to speaking, that he commonly intimates his desire to be left alone, by some signal rather than by any expression. The physicians, however, say there is nothing in his disorder which he may not recover, but do not pretend to say there is any prospect of its being soon.

I am told that even Lord Holland is so much displeased at Lord Rockingham as to prefer Mr. Grenville. I am told, too, that many of his Lordship's friends express their discontent at the point to which he sacrificed their interests.

LORD GEORGE SACKVILLE TO MR. GRENVILLE.

Stoneland Lodge, July 30, 1767.

Sir,—I am greatly obliged to you for permitting Mr. Whately to send me so very distinct and satisfactory an account of the late extraordinary negotiation, and I cannot omit the earliest opportunity of returning you my sincere thanks for your attention to me upon that occasion.

I am persuaded that the part you have taken will meet with the approbation of all your friends; and, as far as my intelligence goes, those who are not personally acquainted with you do justice to your principles and to your disinterested conduct, in making public measures the great object of your consideration. I shall be happy in every opportunity of assuring you that I am with the sincerest regard and respect, &c., &c.

Geo. Sackville.

MR. GRENVILLE TO MR. WHATELY.

Wotton, July 30, 1767.

DEAR WHATELY,—I am glad that you have sent my letters to Lord George Sackville and to Lord Mansfield. I will talk to you of what you mention of the former when I have the pleasure of seeing you. Your conversation with Lord Mansfield will probably be over before this can reach you. I will only say, therefore, that I wish to leave him as fully informed as may be; and I think no part of this transaction can in its nature be a secret after the whole of it has been intrusted to such a variety of persons of different parties and situations. I approve of the communications you have made of the particulars of it, and especially to Sir F. Norton and to Mr. Wedderburn. The language holden by the latter, in his conference with Lord Bute, is in all respects so friendly to me that I beg you will assure him of my kindest thanks for it, and that I am much obliged to him for the justice he has done me in declaring my sentiments, that I would never suffer myself to be forced or obtruded upon the King. This has long been my resolution, and I have made no secret of it to anybody. When the Duke of Bedford and I met Lord Bute at Lord Eglintoun's, the winter before last, it was the only declaration I then made, except what related to the repeal of the Stamp Act, the measure then depending. I am glad that Lord Bute does justice to Lord Temple's opinions and mine upon the present occasion; and I trust, whatever changes may happen in the various systems of parties and of politics, that Lord Temple and I shall always be found on that public ground upon which the honour and safety of the King and of his people equally depend. I agree with you in thinking, from the whole tenor of Lord Bute's conduct and conversation, that he will not appear in any transaction. As to what may be intended, the accounts are so contradictory that I can form no judgment of them; nor do I see the clue which is to extricate the King from the perplexities and difficulties in which His Majesty, and through him the kingdom, is unhappily involved. Any plan formed for that purpose shall certainly have my warmest wishes for its success, but what prospect there is of such a plan I am sure I know not. I will take no notice of the information you have given to me of what passed between Lord Bute and Mr. Wedderburn, except to Lord Temple, from whom I take it for granted nothing in which my name and ideas are mentioned is intended to be concealed. I agree with you in thinking it probable that nothing might be meant by Lord Bute in that conversation except expressions of civility, and to show his friendship for Mr. Wedderburn, in return for the very honourable part which Mr. Wedderburn took towards him personally in the course of last Session of Parliament. I am, &c., &c.

GEORGE GRENVILLE.

THE EARL OF MANSFIELD TO MR. GRENVILLE.

Bloomsbury, July 31, 1767.

MY DEAR SIR,—I am extremely obliged to you for the justice your letter does to the friendship which has long continued between us, and which is not likely to alter, because it is built upon a more solid foundation than the shifting quicksands of modern party and politics.

I heard of the negotiation you mention while it was depending, and the several steps it took. I only *heard*, for, in my private opinion, I never saw through it to the end I wish; which is to restore credit and wisdom to the King's Councils, ease to his mind, and honour to his person. I suspected a snare[1] in the proposition, or that it might be turned into one. I thought it would drop by a negative from the quarter which begun. I did not foresee the precise mode in which it ended, which certainly was a sudden start; but I expected no good from such a meeting, so composed, without any previous preparation, or any system digested. It seemed like throwing the question with the East India Company among the members of the House of Commons.

Since the whole ended, the Duke of Bedford did me the honour of a visit and very long conversation. I have seen Lord Rockingham several times. I have seen and often heard from the Duke of Newcastle, who is strongly and entirely of opinion with the Duke of Bedford, and very much applauds his behaviour.

---

[1] Lord Rockingham also had his share of *suspicion*. In a letter to Mr. Dowdeswell, shortly after, he says, " I am sure you will recollect that on the Monday night (20th July), I said that George Grenville and Lord Temple calling upon us for a declaration on North American affairs, was *a trap;* that whatever answer we gave, they would lay it before the public with whatever colouring they thought proper, so as to throw a construction upon our conduct to our disadvantage."[a]

The Duke of Grafton, too, *suspected* the Rockinghams, as we learn from Horace Walpole, who, in speaking of one of Lord Rockingham's replies to the Duke, says: " Impertinent as the body of the letter and the assumption to himself of forming an Administration were, it seemed but reasonable that the King should see the man whom he had sent for to be his Minister; and to have refused him an audience on the arrogance of his style, would probably be *falling into the snare they had laid for breaking off the treaty.*"[b]

[a] *Cavendish Debates: Appendix,* p. 584.   [b] *Memoirs of George III.,* vol. iii. p. 71.

Though the way in which it did end was the effect of humour, chance, refinement, and a jealousy of the hour, I do not know whether it could have ended better, if there is sense to draw good from evil.

The Duke of Bedford is very temperate; so is Lord Rockingham; they are disposed to continue the intercourse of every civility.

Lord Rockingham has refused to accede to the present set. He immediately communicated to the Duke of Bedford that the King formalized upon the Treasury having been *offered*. Mr. Conway continuing Secretary, I believe is not in concert with him.

I have been so engaged that I could not find a moment to see Mr. Whately 'till last night. Though I had heard from different quarters what passed with Lord Temple and you, yet the letters he showed me to himself and Mr. Rigby, and the account he gave me of your letter to Lord Suffolk, struck me very much. There is not an unguarded word or sentiment in respect of any person or thing. I think, under all the circumstances, your conduct wise, I think it honest, I believe it sincere. After making Mr. Whately read them over a second time, I was confirmed in a thought which immediately occurred to me. It is but doing you justice, and will be of great service to you to communicate them in private confidence. They might safely be printed in the Gazette, but any publication would destroy their effect. Nobody can do what I wish to have done so well as myself. Everybody knows that I am warmly your friend, they talk to me upon that footing; but they do not think me your or any man's follower, beyond my judgment and opinion.

It is very natural that upon this occasion you should

acquaint me in confidence with the resolution you had taken, and the part you had acted. No way could be more ingenuous, and less liable to suspicion, than by showing your letters to your intimate friends writ at the time, and therefore I wish I had that you wrote to Lord Suffolk. Now I see no objection to my exercising my judgment in making a confidence in a place or two, without suffering any copy to be taken.

God knows what is to come next. One faction for another. A series of weak Administrations and perpetual strong Oppositions will lead to destruction. A struggle of places and pensions is scandalous. The cure must come from serious conviction. I have no more room. Ever yours, &c.

EARL TEMPLE TO MR. GRENVILLE.

Stowe, Friday morning, July 31, 1767.

My dear Brother,—Under the seal of the *deepest* secrecy I send you the letter I received last night [1]. As I had before been conjured not to communicate the contents to any one person living, I must beg of you not to take a copy, and to return it to me on Sunday by Lord Thomond. I will make no comments except that I think Lord Bute gave many natural explanations to matters which required them, and that I most perfectly approve of your answer in every particular. I have long thought that this business must end in new plague to one or both of us, and I see no possibility of good. I am ever your most affectionate, T.

---

[1] Probably that from Mr. W. Gerard Hamilton of the 29th instant.

MR. AUGUSTUS HERVEY TO MR. GRENVILLE.

Park Place, July 31, 1767.

DEAR SIR,—Lord Eglintoun going to Stowe, I inclose this to Lord Temple by him, and have begged the favour of his Lordship to let a servant carry this over, that I may with some prospect of security write you what is going on here, as far as I can discern, and from what I learn from very good authority; I came but the last night and go to-morrow.

The Duke of Grafton certainly means to patch this up and go on, and Mr. Conway has undoubtedly determined to stay, and has promised to behave better, and says he will stand by the Duke of Grafton. You will allow this to be a Conway-ish return to the Marquess of Rockingham. But as Lord Hertford has totally the ear of the Closet in a public view, 'tis no wonder this has been so strangely conducted, and I scarce find one man that does not arraign Mr. Conway for his conduct, and not much less the Duke of Grafton for admitting it, but 'tis said, 'tis this or nothing. Mr. Charles Townshend is in the country much dissatisfied, as this arrangement does not answer his purpose, for you may be assured Lord Egmont is sent for, and will be in town Sunday or Monday, and is, they assert confidently, to have the seals in the room of Lord Shelburne, whom they turn out malgré lui. Lord Townshend is sent for to offer Ireland to, as I hear, in the room of Lord Bristol[1], who I know has either resigned or given notice some days ago that he will not keep it longer, which, together with Lord Egmont's

[1] Lord Bristol had just resigned the Lord Lieutenantcy of Ireland, and Lord Townshend was soon after appointed his successor.

being sent for, assures me that the Privy Seal will be taken for the present from the present holder of it. When you weigh this you will be of my opinion: first, Lord Egmont they know would not serve with Lord Chatham, though he supported; this does not answer his Lordship's business, he wants a place, and therefore I think they would not send for him without giving him one without incumbrance, for which he left his other. Another reason is, that Lord Bristol would not resign (and I know for certain he does) if he did not think Lord Chatham used ill, and yet he intends to support the King, he says, but not a word of another place do I hear for him. But I can never think Lord Townshend will be prevailed on to accept with this situation of affairs, what he has long wanted in another: first, 'tis the eve of a Sessions, which will be as troublesome a one as any that ever was; the salary is all gone for the preceding year, and no one can answer for his being there an hour after the Sessions, and not supported perhaps through it. Sure, therefore, of losing 8000*l.* or 10,000*l.*, and not sure of being six months there; and very sure of very disagreeable work at any rate.

Barré I find is to be removed from Vice Treasurer of Ireland, but I have not heard who is to succeed.

The Duke of Roxburgh and the Duke of Buccleuch are to have the Green ribbons. Lord March and Lord Frederick Campbell are competitors for the Admiralty of Scotland; the first has the Duke of Grafton's wishes, but the last is so much pushed by Conway, that at this crisis 'tis yet doubtful if he will not succeed[1].

[1] Lord Frederick was the brother of Conway's wife, Lady Ailesbury; Lord March was the successful candidate.

Sir Thomas Sewell[1] is, I hear, certain to go to Ireland, from which they hope to make some arrangement either to gain Sir Fletcher Norton or Wedderburn.

Young Horace[2], as they called him, is very busy in this time even at Court, where (as I told him) I scarce remember ever seeing him, and Lord Hertford is more in the Closet than ever.

Mr. Stanley remains Ambassador still and Cofferer, as he told me this morning, and has kissed hands to go to Paris for six weeks: what do you think of this?

Now, my dear Sir, I have sent you everything which I have heard and think I can depend on for certain. Chit-chat stuff is not worth wasting your time in reading it.

Eglintoun yesterday came to me, and told me it had been very much reported, and even strongly asserted, that Lord Temple and you made a point of his being out in the arrangement, and that Granby believed it, and wished me to go to Granby and contradict it authentically, which, to avoid his Lordship's very repeated urging, I said I would at a proper time; but I do not intend to go there, but if I meet him at Court, shall tell him I know it to be false, with circumstances that shall convince him; and I believe this to be a properer way for me than the other, but if you think otherwise, I will go to him, though I come to town purposely. But in that general subject I have very openly set all

---

[1] Master of the Rolls; he was mentioned for the Irish Chancellorship.

[2] It will be seen by Horace Walpole's account of these transactions, that he meddled in all the negotiations between the Duke of Grafton, Lord Rockingham, Conway, &c.; and he takes considerable praise to himself for the composition or correction of the letters which the Duke of Grafton had occasion to write to Lord Rockingham at this time. See *Memoirs of George III.*, vol. iii.

your conduct in the light you and your brother wish it, and exactly to those that I believed it necessary, and am sure I very much surprised one person who had been (as he told me) assured of the reverse, in short there is nothing some of the Rockingham party (I do not believe with his knowledge or approbation) have not said to endeavour to make it thought here, that the exclusion of the Butes came from your quarter tacitly, and the Chathamites from the Duke of Bedford's. You will easily believe I was as stout as well armed on this point; and to tell you the truth, by what I find, the *Closet* thinks very differently now of the Rockinghams than they did, and are more exasperated against them than any set.

I think Monday you will see some other pictures in the *Gazetteer* that will not be unlike the originals[1].

---

[1] Mr. Hervey alludes to the same subject in a letter of this date to Lord Temple. "You will in a day or two see a *Briton* you will not dislike, and some pictures 'tis hoped your Lordship will acknowledge as originals as to likeness, though they might have a more masterly hand for finishing." The following are specimens of the "pictures" which are contained in a letter signed A BRITON, dated from "Somersetshire," and printed in the *Gazetteer* of August 3rd—first of LORD CHATHAM:—"Let us suppose now that one man should be presiding as he thought over them all, who is ambitious of everything, yet incapable of anything; too infirm to act himself, too jealous to let others; too proud to ask advice, too recluse to give any; too much distressed in his circumstances to resign, too much devoted to the *Favourite Thane* to be turned out; in short, too strongly supported by *that quarter*, and too little deserving of it from any." Among other members of the Administration, here is a "picture" of GENERAL CONWAY. "Supposing another should be temporizing with different parties through a whole kingdom, and keeping one of the greatest offices of trust in a kingdom, secretly connected with one sect, openly disclaiming of any, irresolutely opposing one day, and peevishly supporting the next, resigning yet holding, and at last proves to be the identical man proposed as Minister in his same department by one of the very

Your Somersetshire friend will never sleep, I assure you. I am ever, &c., &c. A. HERVEY.

MR. WEDDERBURN TO MR. GRENVILLE.

Lincoln's Inn, July 31, 1767.

DEAR SIR,—I have been exceedingly unfortunate in not having been able to command one day even to have paid my respects to you at Wotton. The Chancellor has sat every day without interruption since the Term, and I find myself obliged to set out upon the circuit to-morrow.

Mr. Whately has informed you of an incident that occurred to me lately, as fully as I could have done; I thought it marked a very proper disposition, and I attended the more to it, because the conversation was not brought on by anything that fell from me, but was introduced and carried on by the person I talked with, who appeared very inquisitive about the part Lord Temple and you had taken in the late transaction, of which he had had but an imperfect account, and took every occasion of expressing his strong sense of the propriety of it, and his good wishes towards you in general. I am at a loss what conclusions one ought to draw from it, but I should rather incline to think that it was meant for something more material than mere civility to me, and that idea coincides with a great many other obser-

leaders of opposition to that Administration this very man is now employed in, and has been trusted by."

A few days afterwards an admiring poet sends some verses to the same paper, which end with the following couplet:—

" Thanks, BRITON, to thy nervous pen,
Like Vandyke's art, it *paints the men*."

vations I have heard upon the language that has been lately held by some of his nearest friends.

I have not lived much in the political world for some weeks past, but all those I have seen agree perfectly in their sentiments of the only material part of the late transaction, I mean that which regards Lord Temple and you; the rest was but the folly of a day; but it must be of real consequence to the public some time or other, that this folly has afforded you an opportunity of demonstrating the moderation, the firmness, and the consistency of those principles you have always professed.

As I understand Lord Clive intends to pay his respects to you in his way to Bath, I must take the liberty of troubling you with a few words upon Indian affairs.

My part, you know, has in general been to support the Directors, 'till I thought they took a part against the interests and against the honour of the Company. I had no acquaintance with them, nor no other reason for supporting them (in opposition to almost all the people I knew, who gave themselves any trouble in the Indian meetings), but my desire to support the system Lord Clive had adopted. Since you left town, I took a very warm part in opposition to the Directors and to Mr. Dyson, in favour of the Company's servants, for whom, in the outset of the affair, I had declined to interest myself, notwithstanding the regard I had for many of their friends, who had pressed me very earnestly to assist them. But the state of the question was totally changed; it had blended itself very much with the questions debated in the House of Commons, and I had no difficulty to support the propriety of the act done by the Company as a matter of favour to particular persons, and to insist that it ought not to be rescinded under the terror of the threats thrown out by Mr. Dyson, though I had not urged it formerly as a matter of right. It has so happened that these gentlemen think themselves obliged to me, and I am persuaded it is in my power to be of some weight amongst them, and their numbers and influence in general Courts is not inconsiderable. I wished to have seen Lord Clive, and desired Mr. Whately to explain my sentiments to him; but I understood that he received the civility I meant to him in so cold a manner that it has gone no further on my part.

It gave me very great satisfaction to find that my conduct in regard to the civilities that were shown me by Lord Rockingham has met with your approbation, which will always be the most important circumstance to me in every concern I can have.

As soon as my business is finished in the North, I hope to have the honour of waiting upon you, and to make myself amends for the disappointment I had last year in paying my respects to Lord Temple. I am ever, &c., &c.   AL. WEDDERBURN.

MR. WILLIAM GERARD HAMILTON TO EARL TEMPLE.

Saturday night, (August 1, 1767.)

MY DEAR LORD,—I shall probably do nothing more than repeat what you have heard more satisfactorily from Whately: nor have I any reason to think that the intelligence which I send you is particularly authentic; but what is reported and believed is, that Lord Egmont will have his choice of being President of the Council, or Secretary of State for the Southern Department; that

Shelburne will be First Lord of the Admiralty, and Lord Halifax in some considerable employment.

Lord Bristol, before he went out, made Mr. Phipps, his brother-in-law, an Irish Peer, by the title of Lord Mulgrave[1].

There was likewise a vacancy of the Bishop of Killaloo, which I hear he has declared shall not be given to Sir William Pynsent[2], to whom it was generally understood he had engaged himself for the first ecclesiastical preferment that should be in his disposal, after he had provided for his brother. The dissoluteness of Sir William Pynsent's life is the reason he assigns for this refusal.

The prevailing opinion is, that De Grey will not take the Chancellorship of Ireland; and there are those who think it will terminate in my friend Hutchinson, and be purchased by the transfer of his reversion to some relation of the Lord Lieutenant's.

Lord Townshend has not as yet named his Secretary, and Jenkinson, it is generally believed, will have the offer of it; but his acceptance of it is much doubted.

I am well informed that Lord Verney, at his house in your neighbourhood, within these very few days, attempted to hang himself, but was cut down before any mischief ensued. I need not desire your Lordship to be reserved upon this subject, but my intelligence comes from those who have been lately upon the spot.

---

[1] Constantine Phipps, created Baron Mulgrave of New Ross, county of Wexford. He married the eldest daughter of John Lord Hervey and his wife " the beautiful Molly Lepel."

[2] He means Sir Robert Pynsent, who was in holy orders, and who had succeeded to the baronetcy upon the death of his cousin Sir William, in January, 1765. It was Sir William who bequeathed the estate of Burton Pynsent to Mr. Pitt.

Mr. Conway succeeds Lord Townshend as Lieutenant General of the Ordnance, and continues Secretary of State. I shall not trouble you, my dear Lord, with any letter on Monday, as I hope to have the honour of meeting you at Eastbury; but, if I should be prevented, I shall not fail writing by Mr. Hervey. Yours most faithfully, &c., &c.

MR. WHATELY TO MR. GRENVILLE.

August 1, 1767.

DEAR SIR,—I wish I could spare your eyes the reading of another long letter from me; but I doubt you would hardly allow me to postpone an account of the conversation I had with Lord Mansfield on Thursday night. It lasted an hour and a half, was very open, friendly, and agreeable. He said he had heard from the Duke of Bedford, the Duke of Newcastle, and Lord Rockingham, their several accounts of the late negotiation, and was very glad you had given him the opportunity, by sending me to him, of hearing particularly the part you had taken. I answered that I was able to give him that satisfaction immediately from yourself, by showing his Lordship, at your desire, the letters you had written upon the occasion; for which purpose I produced yours to me of the 12th and 30th; the extracts I had taken from that to Mr. Rigby of the 16th, and to Lord Temple of the 18th; and the copy of Lord Temple's and your joint note to Mr. Rigby of the 18th [1].

When I had gone through them, he desired me to read them all over again, for a reason which he would

[1] See *ante*, pages 43, 57, 59 and 126.

give me; and having done it, he told me his reason was, to watch whether there was a word in any of them which could give offence to anybody, to the Duke of Bedford, the Duke of Newcastle, Lord Rockingham, Lord Bute, or even the King, if he were to see them; that he found there was not an iota which could be exceptionable; that the sentiments were noble and becoming, the expressions most cautiously guarded, the ground you had taken excellent, and your whole conduct and correspondence such as would do you great honour; that he therefore wished he might be favoured with copies of all I had read, except that to me of the 30th, which was not material; but that the others, particularly that to me of the 12th, and to Lord Temple of the 18th, contained your real sentiments, freely delivered at the time of the transaction to your friends; and were authentic testimonies to the probity and the motives of your proceedings.

The use, he told me, which he particularly meant to make of them, was to show them to the Duke of Newcastle, under a charge of secrecy, which he knew his Grace would not keep; and that one reason for wishing to make that communication was to spread the truth, as it appears from these letters, among those to whom the Duke would tell it; but, more especially, to fortify his Grace in the part he had taken; for that, with respect to the late transaction, he was wholly and solely a Bedford, and these letters would support him in the opinions he had entertained already.

I replied to this, that I could without difficulty furnish his Lordship with the copies, having your permission to do so, under the restriction that they were only to himself. He said that he meant to give the communication that appearance; that nothing could seem more natural than for you, with whom he had so close a connection, to send him copies of your letters; and that though they were such as might be read at Charing Cross, yet any ostentatious exhibit of them from yourself would destroy the effect he intended, which was, to produce them as your private letters (those especially to Lord Temple and me), never meant to be shown.

It is needless to say that I promised him the copies he desired: he told me that any time before this day se'ennight would be soon enough, as he should not see the Duke of Newcastle 'till then, for he sets out on the Home Circuit next Monday; but, however, he shall have them to-morrow. In the course of the conversation upon the letters, he said they were such as might be shown to the King. I dropped slightly that I had no channel of conveying them, and he stopped short. I thought by the manner, he took it as I meant he should, and I took care not to mark my meaning too strongly. The other letters, which I had in my pocket, which were the correspondence between the Duke of Grafton and Lord Rockingham, I offered to read, but it was unnecessary, as he was accurately acquainted with the contents; the rest I left purposely at home, and took no notice of.

He went through with me most of the particulars of the late negotiation: I do not repeat to you such as we all know and think of alike: those which he mentioned, and which I had not before so particularly or so authentically as from him, are, that he had himself kept clear of the transaction, because he never saw an end to it, as it was impossible the Court should ever admit a comprehensive plan in such an extent; that Lord Rockingham, before he went to the first meeting, considered the thing as over, and was indifferent as to the point on which it broke off; that he had not then any thoughts of Mr. Conway; that the idea of meaning him for Secretary of State was not Lord Rockingham's, nor was it taken up three hours before the second meeting; that Mr. Conway knew nothing of it; that at the subsequent conferences between Lord Rockingham and Mr. Conway, his Lordship absolutely declined coming in with his own friends only, and declared that if the King ever sent to him again, he would send to the Duke of Bedford; and that he resented very much Mr. Conway's still staying in. He further told me, that by the attentions which had passed between the Duke of Bedford and Lord Rockingham, and by the language he had heard from both, he understood that this affair had not interrupted any regards which the one might have towards the other, but left them just where it found them. I could not determine in my own mind whether in mentioning this he meant to convey a gratulation or an alarm[1]. He

---

[1] Most probably the latter. Lord Mansfield's political sagacity enabled him to perceive how essential the Bedford connection was to the Grenvilles, and that without it their power, as a party, would be materially weakened, if not altogether extinguished. Mr. Grenville and Lord Temple were well aware of this, and it has been surmised that their motive in entering into the recent negotiation was not so much with the view of themselves joining the Rockinghams, as to endeavour to prevent the union of the latter with the Duke of Bedford and his friends, and the events of a few months later proved how ready the Bedfords were, at the first favourable opportunity, to separate themselves from the Grenvilles. In truth, there was not at this time, nor indeed was there at any time, any *real* cordiality between the Grenvilles and the Bedfords, and certainly none was now even pretended between the Rockinghams and Grenvilles. In relating to Mr. Dowdeswell a conversation with Lord Lyttelton some months before, Lord Rockingham said: " In the first place I told him, that an union formed with us on an idea of managing Lord Bute, was a scheme which

said Lord Rockingham's friends spoke with respect of you, but imputed their miscarriage in some measure to Lord Temple. I tried two or three times to get from him the grounds upon which they founded such a surmise: he would not enter into particulars, but said in general that they had no real grounds; that it was refinement and folly, proceeding from old rancours, and upon those refinements he intimated that Lord Rockingham had concluded the affair was at an end, before he went to the first meeting. In order to find out their grounds, I threw out what I had heard, that the explanation upon the American measures was required only

I was sure neither myself nor any of our great friends would have anything to do with; that I did not at all doubt but that Lord Temple and George Grenville were next oars to Administration, because I understood that their language was on a plan of tempting Lord Bute to quarrel with Lord Chatham, and also from various other reasons."

The letters of Mr. Whately and Mr. W. Gerard Hamilton certainly indicate a leaning, at least on the part of Mr. Grenville, if not of Lord Temple also, at this time, towards a reconciliation with the Bute party, or the *King's friends*, and from Lord Bute's conversation with Mr. Wedderburn, there would seem to have been no disinclination on his side.

Lord Rockingham, continuing his account of the conversation with Lord Lyttelton, adds, " I then answered what related to the Treasury In regard to Lord Temple I told him fairly and fully, that his conduct in the matter of *libels*, and in his public *conversations*, had been such, that I believed amongst our friends he was not a man to be talked upon, but that, exclusive of that consideration, I must say truly, that the making either Lord Temple or George Grenville First Lord of the Treasury, was, in fact, making both of them the Minister: that I did not think Mr. George Grenville, *personally*, was quite in the same light as Lord Temple; but that making Mr. Grenville Minister would be the most inconsistent act for us that could be thought of, and that of course we, who were determined to act consistently, would never join in such a plan; that our credit had risen with the public by our opposing Mr. Grenville's measures when he was Minister, and that we had confirmed our credit, by reversing his measures when we were in Administration."—*Cavendish Debates: Appendix,* p. 581.

to raise a difficulty, which supposition, I observed, was contradicted by Mr. Rigby's declarations on that head to Lord Rockingham in town, before he had seen you or Lord Temple. He was struck with the fact, saying it was new to him, and material. I am persuaded that I there hit upon one of their reasons; and yet he told me that Lord Rockingham would, when the subject had come quietly into discussion, have been very easy, and have concurred in almost any measures short of re-enacting the Stamp Act, which he did not suppose you would think of.

I brought up the topic of Lord Temple once or twice more, in order to discover the foundations of their surmise that he had obstructed the negotiation, but he did not mention particulars, was himself perfectly satisfied in his Lordship's conduct and intentions, and treated all suggestions to the contrary as *nonsense*, not worth regarding.

He declared he could not foresee what was next to happen; for the present it seemed determined to go on. He had heard that Lord Northington had been sent for, and was come, but did not know whether the message was from the King, or only to attend some official business, and sent by the Ministers. I hear since from different hands, that he is not come; one of these hands is Mr. Woodcock, who knows as much of Lord Northington as anybody, and who adds that a message has indeed gone, but that his Lordship has refused to come up: this can be true only if it was sent by the Ministers.

Lord Mansfield said he understood some negotiation was on foot, concerning the Chancellorship of Ireland; that Malone[1] and some others there were endeavouring

---

[1] One of the Judges of the Court of Common Pleas in Ireland.

to get it among themselves, and Lord Bristol would probably stickle for their pretensions, but that if the Master of the Rolls would take it, and Sir Fletcher Norton would go to the Rolls, that would more probably be the disposition. He seemed to think that the proposition was actually made to Sir Fletcher Norton, but I believe he was mistaken. Sir Fletcher has been at Guildford ever since Wednesday, and does not return 'till to-morrow: not an hour before he went, his most intimate friend[1] tells me that he had a conversation with him, in which the possibility of such an offer was the subject, and he is positively sure that then it had not been made: he is persuaded that if it should be hereafter, Sir Fletcher will take the part which becomes him, and is even of opinion that he would take no step without consulting you.

I touched with Lord Mansfield on the subject of Lord Bute, asking what part he had taken. He protested he did not know, not having seen him since November, and said that he believed in general that he did less than was imagined; that his greatest fault was not doing so much as he might; for that if the King's mind led him to place his confidence nowhere else, it was incumbent on Lord Bute to give His Majesty proper advice when it was wanting.

He told me that the King and Queen had both distinguished him very particularly of late; that on Thursday it was so marked by the King, that the Spanish Ambassador told him if anybody had been so distinguished at Madrid, they would have said that his fortune was made; and that the Queen was so particularly gracious that Lady Egremont asked him whether

[1] Mr. W. Gerard Hamilton.

he was not proud of the honours done him. I understand this was on Thursday, and that it was as strong a few days before. I *know* that it was designed: *the King regrets that he cannot have the assistance of Lord Mansfield's abilities, and is resolved to make the first advance*, are very strong expressions. I find Lord Mansfield's friends expected that he would have been called in before this, and Ross[1] the agent, to whom he opens himself more than to anybody, says that he will avow the advice he shall give, and doubts not that after the circuit it will be asked. He does not make a question of his Lordship's pointing directly to you[2]. I think from all these circumstances that the intelligence I gave you concerning him, which was from a very different quarter, was not ill-founded, and I am sure the communication to his Lordship has not been ill-placed.

The open language of Lord Bute's friends now is, that he has the same opinion of you as he had four years ago. The similarity of the phrase proves that the conversation with Wedderburn was for a purpose.

---

[1] George Ross; called by Junius "the Scotch agent and worthy confidant of Lord Mansfield."—Vol. ii. p. 58.

[2] Whately's conjecture in this respect is corroborated by Lord Rockingham in a letter to the Duke of Portland, dated September 15th: "Lord Mansfield has the seals in the interim: if his having them affords him opportunities of going to the Closet, and that he does so, and makes long stay, possibly His Majesty and he may enter into conversations which may produce events. I should think it probable that Lord Mansfield would try to incline His Majesty towards George Grenville. And if he does, and it succeeds, I shall think we have had an escape, for I don't believe that any of our friends will avow George Grenville in open daylight as leader of Administration. What I shall most dread is, that if we had the forming of an Administration, some of our friends, on the idea of conciliating the Duke of Bedford, &c., would throw such a weight into the Grenvillian party, as would hamper us in every measure, and blow us up the very first opportunity."— *Lord Albemarle's Memoirs of Rockingham*, vol. ii. p. 59.

The reports of the day are that Lord Egmont is sent for to be a Minister, and Lord Townshend to go to Ireland. I do not much heed such rumours, but you have a test to try them by, for with equal confidence and authority it has been said, and is now believed, that you have been sent for; as you mention nothing of it to me, you may suppose I am hard of belief.

The enclosed from Lord Mansfield he desired me to convey to you; that from Wedderburn, I suppose, is on the subject of Lord Clive, to whom he desired me to speak, offering to introduce him to his Lordship. Mr. Walsh being in the room, indiscreetly threw out that Mr. Wedderburn had shown himself a friend to the prosecuted servants, which I thought made Lord Clive rather cold about seeing him, but still said he should be glad to see any friend of yours. I would not put it on that ground, but stated Wedderburn as a considerable man in this country, both in Parliament and the law, and a respectable India proprietor, on account of the weight his abilities gave him in the Court, and the numbers who followed him; but as Lord Clive did not eagerly advance towards him, the affair was dropped between us; and I should think if, in consequence of Wedderburn's letter, you should mention him to his Lordship, it will be better to take no notice, if possible, of what has passed between his Lordship and me, and my ineffectual attempt to bring him and Wedderburn together.

MR. GRENVILLE TO COLONEL HOTHAM[1].

Wotton, August 2, 1767.

SIR,—I had heard the melancholy news of Lady Suffolk's death[2] before I received the favour of your letter, and though her advanced age, joined to the frequent complaints she has lately had, must necessarily diminish our surprise at the suddenness of this event, yet it cannot lessen the sincere concern which it has given both Mrs. Grenville and myself. I feel very sensibly the kind testimony of the continuance of that friendship to the end of her life, which I have so many years enjoyed, and to which I have been so highly obliged. If there is anything beyond mere matter of form, in consequence of the trust which you inform me she has reposed in Lord Chetwynd[3] and me concerning the disposition of her estate at Marble Hill, I shall be happy in every opportunity of showing my real respect to her memory by the strict performance of everything she wished, and by my regard and attention to those she loved. Mrs. Grenville desires me to make her compliments to you, and we both join in begging the favour

---

[1] Afterwards Sir Charles Hotham: he married Lady Suffolk's niece, Lady Dorothy Hobart; their only daughter, Miss Hotham, was adopted and educated by Lady Suffolk.

[2] "Lady Suffolk closed in July, 1767, a long life, which had been chequered with the vicissitudes of Court favour, and afflicted by constitutional infirmities, but sweetened by the equanimity and moderation of her own mind, and the affection and friendship of the most eminent and distinguished persons of the long period in which she lived."—*Mr. Croker's Biographical Preface to the Suffolk Correspondence.* See also Horace Walpole's account of her death in a letter to Lord Strafford, July 29, 1767.

[3] William, third Viscount Chetwynd: he had very recently succeeded his brother in the title. He died in April, 1770.

of you to assure Lord Chetwynd of our most cordial good wishes for his health under a blow which we know will greatly affect him as well as ourselves. I have the honour to be, &c., &c. GEORGE GRENVILLE.

EARL TEMPLE TO MR. GRENVILLE.

Monday night, August 3, 1767.

MY DEAR BROTHER,—Many thanks for the communication of the various dispatches. I will make no comments upon the various moving sands of intelligence which we daily, not to say hourly, receive; but nothing can surpass the nonsense of laying to my charge the breach of a negotiation in which you and I were only passive, and in which we proceeded with perhaps unprecedented fairness and generosity. I am sorry to hear of the complaint in your eyes, and am ever your most affectionate, TEMPLE.

MR. GRENVILLE TO THE EARL OF MANSFIELD.

Wotton, August 5, 1767.

MY DEAR LORD,—Your letter of the 31st of last month gave me the highest satisfaction which I could propose to myself from the late negotiation, by informing me that you so kindly approved the conduct of Lord Temple and myself in the course of it; and I should not have delayed from the 2nd of this month, when I received it, 'till now, to return you my sincerest thanks for every part of it, if Mr. Whately had not informed me that you was set out upon the Home Circuit, and would not return to your own house 'till the end of the week. My thoughts agree so perfectly with yours as to the other parts of this transaction, that it would only be giving you unnecessary trouble to repeat them.

I am extremely obliged to you, my dear Lord, for the wish you expressed to have copies of the papers which Mr. Whately showed you by my desire, and likewise of my letter to Lord Suffolk [1]. The former, Mr. Whately says he would send to you before this time, and enclosed I transmit to you a copy of the latter, and shall be very happy to give you any further information of what has passed, if there is anything which has not yet come to your knowledge; feeling, as I do most sensibly, those friendly motives which have induc d you to be troubled with them, and knowing that if they were far more secret than from the nature of them they can be, there is no man to whose judgment and to whose affection I would more gladly entrust them. It cannot but appear, therefore, very natural to the world, who are no strangers to the respect I bear to your opinions, and to the sense I have of your friendship, that I should take the earliest opportunity to acquaint you with all circumstances in which my public life and character are concerned. As to the present state of things, the melancholy picture which you draw of it at the end of your letter, is too striking and too true. The cure must come from a serious conviction and right measures, instead of annual struggles for places and pensions, and that cure ought not to be delayed [2]. Private resentments should mix as little as may be with public opinions. In the last negotiation, Lord Temple and I have stood entirely upon the latter, and upon that ground

[1] See *ante*, page 48.
[2] This short confession from such a man as Mr. Grenville, is the true explanation of all the factious confusion of these times, and the fullest justification of George III., the victim of these "annual struggles."

I trust we shall continue, being convinced that the situation grows hourly too critical and dangerous to indulge other passions. This is the only clue to lead us through the present maze of politics, to the King's honour and happiness, and consequently to the public safety. This is, I am sure, the likeliest means for me to obtain your good opinion, which, both as a public and as a private man, I shall ever be most anxious to preserve, from the sincere respect and regard with which I am, my dear Lord, &c., &c. GEORGE GRENVILLE.

MR. WHATELY TO MR. GRENVILLE.

Croydon, Thursday, August 20, 1767.

DEAR SIR,—I came hither this morning to pay my respects to Lord Mansfield at the Assizes, with whom I dined, and as the company was retiring after dinner I took an opportunity, by presenting your compliments, to offer him an opening for conversation, which he readily took, and kept me above an hour and a half after they all were gone. He told me he had received a letter from you, and that he had shown your letters to the Duke of Newcastle, with whom they had had all the effect that could be wished, and his Grace was the more pleased as it confirmed him in his opinions concerning the late negotiation.

I then told his Lordship, that a letter from the Duke of Newcastle to the Duke of Bedford had put us all upon the watch, expecting, on such an authority, that the Parliament would be dissolved at the next prorogation. He assured me, that he knew the Duke, when he wrote that letter, had no fact to go upon; that perhaps he himself might have contributed to fix the Duke in that belief, by saying, just before that letter was written, that he did not doubt the measure would be taken; that since, a person had asked the Duke of Grafton whether it would, and that his Grace protested he knew nothing of it, and promised, if it should, that he would give that person notice, which notice has not been given; that in a conversation he had the night before last, with the Dukes of Newcastle and Richmond, at Lewes, they then thought there was no one in Administration who would undertake to advise it; but that, notwithstanding all this, he (Lord Mansfield) was firmly persuaded that the Parliament would be dissolved, it being so evidently desirable for the King, convenient to the Ministry, even unsettled as they are, and seasonable for the people in their present state of indifference, and it not being now a strong measure for any Minister to advise. He spoke of it with great positiveness, almost to assertion, but not giving me reason to think that he went upon any other ground than speculation, except from the peremptoriness of his manner, and he was very explicit in assuring me repeatedly that the Duke had no other foundation than the probability of such an event. He afterwards entered at large into the state of affairs, lamented the condition of the kingdom and of the King, said that nothing could extricate us but the conviction of the King's mind; that he knew His Majesty was in great distress; saw every step he took plunged him deeper, and that he believed that the whole rested with him now upon his not knowing which way to turn himself; that indeed his difficulty was great; that if his advice were asked, he should hardly know what to advise; that parties aimed only at places, and seemed regardless of measures; that this made the country indifferent to their success; that in the late negotiation you were the only person who had rested at all upon a measure, and that, therefore, the people did not enter into the dispute whether the Duke of Grafton or Lord Rockingham should have the disposal of offices; that, indeed, in the late affair, many of Lord Rockingham's friends were displeased at the point on which he broke with the Duke of Bedford, though in reality that was immaterial, perhaps it was the best ground on which they could have broken, and they never could have gone on, but still many were dissatisfied. This he mentioned, I thought, as a gleam of hope, to extricate the King and kingdom from the difficulties in which it is involved by the interestedness of parties, and he evidently felt as if he had said too much, and endeavoured to divert my attention from what he had let drop[1]. I imagined that he supposed some of Lord Rockingham's friends might be induced to join other parts of the Opposition, if called into Government, though the whole body should not be included; and on that idea, when he launched out into complaints of all parties, that they sought their own advantage only, to the exclusion of all others, I endeavoured in general

---

[1] Mr. Whately here seems to imagine Lord Mansfield's meaning to have been, that if he were called upon by the King for his advice in the formation of a Government (a circumstance at this time by no means improbable), he would endeavour to promote a coalition between Lord Bute's party, or the *King's friends*, the Grenvilles, and some of the *dissatisfied* members of the Rockingham party; and as his (Lord Mansfield's) opinions are described to be so much in accordance with those of Mr. Grenville, who desired that *measures* should be considered more than *men*, he may also point at some conciliatory and comprehensive measures with regard to America, in which he expected Mr. Grenville might be induced to concur.

terms to make our party an exception, but he gave me little credit for it. He, however, repeated again his commendations of your behaviour, if possible, more warmly than in my former conversation. He spoke with great contempt of the present Administration, dwelt much on their internal weakness, laughed at the idea which I told him they entertained of having gained the King, thought that impossible without attention to Lord Bute, talked much of the absurdity of thinking to take the King prisoner, which was, he said, a very common notion; and urged over and over again, that nothing but a conviction of the King's mind, or some accident, could give us relief. I said, that I did not see that accident likely to happen; his answer was, that though he neither did not see it, yet he was sensible that a trifle light as air might prove one.

I had frequent opportunities during the course of this conversation, to throw in several of your sentiments (as having heard them lately from you), where they tallied with his, as you will see they do very much, from the above relation. He went over again much of the same ground he had trod in our former conversation, relative to the late transaction; blamed Lord Rockingham for the notice he had taken of Lord Bute's party in the Closet; and repeated, that Conway stayed in against the inclination of Lord Rockingham. I told him at large what I heard was Mr. Horace Walpole's language; that Lord Rockingham had ruined himself in the Closet, by that, and by the disdain with which he had received the last proposition; that he never would be sent for again, and that it was better to send directly to Mr. Grenville, than to convey a message to him through Lord Rockingham. Lord Mansfield observed upon this, that it signified nothing, and only admitted that it showed Mr. Conway's sentiments. He abused the whole of Lord Chatham's conduct, wondered at Lord Bristol's resignation; and this, with a repetition of much which he had said to me on a former occasion, was, I think, the substance of our conversation.

I hear that Dr. Addington says, he never saw any man's *muscles* so relaxed as Lord Chatham's, but that his head is clear. Lord Mansfield has heard that he says he will recover, but does not believe he speaks his opinion.

I have had an account of Mr. Walpole's language, from two several quarters; I have told you parts of it, both in this letter and my last, and upon the whole it does not seem to me very sanguine. He is the author of the news, that Lord Northington refused to resign; and upon being asked why the Ministers would suffer such a declared enemy to stay in, he said he had asked the same question, and was told that he could do no harm; that the last time he went into the Closet he had met with a reception which was not very pleasing, and if he attempted it again it would be worse; yet, since that, I am told that Lord Northington will soon resign, as I believe I wrote to you in my last.

Lord Mansfield's account agreed with that which I have heard repeated from Mr. Walpole, that the ground upon which Lord Rockingham broke off the second negotiation with Mr. Conway was, that he would not treat with Ministers, though I understand they used the King's name, but he was positive to hear nothing except from His Majesty himself. Lord Mansfield added, that if Lord Rockingham had thought that it amounted to a negotiation, he would have communicated it to the Duke of Bedford.

MR. WHATELY TO MR. GRENVILLE.

[Nonsuch], August 24, 1767.

DEAR SIR,—The letter I sent you last Tuesday was written from *the worst inn's worst room* in an assize town, with noise and hurry and disorder all around me. It partook, I suppose, of the confusion of the place, and was hardly intelligible. Being written, however, immediately after I rose from the conversation which it related, I conclude that it contained all the particulars, nor do any occur to me now which I omitted then, except one expression which his Lordship used when, speaking of the necessity there was that the King's mind should be convinced, he added, and then perhaps his passions, which have been biassed one way, may set as strongly the other; on which subject and on many others his sentiments coincided so exactly with yours, that if I had not known it to be impossible, I should have thought you had been talking them over together; I said as much to him, and I was pleased to find you agreed on those points so entirely.

Upon recollecting all that passed, the general impression which it has left upon me is, that the character he *affects* is that of independency and impartiality; that the distress at present he supposes to arise from the necessity of a comprehensive plan, for the benefit of the kingdom and for the security of the Minister; in opposition to which, he fears the interestedness of contending parties, who may disregard the former of those objects, and the reluctance of the Court to concur in providing for the other; that he presumes a possibility at least, if not a probability, that he may be called upon for his advice; that if he should be, he considers your behaviour during the late transaction, (and I thought he clearly mentioned it) as a pas gagné; and I imagined that the hint he dropped, and endeavoured to retract, of the *dissatisfaction* in some of Lord Rockingham's friends, appeared to him as another facility. You will judge whether the particulars (giving me only a little credit for his manner, which I cannot convey) support these general conclusions; I send them to you because they may be of use to connect the desultory account which I gave you before, and which I could not then, in the midst of so many interruptions, and so much confusion, state with care, or bring into order. I took an opportunity yesterday to call upon the gentleman who first gave me the intimation that his Lordship might be applied to, and whose country house is not above eleven miles from hence. I told him very shortly what had passed, he expressed great satisfaction at the disposition in which I represented his Lordship to be; I presume from thence that his ideas upon the point are the same as they were, though he did not give me any fresh confirmation of them.

I am told *very privately*, but very authentically, that there are many marks which show that the continuance of the present system is certainly not the idea; on the contrary, it is probable that some other arrangement is actually under consideration, though perhaps it may not immediately appear; that it is not understood that the Duke of Grafton means to remain long where he is; that he continues only in consequence of the professions he had made, not to suffer the Closet to be taken by storm; but is as uneasy in his situation as ever, and as much dissatisfied at the absence of Lord Chatham from all public business; that he has contrived lately to offend the Queen by the *manner* in which he has opposed her inclinations; for that on the vacancy of the place of Vice Admiral of Scotland, she expressed her wish that the King might on that occasion bestow a mark of his favour on General Græme[1]; Mr. Conway was at the same time pressing for Lord Frederick Campbell, and the Duke of Queensberry for Lord March; in support of the pretensions of the latter it was urged, that the place was proper only for a Peer; the Duke of Grafton espoused the objection, and it was imagined he did so more particularly against the General than against Lord Frederick. The precedents failing him, as there were many instances produced of its being given to commoners, he made use of other pretences, and at last carried the point for Lord March. I was told also at the same time, that the language with respect to you is much softened, and what alienation there may have been, seems to be at an end; that Lord Rockingham it is supposed has made himself very ill in the Closet; that the Ministry are all disjointed; Mr. Conway is a declared King's man, not the Duke of Grafton's; and the whole seems to be far from a *settled* Administration.

I dined yesterday with Mr. Cooper[2], the Secretary of the Treasury, who spoke of Lord Chatham's case as

---

[1] The Queen's Private Secretary.

[2] Afterwards Sir Grey Cooper. He obtained the revival, in 1775, of the baronetcy of his great-grand-uncle, which had been *dormant* for many years. He was subsequently one of the Lords of the Treasury, and died in 1801. He is said by Almon to have been the author of two Political Tracts: *A Pair of Spectacles for Short-sighted Politicians*, and *The Merits of the New Administration truly stated*, both published in 1765.

very critical; and upon my asking whether he meant dangerous, he said, that he thought a person much reduced, greatly emaciated, and whose only chance was a fit of the gout, must be in a dangerous situation.

He told me that the Chancellor of the Exchequer having been not well of a long time, and he observing that he looked still worse a few days ago, he advised Lady Greenwich to send for a physician; she at first said that Mr. Townshend's disorder was only lowness of spirits; but at last called in Sir William Duncan, who has pronounced it to be a slow fever of the putrid kind; from which he does not apprehend any danger at present, but says that it is a disorder liable to so many accidents that he cannot answer for the event [1]. Mr. Townshend yesterday kept his bed, but I believe rather because he was desired than because he was obliged to do so.

---

[1] " On the 4th of September, 1767," says Horace Walpole, "died Charles Townshend, of a neglected fever, in, I think, the forty-second year of his age. He met his approaching fate with a good humour that never forsook him, and with an equanimity that he had never shown on the most trifling occasions. Though cut off so immaturely, it is a question whether he had not lived long enough for his character. His genius could have received no accession of brightness; his faults only promised multiplication. He had almost every great talent, and every little quality. His vanity exceeded even his abilities, and his suspicions seemed to make him doubt whether he had any. With such a capacity he must have been the greatest man of this age, and perhaps inferior to no man in any age, had his faults been only in a moderate proportion—in short, if he had had but common truth, common sincerity, common honesty, common modesty, common steadiness, common courage, and common sense."—*Memoirs of George III.*, vol. iii. p. 99.

Charles Townshend had been in Parliament for twenty years, and during that period he was successively in office as a Lord of Trade and of the Admiralty, Secretary of War, Paymaster of the Forces, and, at the time of his death, Chancellor of the Exchequer.

MR. WILLIAM GERARD HAMILTON TO EARL TEMPLE.

Monday morning, (September, 1767.)

MY DEAR LORD,—Though my fever has left me, it has left me so extremely low that I am ordered into the country, where I go to-morrow for a few days. A new scene of intrigue and negotiation is opening. Lord Camden left London in his way to Bath on Saturday. Before he went it was clearly his opinion that Lord Rockingham would be the first treated with, and that the thing attempted would be a reunion between the Cavendishes, Conway, and the Duke of Grafton. I know likewise that Dunning was to have gone on a party of pleasure to Flanders, and that his journey is stopped.

Taylor, who purchased part of the Pynsent estate, turns out to have been only an agent in that transaction for Lord Holland and Lord Radnor.

Before Lord Chatham left North-End he sent for his upholsterer (whom I employ) and paid him 2000*l*., in part of a bill of 2700*l*. which he owed him, and gave him many directions about his house, and particularly as to the manner in which the room was to be fitted up, *where he proposed doing business next winter.*

In his way down to Somersetshire he walked ostentatiously before the door of almost every inn at which he stopped, and a servant who went with him into the country is returned, who says he never remembers to have seen his Lordship better in his whole life.

Lord Camden likewise, before he left town, declared that he had received a letter from him, in which he proposed that they should drink a glass of Bath water together in less than three weeks.

Lord North is gone into the country. From the little

that has dropped from the friends of Lord Rockingham now in town, it does not seem as if the admission of the Bedfords, in case of any new proposal, would be, as it was before, an indispensable condition.

It is reported that Charles Townshend has died in very indifferent circumstances.

Lord Mansfield, I hear, is of opinion that my friend will take before the Session opens, with the Ministry that shall be existing at the time.

Mr. Conway is again in one of his fits of doubt and indecision as to his resigning or holding the Seals.

I have the best reason for knowing that the Chancellorship of Ireland[1] has never been offered to De Grey, and I know likewise that De Grey is of opinion Sewel will be the man, and that all is actually settled with Norton to be Master of the Rolls.

Lord Townshend, who did not intend leaving England for a fortnight, now talks of setting out next Friday, which looks as if he was willing to secure the Lord Lieutenantcy against any approaching change. Yours, &c., &c.

MR. WEDDERBURN TO MR. WHATELY.

(September, 1767[2].)

DEAR WHATELY,—I found no opportunity of writing to you from York that I would have preferred to the

---

[1] Sergeant Hewit, one of the Judges of the King's Bench, was soon after appointed Lord Chancellor of Ireland; in June, 1768, he was created Baron Lifford, and Viscount Lifford in 1781. He died in April, 1782.

[2] This letter was probably written while Wedderburn was on a visit to Lord Rockingham at Wentworth, about the beginning of September.

post. Stuart, who sets out from hence to-morrow, has promised to take charge of this. The hint I wished to convey to you in my last letter I find you have perfectly understood. All I meant was, that our friend should keep himself reserved upon the subject, and should not express himself with any degree of hostility. I have reason to think that the Duke of Grafton has given great disgust by his behaviour in that business, and if the account I heard be true, the resentment entertained at his conduct upon it is not unreasonable, for he had first declared himself perfectly satisfied as to the merits, pledged himself to support it, and afterwards drew back upon the pretext of its being very unpopular. This you may easily imagine is not a matter to be soon forgiven, perhaps not to be immediately resented, but that it will be resented I have very little doubt.

Lord Rockingham's conversation on American affairs was very temperate and reasonable, blaming exceedingly the indiscretion of the present Ministers, who had ventured upon strong measures without being prepared to support them, especially after the experience they had had that the powers of Government in that country were insufficient to execute the law, and lamenting the misfortune of the Americans, who had been seduced into resistance by the countenance shown to those who had dared to deny the right of the British Legislature. His idea seemed to be that an application would be made to Mr. Grenville through the Bedfords, and he did not seem to expect that it would be made to his friends. I am going to Richmond to-morrow for a few days, and then I shall compose myself entirely 'till the meeting of Parliament, which I presume will be early. I wish Mr. Grenville would take some opportunity of writing to Sir Laurence Dundas; the Bedfords are extremely attentive to him, and he is apt to be taken with attentions[1]. I ever am, &c., &c.

MR. CHARLES LLOYD TO EARL TEMPLE.

York Buildings, Thursday evening, September 10, 1767.

MY LORD,—Lord North came to town yesterday, saw the Duke of Grafton, and was at the Levée. It was generally understood that he had refused, and yet as generally known that, if forced to the alternative of taking the Chancellorship of the Exchequer, or of quitting his present office, he would yield. Lord Guilford is said to be in a dangerous way, so as not to be likely to live even a few weeks[2]. This may operate on Lord North's conduct. The arrangement much talked of is Lord Barrington to succeed Mr. Townshend, and Mr. Stanley to replace Lord Barrington.

The King did not go from the Queen's House 'till seven this evening. Just before his setting out for Richmond, I saw the Princess of Wales come from him. Lord Bute, it is said, is come to town so ill as to be attended by three physicians. But what would the public get by Lord Bute's death!

Lord Mansfield was in the Closet yesterday one hour and a half. I have the honour to be, &c.

CHARLES LLOYD.

---

[1] Sir Laurence Dundas was an object worthy of attention, inasmuch as he had considerable borough influence. Under his patronage Wedderburn was now M.P. for Richmond, but he vacated his seat for that place in May, 1769, in consequence of his vote in favour of Wilkes on the Middlesex Election question.

[2] Lord Guilford survived many years: he died in 1790, and was then succeeded by Lord North, as second Earl of Guilford.

MR. WHATELY TO MR. GRENVILLE.

September 11, 1767.

DEAR SIR,—The Duke of Grafton wrote to Lord Mansfield on Tuesday night, to signify to him the King's commands, that he should attend him the next day. The order of the Audiences was, the Duke of Grafton, Lord North, and Lord Mansfield. Lord North was in near an hour, and, in the meanwhile, the other two sat conversing in the outer room. Whether anything that passed in that conversation, or some other circumstance, had convinced Lord Mansfield of the certainty of Lord North's being Chancellor of the Exchequer, I do not know; but he was so persuaded of it, that, on his coming out, he went up and wished him joy: others followed the example, 'till Lord North was obliged to declare that he had not accepted, which, they say, seemed to disconcert the Duke of Grafton, as if he had not been aware of it.

After Lord North, Lord Mansfield went in, and received the Exchequer Seal[1]. He expresses great satisfaction in the reception he met with: the particulars of it he does not mention, as I hear.

Lord Chatham has sold of the Pynsent estate to the amount of 28,000*l*. Dr. Addington, who went down with him to Somersetshire, was called back by an express to attend his own son[2], who lies dangerously ill at the school just by us here. He contradicts the accounts

---

[1] When the Chancellorship is vacant, the Exchequer Seal is usually delivered *ad interim* into the custody of the Lord Chief Justice of the Court of King's Bench.

[2] Afterwards the Right Honourable Henry Addington, first Viscount Sidmouth.

of Lord Chatham's health, represents him as in a very shattered condition, but able to go about a little, and even to be amused by being read to.

Lord Bute has been in town for advice, being still much out of order. He has had a consultation of physicians, who, I hear, do not know what the case is.

Lord Barrington, it is said, is sent for, I suppose to have the Exchequer Seal.

CAPTAIN SAMUEL HOOD[1] TO MR. GRENVILLE.

Halifax, September 22, 1767.

SIR,—I beg the honour of acquainting you that I arrived safe here in six weeks and three days, and called at Madeira as I came along, and had the finest weather I ever saw, without an hour's contrary wind the whole way. This was very fortunate for Mrs. Hood, who embarked in poor health, but the sea air and that of this place has been of infinite service to her.

The greatest part of Nova Scotia is a very fine country, capable of every improvement, but in great want of hands. Labour comes high; an artificer will not work under four shillings a day, nor a common husbandman under three; very heavy upon a young colony, where nine out of ten that adventures are driven by poverty from other parts. However, some counties begin to thrive, and, was a communication open to the several interior townships, would soon flourish; the want of which checks industry, and is very severely felt. The

[1] Afterwards Admiral Lord Hood. He was made a Baronet in 1778, Baron Hood in the Peerage of Ireland in 1782, and Viscount Hood in that of Great Britain in 1796. He died in 1816.

inhabitants are not rich enough to make roads. The work is immense, especially for waggons to pass, which is much wanted, as the country near the sea is mountainous, full of trees and large rocks, and further up very swampy. There is no riding above six miles from this town without endangering the neck of man and horse; and the little that is good has been chiefly made this summer, at a vast expense, by the direction of Lord William Campbell[1], the Governor, who sees the necessity of proper roads, and has the making them much at heart. It does him great honour, as nothing can more strongly prove him a good father to the province intrusted to his care than the effecting a work of such great public utility. This to me appears an object highly deserving the attention of Government; and an annual gift of 1000*l.* or 1500*l.* for seven years, to be appropriated to road-making only, would be of infinite more use to this country than the whole vast sum it has received from home, which has not been of the least benefit towards cultivating the lands.

The mother country would I am sure soon experience very ample and happy returns, and without some help this way the sufferings of the poor farmers must continue to be great, and they will be altogether disheartened. For of what use is it, Sir, for a few people to have a large overplus of food beyond their wants, if it cannot be carried to market to buy raiment, &c. And this country will not admit it at present, except in the neighbourhood of Annapolis, and the Bay of Fundy is a very ugly and precarious navigation; it is indeed a very dangerous one in the winter, and as the harvests here are

---

[1] Son of John, fourth Duke of Argyll.

very late, the winter will be far advanced before the grain can be got ready for market.

The province seems to have exerted itself for some years past, but it is now so poor it knows not what to do; for by building a lighthouse at the entrance of the harbour, a church, giving premiums, and making temporary roads, it is now loaded with a heavy debt, the interest of which it cannot pay. From the head of the basin about thirty miles there has been a tolerable path, but it is now impassable, as all the bridges are broken down. Three shillings is an amazing price for a day's labour, which ought to be reduced one half at least, and it certainly must whenever a good communication is open between this town and the interior counties; for that will make provisions as cheap here as at any place in North America, and there can be no doubt but that inhabitants will then flock here from all the provinces.

I am exceeding happy, and much rejoice in an opportunity of relating these facts to you, Sir, as I shall in every other, of testifying the grateful sense I have of the many marks of favour and friendship you have been pleased to honour me with. I am, with the greatest respect, &c., &c. SAM. HOOD.

THE REVEREND DR. MARKHAM TO MR. GRENVILLE.

Bloomsbury Square, September 30, 1767.

SIR,—I have been called to town suddenly by an offer of the Deanery of Christ Church. I did not apply for it, nor can I find that I have been recommended. I am told that it was His Majesty's own doing. If it be so,

I cannot any way account for it so naturally as by ascribing it to the impression which your kind mention of me on a former occasion may have left on His Majesty's mind.

Permit me, therefore, to return you my thanks for it. Your kindness to me has been such, that whether I owe this obligation to you or not, it makes no difference in my duty, or in the sense which I have of it.

I beg leave to add my compliments to Mrs. Grenville, and my sincere wishes for everything that can contribute to your honour and happiness, and am, Sir, your most obliged, &c., &c.   WILLIAM MARKHAM.

MR. WILLIAM GERARD HAMILTON TO EARL TEMPLE.

Friday, (October 2, 1767.)

MY DEAR LORD,—A return of my fever has once more drove me from the country back again to town.

Lord North, it is now universally understood, will kiss hands on Wednesday next. He insisted upon terms in which the Court have acquiesced. Barrington was sent for, but before his arrival the Ministry had agreed with Lord North. What were his conditions I have not learnt.

The paragraph in the newspaper of Lord Chatham's having been desired and having refused to leave the Privy Seal in commission, is true.

Lord Townshend told me that Lord Bute had declared to him his determination to go abroad. The Court, even after all that has passed, cannot satisfy themselves, but that your Lordship, Lord Chatham, and Mr. Grenville will by some means or other be reconciled before the General Election, and the idea that you will not suffer that advantage to be thrown away, I know is at present the cause of great uneasiness.

London never was thinner, or more stifling and pestilential. I hope to leave it again in a few days.

No one is as yet mentioned to succeed Lord North. Yours, my dear Lord, &c., &c.

MR. WHATELY TO MR. GRENVILLE.

October 3, 1767.

DEAR SIR,—The circumstances of the Duke of York's death[1] which have come to my knowledge are, that Colonel Wrottesley having promised if he ever came near Monaco to pay a visit to the Prince of it, whom he had known at Paris, desired leave of the Duke, who intended to cross the Alps, that he might go round that way, and join him on the other side. The Duke there-

[1] Edward Augustus Duke of York, next brother of the King, died on the 17th of September, in his 28th year. Horace Walpole, in mentioning his death, adds, " He suffered considerably, but with a heroism becoming a great Prince. Before he died he wrote a penitential letter to the King (though, in truth, he had no faults but what his youth made very pardonable), and tenderly recommended his servants to him. The Duke of York had lately passed some time in the French Court, and by the quickness of his replies, by his easy frankness, and (in him) unusual propriety of conduct, had won much on the affection of the King of France, and on the rest of the Court, though his loose and perpetually rolling eyes, his short sight, and the singular whiteness of his hair, which the French said resembled feathers, by no means bespoke prejudice in his favour. His temper was good, his generosity royal, and his parts not defective; but his inarticulate loquacity, and the levity of his conduct, unsupported by any countenance from the King his brother, had conspired to place him but low in the estimation of his countrymen."—*Memoirs of George III.*, vol. iii. p. 103-4.

upon said he would himself go that way, and for that purpose went on board an open boat after being violently heated with dancing. From the time he was first seized, he thought he should die, and ordered large drafts to be made upon England for the payment of all his servants, observing to them that if it were postponed, they might be delayed at the least in getting their money.

James's powder drove off the fever twice when they thought him quite gone, and from thence some hopes were entertained of his recovery; but on the third attack, the dose they gave him had so very violent an effect, that they were afraid to repeat it, and of that attack he died. I believe these circumstances are tolerably exact.

MR. WHATELY TO MR. GRENVILLE.

October 5, 1767.

DEAR SIR,—I wrote you no news by the Saturday's post, because then I had seen nobody. I have this morning been with a gentleman who would know all if any were stirring, and he can tell me very little. He hears that Lord North will kiss hands on Wednesday. The reason he has not done it before is, that he desired to postpone it 'till the election of a Mayor at Banbury was over.

Lord Townshend's journey is postponed 'till next Thursday: at a Council on Saturday night, he could get so little satisfaction on the heads he wished, and particularly the Chancellorship, that he burst into a very justifiable rage, said that he would still go, but bid them take notice that if any detriment happened to the King's affairs, they, not he, were answerable for it.

They have desired him to stay for another Council, but in the meantime he complains without reserve of the treatment he meets with. I have several letters from North America, but no very interesting news. Rhode Island has not yet made the compensation. Mr. Ingersol has heard of the motion made by you in Parliament for marks of favour to the sufferers, and of your reference in particular to him, for which he desires me *to present to you his most humble acknowledgments, and to let you know that he has a most grateful sense of your disinterested and truly friendly goodness to him, who has it not in his power to reward it otherwise than by sentiments of unfeigned goodness.*

The measure itself seems to me to be pleasing. I do not learn much of the manner in which the others are received, but in general things seem quiet, and the loyal party gaining strength and credit.

MR. WHATELY TO MR. GRENVILLE.

October 8, 1767.

DEAR SIR,—I have seen Mr. Lloyd, and am glad that I can make you perfectly easy on his account: he has not the least note of any of the letters, but has returned them all to me: he never had any idea of referring to them. He had begun something, but being displeased with it, threw it into the fire. He has now some ideas which he will endeavour to put together, and in the meantime has put a paragraph into the paper to contradict the representation which gave you offence. That I might write this explicitly is the reason of my preferring this conveyance to the post, and I take the opportunity to add the news of the day. I have picked up this morning a very exact account of what has lately passed concerning Ireland, which is so curious that it will entertain you. At the Cabinet which I mentioned to you in a former letter, Lord Townshend was so provoked at their doing nothing, either by way of instruction or support, that he told them he found it was nugatory to wait any longer; that he would go to his post directly, and was careless what happened to himself, but that if any mischief happened to the King's affairs, they should be answerable, not he, and that he would the next morning wait upon His Majesty, tell him the situation, leave it there, and set out immediately. The Ministers then present were so alarmed at this threat, that they begged him to defer his journey 'till a full Cabinet could meet, and yesterday was fixed for that meeting[1]. It was to

[1] This is the meeting to which the author of Junius alludes in his paper entitled *Grand Council upon the Affairs of Ireland, after eleven Adjournments* [a]. It is correctly dated the 7th of October, the day on which the Council mentioned in Mr. Whately's letter was held. The authenticity of this paper has frequently been questioned; but besides the internal evidence and peculiarity of style by which it is distinguished, it is now placed beyond doubt by the acknowledgment of the author in his letter to Mr. Grenville of October 20, 1768, which will be found at that date, and in which he says, " *the Grand Council was mine ;* " and from the circumstance of his directing Mr. Grenville's attention to this piece nearly a year after its appearance, we may presume that it had attracted much notice, and that the author was, as he said upon another occasion, " strangely partial " to it.

The Cabinet Ministers present at the Council are designated as follows :—TILBURY (Lord Northington), JUDGE JEFFREYS (Lord Camden), CAUTION without foresight (Mr. Conway), MALAGRIDA (Lord Shelburne), BOUTDEVILLE, sulky (Lord Townshend).

The business is commenced by Tilbury, who is appropriately introduced by a couplet [b], as coarse as the language in which Lord North-

[a] *Junius*, vol. ii. 482.

[b] The lines are taken from Swift's Poem of " THE PROBLEM : *that my Lord Berkeley stinks when he is in love.*" It was written when Lord Berkeley was Lord Lieutenant of Ireland, and Swift was his Chaplain.

consist of the Duke of Grafton, the Chancellor, the President, the two Secretaries of State, Lord Granby,

ington is said to have habitually indulged. During the sitting of the Council, Tilbury utters five short sentences, and there is an oath in each of them. The name of Tilbury was supposed to have been applied to Lord Northington, because he had once put up at the house of a man of that name who kept the Red Lion at Bagshot; but a more probable reason would seem to be, because the Lord President may have been thought to resemble "mine host" of the Red Lion in the habit of swearing which distinguished his Lordship's conversation. The name was not, however, first applied to him by Junius: I find it in a letter from "Gilly" Williams to George Selwyn, in December, 1764: "Whenever *old Tilbury* resigns the Seals, he (Charles Yorke) will most undoubtedly succeed to them."

The name of "CAUTION" had incidentally been mentioned in allusion to Mr. Conway, in a pamphlet published not long before, and entitled *The Conduct of the late Administration examined, relative to the Repeal of the American Stamp Act*, the authorship of which I have ventured to ascribe to Lord Temple, for reasons already assigned.

MALAGRIDA was the name of an infamous Jesuit priest, well known in Portugal. He was strangled and burnt at Lisbon in September, 1761. This opprobrious designation is given to Lord Shelburne for the supposed insincerity of his Lordship's character. He is made to say, "My Lord Holland, who certainly has had some reason to know me, has done me the honour to say that I was born a Jesuit, and that if all the good qualities which make the Society of Jesus respectable were banished from the rest of the earth, they would still find room enough in the bosom of Malagrida." Horace Walpole, in relating the circumstances attendant upon a rearrangement of the Ministry in 1763, thus mentions Lord Shelburne:—"He (Fox) now broke out against his scholar, reproached him for concealing Lord Bute's intention of retiring, and spoke of Shelburne to everybody as a *perfidious and infamous liar:* these were his usual words. Lord Bute called the secrecy he had observed *a pious fraud.*"

Lord Townshend is called BOUT-DE-VILLE, a jeu-de-mots upon his name, and he is described as "*sulky,*" or as Mr. Whately very appropriately expresses it, "*in a very justifiable rage.*"

It must not be supposed that Lord Camden was named JEFFREYS because he had any qualities in common with Judge Jeffreys of infamous memory. Junius was no doubt intimately acquainted with Lord Camden, and he would probably know that Lord Camden had married a Miss Jeffreys, that his eldest son was named John Jeffreys, and that his half-brother had also married another Miss Jeffreys, so Jeffreys was

Lord Hertford, and Lord Townshend. The Chancellor came up from Bath to attend it, and the questions to be discussed were the disposal of the Chancellorship and the Septennial Bill. They met at Lord Shelburne's to dinner, but an excuse soon came from the Duke of Grafton, who was to have a match that morning at Newmarket, and who said he could not be in town before eight in the evening. At eight another messenger brought advice that he would not be in town 'till to-night. They, however, sat on 'till two, but as companions, not as statesmen. Nothing was settled, nothing done. Lord Chancellor is gone back to Bath, and Lord Townshend waits upon the King to-day, and then sets off in the afternoon for Ireland, the Parliament of which kingdom is to be prorogued from day to day 'till he arrives.

The other news of the day is, that at Newmarket some symptoms appeared of a tampering between the Duke of Grafton and Lord Rockingham, and that since some private messengers are sent to some of Lord Rockingham's friends. The opinion brought away from thence is that Lord Rockingham has resisted all advances, and keeps to his purpose of acting in conjunction with the Duke of Bedford. That a messenger is gone to Mr. Burke seems to me the best authenticated

---

at least well known in his Lordship's family. Some expressions towards the end of this satire, supposed to be uttered by Lord Townshend with reference to the conduct of Lord George Sackville at the Battle of Minden, have been noticed in a recently printed letter, written by the late Sir James Mackintosh, and these expressions have been therein tortured into an "allusion to something of a very *different nature from cowardice.*" I cannot refrain from asserting my entire disbelief and abhorrence of this atrocious insinuation; it is as unjust towards the author of Junius, whoever he may be, as it is injurious to the character of the two noblemen in question: it has no other foundation than the suggestions of an impure imagination.

of any of these stories, but whether from Lord Rockingham to bring him up for his advice, or whether from the Ministers, as some say, to offer him the place of half-paymaster, I cannot say. The first is the more probable speculation, but the last is not ill vouched as a fact, though not certainly true.

While I am writing, Gerard Hamilton calls upon me, and tells me that he has seen Lord Townshend this morning[1]: he confirms most of the particulars I have told you of the yesterday's Cabinet, and contradicts none, except that the reason assigned for the Duke of Grafton's absence was the Cholic, and company in his house[2]. Lord Townshend told him that Lord Mansfield had said to him that a crack would come soon, and as probably in the quarter he was going to as in any other: Lord Townshend further said that he suspected something was going on; he could not guess what; he hoped it was not Rockingham.

Lord Mansfield was yesterday above half an hour with the King, and the show of favour is still kept up as high as ever. The friends of Lord Rockingham do not expect any advances towards them at present: I am not speaking of his particular confidants, but of his followers.

Lord North was observed not to be very happy when

---

[1] Here are two sources at least from which Lord Temple would derive his information relative to the Cabinet Meeting, which formed the subject of his "GRAND COUNCIL." It has been seen that Mr. Gerard Hamilton was his frequent and most confidential correspondent, and if he did not also receive the same information direct from Whately, he would certainly hear it through the medium of Mr. Grenville. The Paper was not inserted in the *Public Advertiser* until the 22nd of October.

[2] "A chair left empty for the High Treasurer (Duke of Grafton), detained by a hurry of business at Newmarket."—*Grand Council: Junius*, vol. ii. p. 483.

he had kissed hands: I missed of him this morning, and I am now going out of town.

The Chancellor and the President I understand are the principal opponents to the nomination of an Irishman to the Chancellorship, and though perhaps the Ministers for it, may be more numerous than those against it, they do not choose to out-vote the Law Officers on such a question.

MR. AUGUSTUS HERVEY TO MR. GRENVILLE.

Bath, October 17, 1767.

MY DEAR SIR,—Your obliging letter of the 27th past, I have not set down to answer 'till this day, that I might give you some better account of my recovery than hitherto I have been able; for this has been as tedious in the convalescence as it was dangerous in the attack: but I flatter myself that a few days more of these waters will entirely set me up, and that the half-year's tax that my detestable constitution (as it is become) pays every spring and fall for its continuance in this delightful world is over for this time, and that I shall not be called upon for any arrears, for I have really paid the full rent.

I lamented much my not being of the expedition with Lord and Lady Temple, and more so, as I think I must make a trip *that way* from hence before I go to town; the particulars you shall know when I see you, and I think you will not disapprove. I find things going on just as usual, with no more steadiness than cordiality among them. What a fate is hanging over this poor ruined country! 'T is a storm indeed approaching that I fear we are not prepared for, and I am sure our present pilots (are) not able to conduct us through.

I most sincerely lament the loss of the Duke of York, and confess to you, that I have been thinking this whole day, that it was this very day month that terminated in depriving me of one of the most friendly, and perhaps useful friends I know; and though there may be some seeming arrogance in making use of that appellation for one in this rank, yet, my dear Sir, you are too just to me, I am sure, to imagine it was dictated by my vanity, or suggested by anything but the affection and respect I really bore him from his constant goodness to me. I know, too, it is an unmanly weakness, which I neither know how to account for or excuse, and as little to conquer, to feel a loss of this kind more freshly, or more heavily on one day of the week or month than another: but this is a circumstance, like many others, in our feeble compositions, where the understanding in vain tries all its strength with the heart, whilst the last recoils as fast as the other can operate; however, I will say no more on the melancholy subject; I think it a loss to *us* all. I am, &c., &c. A. HERVEY.

MR. GRENVILLE TO MR. WHATELY.

Wotton, October 20, 1767.

DEAR WHATELY,—I know no kind of political news, except a confirmation of the uneasiness and discontent with which Lord Townshend set forward for his new government of Ireland, where it is most likely that he will meet with many circumstances to increase both, instead of lessening either. The account of the Cabinet Council meeting to settle the business of that kingdom being put off, first for a match at Newmarket, and secondly, because the Duke of Grafton had company in his house, exhibits a lively picture of the present Administration on the one hand, and on the other, of the supineness and indifference of the good people of England, from whence the Ministry seems to have copied it, as the means of being popular, by adapting themselves to the genius of the nation; and I will venture to prophesy, that the first will never be effectually changed till the latter is. As to any other change merely of persons, you know my opinion, that it is not worth the contest. Nothing but a serious conviction of the evils we labour under, in the minds both of the King and the people, can in any degree operate a cure; and 'till that is effected, at least in one of the two, I own I see no prospect of any public benefit, though a very fair one for private emolument from the present disgraceful and uncertain state. Distresses of many kinds will, if I mistake not, open their eyes at last. The best wish I can form is, that it may not be too late to apply any remedy. I hear that the Duke of Bedford is at Woburn, in better spirits than he has been with regard to his blindness, from the hopes which have been given to him that he may soon be in a condition to be couched. I shall be glad to do any good offices in my power to Mr. D'Oyly[1] wherever an occasion offers. I am, &c., &c.

GEORGE GRENVILLE.

[1] Deputy Secretary at War. He was afterwards, according to Junius, "driven out" of the War Office by Lord Barrington, to make room for Mr. Chamier.

EARL TEMPLE TO MR. GRENVILLE.

Stowe, Friday, (October 23, 1767.)

MY DEAR BROTHER,—You perfectly understand Beardmore's business; expressions of a total devotion to you and me on the part of Mr. M., who is, it seems, a Bucks gentleman, and a desire of our good offices at Aylesbury. The only question is, whether the Duke of B. and Lord G. will forgive him, which is much wished on his part.

As to London, I do not think of visiting it at all 'till after New Year's day, unless pressingly summoned to it by the Bedfordians upon a plan of very determined opposition[1]. If the kingdom choose to continue asleep in the hands of children and worse, I am tired of attempting to wake them from their delightful dreams[2], till they awake themselves with a vengeance. News I hear of none. I am much obliged to Lord and Lady Aylesford for their kind intentions through the vale of sin and death; when they are safely landed here, the rest of their journey will be very good. Respects and

---

[1] As Lord Temple expected a summons from the Bedfords, and was evidently very willing to enter with them into "a plan of very determined opposition," so much the greater was his rage and disappointment when he found, a few weeks later, that the Bedfords had been secretly plotting with the Minister, that they had altogether thrown over the Grenville connection, and were far advanced in making their own separate bargain with the Duke of Grafton. This may be considered as one of the sources of the extreme virulence of Junius against the Dukes of Bedford and Grafton and their political associates, including Lord Mansfield, who was believed to have been one of the persons by whom the treaty was suggested and secretly encouraged.

[2] "The publication of this paper may perhaps come time enough *to rouse him from his dream*, and to prevent his doing a national mischief *in his sleep.*"—*Junius, Private Letter to Mr. Grenville.* See *post*, February 6, 1768.

kind compliments to all, above and below Wottonian ground. Your most affectionate, T.

MR. GRENVILLE TO MR. WALLACE.

Wotton, October 25, 1767.

SIR,—I received your letter enclosing a state of my first and second treasurership of the Navy, by which I find that no more than one-third of the pay-books of the latter are made up and adjusted. I beg that you will press them forwards by every means in your power, that I may be able to show to the Court of Exchequer that nothing has been omitted, and that you may make an affidavit to that purpose. You know how strongly I urged this to you and to all the officers, while I was First Lord of the Treasury, and how constantly I have continued to press them forwards[1]. I am, &c., &c.

GEORGE GRENVILLE.

[1] Mr. Grenville was three times Treasurer of the Navy. He resigned his third Treasurership upon his appointment to be Secretary of State in May, 1762. It appears that no more than *one-third* of the accounts of his *second* Treasurership, which ended in 1757, were made up at the date of this letter, more than ten years after. When his accounts up to the year 1762 were adjusted, it is not my purpose to inquire. I mention these circumstances to show that Lord Holland was harshly treated by the Livery of London, when he was singled out to be stigmatized in their Address to the King as a "*public defaulter of unaccounted millions.*" Although his accounts as Paymaster of the Forces had remained for ten years unsettled, it was no more his fault than it was Mr. Grenville's that *his* accounts were also unsettled, or that the Pay Office accounts of Lord Chatham, or those of the Earls of Darlington and Kinnoul, and of Mr. Potter, were still before the auditor at this time. It was the vice of the system, not of the individuals. Junius, in a private note to Woodfall (July 21, 1769) writes, "I wish Lord Holland may acquit himself with honour. If his cause be good, he should at once have published that account to which he refers in his letter to the Mayor."

Lord Holland had written to the Lord Mayor and mentioned that

MR. AUGUSTUS HERVEY TO MR. GRENVILLE.

Bath, November 3, 1767.

MY DEAR SIR,—I am so much the better for this place and the waters (which I shall leave in a few days) that I cannot help letting you know it, that I may prove by that how sure I am of your friendship, and the part you take in what concerns me. I hope, on my return to town, to hear as good accounts of you and Mrs. Grenville. I have much to say to you about some transactions going on in the West, but do not care to risk it by letter; but I think the gentlemen in Administration have no reason to plume themselves on their success in every place, although I fear they have too well succeeded at Taunton, by what I find from a friend of mine on the spot there. Here Lord Chatham is, and goes out every day on horseback when the weather lets him, and looks rather thin and pallid, but otherwise very well to appearance; he sees no one. Lord Camden is gone, after a very urgent but totally fruitless attempt to bring in your brother, Mr. James Grenville, for this place. They think it very private, but I know the whole transaction, and though he still remains to try on, yet it will not do. They have been told openly that any man that voted for the repeal of the Stamp Act shall never have

Mr. Beckford had the means of showing the utter falsehood of what was insinuated in the Address from the Livery, for that he had communicated to him an explanatory statement of the circumstances, which was subsequently printed in the newspapers. Alderman Beckford, however, until he was applied to in consequence of Lord Holland's letter, had considered it to be a private paper, and did not recollect having shown it to more than a single person. This single person may have been Junius himself, in the person of Lord Temple, with whom, as well as with Lord Chatham and Mr. Calcraft, Mr. Beckford was at the time upon very intimate terms. I have already alluded to the reasons why Junius is said to have "*spared Lord Holland.*"

their interest here, and that Lord Chatham cannot make one single vote in the town, so that Sir John Sebright will (by good luck for him), in all probability, come in, because there are two parties here, the *Smiths* and the *Warburtons*, that are at bay, and do not care to attempt for any other, lest they should either weaken their own party; but both are united against Lord Camden's recommendation, and from some more particulars that I do not care to mention in this, though I shall send this to my sister to forward to you, as I think *these posts* are rather suspicious.

I go to Saltash to-morrow, where I think things are in a very good way; and they have assured me that nothing shall hurt me there, so that I hope (between ourselves) to get young Phipps chose there malgré Monsieur le Duc de G——, [Grafton]; but this yet requires management for him; not the least of it was for myself; I set them at defiance unless they had other heads at the Treasury or Admiralty. I am, &c., &c.

A. Hervey.

MR. AUGUSTUS HERVEY TO MR. GRENVILLE.

Bath, November 5, 1767.

Though I wrote to you, my dear Sir, so lately, you may perhaps be glad to know what is *certainly* passing with a *principal person* here:—First, I suppose you know he has got Hayes again[1], and he goes to town

[1] Lord Chatham's former residence near Bromley, in Kent, which he had sold to Mr. Thomas Walpole some years before; and now ardently desiring to repossess it, Mr. Walpole had, with singular generosity and good nature, consented to gratify his wishes. Lord Camden, who transacted the business on the part of Lord Chatham, writes to Lady Chatham, "If this sacrifice shall prove instrumental to the recovery of Lord Chatham's health, Mr. Walpole will be well paid; and I am afraid that nothing short of that will make him completely happy. It

either Wednesday or Thursday next; and I know, from one *she* said it to, that *he* is not very well pleased with the Ministry above. They certainly sent to him, three or four days ago, to take his part absolutely, either to go up or give it up, and he gave no answer, but keeps the *Seals* here, and I am assured is most extremely dissatisfied with their conduct above. He has no reason to be very well content with them here, Mr. J. G. (James Grenville) being obliged to give up the pursuit of being chosen here.

Lord Clare[1] is here, and is very busy and bustling; but I do not think he has been able to accomplish seeing Lord Chatham: that has been reserved for only Mr. Beckford, who came here the night before last, and is this morning vanished again, and, as I am told, was admitted openly yesterday.

I met my Lord and Lady to-day airing, and both looked very well, I thought.

To-morrow I undertake the journey to Saltash, and you may be assured I should not do that for diversion; and although safe at Bury, yet I think it will answer my purpose. I purpose being back again Sunday, 15th, but sooner if I can, and hope I shall hear from you by that time.

Pray let me know if you go up to the meeting[2], be-

is impossible to describe as it deserves the pangs he felt at parting with his favourite place; but his humanity and regard to Lord Chatham got the better of all his partiality; the consideration of whose melancholy case prevailed beyond the power of persuasion, force, or interest."
—*Chatham Correspondence*, vol. iii. p. 291.

[1] Robert Nugent, M.P. for Bristol, recently created Viscount Clare, in the Peerage of Ireland. Goldsmith's poem of the *Haunch of Venison*, which was probably written about this time, though not published until after Goldsmith's death, was addressed to Lord Clare.

[2] Parliament met on the 24th of November.

cause, in that case, I certainly shall; if not, I think I shall remain some days longer here, as I shall be glad to give the waters quite fair scope, they having lately agreed with me so well. I am, &c., &c.

A. HERVEY.

MR. WHATELY TO MR. GRENVILLE.

November 5, 1767.

DEAR SIR,—I have just received the inclosed from General Irwin[1], which he desired me to convey to you. He will have apprized you of his getting a regiment, which alone is an event very agreeable to me; but the manner of it pleases me much more. He asked it of the King, and received at first no positive answer; notwithstanding repeated hints that if he would apply to the Ministers, there would not be a difficulty, he never mentioned it to any of them, though he saw them all as he waited upon them on his return; he only wrote an official letter to Lord Granby (upon being informed that his Lordship had declared he must have the first regiment) desiring him to lay his pretensions before His

---

[1] He had recently returned from the Government of Gibraltar: he was soon after made a Knight of the Bath, and Colonel of the 6th Regiment of Dragoon Guards. He had previously held for several years the post of Commander-in-Chief in Ireland.

Wraxall describes Sir John Irwin as a man of "imposing personal appearance. It was impossible to possess finer manners without any affectation. The King considered and treated Irwin as a person whose conversation afforded him peculiar gratification. He often delighted to protract the discourse with a courtier, whose powers of entertainment, however extensive, were always under the restraint of profound respect, and who never forgot the character of the Prince whom he addressed, even for a single moment." His pecuniary embarrassments compelled him to retire to the Continent, and he latterly established his residence at Parma, where he died, in May, 1788."—See *Wraxall's Historical Memoirs*, ed. 1836, vol. iv. p. 442.

Majesty, and observing that nine juniors had been promoted to regiments during his absence; and he now declares that he accepts not as a favour but justice, and thinks himself as free in his political walk to-day as he was yesterday.

I am greatly delighted with the spirit of his conduct, and the firmness of his attachment, upon which head he desired me last night to say to you that he knows and will know of no ministerial connection but with you; and he is happy to think that that is not likely to interfere with his old connection with Lord George Sackville[1].

In a very long audience which he had of the King, he took occasion to tell His Majesty that he had been ill advised in recalling the additional troops which had been sent to Gibraltar. The King said he agreed with him, but he was not answerable for it; it was *their* doing. Do you know, says he, how I have been circumstanced; *how many Secretaries of State have you corresponded with?* Five, Sir. *You see my situation; ce métier de politique est un très vilain métier; c'est le métier d'un faquin; ce n'est pas le métier d'un gentilhomme*[2].

Is not this very singular language? It seems to me

[1] General Irwin was at this time the colleague of Lord George Sackville as M.P. for East Grinstead.

[2] This *singular language* had direct reference to the painful position in which all these intriguing factions were perpetually placing the King, by forcing upon him, in rapid succession, Ministers who suspected and hated one another, and to whom he felt himself obliged by the Constitution to give the same countenance and support, to which, perhaps, only a short time before, their antagonists had been equally entitled. The King *seemed*, indeed, to be master, and to have a responsible choice; but it was not so; and in his honest endeavours to act with fairness and even with kindness to all, he has often very undeservedly incurred the charge of duplicity and favouritism.

to be the disburthening of an oppressed heart; you know it is not weakness.

I have met with but one person who has seen Lord Mansfield since his last conference[1]; and to him he said of it, that never was Chancellor of the Exchequer dismissed with more good humour; and that some things passed in the conversation which he never would divulge[2].

The reports of the day are that Lord Bute is very ill, and that Sir Fletcher Norton is to have the Rolls. I believe neither; on the contrary, I hear that Lord Bute is recovered.

Of Lord Chatham I can hear nothing very positive. I believe the story of his having repurchased Hayes; and I have been told that he is really out of his senses:

[1] With the King, when he went to deliver up the Exchequer Seal.

[2] He told Mr. Grenville also that he had promised never to disclose the particulars of that conversation. It seems to have been one of Lord Mansfield's peculiarities always to have a secret; as if he would

> "Still keep something to himself
> He'd scarcely tell to any."

His characteristic timidity frequently prevented him from avowing his political opinions. "Instead of acting," says Junius, "that open generous part which becomes your rank and station, you meanly skulk into the Closet, and give your Sovereign such advice as you have not spirit to avow or defend." On the question respecting the Middlesex election, Lord Mansfield said, "I have never delivered any opinion on the legality of the proceedings of the House of Commons, nor, whatever expectations may be formed, will I now deliver my sentiments. *They are locked up in my own breast, and shall die with me.*" Upon a subsequent occasion, and while quailing under the infliction of one of Lord Chatham's bursts of oratory, and "having pretty well," says Lord Campbell, "disclosed the secret which he said was to die with him, he unaccountably added, 'What part I took previously in this matter shall ever remain with myself. I have, I must confess, deposited it in the breast of one of the Royal family, but resting secure in that confidence, it shall never be disclosed to another.'"—*Lives of the Chief Justices*, vol. ii. p. 473.

a gentleman here does aver, that meeting him as he was riding out, he went up to speak to him; that his Lordship started, and gave no answer, but Lady Chatham coming up, desired him not to interrupt my Lord in his ride. I do not vouch for the truth of my tale, any further than that this gentleman does tell this story, and I know no reason for his telling a lie.

I met Admiral Keppel yesterday; his language was violent and spirited opposition, with great virulence against Conway, for whom, however, he said the Cavendishes have still a strange partiality. He was particularly angry at the offer made to Lord Edgecumbe of half the Pay Office, and quoted Sir C. Saunders for saying that Lord Edgecumbe ought to have asked Mr. Conway what reason he had to think him a scoundrel. I asked what answer he had given: *he did not know particularly, but only knew he had refused.* This made me inquire, and I since hear that his Lordship did so far hesitate as to consult Lord Besborough, who let him understand, that his friends who had resigned on his account could never forgive his accepting.

Admiral Keppel was very hostile too against the Duke of Grafton: he lamented much the conduct of his party last winter; in that I concurred: he hoped we should explain ourselves to each other before the opening of the next Session. To that I said nothing.

Sir Charles Bunbury dined with me the other day at Nonsuch[1]; he does not seem much alarmed at the opposition to him in Suffolk, but is vexed at the expense.

He was at the Duke of Grafton's at the time that his Grace ought to have been at the Cabinet Council upon Irish affairs, and says all the reasons given for his

[1] Whately's residence in Surrey.

absence are true. He had the cholic; there was a race that morning, and the house was full of company; but the cholic was not the most weighty consideration.

Mr. Calcraft is gone down to oppose Mr. John Pitt. There is a rumour to-day that Lord Guilford is dangerously ill. I saw Lord Fife to-day, who is come thus far in order to accompany his lady to the south of France, but she is too weak to proceed, and he is now going to try Bristol.

MR. GRENVILLE TO MR. WALLACE.

Wotton, November 14, 1767.

Sir,—I received the favour of your letter of the 12th of this month, and entirely approve of your attending at the Court of Exchequer with the state of my accounts, and the reasons why they have not been adjusted before now. I think it necessary for me that this should be stated and publicly explained to the Court, together with the repeated and urgent directions which I have given whilst I was in the Treasury, and since I left it, to have them forwarded with the utmost dispatch. For this reason I can by no means approve of any application to be made to the Treasury to stop the process, 'till this has been fully and properly explained to the Court, as that would look like an endeavour to conceal it from the Court. It will be time enough to think of stopping any future trouble when what we have hitherto done is fully known and justified, and I hope we shall soon get so forward as to have no occasion for it. I shall be in town on Saturday, the 21st of this month, and shall hope to see you before this business comes on in the Court of Exchequer. I am, &c., &c. GEORGE GRENVILLE.

MR. WILKES TO EARL TEMPLE.

Paris, Rue des Saints Pères, November 16, 1767.

MY LORD,—I have suffered for some months severely by a fever, but much more from what I heard from some of my friends, that your Lordship disapproved several things in my conduct of late. I have endeavoured to find out the particulars, but I am told only of two charges, which I beg leave to state and to answer.

The publication of the letter respecting the affair with Lord Talbot is said not to be approved by your Lordship. I desire only to state the history of that publication[1].

When I was at Geneva I printed twenty copies only of that letter, which I gave to some friends.

When Mr. Almon had determined to publish the *Political Register*, he wrote to me that he wished for my assistance in that work, and that my friends had already furnished him with several things which he should publish. I have his letter still, and he particularly named the letter in question. I did not choose it should make its first appearance as a piece of politics. I considered it more as an affair of honour, and therefore

---

[1] I have before referred to this letter: it was addressed to Lord Temple, and written by Wilkes from the inn at Bagshot, an hour or two after his duel with Lord Talbot on the 5th of October, 1762. It contains a minute and extremely well written description of the circumstances both before and after that ridiculous affair. It made its first appearance in print in the *St. James's Chronicle*, on Saturday, May 16, 1767, and Lord Temple was generally supposed to have sent it to the press. He was accused of it in the House of Lords by Lord Talbot, and a serious quarrel between them would have ensued, but for the immediate interference of the House. It was subsequently printed by Almon in the *Political Register*.

I sent it myself to the *St. James's Chronicle*, from whence it was copied into the *Political Register*.

The various dates prove this. This is a fact, nor can I be sorry that such a transaction was authenticated during the lives of Lord Talbot and Lord Botetourt[1], for surely such an affair will not be forgot; it is linked to other events of great moment. The consequences of the publication ought to have fallen on me, nor do I see how Lord Temple is interested in a letter only addressed to him.

No man was ever thought answerable for a letter wrote to him, nor can any man prevent it happening, even if the contents were treason. Lord Talbot was rendered ridiculous by the publication, but his conduct since has shown still more impotent rage and folly.

I am again unhappy as a man of letters, in another circumstance which I am told has displeased your Lordship, my epistle to the Duke of Grafton.

I will only say about that, I am very unlucky to have displeased where I meant to compliment.

I regret having been so long silent on some particulars; so did my late valuable friend.

No man in Europe has so much reason to be out of humour with politics as I have; no man has made such sacrifices. I have on several occasions desired to have the advice of my most respectable friend, who would have been my polar star. I was, however, left in the dark, and then if I do miss my way I am told that I go astray. My lot is indeed hard, but, whatever my fate may be, I will preserve to the last moment the high regard and attachment which has always made me, my

---

[1] At that time he was Colonel Norbonne Berkeley, and was Lord Talbot's second in the duel with Wilkes.

Lord, your Lordship's most obedient and devoted servant,
JOHN WILKES.

May I beg your Lordship to assure Lady Temple of my sincere respects?

MR. MACKINTOSH TO MR. GRENVILLE.

Edinburgh, November 16, 1767.

SIR,—I cannot sufficiently express my sense of the obligation you laid me under by the very kind and obliging letter with which you honoured me. Nothing could have prevented my offering you my warmest thanks before now but the continual hurry I have been in, which has totally put it out of my power to write letters at all. The very time taken up in going between five distant towns[1] is more than one can spare in such a business, especially with so active an opponent as I have. You will make all allowances on an occasion of this sort, and I hope I need say nothing to persuade you how much it is my desire to justify both the friendship and the favour of the good wishes you have expressed in my behalf.

Your letter to Lord Panmure[2] I made no use of. I did not think it would have been delicate on my part to have made any application to him, as Mr. Dempster[3]

---

[1] He was canvassing the Forfar District of Burghs, with the intention of becoming a candidate at the ensuing general election, in opposition to Mr. Dempster. He was one of the Senior Advocates of the Scotch Bar.

[2] William Maule, Earl of Panmure, in the Peerage of Ireland; at this time M.P. for Forfar. He was a general officer, and died in 1782, when his honours became extinct.

[3] George Dempster, at this time M.P. for the Forfar Burghs. He was made Secretary of the Order of the Thistle in 1765.

goes with him in his county election. But I am not the less sensible of your goodness in that mark of your regard, and I would be loth in anything to carry your inclinations to show kindness to me beyond consistent bounds. Lord Strathmore [1] is tied up by connéctions, too; but he has acted very genteelly towards me, and does me no harm. I am so connected with his own nearest relations that I have reason to believe I might have had his active friendship in any other circumstances; but less would do if things got fair play otherwise.

I have put it upon friends to tender my most grateful acknowledgments for all your favours, and this will be delivered by one through whom I have taken the liberty to convey my solicitations, both for your opinion and interposition in regard to a Parliamentary proceeding as to privilege, which is likely to spring out of my political contest. I could not take the liberty to trouble you with all I had to say on the subject, but my friend is possessed of the materials necessary to form your judgment; and I hope for your friendly attention in this matter, not the less that, if I mistake not, the question, supposing it made, touches former proceedings, from which I took my line, I thought safely, and to which, I am persuaded, you will think some regard due from yourself on other grounds than good-will and friendship to me. I shall hope by my friend to receive an early communication of your sentiments, and he can inform you of all my concerns. I have the honour to be, &c., &c.

R. MACKINTOSH.

[1] John Lyon-Bowes, ninth Earl of Strathmore, in the Peerage of Scotland. He had been recently elected one of the Representative Peers on the death of Lord Hyndford. He died in 1776.

EARL TEMPLE TO MR. GRENVILLE.

Stowe, November 26, 1767.

MY DEAR BROTHER,—Having pretty near accomplished all my great businesses in this part of the world, Lady Temple and I have amicably agreed to take a trip, by way of party of pleasure, to town for a week. We intend to be in Pall Mall on Saturday before three o'clock, and to the opera at night, dining, according to annual custom, at Lady Betty's[1].

I have not received Lord Lyttelton's letter[2], who, I

[1] Lady Betty Germain's, in St. James's Square.

[2] The letter was dated November 25, and is printed in Phillimore's *Memoirs of Lord Lyttelton*, p. 736. It has an endorsement in Lord Lyttelton's hand: "*Lord Temple coming to town unexpectedly, it was not sent.*" It contains chiefly an account of his conversations with Lord Mansfield and the Duke of Bedford. Of the former, Lord Lyttelton says:—" I found that he wished your Lordship would have been in town at the meeting of Parliament, as the Duke of Bedford intended to say something the first day. I answered him, that if his Grace called you, you would come, and had signified so to his Grace. He said you would not be *sent for*, but he thought you had better have been in town at this time, as the Duke was eager to speak, and your being at his side, and taking the same part, when the tone was to be given in the ensuing Session, might have good effects, and your absence might be liable to misrepresentations." He said also, " That something might arise from the quarter of America, but yet no opposition would signify anything, if the Ministers hold together. That the King mediated between them, and kept them from breaking: that he was the most *efficient* man among them; that he made each of them believe he was in love with them, and fooled them all. That unless that *mad man*, Lord Chatham, should come and throw a *fire-ball* in the midst of them, he thought they would stand their ground; but what that might do he could not tell. That Lord Bute alone could make a Ministry which would last: that if he was dead no other man could do it so well. That he (Bute) had just causes of complaint against Mr. Grenville, but was much less his enemy than Lord Rockingham, or Mr. Conway, or Lord Camden, or Lord Holland.

" He (Lord Mansfield) seemed very desirous that the present Ministry should not continue, but equally unwilling that the King should be

believe, has mistaken the day. We lie at Backwell's¹ to-morrow night.

Pleasure, not political curiosity, brings me among you; and I do not intend to visit either Court or Parliament till after Christmas. Kind compliments to all Bolton *Row*. Your most truly affectionate, T.

MR. WHATELY TO MR. GRENVILLE.

December 9, 1767.

DEAR SIR,—The day began with a motion by Mr. Conway, for leave to bring in a Bill to explain and amend the 10 W. 3, relative to the Irish army, stating, however, doubts whether the Act were temporary or perpetual, and declining at present to open the plan, but resting wholly on the generally acknowledged expediency of some augmentation.

Wedderburn attacked him for doubting of the existence of a law which was so constitutional as being the only authority on which any army at all has been kept up in Ireland, since the revolution; and on his disregard to the jealousies of the House, concerning a standing army, when he proposed an augmentation of it as a matter of course, without opening the extent of it.

A reply from Mr. Conway, and short speeches from

---

forced to remove them: full of contempt for Lord Rockingham and the Duke of Richmond, of hatred to Lord Chatham and all his friends, and of managements for Lord Bute, without much esteem of him, or affection for him. His (Lord Mansfield's) great use to our party is in the House of Lords; for in his intrigues he is warped by many different views, by managements for various connections, by a great attention to the Closet, and by the uncertainty, timidity, and over-refining turn of his mind."

¹ Tyringham House, near Newport Pagnel.

Mr. Townshend and Mr. Burke, finished this business. Then Lord North gave notice that he should bring in a Bill for limiting the East India dividends, which notice he said he thought he was obliged to give, on account of the sudden rise of the Stock, within the last four-and-twenty hours. This passed over with some slight observations by Mr. Wedderburn and Mr. Burke, and then, upon calling for the order of the day, Wedderburn, addressing himself to Lord North, expressly submitted it to his candour whether he would go into it in your absence, declaring, however, that he did not at all know you had any particular ideas to state, but only knew that you were ill, and that the House would, if any general state of the finances were opened, wish for your assistance. Lord North declared he meant to enter into no such state, and with many civil expressions towards you, wishing for your assistance in every matter of importance, said he did not think this could be so, and for the dispatch of business was for going on. In the Committee he only stated the supply voted to be about 2,500,000*l.*, and proposed three shillings Land Tax.

MR. WHATELY TO MR. GRENVILLE.

Monday, December 14, 1767.

DEAR SIR,—I called at your house just to tell you the following particulars concerning the negotiations with the Bedfords, which I take to be authentic[1].

That in the whisper at the Opera, on Saturday night, the difficulty about Rigby's having the whole Pay Office

---

[1] It seems that the negotiation between the Bedfords and the Court party was set on foot by Rigby, and principally carried on by him in the name of the Duke of Bedford, who had personally very little share in

was first started; that the negotiation hitched upon that point yesterday morning, the Ministers being unwilling it. Horace Walpole says that "the precarious state of the Duke of Bedford's health, who was breaking, and on the point of being totally blind, had suggested to Rigby the thought of abandoning Grenville;" and that Grenville's "avoidance of hostilities towards the Court, which alarmed the Bedfords lest he should anticipate them and make his peace first, drove Rigby into immediate negotiation."

Mr. Grenville mentions in his Diary an interview which he had with the Duke of Bedford on Thursday the 3rd, or Friday the 4th, of December, when his Grace first announced the intended separation of his party from the Grenville connection. But if Horace Walpole's dates are to be relied on, the negotiation had actually been then in progress for several days, and it may be presumed that he was correct, because his information was derived from the Duke of Grafton and Mr. Conway. He says:—"On (Sunday) the 29th (of November), opened another new scene. Mr. Conway told me as the greatest secret, that the Bedford faction had offered themselves to the Duke of Grafton on these limited, though few conditions,—that Lord Gower should be President of the Council; that Rigby should have a place; and that Lord Weymouth should divide the Secretary's place with Lord Shelburne, taking either the European or American department. * * * The Duke of Bedford (for the message was sent in his name) demanded a solemn promise that it should never be known if no treaty was concluded. * * * The negotiation being so prosperously advanced, Rigby went out of town for three days, as was his way on such occasions, that if it miscarried, he might, to Grenville, plead ignorance."

Walpole continues:—"Whether Grenville had got wind of the negotiation, or whether he acted in consequence of the separate plan he had formed, he and Lord Temple attempted a private negotiation with Lord Hertford by the means of Calcraft and Governor Walsh; I persuaded him to encourage these overtures. If the Bedfords were not to be had on moderate terms, it would be wise to get the Grenvilles, and break the Opposition that way: that Lord Temple might be President, and Grenville Paymaster. He answered, that Lord Temple's ambition now was a Dukedom. I said that would be a cheap purchase. Lord Hertford readily consented to court the Grenvilles. * * * * * But Rigby got the start by plunging at once into the treaty, while Grenville was preparing to soften the Court by affected moderation."[a]

Walpole pretends that he had "often and often announced to him (Grenville) that the Bedfords would betray him the first instant they should find their advantage in it." And that "many persons ascribed

[a] *Walpole's Memoirs of George III.*, vol. iii. p. 136.

to sacrifice Mr. Cooke, and thinking that another of Lord Chatham's friends, added to Lord Shelburne, Lord Clare, and Colonel Barré, would be too much; that they also drew back on finding that, by putting Lord Gower as President, and Lord Weymouth as Secretary of State, into the Cabinet, at the same time that the Board of Trade was to be given to Lord Hillsborough, with all the powers Lord Halifax had over America, and the whole Pay Office to Mr. Rigby, and the Vice-Treasurership of Ireland to Lord Sandwich, the Bedfords got more power and influence than they chose to part with; that Rigby said, yesterday morning, he should not know on which side to lay an even bet, so doubtful was the issue; that after Court there was a meeting of some of both parties; that one who must have been informed if the difficulties had been got over, said shyly this morning, he did not know that they were; from whence the gentleman who gave me these particulars, and who seldom fails in his intelligence, infers that they still continue unresolved, in which opinion he was confirmed by not

the suggestion of this treaty to Lord Mansfield, and to his weariness of opposition, which was not his turn, and in which his aversion to Lord Chatham had solely embarked him. It had been sufficient cause to Lord Mansfield to promote this new settlement, that it would, as it did entirely, give the finishing blow to Lord Chatham's Administration."

Mr. Walsh then, who was brought into Parliament through the influence of Lord Clive, was the person who, according to Walpole, had been employed by Mr. Grenville, in conjunction with Calcraft on the part of Lord Temple, to attempt a negotiation with the Court party, in order to counteract, if possible, the intrigues in which they suspected the Bedfords to be engaged. They were, however, too late. Rigby, Sandwich, and Weymouth had got the start of them, and the bargain, or at least the basis of it, was already settled: the contracting parties had completed their negotiations on the 18th of December. I have not found any corroboration of this gossip either in Lord Temple's or Mr. Grenville's papers.

having received a note, which was promised him as soon as any certainty could be learned concerning the negotiation. I did not think these circumstances of such importance as to interrupt your conversation with Lord Mansfield, as their only value is that they contradict, with some degree of authenticity, the common reports of the day.

MR. WHATELY TO MR. GRENVILLE.

December 25, 1767.

DEAR SIR,—The Dukes of Bedford and Grafton had their first meeting on Tuesday, in which the latter was profuse in his professions of esteem and regard, declared he had sought for the connection from inclination, not necessity, and threw out his indifference concerning office, saying that he wished to continue in employment no longer than should be necessary for the King's service, and would never stand in the way of more proper arrangements.

On Wednesday Lord Gower took his seat at the Council: neither of the Secretaries of State nor the Lord Chancellor were present; the discontent of Lord Shelburne is as strong as ever; there are strong appearances of ill-humour in Lord Hertford; and Lord Bristol is quoted for saying that the Chancellor went out of town very sulky, so that their absence seems to have been not merely accidental.

General Conway is to have the lead still in the House of Commons, and yet I believe the ill-humour observed in Rigby is owing to his dislike of him, as I hear he has declared he will not accept 'till Conway has actually vacated his office: he will not act under him as Secretary of State, which declaration does not seem to be a very comfortable prospect of support to the Leader of the House of Commons[1]. Mr. Rigby's language is as warm and friendly with respect to you as ever: the rest of the party still continue the same tone; and they have had a precise explanation on the American measures, on which the Duke of Grafton gives way, so that there will be no difference of opinion between

---

[1] Rigby gave himself what Walpole calls airs of "impertinence" with regard to General Conway, who "bade Grafton tell the Duke of Bedford that he ought to send for Rigby and whip him; but the impertinence was so childish, he himself should take no other notice of it." The truth seems to be, that Rigby was discontented with the place assigned to him. The Irish Government had lately imposed a tax of four shillings in the pound upon the places and pensions of all persons who resided in England, and this very materially diminished the profits of his Vice Treasurership, as well as his office of Master of the Rolls, in Ireland. "He now," adds Walpole, "openly paid court to Grenville, and in private disavowed to him having either conducted or approved the treaty; yet on a question relative to East Indian affairs, Rigby left the House, and Grenville, Burke, and Wedderburn, were beaten by 128 to 41." Rigby obtained the lucrative office of Paymaster of the Forces a few months afterwards.

The "blushing merit" which Junius describes as characteristic of Mr. Rigby is thus illustrated by Wraxall:—"The obtrusive manner in which at the Levée he often thrust himself between persons of the greatest rank, in order more expeditiously to approach the sovereign, sufficiently indicated the value in which he held his personal appearance at St. James's. When in his place in the House of Commons he was invariably habited in a full dress suit, commonly of a purple or dark colour, without lace or embroidery, close buttoned, with his sword thrust through the pocket. Corpulent in his person, he was not on that account unwieldy or inactive. His countenance was very expressive, but not of genius; still less did it indicate timidity or modesty. His manner, rough yet frank, bold and overbearing if not insolent, but manly, admirably set off whatever sentiments he uttered in Parliament. His eloquence was altogether his own, addressed not to the fancy, but to the plain comprehension of his hearers. There was a happy audacity about his forehead which must have been the gift of nature. Art could never attain to it by any efforts."—*Wraxall's Historical Memoirs*, edit. 1836, vol. ii. p. 214.

him and his new friends, for he acquiesces entirely in their system.

It is certain that he has carried on this negotiation without concert with the rest of the Administration[1]. I have been told it by one who is glad of their dissensions, and it has been confessed to me by one who is sorry for them. His Grace's attentions to the Bedfords are infinite, and his professions unlimited. He has explicitly declared, upon the direct question being asked whether he had consulted Lord Chatham, that he had had no communication with him upon business these six months, and from the anecdotes I have mentioned, and other little circumstances, it seems at present clear that be means to throw himself entirely upon the Bedfords, disavowing certainly on this, and probably intending upon others to break off, all his other connections.

Lord Chatham avoided going through town in his way to Hayes, and to avoid it lay at Mrs. Pitt's[2] near Putney. Lord Shelburne waited for his passing, some hours at Bromley, and when he went away, left a letter for him[3]. Lord Clare has sent to Hayes a how do you

---

[1] "It is understood by the public, that the plan of introducing the Duke of Bedford's friends entirely belongs to the Duke of Grafton. It is also understood, that if you should exert your influence with the King to overturn this plan, the Duke of Grafton will be strong enough with his *new friends* to defeat any attempt of that kind."—*The Author of Junius to Lord Chatham, Chatham Correspondence*, vol. iii. p. 302.

[2] Probably his sister, Mrs. Anne Pitt.

[3] Lord Shelburne's letter is printed in the *Chatham Correspondence*, vol. iii. p. 300. It is addressed to the *Countess* of Chatham, as indeed had been all letters on business for some months past, from Lord Shelburne, Lord Camden, the Duke of Grafton, Lord Bristol, &c. So many of Lord Chatham's letters were written by Lady Chatham, that she must have been extremely useful to him as a secretary, not only at this time, but in former years, when he was Secretary of State, and particularly during his long and severe illnesses, when probably much of the confidential business of the office was transacted by Lady Chatham and her brother Lord Temple, who was then Lord Privy Seal.

do, to which he has received a very civil answer, and is positive that Lord Chatham's head is as clear as ever, that he will appear at Court again, &c., &c. Mr. Brand[1] is to be a Peer soon; it was made a *sine quâ non*. Wood undertakes the office of Under Secretary of State for the present, Mr. Lynch is to be the other, Mr. Thynne Comptroller of the Household, and the others as you told me. From all appearances it seems now that the Bedfords have in reality the most influence of any part of the Ministry. Their behaviour, as far as I can judge of it, both with respect to measures and to men, seems conformable to the declarations you have had from them; the only interruption of their attentions towards you and Lord Temple was upon the publication of those *Parting Words*[2] from Almon, which I find has given great offence, but that offence taken then seems now to be subsiding.

LORD CLIVE TO MR. GRENVILLE.

Bath, December 28, 1767.

DEAR SIR,—I should long ere this have acknowledged the receipt of your very obliging letter by General Irwin, had I not been seized with so violent a return of my old complaint that I was totally incapacitated from writing, and even now, though I am considerably relieved, I cannot employ my own hand to thank you for your repeated expressions of friendship and regard. The relapses of my disorder are so frequent and dangerous, that Dr. Moysey insists upon my making all

[1] Thomas Brand, at this time M.P. for Shoreham. He died in 1770, without having been made a Peer. His grandson became Lord Dacre after the death of his mother, who had inherited that barony.

[2] See Mr. Grenville's answer, *post*, p. 202.

possible haste to a more temperate climate, and I have accordingly determined to set out in a week or two for the South of France and Italy. This journey I am frankly told is the only chance I have for a perfect recovery. I did flatter myself that my health was so far improved, that I might be able to attend Parliament a little, after the holidays, and I am sure I should have been happy if any communication of the knowledge I have acquired [of affairs] in India could have contributed to an equitable arrangement of them for the mutual advantage of the nation and of the Company. But the establishment of my health must now supersede all other considerations, and my best wishes are all I can offer to you and the public. The time, I think, cannot be far distant when your superior abilities as a Minister will oblige the King to call you again into Administration. For his sake and for the country's, I hope the event is near, but for your own, I ought, perhaps, to wish that you might pass the remainder of your life in the tranquil enjoyment of private friendship, and in pleasing reflections upon that great and unspotted public character which you have already acquired. Lady Clive joins with me in most respectful compliments to Mrs. Grenville, and I have the honour to remain, &c., &c.

CLIVE.

MR. GRENVILLE TO MR. WHATELY.

Stowe, December 29, 1767.

DEAR WHATELY,—I received your packet by the coach very safe, and was so far from having heard all the circumstances contained in it, that some of them surprised me, and if your authority for the strong and explicit declarations of unlimited confidence and exclusive union is not unquestionable, I own I should still doubt of their being carried to that extent; however, a very little time will necessarily explain it, and to that best expositor of these mysteries I leave it.

You will have heard from this house how very unjustly any degree of discontent has been taken up by the Duke of Bedford's friends against Lord Temple on account of the parting words in the *Political Register*, with which, as I always told you, he had nothing to do, either directly or indirectly, being an absolute stranger to it till he saw it in print[1].

[1] The following is the article alluded to :—

"A WORD AT PARTING, TO HIS GRACE THE DUKE OF BEDFORD."
"*Cape dona extrema.*"

"MY LORD,—Your Grace has no occasion to be alarmed at this public address; I mean neither to betray private conversations, nor to reproach you with the breach of engagements. I pretend to no anecdotes of Cabinets, nor will I indulge myself even in conjectures on past stipulations. Shall I say fairly to you, that I have ever disliked juntos and associations of men promising to wade together through every scene of public business? They fetter men of good intentions, and are a feeble barrier to those who have necessities to contend with. The broad tongue of the town has lately been employed in circulating reports of your Grace's declaration (to those with whom it is probable you might think yourself engaged), *that you hoped it would not be considered as a breach of good faith, if your friends thought themselves at liberty to accept of any offers which might be made to them of public employments.* Whether any or what answer was returned to this declaration, it is neither my inclination nor my business to inquire. My only intention is to submit to your Grace's own judgment, whether (setting aside every private contract and agreement entirely out of the question) the accession of your friends to the present Ministry, at this time, is not a breach of the good faith which you owe both to yourselves and to the public?

"All this is to be understood upon a supposition that the change is made upon principles *professed* at least, and not upon the avowal of necessity. If your Grace's followers are starved into compliance, and you will not march them through Coventry, for the same reason with

I took an occasion to assure some of the Duke of Bedford's friends of this before I left London, both on

Sir John Falstaff, they are to be pitied and not argued with. The remedy is a very easy one [a]; refer their cause to the Corn committee, upon whom so much is laid already. I do not see why a distressed patriot should not be relieved as soon as a clamorous weaver; it is a dear time, and both ought to be provided for.

"Your Grace, indeed, who can have no such temptation for yourself, may during the present prorogation be at leisure to consider how far the step you have taken is consistent with the measures to which you are publicly pledged, and with what decency you can now acquiesce with the men whom you have so lately renounced. The time, as well as the measure, is somewhat unfortunate. Have any steps been taken to vindicate and assert ([or] as your Grace would now say), to maintain and support the sovereignty of *Great Britain* over *America?* And, as if every humiliating circumstance was to attend you, is not Mr. Conway still to take the lead in the House of Commons [b]?

"But you have made stipulations, it may be said; it is not all bargain and sale. What stipulations are any men inclined to grant to those who throw down their arms and surrender at discretion? And what can these men grant to you? They would scarcely think you serious in the proposal: they see you sacrificing your personal animosities— your declared, recently declared enmities—for the sake of offices for your friends; and can they imagine that you will stick out for the sake of the public? They see you abandoning men whom you have professed to link with and to like, and, linking yourself to those who wish it to pass for their merit, that they have undone all that your former colleagues advised. Are the Ministers likely to become your converts, or have you resolution enough, having reconciled yourself to the men, to quit them upon the score of their measures?

"It may be worth your while to ask yourself, to what men you are now reconciled? To a Ministry supported (I say it not by way of imputation, but as a notorious fact) and protected by Lord Bute and his friends. What I may think of the noble Lord is beside the question. In Government I would not be his tool; out of Government I will never be his accuser and persecutor. But your Grace may perhaps remember who it was that advised and insisted on the dismission of Mr. Mackenzie, and who have echoed through the kingdom complaints of Lord Bute's influence and resolutions to oppose it. If it is a grievance that his standard is hoisted over these united kingdoms, who is now unfurling and propping it? If it has been his maxim to divide in order to govern, to whom

---

[a] "The remedy will soon be in your power."—*Junius, Dedication,* i. 348.
[b] See Whately's letter to Mr. Grenville, *ante,* pages 198, 199.

my brother's part as well as my own, and it is a piece of justice that I wish you would do to him whenever you have an opportunity. I am, &c., &c.

GEORGE GRENVILLE.

will he now be indebted for an additional subdivision, and by consequence for an additional resource? This, my Lord, is not the language of exaggeration [a] or resentment; I have just touched the topics, and left them to your own reflection. As to men, it is indeed an indifferent matter.

"It is the disease of the present times, that a short experience convinces us, there are scarce any men, how high in rank soever, who are worth the contending for. But measures are permanent, and thence arises my concern, that at no very distant period [b], I trust, when the present heats shall be somewhat subsided, and the people of this country shall, as the mind of one man, applaud the public-spirited few, who, in a venal and profligate age, dared to exert the legislative rights of *Great Britain* over every part of His Majesty's dominions: then alas! there will be wanting the name of *Russell*, which has derived strength and credit on so many glorious undertakings."

I have no hesitation in ascribing the *Word at Parting* to the pen of Lord Temple, and consequently, as I also believe, to that of the author of Junius. The internal evidence from similarity of style (of which I have pointed out in the sub-notes a few striking instances) can hardly, I think, escape the notice of any person who has attentively studied the writings of Junius.

As for the disclaimer by Mr. Grenville on the part of Lord Temple, which may seem to militate against my theory, I can only say it has very little weight with me. If Lord Temple were the author of this, and other more libellous political papers, he involved himself in the necessity of denying them, and it is not incumbent upon me to examine the arguments by which such deviations from strict veracity have been defended or extenuated.

Almon subsequently attributed the authorship of the *Word at Parting* to Charles Lloyd, perhaps even at the suggestion of Lord Temple, in order to divert suspicion from himself. If Lloyd could be proved to be the author of the paper in question, I should then believe in the *possibility* that he was the author of Junius; a fact which, from the well-known circumstances of Lloyd's miserable and protracted state of ill health, if there were no other reasons, I should consider to be, in the words of Junius, "as near to impossible as the highest improbability can go."

[a] " This is not the language of vanity."—*Junius*, i. 342.
[b] " The period is not very distant."—*Ibid.* i. 343.
   " ———— nor will that period be distant."—*Ibid.* ii. 516.

LORD TREVOR TO MR. GRENVILLE.

Green Street, Tuesday morning, December 29, 1767.

DEAR SIR,—Since the low piece of jockeyship of the new Ministry's adjourning, *tanquam aliud agendo,* over the day minuted for the inquiry into the state of the nation, and thereby superseding that motion *sub silentio,* I have heard of nothing curious except Rigby's spirited refusal, notwithstanding the Lord President's example, to kiss hands, until Conway, who had pretended to keep the Seals, and take the lead in the House of Commons to the end of the Sessions, had actually resigned both. Which of the two is to carry his point I cannot say, but the issue either way will in my opinion be significant.

I suspect some appearance of resentment against the Americans is to be the first-fruits and cement of the new alliance, but I much doubt whether it will be such an one as you should have suggested or I approve.

The Duke of Newcastle has had a severe relapse since his return from Bath to Claremont, and, though he has been let blood twice since last Thursday, I cannot learn that his symptoms are much mended. Indeed I think his Grace in a very precarious situation, and not knowing what speculations it may occasion at Lewes, I am just setting off for that neighbourhood. I am, dear Sir, &c., &c.
TREVOR.

The old Speaker[1] is given over of a mortification in his leg.

---

[1] The Right Honourable Arthur Onslow, who had formerly been Speaker of the House of Commons for so many years. He died on the 17th February following.

MR. GRENVILLE TO LORD TREVOR.

Wotton, December 31, 1767.

My dear Lord,—No information which your letter could convey to me concerning our present political state could give me so much pleasure as your kind attention in writing to me.

I have indeed heard very little news since I came hither, but I was informed authentically of the intended alterations the day before I left London, and was then told that Mr. Conway wished to keep the Seals *'till after the adjournment*, that it might not look as if he was turned out. It was not then, I believe, understood that he meant to keep them 'till the end of the Sessions, nor did I hear of Mr. Rigby's refusal to kiss hands for his employment 'till Mr. Conway had actually resigned both his office and the lead in the House of Commons. I should think the latter very difficult to be retained without the former, but whatever the merits of the dispute may be, the decision of it, if it has arisen, will certainly be significant in the present situation.

I shall be curious to know what system is to be adopted for Ireland and America; whether the new Secretary of State for the Colonies will be reconciled to the ideas of their *dependence* and obedience, agreeably to the letter and intention of the British Acts of Parliament, or whether their independence is to be openly avowed: if the former is determined upon, a firm and temperate conduct must be steadily pursued; if the latter, appearances of resentment against the Americans, which you suspect, will only expose the honour of the King and kingdom to fresh insults and contempt.

I am sorry for the very indifferent account you give

of the Duke of Newcastle's illness, because I think that his influence with his friends has of late been well employed.

I am very sorry for my poor old friend the late Speaker; a mortification in the leg at his time of life seems indeed very desperate. He has lived, however, long enough to have the additional mortification of outliving the credit and dignity of that House which had been the great object of his life, and which he had supported with so much reputation. I am ever, &c., &c.

GEORGE GRENVILLE.

MR. GRENVILLE'S DIARY

OF

MEMORABLE TRANSACTIONS.

(Continued from Vol. iii. page 397.)

Saturday, January 21*st,* 1767.—Lord Cardross [1], who was in the most intimate connection with Lord Chatham, was by him named Secretary to the Embassy for Spain, under Sir James Gray. He now is extremely discontented, says he is very ill used by Lord Chatham, refuses to go, and told the Bishop of Carlisle (who told it to Mr. Grenville) that Lord Chatham would not dare to quarrel with him, because he has him in his power, he having been the person who managed the whole of the last negotiation with Lord Bute to bring Lord Chatham into power; that this was first set on foot through the means of Lord Northumberland, by Lord Cardross going to make overtures to his Lordship from Mr. Pitt. Lord Northumberland at first declined it, telling Lord Cardross that he was not so well acquainted with Mr. Pitt as he was; that he would make his way by their means, and then use them ill, and break every tie to which he had engaged himself. This did not discourage Lord Cardross, who still continued to go between Lord Northum-

---

[1] David Stewart, Lord Cardross: at the death of his father, on the 1st of December following, he succeeded to the Earldom of Buchan, and survived until 1829.

berland and Mr. Pitt; the former at length listened to him, and the promise of the Dukedom was the seal of the bargain.

This is the account Lord Cardross gives: how far liable to doubt is a question; but certain it is that, during the last twelvemonth, he lived in the nearest intimacy with Lord Chatham, who never came to London even for an hour without seeing him. This story seems, in some sort, to agree with Lord Percy's narrative to Mr. Pitt[1]. If Lord Chatham had promised the Dukedom, he had been slow in the accomplishment of it, and the appointment of Lord Hertford appears to have furnished an opportunity to Lord Northumberland not only to remind him of the promise, but to insist upon the immediate performance of it, which accounts for what appears so strangely abrupt in that transaction.

Mr. Pitt[2] told Mr. Grenville a most extraordinary anecdote, relating to the King's attachment to Lady Sarah Lennox. He says that His Majesty came to Lady Susan Strangways (Lady Susan O'Brien) in the Drawing-room, asked her in a whisper if she did not think the Coronation a much finer sight if there was a Queen; she said yes. He then asked her if she did not know somebody who would grace that ceremony in the properest manner: at this she was much embarrassed, thinking he meant herself, but he went on, and said I mean your friend Lady Sarah Lennox; tell her so, and let me have her answer the next Drawing-room day.

Lady Sarah was at this time in love with Lord New-

[1] See Mr. Grenville's Diary, November 13, 1766.
[2] Mr. Thomas Pitt.

bottle [1], and therefore received this news with great reluctance: it was, however, talked over in the family, and, by Lord and Lady Holland's persuasion, she was brought to listen to it. She went the next Drawing-room day to St. James's, stated to the King, in as few words as she could, the inconveniences and difficulties in which such a step would involve him. He said that was his business: he would stand them all; his party was taken, he wished to hear hers was likewise.

In this state it continued, whilst she, by the advice of her friends, broke off with Lord Newbottle very reluctantly on her part: she went into the country for a few days, and, by a fall from her horse, broke her leg. The absence which this occasioned gave time and opportunities for her enemies to work: they instilled jealousy into the King's mind upon the subject of Lord Newbottle, telling him that Lady Sarah still continued her intercourse with him, and immediately the marriage with the Princess of Strelitz was set on foot; and at Lady Sarah's return from the country, she found herself deprived of her crown, and her lover Lord Newbottle, who complained as much of her as she did of the King. Whilst this was in agitation, Lady Sarah used to meet the King in his rides early in the morning, driving a little chaise with Lady Susan Strangways; and once it is said that, wanting to speak to him, she went dressed like a servant-maid, and stood amongst the crowd in the Guard room, to say a few words to him as he passed by.

The House of Commons is very ill attended on both

[1] William John Ker, afterwards fifth Marquess of Lothian. He died in 1815.

sides. The Army Extraordinaries for England and America were passed with no more than about 150 Members present. Mr. Grenville delivered his sentiments, seconded only by Mr. Pitt and Lord George Sackville. Mr. Townshend spoke warmly for making America bear her share of the expense, commended the Stamp Act, and treated Lord Chatham's distinction, between internal and external taxation, as contemptuously as Mr. Grenville had done: nobody got up to justify Lord Chatham but Mr. Beckford.

Lord Hyde told me yesterday (January 21), that the clamour against Mr. Pitt and the universal dissatisfaction increases daily. Many people think Lord Chatham is ill [not in favour] at St. James's. He said he had heard that Lord Shelburne had differed in Council from the rest of the King's servants there present, and had been totally unsupported (this report was never confirmed), and that it is said Lord Bute was lately for near two hours in the King's Closet, that he came out of it with an air of Minister, had a circle immediately round him, and then went down the back stairs.

Thursday, February 26th, 1767.—Yesterday Mr. Townshend proposed the Land Tax, at four shillings in the pound, for one year more. Mr. Dowdeswell opposed it, proposing the taking off one shilling, and reducing it to three; in this he was supported by both the parties in Opposition, and when the question was put, the numbers were 206 for three shillings, and 188 for four shillings.

Lord Mountstuart, Mr. Mackenzie, and all Lord Bute's friends were in the minority, and looked very blank at their defeat. Lady Bute heard the news at Lady Grey's assembly the same evening, and could not conceal her surprise.

The joy in the House of Commons was very great, all the country gentlemen coming round Mr. Grenville, shaking him by the hand, and testifying the greatest satisfaction.

Lord Chatham remains at Marlborough ill of the gout, where he has been for a considerable time. The East India business has been put off from time to time on account of his absence, but it is said will now come on finally on Friday next.

Saturday, February 28th.—The King went as usual to Richmond, but sent for the Duke of Grafton before he went (at eight o'clock in the morning), and, as it is imagined, expressed great uneasiness at the loss of the question the preceding night, but saw nobody else 'till his return in the evening, when Mr. Conway went to him. He tells all his servants that he will support Lord Chatham.

Sunday, March 1st.—Mr. Grenville saw Mr. Augustus Hervey, who told him that Lord Bristol had been that day with the King, that he had never seen him so much ruffled before, that he blamed the Treasury exceedingly, and Mr. Conway also, for having lost the question, but said he was determined to support Lord Chatham to the utmost. He tried the ground of Secretary of State to Lord Bristol, but he declined it, and told his brother he would on no consideration take it.

Lord Chatham came to town at four o'clock; saw nobody that night but Lord Bristol, who seems at this hour the person most in his confidence.

All the intelligence Mr. Grenville has confirms the agitation into which this event has thrown the King, though his exterior is as usual placid and easy.

The Rockingham party make very strong advances to Mr. Grenville, particularly Sir William Meredith.

Friday, March 6th.—Nothing was done in the East India business. Some time was taken up in debating whether or no the papers should or should not be printed, and Mr. Beckford made a motion to lay the proposal made by the Company before the House, for them to judge of the bargain proper to be made for the public, but putting it off 'till that day fortnight. He was seconded by Mr. FitzRoy. The appearance of the House marked confusion and disagreement. Sir Edward Hawke had the imprudence, forgetting his oath of secrecy, to say that there had been a debate upon this business in the Council, where the majority of the King's servants had been for rejecting the proposal made by the East India Company.

Sunday, March 8th.—Mr. Cadogan came to see Mr. Grenville, and told him that the report now was that Mr. Charles Townshend had made his peace with Lord Chatham, and that for the present there would be no change, although he knew Lord Chatham had sent to Lord North, to offer him to be Chancellor of the Exchequer, with all the support and confidence he could desire; that Lord North had declined it properly, and in a very becoming manner, saying, that in the present state of things he could not feel himself equal to the distressed situation of affairs, nor to the eloquence and abilities exerted against the Ministry; but knowing how often His Majesty had been refused by those to whom great situations in Government had been offered, and how prejudicial it must be to his affairs, he humbly begged to have this transaction kept secret. It is said the same offer was made to Mr. Oswald, who likewise declined it.

Mr. Cadogan said the King had spoken with great peevishness to the Duke of York upon the loss of the question, and the disorder amongst his Ministers, saying one was in bed at Marlborough, and another in town with the piles, and this was the way in which he was served. He took notice to the Duke, that in the debate on the Land Tax, Mr. Grenville had conducted himself with great ability.

Monday, March 9th.—The Court carried the question in the House of Commons concerning the printing the papers relating to the East India Company, by a majority of no more than 33. Mr. Charles Townshend was not in the House, saying he chose to be absent, as he had declared his opinion before, and must have voted with the Opposition.

Wednesday, March 11th.—The main question about the printing the papers came on, but the opposition appeared to be so strong, that the Court gave up the question and would not divide. Mr. Charles Townshend cut between the two sides, was for printing the Charters, &c., but not the correspondence on all this affair. The Rockingham party are strongly with Mr. Grenville, and by the daily intercourse between the two parties, it seems as if they would resolve to unite, at least for the destroying this Ministry, whatever may be the consequence afterwards.

Thursday, 12th.—The House of Commons adjourned 'till Monday upon the Speaker's indisposition.

Lord Suffolk came in the evening to see Mr. Grenville, who was ill, and told him that Lord Hyde had desired him to tell him that he knew, from the most undoubted authority, that Lord Bute had said the following words within these few days:—" That he thought Mr. Grenville was the only proper person to be at the head of the Treasury, that he had shown himself to be so, and he was glad to find that mankind was come off from their opinion of that madman, Lord Chatham."

Mr. Grenville has a great deal of conversation at different times with Lord Mansfield, who laments the state of disorder that everything relating to Government is in. Mr. Grenville held a language of temper to him, and conciliation with all parties, as far as his own general principles would admit, saying that whenever the King should think fit to change his Administration, he was of opinion that, to whoever the proposition should come, their only wise conduct would be to endeavour to form an Administration upon a wide and extended idea, taking in all parties without exclusion; that he saw the difficulties with which it was attended, and how much good faith and honour was required to maintain it when formed; but that it was the only means to destroy the perpetual idea of change by destroying the game of fighting one set of men against another. Lord Mansfield highly approved this idea, and commended the moderation and wisdom which Mr. Grenville manifested by it. He told Mr. Grenville that he had seen the Duke of Newcastle, who professed never more to enter again upon the public scene, both from the ill-usage he had met with, and that it became him, at his time of life, to retire. That he was determined, as soon as the Duke of Bedford's first hours of affliction for the loss of

Lord Tavistock[1] were over, he would go to him to give him his last thoughts upon public affairs as a legacy, and to recommend a union of all who wish well to the King's Government and the good of their country.

Mr. Grenville balanced in his own mind whether he should open this idea to Mr. Rigby to put him upon his guard, and thereby to prepare the Duke of Bedford, as it appeared to be a scheme to unite the Rockingham and Bedford party, leaving out Lord Temple and Mr. Grenville, and their party.

Monday, March 23rd.—Mr. Townshend brought the message to the House of Commons, for the provision for the King's brothers. Mr. Grenville said what was decent and proper that day upon the bringing it in, reserving himself to speak further upon it on the Wednesday following.

Wednesday, March 25th.—Mr. Grenville spoke with greater applause than ever upon the Princes' affair, with great respect to the King and his brothers; but showing at the same time how hard it was to lay any additional expense upon the nation, when so much economy was necessary, and so much profusion was shown in everything. He commended the liberal hand of the King, and wished not to restrain his expenses, which were all of a becoming nature, for the encouragement of arts and sciences, and to indulge such pleasures as were fitting to the leisure of a great Prince; but, amongst other articles where saving might be made, he instanced that of so many Ambassadors Extraordinary, viz. the Ambassador

---

[1] The Marquess of Tavistock, the Duke's only son, died on the 22nd instant, in consequence of a fall from his horse: he was only in his 28th year.

named for Russia [1], the Ambassador named for Spain [2], the Ministers for Portugal [3] and Turin [4]; Ministers in time of peace named to Foreign Courts, but who received their pay and continued in England. That we were told last year of mighty schemes for strengthening our alliance in the North to balance that of the South; what had it amounted to but to name an Ambassador Extraordinary to Russia, in the month of July, whose instructions had never yet been made out. That a Minister every way agreeable to the Court of Spain had been recalled from that country at a time when it was most of all necessary to have an able person there, from the ticklish state of that Court, and that important negotiation trusted to the care of a clergyman, left there chargé des affaires. A chaplain (to Lord Rochford) of the Church of England charged with the great and desirable object of breaking the family compact at the Court of the Catholic King, whilst the Ambassador appointed to go there was waiting in England 'till time could be found to give him his instructions. That in saying this he did not mean to throw blame on either of the Ambassadors so appointed, and who he was persuaded were ready to go; neither did he mean to blame the Right Honourable Gentleman who must sign the order for their pay; nor the Secretary of State in that House, and in whose department one of these Ambassadors was. It was true, indeed, that the Secretary of State ought to have the appointment of the Ministers of his department, because he was answerable for their dispatches, and ought to give them their instructions, but he did not believe that

[1] Mr. Hans Stanley.   [2] Sir James Gray.
[3] William Henry Lyttelton, brother of Lord Lyttelton.
[4] Mr., afterwards Sir William, Lynch.

to be the case at present; but if their presence was not necessary at the several Courts, why were they appointed, since it was well known that the expense of an Ambassador Extraordinary for the first year amounted to no less than 13,000*l.* He then asked why a larger proportion of the Princes' provision was not drawn from Ireland, especially as he knew to a certainty that country would see with pleasure a part of the money of that kingdom belonging to His Majesty appropriated to that use. That the pensions charged upon the Irish establishment in the late King's time amounted only to 22,000*l.*, and were now increased to above 88,000*l.*; but that, instead of taking any of these methods to ease the people of England, the Administration had thought fit to absolve America from contributing her share. They were now going to lose the East Indies; and yet, by the provision now settled upon their Royal Highnesses, however small the sum might appear, valued at three per cent., it amounted to 800,000*l.* Mr. Grenville through all this made great distinction between the expenses of the King and the Minister, saying it was in vain for the former to be free from avarice and profusion, whilst the conduct of the Minister subjected him to all the inconveniences arising from both.

Thursday, March 26th.—Mr. Grenville saw Mr. Rigby, who told him that he had lately had conversation with Lord Rockingham, who he met often at Arthurs'; that his Lordship seemed very desirous to talk with him upon public affairs, and to bring the two parties nearer each other; to which Mr. Rigby said he had told the Marquess that he could say nothing upon those subjects without previously speaking to Mr. Grenville, with whom he meant to act, and without whom he would hear nothing ; telling Mr. Grenville, at the same time, that the Duke of Bedford was stronger than ever in those ideas ; that he thought nobody fit to be at the head of Government but Mr. Grenville, and that he would see him, even in this hour of affliction, though he saw nobody else.

He then asked Mr. Grenville what were the outlines of his ideas, and what sort of language he should hold to Lord Rockingham and Lord Albemarle, the latter of which [whom] he knew had the government of the former, and that the sad calamity in the Bedford family often threw Lord Albemarle in his way, and had in some degree renewed the intercourse and friendship which had formerly subsisted between them. Mr. Grenville held much the same language to him as he had done to Lord Mansfield upon the idea of an extensive plan free from exclusions, saying, that if the Duke of Bedford and his party, Lord Temple, himself, and their party, could have the temper to say and mean this, it was still more the interest of the Rockinghams to do so, who were inferior in number, and far less congenial with those who were called the King's friends, and Lord Bute's party, than they were ; that if, therefore, such a general union could be brought about upon an explained reasonable footing, it would be extremely desirable, but if the Rockingham party meant only to unite for the present, availing themselves of that strength to overturn this Administration, in order to put Mr. Townshend and General Conway at the head of the next, it was what he could not hear of.

Mr. Rigby perfectly agreed with him, and renewed his professions of attachment to him in the strongest manner.

Mr. Charles Townshend complained bitterly to him (Mr. Grenville) of the state of things, when he saw him at the House of Commons, vowing he would resign if the report he heard was true, viz. that Sir Fletcher Norton was going to obtain a peerage for his wife. He stated Lord Chatham in the most ridiculous light imaginable, showing how totally inaccessible he was, viz. in a morning, not up; at noon, taking the air; in the evening, reposing and not to be fatigued; in fact nobody is supposed to see him now except Lord Bristol.

Friday, March 27th.—Mr. Grenville saw Mr. Rigby, who came to tell him that he had seen Lord Rockingham again, but that, upon sounding him upon the ideas and expectations of him and his party, he found they went to the wishing to have Lord Rockingham First Lord of the Treasury, Mr. Dowdeswell Chancellor of the Exchequer, Mr. Yorke Chancellor, and Mr. Charles Townshend Secretary of State: this at once destroyed all idea of union, as being of too exclusive a nature, and Mr. Rigby stated the impossibility of Mr. Grenville finding any proper station under such a plan. Lord Rockingham spoke civilly and with regard of Mr. Grenville, but more slightingly of Lord Temple. Mr. Grenville agreed with Mr. Rigby that no such proposition could be admitted, and as a middle way, mentioned the situation in which Mr. Pelham formerly acted, which was that of being First Lord of the Treasury, with the disposal of the House of Commons' offices, leaving the Chancellor and the House of Lords to them.

Saturday, March 28th.—Mr. Rigby told Mr. Grenville that the Duke of Newcastle had sent to him, and had a long conversation with him, in which Mr. Rigby had convinced his Grace of the unreasonableness of

Lord Rockingham's idea; the Duke himself was more moderate.

Lord Mansfield was with Mr. Grenville in the morning, who seemed to think from various reasons that the King would not leave Lord Chatham.

Mr. Grenville went in the evening to Bedford House. The Duke spoke a little upon public affairs, and entered very much into Mr. Grenville's ideas.

Wednesday, April 1st.—Mr. Grenville went to Lord Mansfield, with whom he had a long conversation, chiefly relating to a motion intended to be made in the House of Lords relating to America, of which Lord Mansfield approved. He told Mr. Grenville, under the seal of secrecy, and saying he had it from the most unquestionable authority, the following anecdote of Sir Fletcher Norton, who some time ago signified through Mr. Hussey his desire to support Government, in consequence of which Sir Fletcher Norton saw Lord Chancellor, and after a long conversation with him, the particulars of which were not known to Lord Mansfield, but that a proposition was made for Sir Fletcher's acceptance of the office of Master of the Rolls, to which Sir Fletcher had said that he had no objection to the office, but that he could not accept of it without Lord Bute's approbation, advice, and desire, for 'which he desired Lord Camden to apply. His Lordship said he was in no intercourse with Lord Bute, and therefore wished Sir Fletcher to do it himself, but he still insisted upon its being done through the Chancellor, and accordingly a message was sent to Lord Bute to that purpose by Lord Denbigh, and delivered to Lord Bute in presence of two of his friends. Lord Bute seemed surprised at receiving it, and insisted upon its being put into writing, which it was, to the following effect: " that a proposition having been made to Sir Fletcher Norton upon his having signified his desire to support Government, to make him Master of the Rolls, Sir Fletcher had said he could not accept that office unless he had Lord Bute's approbation and desire for so doing, and therefore had desired that application should be made to Lord Bute to that effect."

Lord Bute wrote a letter to Sir Fletcher Norton, saying that he himself had always wished to support Government, and was desirous that all his friends should do the same, and particularly Sir Fletcher Norton, both from the assistance he was able to give, and the honour he should do himself by it, but that he himself was an utter stranger to the plans and purposes of the present Administration, with whom he had no communication; that as to any particular office which Sir Fletcher might accept, he could give no opinion about it, as Sir Fletcher must be the best judge for himself.

The Duke of Bedford is very warm and strong in his professions to Mr. Grenville, both from himself and through Mr. Rigby.

Mr. Charles Townshend comes every day in the House to talk with Mr. Grenville, and to abuse Lord Chatham, and laugh at the Administration; and speaking in relation to what would be proper to be done in America, he said Mr. Conway was upon that subject below low-water mark.

Friday, April 10*th*.—The Duke of Bedford made a motion in the House of Lords (the Lords having all been summoned to attend [1]) relating to America. It

---

[1] The Lords were summoned at the instance of Lord Temple. The Duke of Bedford moved, to address the King to order the Privy Council to take into their consideration a recent Act of the Assembly of

was debated for some time with great insufficiency on the part of the Administration. Lord Mansfield distinguished himself extremely, and many others of the Opposition. Lord Botetourt was eagerly warm on the side of Government, with a personal attack upon the Duke of Bedford's *connections* and *associates*, and likewise upon the Stamp Act (which he had formerly supported) with reflections apparently aimed at Mr. Grenville [1].

The previous question, for putting off the business, was proposed; the numbers for the Court were 63, against 36.

Saturday, April 11*th.*—Lord Lyttelton saw Lord Hardwicke, who had voted with the Opposition, and in a long conversation with Lord Lyttelton he expressed great civility and approbation of Lord Temple and Mr. Grenville, and the direct contrary of Lord Rockingham and his friends, who had one and all declined voting on either side the day before, for which they are universally blamed, and the more as it was manifest the question might have been carried if their body had joined the Duke of Bedford and Lord Temple.

Massachusetts, in which they had taken on themselves to pardon the leaders of the late insurrections, and to couple with that Act an ordinance for raising of money. Lord Bristol, writing to Lord Chatham at this time, mentions the debate, and a conversation with the King upon the subject: he says, "there were some comparisons made of the difference between the conduct of your Lordship and one whom you may guess, but I might be wanting in respect to you to name." The person alluded to is doubtless Lord Temple, and furnishes another instance of the King's dislike of him. See Horace Walpole's *Memoirs of George III.*, vol. ii. p. 454, and *Chatham Correspondence*, vol. iii. p. 248.

[1] Lord Botetourt, when Colonel Berkeley, had been an intimate friend of Lord Temple and Mr. Grenville. He presumed upon this occasion to attack Lord Temple, and this was probably not forgotten when Junius was discussing the Government of Virginia, and the dismissal of Sir Jeffrey Amherst to make room for Lord Botetourt.

Lord Hardwicke went so far as to say he knew of no engagement that his brother and he were under to the Rockingham party, that could prevent their holding offices in conjunction with Lord Temple and Mr. Grenville, especially as the Great Seal was not given to his brother when that party came into Government, though it might have been expected.

The Duke of Newcastle arraigns Lord Rockingham, &c., for their defection on Friday. He goes on Tuesday to talk with the Duke of Bedford.

Sunday, April 12th.—The Court party seemed in spirits, and Mrs. Grenville heard from a *great quarter* that it had been said ironically that on Tuesday Mr. Grenville was to try his strength. Great industry has been used to detach the country gentlemen from Mr. Grenville, in which Lord Denbigh, Lord Litchfield, and Lord Botetourt have been very forward, giving out that the King was utterly irreconcileable to him.

Saturday, May 23rd.—The House of Lords sat yesterday 'till ten o'clock at night, on a question proposed by Lord Gower, and supported by Lord Mansfield, relating to the disobedience of the colonies upon the indemnification.

The numbers on the division were 62 to 56. The Duke of York spoke on the side of the minority, saying that the rambling minds of the Americans ought to be restrained. He went away before the division. His two brothers voted with the majority. This is the more memorable as Mr. Cadogan told Mr. Grenville that the King wrote to the Duke of York to desire him to go down to the House of Lords to support *his* Administration, and to speak to his other brothers to do the same; at which the Duke of York was much hurt, and went to the King and told him he hoped His Majesty's Ministers would propose such a question as a man of honour could support, for that for his part he had a character to maintain in that House to which he must have regard.

All Lord Bute's friends voted to a man with the Court, in direct contradiction to their opinions in the last Session.

In the House of Commons there is greater confusion than ever, Mr. Charles Townshend thwarting and abusing the Administration on all occasions, and declaring that he shall be out of employment shortly.

Mr. Dyson, Sir Gilbert Elliot, and Lord Bute's friends, seemed to take the lead in the business concerning the East India Company on Thursday last. Mr. Townshend differed totally from them. Mr. Grenville took the middle way between the two, and Mr. Conway adopted his opinion.

The cards are daily more and more embroiled, but at the bottom the main point now in view is to have them so played as to let Lord Bute choose the new Parliament, but the specific mode seems not yet absolutely settled.

Sunday, May 24th.—Mr. Cadogan came to Mr. Grenville and told him with great precision what had passed between the King and the Duke of York, which was as follows:—that on Thursday the 21st Lord Chancellor Camden went into the King's Closet, where he stayed near an hour, and was observed to come out pretty much ruffled. As soon as the King returned to the Queen's house, he wrote a note to the Duke of Gloucester in these terms:—"Dear brother, as you are more staid and sedate than my other brothers, I think you are the most likely to be found; I therefore write to desire you will attend the House of Lords to-morrow, and that you will stay and divide in support of my Administration, and that you will likewise inform my brothers Edward and Henry of my wishes, and tell them to do the same." (Signed) "GEORGE R."

The Duke of Gloucester was not in town, so that it was not 'till twelve o'clock on Friday that the note was communicated to the Duke of York from the Duke of Cumberland, whilst Mr. Cadogan was with the Duke of York. His Royal Highness immediately ordered his coach and went to the King, telling His Majesty with how much concern he had received his commands, desiring to know what the question would be (of which the King seemed totally unapprized), and saying that he had a character and reputation to maintain in the House of Lords which he could not give up, but hoped the question would be such as a man of honour could assent to.

When he came to the House of Lords His Royal Highness desired to know from Lord Northington who it was that had advised the King to take such a step. Lord Northington answered him that he hoped His Royal Highness had too good an opinion of him to believe him to be the adviser of so silly a measure. The Duke likewise taxed the Duke of Grafton with it, who denied it. The Duke of York spoke for the question, which was—"That it should be put to the Judges to give their opinion whether or no the Act for pardon passed by the Governor, Council, and Assembly of Massachusetts Bay, ought to stand."

He ended his speech by recommending to the Lords not to divide, but to be unanimous, and then went to ask the Duke of Grafton whether his Grace meant to divide. The Duke said, "Yes;" upon which the Duke of York said, the most respectful thing for him to do was to withdraw, since he must differ from the King's servants, and accordingly he went away. The next morning His Royal Highness went to Richmond by six o'clock, meaning (as he told Lady C. Edwin) to tell his own tale; but the King was already apprized of it, and received him coldly, telling him that question had been meant to be the push of the whole Session.

The Duke of York asked His Majesty what the question was likely to be on Tuesday[1], of which the King could give him no account, but desired him to support his Administration, and repeated that it would be the push of the Session.

The Duke of York invited Lady C. Edwin to his play on Saturday. He told her a good deal of what had passed between the King and him, but the thickness of his speech prevented her hearing it distinctly, but she picked up, amongst other things, that he had told the King that he hoped His Majesty would one day see the propriety of his conduct. Everybody denies the having advised the King to this step, which is generally believed to have been Lord Camden. The Duke of York intends to question him about it.

Thursday, June 4th.—Mr. Grenville went to Wotton.

For news and political events, *vide* Mr. Whately's letters, Mr. Augustus Hervey's, Mr. Charles Lloyd's, &c., &c.

Friday, July 10th.—Mr. Grenville returned from his Western progress, and found Mr. Rigby waiting for him

---

[1] Another motion on the Massachusetts Act. The Duke of York was absent. The Court had a majority of only 3. The numbers were 65 to 62.

at Wotton, who told him, that after many conversations passing between the Duke of Grafton and Lord Gower, in which the former had expressed a desire that the King should send to the Duke of Bedford and Lord Temple to make a part in a new Administration, Lord Gower and Lord Albemarle, being at Woburn on Wednesday morning, the 8th, the latter showed Mr. Rigby a letter (dated "Tuesday, 11 at night"), which he had just received from Lord. Rockingham, informing him that Mr. Conway had desired Lord Rockingham to give the Duke of Grafton the meeting, at his house, at two o'clock that day, which he accordingly did; and that, after some civilities, the Duke told him he had a message to deliver to him from the King, " to desire that he and his friends should compose a new Administration, his Lordship holding again the office of First Lord of the Treasury."

Lord Rockingham asked the Duke whether this was to be composed of his friends alone, or whether he was at liberty to communicate it to others whom he might think necessary to give strength to it; to which the Duke answered, the question had been foreseen, and that he was at liberty to communicate it, but that it seemed to be intended, that if this should be confined to the Duke of Bedford and his friends, that something had been said with regard to the keeping in the Lord Chancellor, but that he (Lord Albemarle) knew Lord Rockingham's sentiments upon it, though he did not then enter upon it at large with the Duke of Grafton; that Lord Rockingham wished to know whether the Duke of Bedford and his friends were disposed to act, and take a part with him in an Administration; and wished to have the honour of waiting upon his Grace, at

Woburn, the next day, being Thursday, either at dinner or in the evening, to know his sentiments. To this, Mr. Rigby answered, that in his opinion nothing could be done by the Duke of Bedford and his friends, without first consulting Mr. Grenville, in which both the Duke of Bedford and Lord Gower agreed; for this purpose, Lord Rockingham's visit was postponed, and Mr. Rigby was to go to London to meet Lord Rockingham that night, and to inquire whether Mr. Grenville was returned from the West, and where he could be found. Mr. Rigby met Lord John Cavendish at Arthur's, with whom he had some talk, and who told him he doubted much whether anything could come of this negotiation, as it appeared strange that it should be carried on through Mr. Conway's and the Duke of Grafton's hands, each of whom had declared to the King that they could no longer go on; that Lord Rockingham had never seen the King, and he (Lord John) suspected that the Duke of Grafton would be disavowed.

Mr. Rigby saw Lord Rockingham in the evening, in Grosvenor Square, who held a language to him conformable to the letter he had written to Lord Albemarle. Mr. Rigby expressly declared to him, that the Duke of Bedford and his friends would do nothing but in concert with Mr. Grenville, and that for his own part, he should never depart from his opinions with regard to America, and that he knew Mr. Grenville's ideas were the same on that subject as they had ever been. Lord Rockingham held a moderate language upon that article. Mr. Rigby suggested to him the singularity of manner in which this negotiation was set on foot. They did not descend into particulars, but in general the idea of an extended Administration was the ground.

Lord Rockingham said, the Duke of Grafton, in the talking, had made no difficulty as to the removing Lord Chatham and his friends; but if he made any pause, it was as to the turning out Lord Bute's friends, against both which the Marquess declared great hostility.

Lord Rockingham said he would dine the next day, Saturday, at Woburn, and Mr. Rigby, having heard that Mr. Grenville was to come to Wotton on Friday, came there to meet him, and was to return to meet Lord Rockingham at Woburn.

To all this Mr. Grenville said, after acknowledging the friendship and attachment shown to him by the Duke of Bedford and his friends, that it seemed scarcely to amount to a proposition, and that in all probability all that was meant by it was to endeavour to divide the Opposition; that as there was no message to him, so he could give no answer, nor would he have given one without Lord Temple, but that in general, if the King thought fit to call Lord Rockingham into his Government, upon a great and extended plan, carried on with vigour, and asserting the sovereignty of Great Britain over her colonies, he had no factious dispositions to disturb it, but that he could never alter his opinion on the subject of America; that with regard to the forming the Administration, he only desired that no pretensions of his should in any way stand in the way of his friends; that, on the contrary, he was willing to waive them entirely, provided he could see his friends properly placed; that he would never on any account or in any situation obtrude himself upon the King, and earnestly desired that his name might not even be mentioned for any office whatever.

Mr. Rigby went back to Woburn, and Mr. Grenville

went in the evening to Stowe, where he found Lord Temple exactly in the same sentiments.

Sunday, July 12th.—Mr. Rigby came at ten in the morning, to tell Lord Temple and Mr. Grenville what had passed at Woburn, where Lord Rockingham had very much holden the same language of a general plan conformable to what had passed before. Mr. Rigby delivered Mr. Grenville's sentiments, and marked to Lord Rockingham the moderation and temper of them. The Duke of Bedford, Lord Albemarle, and Lord Gower were so much of the same opinion in regard to measures, that Mr. Rigby said to Lord Temple and Mr. Grenville that it was as if they had heard the conversation and used the same words.

They alarmed Lord Rockingham on the manner in which all this was transacted, and showed him the indispensable necessity of his seeing the King himself, which had not yet happened, but, on the contrary, it was publicly known that the King had sent for Mr. Charles Townshend on the Thursday, and had a long conversation with him. Lord Temple and Mr. Grenville still desired to waive their own pretensions, and desired to be at liberty to support or not, according to the measures.

Mr. Charles Townshend died on the 4*th of September*.

Lord North was appointed Chancellor of the Exchequer towards the end of the month, after having once declined the acceptance[1].

---

[1] The following is in the handwriting of George, Lord Lyttelton, and is described by Mr. Grenville as "*Lord Lyttelton's account of what Mr. Dowdeswell said to him at Worcester, in September,* 1767, *delivered to me at Hagley, September* 16, 1767." It is entitled, "*Supplement to Mr. Grenville's account of the late negotiations.*"

"Mr Dowdeswell told me (Lord Lyttelton) that after the negotiation

The Duke of York died at Monaco, in *September*.

Saturday, November 21st, 1767.—Mr. Grenville came to town; saw the Duke of Bedford in the evening, whose language was most perfectly friendly to him, and agreeing entirely in his political ideas, but taking no notice whatever of the last letter he wrote to his Grace from Wotton [1]. From thence Mr. Grenville went to Lord Mansfield, whose language was full of contempt of the present Administration, temperate with regard to measures of opposition. He told Mr. Grenville that he had a long conversation with the King when he gave up the Exchequer Seal to him, the particulars of which he had promised never to disclose, but assured Mr. Grenville that nothing memorable had passed, and His Majesty had waived the entering upon past transactions. Lord Mansfield spoke with great derision of the appointment of Sergeant Hewit to the Chancellorship of Ireland. Accounts come daily from that kingdom of the ludicrous manner in which the Lord Lieutenant treats his own situation with respect to the Ministers in England, and draws his own caricature with his hands tied behind him and his mouth open [2].

Monday, November 23rd.—Mr. Grenville saw Mr.

was ended, and Lord Rockingham had had his audience of the King, he was pressed by Mr. Conway to come in with his own connection only, which he declined, but said that if the King should send for him, and tell him clearly *himself*, that he desired to put him at the head of the Treasury, and empowered him to endeavour to form a Ministry, he would apply again to the Duke of Bedford, and offer his Grace such terms as would put him in the wrong, if he did not accept them; which having done, if he met with a refusal from his Grace, he believed he might then come into the present Ministry with his own friends alone."

[1] See *Bedford Correspondence,* vol. iii. p. 396.

[2] In one of the Miscellaneous Letters attributed to Junius, Lord Townshend's "singular turn for portrait painting" is mentioned, and

Rigby, who was just returned from Ireland[1], and confirms all the stories told of Lord Townshend.

General Irwin came to Mr. Grenville, and repeated to him the extraordinary conversation related in a letter of Mr. Whately's[2], upon the subject of withdrawing some of the troops from Gibraltar. He likewise told him an anecdote still more surprising, which is, that General Græme told him, that he, General Græme, had leave from the Queen to go into open opposition to the present Administration if he chose it; that his " excellence in that good-natured species of painting called caricatura." In the *Grand Council*, also, he is introduced under the *sobriquet* of *Bout-de-ville*, a French translation of his name. In the *Public Advertiser* for Friday, June 5th, 1765, there is a letter which is very probably from the same pen: it is signed GEORGE BOUT-DE-VILLE, and complains of the excessive liberty of the *rolling press* in disseminating caricatures. He adds:—" One arch libeller in particular has rendered himself more than a hundred times liable to prosecution for *scandalum magnatum*. There is scarce a distinguished person in the kingdom whom he has not exhibited in caricature. He has dealt his grotesque cards from house to house, and circulated his defamatory pictures from Towns-end to Towns-end. Is there a great general of the highest rank [a], and most eminent military abilities, who has rescued us from the horrors of popery and slavery, and delivered down to posterity the blessings of the Revolution—if the size of his person as well as fame should be larger than ordinary, this malicious libeller at three strokes of his pencil scratches out his figure in all the ridiculous attitudes imaginable. Is there a nobleman distinguished for wit, eloquence, and learning—if his person be long and lank, and lean and bony, he also is in like manner exposed to ridicule." [b]

[1] " Rigby had passed over to Ireland in hopes of obtaining to have his place of Master of the Rolls there, confirmed in the Act for establishing the Judges for life, but had not succeeded."—*Horace Walpole's Memoirs of George III.*, vol. iii. p. 118.

[2] See *ante*, p. 184.

[a] The Duke of Cumberland.
[b] Lord Lyttelton. Under this caricature were inscribed the following lines:—
"But who is this astride the pony,
So long, so lean, so lank, so bony?
This is the great orator, *Lytteltony*."

he had talked much to him of the King's uneasiness and embarrassment, feeling the weakness and insufficiency of the present Ministers, but not knowing well how to get rid of them, and therefore wishing Lord Chatham would come to town in order to set them a quarrelling among themselves; that everybody saw and knew that it must end in the King's sending for Mr. Grenville; to which General Irwin said he thought his Majesty was angry and displeased at Mr. Grenville. The General answered him that had been so, but all was forgot, and that matters would go very easy with regard to Mr. Grenville, and still more so with Lord Temple. But words like these are and have been frequently circulated, possibly with no other meaning than to keep up a degree of good humour.

Tuesday, November 24th.—Lord Lyttelton was with Mr. Grenville last night, and told him some memorable things which had passed between his Lordship, the Duke of Bedford, and Lord Mansfield, in two conversations he had held with them separately [1].

The Duke of Bedford told him that he heard from the Duke of Bridgewater [2] that Lord Rockingham had declared that he would never be of any Administration in which any Grenville was to have a part. The Duke of Bedford expresses great indignation at it, and seemed throughout all his conversation relating to the summer negotiation, to have been determined to have stood middle man, to moderate between Mr. Grenville and Lord Rockingham.

---

[1] See an account of these conversations in a letter written, but not sent, to Lord Temple, in Phillimore's *Memoirs and Correspondence of George Lord Lyttelton*, p. 736.

[2] Francis, second and last Duke of Bridgewater: he died in 1803.

Lord Mansfield in his discourse seemed strongly to adopt the idea of Lord Temple and Mr. Grenville staying out of office, and their friends to come in and support in case of a change of Ministers, saying that there must be difficulties with respect to Mr. Grenville upon his American plans, and that as things now were he could not easily be the person to restrain the colonies. Lord Mansfield talked much to Lord Lyttelton upon the plan of his being President of the Council, which Lord Lyttelton told him could never be without Lord Temple and Mr. Grenville; and upon Lord Mansfield pursuing the idea relative to those two, he said it was what the Duke of Bedford had understood, for that upon his Grace being asked whether that was likely to be agreed to, his Grace's answer had been, "I would have kept them to it."

Wednesday, November 25th.—Mr. Grenville went to the King's Levée, was very coldly received, and a very gracious reception given to Mr. James Grenville. Lord Suffolk, Lord Buckinghamshire, Lord Hyde, and others of the Opposition, were received with the same coldness as Mr. Grenville.

Mr. Grenville, in the speech he made yesterday at the opening of the Sessions of Parliament, upon the general state of things, took occasion to make such declarations upon his American ideas as plainly showed that he was upon very different ground from the Rockinghams. He had an altercation with Mr. Conway, in defence of himself, in an unjust and unfair reflection which Mr. Conway had cast upon him touching the Manilla ransom, but upon his showing by an account of the fact how grossly he had been misrepresented, Mr. Conway, with temper and civility, made him an excuse. Mr. Bourke and some other of the Rockingham party made an angry speech to-day at Mr. Grenville, declaring a division from his party as strongly as Mr. Grenville had done it from theirs the night before [1].

The House sat to-day 'till between six and seven, disputing a point of order with Mr. Grenville.

It was observed, yesterday, in both Houses, that the Ministry seemed low and dejected. The Duke of Grafton made a panegyric upon every one of his associates, describing them severally 'till he came to Lord Chatham, and of him he said, he was sorry to say he was no longer "an effective Minister."

It is said to-day that Mr. Thomas Townshend is to succeed Lord North in the Pay Office, and that Mr. Jenkinson comes into the Board of Treasury in Mr. Townshend's room.

Friday, December 4th.—Mr. Grenville went to make the Duke of Bedford a visit on Wednesday (in order to see his Grace before he was couched, which operation is to be performed on Saturday), but he did not find him at home. He received a note from his Grace yesterday, desiring earnestly to speak to him, and appointing to meet him in the Princes' Chamber. His Grace began by entering into a general discourse upon the state of things, which Mr. Grenville soon perceived drove at

---

[1] See an account of this debate in Walpole's *Memoirs of George III.*, vol. iii. p. 112. He says, "The conduct of Grenville in this debate was extremely remarkable. He not only seemed transported into very impolitic separation from the Rockinghams by his violence against the Americans, but even by personal resentment against the former: while, at the same time, his affected moderation had the appearance of having taken a new part, that of standing detached and waiting to see whether he could not penetrate with more facility into the Closet when standing alone, than by the joint effort of two discordant factions. Whatever were his motives, he soon fell a sacrifice to this very conduct."

the idea of separating from him in party, though he still declared the most thorough approbation of all Mr. Grenville's opinions, saying, "that Mr. Grenville was the only Minister who had ever given him their political creed in writing," by which he referred to Mr. Grenville's letter [of Nov. 6th] to him from Wotton in answer to one from his Grace.

The Duke said that Lord Temple had told Lord Gower, that in the present state of parties there could be no effectual opposition[1]; that he thought so too; that it had been understood from Mr. Grenville's declarations, that he never would come into Government except as First Lord of the Treasury; that he saw at this moment little prospect of forcing that, however strongly he (the Duke of Bedford) wished it. He spoke throughout with the highest regard and approbation of Mr. Grenville, bearing the strongest testimony to the fairness of his conduct; said that as to himself he would never come into office again, but that possibly some of his friends might wish to take offices with the present set of Ministers, for that he did verily believe the interior of the Court and the general distress must necessarily bring on some proposition either to the Rockingham party, Mr. Grenville and Lord Temple's, or his own; that he thought it a fair proceeding towards Mr. Grenville to apprize him (and, through him, Lord Temple, with whose behaviour towards him and his friends he had much reason to be satisfied), that in the latter case his friends should think themselves at liberty to take offices, as, on the other hand, should the pro-

---

[1] A frank confession that public men were so divided into petty personal factions, that it was even more difficult to make an *Opposition* than a *Government*.

posal come to Mr. Grenville, he would likewise be free to act in that case as he should think best.

The Duke, in the course of this conversation, spoke with great contempt and dislike of the Rockinghams, and said no negotiation was at that time on foot from the Court[1].

Mr. Grenville received this communication with great civility and temper; said he never had made any declaration himself for coming in again First Lord of the Treasury, or not doing so; that what he had most invariably said and meant to adhere to was, that he never would in any shape whatever be forced upon the King; that he should ever make measures his point, more than men; that he wished no men to make any sacrifice of their wishes or pretensions to him; that he left his Grace and his friends entirely at liberty to take what part they pleased, as he and his were likewise.

They parted with great civility, and Mr. Grenville saying that he would go to see the Duke during his confinement.

Mr. Grenville had, prior to this meeting, observed that Mr. Rigby was distant and sulky in the House of Commons; he had asked him the reason of it, but he hung his head, and would enter into no explanation.

Arrangements were now daily talked of, by which some of the Duke of Bedford's friends were to be taken in, namely, Lord Gower to be President; Lord Wey-

---

[1] I have already mentioned in a former note, upon the authority of Horace Walpole, that the negotiation with the Court had been commenced by Rigby some days before this time : I do not mean to assert that it was then with the concurrence of the Duke, although his name had been used by Rigby in his communication to the Duke of Grafton, but it must of course have been subsequently sanctioned by the Duke of Bedford.

mouth, Secretary of State; Lord Sandwich, one of the Vice Treasurers of Ireland; and Mr. Rigby, Paymaster with no colleague.

These posts were to be vacated by Lord Northington, Lord Shelburne, Mr. Barré, and Mr. Cooke, all of whom are the immediate friends of Lord Chatham; it therefore remains to be seen whether his power is sufficient to stop it, and to overrule the Duke of Grafton in this attempt[1].

Sunday, December 13th.—Lord Mansfield came to Mr. Grenville, who had been confined at home for a week with a cold. His language was extremely friendly to Mr. Grenville, and lamenting with him the sad disordered state of things in general, and the languid turn of the King's mind, who seemed indifferent to everything, tired of change, and yet dissatisfied with the Ministers and their Administration; and Lord Mansfield seemed to blame Lord Bute for standing still at so critical a moment, after having inspired the King with general mistrust of everybody, and with ideas that frequent changes of men, in order to break all parties, was the wisest plan of Government; and that now he really believed he intermeddled but little, though he still preserved his influence over the King's mind; that he blamed him for not interposing that influence to put some spirit and activity into a weak insufficient system, which by slow degrees was bringing the kingdom to its ruin, and that if the remedy was delayed 'till danger was actually at the door, it would be then too late to call out for assistance.

[1] "It is also understood, that if you should exert your influence with the King to overturn this plan, the Duke of Grafton will be strong enough, with his new friends, to defeat any attempt of that kind."—*The author of Junius to Lord Chatham.*—*Chatham Correspondence*, vol. iii. p 3.

Wednesday, December 16th.—Mr. Grenville went to the House of Commons, where a Bill was proposed by Lord North to settle the East India Dividend.

Mr. Grenville opposed the Bill, but the Court carried it by a great majority[1].

Mr. Conway was rather inclining to Mr. Grenville's opinions, and very civil in his manner towards him.

MR. WHATELY TO MR. GRENVILLE.

January 1, 1768.

DEAR SIR,—I received your favour of the 29th of December in the country, from whence I returned but this morning, and I have already taken care in more places than one to mention Lord Temple's disavowal of the *Word at Parting :* I read part of his Lordship's letter to me to Sir Laurence Dundas, and have besides conveyed to Brand the substance of it: these two channels will, I believe, be sufficient, but if I meet with any more of the Duke of Bedford's friends in town, I shall give them the same information.

I find both Lord Temple and you received the intelligence I sent you last week with some doubt and surprise; it is, however, true, and most of the material circumstances have since been confirmed to me[2].

[1] The numbers were 128 to 41.

[2] Mr. Whately here refers to his letter of the 25th ultimo (see p. 197) to Mr. Grenville, and if he did not write the same information to Lord Temple, this is one of the many instances which might be cited, that whatever political news Mr. Grenville received from his correspondents was immediately communicated to Lord Temple, and *vice versâ*[a]. The

[a] Whately says to Mr. Grenville—"I suppose you saw my second letter to Lord Temple." Lord Lyttelton's letter of this date furnishes, also, a sure proof of this inter-

That the Duke of Grafton settled the whole plan of arrangement with the Bedfords, without the partici-

letters from Whately to Lord Temple are not extant, indeed it is obvious that the latter preserved very little of his correspondence at this time. It will be found that the information contained in these letters, and in the following one from Lord Lyttelton to Lord Temple, corresponds very minutely with the subjects chosen by the Author of Junius for his communication to Lord Chatham, *dated on the following day, January 2nd,* 1768 [a], and therefore they may be considered of some importance in the question of identifying Junius with Lord Temple. Thus, for instance:—Whately confirms the statement in his letter of December 25th, that "the whole arrangement with the Bedfords was settled by the Duke of Grafton himself, without the participation of his brother Ministers."

So Junius writes to Lord Chatham:—"*It is understood by the public that the plan of introducing the Duke of Bedford's friends entirely belongs to the Duke of Grafton, with the secret concurrence, perhaps, of Lord Bute, but certainly without your Lordship's consent, if not absolutely against your advice.*"

Whately has said:—"Lord Bute's friends seem in general pleased with the coalition;" and Lyttelton adds:—"Lord Mansfield told me that he (Bute) was well pleased with the taking in of the Bedfords." With respect to Lord Chatham, Lyttelton reports that he "is better; that his thoughts are full of returning, not only to Ministry, but to omnipotence; that he is coming to town, and will do some great thing there, but nobody knows what." Of Lord Camden, Whately says:— "I know no particular reason for Lord Camden's being displeased, and yet he certainly is so to the highest degree." Lord Lyttelton also:—"I hear that Lord Camden has publicly said that the Duke of Grafton and Lord Chatham are one and the same man; that the act of the former must be always understood to be the will of the latter, and other expressions to the same effect."

And Junius writes,—"*The Chancellor* (Camden), *on whom you had particular reasons to rely, has played a sort of fast and loose game, and spoken of your Lordship with submission or indifference, according to the reports he heard of your health; nor has he altered his language*

---

change of correspondence and intelligence between Lord Temple and Mr. Grenville, for the latter, writing to Whately on the 9th instant, *quotes the very words used by Lord Lyttelton* in his letter of the 1st, with respect to Lord Camden:—"I have heard from good authority, that he (Lord Camden) has on the contrary devoted himself to his Grace (the Duke of Grafton) *without any reserve of fidelity to his former master.*"

[a] See *Chatham Correspondence*, vol. iii. p. 302.

pation of his brother Ministers, is hardly now an anecdote. It is very well known, and you may well

until he found you were really returning to town." As an illustration of Camden's "*fast and loose game,*" the Duke of Bedford himself told Lord Lyttelton " that the basis of the late treaty with the Duke of Grafton was a supposition that Lord Chatham was politically dead, and that Lord Camden had devoted himself to the Duke of Grafton, without any reserve of fidelity to his former master, even if he should revive and act."

Then, Lyttelton's expressions of uncertainty as to the capability of the Duke of Grafton to sustain himself in power :—" The real inclinations of the Court towards the new comers, the degree of favour the Duke of Grafton is in himself, how far Lord Chatham's anger, if he be angry, could shake it, are matters far from being sufficiently ascertained." Upon this Junius says, as if to pique Lord Chatham :—"*It is also understood that if you should exert your influence with the King to overturn this plan, the Duke of Grafton will be strong enough, with his new friends* (the " new comers ") *to defeat any attempts of that kind: or if he should not, your Lordship will easily judge to what quarter his Grace will apply for assistance.*"

The "*quarter*" alluded to must mean the Grenville party: the Ministry had already the support of Lord Bute and his friends, who were well pleased with the coalition, and the Duke of Bedford had spoken " with pleasure and a kind of triumph of the total exclusion of Lord Rockingham and his friends from this treaty." He had also expressed " great esteem and love " for Mr. Grenville, " and wished to see him at the head of the Treasury." Junius certainly points to a reconciliation between the Grenvilles and Lord Chatham: and here is another concurrence with Whately's letter:—" Lord Bristol has more than once or twice expressed his dissatisfaction in the strongest terms to Lord George Sackville, with whom, I believe, he has no very intimate acquaintance, ending every time with heartily wishing that Lord Chatham and his family could agree." Lord Bristol, it should be remembered, was in the most intimate confidence of Lord Chatham, and had access to him when he would scarcely see any other person.

Horace Walpole, too, about this time, says, " I asked Lord Temple's friend, Mr. W. Gerard Hamilton, if the Grenvilles and Lord Chatham would not now be reconciled ? He replied, Lord Temple and Lord Chatham might, but George Grenville never would ; that his love of business, and love of money, would both yield to his obstinacy."

" It is certain," says Lord Lyttelton, " that the world considers us

suppose not very agreeable. The discontent among Lord Chatham's friends seems to be, as far as I can

as forsaken by our only formidable strength the [Bedfords], *et pris pour dupes:*" and therefore it seems to have been the policy of Junius to bring about a reconciliation between the Grenvilles and Lord Chatham, with the view of weakening, or destroying if possible, the Duke of Grafton's Administration.

From this time until after the reconciliation had taken place with Lord Temple in the following October, Lord Chatham is very seldom mentioned by the Author of Junius, and never in the opprobrious terms which had been previously applied to him. In a letter dated the 16th of February, 1768, on the subject of the Privy Seal being put into Commission for six weeks, he is only slightly alluded to. (*Junius*, vol. iii. p. 3.) And again when writing to Lord Hillsborough on the 29th of August following. (*Junius*, vol. iii. p. 108.)

Junius, in furtherance of his scheme for the destruction of the Duke of Grafton, wished to excite Lord Chatham to resign the Privy Seal, which indeed was his own desire, and it was only retained at the earnest entreaty of the King, that he would continue in his service, and thus enable the Administration to proceed. When Lord Chatham did at last determine to resign his office in October, his reconciliation with Lord Temple immediately followed, and Junius soon after acknowledged that *he began to like him;* that he had *grown upon his esteem,* &c.

Even the protection of Lord Chatham did not avail to save Lord Shelburne: the Duke of Bedford, it appears, told Lord Lyttelton that " Shelburne had been mortified by the American department being taken from him, and was gone out of town in ill humour."

Therefore Junius writes to Lord Chatham:—" *Many circumstances must have made it impossible for you to depend much upon Lord Shelburne or his friends; besides that, from his youth and want of knowledge, he was hardly of weight by himself to maintain any character in the Cabinet. The best of him is, perhaps, that he has not acted with greater insincerity to your Lordship, than to former connections.*"

In short, the whole tenor of these letters from Whately and Lord Lyttelton, which seem to have been the text upon which Junius formed his communication to Lord Chatham, is embodied in the following sentence:—" *During your absence from Administration, it is well known that not one of the Ministers has either adhered to you with firmness, or supported with any degree of steadiness those principles on which you engaged in the King's service. From being their idol at first, their veneration for you has gradually diminished, until, at last, they have absolutely set you at defiance.*"

trace it, general. Lord Shelburne's ill-humour might be supposed to be personal; but I know no particular

The motives of Junius then, in writing this letter to Lord Chatham, were to endeavour to excite in him hatred and distrust of his colleagues, and to inform him that the Duke of Grafton considered "*his influence to be removed,*" and that he was "*entirely out of the case.*"

The motives of Lord Temple, were he writing to Lord Chatham at this time, would be precisely the same: the Grenvilles having lost the Bedfords, *et pris pour dupes*, Lord Temple was now desirous of recovering the position and influence of their party, by renewing the alliance with Lord Chatham.

But the opinions of Junius, or rather, to speak more correctly, of the anonymous writer who afterwards adopted that signature, were in direct opposition to those of Lord Chatham upon the American question, and there is an apparent inconsistency in Junius seeking the alliance of Lord Chatham, and declaring his conviction that, "*if this country can be saved, it must be saved by Lord Chatham's spirit, by Lord Chatham's abilities.*" That which would be inconsistent in any other politician, assumes a different aspect as regards Lord Temple, when he and Junius are supposed to be identical, and when it is considered that their opinions on that important subject exactly coincided.

Lord Temple sought the alliance of his brother-in-law, as well from returning affection, as for political reasons: their mutual opinions respecting America remained unchanged during their lives, and yet, after their reconciliation in the ensuing autumn, those opinions were never again the cause of any misunderstanding between them.

Nor is there any reason why Lord Temple should not now express sentiments of respect and veneration for the character of Lord Chatham, or warmth and attachment to his person. There would be no great inconsistency, for although those sentiments might have suffered a temporary suspension, they had always existed in his bosom towards the friend of his youth, and the husband of a sister to whom he was tenderly attached. It is true he had abused him, and had perhaps incited others to do so, but he had great cause—he had great provocation—he had all the motives which political hatred had engendered—but those motives were now removed; there was a prospect of their reconciliation: the coalition of the Bedfords with the Ministry had entirely changed the aspect of party politics. "Lord Chatham," says Almon, "had unceasingly lamented his difference with Lord Temple from the time it happened, and as soon as he was emancipated from the connections of office, and even from the suspicion of a connection with the Court, he sought the friendship of his brother with anxiety and sincerity. He confessed to Mr. Calcraft that almost everybody else had betrayed him:

reason for Lord Camden's being displeased, and yet he certainly is so to the highest degree. Lord Bristol has more than once or twice expressed his dissatisfaction in the strongest terms to Lord George Sackville, with whom I believe he has no very intimate acquaintance, ending every time with heartily wishing that Lord Chatham and his family could agree; and, as far as a judgment can be formed by looks, Lord Granby is far from contented.

Lord Bute's friends seem in general pleased with the coalition; I hear it particularly of Mr. Mackenzie; I do not pretend to account for this, but on looking back to times not long past, perhaps you may think the contrast entertaining.

Sir Laurence Dundas informs me that Rigby told

his brother, he said, had indeed abused him; but it was in the warmth of his temper and in the openness of his nature, which was superior to all hypocrisy or concealment of disapprobation." After their reconciliation, they were, if possible, more affectionately united than ever they had been, as their correspondence in these volumes, and in the *Chatham Papers*, abundantly testifies.

Some other circumstances are to be observed in these letters which would certainly tend to inflame the animosity of Lord Temple against the Duke of Bedford and Lord Mansfield, two persons against whom the virulence of Junius was constantly directed.

The former, in his conversation with Lord Lyttelton, treated Lord Temple with contemptuous silence, as a person considered of no importance in these transactions:—" Of your Lordship he said nothing." *Nothing!* of Lord Temple!—No abuse or condemnation could possibly have been more offensive.

Lord Mansfield, too, " had been so good as to promise Lord Weymouth and Lord Gower *his kind assistance whenever they should want it.*"

"I have reason to think," adds Lord Lyttelton, "he (Lord Mansfield) is gone with his whole heart into this arrangement, rather in hatred to Lord Chatham, who, he thought, would be ruined by it, though his health should return, than out of affection to the system on any other account."

him he should not kiss hands 'till Lord Weymouth did; and Lord Weymouth cannot while Conway is in; perhaps that may be the foundation for Rigby's declaration that he would not accept till Conway was out, or both may have been his declarations to different persons. I asked Sir Laurence whether upon these occasions the Ministerial animosity against him in his Elections was appeased, but hitherto he says he has heard nothing about it either way; my reason for asking was because I had heard that he was now more a Bedford than a Grenville, and I thought by that test to try whether he was 'listed: I did not find that he was, and, from comparing all the accounts I have had of the language he holds, I think his idea is to consider the Duke and you as not broken, and so to quarrel with neither.

The Duke of Grafton's distance from Lord Chatham is more marked since I wrote to you than it was then, and he enters with eagerness into the opinions of the Duke of Bedford concerning America: on the other side, the Bedfords speak with great encomiums of the Duke of Grafton. His Grace has proffered his personal friendship to Rigby, who is pleased with his behaviour, and you may depend upon it that at present the union is very close, and I am persuaded exclusive of Lord Chatham. These may be all fallacious appearances, but they must so soon be brought to a test, that his Grace must be very weak if he is not sincere. If they are not tried by some little party manœuvre, they will be by the public measures, and probably some of the Bedfords will, before they propose any respecting America, take an opportunity of speaking to you: it may, therefore, be worth your while to consider what you would in the present circumstances say they ought to do, in case they should ask you.

Lord Camden, in an accidental conversation which he had with Mr. Forrester, observed that Mr. Wedderburn had been very flippant, both in public and in private, and that *that gentleman* would do well to consider whose gown he wore. Lord Mansfield, on hearing this, diverted himself much with the idea of taking in such times as these a patent of precedency from a lawyer, and took notice how absurd such a threat was from Lord Camden to Wedderburn, who would soon be the more capital card of the two in this country. This little anecdote, however, is not to be mentioned. Forrester desires that it may not be said of him that he repeats such conversations.

Lord Camden's friends say that he has seen Lord Chatham: I do not find that anybody else has; Lord Bristol has not, but has only received a letter from Lady Chatham, in which she places great reliance on the air of Hayes for the recovery of his health.

It is now said that Lord North is to have the lead in the House of Commons: I think this a more likely idea than that of giving it to Conway, but I do not understand that it is certainly settled.

Lord Hillsborough's common language intimates his doubt whether the arrangement, so far at least as relates to him, will hold six months.

Lord Mansfield, I hear, is rather out of spirits, more so, I mean, than he seemed to be in his conversation with you on the new coalition: from another I hear that he is to take a leading part in Council, and will be consulted in everything by Lord Gower: my authority for the former is the better of the two; yet his great objection to interfering with the influence of Lord Chatham is, if he believes appearances, removed; he being now represented with greater confidence every day by the Ministerial people, I mean of the Grafton Ministry, to be entirely out of the case.

By all the circumstances which I have mentioned in this letter, the representations I gave you in my former are confirmed[1]. It seems to me clear that the Duke of Grafton means to gain the Bedfords entirely: whether the consequence will be that he will get them as an accession to his party, or they get him as an accession to theirs, is, I think, very doubtful: circumstances which neither can command must determine; but without the intervention of *particular* circumstances, I should be inclined to think that, the party of the Bedfords being of more real weight than the *individual* Duke of Grafton, they would rather draw him to them, than he them to him.

I suppose you saw my second letter to Lord Temple, in which Dunning's appointment was accounted for[2]. I now hear that it is not to take place immediately, but Willes is to have at least one term to close his business, and perhaps Dunning may not be sorry to

[1] Mr. Grenville, in acknowledging these letters, writes to Whately on the 9th instant,—"I find that they all confirm the former account which you gave me of the entire confidence and union between the Duke of Grafton and the Duke of Bedford and his friends, and the separation of the former from Lord Chatham and his part of the Ministry; how far this may be true with regard to Lord Shelburne and some others, I know not," &c.

[2] Dunning was soon after made Solicitor-General, in the room of Edward Willes, son of the Lord Chief Justice Willes, who was promoted to the Bench.

have a little time to see the certainty on which he engages.

LORD LYTTELTON TO EARL TEMPLE.

Curzon Street, January 1, 1768.

My dear Lord,—Be pleased to sign, as trustee, the mortgage deeds for raising my daughter's fortune, which the bearer of this brings to you in his way to Hagley.

I presume you have been informed by your brother of everything I could tell you concerning the political state of the world before he left London.

Since that time a great cold has confined me to my house, except one morning when I made a visit to his Grace of Bedford. From him I learnt that the basis of the late treaty with the Duke of Grafton was a supposition that Lord Chatham was politically dead, and that Lord Camden had devoted himself to the Duke of Grafton, without any reserve of fidelity to his former master, even if he should revive and act; that Shelburne had been mortified by the American Department being taken from him, and was gone out of town in ill humour; that the Ministry meant to *widen their bottom*, as occasions should offer, and that he had a great esteem and love for your brother, and wished to see him at the head of the Treasury, for which place nobody was so fit. My answers were civil, cool, and doubtful. He spoke warmly of the necessity of doing something to mend the state of our colonies, and said the Duke of Grafton was entirely of the same mind, but opened no plan for that purpose. Of your Lordship he said nothing. I hear that one of the Ministers of that connection had declared at Arthur's, within these two or three days, that *they were trying (if possible) to find a medium between the violence of George Grenville and the madness of Lord Chatham.*

On the other hand, I was assured from two or three different quarters that Lord Chatham is better, and that the report of his having had the gout in his head and stomach was false; that he has had a little in his fingers; that a good natural fit, to which nature is tending in him, would quite restore him; that his thoughts are full of returning, not only to Ministry, but to omnipotence; that he is very angry at Lord Hillsborough's promotion, or rather at the creation of that new office, which he had always opposed; that he is coming to town, and will do some great thing there, but nobody knows what. At the same time I hear that Lord Camden has publicly said that the Duke of Grafton and Lord Chatham are one and the same man; that the act of the former must be always understood to be the will of the latter, and other expressions to the same effect.

I have seen Burke, who talked warmly on the East India Company's business[1], which he supposed would be regulated by Mr. Dyson's plan, notwithstanding the alteration that has happened in the Ministry, and I believe he says true. He said nothing from or of the Marquess of Rockingham, and I avoided the subject; but from other quarters some overtures have been thrown out of coalition and union, between the Marquess and us, against the present powers.

Lord Hardwicke sent me a message the other day

---

[1] The renewal of the Bill for restraining the dividends of the East India Company, which, after much debate, was carried by large majorities through both Houses.

that he wished I would call upon him, not being well enough to come to me, but as I was also indisposed we have not met.

Mr. West has been here upon a report of a reconciliation between us and Lord Chatham, which he seemed to believe 'till contradicted by me. He told me it was understood in town that the Bedfordians had not treated with the Duke of Grafton upon any foot of equality, but had sworn allegiance to his Grace, and would be very good servants. Yet he admitted, that, as much business would be done at table and over a bottle, they were likely to make themselves so agreeable to his Grace in those Cabinet Councils, as to gain an ascendant over him, and that to this they trusted. He added that their present great object was, to get the better of Lord Hertford's credit in the Closet, which would not be easily done, as his Lordship had a strong root of personal favour there, which he cultivated and improved by being a most assiduous courtier to Lord Bute. Of that great man I hear nothing but what Lord Mansfield told me, that he believed he was well pleased with the taking in of the Bedfords.

I presume your brother has told you what I related to him of the conversation between Lord Mansfield and me the night the treaty was settled. I have only to add now, that having heard he was *called to the Cabinet*, I asked the Duke of Bedford whether it was true, who said not as he knew of, but that his Lordship had been so good as to promise Lord Weymouth and Lord Gower *his kind assistance whenever they should want it.*

I have reason to think he is gone with his whole heart into this arrangement, rather in hatred to Lord Chatham, who he thought would be ruined by it, though his health should return, than out of affection to the system on any other account.

I forgot to mention, in giving your Lordship the substance of my conversation with the Duke of Bedford, that he spoke with pleasure, and a kind of triumph, of the total exclusion of Lord Rockingham and his friends from this treaty.

This, my dear Lord, is the general state of things, so far as I can gain any knowledge of it, which is very imperfect. The real inclinations of the Court towards the new comers, the degree of favour the Duke of Grafton is in himself, how far Lord Chatham's anger, if he be angry, could shake it, are matters far from being sufficiently ascertained. It is certain that the world considers us as forsaken by our only formidable strength, *et pris pour dupes.*

But what should we gain by complaining, or showing any resentment? Some think that a promise to pay the Civil List debt next year was the secret article of this treaty. If so, it will not hurt our credit with the public, that we are no parties to it.

A happy new year, and many of them, to your Lordship, Lady Temple, and all the family at Stowe, which I suppose at present includes that of Wotton, is the most ardent wish of, my dear Lord, your most affectionate and most faithful Servant, LYTTELTON.

If my illness had not damped my poetical fire I would have sent Lady Temple a New Year's ode.

Be so good as to let the bearer pass through your Ridings to Towcester. His name is Bateman.

Since I wrote the account of Lord Chatham before given, I hear from one to whom Dr. Addington told it, that he has been worse, which much alarmed Lady Chatham, but not the doctor, who still says he will be well as soon as he can get a fit of the gout. He is removed from the dairy house to the house at Hayes, and is still in treaty about the house in Pall Mall that belonged to the late Mrs. Harris.

Old Onslow is dying of a mortification. The Duke of Newcastle will recover, but probably so broken as not to hold it long.

The sending of this letter has been delayed by the snow's retarding the arrival of the Exeter coach, which brought back the deeds from Lord Fortescue.

I have had a visit from Lord Hardwicke, but it produced nothing worth writing, his conversation being only of the same colour as all his former ones with me, blaming the extravagance of Lord Rockingham's pretensions, wishing well to our system and connection, but not seeming determined to run all fortunes with us, if other doors should open to let in his brother, whose promotion to the Seals appears to be his main object. He spoke of the Bedford connection coming in, as an act of hungry impatience for places and emoluments, but thought that the Duke of Grafton had done well for himself, unless he should suffer them to beat him in the Closet, and so become his masters[1].

[1] "It would be unjust to the Duke of Bedford's friends to attribute their conduct to any but the motives which they themselves profess. Mr. Rigby is so modest a man, that the imputation of public virtue or private good faith would offend his delicacy, if he did not feel, as he certainly does, the genuine emotions of patriotism and friendship warm in his breast. They argued not ill for ambition, while they asked for nothing but profit; and when the Duke of Grafton has exhausted the Treasury, he will find that every other power departs with the power of giving."—*Junius*, vol. iii. p. 188.

C. [THE AUTHOR OF JUNIUS] TO MR. GRENVILLE[1].

London. 6 February. 1768.

SIR—the observations contained in the inclosed paper are thrown together and sent to you upon a

[1] Endorsed in Mr. Grenville's hand, "Anonymous, C, with the enclosed paper, Feb. 6th, 1768." This is the first of three letters sent during the present year to Mr. Grenville, by the writer who afterwards became so well known under the signature of Junius. They are written in a hand very carefully disguised, nevertheless it must be confessed that these communications furnish a *primâ facie* case of some difficulty in opposition to the theory of assigning the authorship to Lord Temple.

It would seem to most persons extremely improbable that Lord Temple should anonymously address such letters to his own brother, and assure him therein, that he, the writer, was *a man quite unknown and unconnected;* that he had *no connection with any party;* that it was not *either necessary or proper to make himself known* to him *at present.*

I think, however, that upon a closer and more careful examination of all the circumstances, these difficulties will appear less prominent, and that which has seemed impossible at the first glance, will be found, upon reflection, to be only the peculiar contrivance which the author thought would be most conducive to his purpose of absolute concealment; for he may have had many reasons to believe that his brother, as well as others, suspected him to be the writer of certain articles in the newspapers, and therefore he would deprecate all attempts to discover him, by the promise:—" *At a proper time he will solicit the honour of being known to you: he has present important reasons for wishing to be concealed.*"

Now, it appears to me that he adopted the most effectual means of obtaining that absolute concealment by the bold determination of appealing as he did to the honour of his brother, who would either be entirely thrown off his guard by this apparently improbable and almost impossible step on the part of Lord Temple, or that if he had still any suspicion of the writer being his brother, he would understand it as a hint that he was expected to abstain from any observation or inquiry, or any attempt to remove the veil of mystery under which he desired to conceal himself. The condition that Mr. Grenville should not only not show these papers to *anybody,* but that he should never mention his having received them, was probably intended most impressively to imply, that he should not show them, nor even

supposition that the Tax therein referred to will make part of the budget. if Lord North should have fallen

mention them to Lord Temple, to whom he was now known to be most affectionately attached, both privately and in politics, in order that, in any conversation upon the subject, he, Lord Temple, might not be placed in an embarrassing position by affecting to be ignorant of them.

It is remarkable that Junius made no such condition to Lord Chatham, to whom he had written in the previous month, because as he and Lord Temple were not upon good terms, he was not so likely to meet him, but the same condition is repeated with still stronger emphasis in a subsequent letter to Mr. Grenville, in which he says:—
"*If an earnest wish to serve you gives me any claim, let me entreat you not to suffer a hint of this communication to escape you to* ANYBODY."

It is not in the least probable that a mere political writer—a stranger—professing to be unknown to either party, should privately express at the same period of time equal warmth of personal attachment to two men so distinctly separate in politics and in private life, and yet with the peculiarity of being in some respects so connected, as Lord Chatham and Mr. Grenville. As politicians, they were opposed on almost all questions of public interest; as private men, there had been between them great animosity for several years; they had scarcely met but in public places; and in the House of Commons, Lord Chatham (when Mr. Pitt) had treated Mr. Grenville with ridicule and contempt.

From Lord Temple alone could these expressions be expected, or be in any way consistent. Who so likely as Lord Temple to profess, and to feel, *a voluntary disinterested attachment* to the cause and person of his brother, Mr. Grenville, or to write almost at the same period to Lord Chatham, his brother-in-law, with *sentiments of respect and veneration for his character, and warmth of attachment to his person?*

In the event of a reconciliation with Lord Chatham, Lord Temple would certainly not wish it to be known, or even to be suspected, that he had been the author of some of the most virulent abuse which had so recently been levelled against his character and conduct.

After an interval of seven months, he again writes to Mr. Grenville, in September and October following, and knowing that in the meantime his confidence had not been misplaced, he becomes more communicative, and though he disclaims all motives of vanity, yet he avows himself to have been the author of THE GRAND COUNCIL, of some other papers under the signatures of LUCIUS and ATTICUS, and a multitude of others; in short, everything which for two years past had attracted the notice of the public.

Still it was not, perhaps, for what he had written, as for what he

upon any other scheme, they will be useless. but if the case happens, and they shall appear to have any weight, the author is satisfied, that no man in this Country can make so able a use of them, or place them in so advantageous a light as Mr. Grenville.

It is not, Sir, either necessary or proper to make myself known to you at present. hereafter I may perhaps claim that honour. in the mean Time be assured that it is a voluntary disinterested attachment to your person founded on an esteem for your Spirit and Understanding, which has, and will for ever engage me in your Cause. A number of late publications, (falsely attributed to men of far greater talent) may convince you of my zeal, if not of my Capacity to serve you.

The only Condition, which I presume to make with you, is that you will not only not show these papers to any body, but that you will never mention your having received them. C.

THE FOLLOWING IS THE ENCLOSURE REFERRED TO IN THE PRECEDING LETTER.

It is a melancholy consideration that, when every commodity, which can admit of a Tax, is loaded to the last point, it sh^d still be necessary for Government to contrive new taxes. The necessity of doing so in time

---

intended to write, that he again imposed upon Mr. Grenville the condition of secrecy, and that *until he is Minister, he must not permit himself to think of the honour of being known to him.*

I have already made some remarks upon the handwriting of these letters, and therefore I need only now repeat that it was very carefully disguised, and my belief that it was such as would not alone have awakened in the mind of Mr. Grenville any suspicion with respect to the author of them.

of peace makes our situation still more alarming. But if we saw ourselves at the mercy of Bunglers, who might recommend Taxes, without the smallest conception of the manner in which they are to operate, or even of the first principles of taxation, we sh^d. be really reduced to a state of despair. In such unskilful hands, every drug is a poison, every weight an oppression. It is now generally known that the Ministry will be obliged to borrow one million eight or nine hundred thousand pounds for the service of the year, and that a new Fund, to be appropriated for part of the interest of this sum, or in aid of the whole, is to arise from a tax or duty of 3^d. in the pound on every species of thing sold in this country by public Auction[1], with a very unreasonable exception in favour of the East India Company's sales. This I am well assured, (and if I were not well assured I co^d. hardly believe it) is the main foundation of the intended tax, tho' I may not be exact in minuter particulars. Now, Sir, without entering into the merits of the Contriver, permit me to state to you some objections to the scheme itself, which tho' not less obvious than important, I presume have never once occurred to his mind. The publication of this paper may perhaps come time enough to rouse him from his dream, and to prevent his doing a national mischief in his Sleep.

I believe it will be admitted that to lay a new tax indiscriminately & equally upon almost all saleable Commodities, which have been severally taxed before, some heavily some lightly, shows a great want of Judgment

---

[1] The Auction Duty did not form part of Lord North's Budget on this occasion, and therefore the observations upon it were of no use to Mr. Grenville. The tax referred to was first imposed in the year 1777.

as well as a poverty of Contrivance in the first formation of the tax. To make no distinction between things, which have already different burthens laid upon them, & to distribute the new burthen indifferently upon them all, may be short work indeed, but it is a sign of a bungling confused plan, and just as absurd as if a waggoner, who had a hundred weight of goods to carry more than he expected, were never to examine which of his waggons were laden before & which not, but to divide the last load equally among them all, & so let some break down, while the rest travelled empty. So much for the generality of the Tax. The next thing to be considered, particularly by gentlemen of landed estates, is that, as the mode of selling estates by auction is become very general, a tax on that mode is in effect an additional land-tax, & will be found a heavy clog upon a most eligible way of alienating landed property. It is unnecessary to say that every impediment of this kind ought to be strongly discouraged in a commercial Country, whose welfare depends on the number of moderate fortunes engaged in trade. Whether the landed gentlemen, who thought it necessary to take off one shilling in the pound last year, will submit to this indirect reimposition of a part of it, is a point, which I shall leave to them to consider. Permit me only to observe that this method of encreasing the land tax will be particularly grievous, as it must fall chiefly on persons, who may be compelled by distress of Circumstances, or the call of some sudden Emergence to part with their Estates.

My third Objection is that this tax will fall heaviest upon that part of the people, who stand most in need of ease & relief from the legislature & whose distresses, if they cannot be relieved, certainly require no aggravation. It must fall upon the creditors of Bankrupts, whose effects, tho' they may not produce half a Crown in the pound, are to be liable to a further defalcation; as if the loss of a considerable part of the debt were not sufficiently severe, or as if it were the office of the legislature to encrease the load of Misfortune, and to combine with the bankrupt in compleating the Creditor's destruction. But this is not the only blow levelled at the poor. Let it be considered that it is chiefly the lower rank of mechanicks & tradesmen, who, to raise ready money, have recourse to auctions where their goods find a quick, if not a profitable vent[1]. If you Deprive them of this resource, by laying a new tax upon their labour (the materials of which have probably been taxed in various shapes before) what can be the consequence, but that their goods will perish in their shops, or be seised by their Creditors, or be sold at such a loss as Necessity & despair may force them to submit to; besides that, in many instances it may be more advantageous to sell a thing for two thirds of its value to-day, than for its full value six months hence. But I suppose the Chancellor of the Exchequer has never once considered what the addition of three pence in the pound to the present exorbitant demands made by Auctioneers, will amount to, nor how the industry of a poor man can bear such an accumulated oppression.

[1] This word, derived from the French *vente*, and here used in the sense of *sale*, is not very common. It occurs again in Junius, thus:—
" Our manufactures no longer find a *vent* in foreign markets."—Vol. ii. p. 515.
In *Another Letter to Almon*, also:—" And was pretty indifferent about his personal liberty, provided his press moved freely, and found a large *vent* for his productions."—p. 191.

I have often heard it said & by judicious people, that the suffering a number of small auctions in this town is a perpetual Source of Fraud, & an impediment to trade. perhaps it may be so; but I fear it is an inconvenience we must submit to, untill some other method of raising ready money upon the produce of their industry, be laid open to the poor. at all events the Tax in question will rather confirm and sanctify this fraudulent mode of traffick, by placing that which was only connived at before, under the immediate notice and protection of the legislature; or if it should operate as a prohibition, the tax will defeat itself as a fund of revenue, & the deficiency fall on the sinking fund, which we are told it is the object of Governm^t. to relieve.

A fourth objection, which appears to me more considerable than any of the former, arises from the method, in which all auctions are & must be conducted. When the seller finds that there is less bidden for his property than he can afford to take for it, he is of course obliged to buy it in himself; so that, besides the Auctioneer's profits, he must pay a tax to Government, on account of a supposed sale of goods which never were sold; nor do I see a possibility of framing a Clause to relieve such a Case, without giving occasion to a multitude of frauds & perjuries. These are matters however, which it is no wonder great folks should be unacquainted with. Exempt as they are from the wants and distresses of life, they know nothing of the shifts, to which the poor man & his poverty are reduced. But there is another point, which I am astonished that the great persons, who frame & recommend this tax, should not understand. I am astonished that a Chancellor of the Exchequer sh^d. know so little of the laws relative to buying &

selling as to attempt an act which directly invades this whole branch of the common and Statute law of England, & forms a Contradiction, no less daring than absurd, to all the wisdom of our Ancestors. Untill this day it has been a Maxim of the English Legislature to give every possible encouragement to the most open & publick methods of disposing of property by bargain & sale. to this End fairs and markets have from time to time been Established, with grants of particular immunities & of exclusive privileges. Perhaps our Ancestors were mistaken, but it has been the prejudice of more than a thousand years, that the more publick and notorious the transaction of Sales was made, the more likely it would be to prevent Collusions & Frauds in traffick & consequently the more deserving of *favour & indulgence* from the legislature. Now, Sir, it cannot be denied that an auction, next to established fairs & markets, is the most open and publick method of sale that can be imagined. At least if Frauds are committed in this way, they ought to be corrected by regulations, not the thing itself restrained or suppressed by a tax, which, in many instances must amount to a prohibition, & when that happens, will at once defeat itself & injure the publick [1].

[1] The original orthography, abbreviations, capital letters, and punctuation in these papers by the author of Junius, have been very carefully preserved.

MR. WILKES TO EARL TEMPLE.

Saturday, February 13, (1768.)

MY LORD,—I desired Mr. Cotes, the day of my arrival here[1], to assure your Lordship of my regard and

---

[1] Wilkes returned to London from Ostend about the 6th or 7th of February. In a letter from Humphrey Cotes to Wilkes, dated January 28th, he mentions having seen Beardmore (Lord Temple's attorney) and he says also,—" Our friend [Lord Temple] you may be very certain, has nothing to do with these men [the Ministers]: he really wishes you well." Whether Wilkes had any interview with Lord Temple at this time, is uncertain. I find no information on the subject in the Grenville Papers.

Immediately after the dissolution of Parliament on the 11th of March, Wilkes offered himself as a candidate to represent the City of London. In this he was unsuccessful. He then announced his intention of standing for the County of Middlesex, and he was elected by a large majority. He presented himself before the Court of King's Bench on the first day of the ensuing term, the 20th of April, but as he was not there by any legal process, Lord Mansfield refused to recognise him. A writ was afterwards issued, and he was brought before the Court as an outlaw on the 27th of April, and, bail being refused, he was committed to the King's Bench Prison. On his way thither, the people took the horses from the carriage, and drew it to a public-house in Spitalfields, from whence Mr. Wilkes contrived to make his escape, and went immediately to the King's Bench Prison, where the Marshal, who was forced out of the coach at Temple Bar, had arrived before him. The outlawry was reversed by Lord Mansfield on the 8th of June, and Wilkes was soon after brought up for judgment, for the publication of the *North Briton*, No. 45, and the *Essay on Woman*; he was sentenced to two years' imprisonment, and fined 1000*l*.

The new Parliament being appointed to meet on the 10th of May, there was an expectation that Wilkes would proceed to take his seat in the House of Commons, and a great crowd of people assembled near the prison: a riot ensued, the military were called out, and some lives were lost: a young man named Allen was shot by the soldiers in mistake. Lord Barrington's letter, as Secretary at War, to the Field Officer in waiting, conveying an expression of the King's approval of the conduct of the officers and men upon this occasion, was the subject of much comment by the Author of Junius.

It will be seen by a letter from Lord Temple, that he visited Wilkes

attachment. I have waited 'till the end of term the resolutions of Administration. I am now to take a decided part with respect to the next Parliament before the ensuing term.

May I so far hope for your Lordship's indulgence, as to be gratified with the opportunity of submitting my own sentiments on some delicate points, and of hearing the opinion of my best friend as to my future conduct in the present situation of my affairs? I shall be most happy to attend your Lordship any half-hour you will please to appoint, in any place you choose, and my brother in St. John's Square would be so kind as to take the charge of your Lordship's commands for me. I am, with the truest respect and gratitude, my Lord, your Lordship's most obedient humble servant,

JOHN WILKES.

MR. WEDDERBURN TO MR. GRENVILLE.

Morley, April 3, 1768.

DEAR SIR,—The elections in this part of the world have been very quiet, not even excepting Pomfret, which, according to the account I have of it (from Walsh's opponents indeed), has only been an instance of very gross misconduct on his part[1].

in the King's Bench Prison soon after his committal; and subsequent to that time, I do not find any more letters either to or from Wilkes among Lord Temple's papers. Almon states that he offended Lord Temple by some remarks which he printed on George Grenville's speech on the question of his expulsion from the House of Commons in February, 1769, and that he never spoke to him afterwards. This statement is, however, probably incorrect. In 1771, there is an allusion to Wilkes in a letter from Mr. Dayrell to Lord Temple, but I have noticed that communication in another place.

[1] Walsh was M.P. for Worcester in the new Parliament, through the interest of Lord Clive. Lord Galway and Sir Rowland Wynn

How different has the scene been in the south, and how little reason can any man have for leaving a country of plenty, frugality, and sobriety, as this is, where the laws execute themselves, and where the name of Wilkes is never profanely joined with liberty, nor mentioned but with detestation; to inhabit a great bedlam under the dominion of a beggarly, idle, and intoxicated mob without keepers, actuated solely by the word Wilkes, which they use as better savages do a walrus, to incite them in their attempts to insult Government and trample upon law. Wilkes, I dare to say, is vain enough to imagine that he has raised all this tumult, but in my opinion he is as innocent of it as the staff that carries the flag with his name upon it. The mob has been made sensible of its own importance, and the pleasure which the rich and powerful feel in governing those whom fate has made their inferiors, is not half so strong as that which the indigent and worthless feel in subverting property, defying law, and lording it over those whom they were used to respect. A Jack Straw, or a John Wilkes, are but the instruments of those whom they seem to lead; the leading principle of every mob is that impatience of legal rule which the relaxation of just authority, and the mutability of Government, that we have for some time experienced, never fail to produce in the minds of the inferior people. Has not the mob of London as good a right to be insolent as the unchecked mob of Boston? Was not the attack on Bedford House an encouragement to pull down any other house in London? and is it wonderful that the

---

were chosen for Pontefract; but the latter having been unseated upon petition, Mr. Strachey, Lord Clive's Secretary, was elected in November following.

populace should at last assist the endeavours of those who for five years past have been making interest for Mr. Wilkes? His best friends have not been a Mr. Lewis Gilbert of Spitalfields, but if I were to name them, I should reckon up one-half of the Ministers canvassing for him as a fit colleague for Mr. George Cooke, for I really think when he was appointed Joint Paymaster, Wilkes was very fairly pointed out to the mob of Middlesex, and he was as certainly recommended on many other occasions by many people who little thought they were espousing Wilkes's resentments, while they imagined they were only gratifying their own. I am perhaps writing in a very unfashionable style to you at present, for I should not be surprised to hear that Mr. Wilkes had not only a pardon under the Great Seal, but the Great Seal itself bestowed upon him. But I have the pleasure to know, that whatever extraordinary scene the present distraction may exhibit, you can view it with no concern but for the public; you have no part of the blame to impute to yourself; your conduct will be, as it always has been, clear, steady, and determined in support of the laws and constitution of the country[1]. I am ever, &c., &c.

AL. WEDDERBURN.

[1] In less than a year after this time, Wedderburn exerted himself as much in the defence of Wilkes as ever he did in his condemnation. His vote on the popular side of the Middlesex Election question, in February 1769, lost him his seat in Parliament. Having been elected for Richmond as a Tory, under the patronage of Sir Laurence Dundas, he was bound in honour when he set up as a patriot to vacate his seat, by accepting the Stewardship of the Chiltern Hundreds. Lord Temple, writing to Lady Chatham an account of that debate, mentions that "Wedderburn made a most excellent speech with us." At a great dinner given shortly after at the Thatched House, by the leaders of Opposition, his health was drank as Steward of the Chiltern Hundreds, and he was looked upon as a martyr to the cause. He made

MR. GRENVILLE TO MR. WHATELY.

Wotton, April 13, 1768.

DEAR WHATELY,—I do not see how the conduct of the Assembly of New York, in giving a sum of money to the Crown, but refusing to take the least notice of the Mutiny Act, can be called a submission to that law, or represented as a discouragement to the popular opinions of America not being bound by our laws. It seems to me the very reverse; but I have done with talking to the deaf: they must feel before they believe, and I think that period of conviction is not far off.

If different factions prevail in the management of the East India Company's affairs abroad, as much as they seem to do in their general courts at home, the former will lay them open even to a weak attack in India, as the latter will infallibly do to the weakest Administration at

---

a very inflammatory speech in reply, denouncing in no measured terms the usurpation of the rights of the people by their own representatives, concluding with the following oath of abjuration: "I do from my soul denounce, detest, and abjure as unconstitutional and illegal, that damnable doctrine and position, that a resolution of the House of Commons can make, alter, suspend, abrogate, or annihilate the law of the land." Whereupon he kissed the bottle.

Through the friendship of Lord Clive to Mr. Grenville, and at the recommendation of the latter, Wedderburn was elected for Bishop's Castle in November following. While he was out of Parliament he went about making harangues, and supporting violent resolutions against the Government, and he was more a Wilkite than even Wilkes himself.

Wedderburn acquired a considerable fortune by his marriage in December, 1767, with the daughter and sole heir of John Dawson, Esq., of Morley in Yorkshire, from whence this letter is dated.

Lord Campbell's biography of Wedderburn, in his *Lives of the Chancellors*, is written in his usual comprehensive style. I have been frequently indebted to that amusing work, in which, however, an accurate observer will perhaps detect too many allusions to the personal and party feelings of our own times.

home. I am glad you have seen Mr. Walsh and Mr. Strachey, and that you approve so much of their cause. I hear that Mr. Wilkes has met with a very mortifying reception at Bath, being universally avoided by all degrees of men [1]. If this account be true, it may possibly have given courage to our Ministers to hold, as I am told they do, a higher language at this moment. I will, however, foretell, without the gift of prophecy, that this language will be exactly similar to what has been holden out about America, and fall again under low-water mark on the appearance of any difficulty, or any disapprobation from the mob. For my own part, I agree with our friend Mr. Wedderburn, that the populace of London have a better right to give the law to the King and the Government of Great Britain, than the populace of Boston, and I can hardly believe that those who tremble at the latter will be bold enough to encounter the former. I should not wonder if what you tell me of Sir William Beauchamp Proctor's audience should be true; and yet if it were, I should not draw any consequence from it. I am, &c. GEORGE GRENVILLE.

MR. WHATELY TO MR. GRENVILLE.

April 18, 1768.

DEAR SIR,—I could not write you by the post the anecdotes upon which I grounded the positive assertion that none of the Ministers would venture to propose a pardon for Wilkes, but have been obliged to postpone

[1] "The Chancellor met him in the Pump-room; neither of them spoke or bowed to the other, but both stopped and stared in such a manner as to set the whole room in a titter."—*Whately to Mr. Grenville.*

them, and some other particulars, 'till I could send them by a more private conveyance.

The manner in which the late transactions have been, and [the] present situation is, considered, by the person[1] who is principally affected by them, has, you know, been differently represented: one fact will tend to fix it; for he certainly sat up all the first night of the illuminations, the Monday night, full of indignation at the insult, and saying to those about him, who expressed apprehensions of the mob coming to the Queen's house, that he wished they would push their insolence so far, he should then be justified in repelling it, and giving proper orders to the Guards: he spoke with great discontent of the Lord Chancellor and the Duke of Grafton, to Lord Weymouth[2]. He still retains the same sentiments, holds a language of vigour, and though he has resolved to put *a good countenance* on the matter, yet shows that pardon is not to be mentioned. The speculation of my friend[3], from whom I have this intelligence, and whom you will easily guess, is, that it is resolved to let these people go on for the present; that it is desirable in the present circumstances they should involve themselves inextricably; that, however, it is impossible they should continue long; and he recurs again to his former idea, that Lord Mansfield will be consulted. This was his information on Wednesday evening; on Thursday, Lord

---

[1] The King.

[2] Lord Weymouth recommended himself to the King by punctuality and activity in the business of his office, at a time when the Duke of Grafton, inclined to moderation, neglected everything and went to Newmarket, while the Chancellor, to avoid difficulties, betook himself to Bath. "In the midst of all this tumult and confusion, the Chancellor of Great Britain and the First Lord of the Treasury retire out of town, and leave the whole executive power of the Crown to fall to the ground."—*Junius*, vol. iii. p. 31.

[3] Wedderburn, or Augustus Hervey.

Mansfield had a long audience, and though I do not positively know yet, I have great reason to believe he was sent for, at least so far as this, that if he was not brought to Court by a particular message, he was ordered after Court to go in to the Closet. Lord Trevor dined with him afterwards, and observed he was very thoughtful, from whence he concluded that he was displeased at what had passed: I rather suppose he found that he would be involved, and had either been asked or had given advice. The accounts I have since heard confirm that supposition; for on Friday morning, Lord Mansfield called himself on Sir Fletcher Norton, was in high spirits, and very resolute: if his absence of the day before had been dejection, it would have continued; but supposing it to be perplexity, as soon as he had made up his mind it would turn to alacrity. He told Sir Fletcher that he had been in the Closet, and, without entering into particulars of the conversation, said that it was doing great injustice to the King to believe that he was indifferent; that nobody in the kingdom was more sensible than the King, both of the present insult, and of the general dissolution of Government, and that he would certainly, though perhaps not immediately, change his Administration: his expression was that it was *out of doubt.*

His Lordship being so very communicative, Sir Fletcher in return laid before him the difficulties he was under about his own conduct, the Attorney-General having desired him to be of Counsel for the Crown against Wilkes, and told him that, having consulted Wedderburn, D'Oyly, and me, we had advised him against accepting the invitation, because it would draw on him all the odium, and engage him to support all the weak measures of people who did not understand the business, who would push him into the lead, and yet not follow his advice. Lord Mansfield said, he differed from us all in opinion; that besides Sir Fletcher's duty as King's Counsel, his duty as a citizen obliged him to accept, but did not oblige him to take the most forward part, nor if he disapproved of their conduct, to take any part at all, and that when they took wrong steps, he might then refuse to be further concerned, with more credit to himself than he could now decline to be concerned at all. Upon this advice Sir Fletcher went to the consultation on Saturday; he found them totally ignorant of all the proceedings. The Attorney and Solicitor General thought that when Wilkes appeared, they also were to appear, and then the Court would be under a necessity to dispose of him, without their making any specific application. Sir Fletcher asked them whether they had ever been in the King's Bench, that they could suppose the Court would act without an application from the prosecutor. They then suggested that they might admit error: there again Sir Fletcher told them they were wrong, for they could admit only errors of fact; but if errors in law should be assigned, the Court would not take their admission: they then went through all the errors which they have heard of, all which Sir Fletcher insists are of no consequence; the principal is, that Mr. Wilkes was beyond seas at the return of the Exigent; the answer to which is, that he cannot avail himself of his own *laches*, and be protected by flying from justice: at last the Attorney asked Sir Fletcher, and begged him as a friend to tell him, whether he would advise him to take out a *capias* before the first day of term, in order to bring Wilkes properly before the Court: to which Sir Fletcher said that he should answer that question by another, why he had not taken one out before? He said he had not been directed; and was told by Sir Fletcher that he should not have waited for directions; that this was a process of execution, not of prosecution, and thus ended this doughty consultation; since which I hear that at a more private meeting, to which Sir Fletcher was not invited, they have recurred to their first idea of doing nothing, but waiting to see what the Court will do, which certainly, as the affair now stands, will be nothing, except what may arise from Wilkes's writ of error which he has taken out. A great concourse of people is expected on Wednesday[1]: the very expectation will alone make it; but besides, I was told yesterday, that Mr. Fitzherbert said the day before at table, that he had advised Wilkes to prevent all crowd on that day, and that Wilkes in answer swore, that he would be carried down to the Court on the shoulders of the City of London.

There is a well-invented phrase handed about for Lord Chatham, that *he is for vigorous, not rigorous measures.*

MR. WHATELY TO MR. GRENVILLE.

April 22, 1768.

DEAR SIR,—I had this morning a visit from my friend[2] whose information I much rely on, who called

[1] The 20th instant: the day on which Wilkes was to surrender to his outlawry.
[2] Mr. Whately's "friend" most frequently means Wedderburn, but upon this occasion I believe that Augustus Hervey is the person indicated: the "domestic affair" alluded to is mentioned by Horace

partly, I believe, to communicate to me a domestic affair in which he is much concerned, but more to relate to me the substance of some conversations he had lately had, the most material of which was this morning. He first asked me whether I had heard of Lord Mansfield's audience. I told him I had, and gave him the account which I sent you of it. He had not been informed of any particulars, but only told that his Lordship had had such an audience, and the information was accompanied with the warmest wishes that the King would follow that noble Lord's advice, saying, that the King had the highest regard for it, and would never be satisfied with a system which his Lordship did not approve of; but still did not positively say that he had asked, or when he asked would certainly adopt his opinion. My friend took the opportunity to extol Lord Mansfield's abilities and principles, and then to say, that if the King would take his advice in the framing of an Administration, and would place Mr. Grenville at the Treasury, it would be the only means of recovering the authority of Government; that he believed Lord Mansfield's opinion was, that there had been no Government since Mr. Grenville was dismissed; that the King had tried great numbers, and every one had been worse than the other; and that if anything displeasing had fallen from Mr. Grenville while he was in office, he hoped that he was not the only man who could not be forgiven, especially when the public good required the assistance which he could, and he alone could, give. His answer to this

Walpole in a letter to Conway some time after: "Augustus Hervey thinking it the *bel air*, is going to sue for a divorce from the Chudleigh. He asked Lord Bolingbroke t' other day, who was his proctor? as he would have asked for his tailor."

was a very warm complaint of the conduct of the present Ministers, particularly of the Duke of Grafton; *that a man in his situation should propose a pardon*[1] was one of the expressions, but said the King had stood against that proposition, and would continue firm against it. Besides this conversation, the same friend told me, that having had occasion to mention to a person he did not name, but whose intelligence he says is the best and most confidential, some business of his own (I fancy some electioneering connections), and talked to him of the part he intended to take; that person advised him not to stir a step, for that *the Duke of Grafton would not long continue where he now is,* which information my friend relies upon very much. He likewise said, that he had been told by another person, to whom he did not give such implicit credit, *that there was still a hitch on Lord Chatham;* to which he answered, that such a regard as would save to Lord Chatham an honourable, lucrative, inactive situation, was very proper, but he could not conceive the obligation should extend to the keeping in office men who had been proved inefficient, merely because Lord Chatham had once recommended them. I observed upon that, that he had certainly taken the right distinction, and that whether Lord Chatham should keep a valuable sinecure could never be a question with the family he was so nearly related to. I then asked him whether he had ever explained the situation in which the Bedfords stood with you; he told me that before he went out of town he had mentioned it, but there was no occasion to dwell upon it, as he believed the King understood it thoroughly,

---

[1] For Wilkes; it is well known that the King always refused to listen to any proposal of that kind in favour of Wilkes.

and there was the less reason for taking it up now, as Lord Weymouth was the *only* one of the Ministers who was thought to have behaved *tolerably* on the present occasion. I answered that I was, notwithstanding, of opinion, that taking great care on the one hand to show how easily Mr. Grenville could, if His Majesty's service required it, act in concert with them, with whom he agreed in principles, it was, on the other hand, of moment to state the utter impossibility of our ever again banding with men whom we could never absolutely trust. He hoped, he said, we continued upon the same fair terms as we had parted, and observed, this was the time for them to interpose, when the King's mind is alienated from the others[1]. I assured him, that we remained in

---

[1] Whately implies that Mr. Grenville would not be unwilling to act again with the Bedfords, "if His Majesty's service required it;" but he speaks more of his own wishes than of Mr. Grenville's intentions, for the latter in his reply evidently evades the subject as one "upon which every man's mind must suggest more than he can write." Walpole relates the state of affairs at this time, from the information of Lord Hertford and Mr. Conway, and he says: "I believe these last good folks (the Bedfords) are still not satisfied with the satisfaction of their wishes. They have the favour of the Duke of Grafton, but neither his confidence nor his company, so that they can neither sell the places in his gift, nor his secrets." And again: "The Bedford faction, who had almost got entire possession of the Duke of Grafton, began to perceive how little security there was in that tenure. They found that every disgust inspired him with thoughts of resigning. They saw the immediate necessity of strengthening themselves, lest some sudden caprice should hurry him to resign, and leave them weak at Court, or exposed to the dislike of the next Minister, whoever it should be. Rigby in particular had not attained the Paymastership which Grafton had engaged to him on the first opportunity, and was sure of being the first victim, if Grenville, whom he had sacrificed, should return to power. With as little decency as he had abandoned him, Rigby now made secret offers to Grenville to support him, if the Duke of Grafton should quit; but they were rejected, both from the haughtiness of Grenville's nature, and by the positive injunction of Lord Temple, who sent Calcraft to Lord Hertford with an account of that

the same dispositions as we were, but doubted of the Bedfords' interposition, if any risk of losing their places attended it. He told me, further, that it was certain the Duke of Grafton had lost ground very much lately; that the Ministers had been obliged to acquiesce in the determination against the pardon, but that still the King was every day more and more disgusted, as he saw blunder following blunder, and that no part of the whole transaction had pleased him but Lord Weymouth's behaviour. He did not distinctly tell me whether this part of his information came from his best authority directly, or from the other quarters in whose intelligence he confides; I only know that none of it was immediately from the King, whom he has not seen, and he seemed very certain of the truth of it.

It is impossible to conceive the disgust which the Duke of Grafton's appearance at the Opera with Mrs. Hoghton[1], last Saturday, has given: a Minister, a mar-

---

transaction, adding that his Lordship had sworn to his brother, that should he ever join the Bedfords, he (Lord Temple) would persecute him to the last hour of his life. This Lord Hertford was desired to communicate to the King, with offers from Lord Temple to serve His Majesty whenever he should be wanted."—*Memoirs of George III.*, vol. iii. *passim.*

Lord Temple never again relaxed in his hatred and distrust of the Bedfords,—"the Bloomsbury gang:" the burden of his song, as Junius, was ever the same. "*Barrington, Weymouth, Gower, Rigby, Jerry Dyson, and Sandwich.*" I have not found any particulars of this alleged communication from Rigby; but as Walpole's information came from Lord Hertford, that Calcraft was sent to him by Lord Temple, I think it may be depended upon; and as Temple knew that Lord Hertford was an active partisan, and much in the King's confidence, it gives a clue to the passage in Junius's private letter to Lord Chatham, in which he says, "*Lord Hertford is a little more explicit than his brother, and has taken every opportunity of treating your Lordship's name with indignity.*"

[1] Horace Walpole calls her "the Duke of Grafton's Mrs. Hoghton,

ried man, the Duchess there in the Pit, talking to her only, waiting upon her out, are the changes rung by

the Duke of Dorset's Mrs. Hoghton, everybody's Mrs. Hoghton;" but she is more commonly known by the name of Nancy Parsons. If it had not been this lady's misfortune to be embalmed in the pages of Junius as the mistress of the Duke of Grafton, her charms as the "*lovely Thais,*" or her "*faded beauty,*" together with her name and memory, would long since have been forgotten, although she was subsequently "*made an honest woman,*" and a Peeress of Great Britain, by her marriage with Viscount Maynard, in 1776. Anne or Annabella Parsons is said to have been the daughter of a tailor in Bond Street. She obtained the name of Hoghton from a West India captain and merchant of that name, with whom she lived for some time, and accompanied him to Jamaica, but she was not married to him. Miss Parsons soon became weary of a residence in the West Indies: she escaped from her lover by stratagem, and, returning to London, took lodgings at a perfumer's in Brewer Street, where by some strange chance she soon became acquainted with the Duke of Grafton. An account of their amours is given in the *Town and Country Magazine* for 1769, under the names of Palinurus and Annabella, where are also printed the letters which are supposed to have passed between them on their separation, and the Duke's marriage with Miss Wrottesley.

Her appearance at the Opera House, as mentioned by Whately, was probably witnessed by Lord and Lady Temple, who were constant visitors there, and only a few days afterwards it is alluded to by the author of Junius in a letter to the Duke of Grafton. " Highly as I thought of you, your Grace must pardon me when I confess that there was one effort which I did not think you equal to. I did not think you capable of exhibiting the lovely Thais at the Opera House, of sitting a whole night by her side, of calling for her carriage yourself, and of leading her to it through a crowd of the first men and women in this kingdom. To a mind like yours, my Lord, such an outrage to your wife, such a triumph over decency, such insult to the company, must have afforded the highest gratification when all the ordinary resources of pleasure were exhausted; this, I presume, was your *novissima voluptas.*"—*Junius*, vol. iii. p. 40.

The name of Miss Parsons was used by Junius as a fertile source of annoyance to the Duke of Grafton; and the suggestions of Lady Temple may surely be traced in the unmanly and frequently recurring allusions to her "*faded beauty ;*"—" I will not insult the memory of *departed beauty ;*"—" Miss Parsons had at this time *surpassed the prime both of her youth and beauty ;* "—and again as Philo-Junius :—" Did not the Duke of Grafton frequently lead his mistress into public, and

everybody. Libertine men are as much offended as prudish women; and *it is impossible he should think of remaining Minister who thus defies all decency*, is almost the general conclusion.

The diversion of to-day is to laugh at the Chancellor's being called upon to interpose in Wilkes's affair; it is a whimsical piece of justice, and no man, I suppose, would feel it more sensibly than himself.

That the present system will not do seems generally agreed; that Mr. Grenville must be the Minister con-

even place her *at the head of his table* as if he had pulled down *an ancient temple of Venus*, and could bury all decency and shame under the ruins?"

When Lord Temple was writing this passage, the Temple of Venus in his own Gardens at Stowe might have occurred to his mind, and still more likely the following from one of Lady Temple's notes: "The Duke of Grafton's female friend sits at the upper end of his table, and he brings everybody to dine with him: some do like it, and some do not. She is very pious, a constant churchwoman, and reproves his Grace for swearing and being angry, which he owns is very wrong, and with great submission begs her pardon for being so ill bred before her. Would he have done so to the Duchess of Grafton? but I am afraid she has lost him by her own fault, and is now very miserable."

Junius also takes occasion to allude to the *age* of Miss Parsons, in his poem called *Harry and Nan*.

" From fourteen to forty our provident Nan,
Had devoted herself to the study of Man."

I have already noticed this poem in the Introductory Notes to vol. iii.

A year later Junius says,—" The Duke [of Grafton] about this time had separated himself from Ann Parsons, but proposed to continue united with her on some Platonic terms of friendship, which she rejected with contempt. His baseness to this woman is beyond description or belief."—*Junius*, vol. i. p. 478.

As the fame of Nancy Parsons has been preserved by Junius, so also, it may be remarked, says Mr. Mathias, in the *Pursuits of Literature*, that the Duke of Grafton had the singular fate of having been *celebrated* by the first prose writer and the first poet of the age.

" Or Grafton's virtues, to their latest day,
Expire in JUNIUS and revive in GRAY."

tinues and gains ground; men who were your enemies say so. Lord Talbot held that language very strongly to Lord Suffolk last Monday, but I have not heard it from any others of his class, though all agree to acknowledge there is no Government in this country. At the same time, no steps appear to be taking towards an immediate change; the answer is, that a change now is not desirable, and all changes have been sudden[1].

[1] Thomas Whately was a very profound politician, as well as an industrious and very intelligent purveyor of news. His information is not to be despised, though it might not be *always* correct. Having been Secretary of the Treasury during Mr. Grenville's Administration, he was well known, and had familiar access to some of the principal men, and was undoubtedly much trusted by them. Junius was very severe upon him, because he followed the example of some of his betters, and very soon, too soon, after Mr. Grenville's death, he went over to the Ministerial ranks. No one knew Whately better than Lord Temple, or how much he had been trusted by Mr. Grenville; and all those who left the Grenville connection sooner or later felt the lash of Junius:—" To be corrupted by such a *maquereau* as Whately would turn the appetite of Moll Flanders. This poor man, with the talents of an attorney, sets up for an ambassador, and with the agility of Colonel Bodens, undertakes to be a courier. Indeed, Tom, you have betrayed yourself too soon! Mr. Grenville, your friend, your patron, your benefactor, who raised you from a depth, compared to which even Bradshaw's family stands on an eminence, was hardly cold in his grave, when you solicited the office of go-between to Lord North. You could not, in my eyes, be more contemptible, though you were convicted (as I dare say you might be) of having constantly betrayed him in his lifetime. Since I know your employment, be assured I shall watch you attentively. Every journey you undertake, every message you carry, shall be immediately laid before the public. The event of your ingenious management will be this; that Lord North, finding you cannot serve him, will give you nothing. From the other party, you have just as much detestation to expect as can be united with the profoundest contempt. Tom Whately, take care of yourself."—*Junius*, vol. iii. p. 310.

The whole of this passage is eminently characteristic of Lord Temple's knowledge of Whately. He knew that Whately had often been employed as a sort of *courier* to Mr. Grenville. Pending some of the important political negotiations, it will be seen from his corre-

EARL TEMPLE TO MR. WILKES.

(April 28, 1768.)

SIR,—I little thought that I should ever pay a visit to the King's Bench Prison; but the same opinions which carried me to see you in the Tower now incite me to take an opportunity (before I leave town for the summer, which I purpose doing forthwith) of returning my thanks to you in person for your sober and discreet conduct of yesterday, manifested in a dutiful submission to the law, though carried on against you with the most unnecessary rigour, by refusing bail [1].

spondence in these volumes, that Whately held himself in readiness to leave London for Stowe or Wotton at a moment's warning: he offered his services to Lord Temple for that purpose [a]. If a *journey* was to be undertaken; if a *message* of importance was to be conveyed, or the details of a negotiation to be explained, either personally or by letter, to some influential member of the party, Whately's *talents* as an *attorney* were called into requisition; he was the *ambassador* employed. His numerous well-written letters in this collection sufficiently display the *ingenious management* of which he was capable. I am not aware that any portrait of Whately is extant, or that anything is now known of his personal appearance or activity, or whether it had any resemblance to *the agility of Colonel Bodens* [b], to which Junius ironically refers.

Poor "Tom Whately" did not long survive Mr. Grenville. He obtained the post of Under Secretary of State to Lord Suffolk, and an appointment about the King's person as Conductor of Royal Progresses, &c., and died in June, 1772.

[1] Mr. Adolphus says, "A writ of *capias utlagatum* was issued, and as no precedent could be found of a person in his circumstances being delivered to bail, he was ordered into custody."—*History of England*, vol. i. p. 340.

[a] See *ante*, vol. iii. p. 262.

[b] This Colonel Bodens had probably been well known in the neighbourhood of St. James's and the fashionable clubs for his unwieldy size, and consequent want of activity. He died in 1762, and his death is recorded as follows in the obituary of the *Gentleman's Magazine* for December of that year:—"Colonel Bodens; in St. James's Place; a remarkably large man."

I applaud your wise and humane discouragement of all tumult and disorder, in which I doubt not but you will persevere.

Though I have not seen you for many years, yet I shall bring with me the same heart warm for the support of the just rights and dignity of the Crown, and for the defence of the constitutional privileges of Englishmen, violated in so many instances in your person [1].

What will be the most convenient and quiet time for you to receive me. I do nothing in the dark, and am in the face of day, Sir, your most obedient humble servant,

TEMPLE.

THE COUNTESS OF CHATHAM TO EARL TEMPLE.

April 28, (1768.)

You are *not right* in your guess, but that is of no consequence, since my purpose is equally answered, which was, that should any *arising* circumstances bring the matter to your mind you might be secure with regard to it. Your answer, dated *at night*, did not reach its *direction* 'till about noon the day after, and was brought late to me by the accidental return of a servant. I mention it only, because if it was your intention that it should have been carried earlier, the person intrusted did not execute your orders punctually, and possibly it was retarded for inspection somewhere or other.

I thank you sincerely for the feelings you express for me, and the best return I can make you is to wish your

---

[1] "The Rockinghams," says Charles Lloyd to Mr. Grenville, "affect to take up Wilkes, and to complain of the continuance of his persecution. The Burkes went to see him yesterday in the King's Bench."

feelings for me may never bear any proportion to my sad affliction, and that you may think as little as possible how it has been caused [1].

EARL TEMPLE TO THE COUNTESS OF CHATHAM.

(April 28, 1768.)

I THINK I am not out in my guess, though perhaps I might not be intelligible to yourself.

There is a material difference betwixt words spoken

---

[1] There is nothing, either in the Grenville Papers, or in the printed volumes of the *Chatham Correspondence*, which throws any light on the subject of these secret letters between Lord Temple and Lady Chatham. They show that Lord Temple was upon very affectionate terms with his sister, for at least six months before his reconciliation with Lord Chatham; indeed it is not probable that there was ever any cessation of kind feelings between them. One of these letters furnishes a very curious illustration of the manner in which Junius carried on his correspondence with Woodfall. It appears that the confidential person to whom the letter was entrusted did not deliver it himself; he gave it to a porter to deliver, but he ("the safest hand") saw the porter deliver it safely, because he watched him. This, therefore, was probably the mode in which the "conveyancing part of the correspondence" was managed by Junius, and it may be inferred that "*the safest hand I could place it in*," and "*the person whom the waiter twice attempted to see*," [a] was one person only, and that person Junius, that is, Lord Temple himself. The letters or parcels from Woodfall were usually sent for *at night*, or *in the evening*, and the method might be to employ a common porter or chairman whom he might accidentally meet, and wait for, or watch him while he executed his commission. Many of the letters from Junius to Woodfall were sent by the penny post, but Junius could not receive his communications from Woodfall through the same medium [b].

[a] *Junius*, Private note to Woodfall, No. 58.

[b] I do not attach the slightest importance to the story of a *tall gentleman* who was alleged to have thrown a letter into Woodfall's office door, but it may be as well to mention that a portrait of Lord Temple formerly preserved at Stowe, represents him with a bag, wig, and sword, and in a light brown coat, similar to that described by Mr. Jackson.—See Woodfall's *Junius*, i. 43.

by a person, and committed to writing by him. Be that as it may, I shall be happy, whenever the proper time comes [1], of speaking to you with that real affection and esteem which I bear to you, enhanced, if possible, by this kind attention. Had you been of a certain journey, perhaps things had turned out better.

The latter part of your letter is grievous to me. Though my note was dated at night, yet it was not sent till after breakfast. It was disposed of to the safest hand I could place it in, who gave it to a porter, and saw it delivered in at your house. What will these strange times produce! This will be sent the same way, and probably about the same time.

THE COUNTESS OF CHATHAM TO EARL TEMPLE.

Sunday evening, (May 1, 1768.)

MOST happy in being mistaken, my dear brother, I have only to thank you for the kind dispatch with which you have removed the idea that pained me. I will not be sorry for what has occasioned my receiving that which affords so much comfort to my mind, as the assurance of your kind affection and tenderness, where I thought myself wounded.

A wrong construction of an expression, now not worth

---

[1] " Act honourably by me, and *at a proper time* you shall know me."
—*Junius, private note to Woodfall.*

" *At a proper time* he will solicit the honour of being known to you."
—*Junius, private note to Mr. Grenville.*

" It is not, Sir, either necessary or *proper* to make myself known to you *at present.*"—*Ibid.*

" The *proper time* for our meeting again is certainly not *the present.*"
—*Lord Temple to Lady Chatham,* May 8, 1768.

the naming, urged the writing the lines you received. Whether I *misheard*, or whether the word bore a *different* sense, is now perfectly equal, since nothing can hurt that is not intended. I would ask your pardon for what has passed, if it did not mark a jealousy of your love and of my own dignity, which I trust you will not be displeased to have found in *your* sister.

I will not delay long coming to town, and in the meantime am a petitioner that you will not remember anything of what occasions you this present trouble.

I write in infinite haste, that I may have no questions asked, having happily received your letter whilst I was at dinner below stairs, for on no account would I have my Lord conceive the smallest idea of what has so much touched me, and which entirely ceases to be felt by your most affectionate sister, HESTER CHATHAM.

THE EARL OF SUFFOLK TO MR. GRENVILLE.

Duke Street, Westminster, May 2, 1768.

MY DEAR SIR,—As I do not depend on your accepting Lord Hyde's invitation to the Grove, where I am going to-morrow, and Whately having undertaken to provide a safe conveyance for a letter to you, I am induced to express in this manner my satisfaction at your intentions of attending the opening of Parliament in support of Government, properly understood, against the open attacks of some, and the folly and incapacity of others.

The conversation I had last night with Lord Mansfield will tend to confirm you in them. After his company was gone, he expressed to me much curiosity to know whether you would be in town. Professedly taking for granted that you would, and alluding to intimations he had received from you some time ago of your inclination to attend business if there was any, which he said must unavoidably happen, as a member of Parliament could not be in confinement without a communication of it from the Crown to the House.

He was full of the propriety of your attendance, and repeated several times over, that "there was an opportunity for Mr. Grenville to appear in a very great light." He launched out much on the folly of Administration, professed having nothing to do with them, and treated the private indiscretions and indecencies of the Duke of Grafton as they deserve. He showed anxiety that you might not be under any restraints on account of Lord Temple, who, he was fully persuaded, 'till I convinced him of the contrary, had seen Mr. Wilkes[1], and apprehensive that he had too strong leanings towards him, which he earnestly hoped would have no effects upon your conduct. He said he spoke from regard to the public, to you, and to myself. My answer was in the general. I told him that if there was business I made no doubt but you would attend it; that I believed Mr. Wilkes was one of those subjects which you and Lord Temple most seldom conversed upon; that I was confident the latter had never seen him, and that his Lordship knew how unlikely you was to deviate from your opinion and principles upon any occasion whatever. He added, that he was assured there would be a contest for the Speaker, in favour of Mr. Dowdeswell, which (if there was one) he did not think worth a wise man's interference.

[1] See Lord Temple's Letter to Wilkes, *ante*, page 279.

I could collect from him that the errors assigned in Wilkes' outlawry were likely to be admitted; but he scouted the complaint of the informations being filed by the Solicitor instead of the Attorney General. This is pretty accurately the substance of what passed worth your immediate notice; and I was extremely happy to find it so consonant to your plan, which I kept to myself.

It has struck me that a motion of Address to the King, for some mark of favour to the Lord Mayor for his vigilance and conduct in the late disturbances, would not come improperly from us at the opening of the Sessions [1]. It is the only respect in our power to show him, and he deserves the utmost. I am not fond of making propositions, especially at this moment; but whether one of the nature I hint at would not tend to show our abhorrence of the late disorders, and our inclinations to support Government, by rewarding the only man who has maintained its authority, not to speak of the reproach which such a motion would throw upon those who, in desertion of their duty, have neglected to maintain it, is submitted to your consideration and opinion. I don't mean to make it the object of a division and trial of strength. Let the Ministry negative it, if they please; the disgrace would not fall on Lord Mayor, but themselves. What think you. Yours sincerely,

SUFFOLK.

[1] Lord Suffolk did make a motion to that effect, and it was met by the Duke of Grafton saying, that the King intended to confer some distinction on Harley, the Lord Mayor, and that the subject was under consideration. The same motion was made in the House of Commons and carried unanimously. Harley was soon afterwards made a Privy Councillor, and it was said that the City of London had not had a Chief Magistrate in the Privy Council since the time of Sir William Walworth.

MR. WHATELY TO MR. GRENVILLE.

May 3, 1768.

DEAR SIR,—The enclosed from Lord Suffolk contains the intelligence, for which this conveyance is chosen. He has, I dare say, given you very fully the particulars of his conversation with Lord Mansfield. We had agreed at noon that I should purposely avoid paying my visit in Bloomsbury Square yesterday, that Lord Mansfield might not perceive any reserve, which he would have taken much notice of, when he had known that I was just returned from Wotton, and yet we both agreed that it was proper to keep your dispositions an absolute secret from him, lest he should communicate them to the Bedfords at least, and perhaps still higher, meaning to do you service: we wished that you should be quite at liberty to take what conduct you please, free from all declarations, and even expectations, and should your sentiments be misrepresented, as probably they will be, and as I have reason to believe they are already, the falsehood must be detected in a fortnight; the part you take in Parliament must be known, and perhaps this misrepresentation in such a personal affair to the King, may at once suggest that there have been misrepresentations in others. I shall therefore leave every thing absolutely doubtful. Lord Suffolk, Lord George Sackville, and Wedderburn are sensible to the highest degree of the necessity for secrecy. They are all delighted at the accounts I have given them separately of your sentiments, think the ground on which you stand excellent, and see the situation just in the light you wish it should appear to them. The opinions, the confidence, the apprehensions of Lord Mansfield, all concur to encourage that plan of conduct which you have adopted; and he, perhaps, in the end will be more flattered by having it to say he knew you would act so, without being informed of your intentions, than he could be by any communication.

I have, however, taken care not to represent you as having formed any determination upon any of the points likely to be made the foundation of the proceedings in Parliament; but only stated that you feel yourself called upon to attend, that you will disclaim all personal considerations in the part you take, and as a public man freely give your opinion on questions affecting the King and the kingdom, which, if they happen to fall upon subjects on which you have formerly held opinions, will certainly be consistent with those former opinions. I have gone no further to the three persons above mentioned, and I have not said a syllable to anybody else.

The errors assigned upon record are, that there was no information, no proclamation, no judgment: no information because it was filed by the Solicitor-General; no judgment because it is in the third, instead of the first person. What are the exceptions fixed upon out of all which we have heard against the proclamations, I have not been able distinctly to learn; I only know that there are three; so that upon the whole there are five errors asigned.

Sir Fletcher Norton being now apprized of all, declares positively that there is no error; Mr. Thurlow is to argue for the Crown; Mr. Mansfield for Wilkes; the leaders on each side reserving themselves for a second argument if it should be required by the Court. When Lord Suffolk wrote the enclosed, he did not, I believe, know for certain whether Lord Mansfield had had a second audience. I this morning hear authentically that he was in with the King on Friday, and on the mere report an abuse upon him has been built, for the unseasonableness of it, when a matter so personal to the King is before him as Judge.

I understand that the thought of proposing Mr. Dowdeswell to be Speaker is dropped. They say, but without any positive authority, that Wilkes's affair will be brought before the House on Tuesday se'nnight.

MR. WHATELY TO MR. GRENVILLE.

May 7, 1768.

I HAVE not time to-night to give you the detail of the arguments in the King's Bench to-day on the writ of error; for the present I can only tell you that all the lawyers whom I have seen agree in thinking there is no error, that it stands over for further argument to the next term, and that this delay was received with great displeasure by the crowd in the Hall, which was considerable.

I met Mr. Dyson to-day, and asked him when, by the usual forms, the King's speech would be reported, and business begun; he said *he did not know what was intended, but he took it for granted* that the precedent established in 1754, and then settled with much consideration by Mr. Onslow, would be followed, unless a greater or less number of members to be sworn should make the difference of a day, and therefore said that by looking into that precedent I should be a better judge than by any information he could give me. I have accordingly looked into it, and I find that then the

House met on a Friday, and chose their Speaker; on the Saturday he was confirmed by the King, and upon his return from the House of Lords took the oaths; the other members did the same the rest of that day and the beginning of Monday, but having finished before four o'clock on Monday, the Speaker on that day reported the King's speech, and business immediately began. If the same track is followed, business will begin this time on Thursday[1].

THE COUNTESS OF CHATHAM TO EARL TEMPLE.

May 8, (1768.)

I COULD not, from the want of a proper opportunity, convey to you before that your note had been delivered as you intended, or tell you how much I was touched with it, in spite of the many cruel circumstances which continually make me feel all the grievous wounds that have been given to every part of my happiness.

Was I the single sufferer from the consequences, the seeing you again, with the sentiments you express for me, would be a balm that would cure my affliction; but as things at present are I must wait 'till some favourable incident or happy change may take off my difficulty, which I am persuaded you too well understand to disapprove.

Accept of my real wishes for your health and happiness.

---

[1] Parliament met on Tuesday the 10th instant, and was opened by commission; the King making no speech, as the Session was to be so short. Sir John Cust was re-elected Speaker. The Parliament was adjourned on the 20th, met again on the 2nd of June, and was again adjourned.

EARL TEMPLE TO THE COUNTESS OF CHATHAM.

May 8, 1768.

From the contents of my notes in answer to yours, you cannot be a stranger to the sentiments I entertain of you, and I am glad I have had such an opportunity of expressing them; they have been invariably the same towards you. The amiable part which you have taken I shall ever reflect upon with much affection.

The proper time[1] for our meeting again is certainly not the present, for many many reasons.

I have felt too well your situation, not to have done a violence to my own inclination towards you in many instances. I return you, with great kindness, every real wish for your health and happiness. My letter to you from Stowe was expressive of the same sentiments with regard to you as those I have lately marked, and now convey to you. It is extremely difficult for me to say neither too much nor too little upon the subject of your difficulty and affliction, &c. I therefore waive it entirely, and approve your conduct; with wishes for that recovery in which you are so deeply interested.

MR. WHATELY TO MR. GRENVILLE.

May 9, 1768.

Dear Sir,—I promised in my letter of Saturday last to send you a detail of what passed in the King's Bench that morning, and I will begin with that subject, while I wait for some additional intelligence to that which is

---

[1] See *ante*, page 282, *note*.

more immediately the cause of my choosing this conveyance.

The business there was opened by a motion that Mr. Wilkes should personally attend. The motion was intended, but neglected to be made the day before, and now the Court said it was too late for that day; if it was desired, they were, however, willing to put off the business 'till Monday, when he might be present; but Sergeant Glynn chose rather to go on in his absence than defer the argument, and therefore stated five objections to the outlawry. That no process of outlawry lay on an information, because the original proceeding was a subpœna, and a capias could not follow upon the judgment when it could not be taken out on the mesne process: on which objection Sir Joseph Yates observed that in informations of quo warranto it was true, for the original process in them was by subpœna and distringas only, but in all criminal informations it was by subpœna, distringas, and capias, so that the objection was founded on a mistake in fact, and the counsel besides quoted many precedents of outlawries on informations. The next error assigned was, that the information was filed by the Solicitor General, without any averment that there was an Attorney General at the time; and supported by saying that if the Solicitor General might, so might the Prime Sergeant file informations. The answer was a multitude of precedents; near seven hundred in the five years of Queen Anne, when there was no Attorney General, and above half of them without such an averment. The next error was, that there were no proclamations set forth at the times and places required by the statute. Sir Joseph Yates said that before verdict such an objection would be fatal, for then proclamations were required to prevent a surreptitious proceeding, but that a verdict could not be obtained unless the party had appeared, and was therefore a sufficient notice. In outlawries upon civil actions no proclamations were then necessary, and the statute directed those on criminal proceedings to be the same.

The fourth error was, that the County Court was not said to be *for* the county of Middlesex, which was an ambiguity, proved by many cases to be fatal. The answer was, that in every other county it would be so; but in Middlesex only, two persons made one sheriff, and this being signed by two, and yet all spoke in the singular number, ascertained it without a doubt to be Middlesex.

The fifth error was, that it was not held *within* the county, for though Holborn might be, Brook Street might not be within it. The Court asked whether Brook Street near Holborn might not be one name, as George Street, Hanover Square, to distinguish it from the other Brook Street.

Upon the whole, the lawyers whom I have seen think the errors not maintainable, and that the Court, by what dropped from Sir Joseph Yates and Sir Richard Aston, were inclined to be of that opinion. Lord Mansfield did not say a word which could lead to his, but with the other judges desired a second argument. Wilkes's counsel declined it, declaring they had nothing further to urge, and even intimating they they would not argue it again, but the Court insisted upon it; and as two arguments on the same case are never allowed in the same term, this stands over to the next.

The delay has given great offence; the people seem more exasperated than at anything which has happened, and, in general, the judges are blamed.

Some of the sailors went on Saturday to Richmond, where two of them were admitted to the King, and presented their petition. The King's answer, as I have heard it, was, that he could not relieve them; that, however, he was ready to do what he could; and that the Parliament was to meet in a few days.

Wedderburn met Rigby on Saturday morning, and asked him whether there would be any business, in order to inform you. Rigby's answer was, that he should be sorry to mislead you, and therefore desired he might be quoted to you for what he said, that you might form your own judgment. He said he believed there would be no proposition made by the Court; at that minute he knew they had come to no resolution; that Camden, Grafton, Shelburne (who, by the-bye, is very much out of humour), and Conway, on account of their former conduct, were inclined to avoid it, and had rather it should be brought in by chance than by them; that Lord North could not in such circumstances take the lead, and that the Administration was distracted among themselves, and incapable of acting; that, however, nobody knew what might happen, and possibly the business would force itself in; that all that has been said of the King's displeasure against the Duke of Grafton is true; that, however, from a conversation he has had with his Grace, he does not believe the Duke intends to resign, or wishes to be dismissed; though, says he, I differ from many of my friends in that opinion, and I must own that his conduct is on every other ground unaccountable.

On Saturday, at the Opera, he industriously sought an opportunity of saying the same to Lord Temple, telling him that he had mentioned all this to Wedderburn, that he might repeat it to me for your information; adding a violent invective against the Court, and saying repeatedly, that though there was every reason to suppose a change, he saw yet no step tending that way.

Last night I was alone some time with Lord Mansfield; he was not very open, but he spoke hostilely against the Ministers: said, never was any conduct so bad; that they were disunited and irresolute; that though they might not wish to bring the business on, he did not see how they could avoid sending a message on Wilkes's commitment, and nobody could answer for what might arise: he therefore thought you should attend; your dignity required it; there was reason enough to expect business, and there could be no harm in it.

Lord Temple says that he sees no objection to your coming up, but that it exposes you to conversations, which may lead to a discovery of your opinions; you may, however, avoid the discussion, and, let the Court mean what they may, the questions on Wilkes, his mob, the sailors' mob, and the news from America, which is worse and worse, will probably occasion business, from which you would be very sorry to be absent.

MR. WHATELY TO MR. GRENVILLE.

May 21, 1768.

DEAR SIR,—It is the opportunity which Lord Temple's visit at Wotton to-morrow gives me, and not the importance of any news I can send you, which occasions

you this trouble. He will tell you how very little is
stirring, but if we have no anecdotes to boast of, the
Rockinghams have as few to whisper. 'Till now they
say they have always had some little line held out, some
appearance of something, but now all is absolutely shut
up, and from that closeness towards them, they concluded that an opening was made towards you, not believing it possible that the Court could be without a
shadow of a negotiation. We too, you know, have had
our little lines from time to time, and as they are withdrawn from both parties all at once, and altogether, the
doing so appears evidently to be a measure: I might
even call it a change of measures; the effect of which is
certainly to keep things entire for the present, but with
what view I do not guess; not, I believe, for Lord Holland's advice; I am convinced he has not been sent for,
as he proposed when he set out to return at this time,
and is not come a day sooner than he intended[1]. He
has besides, sent from France to inquire whether the
Parliament is sitting, being determined to stay in Kent
'till it rises. I told Lord Temple this morning, that I
understood the disgust of the Duke of Grafton was
returned upon him, and that he wished, if he decently
could, to retire. I since hear, that if he should show
an inclination to go, he will hardly be pressed again to
stay. I the rather believe he is so disposed, because
the more I see into his situation, the more eligible does

---

[1] Lord Holland, writing to George Selwyn from Nice, in the January
of this year, says, "I cannot help sometimes asking myself, dear Selwyn, why I am in such disgrace with the King? Have I deserved it?
I am now the only mark left of irrevocable displeasure, and I vow to
God, I cannot guess why, any more than I do why Ellis has refused
the offer I hear the King most graciously made him very lately to be
Joint Paymaster."—*Selwyn Correspondence*, vol. ii. p. 247.

a change of it appear. He is now literally unsupported, for even the Chancellor no longer considers his Grace and Lord Chatham as one, and makes his option for Lord Chatham[1]. The Bedfords, I take it for granted, have been disappointed in their attempts to gain him, and it is expected every day that Lord Shelburne will be out. Thus alone, a bolder man might be alarmed at the circumstances which a Minister is now in.

The Corsican affairs add to the general distress. A Cabinet was held upon that subject on Thursday night, to which I know the Ministers went with great anxiety and doubt upon their minds; the result of their deliberations I know not, but I take it for granted that as usual no determination was agreed to, and in the meanwhile the French are sending twelve battalions in addition to those troops already there. They propose to make up in all a body of 12,000 men. The Genoese approve of their going; Paoli had agreed to it on certain conditions, but those conditions have not been granted, so that it is still uncertain whether he will oppose or submit to them.

The Irish Bill for securing the independence of their judges by making them irremoveable quamdiu se bene gesserint, was drawn exactly upon the plan of our Act, with the clause of an Address from both Houses of their Parliament. The Council here sent it back with an alteration, requiring that such address should be certified by the Privy Council there, and pass under the Seal of Ireland, in the same manner as their Bills do; and also made the judges liable to be removed on an Address of the British Parliament. The Irish House of Commons, upon this amendment, have rejected the

[1] This is what Junius calls Lord Camden's "fast and loose game."

Bill, not choosing that their Privy Council should interfere with their Address, or that an Address of the Parliament of Great Britain should have the same weight as an Address of the Irish Parliament.

MR. KNOX TO MR. GRENVILLE.

London, May 24, 1768.

DEAR SIR,—Two days since I had a conversation with Lord Hillsborough, which his Lordship seemed willing I should communicate, and as I imagine you will be pleased to hear something is doing, I take the liberty of setting down the substance of what he told me.

The resolutions of the Assembly at Massachusetts, his Lordship said, had been proposed at the beginning of the Session, and then rejected by a great majority, which was the foundation for saying the American subjects were returning to their duty; but when many of the county members were gone home, the same resolutions were again moved and agreed to. So soon as this transaction came to Lord Hillsborough's knowledge, his Lordship writ to Governor Bernard to call the Assemblies together, and require them in the King's name to rescind the resolutions of the last Session[1], and, if they refuse so to do, then to dissolve them instantly, and when their Charter requires a new Assembly to be

---

[1] "The continuance of one of their principal Assemblies rested upon an arbitrary condition—that they should retract one of their resolutions and erase the entry of it—which, considering the temper they were in, it was impossible they should comply with, and which would have availed them nothing as to the general question, if it had been complied with."—*Junius*, vol. i. p. 396.

called, he is to make the same demand, and, upon refusal, dissolve them likewise, and in no case to suffer an Assembly to sit or do business until they shall comply with this demand. His Lordship has also written to the Governors of the other colonies, acquainting them that a certain seditious letter is said to have been written by the Assembly of Massachusetts to the several Assemblies on the Continent, which letter the King hopes and expects their respective Assemblies will treat with great contempt and indignation, and if they do so His Majesty thanks them. But should the Governors perceive an inclination in their Assemblies to adopt the measures of the Massachusetts Bay Assembly, they are to dissolve those Assemblies, and, by repeated dissolutions, frustrate such combinations. The civil expense in the several colonies which by this proceeding may be left unprovided for, is to be defrayed out of the American revenue, and the Governors are directed to draw on the treasury for it.

I think this measure will bring matters to a crisis very speedily, and if the colonies see this country is in earnest, they will presently make their option, and take the part of peaceable subjects in future. It is said today the Duke of Grafton gives up, and Lord Gower succeeds him at the Treasury. The occasion is variously spoken of. Lord Barrington's moving the Militia Bill contrary to his Grace's injunctions, and a disagreement with Lord North, are assigned as causes; but it is not impossible that a much more insignificant circumstance than either may have led him to take that resolution, if he has taken it. Lord Hertford sent to the Duchess of Grafton to walk as chief mourner at the

Princess's[1] funeral without first acquainting the Duke. Miss N. P.[2], it is said, thought the honour too great for a discarded wife, and insisted the Duke should interpose and prevent it. An altercation between Lord Hertford and the Duke followed, and who can tell but N. P. insists upon the Duke's obtaining Lord H.'s dismission in revenge, or the Duke's resigning in disgust. Such is the chat of the town, and for your amusement I send it to you. I have the honour to be, &c.

WILLIAM KNOX.

MR. WHATELY TO MR. GRENVILLE.

[Nonsuch,] June 4, 1768.

DEAR SIR,—I came yesterday into the country for the summer, and though I shall very frequently go to town, yet I shall not from henceforward see so closely or so immediately as I have hitherto seen into what passes there. I shall therefore endeavour to give you an exact state of affairs as I left them, and though I have few anecdotes to communicate, I may have some things to say which I would not tell the postmaster, and for that reason have chosen this manner of conveyance.

The necessity of a change and of a change in your favour, is perhaps more generally than ever the public opinion, and that opinion is not founded on any obser-

---

[1] The Princess Louisa, one of the King's sisters: she died on the 13th instant. Whately, writing to Mr. Grenville, says,—" The Duke resented it as an affront to him, and forbid it. I have heard that his expression was, ' *If this be the King's doing, I will never again step into St. James's; if it be Lord Hertford's, either he or I must never go there.*' I look upon it as certain that he did interpose, in consequence of which the Duchess of Manchester was appointed Chief Mourner."

[2] Miss Nancy Parsons; see *ante*, page 275.

vations of the disposition of the Court towards you, for there is not the least appearance of such a disposition. The national distress is the only ground for the expectation.

Admiral Keppel told me two days ago that his party have not the least opening, and that Lord Rockingham goes out of town next Monday for the summer; but the difference is, that nobody except his own friends wishes his Lordship may be sent to, and they do not expect it. I believe there has never yet been a time of so much reserve; one or other or both of the parties in opposition have always had some token held out to them; neither of them is flattered now; from whence it is evident to me that the reserve is a measure, and different from the conduct which has been hitherto observed during the continuance of this Administration: so long as that other conduct was pursued, they have been supported; perhaps the change may predict their downfall; but such a speculation is too refined to rely on, though it probably may prove true. About ten days ago Lord Chesterfield (who has been always remarkable for his intelligence) said to Irwin, "*I think I smell a change, I rather mean two changes; the first inconsiderable, introductory to a greater: during the interval I fancy Lord Barrington will be Secretary of State, but whatever is done, Mr. Grenville must be Minister before the meeting of Parliament.*"

Irwin thought by his manner that he spoke from some information which he did not explain; but it is certain that part of what his Lordship smelt ten days ago, was become a general report just before I left London, where it was confidently said that Lord Shelburne was immediately to go out, and to be succeeded by Lord Barrington.

If I had not so often believed that Lord Shelburne was going out, I should be sure of it now; but as it is, I will wait till I see, and if it does not happen within a very few days, I shall think I am again deceived as before.

The report of Lord Gower's going to the Treasury has in a great measure died away: among some few, however, it is still current; and they add that Mr. Yorke will be Chancellor, and Sir George Macartney Secretary at War. The last seems to me too bold a step for his friends to take at present; as to the other, I found it news to Mr. John Yorke, four-and-twenty hours after I had heard it, and I can hardly believe that to have been, instead of being Chancellor, will so entirely satisfy Mr. Yorke's ambition, as to make him leave all his connections and his attentions, and his coalitions, to engage in a precarious situation.

That Lord Gower may have an offer of the Treasury seems to me not unlikely. It will not appear to amount to a change of Administration, and of the people now in, the Bedfords are certainly forward candidates for favour. They are outwardly well with Lord Bute's friends; the Hertfords have certainly little to say; the Duke of Grafton, though we may not know to what degree, yet to a certain degree, has undoubtedly given disgust by his late behaviour. The dismission of Lord Shelburne is at least no compliment to Lord Chatham, and the Chancellor is uneasy. The Bedfords then are the only set who have not something against them, and Lord Weymouth has given great satisfaction by his conduct during the late riots; but should the Administration be offered to them, the question still remains whether they should choose to accept; for my part I believe they may be withheld by the fear of losing their back game, though not by other considerations. They must be sensible that every Administration is precarious; they know that in the most quiet times they were unpopular, and now the people are in a ferment; they could not but see the ill-humour of the House; everybody who attended observed it, and the idea of dissatisfaction carried into the country during the summer, will increase that dissatisfaction; the public difficulties are great; the Bedfords really hate, and are hated by, those with whom they are now connected, and, even with the assistance of all that connection, are weaker in debate in the House of Commons than any other party. These considerations would not restrain mere ambition, but they have a still stronger passion for good places, and to secure lucrative situations, at all events, is the great principle of their politics; no other can reconcile their accepting as they did, and still keeping their attentions towards you. I do not doubt that if they were to take the Administration now, they would again pay you the compliment of a communication, and flatter themselves with meeting with the same moderation. I do not wish for any intemperance, but a clear explanation that you are, and they have set you entirely at liberty; and that you will not be restrained by the consideration that you are opposing them, seems to me so inevitable, not only with a view to deter them from engaging, after they have left you out, to keep you out, but also for your own situation; that if the subject were started to me, I should make no scruple of expressing these as my sentiments: I have found your friends in town entirely agreeing with me; and I write them to you to know whether such a language would be agreeable to your ideas; I mean to hold it very temperately; for some think, and not without reason, that if the

Bedfords were to accept now, they would endeavour only to secure the good things to themselves during the summer, and would wish to throw the whole afterwards into your hands, from a consciousness of their weakness in the House of Commons. I would not desire a breach before the meeting of Parliament makes it necessary to take a part, but I should not, on the other hand, encourage them to suppose that they have an advantage over other Administrations in your pacific dispositions towards them, which they must imagine now; for if they had not expected that your attentions towards them would have screened the Ministry from your censure, they would have disavowed Mr. Wood's attack upon you. Should they accept, they will, I think, bid high for Sir Fletcher Norton and Wedderburn: Wedderburn is not to be gained, if he does not suppose that taking part with them will be entirely agreeable to you: if they fail there, I am told they will push Thurlow against him at the Bar, and they may give Thurlow a place, but they cannot give him established business. The present Solicitor General[1] seems even now in a doubtful situation; his principal connection I suppose to be Lord Shelburne, and the part he has taken in Wilkes' affair cannot recommend him. The ideas of the King's friends (as they are called) upon that subject seem to be the same as they were. Lord Holland (who, I take it for granted, sounds them before he speaks himself) is very inveterate against Wilkes: Gerard Hamilton has had a long conversation with him, in which his Lordship affected to know nothing, but was perfectly informed of everything. Hamilton thinks that some attempts towards a recon-

---

[1] Dunning, afterwards Lord Ashburton.

ciliation are making between him and the Bedfords, through Lord Ossory. I take this to be only a surmise, nor do I apprehend that Lord Holland is now a very great card. It appears clear to me that he was not sent for: I do not say he will not be consulted, but I see no reason to suppose he will be, and though his health is much mended, there are many difficulties attending his interposition.

In my conversation the other day with Admiral Keppel he spoke with eagerness of their party being quite clear of Lord Bute, and took merit on that score, whatever might be the consequences of keeping them at a distance from Court. I bid him recollect that this time twelvemonth the Bedfords were to the full as hostile to his Lordship; he answered, much more so, for when Lord Rockingham declared he was unwilling to carry in to the King a total proscription of that party, and proposed to save some of them, not exceeding three, Keppel told me, of which Mackenzie was one, and the other two were in insignificant offices, the Bedfords objected to it, as granting too much.

This anecdote confirms the suspicion you always had of their not telling you how far they had settled the arrangement, in which they must have made a considerable progress before they came to such a discussion.

I sat next to Jenkinson yesterday in the House, and upon my asking him whether he was going far into the country, he told me he could not, for the First Lord being seldom present at the Board, the attendance of the others was the more necessary. The business is almost entirely in Lord North's hands, who even carries the warrants to the King, the Duke of Grafton trusting in him much more than he did in Charles Townshend.

This shows that his Grace's neglect is very general, and that small matters are as much below his attention, as the greater are above his abilities.

To the account I have given you of the state of the Court, and of the Treasury, I will add that of the Army, and then you will have a tolerable view of the whole; and upon this last, General Harvey [1] said to me, that if it were not for the reviews the army would go to ruin, for want of a proper authority, which the King would not, Lord Granby would not, and he in his subordinate situation could not exercise; that he had represented to the King, that if His Majesty received equally well the deserving and undeserving officers, it would be impossible to preserve a distinction between them; but that his representations had not all the effect he could wish; and the emulation of the reviews alone, now kept up attention to discipline. It was indiscreet of Harvey to say so much to me, and I would not therefore repeat it except to yourself; but the observation is obvious, that civilities and even kindness which is attributed to design, is often the effect only of too great easiness of temper: it is not worth the while to flatter a Lieutenant-Colonel or Major at the expense of the service; but bystanders are apt to ascribe all actions that are similar, to the same principle; whereas different motives often produce the same effects; and that knowledge of a character is very imperfect, which does not comprehend all its principles.

To the state I have given of the interior as far as I have been able to learn it, I will only add, concerning outward circumstances, that the river is again in possession of the sailors, who prevent ships from sailing if the masters do not agree for an advance of wages. The

---

[1] Adjutant General.

merchants abide by their refusal not to interfere in it, and that affair is far from being in a way to be settled. The neglect of Corsica begins to make a great noise, the importance of that island being now much insisted on, and our supineness, it is said, makes us contemptible all over Europe. The King of Sardinia and the Great Duke of Tuscany, it is pretended, are alarmed, and probably they may be, but I have not heard authentically of any representations made by them.

My conclusion from all I have seen is, that no change is immediately in view, but that the ill health of the Duke of Grafton, the divisions of the Ministry, the brouillerie of parties, and the public distress, will make it necessary before the end of the summer.

COMMODORE HOOD TO MR. GRENVILLE.

Halifax, July 11, 1768.

SIR,—What has been so often foretold is now come to pass. The good people of Boston seem ready and ripe for open revolt, and nothing, it is imagined, can prevent it but immediate armed force.

I do myself the honour to give you, Sir, a little detail how matters have gone, and how far the force entrusted to my care has been employed in the support of the Commissioners of the Revenue, on the applications they have made to me.

On the 24th of March I received a letter from the Commissioners, setting forth, that from the conduct and temper of the people, and adverse aspect of things in general, the security of the revenue, the safety of its officers, and the honour of Government, required immediate aid, and hoping I should find it consistent with the King's other services, to afford them such assistance.

I ordered the *Romney* of 50 guns to be fitted with all possible dispatch, and as soon as the season would give leave she sailed for Boston, accompanied by two armed schooners. The commanders were strictly directed to be aiding and assisting to the Commissioners to the utmost of their power, in the due and legal execution of the laws of trade and navigation, according to the true intent and meaning of the said laws, and the several Acts of Parliament made in that behalf.

On the appearance of the *Romney* before the town, the riot and disorder seemed to subside, but on a vessel's being seized for illicit trade, belonging to a Mr. Hancock (by far the richest man in the province, and the known abettor of tumultuous proceedings), by the Comptroller (who went for England about a fortnight past), a numerous and violent mob assembled, and the Collector and Comptroller, with other officers, were beaten and wounded, the Collector's boat burnt, and other acts of a most outrageous nature committed. The lives of the Commissioners were threatened, and they were happy in taking shelter by stratagem on board the *Romney*, where they tarried some days, and then landed at Castle William. They then wrote to me for more aid, and I immediately sent two more ships, which has secured the castle from all attempts of surprising it.

On the 21st past, Governor Bernard, by command of His Majesty, acquainted the Assembly that it was required to rescind the resolves of last year. This has been refused, with the most scurrilous abuse of all His Majesty's servants in England as well as those in America, and even the person and office of the King was not spared by some of the demagogues.

The Governor gave the Assembly a longer time to

reconsider the matter, which still refused, and it was dissolved on the 2nd instant, as you will see by his Excellency's proclamation in the newspaper I now send, which contains the several messages between the Governor and Assembly previous to the dissolution.

On the 5th instant, orders were received here to prepare temporary coverings for the six companies of the 59th regiment, on the islands of Cape Breton and St. John, and the four of the 29th at the other outposts of this province. Upon information of these orders from Colonel Dalrymple, I ordered the equipment of the *Launceston* to be hastened as much as possible, and she is now ready for service; and as I had a letter yesterday from General Gage, requesting my assistance for transporting troops, and Colonel Dalrymple having orders to repair to Boston with those now here, if a requisition should be made by Governor Bernard before a junction of the whole can be effected, I hold the *Launceston* in constant readiness to take troops on board. I have sent an officer with my letters to the Admiralty, and I could not let him depart without being the bearer of a letter to you. I have the honour to be, &c., &c.

SAM. HOOD.

MR. WHATELY TO MR. GRENVILLE.

July 12, 1768.

DEAR SIR,—I feel myself so much more at liberty in writing by this conveyance, that I hope you will excuse the trouble I give you of sending for my packet to Aylesbury.

I will in return endeavour to send you a state of affairs as they stand at present, which seems to me different from that in which they stood when I left London, or as they then appeared to be; the best authorities agree that Lord Shelburne will carry his point in the nomination to Turin; and as the idea of Mr. Lynch was avowedly adopted on purpose to thwart him, his prevailing against them shows they mistook the quarter to which the favour inclines.

The King, it is said, declares that he will not interfere, but leave his Ministers to decide it among themselves; if such a declaration has been made, the consequence must be, that the Ministers to whose department the nomination belongs must nominate, and what part the Duke of Grafton takes is by no means clear. I believe that he wrote to Lord Shelburne the letter directing him to make out the appointment for Mr. Lynch, and that the order was conveyed in a very high tone, telling him, that he, the Duke, had spoke of the affair to the King, and recommended Mr. Lynch; that His Majesty had approved of the recommendation, and, therefore, his Lordship would be pleased to make out the appointment.

So far his Grace was committed; and Lord Shelburne's answer, that the King had never mentioned the affair to him, but that when he did he should recommend Lord Tankerville instead of Mr. Lynch, was as clearly directed to the Duke only: but these letters passed long ago. I have heard it surmised, that the Duke now wishes well to Lord Tankerville, because of the relation between them, and that he is by no means inclined to support pretensions made by the Bedfords. He has, I believe, declared that they have enough; that they shall go no further; that as long as he holds the office he will retain the power of a Minister, but that he is sick of the whole, and wishes he was clear of it. That Lord Shelburne and he are hardly upon speaking terms, is true; but that there is no cordiality between him and the Bedfords, seems almost as clear; and even if he be in earnest with them in this point, the conclusion is only that he is involved in the disgrace: not that I suppose any favour intended to Lord Shelburne; it is certain that he is, personally, ill in the Closet; but if he should prevail, I shall think it clear that an attention is kept up towards his connections, and that against them neither of the Dukes nor their friends stand in competition.

As to Lord Chatham himself, I have been told a strange story concerning him, too long to repeat, and too extravagant to deserve a particular repetition; but as my authority for it would be good, if the tale were not so extraordinary, I will just give you the outline of it. The Duke of Grafton, I am told, ordered Mr. Taylor the architect to go down to Hayes, and estimate the alterations Lord Chatham wished to be made there. Mr. Taylor went, was shown all over the house by Lord Chatham himself, who pointed out the several alterations he proposed, of which Mr. Taylor took notes, and when he had thereon formed his estimates, waited on the Duke, who bid him return to Hayes to receive his Lordship's directions, inquiring however, anxiously, how he had found him in health; to which Mr. Taylor answered, that he thought him very well, very intelligent upon the subjects on which they conversed, and alert in going about with him; but on his return to Hayes he did not see his Lordship. Lady Chatham only appeared, and with great marks of displeasure asked him the reason of the representation he had given of Lord

Chatham's health; said that it was not a true one; that his Lordship was indeed better on some days than on others, and that he had seen him on one of his best; but that he was upon the whole in a very different state of health from that which he had reported. You have the story as I had it. It came to me from one who is much about the Court, and who said he had taken pains to inform himself from Mr. Taylor's friends, of the facts, from which he inferred that Lord Chatham was acting a part, but was ready, when he saw occasion, to take any other, and in the meanwhile was possessed of a great share of personal favour.

Wedderburn has had a long conversation with Mr. Burke, whose language with respect to you, he observed, was very different from any he had ever heard from that quarter. Mr. Burke took notice that the language which he heard you held, was that of a very wise man; the particular topic to which he alluded was, that no Minister could be safe, or be active, who was not sure of the King, and of the persons with whom he was connected, which he had been told had been a principle you had much insisted on lately: he added, that you were certainly a most excellent party-man; that your behaviour to the Bedfords had proved you might be relied on; that you would not desert those who would abide by you, and were steady to all your purposes; that it was pleasant to be connected with such a man, and the party would act with confidence who acted under him. Upon the whole, Wedderburn thought he saw a disposition in that party to follow your lead in the House of Commons; a difficulty was started, but soon waived, about America; and in everything else there seemed more inclination than he has hitherto seen towards you.

This is no otherwise important than as it tallies with the intelligence you have had of Lord Rockingham's having lowered his pretensions, and greatly corroborates that information.

A gentleman who sees a variety of all sorts of connections, told me this morning, that the idea of the impossibility that this Administration should continue, and of the necessity of sending for you, gained ground every day, and the reports about it I find as current and as confident as ever; I hear, on the other hand, from the same authority, that a persuasion of the Bedfords meaning only themselves prevails; but it cannot escape your observation, that when any man spreads the former of these reports he speaks his own opinion; when the latter, he only believes his information: and as to the Bedfords, the speculation which I have heard is, that should they be foiled by Lord Shelburne, it will diminish their confidence, shorten their views, and make them recur to you.

The Duke of Bedford you know is going to Ireland, and, as I hear, takes Lord Weymouth with him, it being his Lordship's principal object to be hereafter Lord-Lieutenant of that Country.

MR. POWNALL[1] TO MR. GRENVILLE.

Westthrop, Marlow, July 14, 1768.

DEAR SIR,—The fourth edition of the Administration of the Colonies is in the press, and printed off to

[1] Thomas Pownall, M.P. for Tregony, and Secretary to the Board of Trade. He had been successively Lieutenant-Governor of New Jersey, Governor of Massachusetts Bay, and Governor of South Carolina, and was afterwards appointed Director-General or Comptroller, with the rank of Colonel, in the army in Germany, from which he retired in 1763. He was a man of profound experience and learn-

the last sheet. I have continued the Dedication of it to you, by a new and particular Address, stating the views of men, and the certain consequences of things as matters are at present circumstanced; also pointing out a measure, which I am from conviction persuaded ought to be taken up at least, not on the grounds of policy, but from necessity.

As the tenor of this Address may carry with it suggestions that may or may not be proper, as it may or may not be found expedient to adopt the idea of this measure, as it may or may not be proper to avow it, if taken up, I have taken the liberty to send the draught of it to you before it goes to the press. For as I sincerely mean, to the utmost of my abilities, to aid those whom this country must look up to, if ever it again returns or is forced into a spirit and temper of doing business, so I am sure I would not, in the most distant point, say or do anything respecting yourself that might be occasion of embarrassment to you.

If you conceive that any proper use may be made of bringing forward the proposal referred to, in Parliament, I shall be very glad to communicate with you upon it. I am very shy of obtruding myself or my views upon any one, especially on such who I conceive have sentiments of friendship towards me, and that is the true reason that I did not take a ride over on this errand myself; but if you wish to have a conversation on these American matters, either as to facts or opinions, I think I can not only point out how they might be taken up

ing, both as a politician and an antiquary; he was the author of the *Administration of the Colonies*, and wrote many pamphlets, chiefly on subjects of antiquarian interest: a list of his works is given in the *Gentleman's Magazine*, vol. lxxv. p. 288. He died in 1805 at the age of eighty-five.

as concerns the business itself, but particularly how, as they respect the situation in which you stand towards them, and towards the various clanships of factions which take a part in them.

Whatever is settled as the measure to be taken up, ought to be agreed upon early, that the various grounds on which the various parties might be led to join in it, should be prepared and laid.

There is now open to you, and to you only, with consistency, a noble track of politics. I am an enthusiast for your striking into it: it would do you honour, and establish you as a Minister of this country, and, what is more, it would lead to the establishing the peace and prosperity of this country.

I have a thousand things to say that I neither can nor will write about.

As to the part I shall myself take, both here and in America, I have, upon very serious and deliberate resolution, determined unalterably. In one other thing I am unalterable, my regard and attachment to you, and I have the honour to be, &c.   T. POWNALL.

MR. WILLIAM GERARD HAMILTON TO EARL TEMPLE.

July 14, (1768).

MY DEAR LORD,—It is now universally understood by those who have a right to know the transactions of the Administration, that the Duke of Grafton, in the course of last week, proposed in the Closet the dismission of Shelburne, but that he did not succeed in his request, notwithstanding the importunity with which he pressed it. The construction put upon this refusal is, that the Court are unwilling to do anything which may, by any possibility, be unacceptable to Lord Chatham, 'till they have formed an Administration which may be capable of resisting him, in case he should be able to make his appearance again in public, and be offended at the measures which may have been taken during his illness. Sir Richard's intelligence is, that Mr. Grenville is at present the only object of the Court, and that the wish is to bring him to the head of the Treasury, avoiding, if possible, any negotiation with your Lordship, and those who are more particularly your friends. The not knowing very well how to accomplish this plan, he thinks is the reason why no proposal has as yet been made to Mr. Grenville.

Lord Mansfield had yesterday a very long interview with the King.

The Administration triumph exceedingly upon the acquittal of the Justice of the Peace[1], and upon his obtaining a copy of the indictment from the judges. I think I can perceive that they are not without hopes of reaching Wilkes himself, or at least some of his agents, for spiriting up the widow of the person killed, to carry on the prosecution, and for supporting her in the expense of it.

The Duke of Bedford goes in the beginning of August to Ireland, to be installed as Chancellor of the University of Dublin; but what appears extraordinary is, the report of Lord Weymouth's going with him. Should this prove true, I shall conclude his Lordship means to succeed Lord Townshend, and that this is to make part of a more general arrangement.

---

[1] Gillam, the Justice of Peace, who had ordered the soldiers to fire when the mob attempted to release Wilkes from the King's Bench prison. Upon this occasion, it will be remembered, an innocent man named Allen was shot by mistake.

A friend of mine had yesterday seen Lord Egmont, who informed him that the Duke of Grafton had lately expressed in the Closet his sense of the difficulties of his situation, his wish to resign it, and his concern at not being able to recommend a proper person to succeed him. Lord Granby's opinion is, that there are at present not the smallest thoughts of a change in any department.

These are the contradictory ideas which prevail amongst the few people who are still in town, and it is the whole I can send your Lordship for your entertainment in the country. Adieu, my dear Lord; do me the justice to believe me upon all occasions, yours most faithfully and affectionately,   W. G. H.[1]

MR. GRENVILLE TO MR. POWNALL.

Wotton, July 17, 1768.

Sir,—I am very sensible of the honour which you do to me, both in this and in the Address prefixed to the former edition of your Treatise upon the Administration of the Colonies, and am much obliged to you for the expressions of your regard and good opinion.

You say very truly in the beginning of your present

---

[1] In this single instance, the latest letter I have found from Mr. Hamilton, he has subscribed his initials instead of the three *dashes* which he usually substituted for his name. Nearly all his letters to Lord Temple are ended in the same manner as above:—*Yours most faithfully and affectionately:*—sometimes *unalterably.* These expressions denote a very close and intimate friendship. I may take this opportunity of observing, that I have frequently in these volumes found it necessary to abridge the subscriptions to the Letters, in order to avoid the tedious repetition of *Your obedient humble Servant,* or *Yours truly, &c., &c.*, but I have carefully retained those which I considered to be in any respect significant of the degree of intimacy between the writer and his correspondent.

Address, that our opinions differed on several points, but we agree entirely in our wishes that the constitutional powers of this kingdom and the fixed government of the laws may prevail, and the rights of the subject be established upon true political liberty.

As to the great question of our Parliament's granting to America a competent number of representatives to sit in our House of Commons, you are no stranger to the declarations I repeatedly made in the House, at the time when the repeal of the Stamp Act was agitated, " that if such an application should be properly made by the Colonies to Parliament, in the same manner as those which were made from Chester and Durham, and probably from Wales, it would in my opinion be entitled to the most serious and favourable consideration."

I continue still in the same sentiments, but I am much afraid that neither the people of Great Britain nor those of America are sufficiently apprized of the danger which threatens both from the present state of things, to adopt a measure to which both the one and the other seems indisposed.

Some of the Colonies in their address to the *Crown* against some late *Acts of Parliament,* have, if I mistake not, expressly disclaimed it, and I do not think it has been kindly received in Great Britain, when it has been thrown out in Parliament, or started in any pamphlet or printed paper.

The fullest conviction of its necessity, and the hearty concurrence both of the Government and of the people, are indispensably necessary to set so great a machine in motion, as that of uniting all the outlying parts of the British dominions in one system.

As to what relates personally to me, I have done my

duty by endeavouring to assert the sovereignty of the King and Parliament of Great Britain over all the dominions belonging to the Crown, and to make all the subjects of the kingdom contribute to the public burthens for their own defence, according to their abilities and situation.

I thought that we had the clearest right imaginable, and that we were bound, by every tie of justice and of wisdom, to do this; and I am convinced it would have been accomplished, without any considerable difficulty, if America had not received such encouragement to oppose it from *hence*, as no other people would have resisted. To this the present confusion is entirely owing, nor will it now cease if we shall run into the contrary extreme of violence on the other side. Nothing but a plan of wisdom, justice, moderation, and firmness can now extinguish the flame which has so weakly and so wickedly been raised both within and without the kingdom. For my own part I shall wait the event with concern, and shall be ready to give any assistance I can whenever I see any practicable road opened to our safety.

As to what you obligingly mention in your letter respecting me, that you would not do anything which might be the occasion of any embarrassment to me, I desire to return you my thanks for this kind mark of your attention to me, but I do not see how I can be affected by it, if it is fully understood and explained in your Introduction, that you speak your own sentiments and not mine; and if I keep myself at full liberty as to my own conduct and opinions, which I am determined to do, I certainly ought not to put any restraint upon yours. I shall always be glad to receive from you in any manner which is most convenient and agreeable to you, such information upon these American matters both as to facts and opinions, as your knowledge and experience may enable you, and your kind dispositions towards me may incline you, to give to me. I am, &c., &c.

GEORGE GRENVILLE.

MR. KNOX[1] TO MR. GRENVILLE.

London, July 23, 1768.

DEAR SIR,—The newspapers will have told you upon your tour, what I am now sending better authenticated to meet you on your return. The Comptroller of the Customs at Boston is arrived, and I met him this morning at Lord Hillsborough's office.

The riot began upon account of a vessel laden with wine, which the searcher refused to be bribed, as usual, to admit to an entry. The master of the vessel thereupon confined the officer in the ship, and discharged the cargo, and was preparing to take in another and proceed on his voyage when the surveyor detected him, and seized the vessel, and set the searcher at liberty.

The prize was sent alongside the *Romney* man-of-war, and the mob finding her out of their power, vented their indignation upon the revenue officers, by demolishing their houses, and beating those they got hold of in

---

[1] Mr. Knox was at this time Under Secretary of State to Lord Hillsborough, and, subsequently, to Lord George Germain. He was the author of the pamphlet, entitled, *The Present State of the Nation, particularly with respect to its Trade, Finances, &c.*, which, being ascribed to Mr. Grenville, produced a reply from Burke, in his *Observations upon the State of the Nation.*

Mr. Knox was also the author of several tracts on American subjects, and he published two volumes of *Extra-Official State Papers*. He died at Great Ealing, in August, 1810, at the age of 73.

a terrible manner. Even their own excise officers were obliged to fly from the general outrage against revenue officers, and the Commissioners of the Customs took refuge on board the *Romney*.

The town after this addressed the Governor, not to interpose, but to allow them to save themselves the reproach of having parted with their liberties without one struggle. They say, as they have so happily rid the land of those vile vermin the Commissioners, they are determined never to suffer them to set foot on it again.

Councils were summoned for Thursday and Friday last, but the Duke of Grafton not choosing to come to town 'till to-morrow, they were put off 'till then.

Mr. Pownall tells me the troops lately ordered for Quebec, which it was said were ordered to call at Boston, are not to do so, but the Commissioners have applied to the Commander-in-chief at New York, and the commanding officer at Halifax, for troops and ships.

Lord Hillsborough's letters were not arrived at the time of this riot, so that when they came we may imagine the uproar was general.

Surely these things will at last open the eyes of the King, and lead him to think the Government of a great nation is not to be played with; but I much fear matters will be too bad for even you, Sir, to retrieve them before that happens, and that it will not be in your power to prevent them coming to extremities. How much would the public be obliged to you if you would permit me to introduce an extract from the last letter you honoured me with, in the answer I am preparing to write to the Farmer's Letters. I would only do it as a third person who had seen such a letter. I have left out entirely what I had said in regard to a repeal of the duties, and what you thought would be taken for a declaration to impose no more taxes. I have mentioned domestic taxes as the most proper by which to raise a revenue in the colonies, and said that perhaps, if Parliament assessed the colonies particular sums, as is done in the case of the Land Tax, and left it to the Assemblies to raise it as they thought fit, it would be the most expedient manner. These are not the words, but it is to this effect.

The paper is now in Almon's hands, and part of it already composed, but I shall not suffer it to be published 'till near the meeting of Parliament, which I am told will be much sooner than was expected. I am, &c., &c. WILL[M]. KNOX.

MR. WHATELY TO MR. GRENVILLE.

July 26, 1768.

DEAR SIR,—I came to town this morning. I find the alarm about America very great. The Stocks have fallen two-and-a-half per cent. upon it. The Ministers are in great confusion. I am told they differ in opinion. Lord Shelburne and Lord Camden, they say, do not agree with the Bedfords, and the business itself would puzzle Ministers of abilities equal to theirs in perfect unanimity[1]. No measure is yet taken; none indeed can

---

[1] This is one of the many instances in which the intelligence conveyed by Whately to Mr. Grenville or Lord Temple, is almost immediately repeated by Junius. In his letter of the 30th July, this want of unanimity, and the fall of the stocks, are both alluded to:—

"A resolution adopted by a small majority *in a divided council*, can be but little depended upon."   *   *   *   *

"In this situation I am rather afflicted than surprised at the shock which public credit has just received. The weight of the funds is of itself sufficient to press them down."—*Junius,* vol. iii. p. 78.

be resolved on, for the Duke of Grafton has not yet been in town since the news arrived. He has, they say, been sick; but to-morrow he comes, and then there is to be a full Cabinet Council. The accounts you have already had of the affair were not at all exaggerated. I now know the circumstances on which the Commissioners determined to retire on board the men-of-war, and think they had very good reason for so doing. Governor Bernard, you heard, sent them word that he apprehended he should soon follow them; this was not on account of the disturbance which then subsisted, but because he had just received the orders you heard of some time since for the dissolution of the Assemblies, if they would not erase certain resolutions[1]. He deferred to execute these orders 'till the town meetings were over, but had, when the ship sailed, summoned the General Court, in order to communicate these instructions, and expected they would meet with a reception which would make his stay impossible.

COUNTESS TEMPLE TO LADY BROWN[2].

Stowe, (about the end of July, 1768.)

I was very happy to hear from my dear Lady Brown at last, and cannot be angry with you for saving me from

[1] See *ante*, page 297, *note*.
[2] Probably Horace Walpole's friend and correspondent, "the merry Catholic, Lady Brown." She was his neighbour at Twickenham, and in one of his letters to Lady Ossory, he relates that going one evening with Lady Brown in a chaise to visit the Duchess of Montrose in the same neighbourhood, they were stopped by a highwayman, who demanded and received their purses. The man offered no violence, and was very civil. After he had departed, Walpole hoped Lady Brown was not frightened "No," said she, "but I hope he won't return,

the uneasiness you certainly would have given me in not being able to have ascertained your bodily health, had you writ some time before. I am very much obliged to your Cokam [Cookham?] friends for mentioning Stowe in so kind a manner. They made it agreeable by their enlivening conversation, and nothing could have added to our happiness but the presence of a person on the other side of the water. I must explain myself, for fear of being thought guilty of writing treason by innuendos. I mean a relation of theirs, who is always a help to society from her cheerfulness and good humour.

We are but just arrived from various excursions. We have been at Lord Aylesford's, Lord Coventry's, Lord Lyttelton's[1]; at the latter place Queen Mab appeared to me in a very romantic spot in the Park. This remarkable event was preceded by soft music from the clouds. Queen Mab was properly dressed in green, with a very long train supported by little fairies, and two little fairy boys, dressed in white, walked on each side with baskets of flowers in their hand. Her head was ornamented with flowers, and she held her magic wand. She made me a pretty compliment upon my coming to Hagley, and presented me with a basket of flowers taken from one of

because I have given him a purse with only bad money that I carry on purpose."

[1] This letter is from a draft in Lady Temple's hand: it is without any date either of month or year. I have presumed it to have been written about the time above-mentioned, because I find in Phillimore's *Life of Lord Lyttelton*, a letter from Lord Temple to that Lord, dated from Stowe, August 14th, 1768, in which he says, as if in remembrance of the *Masque of Fairies*, and of his recent entertainment at Hagley:—
" I cannot find in my heart to let the Grenville cargo depart for Hagley without bearing along with them a testimonial under my hand of my kindred regard for all *Fairy Land*, and the Apollo thereof, for Fairy Land has its Apollo as well as other regions."

the little white elves, at the bottom of which I found these verses, which I enclose [1]:—

[1] To Lady Temple.

In me behold the Fairy Queen!
Oft have I traced thy steps unseen
O'er all the gay, delightful round
Of lovely Stowe's enchanted ground.
Oft has my wand, extended there,
Raised lofty domes and Temples fair,
Has bid meandering rivers wind
Thro' vales once dry, or flow combined
In spacious lakes, where erst his sheep
The farmer's boy was wont to keep,
Or ploughman forced the furrowed field
Its annual crop of corn to yield!
Oft have I led my sportive train
To smiling Concord's [a] beauteous fane,
And seen bright Cynthia's silver beam
On all its stately columns gleam!
Sometimes to shun the noontide hour,
With thee I sought the Elysian Bower [b],
Or helped when darkness veiled the sky
To light the Grot for Emily [c].
Now, more retired, the secret shade
I haunt, of this sequestered glade,
And call my wanton elves to rove
Through every lawn, and every grove
That decked by Nature's hand alone,
To Kent or Brown was never known.
Nor thou disdain with us to dwell
In woodland wild and mossy cell,
For though nor Prince, nor Princess here
Will share thy walks, yet Love sincere,
And tranquil peace, and glad content,
And pleasure gay but innocent,
And mild philosophy, will meet
Thy wished approach to this Retreat.
The Muses too, whom oft the shade
That pendent waves o'er yon cascade

[a] [b] [c] The Temple of Concord, the Elysian Fields, and the Grotto in the Gardens at Stowe. The Grotto was frequently illuminated for the visits of the Princess Amelia.

The same ceremony was performed to Lord Temple, who was on the spot. If you were to see the particular place, you would say it was the best calculated for a fairy scene of any you ever saw or could have a notion of. There is a cascade that comes tumbling down a piece of rude rockwork, and runs into a rivulet at the bottom, which loses itself among the stones. The ground is enamelled with different flowers wildly dispersed, and here and there they peep out between the stones on each side, for the rock is continued on to the right and left, so as to admit of several benches cut into it, which are covered with moss; very large trees hang over, which shut out the rays of the sun; and this rock or grotto, or both, opens on a fine green lawn, from whence the fairies were seen to come, and where I believe they chiefly reside, if one may judge by the fairy rings upon the grass, for they are innumerable: but I leave this to the virtuosos; I only know there are such beings. You will excuse my damaging any more white paper, as I send you so much better a performance. Lord Temple desires to be remembered to your Ladyship in the kindest manner, and I hope you will believe that I am, most

> Has seen, beneath this verdant slope,
> Playing with Thomson and with Pope,
> Shall come, obedient to thy call,
> Fair boast and darling of them all!
> Here, for thy brows their hands divine
> Of never-dying Bays shall twine
> Such garlands, as, in days of yore,
> Their favoured Votress Sappho wore:
> And TEMPLE here may find with me
> His best-loved Nymph, sweet Liberty![a]

[a] The lines addressed to Earl Temple by Queen Mab, beginning,—

" By magic wheels thro' air conveyed,"

are printed among the poems of Lord Lyttelton, and therefore it is unnecessary to repeat them here.

sincerely, your Ladyship's very affectionate, humble servant,
ANNA TEMPLE.

MR. WHATELY TO MR. GRENVILLE.

August 4, 1768.

DEAR SIR,—The dismission of General Amherst [1], and the manner of his dismission, begins already to occasion

[1] The dismission of Sir Jeffry Amherst from the Governorship of Virginia was a subject upon which the author of Junius, in several letters, but more particularly under the signature of *Lucius*, devoted much of his attention at this time. Sir Jeffry Amherst was a very old and intimate friend of Lord Temple. He had been appointed to the chief command in America, and had obtained all his great successes in that country, during the war under the Administration of Mr. Pitt in the last reign, in which it is well known Lord Temple took so active a part.

Sir Jeffry was a frequent visitor at Stowe: he was there with the Princess Amelia in 1764, and he is again mentioned in a letter from Lord Camden as being there in 1766:—" There are now, or will be in a few days, at Stowe, the two Dukes of B. [Bedford] and M. [Marlborough] with their ladies, Sir Jeffry Amherst, and the Royal guests."[a]

Besides, that Lord Temple might have derived the fullest information from Sir Jeffry Amherst himself with respect to his interview and communication with Lord Hillsborough, some letters from Whately to Mr. Grenville appear to have furnished him with materials for the letters of Lucius, particularly that of August the 29th, in which several passages in Whately's letters of the 4th, 10th, and 24th inst. very pointedly apply.

It was subsequently discovered that an error had been committed by assigning an incorrect date to the chief transaction, and it was acknowledged by Lucius that he had by mistake advanced the communications between Lord Hillsborough and Sir Jeffry Amherst, too forward by *one complete week*, but the days of the week, the facts, and the order in which they succeed one another, are the same [b]. I think it may not be

[a] Lord Campbell's *Lives of the Chancellors*, vol. v. p. 259.

[b] I have already mentioned a similar instance of incorrect dating in an interesting and important document, recently printed by Lord Albemarle in his *Memoirs of the Marquess of Rockingham*. I allude to the account drawn up by the Duke of Cumberland of his negotiations with Mr. Pitt and Lord Temple, in his endeavours to form an Administration in the summer of 1765. See *ante*, vol. iii. p. 175, *note*.

much talk, and will not, I think, pass even without clamour. It was determined, without his knowing the

difficult to account for that error, but it is quite unimportant, except as it would tend to strengthen the probability that these letters from Whately had been communicated by Mr. Grenville to his brother, and that they had been used by the latter, as materials for his own, under the signature of Lucius.

It was Whately's usual habit, in his correspondence with Mr. Grenville, neither to sign his letters, nor to make any other ending to them, than by placing the date of the month immediately after, and quite close to, the last words [a].

Mr. Grenville was at Wotton when he received Whately's letter, dated "August 4th," either on the Friday or Saturday following, but it may not have been sent or shown to Lord Temple at Stowe for some days later.

"The dismission of Sir Jeffry Amherst," says Whately, "was determined without his knowing the least of it, on Tuesday or Wednesday *in the last week*: he came to town accidentally on Thursday, and found at his house a letter from Lord Hillsborough, to desire to speak with him, &c."

Now, a person reading this letter some days after it was written, and either not observing its date, or not particularly considering that the 4th, the day of its date, was Thursday, might very easily understand the words, "on Thursday," to mean *Thursday last*, instead of *Thursday in the last week*, and this I conceive to be the way in which the error may have arisen.

The letter in which Lucius first mentioned the dates of this transaction was not written *until more than three weeks had elapsed*, and although Lord Temple may have been very exactly informed of all the circumstances, yet he may still have adopted, as he thought correctly, the dates from Whately's letters, as I shall endeavour to show he used other information contained in them.

In the letter signed Lucius, of the 29th of August, Lord Hillsborough is called upon to answer six questions, all of them relating to facts previously mentioned in Whately's letters :—

1st —*Was not Lord Botetourt's appointment absolutely fixed on or before Sunday, the 31st of July?*

2nd.—*Had Sir Jeffry Amherst the least intimation of the measure before Thursday, the 4th of August?*

3rd.—*Was it not then mentioned to him in general terms, as a mea-*

---

[a] In a letter written by Whately to Lord Temple on the 6th of July, 1767, he said, "In all letters which I write to Mr. Grenville, I omit my name, and can therefore write more freely : for the same reason I will, if I have occasion to trouble you again by the post, and your Lordship will permit me, put the date in the place of the signature, and hope that by this time you may recollect the hand of your correspondent."

least of it, on Tuesday or Wednesday in the last week. He came to town accidentally on Thursday, and found

sure merely in contemplation, without the most distant hint that Lord Botetourt, or any other person, was actually in possession of his Government?

4th.—Did not Lord Botetourt kiss hands the next day, that is, on Friday, the 5th of August?

5th.—Did you not dare to tell your Sovereign that Sir Jeffry Amherst was perfectly satisfied, when you knew your treatment of him was such as the vilest peasant could not have submitted to without resentment?

6th.—Is it not a fact that Sir Jeffry Amherst having been called upon some time ago to give his opinion upon a measure of the highest importance in America, gave it directly against a favourite scheme of your Lordship: and is not this the real cause of all your antipathy to him?—Junius, vol. iii. p. 110.

Without again referring to the dates of the month, it is distinctly stated by Whately, that Sir Jeffry received the first intimation of the matter from Lord Hillsborough on *Thursday:*—the next day, *Friday,* Lord Botetourt kissed hands for the appointment.

" It has been given out," says Whately, " that he was, or would be, satisfied. The fact is directly the reverse: he is as outrageous as his nature can be: on the Friday, Lord Botetourt kissed hands: on the Saturday, General Amherst did not know that the business was actually done, so little was the state of the affair explained to him at the only communication he has had of it;" until " he went to Lord Botetourt himself, who confirmed the fact, expressed his concern, &c., and assured him that the thing had not been settled till the *Saturday before.*"

The sixth and last question refers to the following passage in Whately's letter of the 10th:—" Upon this occasion an anecdote is come out, which before I was not aware of: that Sir Jeffry, in the advice he gave, *strenuously opposed the repeal of the Stamp Act.* Admiral Keppel tells me so, and it is confirmed to me by one of Sir Jeffry's most intimate friends. He was consulted because it was supposed that the Government of Virginia and the two American Battalions were left to him in consideration of his taking any part he could take here in American affairs, but his opinion was over-ruled."

To Lord Hillsborough, Lucius says,—" *The world attributes to your Lordship the entire honour of Sir Jeffry Amherst's dismission, because there is no other person in the Cabinet who could be supposed to have a wish or motive to give such advice to the Crown.*" * * * *

" *The Duke of Bedford and his friends have uniformly held forth Sir Jeffry Amherst as the first military man in this country; they have quoted him on all occasions when military knowledge was in question,*

at his house a note from Lord Hillsborough to desire
to speak with him. He supposed it was to desire him

*and even been lavish in his praise. Besides, they openly disclaim any
share in this measure, and they are believed."—Junius, vol. iii. p.* 106.

And the parallel passages in Whately's letter are :—

"Mr. Rigby (*the Duke of Bedford and his friends*) has upbraided
Lord Weymouth for concurring in his dismission: his Lordship's
defence was that the King and the King's servants understood that he
would be satisfied, but now they find themselves egregiously mistaken."
* * * * * * "His services and his abilities were at the same time
another reason for his having those emoluments, and on that ground I
understand Rigby reproached Lord Weymouth, for joining to disgrace
a man whom they had always held up as a General equal to great
commands, and whose services might be wanted on future occasions."

I have assumed that Mr. Grenville communicated these letters to
Lord Temple, but Whately may also have written to the latter in the
same strain. He corresponded with both, and he very frequently sent
the same information, with but slight alteration in words, to each.

Other passages might be selected : such for instance as this :—" You
know he is a temperate man, and I suppose spoke with moderation,"
&c.

Lucius says:—" *Sir Jeffry Amherst is one of the mildest and most
moderate of men:* ERGO, *such a man will bear anything.*"

Again, Whately writes:—" The next day Colonel Amherst heard
at Court *that Lord Botetourt had that morning* (Friday) *kissed hands*
in the Closet, *and he directly sent an express with the news to his
brother.*"

Lucius says:—" *Yet Lord Botetourt kissed hands the next morning
(Friday), and the first notice Sir Jeffry Amherst received of his Lordship's appointment was by an express sent to him that evening by his
brother."—Junius,* vol. iii. p. 147.

In Whately's letter of the 24*th of August,* is the following :—" But
the King is desirous to make you amends in any other way, by way of
annuity, or, &c., &c. Annuity ! says Sir J. Amherst, turning it in his
mind, but speaking aloud : an annuity is a pension : the word pension
is *grating to my ears:* if, my Lord, the King would bestow upon me
some mark of honour, or something in the military line, I should be
happy in the distinction; but a pension, my Lord, *is grating in my
ears."*

A week later, Sept. 1*st,* Lucius writes:—" *For the matter of a recompense equivalent to his government, he repeatedly told your Lordship that
the name of pension was grating to his ears, and that he would accept of
no revenue that was not at the same time honorary. Your Lordship does*

to go to take the command in America; but it was to tell him of the design to appoint Lord Botetourt, and to offer him any equivalent. His answer, I understand, was, that if his age and infirmities obliged him to retire, he might be glad to accept any mark of distinction, though in the shape of emolument, if his services were thought to deserve a reward, but as long as he was able to serve he could not take a pension.

You know he is a temperate man, and I suppose spoke with moderation; he was therefore either mistaken or has been misrepresented, for it has been given out that he was, or would be, satisfied. The fact is directly the reverse; he is as outrageous as his nature can be. On the Friday Lord Botetourt kissed hands; on the Saturday General Amherst did not know that the business was actually done, so little was the state of the affair explained to him at the only communication he has had of it. The King has since asked Lord Botetourt when he should be ready to go. *To-night, Sir,* was his answer[1]; and yet, after all, I think it not certain that he

---

not know the difference, but men of honour feel it."—*Junius,* vol. iii. p. 122.

" He *repeatedly* told your Lordship that the name of pension was *grating to his ears.*" It is remarkable that Whately reports him to have used that expression *twice* in the above extract.

In short, all the letters written by Lucius during the months of August and September will be found, upon close comparison, to contain, at various times, the same information upon the subject as Whately's letters, and expressed in very similar terms.

[1] Lord Botetourt was one of the King's Lords of the Bedchamber: described by Junius (Lucius) as a "cringing, bowing, fawning, sword-bearing courtier;" and Walpole, mentioning him at this time, says,— "Lord Botetourt is like patience on a monument, smiling in grief. He is totally ruined, and quite charmed. Yet I heartily pity him. To Virginia he cannot be indifferent: he must turn their heads somehow or other. If his graces do not captivate them, he will enrage them to fury: for I take all his *douceur* to be enamelled on iron."

will go. I find some doubt whether Lord Chatham will put the Privy Seal to such an appointment. I can easily perceive an alarm taken at finding it impossible to satisfy General Amherst, and I believe they will not be fond of the reproach of dismissing General Amherst from a command which, though not necessarily, has been constantly given in the military line, in order to provide for Lord Botetourt.

The defence is, that in these times the American Governors ought to reside; and perhaps they may imagine the step may be popular in the colonies; but Amherst has not been asked whether he would go, and the colonies will receive not the least satisfaction. Their complaint has been that a settled stipend provided for a Governor has been converted into a pension for some resident in England. Virginia is the only colony which ever made such a provision, and the others have constantly, when required to do the same, urged this instance against it, saying that the consequence to Virginia has been that their money has been spent in England, while they have been governed by a Lieutenant-Governor. They have not by this appointment the least security that Lord Botetourt will not some time hence do as all other Governors have done, and I doubt whether they will think his Lordship more deserving of a sinecure at their expense than a General whom they know and respect. It is said, but I do not know with what truth, that as a further mark of favour he is to have the same quantity of plate as is usually given to Ambassadors, upon which a joke is raised of his going Plenipo. to the Cherokees.

Besides this notable measure for reconciling America, I know of none likely to produce any decisive effect;

two regiments indeed are ordered from Ireland, the 60th and 61st. They lie at a distance from Cork, and the regiments to be drafted in order to make them up from 300 to 500 men, are dispersed about the kingdom, so that it is hardly possible these regiments should get away by this day month. Three men-of-war of 60 guns each are also ordered to sail, and they will probably get there just in the stormy season, and a little before the frost will make the harbour of Boston untenable. No orders are yet prepared for the troops about their conduct when they arrive there; none, as I can hear, sent to those already in America; and the letters now going out to the several Governors (except perhaps Bernard), are in the same careless style, and on the same trivial subjects as usual in times of tranquillity. The Ministers seem to have no other idea than to save themselves from the reproach of doing nothing; but they will not venture to do anything, if I can judge of their intentions. I have even heard it surmised that they begin to repent of doing so much. They made the proposition for troops, as some imagine, only in hopes that Lord Shelburne would oppose it. He did not, and they are disappointed of that pretence for pressing his dismission, in which, it is said, they would then have succeeded.

COMMODORE HOOD[1] TO MR. GRENVILLE.

Halifax, August 8, 1768.

SIR,—I did myself the honour to address to you a short detail of the situation of affairs at Boston on the

[1] He was at this time Commander of His Majesty's ships and vessels on the Boston station. He was subsequently well known as a most distinguished Admiral. He was created Viscount Hood in 1796, and died in 1816.

11th past, by an officer I charged with dispatches to my Lords Commissioners of the Admiralty; since which the aspect of things is not in the least mended—indeed the ferment amongst the people seems at times to be smothered, but then diligent search is ever making by the demagogues after fuel to kindle the flame afresh.

Mr. Williams, the Inspector-General of the Customs, who was from home in the late riots, had his house beset on the evening of his return by a vast mob, who, in a tumultuous manner, insisted on seeing Mr. Williams, and his appearing at the window. It was demanded that he should immediately go to Liberty Tree, there resign his office, and take an oath never to resume it, which he refused, assuring them, at the same time, that he had friends in the house ready to defend him if his doors were forced. They then insisted he should go to the Castle to the Commissioners, where they have been prisoners at large many weeks, which he also refused, when much clamour ensued, and much vengeance was threatened; but on assurances being given by Mr. Williams that he would meet them at the Town House next day at noon, they dispersed without doing much mischief.

At the appointed hour Mr. Williams went through a mob of many thousands, who opened a passage for him, and, from a window, he repeatedly told them of their proceedings last evening, that he was come agreeable to his promise, and demanded what they had to say to him: not a word of reply was made by any one; *all* were silent. His resolute behaviour had quite disconcerted them; but he has often since received anonymous letters threatening his life unless he resigns his office.

Governor Bernard was very apprehensive that the

Castle would be attacked, and wrote to Captain Corner of the *Romney*, requesting his assistance by all means in his power for the defence and protection of it. Thus things at present are: from the information I have received, all is confusion, and Government without authority.

In the latter end of last month, Mr. Bernard pressed his council to advise him to call for troops: the whole except *three* opposed the measure, so that his Excellency is now left to act upon his own judgment solely, which may possibly make him less timid.

Colonel Dalrymple, by General Gage's order, holds two regiments in constant readiness to embark from hence, whenever they are required by the Governor, or directed by the General. Had this force been landed in Boston six months ago, I am perfectly persuaded no address or remonstrance would have been sent from the other colonies, and that all would have been tolerably quiet and orderly at this time throughout America. Every day's delay of the only remedy that can prove effectual, has manifestly tended to an increase of bad humour, by which, what would have been without difficulty effected early in the spring, will become an arduous, and probably a fatal undertaking late in the year.

The giving to the Colonies such time and opportunity for uniting in opposition to the British Acts of Parliament, ought, in my humble opinion, by all possible means, to have been prevented. But I forget to whom I have the honour to address myself, and must entreat your goodness, Sir, to excuse my presumption in saying what I have, in matters of such high importance, and to one who is so perfect a judge of them; I meant only to relate facts as they were transmitted to me. This goes by one of His Majesty's armed schooners, whose defects are too great to be repaired in this Yard, and, as soon as I determined on sending her to England, I made it known to Governor Bernard, who was happy in so favourable an opportunity for his dispatches, which were yesterday brought me from Boston.

Almost the whole trade of America is more or less illicit: three vessels have been this summer seized in the Gulph and River St. Lawrence, by His Majesty's cruisers under my command; and if Government is determined to put a stop to it, a greater number of small armed schooners, upon such an establishment as the cutters are at home, must be employed, which I have taken the liberty to recommend to my Lords Commissioners of the Admiralty, and am perfectly persuaded they would give a vast annual increase to the King's revenues. Only four are at present within my district, and I am of opinion there ought to be a dozen at least.

I have taken the liberty to send by this opportunity a small box of seeds of a fine tree called the Catawba, which I hope will be acceptable, and the more so, as I am told there are very few in England. I have the honour to be, &c. SAM. HOOD.

MR. KNOX TO MR. GRENVILLE.

London, August 9, 1768.

DEAR SIR,—Upon looking over the Papers at the Board of Trade, I am filled with astonishment at the multiplicity of evidence I meet with, not only to prove the right of Parliament to tax the Colonies, but their acknowledgment of it, and even application for Parliament to exercise it.

The letters of correspondents I am not, however, allowed to take extracts of, so that the publication will want that degree of evidence which arises from the opinion of the Governors, in the several periods taken notice of. But there is one thing which is very singular, which I shall have a copy of. A Bill prepared in 1710 for laying taxes upon New York, because of the Assembly there having neglected to make the usual provision for the support of Government. This Bill is signed by Northey and Worge, but it seems it never passed. Perhaps you can tell me the history of this Bill. Another thing which I must beg from you is, the counter proof to Dickinson's[1] assertion, that, until your Administration, no duty or tax was laid in the Colonies, but as a regulation of trade.

The point of Lord Camden's speech is, that the right of Taxation flows from Representation. I have no more of his speech than Dickinson quotes in his letters. If you will take the trouble of showing how that matter stands, you will do great good.

For my own part, I am tempted to deny that there is any such thing as Representation at all in our Constitution, but that the Commons are taken out of the people, as the democratic part of the Government, not elected as representatives of the people, but commissioned by them in like manner as the Lords are commissioned or appointed by the Crown. If the Commons were the representatives only of the people, the people might control them, and the instructions of the electors

---

[1] John Dickenson was the author of the *Farmer's Letters from Pennsylvania*, which were by some attributed to Franklin.

would be binding upon the Members; whereas in the very article of taxation, the Commons exclude the people even from petitioning, much more deny them authority to control their deliberations. If there be any truth in this idea, I am sure you can extend it, and, if you will be so good to take the trouble, trace the origin of this notion of representation; for, until that is overturned, it will be very difficult to convince, either the colonies, or the people in England, that wrong is not done to the colonies.

The Duke of Grafton has lately trimmed the balance a little, which was preponderating on the Bedford side so much as to alarm him, especially as you were mentioned by some of the friends of that House, and his Grace is now in better concert with Lord Shelburne than he has been since he first came into office.

I am sure I ought to beg pardon for the frequent trouble I give you; I have no excuse to plead, but that I am, &c., &c. WILLIAM KNOX.

MR. WHATELY TO MR. GRENVILLE.

August 10, 1768.

DEAR SIR,—I was in town for a few hours on Monday: a friend of mine, who is always there, showed me the two enclosed publications, one without signature in the beginning of the second page of the *Public Advertiser* of the 6th of August, and the other signed L. L. of the 5th of August[1]. Surprised that I had not seen

---

[1] See Letters xxx. and xxxi., *Junius*, vol. iii. pp. 80-83. They are also preserved in Mrs. Grenville's collection of cuttings from newspapers, before mentioned.

them, he asked whether you also missed of those which appeared only in the morning papers, and whether it would be agreeable to you to send such as might seem to him worth your perusal. I told him you would certainly be amused by any well-written papers sent to you in the country: you are not to know from whom they come, though you may easily guess; nor to trouble yourself with acknowledging the receipt of them.

That without a signature, he told me was evidently from a hand who had written on the same subject about ten days before, but I could not get that former paper[1]: I could only get that one of his opponent's signed Tandem[2], of 4th August, to whom the turn of his answer seems masterly; but who this good writer is I cannot guess. I enclose Tandem's, that you may see how well he is refuted, though I perceive you have already seen some paper in the same strain of abuse. It is to be expected from those who are guilty of the present confusions in America, that they should endeavour to divert the attention of the public to any other object than themselves: the attempt proves their consciousness that they are exposed to the resentment of the people they have betrayed, and, in fact, it now falls upon them. The general opinion that Mr. Grenville must be Minister has no other foundation: we know that no step has been taken to give rise to such a report; we have reason to believe that all who are now in, wish to keep you out; and yet every day the reports of your coming in are revived. I am told that even your enemies acknowledge the necessity for it: in the city, for

---

[1] This was probably Letter xxix. in Woodfall's Miscellaneous Collection, *Junius*, vol. iii. p. 73.

[2] The letter of *Tandem* is in Mrs. Grenville's collection.

instance, Mr. Maitland tells me, that many who were forward for repealing the Stamp Act, confess now that you were in the right from the beginning, and when they exclaimed against the Americans, he bid them thank themselves, whose weakness had encouraged the insolence of the colonies, the truth of which reproach they admitted. These have been for some time very general sentiments, and, you may depend upon it, they do not grow weaker. Just at present the dismission of Sir Jeffry Amherst occasions much noise, and gives the Administration great anxiety. He did not say what in my former letter I told you he had said to Lord Hillsborough, about not accepting a pension, but, however, he showed no symptoms of being satisfied. I know he is highly exasperated, and I believe will soon show that he is, but I do not exactly know yet in what manner.

Mr. Rigby has upbraided Lord Weymouth for concurring in his dismission : his Lordship's defence was, that the King and the King's servants understood that he would be satisfied, but now they find themselves egregiously mistaken. Upon this occasion an anecdote is come out which before I was not aware of; that Sir Jeffry, in the advice he gave, strenuously opposed the repeal of the Stamp Act : Admiral Keppel tells me so, and it is confirmed to me by one of Sir Jeffry's most intimate friends. He was consulted, because it was supposed that the government of Virginia and the two American battalions were left to him, in consideration, partly of his taking any part he could take here in American affairs, but his opinion was overruled. His services and his abilities were, at the same time, another reason for his having those emoluments, and on that ground, I understand, Rigby reproached Lord Weymouth for joining to disgrace a man whom they had always held up as a general, equal to great commands, and whose services might be wanted upon future occasions.

A family in this neighbourhood were on a tour at Dover, when Lord Bute came there to embark: they observed a bustle in the streets, and heard *Wilkes and Liberty*, more than they expected, before they knew the reason: a considerable number of people were assembled to see him go into the boat at the usual place for taking water; but he went off from another part of the shore, to his vessel which lay without the pier, and one of the watermen who rowed him told this family, that, having intelligence of an intended insult, and that many of the persons assembled to see him go had filled their pockets with stones, to pelt Lord Bute, Minet's people had advised his Lordship to go off from the other place; the waterman added, that, had he stayed in the town all night, he would certainly have been murdered, but he was there only an hour.

MR. AUGUSTUS HERVEY TO MR. GRENVILLE.

Park Place, Saturday, August 13, 1768.

DEAR SIR,—I would not have troubled you with my thanks for your kind letter in answer to mine, but that I imagined you would like to hear what is going on, as some of your better-informed correspondents may not be in town; and indeed I am so little about, that I scarce hear anything, but I know, and have seen (not read it) a letter handed about, that was yesterday wrote from Lord Hillsborough to Sir Jeffry Amherst, a very guarded one, yet excusing their taking away the government of Virginia, and on *his offer to resign his regiment* (which has been made), expressing their concern for his having so misconstrued the King's intentions, which are therein described as all gracious and well-meaning to Sir Jeffry Amherst, with hints (not offers) of anything to accommodate and gild the pill. I am told there is a kind of proposal to be made to him (if he will not accept the pension), which is, to give Lord Tyrawly the pension, and his government with additional emoluments to Sir Jeffry Amherst, but 't is thought that he will be deaf to all proposals of that kind, as Lord Albemarle, and others of that set, have been constantly with him to rouse and keep awake his present resentment and indignation. This letter was showed yesterday to several people, and is to be shown to Lord Mayor to-day, that the people in the city may be made acquainted that Sir Jeffry Amherst was not deprived of his government in the manner that has been reported there. I find Sir Jeffry's letter makes a great noise, and they do not seem to like the bustle it makes among the military. Lord Botetourt *keeps the Bedchamber,* although he says he *never* desires to return, and certainly *will not for seven years.*

This discourse, and the arrival of the King of Denmark, employs the Court, of which every man must be tired who is not tired of himself, and can bear his own company. The Duke of Bedford is at Court for ever, and the Duchess and Lord Weymouth seem to me to be the oracle here; the Duke of Grafton has not been very often, I think, since I have been in town.

Lord Robert Bertie[1] told me he met Lord Chatham

---

[1] Son of the first Duke of Ancaster, and at this time M.P. for Boston. He was on board the *Ramilies* (proceeding to join his regiment at

the other evening on horseback, and seemed as well as ever; he saw him, and stopped and spoke to him a good while, cheerful and alive.

The King of Denmark was at Lady Hertford's last night, and afterwards went to Ranelagh. His people were introduced to the King at the Levée yesterday, and Lord Chamberlain waited on His Majesty from the King in the morning, to desire to see him at the Queen's house at half-past five, where the King of Denmark went privately, and about eight to the Princess Dowager's; at nine he came to Lord Hertford's, and then to Ranelagh: he was very affable to every one, and as I know others will describe his figure and his manner[1], I will not take up your time. Mrs. Grenville will have all that from Lady Egremont, who I saw there; for my part, I believe, I have the honour to think as you do about the *conferences* and *conversations* of kings. With most people the words of kings are

---

Minorca) with Admiral Byng in the engagement with the French fleet, and was one of those officers who gave evidence in favour of Byng, "that, being near the person of the Admiral, they did not perceive any backwardness in him during the action, or any marks of fear or confusion either from his countenance or behaviour, but that he seemed to give his orders coolly and distinctly, and did not seem wanting in personal courage."—*Walpole's Memoirs of George II.*, vol. ii. p. 292.

[1] Horace Walpole has left us a minute description of him. "The puppet of the day is the King of Denmark; in truth, puppet enough: a very miniature of our late King, his grandfather. White, strutting, dignified, prominent eyes, gallant, and condescending enough to mark that it is condescension." The King was accompanied by a "Lord High Favourite, Count Holke, a pert young gentleman of three-and-twenty, who seems rather proud of his favour than shy of displaying it." Count Bernsdorff, his Prime Minister, was the Mentor of the party: "a grim old man, bowing and cringing at every word of the King with Eastern obsequiousness." They hurried through most parts of England without attention, took notice of nothing, took pleasure in nothing, dining and supping at seats on the road, without time enough to remark so much of their beauties as would flatter the great Lords who treated him."—*Walpole's Correspondence;* and also his *Memoirs of George III.*

more amusing than those of other men, at least men are amused with the same things from lips of that consequence, that would lay them to sleep uttered from any other; but now-a-days, when princes are so lavish of their conversation, a scrap of it is like a rag of their royal garment, that contracts its value from that stamp only, whereas if the one had been uttered, or that worn by a person of less eminence, the first had never been remembered, nor the last ever preserved.

To-day I hear his Danish Majesty is to have a Levée. I am told his expenses are just 25,000*l.* a month, and Lord Talbot told me it would cost the King 150*l.* a day for his tables, &c., whilst he was here; much good may it do them both.

I am unfortunately plunging myself in a very troublesome, disagreeable, yet I think (for me and my family) necessary business[1], which has long employed more of my thoughts and time than my health could bestow, but to my astonishment a few months' labour (and great labour) have given me what many years I could not obtain; and if I succeed in the great point, I shall think myself well repaid, and do not doubt but my health will be restored. As yet we are not quite forward enough to be quite certain for the last determination, and yet were we to consult ten thousand rational thinking people, I am certain there would not be one *contre;* but where law is concerned, there may be delicacies in points of that which are not known in equity. Excuse me saying no more; you have ever been so much my friend, I could not say less, and were I with you, I

---

[1] Mr. Hervey alludes to the pending suit for a divorce from his wife, formerly Miss Chudleigh, who, it will be seen subsequently, married the Duke of Kingston.

should not hesitate saying more, though my lips have never been opened about it but where it was necessary. I am, &c. A. HERVEY.

MR. KNOX TO MR. GRENVILLE.

London, August 20, 1768.

DEAR SIR,—You have made me rich indeed, by the ample discussion you have been so obliging to give the several points I wanted instruction upon, and I think I am now furnished with such materials and arguments as will convince mankind of the weakness of the American cause, and the wickedness of its advocates.

I have got both Lord Chatham's and Lord Camden's speeches [1], and it will surely be very great want of abilities in me, if I do not make theirs exceedingly contemptible.

I was yesterday honoured with a pretty long conversation with Lord Hillsborough, who related to me the whole transaction respecting General Amherst, with permission for me to communicate the story to you, but not as from him.

There have lately been sent over by the President of the Council for Virginia, a petition to the King, and a *Remonstrance* to the Parliament; the latter conceived in terms which imply a total disavowal of the supremacy of Parliament. When Lord Hillsborough received these

[1] In a letter to Whately on the following day, Mr. Grenville writes,—" I hear that the common report in London is, that Lord Chatham is well in health, but not in mind. He has reason to be uneasy for the unhappy consequences which his and Lord Camden's speech against the authority of the Legislature have had, and will have, both here and in America. The seeds of that mischief which they have sown now show themselves; but this, I fear, is but the beginning of the greatest evil which this kingdom ever felt, and the deepest wound it ever received."

papers, he laid them before the rest of the King's servants, who were all of opinion that the Governor in Chief of that province should be resident. The King approved of this resolution, but desired Lord Hillsborough not to press General Amherst to go if he declined it, but to offer him an equivalent. Lord Hillsborough called upon the General, but he being out of town, he writ to him to the following effect, as well as I can recollect, having read the letter:—"That the King had come to the resolution that his Governor in Chief should reside, and that nothing would be more agreeable to His Majesty than to be able to avail himself at this time of General Amherst's abilities in America, but that His Majesty did not forget that the Government of Virginia was given to General Amherst as a reward for his great services, and that therefore he had the King's orders not to press him to go there, if it should from any reason be disagreeable to him, but that it was His Majesty's gracious intention, from the high sense he had of his merit, to make good to him the whole emolument he now received out of that Government, in another manner."

The General came to town, and waited on Lord Hillsborough: he said it would be very disagreeable to him to go to America, and that having been Commander in Chief of the whole, he could not submit to be a Governor of a single province, and commanded by General Gage. Lord Hillsborough replied, that, as his orders were not to press him to go, he did not know whether he ought to answer his objection, but that nothing could be more distinct than a civil governor and a military commander, and that every Governor was superior to all persons in his own province. However, as it was disagreeable to him to go, that was sufficient, and he desired to know what emoluments he received out of the Government, that he might acquaint the King, in order to having his orders to make out a grant for an annuity equivalent to it. The General replied, that he received 1500 guineas; but, says he, does your Lordship mean a pension? Yes, says Lord Hillsborough, I do mean a pension, and, however grating the name of a pension may and ought to be, when it is given merely as a pension, yet when it is given as a reward for services performed, it becomes a testimony of public approbation. Witness Lord Chatham's pension, granted to him for directing those services you performed. Witness, too, Sir Edward Hawke's pension, for saving Ireland, and why not yours for adding Canada to the British dominions? The General continued to say he should dislike a pension, but must submit to the King's pleasure, and so went away.

When Lord Hillsborough reported this to the King, His Majesty was pleased to order a grant of 1500 guineas per annum to Sir Jeffry, during his life, free of all deductions, out of the $4\frac{1}{2}$ per cents. But Sir Jeffry's letter to the Duke of Grafton, acquainting him that, unless he was made a peer, together with that pension, he should resign his regiments, prevented it from being made out. His Lordship disclaims any purpose of giving the Government of Virginia to Lord Botetourt at the time of this conversation, and disavows that Lord's having ever applied for it, but that in his difficulty he thought of him, and he, from the principle of going wherever the King should think it for his service to send him, accepted of it.

I have sent this story to the *Political Register*, and

contrasted it with the General's, which says, that he did not receive Lord Hillsborough's letter, but had come to town on business, and hearing that Lord Hillsborough had been at his house, he immediately waited on him, and that his Lordship read to him his letter. That he determinedly and repeatedly refused the offer of the pension, and, when he went away, expected nothing more would be done in it until he was again consulted with; but that when his brother writ him word that Lord Botetourt had kissed hands, he then thought himself slighted, and had put forth his whole claim, that, if right was not done him, he might take the other only means of avoiding becoming contemptible.

It is pretty plain to me that there was no purpose of sending out General Amherst from the first, else why was not the Command in Chief of the Military offered to him? But it seems he had lately been called to Councils upon American affairs, and his ideas did not at all accord with those of the Administration, and therefore theyd id not choose to employ him.

Lord Hillsborough told me he wished the public would avail itself of your abilities, but that he saw no likelihood of it at present. I am, &c., &c.

WILLIAM KNOX.

MR. WHATELY TO MR. GRENVILLE.

August 24, 1768.

DEAR SIR,—I find, upon inquiry, that most of the intelligence which in a former letter you sent me, as received by Lord Temple[1], has in its day had some

[1] Mr. Grenville, in a reply to Whately on the 14th, said,—" Lord Temple, whom I saw yesterday, told me that his intelligence says, that

foundation; it takes its turn even now: but that of the Duke of Grafton's indisposition towards his situation, and frequent wishes to quit it, continue more or less at all times, though one would imagine he was immoveably fixed, by the adulation paid at the Ridotto to Mrs. Parsons[1], who was surrounded all the time by men of all ranks pressing for the honour of paying their respects to her; so much more profligate is the world become, since all neglected even her paramour[2] when he appeared with her at the Opera, last winter.

The story of Sir Jeffry Amherst's dismission is represented in the manner you have heard it, but with little effect. All men are enraged at it, though the precise facts are not known, but it is only said generally that he was dismissed in a very unhandsome manner. The exact account of it is this:—On the Thursday, he accidentally came to town from Yorkshire, and was told that a letter had been left the day before from Lord Hillsborough, which had been forwarded to his house at Riverhead. Sir Jeffry, hearing at the same time the news from America, concluded that his Lordship's business must be to propose his taking the command there, and therefore went immediately to wait upon him, resolved to accept the command, and not dreaming of his

---

the Duke of Grafton had declared himself so tired and disgusted, that nothing on earth should make him *go on* another year." And in a letter probably written about the same time, and published on the 19th instant, Junius (Atticus) says:—" One day, he (the Duke of Grafton) desponds and threatens to resign. The next he finds his blood heated, and swears to his friends he is determined to *go on*."—*Junius*, vol. iii. p. 167.

[1] Horace Walpole, writing to Conway, says,—" I was thinking it would make a good article in the papers, that three Bishops had supped with Nancy Parsons at Vauxhall, in their way to Lambeth."

[2] The Duke of Grafton.

having any pretensions to build any extraordinary demands on his acceptance. When he came, Lord Hillsborough showed him the copy of the letter, which was, that the late dispatches from America made it necessary that all Governors should reside there, but that he would not be pressed to go if it was not perfectly agreeable and convenient to him; some civilities on his services and expressions of regard made up the rest of the letter.

Sir Jeffry, as soon as he saw it, said he wanted no time to think of an answer, for that it was impossible he could go to Virginia while General Gage was Commander in Chief. I took it for granted you could not go, was his Lordship's reply, but the King is desirous to make you amends in any other way, by way of annuity, or &c., &c. Annuity! says Sir J. Amherst, turning it in his mind, but speaking aloud; an annuity is a pension; the word pension is grating to my ears: if, my Lord, the King would bestow upon me some mark of honour, or something in the military line, I should be happy in the distinction, but a pension, my Lord, is grating in my ears. This is the substance of the whole conversation at that time.

At Court, the same day, Lord Hillsborough asked Sir Jeffry how much his Government produced; his answer was, 1500*l*. per annum, and no more passed between them: in the evening Sir Jeffry went into the country. The next day, Colonel Amherst heard at Court, that Lord Botetourt had that morning kissed hands in the Closet, and he directly sent an express with the news to his brother. Sir Jeffry immediately took his resolution, framed his letters to the Duke of Grafton and Lord Barrington, and then came to town on the Saturday; but not finding anybody who had seen Lord Botetourt kiss hands, to satisfy himself of the truth before he sent any letter, he went to Lord Botetourt himself, who confirmed the fact, expressed his concern, &c., and assured him that the thing had not been settled 'till the Saturday before.

Being now sure that his Government had been actually disposed of without leaving him an option to go to it, which, indeed, the words of Lord Hillsborough's letter had sufficiently intimated, he sent his letter to the Duke of Grafton, in which, after modestly stating his services, he said that he had not expected a disgrace in return for them; that he considered his dismission as a disgrace; and that he could be restored only by a compliance with the terms he should prescribe, which were, to be created an English peer, with remainder to his brother, to have a grant of some mine and a tract of land in America, and if there should be any American peers created, that he should be first American peer. These high demands were, however, founded not on his services, but on the reparation due to him after such a disgrace, and were never hinted at 'till after Lord Botetourt had kissed hands. I do not exactly know the day the Duke sent to desire to speak with him; he received the message in the morning of a day on which the King was to come to town, and therefore wrote in answer, that, should he obey his Grace's commands, he might detain him from Court 'till it would be too late to lay his requests before His Majesty, which he desired might be done that day; and having nothing to add to the letter which he had already written to his Grace, he would not trouble him with waiting upon him.

The Duke, on his return from Court, acquainted Sir Jeffry that he could not mention his requests to the King 'till he had spoke to him, upon which he sent word that he would wait on his Grace in the morning; but in the morning the Duke called upon him, and endeavoured to dissuade him from insisting on his demands. Sir Jeffry, still keeping to the necessity of extraordinary distinctions to wipe away the disgrace, persisted; and upon the Duke's urging his arguments against them, he told him he was sorry to find his Grace so averse to laying his requests before His Majesty; that, however, they must be laid, and if his Grace did not choose to do it, he should find somebody else who would: upon which the Duke undertook it, and on his return from Court, wrote Sir Jeffry a note to tell him that the King was highly sensible of his services, and desirous to reward them, and would readily make him any grant of lands in America[1]; the mines he mentioned could not be granted, the Crown not having the power to grant them[2].

Sir Jeffry then wrote directly to Lord Barrington, to desire leave to resign his battalions in America and his regiment here; but the King's pleasure being signified to him, that His Majesty wished to hear his reasons from himself, he had an audience, and at coming out from it he told Lord Barrington, that His Majesty had been graciously pleased to accept of his resignation.

I believe you may depend upon all these particulars;

[1] "His Grace is wonderfully bountiful in the article of lands. I doubt not he would with all his heart give Sir Jeffry Amherst the fee simple of every acre from the Mississippi to California. But we shall be the less surprised at his generosity when we consider that every private soldier who served a certain time in America was entitled to two hundred acres, and that not one man, out of perhaps twenty thousand claimants, has yet settled upon his estate."—*Junius*, vol. iii. p. 123.

[2] "If reasons political and commercial forbid working the coal-mines in America, *that*, I allow, is an answer *ad hominem*. It may be a true one."—*Ibid.*, vol. iii. p. 122.

there are other little anecdotes attending the story, which concern only individuals, and which I will tell you when I see you, but cannot write.

Now was Sir Jeffry Amherst dismissed because he refused to go to America, or because his demands were extravagant, or because his Government was wanted for Lord Botetourt[1]?

Several letters arrived yesterday from America, dated 10th and 12th July. They contain accounts of the proceedings with respect to Lord Hillsborough's orders, which were, that the Assembly should be required by the Governor to annul their vote for the circular letter, and in case of non-compliance be dissolved. Several messages passed, of little consequence, concerning copies of these orders and of the letters from Governor Bernard, which gave occasion for them; they desired a recess to consult their constituents, which he refused, as being contrary to the spirit of his instructions to dissolve if they did not immediately comply. They therefore debated the point, and it was carried not to comply, by 92 to 17. They then drew up a representation of their reasons, in which they are very impertinent to Governor Bernard personally, assert that the circular letter contains nothing which is not in principle perfectly constitutional, and in expression perfectly decent; take it for granted, that a tax for the purpose of revenue only is an infringement of their rights, and complain of grievances. They were then proceeding to prepare a charge of mal-administration

---

[1] "The manner of filling the vacancy made by the removal of Sir Jeffry Amherst, sets in the broad glare of daylight the true reasons for making it; it was not done to reform a public abuse, but to accommodate a private job; it was not Virginia that wanted a Governor, but a court favourite that wanted the salary."—*Junius*, vol. iii. p. 103.

against Governor Bernard, from the very beginning of his Government, but he first prorogued and then dissolved them, declaring to them that he thought he was restrained by his instructions from calling another Assembly 'till he had special orders for that purpose from England. The reason he assigns to his friends for deviating so far from his instructions, as to prorogue before he dissolved, is, that he did it out of regard to the 17 who voted for complying, and to give them an opportunity of providing for their safety, as he thought they would be exposed if the people were exasperated by an immediate dissolution.

The same letters bring an account of a ship seized for having some unentered molasses on board; but a day or two after, about fifty armed men came on board, confined the officers, and carried off the molasses. The merchants in general were much alarmed at this; they said it was putting the Commissioners in the right, for as on the great riot of 10th June, the mob had pretended that their resentment was raised, not by the seizure, but by putting the ship seized under the protection of the *Romney*, this rescue justified that measure, and they, therefore, began to inquire after the persons concerned in this outrage, whereupon all the molasses were carried again on board.

There were, when the letters came away, the *Romney* of 50 guns, and four sloops of 12 and 14 guns in the harbour of Boston, and more expected. Reports of troops coming were circulated about the town, but not believed. The Commissioners of the Customs were still at the Castle, where they held their boards, but kept their office open in the town as usual.

General Gage had called in the outposts, which was

the only preparation for the motion of troops towards Boston. A letter from a lieutenant-colonel at Halifax, dated 12th July, says, that he had received orders to keep three regiments there, with some companies of artillery ready to embark, but mentions no orders actually to go; now, when Mr. Hollowell arrived with the news of the riot at Boston, on the 18th July, he was told that such orders had been sent so long ago for one regiment, the 14th, that they must have arrived at Boston a fortnight before he got to England. Candour obliges one to admit, that the ship which carried these orders might have a long passage, but it is very candid to suppose so long a one.

It is much to Sir Jeffry Amherst's honour that he retires on 800*l.* per annum in land, a house in town for which he gave 4000*l.*, and having furnished he expects to let for 400*l.* per annum, and 4000*l.* in money. His paternal estate was that 800*l.* per annum; he has received 10,000*l.* with his lady; he got nothing, therefore, by his command.

C. [THE AUTHOR OF JUNIUS] TO MR. GRENVILLE[1].

London. 3ᵈ. September. 1768.

SIR.—It may not be improper you should know that the publick is entirely mistaken with respect to the Author of some late publications in the Newspapers. Be assured that he is a man quite unknown & uncon-

---

[1] Endorsed in Mr. Grenville's hand, "Anonymous, Sept. 3, 1768." This was the second of the three letters addressed by the Author of Junius to Mr. Grenville.

nected[1]. He has attached himself to *your* cause and to *you* alone, upon motives, which, if he were of Consequence enough to give weight to his Judgment, would be thought as honourable to you, as they are truly satisfactory to himself. At a proper time he will solicit the honour of being known to you[2]: he has present important reasons for wishing to be concealed.

[1] It is evidently here the policy of Junius to induce Mr. Grenville to believe that the writer was a person of obscure condition, and unknown to fame; and such I know to be even now the opinion of those for whose information upon this subject, and for whose extensive knowledge and critical acumen, I have the greatest respect and admiration; but, after long reflection, I cannot arrive at the conclusion that Junius was otherwise than the exact reverse of that which in the present instance, and for his present purposes, he professed to be.

In ascribing the authorship of these famous papers to Lord Temple, I have sufficiently avowed my conviction that Junius was, as he has elsewhere described himself, far above all pecuniary views: that he was a man of rank and fortune to an extent that placed him above the suspicion of a common bribe: that he was a man of ardent, but disappointed ambition: and that, although in his assumed character, and as an anonymous writer, he may have had ample reasons for wishing to be concealed, and for choosing to be thought unknown and unconnected; to be retired, and live in the shade; to have only a speculative ambition; to have no motives of vanity but those which were confined to a very narrow circle; yet with all these pretended negatives, his writings prove him to have possessed such ample knowledge and experience, as could only be derived from mixing largely with the world; to have been conversant with the language of Courts and Cabinets, and intimately acquainted with the leading politicians of his time; to have known their private characters and habits, as well as their public capacity and conduct; to have had strong motives of personal pique and resentment, not only against the King, but against the principal men who were by turns the objects of his vituperation or his sarcasm: all these reasons form a combination of circumstances which render it, to my understanding at least, almost an impossibility that Junius could have been a man "entirely unknown and unconnected."

[2] More than three years later, in November, 1771, he said the same to Woodfall, and almost in the same words:—"Act honourably by me, and at a proper time you shall know me." But he never intended to make himself known, and therefore the *proper time* never did arrive

Some late papers, in which the cause of this country, and the defence of your Character and measures have been thought not ill maintained;—others, signed Lucius, and one or two upon the new Commission of trade, with a multitude of others, came from this hand[1]. They have been taken notice of by the Publick.

May I plead it as a merit with you, Sir, that no motives of vanity shall ever discover the author of this Letter. If an earnest wish to serve you gives me any claim, let me entreat you not to suffer a hint of this Communication to escape you to *any body*[2]. C.

MR. AUGUSTUS HERVEY TO MR. GRENVILLE.

Park Place, September 5, 1768.

DEAR SIR,—As you will see the death of my poor mother[3] in the papers, I dare swear you will be im-

---

either to Mr. Grenville or Woodfall. Even at the time he was writing the words I have quoted, to Woodfall, he had probably also written, or was just about to write, that passage in his Dedication in which he declares,—"*I am the sole depositary of my own secret, and it shall perish with me.*"

Upon occasions, when Junius makes a solemn asseveration, there is something in his mode of expression that carries conviction with it, and I confess myself, in this instance, to be fully impressed with the truth and sincerity of his assertion.

[1] *Junius*, vol. iii. p. 89, *et seq.*, eight Letters under the signature of LUCIUS, chiefly devoted to the case of Sir Jeffry Amherst's dismission; and *Junius*, vol. iii., p. 63, *et seq.*, in ridicule of the new Commission of Trade, under the signature of C.

[2] There is every reason to believe, that both this and his former injunction to secrecy, were most honourably kept by Mr. Grenville. The words printed in *Italics* were so marked by the author.

[3] Mary Lepel, Lady Hervey, once so celebrated for her beauty:—

" Youth's youngest daughter, sweet Lepel."

At a very early age she had been Maid of Honour to the Princess of

patient to know how it may have affected my situation, since your last so kindly expresses your feeling obliged by any communication of what concerns me.

I dined with Lady Hervey, Saturday, at Sunning Hill, where she had been complaining some days of a cold, which obliged her to come to town the Monday following late, and very much oppressed. She felt herself going some time before, as my brother tells me, in a letter she wrote him. She was blooded and blistered, and Mr. Hawkins and myself at last persuaded her to have a physician, when she consented, provided 't was James.

I never left her, though but very indifferent myself, 'till she expired at four o'clock Thursday afternoon; in the course of her illness she never mentioned any one of her children or acquaintance, nor ever spoke to any one but Mr. Hawkins and me, when we advised about the physician; only on Wednesday, she squeezed my hand, and said, *Poor dear Augustus*, and never spoke afterwards, even to her maid: she felt, thank God! no pain whatever. I sent an express for my brother, Wednesday, who came up Thursday night; and with me went Friday morning to the House, *he and I being reconciled* first entirely, and he has dined with me every day since.

My mother *has left her house, plate, furniture, &c.*,

Wales, afterwards Queen Caroline. She was married to John Lord Hervey in 1720. He died in 1743. Their three eldest sons, George, Augustus, and Frederick, became successively Earls of Bristol; the latter was also Bishop of Derry. Her youngest son, William, was a General in the Army. She had also four daughters, the eldest of whom was the grandmother of the present Marquess of Normanby. A volume of Lady Hervey's Letters, addressed to Mr. Morris, a clergyman who had been tutor to her sons, was published in 1821.

and all her jewels, to my brother Bristol and his son; then to me and mine; and then to brother William for ever, cutting out the Bishop. Her money in these and other funds equally between William and myself; to my sister Mary a little ring, and never mentioned my other sisters at all. There were two wills, the one of 1763 that left all to me, and this of last May in the manner I tell you. Some small legacies to Lady Bute, Lady Jane Macartney, Lord and Lady Holland, Mr. Walpole, &c., whom (between you and I) I believe have in some degree influenced that opinion which may have occasioned the unexpected change, but which my brother saw had no effect, nor has on me; he could not read the rest of the will for surprise, and I did without the least; I only know I have a satisfaction in having been the one here to continue that invariable filial affection and duty I had ever shown her, to her last sigh, and hope she is happy now; God knows how all these things are, or why anything is: I can only say, like Desdemona, "*'t is strange, 't is wondrous strange*," and in any sense of the word, our whole conditions and dispositions seem, as she also says, "*pitiful, 't is wondrous pitiful.*"

I thank God my health is surprisingly recovered, and if I have better success in *another point* of life[1], I shall not let the disappointment of affluence affect me whilst I have the conveniences as well as necessaries of life; I never loved money for the sake of money in my life, and as I never wanted it less than at present, the lucre of gain could never induce me to follow opinions that avarice might put other people upon undertaking; to be thought enough beloved by her to have distinguished

---

[1] Alluding again to his suit for a divorce from his wife, who afterwards married the Duke of Kingston.

me, and to be thought considerable enough by the friends I am unalterably attached to, to receive distinction through them whenever they could, is what I own I have had pride and vanity enough to desire, but for the rest, fortunæ cætera mando.

Forgive this scrawl, and be assured, I am, &c., &c.

A. HERVEY.

MR. KNOX TO MR. GRENVILLE.

London, September 8, 1768.

DEAR SIR,—The last page of *The State of the Nation* is now before the compositor, and I have the prospect of a speedy deliverance from the tedious business of correcting the press, at least for that performance. I am, however, unable to complete it for want of the account of the deficiencies of the malt-tax during the last Peace. You were so good as to put it into my hands once, but I somehow or other neglected to make extracts from it. I think the medium deficiency was between 40,000*l.* and 50,000*l.* If you can supply me with it, my work will be the less exceptionable, but if you have not the account at Wotton, I must beg your opinion what the medium may be, and I will venture to insert it, and when you come to town in the winter, if I find we have been mistaken, it may be corrected in the octavo edition.

I have very good authority for thinking the story Lord Hillsborough told me of the transaction with Sir Jeffry Amherst was not the whole of what passed between them. It seems that after the Generàl left him, he went to Court, and there they again met before Lord H. had gone in to the King, and the General called his

Lordship aside and told him, that lest he had not been sufficiently explicit before, he would now repeat to his Lordship, that he desired if he mentioned anything of what had passed to the King, he would acquaint His Majesty that he expected some mark of honour from him at the time his Government should be taken away. Lord H. then asked him what mark of honour? Sir Jeffry said he left that to his Lordship and the King. This part of the conversation Sir Jeffry complains was not reported to the King, and it is upon that ground Lord H. is to be attacked in the House of Lords.

Our last accounts from America contain only details of the spreading of the malignant disposition among the other colonies from Boston, but there is no appearance of acts of violence anywhere. The stocks continue to decline nevertheless, and yet money is so plenty, that all the bankers' shops are full; but people are so unsettled in their minds, and have so little confidence in the wisdom of Government, that they don't know what to do with their property.

Lord Shelburne is again on the hinge, and Lord Barrington is talked of for his successor, but Lord Hillsborough is now the active Minister, and is said to have acquired great favour in the Closet.

I am, &c., &c. WILL. KNOX.

THE PRINCESS AMELIA TO COUNTESS TEMPLE.

Gunnersbury, September 6, (1768.)

ALL the intelligence that I can pick up about the King of Denmark is, that he leaves London again next Saturday for another progress; where he intends going after he has been at Oxford, Portsmouth, Bath, &c., is more than I can inform you, dear Lady Temple, but I think nineteen too young to see all the beauties of Stowe; if he was acquainted with the masters of it, I should hope he would find great pleasure in it, though he is so young.

I suppose you have heard that the foreign Ministers have complained of me to the King, and that his answer to them was, he could not help it: the town thinks the wifes are the chiefs in this affair [1].

I am very sorry you felt so much inconvenience from giving me so much pleasure, in coming to town, and I desire you, my dear Lady Temple, to make my compliments to your Lord, and believe me most sincerely your friend,   AMELIA.

COMMODORE HOOD TO EARL TEMPLE.

September 14, 1768.

MY LORD,—I return you a thousand thanks for the very obliging letter you did me the honour to write me on the 11th of May, and my feelings of pleasure are not to be expressed, at your so kindly accepting the seeds and trees, as a small token of my gratitude and respect.

On the 11th instant, at midnight, I received a letter

---

[1] There is no explanation of the cause of complaint which the *wifes* [wives] of the Foreign Ministers are supposed to have had against the Princess Amelia. It would seem that Her Royal Highness used the same mode of spelling as that adopted by Lady Temple, as the amanuensis of Junius, in the word *difforce* [divorce]: there is the same substitution of the letter *f*, for *v*, and if it were a fashion among the middle aged ladies of the period, it is all in favour of my theory upon the subject of the *autograph* of Junius.

from General Gage dispatched by express, signifying that he had, in consequence of the King's orders, directed Colonel Dalrymple to embark from hence with His Majesty's 14th and 29th regiments of foot, as soon as possible, and proceed with them to Boston, and desiring my utmost aid in transporting them thither. I was well convinced, in my own mind, that such a measure must take place sooner or later, and had collected together the small squadron entrusted to my care, for that reason; and it is infinite satisfaction to me, that I have been able to embark the whole in His Majesty's ships, which I hope will be landed in Boston in a few days, as the ships are now preparing to sail.

It is also matter of most singular pleasure to me, that the countenance, protection, and support, which I have given to the Commissioners for managing His Majesty's revenue in America, has been so handsomely approved at home.

The moment application was made to me by the Commissioners for assistance from the King's ships, I ordered the *Romney*, of 50 guns, to Boston; a lucky event for those gentlemen, as she proved an asylum for them in time of need, and, from time to time, I continued to throw in additional force, 'till they said no more was wanted. Disquiet at home as well as in the colonies is very alarming; but I hope and trust that order will be restored both in England and America ere long. I am very confident the spirited measures now pursuing will soon effect it in America, as also I am that, had the two regiments now on shipboard been sent to Boston in the spring, it would have prevented any address, petition, or remonstrance, from the other colonies, and must have had very favourable consequences for Great Britain. I have the honour to be, with the greatest deference, and most perfect esteem, my Lord, your Lordship's most highly obliged and ever faithful humble servant,   SAM. HOOD.

EARL TEMPLE TO MR. GRENVILLE.

Stowe, Wednesday morning, past 1, September 14, 1768.

DEAR BROTHER,—An express brings me word that the King of Denmark will accept of an early dinner; this changes my whole plan, and distresses me most exceedingly. I must beg the loan of your cook, your plate, and will accept of a dozen or so of your hermitage. The plate I will send for, but beg you to dispatch the cook in your one-horse chaise as fast as possible. Your most truly affectionate,   TEMPLE.

MR. KNOX TO MR. GRENVILLE.

London, September 15, 1768.

DEAR SIR,—Mr. Whately brought me the letter you were so good to write to me the 11th instant, yesterday.

I have not seen Mr. Pownall's second edition, for indeed the confusion of his first made me expect little from it. I shall now, however, take it into my review of the American controversy, as he has given it importance by addressing it to you.

I now particularly trouble you with a letter, because of the confident assertions you will find in the newspapers of the arrival of an express, with letters from Governor Bernard to Lord Hillsborough. I had it yesterday from his Lordship that the whole was false, no express being arrived, nor any letter of a late date to Administration.

I was told this day in the city that there are accounts from Boston, so late as the 4th of August, by way of Halifax, which say all was quiet, and the duties regularly paid. I find the Administration are all, except Lord Shelburne, agreed upon coercive measures. The Chancellor wholly and absolutely of that opinion. Lord Shelburne must therefore withdraw, which he chooses to make involuntary, though from his conduct he certainly means not to continue. On Tuesday, when the Parliament was to be prorogued, there was a scarcity of Commissioners in town, and the Chancellor sent to Lord Shelburne to come; his answer was, that he neither could nor would come. These anecdotes I learned from Lord Hillsborough. I think he has no design of making a sort of use of me, which neither my nature, my principles, nor my obligations could ever suffer; but whenever I am *desired* to communicate anything to you, I shall always think myself at liberty to mention from whom I had it, whether I am desired to say so or no, and then you, Sir, will judge whether to give me any or what answer, for I beg you to believe me on every motive, and in every instance, very truly, &c., &c.

WILL. KNOX.

MR. GRENVILLE TO MR. WHATELY.

Wotton, September 18, 1768.

DEAR SIR,—Your two last letters of the 13th and 15th of this month were brought over to me to Stowe, to which place we went on Wednesday last, by my brother's desire, to be present at the reception of the King of Denmark, who came thither, according to his appointment, on Friday morning to breakfast. We afterwards walked out, and attended him all round the Gardens. Dinner was ordered, by his directions, to be ready a little before one, and, between three and four in the evening, he set out on his return to London, where he was to be that night. He was extremely gracious, and seemed to be very much pleased with the place, and with all the marks of attention and respect shown to him; and, indeed, my brother omitted nothing which could contribute to make his reception agreeable and convenient to him. There were nine other gentlemen who attended him, and dined with us; amongst others, his Minister, Count Bernstorff, and Count Holcke, who came with his Danish Majesty in the same chaise, and is said to be his favourite. I had a great deal of conversation both with the one and the other, and I thought they behaved extremely well. I understand that the King of Denmark leaves this country on the 7th of October, and then goes to France. I sincerely wish that he may have taken a favourable impression of the manner in which he has been received here in general, and am very sorry to see, by your letter, that any part of the behaviour towards him should be thought deficient, and liable to censure, especially if it is in the Government itself, where it must be of most importance.

I have received from America the same account with that which you sent to me, of the state of things there, which is the natural and certain consequence of what has been done here. I have nothing new to say to you upon that subject. You know my opinions, which every day confirms me in. I believe no plan of operations is yet formed, though I am assured that all the Administration except Lord Shelburne (who must soon withdraw) are agreed upon coercive measures; what those measures are to be, we shall see, I suppose, when the Parliament meets, and not till then. If the petition, which you mention to be preparing by the Americans here, against the dissolution of their Assemblies, goes on, that will probably be presented about the meeting of the Parliament, and will furnish matter of debate immediately, especially if it shall be true, as you have been informed, that the idea of the present Ministry is, that the Crown and not the Parliament is the proper authority to reduce the colonies to obedience. I am, &c., &c.

GEORGE GRENVILLE.

MR. KNOX TO MR. GRENVILLE.

London, September 27, 1768.

DEAR SIR,—I find there was no other difference in our accounts from Boston, than in the description of the vessel which brought them; for what you mentioned in respect to Mr. Williams, was told me by Lord Hillsborough before the express was said to have been arrived, and came by a merchant vessel from Halifax, by which your letters also came. There is, however, a ship this day from Boston, which brings accounts to the 24th of August, when all was quiet, that is, there was no riot.

The town had come to a resolution not to import any British goods in the course of next year, and had pressed the people of New York and Philadelphia to join them in it, but I don't find they have done so, any farther than to avoid importing any of those articles on which the late duties have been laid. I looked over all the Boston newspapers, and did not find one rash or violent expression, and the entries, inwards and outwards, at the Custom House are as many as usual. There are advertisements, also, for the sale of English goods and Madeira wines, and notices for the meeting of the county courts, and such sort of things as are commonly transacted in times of tranquillity.

The rendezvous of the troops, I learn, is at Halifax, where there were three regiments collected, and the detachments from the southern colonies, which had arrived at New York, were ordered from thence to Halifax; but whether they are to proceed directly to Boston, or to wait the arrival of the two regiments from Ireland, I do not know. I should think the latter, from an application having been made to Sir William Draper, to go out with them to command the whole, but it seems that purpose was afterwards changed with regard to him.

It is said a plan of accommodation has been proposed by Lord Chatham, which will render all military proceedings unnecessary, and on that account it was not thought expedient to send Sir William Draper with the troops. My paper would have been ready for this post, but for an addition which I made, on account of the papers published in the administration of the colonies. I think I have discovered in them pretty strong evidence of the right of Parliament to tax those who don't send Members to Parliament, or I would not defer so material a proof until I should make up my American paper.

I have made some other additions at the conclusion,

and when the whole is executed, I shall beg your observations upon it before it comes abroad, lest I may have committed some error, or advanced something which is not founded. Stocks continue to decline, and all mankind seem disheartened and uneasy.

War is apprehended from every quarter, and nothing less than preparation for it is found in this country. One of the Boston toasts, is an able and permanent Administration to Great Britain, in which I most heartily join them, but much do I fear we shall both be disappointed in almost the only thing we mutually desire. I am, &c., &c. WILL. KNOX.

MR. KNOX TO MR. GRENVILLE.

London, October 4, 1768.

DEAR SIR,—By this night's post I have dispatched to you the compleat *State of the Nation*, at least as compleat a one as I could frame, aided by the many materials you were so good to furnish me with.

The whole impression is struck off; but yet I shall suffer none other to go abroad, until I am favoured with your opinion whether there be anything materially amiss. I do not look for your approbation of the work, with all its imperfections on its head, nor would I wish to engage your countenance to it, any further than it consists with your own purposes; but I wish to have your opinion both of the performance and the matter, in so far as it may affect the public or myself, should I come to be known for the author.

Almon has general orders from a great number of Members of Parliament to send them whatever comes out in the recess, and he intends taking the opportunity of the intervening fortnight, between the meetings at Newmarket, to convey this pamphlet to them. He thinks of sending one elegantly done up to the King, as he has done with some other such matters. He is an excellent fellow at circulating a work, and understands all the mystery of raising its character, and exciting purchasers.

I thought it best to keep the American controversy for a separate work, and I have it in such forwardness, that, if I get the supply I am promised from the Board of Trade, I shall have it ready for the press as soon as the Parliament meets. I follow Mr. Locke's method non passibus æquis, and first examine all the American pretences, and then give a political history of the colonies, and from thence deduce their real connection with the mother country. I am, &c., &c.

WILL. KNOX.

MR. WHATELY TO MR. GRENVILLE.

October 11, 1768.

DEAR SIR,—I agree with you entirely in believing that the Ministry have no plan settled for America. Lord Hillsborough is greatly elated, I hear, at Philadelphia and Rhode Island having refused to join with Boston in the agreement not to import goods from England; it was natural they should refuse, because now they will supply Boston: New York therefore has, I understand, also refused; but we are in a miserable plight when we rejoice only that things are not worse, and if we triumph in such an advantage, we shall be content in the end with very slight advantages. It was thought a symptom of the ruin of the Spartan State, that the people exulted in the retreat of the enemy from their gates; they before had not an idea that an enemy could set foot on the most distant part of their territories; we are humbled indeed if we are pleased to hear that some of the Americans will condescend to trade with us; the question of sovereignty is not at all decided by it; on that point Philadelphia, Rhode Island, and New York still agree with Boston; but before their dissent was known, the agreement had very little effect in the city. Lord North tells me there will be no petition from the merchants, and at the same time assures me that no pains has been taken by Ministry to prevent one; from whence his inference was, that pains had been taken by the former Ministry to procure the petitions which led to the repeal of the Stamp Act.

You see in the papers that Mr. Ingersol and Mr. Johnson are appointed Judges of the Vice Admiralty Courts, with salaries each of 600*l.*: two more proper men could certainly not have been chosen; but Lord North, whom I saw on Sunday at the King of Denmark's Levée, told me that, those offices being filled, he feared the other meritorious sufferers must wait some time for opportunities to provide for them; I said there were other means of gratifying them; his answer was, that pensions might be assigned them on the quit rents; my inference from which hint was that the American revenues must have produced miserably if no salaries to civil offices can be laid upon them, for hitherto they are only charged with the expenses of their own establishment and the poor pittance to Governor Hutchinson, and the Ministry do not consider them as able to bear more. I thought, too, that in the present state of the

Civil List, the Ministers might as well let the quit rents alone: however, I took no notice of any of these considerations, but told his Lordship I did not mean pensions; that many of the friends to Government in America would be satisfied if their sons were provided for as collectors and controllers of the customs; he caught the idea eagerly, and desired me, if I knew any such, that I would mention them; too little, he said, had been done, and that had been shamefully delayed so long, he should be glad of the means to do more, and would be much obliged to me, as I was better informed than others upon the subject, if I would from time to time let him know of any of the meritorious sufferers who could thus be marked with attention. I answered that, as his Lordship and I meant the same thing, I should readily at any time, on a public account, give him the information he desired, and I believe that on inquiry I shall find several very deserving of the favours of the Crown, to whom such settlements will be very acceptable; it will encourage them, and check the enemies of Government, to see that in every branch promotion depends on attachment to the cause of Great Britain. I heard when I was in town that Lord Egmont has declared he cannot act in a Ministry of which there are not three of a mind, and Lord Rochford now is talked of to succeed Lord Shelburne, but I do not see that Lord Shelburne is yet likely to be out: who is to turn him out? nobody seems to have any power; and the others, though they do not differ with one another as he does with all, yet they have no communication together, and there is no union between them. Lord Shelburne, it is said, is the only one who is against expelling Mr. Wilkes on the ground of blasphemy; suppose he is; they have been long used to have a Solicitor-General withdrawing himself from this Crown cause, and that I think is the most material circumstance which can attend Lord Shelburne's difference of opinion.

But we are very much out of the fashion, Sir, to be thinking of politics; the King of Denmark is the only topic of conversation: Wilkes himself is forgotten even by the populace. I saw His Majesty, for the first time, at the review on Saturday; Mons. de Diede, seeing me in the company, called me out to tell me that the King would see company the next day at St. James's; Mons. de Bernsdorff joined in telling me the time and manner of it. I thought myself much honoured by the civility, and to show my sense of it to Mons. de Diede, went up on purpose to attend his Danish Majesty's Levée. He went through the ceremony with great decorum, bowed separately to every person as they were introduced to him, spoke to all whom he knew, and something personal to each; and he had an opportunity of showing one act of graciousness; the Levée being over sooner than was expected, many were too late; the King was retired; but on hearing that several whom he had not seen were in the room, he came out again and went round to them all. The attendants speak with great pleasure on the reception he has met with in England; M. de Bernsdorff particularly assured me that the King would be happy to know that he was as agreeable to the nation, as their behaviour was satisfactory to him. You must have heard all the particulars of the Duke of Northumberland's entertainment: perhaps you may not have heard George Selwyn's bon mot; the open court at Sion, you know, was turned into a circle and finely illuminated; Lord Huntingdon, on entering it, cried out, that he had never seen that apartment before. If your Lordship, says George Selwyn, will look up, perhaps you may recollect the ceiling.

While I am writing I receive a letter which tells me that the *Pocock* East Indiaman, just arrived, brings advice, that we have, contrary to our usual custom, purchased a peace from the Country Powers on the Coast of Coromandel, instead of making them reimburse the expenses of the war, which is thought a dangerous precedent.

COMMODORE HOOD TO MR. GRENVILLE.

Halifax, October 15, 1768.

Sir,—By a private letter of the 5th of August, I have received intimation that my command is extended a little to the southward so as to take in Lord Botetourt's government. This I look upon as a handsome mark of approbation of my past conduct, as well as of confidence that I have inclination to do my duty in future with becoming spirit and firmness; as such I shall receive it with great pleasure, though I think it would have been for the King's service had the limit ended, as in the last station, at Cape Florida, because all the ships thus far, come here to clean and refit; and as, in the present posture of affairs in America, it will of course happen that I shall be under the necessity, for the public good, to employ the ships to the southward of Virginia, upon services not appertaining to their stations, I must do it under my present commission at the risk of its being approved or not, which is by no means an agreeable situation to be in; and if I should see occasion for it, I should in all probability be very soon able to fill their stations by other ships, as they may chance to come to me, supposing the whole to be under my command. However, I shall continue to do what appears most eligible for His Majesty's service, and abide the consequences without fear; an officer should be a stranger to that idea, in every instance, to do his duty properly, and he will ever be so, as long as he is conscious of acting with integrity and to the best of his judgment.

I laid hold of the southward ships as well as all those under my command for transporting the troops, by which I saved to Government near 3000*l*., and was able to send the whole with great expedition, for on the twenty-seventh day from the date of General Gage's order for the troops at New York, they were all on shore at Boston; you must therefore be sensible, Sir, there was no delay in any respect.

Affairs in America by no means wear a pleasant complexion, but I hope and fully trust that peace and good order will be restored in no long time.

God be praised! the troops are safe landed, and very critically too, as you will see by an extract of a letter sent to me, as well as by a short diary of Captain Corner's, from his sending away the *Senegal* with the requisition for troops 'till their arrival, by which you have the best accounts I can give how matters really are.

" I embrace the opportunity of the *Magdalen* to return you my most sincere thanks, and to congratulate you on the very important service you have been so instrumental in rendering to the public.

" On the intention of a force being introduced into this province being made public, a convention was formed, as I am told, in direct opposition to law: those that composed it, seemed to warrant the measure, and you will judge of their tempers by their publications. Agreements of mutual defence were entered into, as were also, it is strongly reported, some secret articles of an uncommon nature.

"At this period we arrived: the convention were planet-stricken, and this very favourable occasion I entreated the Governor to improve. It is beyond the power of my pen to paint anything so abject; far from being elated that the hands of Government were rendered so respectable, he deplored the arrival of letters that made his setting out improper, and with earnest looks he followed a ship that he had hired for his conveyance, and in which he declared his fixed intention of going the moment the troops arrived. His actions were entirely of a piece with his words, for, on a requisition for quarters, he declared himself without power or authority in his province. The Council assembled, and they declared they would find none. An express arriving from General Gage, gave me no room to hesitate; his information of the dangerous tendency of the people's intentions rendered an immediate landing necessary. All their bravadoes ended as may be imagined; the Governor prudentially retired to the country, and left me to take the whole on myself. I encamped the 29th Regiment immediately, the 14th remained without cover: by tolerable management I got possession of Faneuil Hall, the School of Liberty, from the Sons thereof, without force, and thereby secured all their arms; and I am much in fashion, visited by Otis, Hancock, Rowe, &c., who cry peccavi, and offer exertions for the public service, in hopes by this means to ruin the Governor, by exposing his want of spirit and zeal for the public advantage. This I have endeavoured, not without success, to turn to the use and advantage of the cause. We have had council after council, and nothing done; the service of the Crown is not much attended to: I spoke my sentiments, full as plain as pleasant.

"What turn matters will take I know not, but thus far, my good Sir, you may rest satisfied, that the arrival of the squadron was the most seasonable thing ever known, and that I am in possession of the town, and therefore nothing can be apprehended; had we not arrived so critically, the worst that could be apprehended must have happened. I have entreated Captain Smith, to continue here in force 'till matters are a little settled. I want words to express our ideas of the very great friendship we received from all the gentlemen of the squadron, I shall not therefore attempt it."

Just as the *Magdalen* was about to sail the next day, the Colonel added the following note:—

"We are, my dear Sir, in a fair way to do very well, prejudices are giving way fast, they neither think us cannibals nor street robbers. In justice to Captain Smith, I must acknowledge his constant readiness in affording us every possible assistance, as have every officer in the squadron. I entreat you will make us as powerful as possible during the winter, much depends upon it."

As the *Romney* is not come to me agreeable to my expectations, I propose going to Boston in the *Viper* sloop, as soon as she is ready for sea. I was under the necessity of careening her, as she was twice ashore, but has received no damage. I inclined much to have gone with the troops, but all the ships were so crowded, there was not room for me without adding to the inconvenience of all the officers.

I propose to remain at Boston during the winter, if I think the service of His Majesty can thereby be in the least promoted.

By what I have related you will pretty plainly see how matters stand, and how little is to be expected from Governor Bernard. I have long and often lamented his timid conduct, and yet would not willingly bring on him more contempt than he must of course feel, when the duplicity of his behaviour is brought to light; but I could not refrain giving you for your particular information my opinion of things in general. A governor of spirit and dignity, and who preferred the honour of his King, and the interest of his country, to his own *little* views, would have prevented almost the whole that has happened; and had Mr. Bernard taken courage to ask General Gage for the very troops now in Boston nine months ago, and which I have authority for believing openings were given him to do by the General, things would now have worn a very different complexion, and the Commissioners never have been forced to leave the town, but have been in a condition to carry on their business in peace and quietness.

They were, as I am told, never properly supported by the Governor, and in no one instance did he ever have recourse to the civil magistrates for putting a stop to any riot or unlawful meeting; and what is yet more extraordinary, he suffered a declaration to be extorted from him, that he had not applied for troops, nor would not do it, which I am afraid led the lower class of people to greater lengths than they would otherways have gone, as well as the demagogues also.

Mr. Bernard is without doubt a sensible man, but he has a vast deal of low cunning, which he has played off upon all degrees of people, to his own disgrace. His doubles and turnings have been so many, that he has altogether lost his road, and brought himself into great contempt. I cannot help mentioning one circumstance which has come to my knowledge as an officer. He frequently lamented to Captain Corner (whom I sent to Boston early in May for the support of the King's revenue) the distressed condition of Castle William, and was afraid of its being attacked, [of] which Captain Corner (knowing his man) took no notice. At last he spoke out, and said if he did not send his marines to the Castle the populace would certainly take it. Captain Corner replied that he would not only send his marines, but every man in the *Romney* in support of the Castle, if his Excellency would request it of him in a proper manner in writing; his orders from Commodore Hood enjoined him to it in the most express terms; to which Mr. Bernard answered, I cannot do that, Captain Corner, but I will tell you what you must do, you must write me a letter that the marines on board His Majesty's ship under your command stand in need of being refreshed, and desire my permission for their being landed on Castle William Island, which I will grant; Captain Corner begged to be excused, and withdrew. In a few days after he wrote Captain Corner a proper letter, and ante-dated it. I think this proves the man very clearly.

I had a letter from him, dated the 27th of August, desiring I would grant him a ship to carry him to England, having the King's leave to return. I was very sorry it was not in my power to comply with his request, for most certainly the sooner he is out of America the better.

I hope the command of the troops will continue in

Colonel Dalrymple after the arrival of the two regiments from Ireland, as he is a very excellent officer, and quite the gentleman, knows the world, and has a good address, with all the fire, judgment, coolness, integrity, and firmness that a man can possess. I account myself very fortunate in having such a man to act with, on so critical and delicate a service.

I fear I have trespassed on your patience and goodness by so long a detail, and shall only add my most unfeigned wishes for your health, &c. I have the honour to be, &c. SAM. HOOD.

ANONYMOUS, [THE AUTHOR OF JUNIUS,] TO MR. GRENVILLE[1].

London. 20th October, 1768.

SIR.—I beg leave to offer you a letter, reprinted in the inclosed paper[2] under the signature of Atticus, as

[1] Endorsed in Mr. Grenville's hand, "Anonymous, Oct. 20, 1768."

[2] The enclosure referred to is the letter signed Atticus of the 19th October (*Junius*, vol. iii. p. 165). The Author with scrupulous accuracy calls it *reprinted*, because it had originally appeared in the *Public Advertiser* of the previous day, and that which he has sent is cut from the *Gazetteer* of October 20th. This paper was not preserved by Mr. Grenville with the letter which it accompanied, but he appears to have given it to Mrs. Grenville to paste down in a small quarto book, which she kept for the reception of political letters cut from the newspapers[a]. In this collection I found it, and its identity is sufficiently established by some corrections in the handwriting of the author; thus the sentence, "He is now what they call a K——s man," has the intermediate letters " ing," placed over the blank space. The following sentence is corrected, and an important alteration made: the printer has given it thus:—"The other Ministers were *foreseeing* in their usual course,

[a] This collection of cuttings marks, in some degree, the estimation in which these papers were held by Mr. Grenville, and it may be observed that most of them are either by the Author of Junius, or immediately connected with subjects which he touched upon. Some of them are dated in Mrs. Grenville's handwriting. The collection was not continued after her death in December, 1769.

finished with more care than I have usually time to give to these productions[1]. The town is curious to know

without *proceeding* or regarding consequences; but this nobleman seems to have marked out, by a determined choice, the means to precipitate our destruction."

The Author has transposed the two words in Italics: he has added the word "*been*," and taken away the words "*the means*," by which it will be perceived that the sentence is completely changed, and the significance of it much improved. As corrected it would run thus:—

"The other Ministers were proceeding in their usual course, without foreseeing or regarding consequences: but this nobleman seems to have been marked out, by a determined choice, to precipitate our destruction."

The correction of a single letter in another word, *some* for *same*, is merely mentioned to show the care with which the Author had read the paper, and his wish that it should be presented to Mr. Grenville with the sense perfect.

[1] It has been fancifully supposed that the Author assumed the signature of Atticus from his own opinion of the purity of his style. Only four letters bearing this signature, and written between August 19th and November 14th, in the year 1768, have been hitherto attributed to the Author of Junius, but a great number of other letters so signed are to be found in the newspapers both before and subsequent to that year. The selection of these four letters was originally made by Almon for the *Political Register*, before the end of the year in which they were written and printed in the *Public Advertiser*. They were afterwards included in a separate publication by Almon in 1769, entitled, *A Collection of the Letters of Atticus, Lucius, Junius, and others*. Whether they were so selected by Almon from his own knowledge, or judgment from internal evidence that those of Atticus, Lucius, and Junius were by the same writer, is a question not in my power to determine, but I would hazard a conjecture that the selection was made by the indirect suggestion of the Author himself, whose vanity, though confined, as he said, "within a narrow circle," might still very naturally be extended to the desire of disseminating his writings as widely as possible. He was, no doubt, personally acquainted with Almon, but certainly not known to him as the Author of Junius. That the latter did also write under the signatures of Atticus and Lucius, is now placed beyond a doubt by his own admission in the letters addressed to Mr. Grenville, and now first printed in these volumes. It would lead me, I fear, far beyond the scope of my present purpose to enter into the inquiry, whether any or all the letters signed Atticus and Lucius which may be found in the newspapers for several

the author. Every body guesses, some are quite certain, and all are mistaken. Some, who bear your character, give it to the Rockinghams; (a policy I do not understand;) and Mr. Bourke[1] denies it, as he would a fact, which he wished to have believed.

It may be proper to assure you that no man living knows or even suspects the author. I have no connection with any party[2], except a voluntary attachment to *your* cause and Person. It began with amusement, grew into habit, was confirmed by a closer attention to your Principles & Conduct, & is now heated into Passion. The *Grand Council*[3] was mine, & I may say, with truth, almost everything that, for two years past, has attracted the attention of the publick. I am conscious these papers have been very unequal; but you will be candid enough to make allowances for a man, who writes absolutely without materials or instruction. For want of hints of this kind, I fear I frequently mistake your views, as well as the true point, whereon you would choose to rest the questions, in which your name is concerned. But this is an inconvenience

years, were also written by the Author of Junius. The question is curious and interesting, but it is one which rather belongs to a future editor of the collected writings of Junius. It has been mooted with some very judicious and pertinent remarks both in the *Athenæum* and in the *Notes and Queries,* and it is an inquiry which deserves very particular attention.

[1] Whately writes to Mr. Grenville a week after this date,—"Atticus is said to be Mr. Burke, Mr. Mauduit, or Lord George Sackville." The name of Edmund Burke was frequently written Bourke in the private correspondence at this time, as well as in the newspapers. I have found it so written occasionally by Mr. Grenville, by Whately, by Horace Walpole, and in a letter from Beckford to Lord Chatham he is called O'Bourke.

[2] In a debate on the Regency Bill in 1765, Lord Temple said, "*He was himself of no party, nor connected with any party.*"

[3] See *ante,* page 171, *note.*

without a remedy. I must continue to argue for you, as I would for myself in the same circumstances, as far as I understand yours. Untill you are Minister, I must not permit myself to think of the honour of being known to you. When that happens, you will not find me a needy or a troublesome dependant. In the mean time, I must console myself with reflecting that, by resisting every temptation of vanity, & even the great desire I have of being honoured with your notice, I give you some assurance, that you may depend upon my firmness and fidelity hereafter[1].

MR. CHARLES LLOYD TO MR. GRENVILLE.

Thursday, October 20, 1768.

DEAR SIR,—Lord Shelburne, after an hour's audience of the King, resigned the seals yesterday. Lord Northington was in the Closet an hour and a quarter. Lord Camden was with the Duke of Grafton yesterday, and has given orders, as his brother tells me, to suspend the making his liveries. The report to-day, at Betty's[2], is,

[1] This letter is written upon a quarto sheet of paper, bearing in the water-mark the maker's name, *J. Portal*. It corresponds so precisely in this respect, as well as in size, quality, and gilt edges, that it may have formed part of the same quire as the paper upon which a letter from Lord Temple to Mr. Grenville was written just one week before, dated Pall Mall, October 13. I have not found any other letters from Lord Temple upon similar paper, but it was used by Junius for his letter to Lord Chatham in January, 1772. The letter from Junius to Lord Chatham, dated in January, 1768, is written upon a half sheet of rough-edged foolscap paper, folded into quarto, and is exactly similar to that used for the paper on the Auction duty, sent to Mr. Grenville in February, 1768.

[2] A noted fruit shop in St. James's Street, and a well-known rendezvous for the political gossips of the day. There is a portrait of Betty the fruit girl, by Gillray.

that Lord Weymouth is to be Secretary for the Southern Department. I should have known all the manœuvres from one or two dejected people who were apprehensive of soon being forced to turn patriots, but we were interrupted by the Duke of Cumberland. I am, &c.,

C. LLOYD.

Wilkes wrote the paper describing the characters of the Administration, which I sent you yesterday[1].

MR. AUGUSTUS HERVEY TO MR. GRENVILLE.

Park Place, October 21, 1768.

DEAR SIR,—I came to town late last night from my brother's, and found all the *Levée* to-day in its usual confusion, and most people much surprised at Lord Chatham's resignation; but not so at Lord Shelburne's, which is supplied by Lord Rochford, and 't is said the *Duke of Marlborough* will have the Privy Seal, so there is an end of those *negative declarations*.

I hear the Chancellor continues, but that Sir Edward Hawke must soon give way to the Earl of Sandwich. That is the talk at St. James's; and that Barré is to be turned out of the Vice-Treasurership, so that it will be

[1] It appeared in the *Public Advertiser* on the 18th instant, signed *A Dreamer of Dreams*, and contains an imaginary account of the Masquerade given by the King of Denmark at the Opera House on the 10th instant. The Duke of Grafton is described as *Janus:* Lord Chatham as *King Lear:* Lord Shelburne as *a Jesuit:* Lord Weymouth, *Landlord of the Bedford Arms:* Lord Hillsborough, *a wild Irishman:* Lord Gower, *a French Harlequin:* Lord Barrington, *a bright active little being in the skin of a cat, with all the cat's dexterity, eternally leaping on, and clinging to, some of the great personages.* The writer adds, that " Mr. Wilkes's daughter was there in the character of *Liberty*, and her appearance was truly amiable, but she retired early, being but little countenanced by the nobility."

a fine mixture at last. There is a meeting to-night to think of the Speech.

Lord Harcourt and Lord Holdernesse are competitors for the embassy to France, but 't is thought the first will have it. Poor Colonel Brudenell died last night[1]. There seemed more candidates for his Regiment than for his place at Court to-day. Would you believe the pious, virtuous, and sober Lord Northington was again sent for to play the harlequin in all this farce, and was above an hour and a half in the Closet to-day before any one else? What a melancholy scene is all this for this poor country! I am told you will shortly see a letter to a *Great Duke*[2] on the present situation he has brought

---

[1] Colonel Robert Brudenell, brother to the Duke of Montague, Vice-Chamberlain to the Queen, Colonel of the 4th Regiment of Foot, and Lieutenant-Governor of Windsor Castle.

[2] Mr. Hervey here, I think, alludes to a letter of which there can be no reasonable doubt, from general similarity of style, as well as from particular expressions and opinions, that he was himself the Author. It appeared on the 1st of December following in the *Political Register*, and it is addressed to the Duke of Grafton under the title of *the Man who thinks himself Minister*: signed—*To my King and Country a* TRUE FRIEND. The following is an extract:—

"I will acknowledge, and in some degree allow, that there might be too great a stoicism or contempt for *American popularity* in that very able *Minister* who (like a true *Englishman*, and an honest one too) would have made them contribute at least towards their own expenses, when he proposed that *very Stamp Act* which the King and Parliament approved: and at the same time I believe his reason for not more industriously courting the vulgar applause of the colonists, at the expense of this country, was the consciousness of his being right in not doing so. It were to be wished he had stood as well in the opinion of that crowd, as in that of all impartial people, and all real well-wishers to this country; nay, I wish with all my soul, *he* and his friends had stooped a little, *ad captandum vulgi*, to take in those fluttering hearts which are to be caught by anything baited with the name of *Liberty*. But perhaps the times would not admit of it, nor the situation of things; and perhaps, too, there was no way to avert the impending fate of that despicable, humbling figure we have made, ever

this country into; but, alas! what signifies any one's painting what is so sensibly felt by every one? How can a Grafton supply the seat of a Walpole or a Grenville? Indeed, my dear Sir, you are universally prayed for by all sets now, except a few dependent hirelings that surround the gilded Pagod. God knows whether one can wish you at such a time in such a crazy sinking vessel, though it can only be such a pilot that can conduct us into safety. I am, &c., &c. A. HERVEY.

MR. CADWALLADER COLDEN [1] TO MR. GRENVILLE.

New York, October 22, 1768.

SIR,—I cannot express the pleasure I received by the honour you have done me in yours of the 28th of July. You may assure yourself, Sir, that there is not one single fact, in the Vindication which I published of my conduct, but what may be proved by the proceedings of the Council and Assembly, copies of which are continuedly sent to the Plantation Board, or were notoriously known at the time. No man in this place has, at any time, attempted to expose any of it as false, which

since that *Minister* was displaced. It has been as a scourge from Heaven for our pride and luxury, and the terrible situation of our affairs at present shews it—the confusion we are in at home, the contempt we are in everywhere abroad, proves it. But alas! nothing can make it more evident than your Lordship being placed in that chair where a *Walpole* and a *Grenville* had been seated."

[1] Cadwallader Colden was a Scotch Physician. He was born in 1688, and, after finishing his studies in Edinburgh, he went to Pennsylvania. He settled at New York, and was made Lieut.-Governor, and subsequently Governor, of that Province. He was the author of a *History of the Five Indian Nations,* and of several medical and scientific works. Botany was his favourite study, and on that subject he corresponded with Linnæus. He died at the age of 88, in 1776.

no doubt some would if they could. I am well assured that no one fact was pointed out to the grand jury, who found it a false libel, nor was any kind of proof attempted to be given, other than of the person who printed it at New York. You may judge, Sir, by what principle our judges are directed. If the Vindication had given any just reason of complaint, as it related to my administration of Government, it ought to have been made to the King, where a proper redress could be obtained, but they chose to make themselves both accusers and judges.

I must own, Sir, that when I wrote to you in January last, I was alarmed, by the attempt to join the Council and Assembly with the Courts of Justice against me, not knowing to what lengths their malice might lead them; but I was soon afterwards freed from that uneasiness, by the general abhorrence, publicly expressed, of the method taken to calumniate an innocent person. Since which time all discourse on the subject, I am told, is avoided by those people who were the authors and promoters of this iniquitous proceeding.

It is very improper to give the characters of men in public authority when it is not accompanied with the proper proofs. I wish you knew the general sentiments of the people, in respect to the integrity and ability of our judges: perhaps you may learn it from some who cannot be suspected of partiality.

There is one thing of which I think it now proper to inform you, and which I have not hitherto done. Major James, of the Artillery regiment, in 1765, carried into the Fort without my knowledge, while I was in the country, several howitzers with their shells, and other artillery ammunition and stores. This gave the first uneasiness to the people, and some imprudent discourse he used at that time raised their resentment more against him than any man in the Province, so far that he did not think it safe to continue in it. He desired leave of the General to go to England, and carried the General's and my dispatches on that occasion.

It may be asked, how came it that the Assembly of this Province should recompense Major James to the utmost of his demands, when, at the same time, they refused to make any recompense to me, or to pay that part of the salary which was due to me? You may judge, Sir, by what follows. Major James, after his return to this place, told me, in private conversation between ourselves, that he had 400 guineas given him in England; that he had a paper of directions how to answer in his examination before the House of Commons; and I suppose the agent of the Assembly had directions to advise the Assembly. These things I cannot prove otherwise than as I tell you; but you may be able to judge of the truth of them.

When I applied to the Assembly, in consequence of the Address of the House of Commons, which you mention, for reimbursement of the losses which I had sustained, and for payment of the salary due to me, they at first seemed to avoid it, by passing over my application without notice, which induced me to write to the Speaker, and then their answer was, that I had brought it upon myself. To this day I remain without one farthing of the reimbursement, or of the salary due to me.

In my letters to the Secretary of State, I gave my opinion, that the faction, in opposition to the authority of Parliament, placed their hopes in intimidating the Ministry by bold assertions, without the least regard to truth, and by intimidating every officer of the Crown from their duty; but that if the Parliament resolved to support the authority of Great Britain over the colonies, the opposition would soon subside. Perhaps I gave my opinion too freely, and thereby gave offence. Now it will appear whether I judged rightly, when the Ministry are resolved to support that authority. Indeed it never entered my imagination that the Stamp Act would be repealed. The success, since that repeal, which has attended the measures taken in the colonies, and the numerous papers continuedly published, in vindication of those measures in opposition to the authority of Parliament, may make it more difficult to convince men of their errors than it would have been by enforcing the Stamp Act.

I informed the Secretary of State likewise of the matters which were the subject of my letters to you; and after I knew that my Lord Hillsborough was appointed Secretary for the Colonies, I had more confidence in him, having corresponded with him while he presided at the Plantation Board. I particularly informed him of several transactions in this Province, which may be needless to repeat to you; and of some Acts to which the Governor had given his assent, in direct breach of his instructions, and which tended greatly to increase the power of the Assembly, in prejudice to the constitutional prerogative of the Crown. I am told that my Lord Hillsborough mentioned me in private discourse very favourably, but as to anything farther I remain entirely ignorant.

The sentiments with regard to the Colonies, which you have done me the honour to communicate to me, I am persuaded will, in the end, be adopted by every honest man, and give me confidence of your endeavours, in whatever situation you be, that justice be done me. I think good policy likewise requires it, that His Majesty's faithful servants may not hereafter be deterred from their duty. I wrote to my Lord Hillsborough, that my only wish with respect to myself is, that I may close my days in ease with reputation, and that my children may not suffer, by my performing my duty in a long series of years, of which I can give many instances, but that they may receive some benefit thereby. May I beg the honour of a line, when you can inform me of what I may expect? I am, with the highest respect and sincere gratitude, &c., &c.

CADWALLADER COLDEN.

MR. WHATELY TO MR. GRENVILLE.

October 27, 1768.

DEAR SIR,—I have only time to tell you that a town meeting at Boston having first required of the Governor to call an Assembly, on his refusal they have chosen four representatives to meet in convention with such deputies as shall be sent by the other towns, and have resolved that the King has no right to send troops thither without the consent of the Assembly; that Great Britain has broken the original compact, and that therefore the King's officers have no longer any authority there: they, besides, have recommended to the inhabitants to provide themselves with arms, and be ready to array that day se'nnight, I suppose with a design to seize the castle before the troops arrive; which is another good effect of our Ministerial delays. The news has sunk the stocks three and a quarter per cent. Everybody one meets now says they wish the Stamp Act had never been repealed.

I do not find it absolutely, though I think it is generally, agreed, that Lord Chatham, in his letter of resignation, mentioned Corsica, the family compact, and Sir Jeffry Amherst[1], but the terms of the letter were so respectful, that the Duke of Grafton has been to Hayes to persuade him to continue; all, however, in vain. I do not find that his successor is at all settled. Lord Camden, I believe, will continue; it is not yet true that Barré has resigned, but I take it for granted that he will. Lord Shelburne, I am told, has, some time since, made advances to the Rockinghams, which were but coolly received. If I was to believe common report, I should suppose you were to be sent for immediately, but I know no more than common report. From the same authority, I hear that the meeting of the Parliament is to be postponed, which I believe not at all.

Lord Shelburne's resignation was cavalier: he did not hint his design to any of the Ministers; he only desired Lord Weymouth would let him go in alone, as he had something particular to say to the King, and, at coming out, told Lord Northington that he might, if he pleased, tell the Ministers a piece of news, for that he had just resigned the Seals.

The author of the *State of the Nation*[2] is said to

---

[1] Lord Chatham mentioned only the removal of Lord Shelburne and Sir Jeffry Amherst.—See *Chatham Correspondence*, vol. iii. p. 338.

[2] The reader will have already observed that Mr. Knox was the author of this Tract, but it was replied to by Burke in one of his famous compositions, entitled *Observations, &c.*, upon the supposition that it was written by Mr. Grenville.

be yourself, your humble servant, Mr. Knox, or Mr. Mauduit.

Atticus is said to be Mr. Burke [1], Mr. Mauduit, or Lord George Sackville.

MR. WHATELY TO MR. GRENVILLE.

October 28, 1768.

DEAR SIR,—I have little to add to the printed accounts you will see of the Rebellion at Boston. General Gage writes to the Ministers, that he shall consider it a direct rebellion, and treat it accordingly; that he, therefore, intended to have sent troops to New York, but that the merchants would not let him any ship to transport them, he must, therefore, send for the two regiments from Halifax. I have now found out the mystery about those regiments, which has puzzled me all the summer. It was said on the 18th of July, that they were probably at Boston by that time, in consequence of the orders sent from hence. Those orders, I find, were only to be ready to go in case their assistance was required, leaving poor Governor Bernard, as usual, to be responsible for the measure; he proposed the requisition to his Council, they did not dare to advise it; he writes word, that if one of them had been for it he would have taken the step, and now they blame him for not doing it on his own authority; this is very hard indeed.

Wedderburn arrived last night from Yorkshire; he has been sounded whether in case the Solicitor General's

---

[1] "Mr. Bourke denies it as he would a fact, which he wished to have believed."—*Junius* [*Atticus*] *private note to Mr. Grenville, 20th October*, 1768.

place should become vacant, he would take it; his answer was, that no man in his senses could think of engaging in the present system. He saw Lord Rockingham just before he came up: his Lordship's language was, that it was impossible the several parts of the Opposition could differ now on American measures; that in Opposition they should entirely agree, but that if they ever were called upon to form a Ministry in concert, as Mr. Grenville would naturally expect the first place, there would be difficulties in giving securities to his Lordship's friends.

He expressed himself a little hurt with the *State of the Nation:* Bourke [Edmund Burke] mentioned it to me yesterday in the same manner; I find they are very hostile to the Administration, condemn their whole conduct with respect to America, and seem inclined to attack Lord Hillsborough's letter for rescinding. That letter was, I find, approved of by all the Administration; they say, that in writing it they only meant to comply with the intentions of Parliament to enforce the laws of revenue.

A strong memorial is come over from the King of Sardinia, representing the dangers of the Family Compact; I suppose Corsica is the occasion of it.

I do not see any likelihood that the Chancellor will resign; if he should, it is said that Lord Mansfield has recommended Lord Chief Justice Wilmot;—that would be probable, if it be true that his opinion has been asked.

I have let my house to Lord Rochford for the winter; if you have any commands for me, please to direct at Mrs. Corage's, Suffolk Street, Charing Cross, where I have taken a lodging.

There were illuminations in the Strand last night,

and some small mobs I met in other streets, to celebrate Mr. Wilkes's birth-day, but the rejoicings seemed faint and forced.

MR. AUGUSTUS HERVEY TO MR. GRENVILLE.

Park Place, October 31, 1768.

DEAR SIR,—I hope you received my two last letters; this will a little surprise you, when I tell you Lord Chancellor wrote to my brother by the King's desire, to offer the Privy Seal, which my brother is come to town to accept, having sent to Lord Chatham to know his inclinations about it[1]. My brother sent immediately to tell me of this, and that he would be in town directly; he came yesterday, and tells me 't is now all settled. I cannot in this tell you the particulars, but it has determined the Chancellor's stay, and I suppose is to serve as a counterpoise to the Bedfords, who would have been [too] powerful had they got it for the Duke of Marlborough, as they wanted. All this is nothing or little to the public, but every individual thinks of his own situation, and therefore as one, I find in mine I must now take a different part from what I intended, and support my brother as long as I can, and wherever it is not absolutely contrary to those opinions I have already given. You have recommended this so strong and so repeatedly to me, that it would be ill paying my court to you not to follow your advice in it, had I not even other calls. But, however that may be, I can never alter my wishes nor my opinions. It makes me very tired indeed of the whole, as I see very little good

---

[1] See Lord Bristol's letter in the *Chatham Correspondence*, vol. iii. p. 347.

to arise from these arrangements, nor shall I ever expect any 'till the reins are again placed in your hands; these are temporary salves that may soften for a short time, but not heal. However, the Duke of Grafton must not like this, as he had no naming, nor any one appearance in it. How, then, is he the master? and yet this is the man that thinks himself master [1]. I do not find that Barré goes out, nor who is to succeed Lord Harcourt. Everything in America is as bad as it can possibly be, and what they'll do is yet undetermined. There has been a sort of doubt if the meeting of Parliament should not be put off for a few days, but I think they say it is at last determined otherwise.

I find this town has made me a much more intrepid person than I really am, for they have already given me another person for a wife, and such a one as I am sure I should never have thought of; very likely the report may have reached you, and I am sure you will treat it as it deserves, but it has been very industriously put about here [2]. My suit comes on this term, and I hope to have success. I am sure of your wishing me well. I am, &c., &c. A. HERVEY.

MR. KNOX TO MR. GRENVILLE.

London, November 1, 1768.

DEAR SIR,—The *State of the Nation* has risen to more importance than I ever imagined it could have attained. It has already run through two editions, and

[1] See *ante*, page 384, *note*,—Mr. Hervey's letter to *The Man who thinks himself Minister*.

[2] Horace Walpole says he had fallen in love with a physician's daughter at Bath, but the doctor disapproved of the match, and gave the girl 5000*l*. not to marry him, and so Mr. Hervey was disappointed.

the third goes to the press this night; but what is of still more consequence, the King seems to have changed his plan of government in conformity to it in one particular. The idea of an unconnected independent Administration is given up, and the Duke of Grafton is declared first Minister, with full confidence and ample powers.

The public opinion gives this Tract to you, and as it is so much approved of, and derives all its merits from your assistance, I did not think you would be displeased with the imputation, and did not for that reason discountenance the supposition.

Mr. Lloyd has, however, published an advertisement disavowing your concern in it, but it is not credited.

Observations upon it[1] have been advertised these three weeks, but have not appeared as yet, and I fancy they are kept back until there will not be time to answer them between their publication and the meeting of Parliament.

The revolt of New England is now unquestionable. Private advices since the 22nd of September, say the Convention had met and agreed to all the Resolves of the town of Boston, and appointed inspectors to see that all the militia of the country were properly armed.

The paper republished in the *Political Register* of this day, written in Pennsylvania, is the fullest and openest declaration of the independency of the colonies that I have seen, and well deserves notice[2].

We have a report that Lord Lyttelton is to have the Privy Seal, but he must go to Lord Chatham for it, as

---

[1] By Edmund Burke.

[2] The paper alluded to is signed "A Citizen," and is entitled, "American Considerations on the Nature and Extent of the British Parliamentary Power. Written and printed at *Philadelphia* in the year 1768."

his Lordship, notwithstanding his letter of resignation, still detains the Seal. I shan't put my name to this letter, as I have some reason to suspect letters to or from you don't pass without inspection.

MR. JOHN TEMPLE[1] TO MR. GRENVILLE.

Boston, New England, November 7, 1768.

SIR,—I have had the honour of writing to you several letters since the constituting of an American Board of Customs, and have from time to time taken the liberty to communicate my sentiments upon the state of affairs in this country; they are now become serious and interesting, and I dare say take up much of the attention of the considerate part of the nation.

---

[1] Afterwards Sir John Temple. He succeeded to the Baronetcy as the eighth in succession to the title, on the death of his kinsman, Sir Richard Temple. In 1773 John Temple was engaged in a dispute with Mr. William Whately, respecting some letters addressed to his late brother Thomas Whately, by persons in America, which Temple was accused (and as it would appear unjustly) of appropriating, and of sending them to be made public at Boston. There was subsequently a duel between Whately and Temple; the particulars of the transaction are given in detail by Almon in the Appendix to his *Biographical and Political Anecdotes*, vol. iii. pp. 236-73.

After the duel Mr. Temple sent a statement of the affair to Lord Temple, but the facts are substantially the same as those given by Almon, and therefore I do not insert it. He says that he supposes "Whately to be the mere tool of Lord Hillsborough and his people, to whom I seem to be a *marked man* for sacrifice, as far as they are able." The reply was very short. "Lord Temple presents his compliments to Mr. Temple, laments the situation to which unfortunate circumstances have reduced him, though the probable recovery of Mr. W. affords some alleviation."

Sir John Temple died in America, where he was Consul-General for the United States, in 1798. He was great grandfather to the present Baronet, Sir Grenville Temple, who inherits the Baronetcy created by James I., in the person of Sir Thomas Temple of Stowe.

My particular situation is disagreeable beyond description; I am a Commissioner of the Customs here, without the least weight or influence at the Board; measures are projected and executed directly contrary to my opinion, and I fear destructive of the real interest of the revenue. I have never yet discovered the least view to that service in all our deliberations; they have appeared to me to flow rather from an anxious desire of lighting up a war between these colonies and their mother country, and no means seem to have been left unattempted (by some of the principal servants of the Crown) that might effect it; if this has been the desire or the design of Government, I have not been let into the secret. I have acted upon principle, and in every part of my duty have endeavoured to regulate and settle revenue matters upon an equal, moderate, and practicable system, in conformity to the spirit of the Acts of Parliament that should govern, but in this I have not been happy enough to find myself seconded; and though I have seen my suffrages of no effect, yet I have patiently and constantly attended, and have given my opinion upon all occasions at the Board. From all other society in these troublesome times, I have almost totally sequestered myself, lamenting at the same time that the affections of so many of His Majesty's subjects on this side the water are wasting away from the mother country through the infamy of some, and the ignorance, insufficiency, and avarice of others.

I am perfectly of opinion with General Gage that the King's cause has been more hurt in this country by some of his own servants, than by all the world besides, and time must turn this up to public view. I am, &c., &c.
JOHN TEMPLE.

MR. GRENVILLE TO THE EARL OF SUFFOLK.

Bolton Street, November 25, 1768.

My dear Lord,—You will, probably, before this letter reaches you, have heard of an event relative to Lord Temple, in which I am so nearly interested from the affection which I bear to him, and from many other motives, that you will be glad, I am persuaded, to know the circumstances from myself rather than from any other report. Lord Temple came to me the day before yesterday, and with the kindest and warmest expressions towards me, told me that he intended to go to Lord and Lady Chatham, at Hayes, either as yesterday or to-day, in consequence of some overtures which had been made to him for that purpose.

He said that as the political differences between him and Lord Chatham, he had reason to believe, were in a great degree over, and as his desires not to hang out false colours upon that subject had been a principal motive with him to break off all intercourse, not only with him but with his sister, Lady Chatham, who had always behaved well to him, the affection which he bore to her now induced him to renew it when that obstacle was removed. He assured me in the strongest terms that his public opinions continued, and would always continue, the same; and that his friendship and affection towards me was, and should ever be, unalterable, and that nothing should divide us. My answer to him, after acknowledging and joining with him in those sentiments of brotherly love which he so warmly expressed and I so sensibly felt, was, that it would ill become me in my situation, and at my time of life, to use any argument to prevent his being reconciled to my sister, Lady Chatham, whenever his own opinion or inclinations led him to it; that I was extremely happy in the strong assurances that he gave me, that this change of situation should make no alteration in his public opinions, nor in the inviolable affection which we had borne to each other ever since our union a few years ago. He expressed himself in the most affectionate terms with regard to the manner in which I received this communication, and repeated to me what he had told me before; and that he had determined to take no step in it till he had acquainted me with it, nor would he do so in the course of it if it went any further. These are the outlines of what passed between us. Many comments may possibly be made upon this event at this time, especially as men's thoughts and conjectures travel much faster than human actions can bear pace with, and run to the end of the journey almost before it is begun. I can truly assure you, that I know of no state mystery in this transaction beyond what all the world must see in this time of universal confusion and distraction. I am, &c., &c.

GEORGE GRENVILLE.

THE EARL OF SUFFOLK TO MR. GRENVILLE.

Charleton, Wednesday night, November 30, 1768.

MY DEAR SIR,—I happen to have an opportunity, by a servant going to London, of acknowledging the most kind instance of your friendship, which I received this evening in Whately's packet, and I shall prefer that conveyance to the post.

I hear of any event with pleasure which is productive

of happiness to one so dearly and nearly connected with you as Lord Temple; nor should I have been sharp-sighted enough had you mentioned nothing about the matter, to have seen state mystery in a transaction which can be only of a private nature.

You know how earnestly, as a public man, I have formerly wished your family union. I think if it had taken place some time ago, many mischiefs that have befallen this unhappy country might have been prevented. It is too late to prevent them now; they are upon us; and it makes no part of my creed that the Earl of Chatham can retrieve the mischiefs of Mr. Pitt.

You see I write to you upon all subjects with equal frankness; it is my ambition to merit your confidence, because I know no considerations would give it me without your esteem; and that, Sir, till you are another man, I shall think the greatest honour of my life.

I shall order my servant to call at your house before he returns in case you should have anything particular to communicate, but not to give you the trouble of writing if you have not. Yours sincerely,

SUFFOLK.

MR. KNOX TO MR. GRENVILLE.

December 15, 1768.

DEAR SIR,—I have been told that the colony agents were sent for lately by Lord Hillsborough, and acquainted that if they would *waive* the point of right, and petition for a repeal of the duties as *burdensome and grievous*, Administration were disposed to come into it. The agents, however, declared they could not leave out the point of right, consistent with their present instructions, but should inform their respective colonies, and so it rests. This expounds the riddle of their Resolutions declaring over again the right of Parliament, and doing nothing more, for the people of England are to be made believe that the right is admitted by the colonies, or otherways an Administration who seem to stand so high upon it would never surely have hearkened to them; and the colonies' petitions saying nothing of it, will be interpreted into their tacit submission, and an express one will not be required. This appears to me to be the treacherous composition plan to which all parties have acceded, and the rights of this country are to be sacrificed to their agreement among themselves.

I have no doubt of the truth of my information, but you will be so good to take notice of it in a way that will not point towards me. If indeed you reserve yourself 'till late in the debate, I should imagine you will find grounds for the suspicion in the course of it.

Perhaps Mr. Garth might tell you what passed at Lord Hillsborough's. I am, &c., &c.

WM. KNOX.

MR. GRENVILLE'S DIARY

OF

MEMORABLE TRANSACTIONS.

(Continued from page 240.)

October 1768.—Lord Chatham resigned the Privy Seal, alleging his ill health as the cause, taking notice likewise of the dismission of Lord Shelburne, and Sir Jeffry Amherst.

Lord Camden, upon this event, came from Bath, saw the Duke of Grafton, and said he would resign likewise. The Duke of Grafton desired him to consider before he took this step: he went to Hayes, saw Lord Chatham, and did not resign, nor did Mr. James Grenville.

The Privy Seal was offered, through Lord Camden, to Lord Bristol, who said he could give no answer 'till he knew Lord Chatham's sentiments upon it. He wrote to his Lordship, received an answer written by Lady Chatham, with a postscript from Lord Chatham, upon which he accepted the Seal, pleading Lord Chatham's approbation for so doing [1].

[1] Lord Bristol in his letter to Lord Chatham said:—" I cannot think of accepting the Privy Seal, without your Lordship's approbation. Do you choose, my Lord, that I shall hold it till your health will permit you to resume the reins of government?" And Lord Chatham in reply said, "As my entire loss of health has for a long time disabled

Wednesday, November 23rd.—Lord Temple came to acquaint Mr. Grenville that, upon some overtures having been made to him from Lady Chatham since her Lord's resignation, he was determined to follow the dictates of his affection to her, and put an end to the difference subsisting between them, but giving Mr. Grenville every friendly and affectionate assurance, at the same time, that nothing should ever divide him from him, and begging him to keep his mind void of suspicion.

Mr. Grenville, with the same warmth of affection, assured him that he would entertain no suspicion on that head; that he (Lord Temple) was certainly the master of his own actions, and that he should never find him the person who would foment, or endeavour to keep up family feuds; that his own situation was, in many respects, different from Lord Temple's, to which his Lordship agreed.

Lord Temple made the same notification to Lord Lyttelton, and to Sir Richard Lyttelton, who did not receive it with the same temper and moderation as Mr. Grenville.

Friday, November 25th.—Lord Temple went to Hayes, and did not return 'till ten o'clock at night. The report of his going spread fast through the town, and various were the conjectures upon it.

The King, at this time, was said to have looked cold upon the Duke of Grafton.

---

me from taking any share in public business, I trust I shall easily obtain your Lordship's pardon, if, after having resigned the Privy Seal on that acconnt, I beg to decline any way entering into arrangements of office. Allow me, my Lord, at the same time to entreat that the idea of your Lordship's holding the Privy Seal only for an interim may not, on my account, be farther thought of by your Lordship."—*Chatham Correspondence*, iii. 347–8.

Saturday, November 26th.—Mr. Grenville went to see Lord Temple, who told him he found Lord Chatham in bed, rather weak, though less so than he had often seen him with the gout, but his mind and apprehension perfectly clear; he got up in the evening, and seemed better when up. He disclaimed the Chancellor for having used his name to Lord Bristol and others, denied his having advised Lord Bristol to accept of the Seal, and referred to his letter, which he said Lord Bristol could show if he pleased, but he never has shown it to any body.

Mr. Grenville hears, from many quarters of undoubted authority, that the Bedford party are industriously endeavouring to detach his friends from him, persuading them that Lord Temple and Mr. Grenville mean to come into employment themselves, leaving their friends unprovided. Lord Powis has been gained by these means, and Mr. Rigby has laid close siege to Sir L. Dundas, and Mr. Wedderburn; the latter told Mr. Grenville that he had been many times pressed to take the office of Attorney-General, but that he had no thoughts of it at this time.

Thursday, December 1st.—There was a division in the House of Lords upon the commitment of an Attorney for prevarication, 51 to 5; the latter were, Lord Chancellor Camden, Lord Rockingham, Lord Abingdon, Lord Lyttelton, and Lord Milton. Lord Bristol (Privy Seal) went behind the throne.

The next day being Friday, Lord Chancellor meeting Mr. Wedderburn, desired to speak to him, and told him that he addressed himself to him, as to a person of honour, wishing him to attend to what he said, and to bear testimony to the truth of it. He then broke out, with great agony of distress, upon the charge made against him (bitterly stated in the newspaper of that day) of ingratitude to Lord Chatham, and of having used his name, without his privity, to engage Lord Bristol to take the Privy Seal. He endeavoured to justify himself, saying that Lord Chatham having resigned that office, upon account of his ill health, and having, by a letter in Lady Chatham's hand, pressed him (the Chancellor) to keep the Great Seal, he thought the office of Privy Seal could not be filled by anybody more agreeable to Lord Chatham's wishes than one with whom he had lived in so much friendship as Lord Bristol; that as to the present Administration he (the Chancellor) hated and despised them, and thought himself in many instances personally ill-used by them, particularly in the business of the preceding night, when upon a law question, and notwithstanding his high station, no one court lord thought fit to divide with him. He repeated many times, with infinite grief, the hard charge of ingratitude laid against him, saying his conduct in the transaction with Lord Bristol could only arise from thinking it was conformable to Lord Chatham's wishes, since he could not mean by it to serve the Administration whom he hated, nor would he do it as a means to preserve that bauble (pointing to the Mace), which possibly he might not hold a week longer. He left Mr. Wedderburn at liberty to tell this to whom he pleased, wishing rather to have it told than concealed.

Mr. Wedderburn told it the same day to Mr. Grenville. Soon after he had done so, Mr. Augustus Hervey came to Mr. Grenville, expressing Lord Bristol's great uneasiness and concern at the paragraph referred to before in the newspapers, saying it did not appear to come from a common hand, and seeming to point by his discourse at Lord Temple [1]. Mr. Grenville said that, as to himself, he never had, on any occasion whatever, made use of that channel, either of abuse, or even to defend himself when attacked; that he believed it did not come neither from Lord Temple, but he knew nothing of the matter, and could not say from whence it came. The three parties concerned all differ in some degree in their narration of this affair.

Tuesday, December 6th.—Lord Temple went yesterday to Hayes. Lord Chatham has a severe fit of the gout: the Chancellor has been several times at Chiselhurst, but has not been at Hayes.

The Princess of Wales laments the sad condition of the kingdom, says there is no Government, that she fears the King is insensible to the danger, and will not awake to it 'till it will be too late: she said she wishes

---

[1] Augustus Hervey himself very frequently sent contributions to the newspapers, and no man was more likely to know, or at least suspect, that Lord Temple did the same. In this instance, too, Augustus Hervey knew that his brother, Lord Bristol, had not shown Lord Chatham's letter to any one, and it is evident that the paragraph in question must have been written by some person to whom Lord Chatham had communicated its contents, and to whom so likely as to Lord Temple, with whom he was now once again in close alliance? The letter itself was never made public until its appearance in the volumes of the *Chatham Correspondence*.

The paragraph was inserted in the *Public Advertiser*, and after mentioning Lord Bristol's appointment to be Lord Privy Seal, it proceeds: " It is a certain fact, and no contradiction can be given to it, that the Earl of Chatham never gave his advice in favour of any such measure, nor has he the smallest connection with the present Administration. A certain letter, if it were shown, is the strongest proof of both these facts, and though his name may have been made use of by a *supposed* friend, yet that supposed friend may find he has justly forfeited the noble Lord's esteem who was *his* friend, *his* patron, and *his* maker."

much to see, she will not say Mr. Grenville, nor any other particular person, but some one whose firmness and steadiness would look like Government; she gives to understand that she has no influence over the King's mind, and is told of nothing 'till after it is done.

Lord Bute returned unexpectedly into England in the month of August, after an absence of a twelvemonth. He was perfectly well when he came, but was immediately taken ill of a bilious fever, in which Sir William Duncan attended him. During the course of his illness Sir William met Lord Barrington at a relation of his Lordship's, whom Sir William attended; he asked after Lord Bute, and told Sir William that, whatever he he might think, that Earl's favour was over, and his credit gone: this is the language held universally, and two circumstances seem to confirm it; the first, that upon Lord Bute's first seizure, he desired Sir William to go to the Princess of Wales to apprize her of his situation, who expressed great regard and concern for him, sent daily to inquire after him, and sent him presents of fruit, but the King never sent; the second, that Sir William went, upon a consultation, to visit Lord Barrington's relation at Richmond, where he met Robinson, the King's apothecary, and one who frequently sees him. He asked Sir William how Lord Bute did, and said he had better not have returned to England. Sir William said perhaps so, both for himself and the kingdom. Mr. Robinson said he would do well to advise him to go abroad again, and that *it was* expected that *he* should give him that advice. Sir William said he should not see him again, and should have no opportunity. Robinson again repeated that *it was* expected that he should advise him to go, and that he could do it by writing to Lady Bute, and that *it was expected* he should do so, repeating, several times during the conversation, that he came from Richmond Lodge that morning, knowing he should meet Sir William, who put an end to the discourse, saying he was no politician.

These circumstances concur with the general notion of Lord Bute's credit being gone, and of his having seen the King but once since his return to England. His spirits are very low: the Queen is supposed to have done him ill offices, and to be entirely in the interest of the Duke of Grafton, the King to be grown indifferent to him, but the Princess to be in the same sentiments towards him as before.

MR. WHATELY TO MR. GRENVILLE.

January 3, 1769.

DEAR SIR,—It is hardly news, so much was it in expectation, that the spirit raised in the colonies should break out in other places besides Boston, and show the narrowness of their views who think that preventing riots in one place is restoring order and subordination to Government in all. The assemblies of South Carolina and Virginia have shown their factious spirit so much as to oblige the Governors to dissolve them, in order to prevent their agreeing immediately in the Boston Resolutions.

Notwithstanding these advices, Alderman Trecothick

still persists in endeavouring to get an application from the merchants for the repeal of the duties. I doubt whether he will prevail to get an application, and then I shall doubt again whether it will succeed.

Wilkes's election does not surprise me[1]. I have long expected the event upon the first death of an Alderman, but I cannot persuade myself that there is an intention to allow the error assigned, on the Solicitor-General's filing the information, to be good cause for reversing the sentence; I do not think so ill even of the present Ministry, as to suppose, 'till I see, them guilty of such a subterfuge, to avoid the questions and the difficulties in which they have involved themselves. I give as little credit to the reports of negotiations actually now in agitation, of overtures made by the Bedfords to Lord Temple, and of Mr. Rigby and Lord Gower being gone to Euston, either to settle the propositions or make a breach with the Duke of Grafton. Such steps suppose more importance than I imagine belongs to the Bedfords; they seem to have nothing to offer but a share in the ill-will that attends them.

LORD TREVOR TO MR. GRENVILLE.

Thursday evening, (February 23, 1769.)

DEAR SIR,—You are at liberty to copy the enclosed for your own information:—I am at present clear of all doubt as to their genuineness. I have got a sight of a *third letter* of an anterior date, but whose contents are as curious as those I now send you enclosed. It repeats

[1] He was chosen Alderman of the Ward of Farringdon-Without, by a very considerable majority.

the tenour of a letter from one of our Bostonian patriots, a correspondent of his, who appears to be of French extraction, not only by the language, but by some inaccuracies in his account of the constitution of that colony. You shall likewise have a communication of these papers, as soon as I have copied them. I don't find that the American Secretary, or even our Royal Master, has yet seen these papers. I shall only add, *fas est et ab hoste doceri.* Yours most sincerely, T—

MR. GRENVILLE TO LORD TREVOR.

Bolton Street, February 24, 1769.

MY DEAR LORD,—I return you many thanks for the communication of the two letters from M. de Montcalm [1], and the leave which you have obtained for me to copy them. I will avail myself of it in a few days, and

[1] If these letters were genuine, there is convincing evidence in them to prove that the Americans had notions of Independence long before the Stamp Act and its consequences. I know of no sufficient reasons to doubt their authenticity. They were communicated to Almon in 1777, expressly for publication, both in French and English, by Mr. George Grenville, who had found them among his late father's papers, and it is most probable they were sent to Almon, at least with the concurrence, if not by the desire, of Lord Temple.

In a debate in the House of Lords, May 30, 1777, on Lord Chatham's Motion for putting a stop to hostilities in America, these letters from Montcalm were alluded to, and Lord Shelburne, on that occasion, expressed his disbelief of them, but Lord Mansfield, in maintaining his former opinions respecting the American views of independency, relied upon what had been stated in Montcalm's letters, which he insisted were not spurious.

Almon says that "Mr. Grenville gave full credit to these papers;" but that "all the Americans reprobated them as forgeries, and that they were fabricated to deceive and provoke the English Government against America. This opinion," he adds, "prevailed with the public, and the letters were in general discredited."—*Biographical and Political Anecdotes*, vol. ii. p. 99.

then send them back to you. I shall be very glad to see the third letter which you mention. Those which I already have, contain a melancholy proof of the certainty of our misfortune, and that the seeds of that independency now claimed by our colonies have been long sown, the roots of which by the late encouragement have I fear struck too deep for the strength of our feeble and divided Government to pull up. I wish, however, that the King were to see them, because if he were satisfied that they were genuine (as you tell me you have now no doubt they are), they would show to him the sense of a knowing, able, and unprejudiced foreigner with regard to the situation of our colonies, and might thereby be the means of opening his eyes and of his seeing the danger as it is; and till that is done, every other hope is vain. I am, &c., &c.

GEORGE GRENVILLE.

MR. DOWDESWELL TO MR. GRENVILLE.

February 28, 1769.

MR. DOWDESWELL presents his compliments to Mr. Grenville, and sends him a copy of the Motions for accounts which he intends to make when the Message is brought. Mr. Dowdeswell, after he left the House yesterday, heard that the Message is not to be brought 'till to-morrow [1].

[1] The Message was to demand of Parliament the payment of the King's debts, amounting to 513,000*l*. Mr. Dowdeswell moved that not only the particulars of the expense might be specified, but that the papers might distinguish under what Administration each debt had been incurred, with the intention of bringing out that Lord Rockingham's Government had been the most frugal.

The accounts moved for in the first and third Motion, together with the account of the present debt which Mr. Cowper will be to lay before the House, will probably answer the purpose of the account of the yearly charge mentioned by Mr. Grenville yesterday. If they do not, Mr. Grenville will be so good as to draw a Motion for that account.

It has occurred to Mr. Dowdeswell that it would be better no Motion were made in the House of Lords for accounts 'till these Motions are decided in the House of Commons. They are so much shorter in their debates than we are in ours, that they would out-run us, and perhaps lay open more of our plan than we may think proper to open at first.

On the other hand they have time enough, as they can do no essential act 'till the Bill comes from our House, and the debates on the Motions in our House may perhaps furnish fresh matter for Motions for some other accounts in theirs.

Mr. Dowdeswell has satisfied Lord Rockingham and his friends in the House of Lords in this matter, and if Mr. Grenville is of the same opinion he wishes he would hold the same language to his friends there.

THE EARL OF BUCKINGHAMSHIRE TO MR. GRENVILLE.

March 20, 1769.

DEAR SIR,—You will find my Gazette a miserable one, yet the pleasure of reminding you of me induces me to write. The news of yesterday was, that an alliance, offensive and defensive, had been concluded between you and Lord Rockingham, through the mediation of the Earl of Chatham; this, men in office give a degree of credit to, and thought me uninformed when I presumed to express my doubts.

Colonel Luttrell, resigning his present seat, offers his services to the county of Middlesex; nor need I add, that he is to be supported by all the weight of Government.

The disgrace of the Court of Berlin is confirmed; the Princess Royal urged in her defence, qu'elle se croyoit en droit de disposer d'une terre qu'on laissoit en friche.

I have some reason to believe that the Court of Russia is not greatly pleased with our present Governors, that the Empress is not very confident in the abilities of her own generals, and that the rupture with Sweden is considered as inevitable.

It has happened to me since we parted, to see many men differently connected, they all evidently wish a change of Ministers and measures, yet would not risk the recommendation of a Custom-house officer to obtain it.

The King honoured the Drawing-room yesterday (it was fuller than a birthday) with an universal smile. All men do not smile when they are best pleased.

I cannot conclude the Gazette without informing you that the Duchess of Kingston was presented, not in an embroidery of orient pearl, but in a silver stuff, which she told us cost nothing. As your old acquaintance Madame de Viri stood near her, she appeared a slim genteel figure.

There has been a dreadful fire in Covent Garden; I was there this morning; the portico of the right hand of

Russell Street is level with the ground[1]. Believe me, &c., &c.

BUCKINGHAM.

THE COUNTESS TEMPLE TO EARL TEMPLE.

Tuesday, (March 21, 1769.)

MY DEAR LORD,—Your heart may be at ease about your picture: the Princess will have a copy; refuses with abundance of mighty fine speeches to you, and the picture is gone to Angelica's, who must keep it some time to finish it as high as the original[2]. Mrs. Middleton has been here, and says nothing at all was the matter about the painter, she only wanted to talk with me about the picture; that the Princess did not know it was ready, and that she had not shown my letter to Her Royal Highness; she had left it upstairs, but when she dressed her she told her we had sent to know how she did, but there was nothing else in the letter. I happen to know she kept my man 'till four o'clock, in order to show my letter when Lord Berkeley should be gone, and that the answer must come from the Princess herself; however, I never entered into that part. I have the gout in my foot, and have a party at home to-day.

They say the Bishop of Derry[3] is coming to annul

---

[1] The fire broke out at Bradley's Distilling House in Great Russell Street. Several houses were burnt under the Piazza, including great part of the Bedford Arms Tavern.

[2] A portrait of Lord Temple in his robes as a Knight of the Garter, by Sir Joshua Reynolds. It was formerly in the collection of family pictures at Stowe. A copy of it was probably made by Angelica Kauffmann for the Princess Amelia.

[3] A younger brother of Lord Bristol and Augustus Hervey. Miss Chudleigh having been divorced from the latter, was now married to the Duke of Kingston, and presented at Court, where it is said the King and Queen honoured them by wearing the wedding favours.

this match, and that he has a living witness to produce. The King hardly spoke to the bride, the Queen little more. Lord Bristol did not appear. Augustus chose to be there, and said aloud he came to take one look at his widow. She had a white and silver [dress] and pearl lappets[1], which were the most curious piece of workmanship that ever were seen; they looked like the finest Brussels point, nobody ever saw such before; the pearl gown is not finished.

Politics subside, and nobody talks of anything but the Chudleigh farce, which may end in a tragedy. The Duke of Kingston gets drunk every day with Lord Masham[2], which must be to drown care, for that vice has never been reckoned amongst his faults. I am, your most affectionate, A. T.

You will have a visit from Mr. Aubrey. I complimented him much upon his speaking.

My Lord Bristol was at Court, and wore his favour.

THE DUKE OF CHANDOS[3] TO MR. GRENVILLE.

London, March 23, 1769.

DEAR SIR,—I told you when last I saw you, that if anything worthy your notice occurred I would inform you of it.

Yesterday a most audacious mob assembled in the

---

[1] "As a proof," says Horace Walpole, "of her purity and poverty."
[2] A Lord of the King's Bedchamber. He married Miss Dives, one of the Maids of Honour to the Princess Dowager, and when he died in 1776, the Barony of Masham was extinct.
[3] Henry Brydges, second Duke of Chandos.

morning at the King's Bench prison, from thence they marched to intercept the cavalcade of merchants, who were going to the King with their Address; they abused the gentlemen and greatly hurt many, throwing dirt, stones, &c., into their coaches; they shut the gates at Temple Bar, and would not let them pass, and in Chancery and Fetter Lanes they overturned carts and coaches to obstruct the passage that way; they then came down to St. James's Palace, and vented their rage upon every one who came to Court; everybody was covered with dirt, and several gentlemen were pulled out of their coaches by neck and heels, at the Palace-gate. The Dukes of Kingston and Northumberland had their chariots broke to pieces, and their own and servants' clothes spoiled; and some had the impudence to sing *God save great Wilkes, our King.* The troops beat to arms, and the guards were trebled; many were greatly insulted, the mob coming up to the muzzles of their firelocks, but it was thought proper for them not to fire. The Riot Act was read twice to no purpose, and they did not disperse, but the Horse Guards were obliged to ride over them. Lord Talbot was greatly insulted, but acted with great spirit; he seized two of the rioters with his own hands, and delivered them to the Guards, which, with three more taken, I hope will fully meet with their proper reward. A hearse, painted on one side with two soldiers and an officer shooting at young Allen; on the other side, Balf and McQuirke knocking down Clark, would have fored its way into the Palace, but was prevented: it is said to have been drove by a gentleman.

Out of one hundred and thirty merchants who went up with the Address, only twelve could get to the King, and they were covered with dirt, as indeed was almost the whole Court: where this will end, God knows; I am sure it is high time for every friend of the King to exert himself. A Cabinet Council was held and a proclamation issued immediately, to command every one to do their utmost to suppress riots, and I was told that care will be taken to suppress the several meetings held by Wilkes's friends, the abettors, I fear, of these outrages.

The Duchess and Lady Augusta join in compliments with, dear Sir, your, &c., &c. CHANDOS.

You may read this letter where you think proper, but do not part with it out of your hands.

MR. WHATELY TO MR. GRENVILLE.

Saturday, March 25, 1769.

DEAR SIR,—I can add nothing to the accounts you see in the papers of the behaviour of the mob; all agree that they were more riotous and seemed more determined than any we have lately seen; they pelted not only with dirt, but with the stones laid ready for the paving, and used their greatest efforts at the palace gate. The Duke of Grafton went thither undressed; his friends advised him rather to walk than go in a carriage: he was called into the Closet four or five times, but His Majesty, the courtiers say, was quite calm and serene, and expressed his hopes that this event would be the means of gaining effectual support to Government from all who wished well to their country. The Duke of Grafton held the same language, and the language in the outer rooms was all the while about authority and licentiousness, and that absolute government was better than mob government, and that all possible vigour would be exerted, and that Parliament would address, and that all those things would be done, which people who do not know what to do, always think of doing. The consequence of so much vigour has been to send five brawlers to Bridewell, and to issue the proclamation which I suppose you have seen, and which all who see must own to be the only effectual exertion of the civil authority which can be found in our constitution.

The tranquillity of the capital being thus perfectly secured, the Duke of Grafton is gone to Newmarket, and the few remaining politicians in town wait with less anxiety for his return than for the appearance of Lord Chatham, which they expect after the holidays, and from which they fear still more perplexity: in the meanwhile it is said, and I believe truly, that the Bedfords have promoted this measure of addressing, contrary to the opinion and advice of the Duke of Grafton.

Colonel Luttrell, I hear, will certainly stand for Middlesex, and this is all the news which reaches me.

MR. WHATELY TO MR. GRENVILLE.

March 30, 1769.

DEAR SIR,—If retirement be the joy of the country, there is no place so rural as the neighbourhood of St. James's; I have the whole parish to myself, and am as quiet as if I were a hundred miles from London.

The Ministry are as usual at Newmarket; the Opposition are enjoying leisure and happiness at their several houses; even General Irwin himself, the last man always to leave London, is gone somewhere into Buckinghamshire; nobody is left here to make news or to tell it, and I am obliged for want of intelligence to send you the enclosed dialogue about the Kentish Address, which I think a neat piece of ridicule; but however the author may divert himself with the spirit of loyalty, it would certainly, some say, spread over the kingdom, if the city of London would but give the tone, and a Common Council is therefore called to consider of it; but I hear they will hardly answer the purpose of their summons; I am told that Sergeant Whitaker will be a candidate at the next Middlesex election; it is certain that he now is canvassing; but I can hardly persuade myself that he will persist, or that the Rockinghams will encourage him to proceed. I have heard, but not with certainty, that it has been debated in council whether Messrs. Townshend and Sawbridge should be expelled; I heard it with particulars which would seem to give it credit: the night was named when the question was agitated; the majority of two who negatived it was specified; but still I doubt the truth of my intelligence.

I am much more inclined to believe that the Ministers have now in contemplation an alteration of the Riot Act, to change *one hour* into *forthwith*, for the time of dispersing, and to leave the construction of *forthwith* to a jury on the circumstances. The alteration has been suggested by the respect paid to the present law by the late mob; they obeyed it, and dispersed within the hour; none of them can be tried upon it, and therefore a law must be contrived that they cannot obey; whether the Ministers will persist in such a design I do not know, but I believe they think of it now. Of the rioters who were apprehended, several were suffered to escape by the soldiers; of the seventeen who were effectually secured, twelve have since been dismissed; the remaining five will perhaps be tried for misdemeanors by a Middlesex jury, at the Quarter Sessions, some Westminster Justice in the chair, and this is all the satisfaction to be had for an offence so specially, so literally against the peace of our Lord the King, his crown, and dignity. Are not these sufficient reasons for altering the Riot Act?

Among the Merchant Addressers, of which a list was so pompously inserted in the *Gazette*, I saw the name of Thomas Broughton, Esq., and had the curiosity to ask whether that was the Tom Broughton who was once my father's livery servant, then kept a punch-house, and is now a broker. The answer I received was, that though there were some few very good names amongst them, there were not fifty better than Tom Broughton; and that many were used to see their names in the *Gazette*, having appeared there before, some of them more than once, as bankrupts.

COMMODORE HOOD TO MR. GRENVILLE.

Boston, April 15, 1769.

SIR,—I have received the very obliging letter you did me the honour to write me last November, and feel myself exceeding happy that the part I have taken respecting the affairs of this country has been such as to merit your approbation.

Everything here has been quite quiet ever since I came, and I am very confident will remain so; for though it may not be easy to bring the Assemblies to acknowledge the power of Parliament relative to taxation, yet here will, I dare say, be no opposition by *force*, but an acquiescence to what they call burthens upon their trade, 'till such time as they are relieved by an Act of grace and favour. I have been very cautious, moderate, and circumspect not to widen, but rather to prepare the minds of the people for a healing of the unhappy difference that has subsisted between Great Britain and the Province, and I have singular satisfaction in a consciousness of not having given the least just cause of offence to any one; for though they are sensible of my doing that which appears most eligible to me, for the honour and dignity of the Crown, yet they are convinced of my readiness to show every possible mark of attention and regard, that is reconcileable to the duty I owe to my Royal Master. I have considered the differences unfortunately subsisting between England and America in a most serious light, and I have studied without ceasing to have nothing done by His Majesty's naval force under my command, that should appear in any manner distressing or harsh. My mind has been constantly on the stretch to this end, and I was not easy 'till I got here, so as every movement should be made under my own eye.

Allow me, my good Sir, to express my most sincere joy, at the happy reconciliation that has taken place in your families, and to say, that I can foresee that it must be productive of consequences great and fortunate to my country; in this light it must be viewed and enjoyed by the true friends of England as well as America.

The worst is certainly past here, and I hope and trust all will be well by-and-by. Perseverance from home must ensure a happy issue, which I flatter myself I shall be an eye-witness of before I leave America—and my command will be at an end next summer.

I shall tarry in this province as long as I think my

presence can be of use, though the necessary works carrying on under my direction will call me to Halifax; but the greater services of the Crown must be first attended to, and my leaving Boston must be determined by the instructions I may be honoured with after the final resolutions of Parliament have taken place respecting this country.

The Canada geese are in great plenty in Nova Scotia; I have now some at Halifax which I raised from goslings, and I shall be happy in sending them to you the first opportunity. They never breed till three years old, as they assure me in this country. I am, &c., &c.

SAM. HOOD.

LORD CLIVE TO MR. GRENVILLE.

Westcombe, May 10, 1769.

DEAR SIR,—Inclosed I send you copies[1] of my letter to Mr. Wedderburn, and his answer.

[1] COPY OF LORD CLIVE'S LETTER TO MR. WEDDERBURN.

Westcombe, May 9, 1769.

SIR,—I am sorry that any personal or party motives should have deprived you of that seat in Parliament which you filled with so much honour and unbiassed ability. If another seat be acceptable, I have one at your service, in which you will at all times be at liberty to exert your talents upon your own principles. I am, with sentiments of the greatest esteem, &c., &c. CLIVE.

COPY OF MR. WEDDERBURN'S REPLY TO LORD CLIVE.

Lincoln's Inn Fields, May 10, 1769.

MY LORD,—I cannot be sorry for an incident that has produced to me so distinguished a proof of your Lordship's esteem. The principles which govern your conduct are so truly honourable, that I have not the least scruple to accept the offer you are so obliging as to make me, and I am extremely flattered to receive it at this time from one whose approbation of my conduct the world will respect. I have the honour to be, &c., &c. AL. WEDDERBURN.

I am very sorry my being in the country will not permit my assuring him in person how happy his acceptance of my offer has made me, and I must request you will intimate as much to him; and my wish that his election for another place may remain a secret until the time approaches for my showing him that mark of my respect and esteem[1]. Although I am fully convinced that ministerial influence and power can effect nothing against me, yet, by having six months' notice, they may occasion trouble and delay in the purchase of some estates which I am making in those parts, for the purpose of entirely surrounding the town of B[ishop's] C[astle] with my own possessions. I am, &c. CLIVE.

LORD LYTTELTON TO MR. GRENVILLE.

Hill Street, June 3, 1769.

DEAR SIR,—I have read with infinite pleasure the paper[2] you left in my hands, and will deposit it in Sir Richard's, to be given to you as you pass through London, in your way to Lord Thomond's.

If you have not the leisure to call upon him for it, send your servant, and he will deliver it to him with the six last books of Leonidas.

I have no news to tell you that you will not see in the papers.

My best compliments wait on all the family at Wotton. Mrs. Montagu, who has been ill, is, I hope, recover-

---

[1] Wedderburn had vacated his seat for Richmond, in consequence of his vote in favour of Wilkes. He was elected for Bishop's Castle through the influence of Lord Clive.
[2] Mr. Grenville's speech on the Expulsion of Wilkes.

ing. She is charmed with what you allowed me to communicate to her. I am ever, &c., &c.

LYTTELTON.

MR. GRENVILLE TO LORD LYTTELTON.

Wotton, June 8, 1769.

MY DEAR LORD,—I am much flattered by the kind approbation which you and Mrs. Montagu have given to the papers which I left with you, and which I will either call upon Sir Richard Lyttelton and take from him, or send for, whenever I come into the neighbourhood of London. I have read but cursorily of the six first books of Leonidas, upon which I have made no particular remarks; in general, the language of the additions appears to me less elevated and the verses less *varied* than I should wish them. They seem to me to have the same genius, the same poetical fire; but they want in many places the same elegance and correctness which he gave to the first edition of Leonidas, before he printed it, and which I doubt not but he will give to this. There is, however, a good deal of this kind to be done. If he could prevail upon the writer of the Essay upon Shakspeare to make observations upon this work, every defect would be pointed out to him in a style and manner which would show the striking effect of imagination, elegance, and correctness, when united. We have read that admirable work, by our fireside, over and over, to form the taste of our young people. I know no public news worth attending to. My thoughts and wishes are confined to domestic objects, and to such friends as will always make a part of that domestic happiness. I trust in God that we shall all meet here well and happy in the month of October. The earlier you can come to us the happier we shall be. Mrs. Grenville desires me to make her best compliments to you, and I am, &c., &c.   GEORGE GRENVILLE.

LORD LYTTELTON TO MR. GRENVILLE.

Hill Street, June 12, 1769.

DEAR SIR,—I am extremely concerned that you and Mrs. Grenville have been so ill, and that she continues so weak. Take care of yourself, my dear friend, as well as of her: for though you seem to think your body as strong as your mind, I know it is not so, but can suffer by cold, to which you expose it too much. I flatter myself, that if Mrs. Grenville has no return of her pain it will not be long before she recovers her strength.

Mrs. Montagu, who has been ill in the country with a fever, is got much better, and talks of coming to town on Tuesday next for some days. What you say of her book will make her very happy. What she says of your manuscript you will see by a letter[1] from her to me,

---

[1] The following is the letter from Mrs. Montagu referred to by Lord Lyttelton:—

MY LORD,—I return Mr. Grenville's speech after having read it with great delight, and I desire your Lordship to return my thanks to him, but I shall not attempt to praise it, for every period in it convinced me my praise is far below his acceptance. I long to see the time when the wisdom that dictated what I read shall be employed in active measures to save this poor country.

I hope I shall find all my friends safe and well at my return to town, but indeed a wicked mob and a foolish ministry may produce strange events. It was better in old times, when the Ministry was wicked and the mob foolish. Ministers, however wicked, do not pull down houses, nor ignorant mobs pull down Governments. A mob that can read, and a Ministry that cannot think, are sadly matched.

Pray make my compliments to the ladies you have invited for this

which Mrs. Stapleton will bring you inclosed in that manuscript.

I entirely concur in your judgment of the additions Mr. Glover has made to his Poem, and believe you will form the same upon those you have not yet seen in the six last books, which I have now sent. I am ever, &c., &c.
LYTTELTON.

THE EARL OF CHATHAM TO EARL TEMPLE.

Hayes, July 7, 1769.

MY DEAR LORD,—I have now the pleasure to be able to tell you, what, I know, you will have no small pleasure to learn; it is, that I have recovered so much strength and general health in the course of the last month, as to be much the same I used to be for ten years past. My legs are still weak and not without swelling, but upon my horse's legs I am as strong even, and ride my six or seven hours a day, without the least fatigue.

I yesterday made trial of my bodily force by going in the morning to town, in a coach, and paying my duty to the King at the Levée, and back to Hayes in the evening; all this with the utmost ease.

His Majesty was pleased to receive me most graciously at the Levée, and to order me (there) to stay, that he might see me in the Closet, where His Majesty again condescended to express in words of infinite goodness the satisfaction it gave him to see me recovered,

evening: it was pure malice in your Lordship to make such a party, when I could not be one of it. The chaise is ready to carry me to my nightingales, so I will only add that I beg your Lordship to send for Mr. Hawkins, if your leg does not grow better. I am, &c., &c.
E. MONTAGU.

as well as the regret His Majesty had felt at my retiring from his service.

I remained in the Closet about a quarter of an hour, during which time His Majesty deigned to use words so expressive of the good opinion he is pleased to entertain on my subject, that I must choose rather to be guilty of vanity, by mentioning this to your Lordship, than to hazard the charge of too little sensibility by suppressing it[1].

The account I have to send to your Lordship of your little friends here, which you are so good to interest yourself for so kindly, is but very indifferent with re-

---

[1] "Lord Chatham's first appearance," says Lord Mahon, " beyond his own domestic circle was at the Levée in July, 1769, to present his duty to the King. Men gazed at him with eager curiosity, as on one risen from the grave; above two years and a half had elapsed since he had last showed himself in public. The King was very gracious, and whispered him to come into the Closet after the Levée, which Lord Chatham did accordingly, and remained in conversation with His Majesty for twenty minutes. He stated his objections to the course pursued both in Wilkes's case and in East India affairs, but added, that with his broken health he could have no desire of office, and that, therefore, if in Parliament he should dissent from any of the Ministerial measures, he hoped His Majesty would do him the justice to believe, that it would not arise from any interested views. To the Duke of Grafton at this Levée he behaved with only cold politeness, much to the chagrin of his Grace, whose feelings of respect and admiration for Lord Chatham had not at all abated." "The fact of Lord Chatham's conversation with His Majesty (the last that ever took place between them) was speedily noised abroad, but its details remained unknown, and thus a large scope was left to rumours and conjectures. Perhaps he was sent for, says Burke, or perhaps he came of his own accord, ' to talk some significant, pompous, creeping, explanatory, ambiguous matter in the true Chathamic style.'"—*History of England*, vol. v. p. 368.

Lord Mahon has also given, in the *Appendix* to the same volume, a very interesting Minute of Lord Chatham's conversation with the King, from the Duke of Grafton's MS. Memoirs, as taken down the same evening, no doubt on His Majesty's report.

gard to poor William, whose state keeps us extremely anxious, though in some respects hopeful enough. The hooping-coughers are, I thank God, almost well.

William's precarious situation will, we fear, hardly allow Lady Chatham to be absent a day from him, which cruelly comes between our ardent wishes towards Stowe. Workmen at the same time must drive us from Hayes, and our purpose is to move as soon as practicable to Chevening, the house of Lord Stanhope, eight miles distant from this place. All loves to you from Lady Chatham. We warmly join in felicitating the happy escape of poor Master W. Grenville[1]. Paper is wanting, and words must be so, to tell you how much we are ever, my dear Lord Temple's affectionately devoted.

THE EARL OF CHATHAM TO EARL TEMPLE.

Hayes, July 18, 1769.

MY DEAR LORD,—Stowe, which is ever in our wish, begins now to be in near view to us. William is, thank God, so much mended as to allow us to hope we may without much anxiety commit him to the care of Mrs. Sparry, while Lady Chatham and I indulge the impatient desire of embracing the Lord and Lady of Stowe. We trust this epistle will find Lady Temple delivered of the fears of gout, and at the same time neither your Lordship nor her engaged in any peregrinations.

If these, our pleasing hopes, should be confirmed by a line of leave from you, we propose to set out about

---

[1] Afterwards Lord Grenville. An accident had happened to him at Eton, from the falling of a piece of lead, which had nearly fractured his skull.

Monday or Tuesday next, and to get to the much-wished end of our journey as fast as the expedition of a convalescent will extend to.

Your goodness has encouraged us to come in the true patriarchal way, and to bring you no less than three children, Hester, Harriot, and Pitt, who are almost in a fever of expectation, 'till the happy day comes. Old and young count the hours with equal impatience 'till the pleasure of a letter from your Lordship fixes our motions[1].

Full of the happy prospect of finding myself again at Stowe, I will only add that I am ever, with the warmest sentiments of attachment, my dear Lord Temple's most affectionate brother and devoted humble servant,

CHATHAM.

LORD LYTTELTON TO MR. GRENVILLE.

Bowood, July 25, 1769.

DEAR SIR,—A quick succession of guests to entertain at Hagley prevented my acknowledging the favour of your last so soon as I ought to have done. I am now at Lord Shelburne's, on way to Boconnock, but he and his Lady are gone to Mr. Beckford's[2], so I have a

---

[1] Burke, in a letter to Lord Rockingham, dated (Sunday) July 30, thus describes Lord Chatham's patriarchal progress to Stowe, to pay his first visit after the reconciliation with Lord Temple:—

"Lord Chatham passed my door on Friday morning in a jimwhiskee drawn by two horses, one before the other. He drove himself. His train was two coaches and six, with twenty servants, male and female. He was proceeding with his whole family (Lady Chatham, two sons, and two daughters) to Stowe. He lay at Beaconsfield, was well and cheerful, and walked up and down stairs at the inn without help." The party therefore probably reached Stowe in the afternoon of Saturday, the 29th instant.

[2] At Fonthill.

night to myself, which I use in returning you my most hearty thanks, and Lord Anglesey's, and my daughter's, for the kind regard you have shown to Mr. Day[1]. Whether he meets with success in his business or not, your goodness is the same.

I am much concerned to hear that the health of Mrs. Grenville remains still unassured, but I hope that as the pain returns with less violence it will soon go quite off, by the obstruction that causes it being removed.

My daughter, I thank God, is got quite well, and I flatter myself will bring me a grandson some time in November, though I am not unwilling to compound for a grand-daughter.

To-morrow I propose to follow Lord Shelburne to the great Beckford's in a return for a visit the Alderman made me last year, at Hagley. I suppose I shall hear a great deal of politics, but the Middlesex and London petitions have so disgusted me of them, that I shall enter but little into that conversation.

There seems to be a competition between the Opposition and Court, which shall play the fool most. What Lord Chatham's apparition at St. James's may produce I am yet to learn; those I am going to, I presume, can form a better guess about it than I, but the best guesser may find himself mistaken. I intend to be at Pitt's about the 8th of next month. Whether I shall call at Eastbury in my way will depend upon what I am not yet assured of, your brother's being there. If he is not, I shall take him in my return from Boconnock. I am ever, &c., &c. LYTTELTON.

[1] A gentleman whom, at Lord Lyttelton's request, he had recommended to Lord Clive for advancement in India.

MR. WHATELY TO MR. GRENVILLE.

August 3, 1769.

DEAR SIR,—I take the opportunity of Mr. D'Oyly's going to Sir William Stanhope's, to send you a letter by a private conveyance, and as I do not know what you may have heard further of the conference in the Closet, I will begin with the particulars which have come to me. That Lord Chatham spoke out his sentiments on the conduct of Administration is certain; he blamed their measures with respect to America and the East Indies, in general terms; he dwelled more on the Middlesex election, and hoped that if he was able to take a part, as he believed he should be, next winter, in the House of Lords, His Majesty would not impute it to faction, that he stood forth in defence of the Constitution, which he thought had been violated; he was very strong and explicit in declaring his opinions on the points which he touched; they were parried, and no direct answer given. The Ministers, it is apprehended, advised the inviting him into the Closet, and such a reception as he met with there: soon after, they held the language you have heard, *he has paid his visit and all is over;* but lately they seem to be more apprehensive of the consequences; they do not hold so high a tone; they apparently grow very anxious, and decline business more than ever, prepare nothing, and have all the marks of people who are not very confident of their continuance.

Some of the best-informed persons go much further, and are positive that the King would be glad of a pretence to send for Lord Chatham; he certainly grows every day more uneasy, the Ministerial people begin to apprehend they perceive a coldness towards their principals, the petitions are particularly grating; that being perceived, was the reason (as is supposed) of the Duke of Bedford's journey into Devonshire, to prevent one there, where, by-the-bye, his journey has fixed it, and his Grace was probably saved from destruction by the interposition of the Bishop, who let him through his palace, from the church, where the people were very outrageous[1].

[1] These circumstances are mentioned by Horace Walpole, and they are also corroborated by the Duke of Bedford's Journal, printed in the Appendix to the *Cavendish Debates*. The Duke was Lord-Lieutenant of Devonshire, and being possessed of considerable property there, it was thought that his presence might be influential in preventing a petition being sent from that county. Lord Temple was one of the most zealous promoters of these popular petitions, which it was now the policy of the Opposition to encourage by every means in their power. Although they were sent from many of the counties, cities, and towns throughout the kingdom, there were still some counties, such as Norfolk, Lincolnshire, Kent, Essex, and Hertfordshire, where the Gentlemen could not be prevailed upon to join in the popular cry. In Norfolk, for instance, Lord Buckinghamshire, in writing to Mr. Grenville, says, that "whatever may be the inclination of the freeholders at large, too many Gentlemen express their disapprobation of the measure, for it to be carried through with an éclat that would give credit and weight to it: they cannot be induced to see the expediency of applying to the Crown, and they obstinately persist in blending what is in fact the cause of the Freeholders of England with that of Mr. Wilkes."

Lord Temple had been very active in procuring the petitions from the cities of London and Westminster, and the counties of Middlesex and Buckingham, and his hostility to the Duke of Bedford would be certainly increased by his endeavours to prevent the success of a petition in Devonshire. In writing to his sister Lady Chatham, on the 14th of September, Lord Temple gives an account of a Meeting of the Freeholders at Aylesbury, and he adds, "all things passed off inexpressibly well, and I hear the holy flame has catched in Dorsetshire, where I suppose I shall find it ready to blaze by the time I get there, which will be by the end of next week."

Besides his Letters, Junius occasionally sent to Woodfall paragraphs for the newspapers. An instance of this occurs in the *Private Note*,

The anxiety in the Closet is so great, that I am assured if any one of the Ministers were to quit, it would probably be a cause for removing them all.

I am also assured that the Lord Chancellor, Lord Granby, and Sir Edward Hawke, have declared to Lord Chatham their readiness to quit, whenever he requires it.

Lord Bute, it is supposed, would also incline to send

No. 29 (vol. i. p. 218), which contains several sentences to be inserted at different times: one of them is headed ("*next day*").

Lord Temple was also in the habit of sending paragraphs to the newspapers: some of these communications have escaped destruction: they are still extant, *in his own handwriting*, and they have the same peculiarity in the directions to the printer. One of them is headed, "*For the Papers*," and another "*For the newspapers another day*." I mention these circumstances now, in order to produce the following sentence, which relates to the Duke of Bedford: it is from the original, in Lord Temple's hand:—

"The Earl Temple we hear is setting out for his seat in Dorsetshire; we shall be to see whether his Lordship's reception in the West will be as *Distinguished* as that of his Grace the Duke of Bedford."

This paragraph was inserted in the *Gazetteer and New Daily Advertiser*, for Monday, September 18, 1769, and the *next day*, September 19th, appeared the Letter from Junius to the Duke of Bedford, in which occurs the following passage:—

"Whither shall this unhappy old man retire? Can he remain in the metropolis, where his life has been so often threatened, and his palace so often attacked? If he returns to Woburn, scorn and mockery await him. He must create a solitude round his estate, if he would avoid the face of reproach and derision. At Plymouth his destruction would be more than probable; at Exeter, inevitable. No honest Englishman will ever forget his attachment, nor any honest Scotchman forgive his treachery to Lord Bute. At every town he enters, he must change his liveries and his name. Whichever way he flies, the *Hue and Cry* of the country pursues him."

Another paragraph relating to the Duke of Bedford, and evidently written for the purpose of annoyance, will be found in the *Middlesex Journal* of the 27th of July, 1769, and it bears marks of coming from the same source:—

"While the Duke of Bedford was at the Bishop of Exeter's Palace, *he cried like a child*, on account of the insults offered him by the mob."

This will at once remind the reader of Junius of a passage having a

to Lord Chatham, but he has had no opportunity to give any opinion; and what influence it might have if it were given, is not quite clear. That he has not seen the King, is certain; that the Princess has pressed for his seeing His Majesty, and been refused, is reported with some degree of credit. I believe the manner of his Lordship's return was this; he intended originally to be back at the beginning of August, then changed his route, which brought him hither sooner than he was expected, or than he himself designed; in the meanwhile, his family, with the concurrence of some of the Ministers, sent three or four expresses to desire him to postpone his return, but the change in his route not being

similar tendency to annoy Mr. Bradshaw, in one of the Miscellaneous Letters, signed "*Q in the Corner*," June 26, 1770.

"When Mr. Cooper mentioned to Mr. Bradshaw an intention of lodging a complaint against him, he burst into tears."

And in the poem of *Harry and Nan*, Bradshaw is the person designated in the lines—

"A friend so obliging, and yet so sincere,
With pleasure in one eye, in t' other *a tear*."

It may not unreasonably be inferred that Lord Temple communicated many such pieces of intelligence to the newspapers, which at that time abounded in paragraphs containing similar information, and generally having a political tendency: such, for instance, as the following:—

"The Duke of Grafton's visit at Stowe was merely complimentary on his marriage. The Earl Temple is steady in his opposition to that violent, wicked, and arbitrary Minister."—*Middlesex Journal, August* 31, 1769.

And again,—

"The publication of Dr. Musgrave's letter, together with the late unsuccessful visit to Stowe, have so disconcerted the *Premier's* intentions, that it is said he will soon retire."—*Middlesex Journal, September* 14, 1769.

Another instance of short paragraphs being sent to Woodfall by Junius, for insertion in the newspapers, is mentioned in the *Private Note*, No. 42: they relate to Lord Hertford, and the marriage of the Duke of Cumberland; and they have a strong resemblance in style to that above mentioned about the Duke of Bedford.—See *Junius*, vol. i. p. 36, *note*.

known, these expresses missed him. He is very ill, his cholics are returned upon him, but I believe nothing will prevail on him to go abroad again.

MR. WHATELY TO MR. GRENVILLE.

August 5, 1769.

DEAR SIR,—I forgot in the letter I sent you yesterday by a private hand to tell you that, however incredible, it is certainly true, that the troops are retiring from Boston. General Mackay, who commanded there, received orders to send two regiments forthwith to Halifax, and to take the directions of Governor Bernard, concerning the third or such part of it as he would wish to keep. Governor Bernard has declined giving any directions, so that what is to become of the few men he was allowed, but I suppose afraid, to retain, I do not know. The same advices represent things as growing worse and worse in America. All the measures of Government are of a piece—inconsistency, inability, and concession.

I enclose you a paragraph out of the *Gazetteer*, which I believe you do not take in, to show you to what lengths the public papers go. It is no less than a direct advertisement for an assassination of Lord Bute [1].

---

[1] The following is the paragraph alluded to, from the *Gazetteer* of Friday, July 28, 1769 :—" It was yesterday reported that a very unpopular nobleman, not the Duke of B——, nor Lord H——, very narrowly escaped being assassinated. But the nobleman here hinted at, suspecting two men who had been seen loitering before his door for upwards of three hours, slipped out at the back door, *à la Bedfordiana*, and for this time escaped that fate which still seems inevitably to hang over his devoted head."

LORD LYTTELTON TO EARL TEMPLE.

Boconnock, August 13, 1769.

My dear Lord,—I most heartily wish your Lordship joy of the success of your endeavours for the reunion of your family, which is a great step towards the reunion of the nation [1].

It would have given me much pleasure to have been a witness of your satisfaction and your brother's on this happy event, in which I share most sincerely. I came hither on Thursday last, and found Lord Guernsey with Mr. Pitt. We propose to-morrow to set out for Falmouth, and the Mount's Bay, and some other parties of pleasure, at the end of which I intend to turn my course towards Hagley, taking Eastbury in my way, from whence about the 28th I shall go to Lord Shelburne's at Bowood. I saw his Lordship at Beckford's, where I passed two days in company with him, with Colonel Barré, with Mr. Cornewall, and the two most illustrious aldermen, Townshend and Beckford; so perhaps I may be soon admitted a member of the Mile-end Society, and outgo your Lordship and the rest of the party at Stowe in zeal for Liberty, &c., &c., &c.

If you don't use me very civilly I will set up against you, and have you and Lord Chatham mobbed by my friends in the city, for joining that oppressor of the colonies, and defender of general warrants, George Grenville.

However, since you are so wickedly got together, I advise you to stick close to one another, and then if this country can be saved, your joint efforts will save it.

[1] In allusion to Lord Chatham's recent visit to Stowe, where he was met by Mr. Grenville.

Pitt desires me to join his congratulations to mine on this auspicious league; but we are sorry to hear that the gout continues so troublesome to Lady Temple. Our best compliments to her, with hearty wishes for the perfect restoration of her health. I am ever, my dear Lord, most affectionately and devotedly yours,

LYTTELTON.

THE EARL OF SUFFOLK TO MR. GRENVILLE.

Charleton, August 19, 1769.

MY DEAR SIR,—You rightly apprehend that every circumstance which contributes to the domestic happiness of my friends, is matter of satisfaction to me. I can receive none higher than from any event which is productive of it to you; in no respect, I am confident, it has been or ever will be obtained, derogatory to your honour and your dignity.

My opinions upon public affairs continue without variation, as I have repeatedly expressed them to you; and I lament the prevailing extremes between which, moderate and constitutional men, who disdain the servility of the Court on one side, and abhor the principles of levellers on the other, wishing to steer, will find themselves in a situation the most impotent and unavailing of any. The choice must be made between actual retirement and that which the disgraceful condition of this deluded country alone can justify. I cannot allow myself to indulge a communication of all that arises on this subject by the common post, or suppress the outline. Your most affectionate and faithful friend,

SUFFOLK.

MR. EDMUND BURKE TO MR. WHATELY.

Gregories, August 21, 1769.

Dear Whately,—I hope you have not entirely forgot your promise of spending a day here, in your way to or from Mr. Grenville's. I wish the pleasure of seeing you from motives as independent of politics as the course of my life and thoughts here have been generally removed from all ideas of that kind.

This I thought not amiss to say, when I am just going to mention a particular that looks a little towards business; I should be glad to have some notion of what your friends think ought to be done at Aylesbury, in the meeting which is advertised for next month; for my own part, I am wholly for a petition, and for as strong a one as can consist with decorum and propriety, but entirely averse from making it a farrago of wild indigested matter.

In Worcestershire, they have confined themselves to one or two points; I think it would be rather awkward to go to the meeting without any distinct idea of what is to be proposed, and I would just hint to you, that some gentlemen, and friends of yours too, on this side of the county, seem rather hurt that no communication has been made to them. I the rather mention this, because Lord Verney moved the meeting in the grand jury, in concurrence with Lord Temple. I am, &c., &c.

Edmund Burke.

COMMODORE HOOD TO EARL TEMPLE.

Halifax, September 2, 1769.

My Lord,—I have taken the liberty of sending you by His Majesty's ship *Launceston* a very fine turtle, which I have had by me near three months; and as he eats heartily and thrives well, I am in hopes he will get safe to Pall Mall, and prove acceptable.

The arrival of some late ships in America, which left London in June, and bringing various letters full of approbation of the conduct of the people of Boston, occasioned a meeting of the merchants, at which they spoke out, and with one voice declared that the repeal of the duties on paper, glass, &c., as mentioned in Lord Hillsborough's circular letter, would not relieve them from their grievances unless the duties on tea, sugar, wine, and molasses, were likewise repealed, without considering whether they were for the purpose of revenue, or a regulation of trade and commerce; and I wish the true meaning of their declaration may not be, that no duty laid on by Parliament must be allowed to exist for any purpose *whatever*.

This step is very surprising to me, and the more so as the very people who repeatedly talked to me in a different language, and took pains to persuade me that a new Governor would soon be able to procure a proper petition for a repeal, waiving the point of *right*, and upon the inexpediency of Revenue Acts in America, now adopt all the violence of the merchants; and it seems to be the general opinion at present, that they can force Administration and Parliament to yield to them in every respect, and that perseverance in non-importation is all that is necessary to procure them all they want.

If this is a truth it is a very melancholy one, as I dare say they will soon show a dislike to the Acts for regulating trade; and by what I am told in late letters, no terms of accommodation will be listened to but such as they are pleased to prescribe. The leading men boast letters from very respectable characters in England, advising them to go on in the plan they have adopted, and that the end would answer their wishes. How then, my Lord, can any conciliating measures take effect here 'till harmony is restored at home? which I hope soon to hear; and, big with mischief as the appearances of things at present show themselves here, I shall no longer regard them than the unhappy misunderstanding prevails amongst His Majesty's subjects in England. When once the nation tastes again the sweets of correspondent sentiment, and has confidence in the King's Ministers, it may do anything with the colonies.

The note here changes with every account received from London; one day the people are very high, the next mighty humble and passive; they take their tone from your side the water, and have all along acted as they have been told from thence. God grant a happy union, and soon, in and with both countries. I have the honour to be, &c., &c. SAM. HOOD.

MR. WHATELY TO MR. GRENVILLE.

September 7, 1769.

DEAR SIR,—It would not have been justice to Mr. Bourke to expose all his political sentiments to the Postmaster, and I therefore give you the trouble of sending to Aylesbury for this packet, if the notice I have given of it to Lord Temple and Mr. Butler should not be the means of saving you that trouble.

I wish that you should be possessed of the particulars of our conversation, because I think it shows a warmer inclination towards you than ever appeared before from that quarter, and a disposition to union in opposition, as you shall judge by the detail.

He began with expressing his approbation, and even applause, of the petition [1] : he was particularly struck

---

[1] Very considerable difference of opinion existed at this time relative to the question of petitioning for the dissolution of Parliament, not only on account of the general inexpediency, but for the impropriety of seeming to force the King's prerogative. Among the many petitions and remonstrances from the Livery of London and other corporate bodies and counties, on the subject of the Middlesex election, and for the dissolution of Parliament, those from Yorkshire and Buckinghamshire were two of the most remarkable: the former was supposed to have been written by Sir George Savile, and the latter by Edmund Burke. It is now known, however, that the Yorkshire petition was written by Wedderburn, and that from Buckinghamshire to have been the production of Lord Temple, the original draught, much corrected and interlined, being still extant in his handwriting. The style and sentiments of Junius are very conspicuous throughout the whole of this composition, and for that reason it attracted the notice of Jeremiah Markland, a critic of considerable eminence in the literary circles of his time, who has alluded to it in his DIARY, thus quoted in Nichols's *Literary Anecdotes*, vol. iv. p. 298, under the date of August 28, 1770 :—" Junius is come to life again; the person whom I always suspected since the Buckingham petition, because I thought nobody could write it but himself. I am sorry to see that he is spoken suspiciously of."

The person suspected by Markland was no doubt Edmund Burke; but as the Buckinghamshire petition was written by Lord Temple, this is a curious instance of indirect suspicion from a contemporary, that he was the Author of Junius, and therefore whatever value may be attached to Mr Markland's opinion, with respect to the style and turn of

with the foundation of the whole laid in the principles of the Revolution; with the notice taken of the fatal thought in the Buckinghamshire petition, it is all in favour of the theory that Lord Temple was Junius.

Some slight alterations, but not improvements, were made in the petition as subsequently adopted, and in the latter form it is printed in the *Gentleman's Magazine* for 1769; but the following is from the original draught in the handwriting of Lord Temple:—

"We, &c., &c., beg leave humbly to approach your Majesty with assurances of our zealous attachment to your sacred person, and to the principles of that glorious Revolution, in consequence of which the Crown was established in your Majesty's family, as the most effectual security for the rights and liberty of the subject.

"Sensible of these invaluable blessings, we shall upon every occasion try to deserve them by our utmost endeavours, on the one hand to repress every tumultuous attempt contrary to good government, and to the known laws of this kingdom, and on the other hand, by our firm determination to maintain those just rights and that liberty inviolate.

"Animated by these principles, we have seen, with the highest concern, the repeated disorders which have arisen, as well within the City as in the adjoining counties, and the unhappy measures which have occasioned them.

"In this critical and melancholy situation we should be wanting in that duty which we owe both to your Majesty and to our country, if we beheld with indifference fresh causes of complaint and disturbance, and could neglect to point it out to your royal wisdom and goodness for redress.

"It is declared by Magna Charta and the Bill of Rights, that no freeman shall be disseized of his freehold or liberties, but by lawful judgment of his peers, or by the laws of the land; and it is declared by the Bill of Rights, that *Election of Members of Parliament ought to be free.* By virtue of these two sacred and fundamental laws whereof all the electors of Great Britain have an undoubted right to elect, by the majority of legal votes, any person for their representative who is not rendered incapable of that high trust by the law of the land.

"Notwithstanding which, two days before the last election for the County of Middlesex, your Majesty's Ministers thought proper, either by their own authority or by their advice to your Majesty, to confer a nominal office upon Lieutenant-Colonel Luttrell to vacate his seat in Parliament, with the avowed purpose of bringing him into the House of Commons as Knight of the Shire for the said county, by a small

effects to the Crown from the claim of one House of Parliament to make ordinances of equal force with laws;

number of voters against the declared sense of a great majority of the legal electors: the plan thus formed [a] hath since been fatally executed, and the return altered in favour of the said Lieutenant-Colonel Luttrell, without hearing any of the parties.

"We are thoroughly sensible that the House of Commons hath a clear right to determine judicially, not arbitrarily, upon the elections of their own Members, and it is certain that the electors have an equal right freely to choose their own representatives in Parliament.

"By the first principles of the Revolution both these rights are to be exercised, subject to no control except that of the law, which is superior to, and cannot be superseded by, any resolution of either House of Parliament. No new incapacity can be enacted, except by the authority of the whole Legislature, and no legal vote adjudged to be forfeited or thrown away, unless given in direct and notorious contradiction to the law.

"The claim of either House of Parliament to make ordinances which shall have the force of laws, hath once already been fatal to the Crown and to the Constitution, and will, we fear, if the exercise of it be encouraged, prove again destructive to both[b]

"Justly alarmed at an attempt of this formidable nature, planned and avowed by divers evil counsellors and Ministers employed by your Majesty, our loyalty and duty call upon us humbly to represent, in behalf of ourselves and all the electors of Great Britain, the dangerous consequences with which it will be attended to the public tranquillity and happiness; to the security of our excellent Constitution, which depends upon the mutual confidence between the electors and their representatives; and lastly, to the peace and glory of your Majesty's reign, which are indissolubly connected with the freedom of your people, and the enjoyment of their undoubted rights and privileges.

"We do, therefore, most humbly implore the intervention of your

---

[a] "Mr. Luttrell has already shown us how far he may be trusted whenever an open attack is to be made upon the liberties of this country. I do not doubt that there is *a deliberate plan formed*."—*Junius*, ii. 156.

" — Since he has been in office *no plan has been formed*."—*Ibid.*, i. 392.

"The whole *plan seems to have been formed*," &c.—*Ibid.*, ii. 185.

[b] "By depriving a subject of his birthright, they (the House of Commons) have attributed to their own vote an authority equal to an Act of the whole Legislature; and, though perhaps not with the same motives, have strictly followed the example of the Long Parliament, which first declared the regal office useless, and soon after with as little ceremony dissolved the House of Lords. The same pretended power which robs an English subject of his birthright may rob an English King of his crown."—*Ibid.*, ii. 83.

with the charge brought home to the Ministers in vacating Colonel Luttrell's seat; with the delicacy in mentioning the part which the House took in that transaction; and with the hint at other grievances, without entering into them: he objected only to the proposition that *no legal vote can be adjudged to be forfeited or thrown away unless given in notorious contradiction to the law*, as being too general, liable to some exceptions, and not necessary for us to maintain. I defended the proposition in all its extent, admitting, however, that it was not a necessary part of the petition; he will I believe mention his objection to Lord Temple, and waive it if his Lordship does not agree to it; he is zealous for the measure, and highly pleased with the mode; eager for an attendance, and anxious for the success: he tells me that Mr. Waller was the person he principally meant, when he said that some of your friends seemed hurt at a want of communication.

We lamented together that there was not time after the meeting at the Thatched House to concert the proper proceedings in the several counties; and we agreed in hoping that at the next meeting there we should settle our Parliamentary proceedings; he added, that before

Majesty's wisdom and goodness, that you will be graciously pleased to withdraw your favour and confidence from those who have been the first promoters of this unjust, unprecedented, and desperate measure, and that, from your paternal affection towards your subjects, you will take such legal and constitutional methods [a by dissolution of the present Parliament or otherwise b] as may effectually remove all just cause of uneasiness, secure to us the continuance of our happy Constitution, and establish your Throne in the hearts and prayers of an united people."

a The words within brackets have been partially obliterated.
b " If he loves his people he will dissolve a Parliament which they can never confide in, or respect."—*Junius*, ii. 221.

that meeting a few of the principal persons in opposition should settle the plan, and propose it at the general meeting; that this previous step should be taken, a day or two before, and only principal persons be invited to it.

After dinner he gave you for his first toast; he did the same after supper; I returned the one with Sir George Savile, and the other with Lord Rockingham; the second day he gave Lord Temple for his toast, and I returned it with Lord Verney. He took an early opportunity to speak in very civil terms of your Parliamentary talents; he frequently expressed the great satisfaction he had felt in the harmony of the Thatched House Meeting, and the important consequences which he hoped might follow from it.

He accounted for the delay in Yorkshire by the death of Lady Fitzwilliam, which had called Lord Rockingham to town. He showed me a short letter from his Lordship promising a full detail of their proceedings and designs.

Mr. Burke, from that and other information, believes that Yorkshire will not only petition the Crown, but add either some resolutions, or perhaps some application to Parliament; of this, however, he is not sure: he says that Lord Rockingham and Mr. Dowdeswell are warm for petitioning; and the county of York furious for it: he has no reason to believe that Sir George Savile is at all cool upon it, he thinks it probable that Sir William Meredith may have objections to it, and he believes the Cavendishes will decline to move it in Derbyshire, as the Duke, their nephew, is so near to being of age, and they make it almost a principle to deliver up the county to him quite clear, and not to involve and commit him in any contest. I bid him remind them that the right of the subject to petition the Crown for the dissolution of Parliament was established by a vote of the House of Commons in consequence of a motion made by the Marquess of Hartington, and that they are therefore particularly called upon to take a part; he answered that nothing was so difficult as to persuade a Cavendish to take a part; it was their fault to miss opportunities of doing right, from fear of doing wrong; but he did not represent their backwardness as proceeding from dislike to the measure; he spoke of it always as strongly espoused by the party, thinks it probable that Lincolnshire and Lancashire will follow Yorkshire, has heard that Gloucestershire intends to take it up at the music meeting, and is persuaded that several other counties will come in.

Though the want of a concerted plan accounted for all that had happened, yet I told him frankly that we had from their delays conceived a jealousy at least of a division in opinions, if not of a general coldness in Lord Rockingham's party; that now their dispositions were explained, and that therefore, to prevent their entertaining any doubt of ours, I would tell him the reasons of your absence from the meeting at Aylesbury. I put it on the difficulties which might occur between you and the knight of the shire; on the peculiarity of your situation, being the only commoner in opposition who had been at the head of His Majesty's affairs; on your rank in the county and the kingdom; on your constantly declining all county meetings whatsoever; and on the advantages your absence would give you in defending the measure in the House. I did not say anything of respect to the King, some words which Burke had dropped plainly showing me that that ground would not do. To the others he answered, that he was sensible there was a rank belonged to one who had been in the situation which you had held, which had not a name, but was apparent to everybody, and which must restrain you upon many occasions; that he was sorry to find you thought it restrained you upon this, for he feared it would throw a damp upon the measure; some people would suppose it was so obnoxious to the King that those who had been in the Closet would not offend His Majesty by taking part in it; and others would, on the other hand, undervalue a measure which men of a certain rank thought below their interposition: that for his part it seemed to him of such a magnitude, that the higher the rank of the person, the stronger the necessity for his attendance; that perhaps the advantage in defending it would be as great if you said, that though you never did attend county meetings, yet the subject of this was of such a moment as to make you overlook all other considerations; and as to county precedency, it might easily have been adjusted with Lord Verney; that for these reasons he wished you should attend; but that, however, it was a step in which you must be governed by your own feelings; if they were against it, he should not allow of a thought even in his own breast that you were wrong; and abroad, would always endeavour to give all the force he could to the reasons I had suggested. I assured him, as from you, that you heartily approved of the measure, that Lord Temple would countenance it by his presence at Aylesbury, and that Lord Chatham was eager to the greatest degree upon it. Though Burke wished for your personal appearance, you will find his ardour not at all abated, and he will in his language try to prevent in others any misconstruction, and to remove that damp which he apprehends your absence may occasion.

After all this had passed, he said that he should accept the honour of Lord Temple's invitation to Stowe, the first opportunity [1]. I then told him that you hoped he would not pass by Wotton without calling: it came in very easily, and he as readily answered that he should be very glad to pay his respects to you there; that he had postponed his journey into Yorkshire, on account of the Buckinghamshire petition; that he had desired Mr. Dowdeswell, who was to go with him, to appoint the time when they should go, after the Meeting at Aylesbury; he supposed Mr. Dowdeswell would name an early day, and that when he returned, which I understood him might be in about three weeks, he would certainly wait on Lord Temple and you.

[1] There was evidently a lurking suspicion in the mind of Burke as to the good policy of too close an union with the Grenvilles, or of their sincerity in desiring to coalesce with the party by whom the Stamp Act had been repealed. In a letter to Lord Rockingham at this time, Burke writes:—"I perceive that Lord Temple and Mr. Grenville seem prodigiously desirous of my paying them a visit. With regard to the former, I have promised it in case of my going to Biddlesden [a], and did not decline it with regard to the latter, but promised nothing. I think they wish to mark in some very public manner that they are on no ill terms with your Lordship, and I expect, in conformity to that plan, a good deal of attention from Lord Temple at the Meeting. I shall avoid going too far, not knowing how all this may end, and indeed because I do not find that your Lordship has at all settled how far you intend coalition with them."

In December following, Burke again writes to Lord Rockingham,—"As to the Grenvilles, I am now satisfied that they have hitherto laboured by every method to give the world an impression that our junction is complete, and that the basis of it is their superiority in the arrangement. . . . . I by no means think that Lord Chatham goes with them as entirely as they think, or will make himself so subservient to the aggrandizement of their family as they wish him to be."

[a] Near Stowe, then the residence of Lord Verney.

He often expressed his desire to form a body in Parliament, whose object should be to balance the designs of those who wished to support the influence of the Court as uncontrollable; and though when we mentioned a particular bond of union, we always kept to the Middlesex election as the text, yet we both in more general conversation, I believe, meant, and I believe understood each other to mean, that the concert might be extended to all other subjects which might arise during the session; he asked whether Lord Chatham and you had gone further than the question of the Middlesex election, and seemed particularly anxious to know whether you had touched upon America: I said that I believed you had discussed many of the present political subjects together; and that with respect to America your conversation had been satisfactory to each other; he said that he did not see what occasion there was for further disputes now about it; that he hoped we should neither of us be caught in the traps which the Ministerial people would endeavour to set for us, with a view to create divisions; and that if we differed in speculative opinions, we had no business to bring them into discussion.

I told him that if the repeal of the revenue laws were proposed, we should certainly not agree to it. He answered, that as for himself, he hardly thought he should oppose; most probably he should absent himself; for his friends, many of them agreed in his principles, and some of them did not go so far.

I told him the particulars you bade me tell him of Mr. Calcraft's intelligence: he placed but little faith in it; he rather thinks the Ministry will stand, 'till some accident happens; he has heard that the Butes and the

Bedfords are at variance about the Ambassador to Spain, the one struggling for Sir George Macartney, and the other for Mr. Thynne. He has heard too of the Duke of Northumberland's ill-humour, &c., &c.; but he gives no credit to any man's language which he does not support by his actions; he thinks these people affect to be dissatisfied only to carry some point, or make the Ministry more subservient, but do not intend to break. He spoke of Dr. Musgrave's letter[1] with great exultation; of Lord Camden with acrimony; said little of Lord Chatham; but showed a great dislike to the Duke of Grafton and General Conway.

In the course of our conversation the place and the establishment at Wentworth happening to be mentioned, he said that if my rambles led me towards Yorkshire, he was sure Lord Rockingham would be very glad to see me there. He told me that the new pamphlet, called, I think, *A Letter from a Member of Parliament to [one of] his Constituents*[2], was Dowdeswell's, but desired it might be kept secret.

At coming away he mentioned again his desire of waiting on you, and Will. Burke being by, I thought I could not do less than say, I was sure you would be very glad to see him too: I do not suppose this will be more than just the civility which could not well be avoided.

Much more conversation passed on the advantages of

---

[1] Dr. Musgrave was a physician at Plymouth. His letter was in the form of an Address to the Freeholders of Devon, and, as is well known, pointed at the Princess Dowager of Wales, Lord Bute, and Lord Holland, as persons who had received large bribes from France for their supposed services in reference to the Peace of 1763.

[2] On the late proceedings of the House of Commons on the Middlesex Election.

harmony, and union, and concert, apparently full of warmth and frankness; it is impossible to repeat the whole; by what I have told you, I think you may be as near and as friendly as you please with the Rockinghams next winter.

Burke will probably pay me a visit here; if you wish to give me any hints, which you do not choose to convey by the post, your servant, when he comes with the young gentlemen to Eton, could bring me a letter, or at any time, if you can convey one to town by a private conveyance, it may be forwarded to me by the Windsor *long* coach, from the One Bell, behind the New Church in the Strand, London.

Augustus Hervey, who is now at Lord Mulgrave's, on hearing of my return, called on me this morning, to inquire after Mrs. Grenville and you; he is himself free from pain now, but much pulled by his last attack. His news is, that Sir J. Lindsay goes out at last with one frigate, and instructions only for the Gulf of Persia, and that another frigate is left to carry out the supervisors if they choose to accept of the conveyance, which service performed, that also is to repair to the Gulf of Persia; so that this measure is frittered like the rest, to nothing.

He further told me that the letter from Dr. Musgrave runs like wildfire, but that he hears D'Eon has been prevailed on to prepare an answer to it. The rest of his news is, that Mr. Trevanion will carry Dover against the Ministry[1], and that the Court has lost the election of a mayor at Saltash by one vote; you see that the Duke of Bedford has lost his mayor at Bedford[2]; some say that county is inclined to petition.

[1] He was, however, unsuccessful. Sir Thomas Hales was elected by a small majority.

[2] " where," says Junius, " the Tyrant was held in such Contempt &

The Russian fleet of eighteen men-of-war of the line has sailed; the report is that they are to be joined by six Danish men-of-war, and that they are to proceed together to Constantinople, under the command of Captain Elphinstone.

The French are much alarmed at this movement, and are fitting out a fleet of observation.

MR. WHATELY TO MR. GRENVILLE.

September 14, 1769.

DEAR SIR,—I have heard no news, but since my return I recollect a circumstance which Augustus Hervey told me passed at a table where he was, and which Captain Phipps[1], who was also present, has confirmed to me.

The language there held by persons of condition was, What has the King to fear? All Scotland and half England are with him; his army and navy are full of Scotch: what signify your murmurs? This is worse than Wilkes, and more likely to set the two nations at variance than all the *North Britons*.

Mons. D'Eon's letter has silenced Dr. Musgrave's charge in the City, for the present.

Captain Phipps is just returned from Lincoln, and says that both the city and county will petition, as he believes, if Lord Monson and Lord Scarborough will exert themselves, though he thinks it rather late; Sir

Detestation, that, in order to deliver themselves from him, they admitted a great number of Strangers to the freedom. To make his defeat truly ridiculous, he tried his whole Strength against Mr. *Horne*, & was beaten upon his own ground."—Vol. i. p. 577.

Parson Horne was one of the newly-elected freemen; the popular candidate for the Mayoralty was elected in opposition to the Duke of Bedford's interest by a very large majority.

[1] Eldest son of Lord Mulgrave, and M.P. for Lincoln.

Cecil Wray is always ready to take the lead there; he has been very busy in that of Yorkshire. Phipps tells me that it was Sir Cecil and Wedderburn and one or two more who first set the petition a-going there, and that Wedderburn drew that which is to be presented at the meeting at York; it is confined to the single point of the Middlesex election, and directly names a dissolution of Parliament as the only remedy. I hear that Norfolk has been sounded, and will not petition.

I find in 1710, Addresses procured then by the Tories similar to those procured by the Whigs in 1701, intimating hopes of a dissolution, and assuring the Queen that in a new election they would choose none but such as were faithful to the Crown, and zealous for the Church.

They seem to have been one of the consequences of Sacheverell's trial. I anxiously watched the weather on Tuesday, and hope it did not interfere with the meeting at Aylesbury. You mention the language held there at the races by Mr. Burke, in terms, which I, perhaps perversely, doubt whether they do not imply that you were not quite satisfied with it, which I should be sorry for.

MR. KNOX TO MR. GRENVILLE.

Watford, September 19, 1769.

DEAR SIR,—I have been every day eagerly expecting to receive the paper which you were so good as to promise me, and my impatience has at last driven me to remind you of your promise. I shall remove to London in the middle of next week, where you will have more frequent opportunities of sending it to me, and there I shall hope to meet it on my arrival.

I find by the newspapers, that the Buckingham petition was gladly assented to by the freeholders at Aylesbury, and I congratulate my young friend[1] upon the

[1] George Grenville, jun., who made his début at the Aylesbury meeting. Burke mentions him in a letter to Lord Rockingham at this time as "a very sensible boy, and as well disposed to a little faction as any of his family."

In a letter from Lord Temple to his sister, Lady Chatham, dated Stowe, September 14, 1769, he says:—" I can now give you a not unwelcome account of the agreeable and triumphant manner in which the day of our Remonstrance and Petition passed at Aylesbury. The particulars, I am told, you will learn from the papers [a]; and the ardent eagerness which was expressed for the union of the three brothers, and the applause with which my assurances that it did exist in the highest degree was received, did indeed give me inexpressible delight."

He did not tell Lady Chatham that he had himself drawn up an account of the meeting for the newspapers: although he had done so the same day on which his letter is dated: the original draft of the communication is still extant *in Lord Temple's hand:* it is written roughly on the back of a letter, and it was probably copied in a feigned hand for the newspapers. It is as follows:—

"FOR THE PAPERS."

"Aylesbury, September, 14, 1769.

"PRO MAGNA CHARTA, the ancient and spirited motto of our Lord-Lieutenant, Baron le Despenser, has set this whole county on fire [b], and it appears happily for the Kingdom that these words are deeply engraved in the heart of every honest elector. The transactions of the 12th instant at the general meeting does infinite honour to all the parties concerned. The Earl Temple dined with the freeholders at 10*d*. per head, and his well-known zeal upon every point of liberty did not desert him upon this great occasion. His Lordship has now stepped forth, and put himself at the head of the stand which is making in support of the very vitals of the Constitution, and the avowed union of the three brothers upon this important object, connected with the whole Rockingham party, almost secures a certainty of success. One most material part of the Remonstrance and Petition agreed upon has not yet found its way into any of the papers. I shall therefore transcribe it for the public attention and use. After setting forth the rights of the Electors, under Magna Charta, the Bill of Rights, &c., it goes on in this manner,—

[a] "An attempt was made to insinuate a great deal of Grenvilleism into the meeting." . . . . . "The ostensible particulars of the meeting Lord Temple took care to transmit immediately to the newspapers."—*Burke to Lord Rockingham, September,* 1769.

[b] — " which has since thrown the *whole continent into a flame.*"—*Junius,* vol. iii. p. 185.

pleasure that day must have afforded him; and I felicitate my country upon such early indications of the part he will one day take in support of her constitution and the public liberty.

I don't hear of any other counties moving, nor is there any talk of its being proposed in this; notwith-

' Notwithstanding which, in defiance and contempt of these our just and ancient rights, coeval with the very being of the House of Commons, *two days* before the last election for the County of Middlesex, your Majesty's servants thought proper, either by their own authority, or by their advice to your Majesty, to confer a nominal office on a Gentleman to vacate his seat in Parliament with the avowed purpose of bringing him into the House of Commons, as Knight of the Shire for the said county, by a small number of votes, against a great majority of legal electors, which purpose of theirs hath since been fatally carried into full execution. Justly alarmed at an attempt of this formidable nature thus planned and avowed by divers evil counsellors and Ministers, duty to our Sovereign and to our injured country calls upon us,' &c., &c.

"Lord Verney, Mr. Aubrey, Mr. Calcraft, Mr. Burke, and Mr. O'Bryan, [O'Brien?] distinguished themselves greatly by their manly eloquence upon this occasion. The satisfaction expressed at the declared union of the three brothers is almost incredible."

The above will be found in the *Gazetteer*, for September 18th, and also in No. 73 of the *Middlesex Journal*, for Tuesday, September 19th, 1769, signed M.

On another half sheet of paper is written, also *in Lord Temple's hand*,—

"As these Petitions do not find their way into the *Court Gazette*, published by authority, should there not be a Country Gazette set up and paid for out of that Civil List which is given in consequence of the great and glorious struggles made by our ancestors in defence of liberty?"

And again, *in Lord Temple's handwriting* :—

"For the Newspapers another Day."

"We are credibly informed that orders have been given to the Lord-Lieutenant of Bucks to change his very offensive motto of Pro Magna Chartâ, into Magna Charta, Magna ——, that being the honourable characteristic of the present despotic and unconstitutional Administration. One paragraph in the Bucks Remonstrance and Petition strikes me much, that wherein the violation of our rights is made clear to the meanest capacity; it is in these words, 'We presume,'" &c.

standing, there is an evident disposition for it, were it called forth.

The Americans have lately shown themselves to be much better friends to this country than have our Ministers. Nothing could be more fortunate than their rejecting with contempt the injurious offer of repealing the late Duty Acts, and insisting upon all the Revenue Laws and the Admiralty Jurisdiction being taken way. As in this demand all the Acts of trade are clearly included, the merchants must see that their interest is struck at, and that the sovereignty of Great Britain is essential to the preservation of their trade. This they ought to have seen, and perhaps did see, long ago, but their regard for self made them hope, that if they sacrificed the sovereignty now, the trade would hold out their time, and they cared not what might become of their successors. I rejoice, however, that the effects follow so quick, and that they who treacherously gave up the one will be driven to give up the other also, or else forced for their own sake to retract their former conduct and make a stand for both. I am not displeased to see the claims of the colonies rising so suddenly to an absolute avowal of independency, for the whole must now come into issue, and the people of England will not sit down with the loss of the whole, however they might give it up by piecemeal; and I think it will be more easy to bring the colonies to submit when the whole is to be contested, than when a part only was agitated. Indeed, I have no fear of settling properly with the colonies, if the people here can be kept from taking part with them, and that I think they now may easily be. I have the honour to be, &c., &c.

WILL. KNOX.

THE EARL OF BUCKINGHAMSHIRE TO MR. GRENVILLE.

Blickling, September 21, 1769.

Dear Sir,—As no man more sincerely wished that a thorough and cordial reconciliation might take place in your family, it is impossible for me not to feel sensible pleasure at an event in every light so agreeable to yourself and friends. These you must know to be my sentiments; it is, therefore, very unnecessary for me to dwell upon them. Since my last, great pains have been taken to promote a petition in this county, and a form has been drawn up, couched in the most decent terms, and confined singly to the point of the Middlesex election; but I fear the idea must be laid aside, as, whatever may be the inclinations of the freeholders at large, too many gentlemen express their disapprobation of the measure for it to be carried through with an éclat that would give credit and weight with it.

All ranks of men except those immediately connected with the Ministers express their abhorrence of them and of their conduct; but many, even amongst the warmest of these, cannot be induced to see the expediency of applying to the Crown, and obstinately persist in blending what is, in fact, the cause of the freeholders of England, with that of Mr. Wilkes. I am, &c.

Buckingham.

MR. WHATELY TO MR. GRENVILLE.

September 22, 1769.

Dear Sir,—I was yesterday in town, where I find some, though not a very strong, apprehension of war prevails; one ground is, the report of some insolence on the part of France, which I do not find to be authentic; and yet some of the Ministerial people, I am told, say, they wonder that France should push us as she does, when the certain consequences will be the bringing in Lord Chatham, which she dreads more than anything. Another ground for the apprehension is the sailing of the Russian fleet

Mons. François, I am told, has said that the French will not interfere; he has, I believe, also said, that the trade to Turkey is their own, and that they will not sit by to see it destroyed by the Russians. The fact is, he has held different languages; he abides now by the latter; at first he was not well instructed. The Russian Minister says that we are all French here, that we pretend to be friends, he is sure we are not allies; that the Prussian Minister says his master has neither friend nor ally here, and that all the foreign Ministers talk of the influence of France over our conduct, not owing to our inclinations, but our imbecility.

Czernichef, on his return, will be created Vice Admiral of all the Russias, as a mark of honour for his behaviour in the affair with Chatelet.

The French Court have given orders to all their Ministers to dispute the rank of the Russian Ministers.

You may depend upon it, that the Duke of Grafton when he went to Stowe[1] hoped to find Lord Chatham

[1] The Duke of Grafton's visit to Stowe was duly announced in the contemporary newspapers. In the *Kentish Weekly Post and Canterbury Journal*, dated Monday, September 11th, 1769, it is alluded to under the head of *Extraordinary intelligence from London*. Bradshaw is mentioned as "one that married a cast-off, who had formerly held no mean rank in the Duke of Grafton's seraglio," and that he had been confidentially intrusted at different times with the most important secrets of Wilkes, D'Eon, and Lord Temple, and therefore a fit person to be intrusted with the opening of a negotiation for a treaty of union

there, and wished to have a conference with him. The Lord Chancellor, who was obliged to be at Court on account of the prorogation last Wednesday, went away during the Chapter of the Garter, when everybody else stayed to wish his Grace joy on the occasion.

I have seen Sir F. Bernard[1], and had a longer conversation with him than any of the Ministers; he has been admitted to none, I understand, but the Duke of Grafton; he did not see his Grace 'till Wednesday last, and then only for ten minutes; the Duke told him, that as Lord Hillsborough was in Ireland he would not detain him from an excursion into the country for a fortnight, so indifferent are the Ministers to the information they might receive from this gentleman.

Sir Francis said to me, that all the heats in America might still be quieted, but it must be by Acts, not resolves of Parliament; that the party at Boston, when he came away, were very alert and triumphant; the inanity of our resolves and the concessions of the circular letter from Lord Hillsborough were the grounds of their joy; and that he doubts whether having now none but Americans in office, the resistance on the part of Government will

---

between Lord Bute and the Duke of Grafton, and Lords Temple and Chatham. It was therefore intended to dispatch Bradshaw to Stowe; but Bradshaw having already forfeited Lord Temple's confidence, though he did not care to acquaint either Grafton or Bute with this secret, he artfully declined going to Stowe himself, adding that the embassy would have greater weight, and probably better success, if the Duke of Grafton went himself to wait on Lord Temple at Stowe. Bradshaw pretended to know the very bait that would tempt Lord Temple: it was nothing less than a Dukedom, but that if he, Bradshaw, were to make the offer, Lord Temple, he said, might doubt the performance. And this, therefore, was said to be the purport of the Duke of Grafton's visit to Stowe.

[1] He had been recently created a Baronet, and was at this time Governor of the Colony of Massachusetts Bay.

be so firm as when he was there. I do not give him so much credit for his personal importance as he assumed, and have myself great reliance on the temper and the steadiness of Hutchinson.

Sir Francis is very happy in the approbation which all Ministers have shown of his conduct, and he expressed himself as greatly obliged to you for the honourable testimony you had given of it in the House.

I find Mr. John Temple is coming home; his business is partly to answer the charge now made in form against him by the other Commissioners, for favouring the popular party, and partly to charge them, together with the Governor, with insolence, indiscretion, and perhaps abuse of their powers.

Letters of 8th August, from Boston, bring advice of messages sent thither from Virginia and Maryland, to ask what lengths they intend to go, and to tell them, that if they mean to proceed beyond the repeal of the last Revenue Law, other colonies will not support them; the Duke of Grafton rejoices much on this event; for my part, I doubt the Bostonians will persuade the others to waive their scruples, and to go along with them.

My intelligence of the language of the Russian and other foreign Ministers, though not from a bad quarter, is not from the best, and must be received with caution.

MR. WHATELY TO EARL TEMPLE.

September 22, 1769.

MY LORD,—I sincerely congratulate with your Lordship on the *triumphant proceedings* at Aylesbury, and thank you for the corrected copy of the petition, though it is rather a tax than a treasure, as the curiosity to see it has more than once obliged me to write it over; but at the same time that I acknowledge my obligations to your Lordship for this communication, I must complain of your reserve upon another point of Buckinghamshire intelligence. Your Lordship never told me that the Duke of Grafton intended by his visit to Stowe to get a conference with Lord Chatham, and yet it is certainly true; but there is such an affectation of secrecy in all who have communication from Ministers, that I doubt whether I shall hear from Stowe of the marked behaviour of the Chancellor, last Wednesday, in going away from Court before the Chapter of the Garter was over, when everybody else stayed to congratulate the Duke on the honour conferred upon him, of which slight I conclude his Grace has complained to your Lordship.

The anecdotes I am possessed of prove that I have been lately in town; I was there yesterday, and find still some apprehensions of war, founded partly on a very doubtful, I believe false report of some insolent messages from France, and partly on a speculation; not, I think, ill-founded, on the consequences of the enterprise of the Russian fleet on Constantinople. The language of the French Minister now (for it has been otherwise, but now it) is, that his Court cannot sit by to see their trade to the Levant destroyed by the Russians; the Russian at the same time says, we are all French, pretend to be friends, but are not allies to his Mistress; the Prussian says that his Master has neither friend nor ally here; and the foreign Ministers in general wonder at our inattention to the proceedings of France; while the Ministerial people in their turn wonder also that the French should push us in this manner, when they must see that the consequences will be the bringing forward Lord Chatham, which they dread of all things.

THE COUNTESS OF CHATHAM TO EARL TEMPLE.

Chevening, September 25, 1769.

WHAT is expressed, my dear brother, in my letter to Lady Temple, on the subject of the triumphs at Aylesbury, might stand as a full answer to your two last letters, but yet neither I nor my Lord can be contented without directly acknowledging them, and returning you our thanks for the pleasing information they contain; besides that we wish to assure you, that we never thought it likely that the expressions put into your mouth by the newspapers were really yours [1].

What did really pass upon the occasion, as mentioned in your last account, is exactly agreeable to what you know of my Lord's sentiments, and the whole of the transaction gave most real joy to us, as you have already fully seen.

We hope you and Lady Temple will have had a safe and pleasing journey to Eastbury, and that you will have found its inhabitants in perfect health. We wish you fine weather for all your sakes. When I recollect my brother Henry's attachment to his flower-garden, by Master Betts's, in ancient times, I feel all his anxiety for being able to show his present improvements with the most advantage.

Your friends here continue their usual exercise and amusements. Hayes calls my Lord frequently thither,

[1] And yet they were most probably communicated to the newspapers by Lord Temple himself. See *ante*, p. 454, *note*.

and I with the young folks visit the different parts of this charming country, see some of our neighbours, and now and then look at a cricket match.

Saturday my Lord Chancellor dined with us, according to promise from the week before. He was very well, and gave us great satisfaction. In a few days he goes to Bath for a month.

The last post brought us a most kind letter from Wotton, proposing a visit to us here from our nephew George, as the deputy of my brother and Mrs. Grenville, whose weak state will not permit them to give us the great satisfaction of their own company.

We never, indeed, once allowed ourselves to think of her undertaking such a journey, and we feel still the more their affectionate attention in doing what they are sure will give us the next greatest pleasure to that of receiving them here themselves. We answered this kind proposal by the post of the same day, and hope we shall welcome young Mr. G. G. on Wednesday or Thursday at furthest.

All the family are impatient for the day, and Pitt's hopes about Eton begin to brighten again; and if they should fail he is at least sure to be a greater personage in his own opinion, from having the honour to be admitted into the society of one who has been so conspicuous amongst the Etonian band. I am, my dear brother, &c., &c. HESTER CHATHAM.

MR. WHATELY TO MR. GRENVILLE.

September 26, 1679.

DEAR SIR,—After so long a letter as I sent you by the last post, you will not expect much news from me;

indeed, I have none to inform you of except a letter from Dr. Musgrave to Lord Bristol, in nearly these words :—

"I have been informed by an anonymous letter, that your Lordship has publicly said, that to your knowledge a sum of money has been issued out of the Privy Purse, as the price of Mons. D'Eon's silence; if so, Lord Bristol's character is too well known to leave the least doubt that he will be ready to declare through whose hands that sum was conveyed, in order to do justice to your injured Sovereign."

Lord Bristol has shown this letter to the Ministers, and told them he should not answer it. The Duke of Grafton's answer was, your Lordship is the best judge "whether to answer it or not, but you may be assured that no such money has been issued."[1]

I have seen a letter from Seymour, before he left Yorkshire, in which he says, that Wedderburn and Lee (the counsel on the Middlesex election) are gone to Wentworth House, which he "hopes will be the means of keeping the petition to one point, against the inclinations of some *immediate* friends to Lord Rockingham."

Mr. Dowdeswell and Mr. Burke are by this time also there, and they, I am sure the latter, and I believe the former, will be of opinion with Wedderburn; I think that Yorkshire business will end right at last, but there has been a puzzle and uncertainty in it, the secret motives of which I do not comprehend.

I have been told that the postponing the Parliament 'till after the holidays gives great discontent in the City,

---

[1] Whately wrote to Lord Temple by the same post, and this is another of the numerous instances in which he sent similar information both to Lord Temple and Mr. Grenville.

but from other hands I hear nothing of it, and, therefore, I doubt whether the discontent be very general.

Attempts have been made to do the same thing at Thetford as has been done at Bedford, but do not succeed[1].

It is supposed that Trecothick will be put in nomination for Mayor, by the Livery, together with Beckford and Baker, in order to force the Aldermen to the choice of Trecothick; the other party wish to put up Sir H. Bankes, who is next in rotation, and if presented will certainly be chosen. The person who repeated to me Dr. Musgrave's letter, could not recollect whether the words were *a sum of money*, or *the sum of* 550*l*., but thinks the latter.

MR. WHATELY TO MR. GRENVILLE.

October 7, 1769.

DEAR SIR,—I came to town yesterday on a summons from Wedderburn, to meet him on his arrival from Yorkshire; he represents the party he has lived with there as now unanimous and zealous on the measure of petitioning: a copy of the Yorkshire petition I inclose: he, with Mrs. Wedderburn, propose to pay their respects at Wotton, about a week hence, but he will write himself to know whether it will be convenient: he left at Wentworth House the gentleman[2] I called on in my way from Wotton, who expressed great satisfaction in the intercourse which had passed between Lord Temple,

---

[1] To choose a Mayor in opposition to the Duke of Grafton's influence at Thetford, as they had succeeded at Bedford, against the wishes of the Duke of Bedford.

[2] Mr. Burke.

yourself, and him; he will probably wait upon you now very soon, as I understand he returns about this time[1]; the conversation of Lord Rockingham was, I understand, similar to that which that gentleman held to me. I hear since I have been in town, that the reason for continuing the poll in the City is to give the Aldermen an opportunity of choosing Sir H. Banks; *Mr. Beckford being under a legal incapacity*, all the votes given for him are thrown away; so mad an attempt, such a confirmation of the present jealousies, so exasperating to the City, is hardly credible, and yet I believe will be made if the Court of Aldermen can be worked up to the spirit of daring to do it. The other party intend, as soon as the poll is over, to move the Resolutions you have seen in the papers, and some others; and at some subsequent Common Hall to propose a second petition, confined to the one point of the Middlesex election, the purport of which, as I am informed, will be, that "the seventh cause assigned for the revolution by the Statute 1 W. and M., entitled an Act declaring the rights and liberties of the subject, &c., was violating the freedom of election of members to serve in Parliament, and it was thereby declared that it is the right of the subjects to petition the King. That the freedom of election of members to serve in Parliament, which is essentially necessary to the preservation of the British rights and

---

[1] Soon after this date, Burke mentions in a letter to Lord Rockingham, that he had paid a morning visit to Stowe, and found Lord Temple alone. He adds:—" We had a great deal of political conversation. He was of opinion that let what would happen, the great point for us and the country, would be to get rid of the present Administration, which could only be effected by the appearance of union and confidence. Lord Chatham, he told me, was exceedingly animated against the Ministry."

liberties, has been notoriously violated by His Majesty's Ministers, and their undue influence in the House of Commons with respect to the late election of a member to serve in Parliament for the county of Middlesex, wherefore the petitioners most humbly pray that His Majesty will be graciously pleased to remove those Ministers from his councils; and that the Parliament, by whom the most sacred and important right of the people has been violated, may be dissolved."

This extract is given me in confidence, that I do not let it be seen 'till it is proposed, which will not be immediately.

Lord Holland is going abroad to Nice, for the recovery of Lady Cecilia Lenox, but it is doubtful whether she will live 'till the time fixed for setting out.

I saw your son, Mr. Thomas, the other day, and, which is more, he saw me too in a very ridiculous situation, for I was riding through Eton with Lady Mulgrave and her youngest boy, who is the least horseman on the least horse that ever was seen. The boys took a fancy to him, and gathered round us; her Ladyship was frightened, dismounted, and fled for refuge into Lord Mulgrave's chaise, leaving me and the little urchin in the midst of the circle. My good friend Tom gave me a wink and a whisper, advising me to make my retreat as soon as possible; I followed his advice, and think he got me out of a scrape[1].

Sir Fletcher Norton was expected yesterday in town I fancy he has been sent for to give his opinion of the

---

[1] An early indication of the sagacity and discretion for which Mr. Thomas Grenville was so eminently distinguished during his long life.

measures proposed concerning the election of Lord Mayor.

I believe the Russian Fleet is by this time at Spithead.

MR. WESTON TO MR. GRENVILLE.

Somerly, near Brigg, Lincolnshire, October 13, 1769.

Sir,—Having been represented to the world in a late newspaper, as the writer of a pamphlet[1] which I never saw, in which my Lord Chatham, to whom I have obligations, and you, to whom I have very great ones, as also some of my former friends and patrons, are grossly traduced; I have thought myself obliged to oppose truth to falsehood by giving a public negative to so infamous a calumny; and being greatly desirous of preserving the favourable opinion with which you have hitherto honoured me, I take the liberty to trouble you with a copy of the answer which I have published for the defence of my own character under those foul aspersions. I am, always with the sincerest esteem and most affectionate respect, dear Sir, &c., &c.   E. Weston.

MR. KNOX TO MR. GRENVILLE.

London, October 18, 1769.

Dear Sir,—The parcel I now send you by the Aylesbury coach will not contain anything new to you, how-

---

[1] Mr. Weston now alludes to a pamphlet, entitled the *Political Conduct of the Earl of Chatham.* Junius had not long before

ever eagerly it will be sought after by the generality of the nation. I believe the execution is correct, and I took special pains that it should be so, which has been the occasion of its being delayed longer than I hoped it would be. The advertisement which I have prefixed will divert the public inquiry from the channel through which it came, and, at the same time, it is so guarded as not to impute it to Mr. Cavendish so strongly as to call upon him to disavow it. Almon, who is a thorough judge of times and seasons for publication, does not intend to publish it 'till the return from Newmarket races, which will be the week after next, when many persons from different parts of the kingdom pass through London. In the meantime he sends it to all those who leave orders with him for every new thing. I send by this night's post a copy to Ireland, to be reprinted and circulated through that kingdom, and I shall supply every American ship that sails, with one, so that in a small space of time every part of the King's dominions will be fully satisfied of the wisdom and uprightness of your conduct.

I was more and more convinced of the propriety of this publication, from the frequent attacks in the newspapers and the general run of conversation in London, since I came here; and however it may provoke the Ministerial writers, yet I am sure it will carry conviction and approbation with it into the minds of every considerate man in the nation. You will see an advertisement on the cover of the last page, containing the title of a new pamphlet on the question of dis-

assumed that he was also the author of *A Vindication of the Duke of Grafton.* The letter of denial appeared in the *Public Advertiser* on the following day.

qualifying by vote[1]. It is written by the author of the letter upon Libels and Warrants[2], who, I believe, is Dunning, though you may believe he does not choose to be known. However, it is some proof of the truth of his professions in regard to the part he will take next Sessions. A dissolution of Parliament is now become a general cry, and the expectation of obtaining it gains ground very fast: before I close my Tempora Mutantur[3], I shall give some reasons for the gratification of the people in that particular.

I inclose a farewell, which I gave Lord Holland, as the paper it was published in does not go to you[4].

A ridiculous story is told about town, as coming from Sir Francis Bernard. He says, he was ordered to come home with the utmost expedition, as he was told that no colony measure could be taken 'till after he was consulted with, and that everything was suspended on that account. He says he has been now here six weeks, and he has not yet seen the Secretary of State for America, nor has he had one conference with the Ministers upon any public measure.

---

[1] The pamphlet is entitled—"*A Fair Trial of the important question: or the Rights of Election asserted against the doctrine of incapacity by Expulsion, or by Resolution: upon true constitutional principles, the real law of Parliament, the common right of the subject, and the determination of the House of Commons.*"

[2] It has no pretence to be so considered, but it may very well have suited Almon's purpose to spread such a report, in order to obtain for it a similar degree of popularity. It is altogether a very dull and heavy production, without the smallest resemblance in the style of composition to the celebrated Letter on Libels, to which it is in every respect greatly inferior. Upon the latter performance I have ventured to make some observations in another place.

[3] Probably some Letters under the signature of "Tempora Mutantur." One of them appeared in the *Public Advertiser* of the 4th instant.

[4] I have not been able to find this *farewell* to Lord Holland.

It is not true that Sir William Draper is appointed to the Government of South Carolina. He is going to that province only in his way to the northern colonies, where he intends spending some time. Sir Harry Moore is dead, which may give him an offer of the Government of New York, if he chooses that line of employment. I am, &c. &c. WILL. KNOX.

MR. GRENVILLE TO MR. KNOX.

Wotton, October 22, 1769.

DEAR SIR,—I was much surprised when I received by the Aylesbury stage coach, the day before yesterday, the favour of your letter, together with a printed copy of my Speech on the expulsion of Mr. Wilkes[1]. I never had the least intention of publishing it, and, therefore, if it is not too late, I beg the favour of you to apply to Mr. Almon, and endeavour to stop the pub-

---

[1] It does not appear in what manner Mr. Knox obtained a copy of this Speech. If it were not for Mr. Grenville's distinct denial, it might be inferred from Knox's letter of the 18th instant, that the Speech had not been printed contrary to Mr. Grenville's approbation and consent. Mr. Grenville is supposed to have corrected Sir Henry Cavendish's report, and had a few copies of it printed for private circulation. It is much more probable, however, that two or three copies were made in manuscript, and it has been seen that one of them was lent by Mr. Grenville to Lord Lyttelton. The Speech, as given in the *Cavendish Debates*, is precisely the same as that which had previously appeared in the *Parliamentary History*, professing to be copied from Almon's pamphlet, and Almon says that "Minutes of the following speech having been taken at the time it was made, and some copies having been handed about, one of them fell into the possession of the publisher, but before he would offer it to the public, he submitted it to the perusal of some gentlemen who heard it delivered, and whose accurate and retentive memories have supplied any defect in the Minutes."

lication, though I am much afraid by what you tell me of Mr. Almon's having sent copies of it to all those who leave orders with him for any new pamphlet, and of his having sent copies of it likewise already to Ireland and America, that it will now be scarcely possible to prevent it. If that is the case, I earnestly desire that you will tell Mr. Almon what you know to be true, that the printing and publishing it is without any direction, participation, or consent whatever from me, and I hope that you will take care to have these words added at the end of the first paragraph of the printed advertisement prefixed to it:—" though, at the same time, he is bound in justice to inform them, that it is published without the approbation, consent, or knowledge of the Right Honourable Gentleman who made it." This I must insist upon his inserting, and I hope that he will make no difficulty in doing it. I am obliged to you for the favourable opinion which you entertain of it, but as to any effect which it may have, or any conviction which you are persuaded it will carry with it, the minds of men are so much heated and so strongly prepossessed on one side or the other of this question, that it may be truly said of them, non persuadebis etiamsi persuaseris. One effect which you seem to foresee it will certainly have, that is, it will cast down upon me a heap of scurrilous abuse from the Ministerial writers, and though I know how to despise as I ought, that worst of all weapons in all cases, where my duty shall make me liable to it, yet I do not wish where it is unnecessary to have a heap of newspaper lies invented of me, to which I have long determined to give no answer. I have heard from America by the last mail, that things go on there worse than ever, and that the colonies rise daily in their demands, from the encouragement which they receive from considerable persons in England; and as my letter comes from one who was strongly of opinion that the disorders there were on the decline, I give the more credit to his intelligence now when he is of a contrary opinion. I am, &c., &c. GEORGE GRENVILLE.

MR. GRENVILLE TO EARL TEMPLE.

Wotton, Sunday, October 22, 1769.

MY DEAR BROTHER,—The letter which you sent to me inclosed from Mr. Walker to Mr. Miller[1], desiring an account of the names and residences of the Bailiff and Burgesses of Buckingham, has surprised me extremely. I return it to you according to your desire. I can see no purpose in it, but with a view, if possible, to make an opposition there, or possibly to furnish an article for the newspapers.

I know nothing of Sir James *Cotter*[2] myself, but have heard that he is an extraordinary personage, and if that is true, I should not wonder that many reports should have been raised either by himself or others in consequence of his having dined with you, though without the least foundation.

I should scarcely think that any places of residence to be now taken up for any of the burgesses can make much difference in the question either way.

---

[1] Miller was an attorney at Buckingham, and an agent employed by Lord Temple in the management of the Borough. The right of election was at that time confined to the bailiff and burgesses, amounting to thirteen persons.

[2] Of Rockforest, county Cork. He was a member of the Irish House of Commons. He became a Baronet in 1763, and died in 1770.

Notwithstanding what Mr. Calcraft writes[1] to you about the directions given to Colonel Burgoyne by the Duke of Grafton to canvass at Preston, I cannot believe it possible that the King or his Ministers think at present of dissolving the Parliament; and if they did, surely such a public letter as this to Mr. Miller, inquiring the *names* and *residences* of the burgesses, and thereby putting you upon your guard, is not the likely means to make a serious opposition, though it may serve to furnish an article or letter in the newspaper, to show by this list that *you* are as great a *tyrant*[2] at Buckingham as the Duke of Marlborough at Oxford or Woodstock, or the Duke of Bedford at Bedford. This is the light in which it strikes me: however I agree with you that every precaution will be proper and necessary, as much as if you believed the other[3].

We trust that we shall see Mr. Wedderburn here as soon as you can part with him. I am, your most truly affectionate, GEORGE GRENVILLE.

[1] I have already stated that no letters from Calcraft to Lord Temple at this time, have been preserved.

[2] This expression had a short time before been applied by Junius to the Duke of Bedford, negatively:—" He would not have thought it consistent with his rank in the State, or even with his personal importance, to be the little tyrant of a little corporation."—Vol. i. p. 577.

[3] This apparent or intended interference, on the part of the Duke of Grafton, with Lord Temple's influence at Buckingham, was perhaps remembered in the pages of Junius, when he soon after denounced the Duke for the "sale of a civil employment," in order to reward Colonel Burgoyne's "activity at Preston."

"Have you a single friend in Parliament so shameless, so thoroughly abandoned as to undertake your defence? You know, my Lord, there is not a man in either House whose character, however flagitious, would not be ruined by mixing his reputation with yours; and does not your heart inform you that you are degraded below the condition of a man, when you are obliged to hear these insults with submission, and even to thank me for my moderation?"—*Junius*, vol. ii. p. 59.

MR. KNOX TO MR. GRENVILLE.

London, October 24, 1769.

DEAR SIR,—The moment I received your letter of the 22nd, I called at Mr. Almon's in hopes to have found it possible to prevent the publication of the pamphlet which he calls your Speech, but I found that he had already circulated so many copies, that although it had not been advertised nor generally sold at his shop, yet it was beyond all probability to call in what were gone forth without supposing that some other printer would get hold of one and republish it. There was, therefore, nothing to be done but adding to the advertisement in the first page, such words as were sufficiently declaratory of your being unacquainted with the publication; and that leaf, in all the copies remaining in Almon's possession has been cancelled, and a proper addition made in the new copy. The words added, are, " though at the same time he is bound in justice to inform them that it is published without the approbation, consent, or knowledge of the Right Honourable Gentleman who made it."

I must confess that I am not sorry to find the people of England out of Parliament in possession of this Speech: none of us were permitted to be present when it was delivered, and for my own part I have heard very strange misrepresentations of it from some of those who were. It was but the morning after you had made it, that a gentleman in office asked me when I had seen Mr. Wilkes's new friend; and very few days have passed since, without giving birth to some new calumny of the same nature, and yet not one of those who heard your Speech has had the honesty to vindicate you by assigning the reasons you gave for your vote; nor has there been a single letter in any newspaper in reply to the various attacks which have been made upon you. What must the public think, but that you are that changeling your enemies have represented you to be, and which your friends do not gainsay? Let them, then, read your argument, and they will do you justice. They will then want no assistance from your friends to enable them to vindicate your conduct, for they will all become your advocates and admirers. His Majesty I am sure will thank you for it, because none of his Ministers have so fully justified his resentment against Wilkes, and the people must see that the King's desire to have him abide the punishment of the laws was highly proper; and that the present evils have their rise from the Ministers' negligence in carrying the laws into early execution, and not from commands to have them executed. The opinion of a speedy dissolution of Parliament gains ground, and if it becomes general it will produce a dissolution.

I don't like the stopping letters in the Penny Post Office, which I have reason to think is practised, and very possibly the letters by the General Post undergo an examination. Such methods may irritate, but they never can reclaim or quiet a discontented people. I am, &c., &c. WILL. KNOX.

MR. WESTON TO MR. GRENVILLE.

Somerly, October 27, 1769.

DEAR SIR,—I have not for a great while had more pleasure in anything than in the receipt of your very kind letter. Having been always ambitious to merit your approbation, the good opinion with which you honour me, with the assurance of the continuance of your friendship, afford me true consolation. I can say with sincerity, that I have suffered as much from the abuse of my friends as from my own, and it was so much the more painful to me to be represented to them and to the public, as the author of that very abuse. But I have now relieved my mind, and will endeavour to follow both your example and advice in abstracting my thoughts as much as possible from objects which suggest nothing but disgust, indignation, and grief. But I doubt they are of a nature not to continue long matters of speculation only. Fuimus Troes: fuit Ilium.

My wife desires leave to join in respects to Mrs. Grenville, and in very sincere wishes for her speedy and perfect recovery. May God grant you that happiness in her and in your children, which no friend to virtue, to religion, and to peace, can much longer have in any view of the present public situation. I am, &c., &c.
E. WESTON.

THE EARL OF CHATHAM TO EARL TEMPLE.

Hayes, November 8, 1769.

MY DEAR LORD,—Your friends at Hayes desire to greet your arrival[1] in the Capital, by this short note of

---

[1] On this same day, Wednesday, the 8th instant, Woodfall received a private communication from Junius, which commences thus:—" I have been out of town these three weeks, and though I got your last, could not conveniently answer it."

Mr. Grenville, in a letter of the 5th instant, to Whately, had mentioned Lord Temple's intention of remaining in London 'till Christmas, which might perhaps have been interrupted only by a journey to Wotton for two or three days on a visit of condolence to his brother,

inquiry after yourself and Lady Temple, who we hope to have the satisfaction of hearing are both in perfect good plight. We should have felt particular pleasure in doing the office of this bit of paper ourselves, in propriâ personâ, but some sensations of gout, though no actual attack, together with the critical season of the year, have checked the execution of our longing desires.

To-morrow we know is dedicated to the honest City and the right noble Lord Mayor, where your Lordship will not fail to give and receive much real joy.

Informations will be a very short chapter from such a recluse as I am: Lord Camden is *graciously* treated since his return from Bath, notwithstanding the full and direct declarations he made to the Duke of Grafton before he left town, touching his determination to explain upon any proper occasion in public, his entire and *invariable* disapprobation of the whole proceedings with regard to Middlesex election.

As to petitioning, his Lordship was also very explicit as to the *right*, as well as to the *illegality* of all prosecutions for the exercise of it. *Between us, be it said*, his Lordship previously consulted me (upon a letter to him from the Duke of Grafton on the subject of prosecution), and well for Lord C. [Camden] it was, for his answer would otherwise have been loosened by *exceptions* as to the *matters* contained in petitions. As he made it at

and to attend the funeral of Mrs. Grenville about the 12th or 14th of December. A letter also from Whately to Mr. Grenville, on the 7th instant, mentions his having been informed by Lord Temple of his intention of being in London at this time. I mention these circumstances because they are of some importance in the question of the Authorship of Junius, for Junius wrote several notes to Woodfall in the months of November and December.

last, his answer was full and manly that the right is *absolute*, and *unquestionable* for the exercise.

Lord Granby is, I understand, in perfectly good dispositions.

Paper admonishes me to make an end.

Lady Chatham and Brats join in all loves and duties to Lord and Lady Temple. Ever yours, CHATHAM.

MR. KNOX TO MR. GRENVILLE.

London, November 10, 1769.

DEAR SIR,—The first edition of your Speech having been almost sold off when I applied to Mr. Almon in order to have the errata inserted which you had pointed out, he has made the corrections in the new one he was then printing, and it is now published.

I cannot agree with you that the present race of men are unwilling to be undeceived, and I can give you some strong instances in proof of my supposition, that they would receive the truth when it was fairly offered to their understandings.

The printer, or more properly the Editor, of the *St. James's Chronicle*, who has hitherto been your sworn enemy from the fine Lord Suffolk moved the Lords to impose on him, and who refused two guineas from me to insert an extract from the American Controversy because it was in defence of your opinions, this very man has voluntarily made a large extract from your Speech, and introduced it with a general account highly commendatory of the performance.

Another American writer, who has published his spleen against you on the colony topic, has declared to

Almon that he was mistaken in his opinion, and that he shall ever honour you. On the other side scarce a dog has moved his tongue; not a single decrying letter has been in any of the newspapers, and a poor catchpenny pamphlet called *Observations on the Present Publication of the Speech*, is all the attack which has been made upon it. Indeed I never knew any publication so well received by all sorts of men, or so universally applauded; and however it may have come to the public against your intention, I am sure it was but just to the people to afford them the means of making a right judgment of your motives and conduct, and I am happy in continually hearing the just use they have made of it. I don't imagine any animadversions will come from the side of Administration. The Bedford people I should think would be rather pleased with the Speech although it censures the act of the day, but it justifies their opinions prior to that Motion, and shows clearly that if they had been adopted, that Motion need never have been made.

Whatever may be said upon it, I apprehend Wilkes will be the author of, for it certainly does him and his cause great dis-service. I know he is resentful and obstinate, but perhaps he may in this instance consult more with his prudence than his other feelings.

Lord Hillsborough gives me hopes that the people in the colonies are in a much more tractable disposition than they appear to be in from the common accounts. His Lordship has no apprehensions of everything doing well, if they be let alone by Parliament, and their affairs not intermixed with opposition points. The duties upon paper and glass, but not teas, are to be repealed from principles of justice, that as the colonies are obliged to take our manufactures, and cannot have others, we ought not to tax them upon their going to them. I like the idea of letting the colonies alone, but I do not approve of starting new divisions, or giving fresh occasions for altercation. However, I have no other concern than as a citizen of the commonwealth, and can therefore wait with patience the issue. I have the honour to be, &c., &c. WILL. KNOX.

MR. WHATELY TO MR. GRENVILLE.

November 14, 1769.

DEAR SIR,—I came to town this morning principally to pay my respects to Lord Temple; he was just returned from Hayes, where he left Lord Chatham quite recovered from a very kindly slight fit of the gout; fully persuaded that though the Ministry yet betray no symptoms of flight, they cannot possibly stand against the distress from abroad and at home, and convinced that the Chancellor's dismission is not yet in motion, though it is imposible for them to go on with him [1].

The resignation of the Duke of Rutland occasions much speculation. He keeps steady to it notwithstanding the many soothing messages sent to him by the Administration; what folly to quarrel with his Grace for two Tory parsons and Lord Denbigh!

Lord Temple told me, and bid me tell you, that Lord

---

[1] Burke writes to Lord Rockingham, " There has been much talk of the Chancellor, his opinions, dispositions, going out, or staying in; but for my part I look upon it all in the usual strain, of distressing the Ministers into some bargain advantageous to him; or in the style of Lord Chatham's politics to keep hovering in air over all parties, and to souse down where the prey may prove best."

Egremont's name was not mentioned at Mr. Wilkes's trial. The verdict is equally unsatisfactory to the Mob and to the Court; Wilkes himself and his particular friends did not, I believe, expect much more[1].

The French are very high upon the subject of the frigate. This was the reason of Lord Harcourt's sudden departure for Paris. The last words of Mons. Choiseul were, les choses commencent à s'envenimer.

The 5000 troops sent by the Court of Spain to take possession of New Orleans has occasioned an alarm both in the Cabinet and in the City.

MR. CAVENDISH[2] TO MR. WHATELY.

Doveridge, November 22, 1769.

Sir,—I received yours last post, and am sorry I cannot furnish you with any satisfactory notes of the Speech you mention[3]. I was so tired that night with the un-

---

[1] The verdict of the jury in the long-pending case of Wilkes and Lord Halifax. "The jury," says Charles Lloyd to Mr. Grenville, "as one of them told me, divided three times. Upon the first division, three were for giving one thousand, five for giving five thousand, four for giving three thousand. It was at length compromised, and ended in four thousand."

[2] Eldest son of Sir Henry Cavendish of Doveridge Hall, Derbyshire. He was at this time M.P. for Lostwithiel. He succeeded to the Baronetcy in 1776, and was soon after made Receiver-General for Ireland, and a Privy Councillor. He married the heiress of Richard Bradshaw, Esq., who was created Baroness Waterpark. Sir Henry died in 1804. The Debates in the House of Commons between May 1768, and June 1774, were reported by Mr. Cavendish. A single volume of them has been printed, and it is to be regretted that the public support did not encourage the publication of the remainder.

[3] Against the admission of

common heat of the House, that I was scarce able to write any part of that most admired Speech. I have often been angry with myself for want of diligence at that time.

The public are much obliged to the publisher of Mr. George Grenville's Speech upon the Expulsion. I shall be glad to see his other Speech published as correctly. I am, &c., &c.
H. CAVENDISH.

MR. HARRIS TO MR. GRENVILLE.

Sarum, November, 23, 1769.

DEAR SIR,—You know you may freely command anything I have. My parliamentary notes the last session were much shorter than usual. As to the motion on the important 15th of last April, I transcribe you word for word, all I have reserved relative to it.

Norton argued that the freeholders of Middlesex were bound by the notice which appeared in the face of the writ, read publicly before them, and setting forth Wilkes to be ineligible, and that voting for him afterwards, they threw their votes away.

Grenville maintained that no Order or Resolution of either House of Parliament bound farther than themselves, and that no vote of the House of Commons, nor anything but an Act of Parliament, could deprive a freeholder of his franchise.

On a division.
Ayes for Luttrell 197
Noes 143

Difference 54

I could not refuse your request, though I think there is little value in what I have sent you, as I dare say your own memory will suggest what passed much more perfectly and fully.

Mrs. Harris begs you to accept her compliments; I remain, with great truth, &c., &c.   JAMES HARRIS.

If you can send me a line of information what reports say is intended for the operations of the ensuing session, I shall be greatly obliged.

MR. CHARLES LLOYD TO MR. GRENVILLE.

Friday evening, December 1, 1769.

DEAR SIR,—The only news I hear is, that Mr. Henry Thynne[1] has a pension of 1000*l*. per annum given him by way of *Indemnity* for his not going Ambassador to the Court of Madrid. As the word Indemnity was not used during your Administration in this sense, you may possibly be as much at a loss for its precise meaning as I am.

I am credibly informed that the story alluded to by Junius in his last letter, relating to Mr. Hynd, [Hine] is a fact. The Customers place at Exeter is said to have been given to Colonel Burgoyne to dispose of, and to reimburse his expenses at Preston[2].   I am, &c.

CHARLES LLOYD.

[1] Henry Frederick Thynne, second son of the second Viscount Weymouth: he was made Master of the Household in March, 1768. Having inherited the estates of his maternal grandfather, John Carteret, Earl Granville, he was created Baron Carteret in 1784. He survived until 1826, and died at the age of ninety-one.

[2] Junius thus apostrophizes the Duke of Grafton on this subject:—
" Come forward, thou virtuous Minister, and tell the world by what in-

MR. WHATELY TO MR. GRENVILLE.

December 3, 1769.

DEAR SIR,—The melancholy apprehensions you entertain for the public are but too well grounded, and too soon will be general; though the alarm of an immediate French war be blowing over for the present, yet it is only for the present, and the pique of Spain, the contempt for England, and the fear in France of a combination against the Family Compact, whenever the Emperor shall be possessed of the power which his mother now withholds from him, may bring on a war soon, exclusive of those motives which may arise from Choiseul's personal and precarious situation. The squabble about the flag seemed to be only seeking a quarrel; the French sloop appeared to me to have been sent only to provoke a subject of complaint, and I suppose it is certain that the remonstrance was in high terms; but of late I have heard nothing of it; whether the French desist from their pretensions, or our Court have made concessions, or the dispute still subsists and I live in ignorance, I do not know. I have letters this week from America; one of my correspondents tells me that a plan has been formed in New York, and he believes is sent

---

terest Mr. Hine has been recommended to so extraordinary a mark of His Majesty's favour; what was the price of the patent he has bought, and to what honourable purpose the purchase money has been applied? Nothing less than many thousands could pay Colonel Burgoyne's expenses at Preston. Do you dare to prosecute such a creature as Vaughan, while you are basely setting up the royal patronage to auction? Do you dare to complain of an attack upon your own honour, while you are selling the favours of the crown to raise a fund for corrupting the morals of the people? And do you think it possible such enormities should escape without impeachment?"—*Junius*, ii. 53.

over hither, for an American Parliament like that in Ireland; but he informs me the scheme is not approved of at Boston, and he supposes it will be scouted here. He also tells me that now the combinations against importing are become serious; that at first they were set on foot at Boston merely to frighten, and many of the subscribers had no idea of abiding by their agreement; but that the Southern Provinces, thinking the Bostonians in earnest, have been so themselves, and this has forced the subscribers, who meant to evade, now to execute their agreement; that they have therefore, and to preserve their lead over the other colonies, proposed a fresh combination against importing till the *Revenue Acts* are repealed, by which loose term he apprehends they intend to reserve to themselves the option of being satisfied if more than *one* Revenue Act is repealed, or of being dissatisfied 'till *all* are taken away, according as they find it convenient.

He thinks that they will be pinched during the course of this year for many commodities which have hitherto been deemed necessaries, but that some supply will be got from their own manufactures, and from illegal importation. Another correspondent (the same gentleman, one of whose letters I lately sent you) thinks they will be able to hold out another year, and that they will succeed in establishing some manufactures which we shall never recover; but he says it is impossible Parliament should sit a week without taking some measures to break these illegal combinations. I am afraid his zeal for Government is greater than his knowledge of the present Administration.

MR. WHATELY TO MR. GRENVILLE.

Epsom, December 8, 1769.

DEAR SIR,—I could not believe, when I first heard of the melancholy event[1]; I was loth to think it true, and your last letter had not prepared me to expect it. I need not tell you how much I regret the merit that is lost, or how largely I share in your affliction: it has been ever in my thoughts since it came to my knowledge; but I will not dwell upon it now, though I trust that it is not aggravated, I wish it could be alleviated, by my participation.

I hope, too, that you will not give yourself the pain of answering a letter from me upon the subject, but whenever you come to town, only let me know, and permit me to attend you. I have the honour to be, with the greatest regard and respect, dear Sir, your most faithful and obedient servant, THOMAS WHATELY.

LORD CHETWYND[2] TO MR. GRENVILLE.

Mare, December 11, 1769.

ALLOW me, my dearest Sir (though scarce able to hold a pen in my hand), to lament the death of the most valuable and amiable woman that ever existed; as a parent, what a peculiar discernment in the education of her children! as a wife, what an inviolable attachment

[1] The death of Mrs. Grenville, which had happened on the 5th instant.
[2] William, third Viscount Chetwynd; he had recently succeeded to the title, having been previously Member for Stafford. He was the very intimate and confidential friend of Henry St. John Viscount Bolingbroke. He died in 1770, at a very advanced age.

for her husband! Being no more, the loss is inexpressible, because inconceivable. From a long and intimate friendship with the late Sir William Wyndham, I loved the daughter in her cradle, I admired her when advanced in life, I honoured and revered her when she changed her name, espousing the man of whom I had, and ever shall have, the highest opinion. God long preserve you to train up a most lovely race of infants; may the same Providence preserve their lives to your present and future real comfort, is the ardent wish of, dearest Sir, your most obedient humble servant, CHETWYND.

THE HONOURABLE AUGUSTUS HERVEY TO MR. GRENVILLE.

Lisbon, December 14, 1769.

DEAR SIR,—I scarce think I could have been tempted to have troubled you with a letter from this remote melancholy corner of the globe, had not an incident happened here which will certainly be much canvassed in Europe, and consequently you might like to know the particulars from the spot, but that is all I can tell you, for the suggestions of the Court and the examinations are as yet kept a profound secret. The 4th of this month (being St. Ignatius' day, and the patron of the Jesuits) a peasant (formerly an artillery-man) of Villa-Viciosa (where the royal family have been these five weeks all hunting), attempted and very nearly missed killing His Majesty. The King always gets on horseback first, and rides off by himself full gallop, as none can mount before His Majesty, and the same ceremony is observed whilst the Queen is mounting, who, in all weathers and times, accompanies the King, and the struggle is always which of them kills most game. The train is, therefore, generally some hundred yards from the King at first setting off. In this situation, as he was going through an arch that led to the ground, where 500 of these miserable wretches are employed to beat instead of dogs, one of them waited in this archway, and, with a long bludgeon, that is a very desperate weapon in their hands, and which they are as expert with, and as fond of, as a Highlander of his broadsword, he struck at the King; the horse starting, the blow fell on the King's shoulder, and he received a second on his wrist, before the Count de Prado, who was one of the Lords-in-waiting, could throw himself in, between the King and this desperate fellow. The Count was much bruised, and knocked from his horse in an instant, but saved His Majesty. The man would then have escaped, but was easily prevented by the numbers that got up. The Queen instantly called for her gun, and would have shot the man, but the King gave directions to secure, not to hurt him. Various are the conjectures: the man will undergo everything that can be invented. They say, he makes himself mad; others, that he speaks very well, and says he did it to revenge himself for two mules taken for the King's use, and which were his only subsistence; that his arrears had not been paid him for ten years; that is the case of all the King's servants in the country [1]. However, it will be a melancholy field opened again, if there is any one left to whom any *grudge* of old is owing, or any order that is to be extirpated. The King arrives to-day at the Ajuda, but, I dare swear, we shall hear no more of this, 'till whatever stroke is given is struck.

[1] Wraxall has given an account of this affair (*Historical Memoirs*, vol. i. p. 32). It was nothing more than the rage of the poor individual for an injury, real or imaginary.

The Condé D'Ocyras has lost one brother, Secretary of State, a few days ago; and this morning, his other brother, Don Paolo de Caravalo, Chief Magistrate and Justice of the whole city, has received the Viaticum, and cannot live 'till night. The Condé himself is and does everything; the King has an implicit faith, and lodges an unlimited power in him; and, indeed, he is, as to the King, worthy of the first, and, in himself, very capable of the last. He is much advanced now, and his health will not permit his constant application as it used to do, and as he does not care to trust others, many things must of course move slowly; which, in the situation of the Army and Navy, I cannot say has advanced much since I was here: I shall reserve all particulars 'till I have the pleasure of seeing you. *Mello* is talked of by some to succeed Francisco Xavier de Mendoça (the Condé's late brother), Secretary of State for the Marine; but others, who observe more minutely, do not think he will be brought over yet, as 'tis thought he looks out to succeed the Condé, which is no recommendation for him. I am, &c., &c. A. HERVEY.

LORD VERE TO EARL TEMPLE.

St. James's Square, December 19, 1769[1].

MY DEAR LORD,—I have been extremely sorry the post would not allow me sooner to return you my sin-

[1] Whether Lord Temple was in London upon the receipt of this letter, I have not the means of ascertaining. He had no doubt been recently in Buckinghamshire, to attend the funeral of Mrs. Grenville, at Wotton, and from whence he had probably returned some days before this date. It is equally probable that Lady Temple had remained in London to wait upon the last moments of her very old and

cere thanks for your very affectionate letter and kind wishes, and at the same time inform you of the disposition poor Lady Betty has made of her estates. Great part of the world, we hear, are extremely angry at her having left Drayton to Lord George Sackville, and, I conclude, will not believe neither Lady Vere nor I are the least disappointed, though we can, with the greatest truth, affirm we never one hour in our lives ever expected it, not only from the ascendant we daily saw the Duke of Dorset had with her, but from its being the wish and desire of Sir John; but, in short, he has it, and 20,000*l.* to lay out, to add to it, to change his name to Germain, all the goods, heir-looms: and, in case he dies without sons, or comes to the title of Dorset, it devolves to Aubrey and his sons. She has left Lady Vere 20,000*l.*, Lady Granard and Lady Craven 3000*l.* a piece, and their brother George 5000*l.*; Lady Temple 400*l.*, to lay out in something to remember her: Mrs.

nearest friend and relation, Lady Betty Germain, whose death was daily expected, and which did in fact take place on the 16th instant.

On Tuesday the 19th instant, the celebrated Letter containing the Address from Junius to the King, that "capital piece" which he had long been "meditating," appeared in the *Public Advertiser*, and on that same day Woodfall is supposed to have received a communication from Junius, as follows:—"for *material* Affection, for god's sake read *maternal*. it is in the 6 Par.—the rest is excellently done."

The note is without any date, but the correction to which it refers was actually made in the *Public Advertiser* of Wednesday the 20th, and therefore it would seem to be unquestionably certain that either Junius or his amanuensis must have been in, or in the neighbourhood of, London, on the previous day. There is, however, just a possibility that Woodfall may have sent to Junius a proof of so important a document as this Address to the King, some days before, and that either the error had hitherto escaped his notice, or that circumstances, respecting which we can now form no judgment, may have prevented him from sending the correction to the printer in time to enable him to make it on the day of publication.

H. Grenville 100*l*., and Mrs. Felton Harvey 500*l*. She has left annuities to her servants, continued others she had given before: 100*l*. a year to Mrs. Dansey, and 40*l*. to Mrs. Dyve at Ipswich; so that the small legacies amount to upwards of 15,000*l*. and the annuities about 700*l*. a year: she has 120,000*l*. in the stocks, which, with the other part of her personal estate, are to be divided betwixt Lady V. and myself, her two executors, and Lord George, who is joint residuary legatee.

I forgot to mention her having left Aubrey 1000*l*. in India Bonds, and a fine pink-coloured diamond, and a very large diamond, she once wore in a ring, to Lady Charles. She has left a picture to Lord Bristol, and another to Mr. Hamilton, who is at Naples; and now I think and hope I have omitted nothing material for your information, and from that you will think I have abundant reason to be thankful and satisfied.

I have sent to the landlord of this house to discourse him, as we wish to stay in it; for though we can't hope to live another thirty-one years in it, or to pass half the number of agreeable hours we have already, yet it will be some comfort to be near those friends that are left us, as long as it shall please God to permit us to remain here. All I mean to guard against is being obliged to remove again, as I feel myself too old for that.

As the whole load of business is upon Lady V. and myself, your Lordship will believe we have not much leisure to see many people were we inclined; in consequence, we know no more of the world than if we were in Japan; I can, therefore, send you no news, only our best wishes that we may see you and Lady Temple soon in perfect health, and that your Lordship will be assured of my sincere affection, &c., &c. VERE.

MR. WHATELY TO MR. GRENVILLE.

December 19 and 20, 1769.

Dear Sir,—I have been in town since I wrote to you. The Chancellor still holds the Seals, and is likely to hold them; that is agreed on all hands, and he seems perfectly at ease, but the ground of this security is not clear. The general opinion is that the Ministry cannot turn him out, and this is probable; but I have heard circumstances which indicate some transaction between him and the Duke of Grafton: he has dined lately with his Grace; his friends, Messrs. Pratt, &c., have also dined there: he has had a conference of an hour and twenty minutes in the Closet. I strongly suspect some negotiation; the nature and extent of it I do not know; I rather believe it is not brought to a conclusion, but I can give you no more information about it, and even this you must receive with some caution.

The other great friend of Lord Chatham [Lord Granby] holds a language not at all equivocal: he is eager in opposition, and, I believe, will be firm. The report of a further prorogation of Parliament seems to have arisen from a surmise of some bustle among the Ministry, for which I can find no sufficient foundation, unless this affair of the Chancellor will bear such a construction.

The Yorkshire Petition will be presented about the second of January: this brings up several of the Rockinghams; and others who are not immediately engaged in it will be in town by that time; their language, I understand, is concert.

I do not find the Ministry have formed the least plan about the Petitions, or about America.

The gentleman who, I told you, had called lately on a friend of ours, at which you expressed your surprise, said, in that conversation, that he was for a strong measure about Petitions: expel all who were concerned in them, and then you are sure of a majority, was the ludicrous answer. *Why, there are but sixty-seven!* was his reply. Is it possible to conceive, that any attack upon those sixty-seven has been in contemplation? and yet, why otherwise be so well informed of the number? The language of Ministry is full of confidence, both as to numbers and support: I doubt the zeal of the former, and the certainty of the latter. The only two who are known to be gained, stipulate only to absent themselves. *They have not more wisdom than they had before*, was an expression which dropped, amongst many other grumbling reflections, from the same gentleman, in the above-mentioned conversation. Even your old acquaintance, a noble Lord, who used to play at chess with you, complains of the neglect and inertness of Administration, and a large set who support the Ministry, are out of humour upon being, as they think, less attended to than formerly. All this I know is of little consequence, but it is part of the state of affairs.

The enemies of Wilkes reckon the election of Mr. Harley, to be President of the Hospital[1], a second triumph: his friends tried what they could do, but, finding it to no purpose, proposed no candidate. His cause, I am told, is very dead in the City. Many of the meetings advertised for the nomination of new Common Councilmen, have been neglected, and failed for want of attendance: there will, however, be a considerable alteration in the Common Council.

[1] St. Bartholomew's.

The opinion that Wilkes was Junius has been very general, but the Junius of to-day will, I think, destroy the supposition. The affair of Hine's patent makes a great noise: the part which the Duke of Grafton had in it, I am told, was this :—Colonel Burgoyne asked him for the reversion of something in Virginia, for a person he named: the Duke answered, he could not have that, but he might have this place at Exeter. The Colonel proposed it to his friend, who declined it; upon which the Colonel desired leave of the Duke to change that person for Mr. Hine, and his Grace answered, that the person was indifferent, he meant to give Colonel Burgoyne the nomination. As to the transaction between Colonel Burgoyne and Hine, I know nothing of the particulars. I am told that Mr. Harbord intends still to move a petition in Norfolk, but I do not know this with certainty.

I never saw so extraordinary a Paper as the Junius of to-day : I conclude you have it in your newspaper, or I would send it you in mine.

The above was too late for the post last night, and, on receiving yesterday evening's paper this morning, I find the Junius is not inserted, I therefore enclose it, together with a paper signed a Freeholder, which is almost as daring as the other, and is published in the *Morning Chronicle* [1].

On the 4th instant, as the King of Portugal was going to hunt in the Chase of Villa Viciosa, and had rode on, according to custom, a little before his attend-

---

[1] On the same day as the Letter of Junius, containing the Address to the King, and it has been attributed by some to the same Author: the supposition is altogether most improbable : it is very inferior to Junius, and I cannot discover the slightest resemblance in the style of composition.

ants, he was attacked by a peasant, with a kind of Club which the countrymen in that neighbourhood use with great dexterity, and prefer to all other arms. The blow glanced on the King's arm: the Count de Prado coming up, threw himself between the assassin and the King, and received two severe blows: the Chief Praedor also received one: the other attendants drawing their swords, the King called to them not to hurt the fellow, but secure him, which was done. Whether he made the attempt of his own accord, or at the instigation of others, is unknown. Perhaps this incident, by keeping everybody to their posts, may detain my friend [1] in Portugal, who, before it, had asked for leave of absence; he desires that none but yourself may know this account comes from him.

THE COUNTESS OF CHATHAM TO MR. GRENVILLE [2].

Hayes, December 26, 1769.

WE would not break in upon you, my dear brother, in the more early part of your affliction, with the expression of how greatly we shared in your deep distress; but we are desirous now that we may be allowed to say to you, that none of your friends have felt more for you, or have had stronger impressions of the greatness of your loss [3]. Our anxiety for you has been proportioned

[1] Augustus Hervey.

[2] Mr. Grenville's reply to this letter is printed in the *Chatham Correspondence*.

[3] The following letter was enclosed to Mr. Grenville at this time by Lord Lyttelton:—

MRS. MONTAGU TO LORD LYTTELTON.

Hill Street, December 23, 1769.

MY LORD,—I received a letter from your Lordship yesterday, and half a buck to-day. I hope you do so much justice to my taste, as to

accordingly, and our solicitude great to know how you and all the young people bore up under so heavy a

believe it greatly prefers the first bounty. I desired your Lordship's porter to carry the haunch of venison to poor Miss Talbot in your name. She is in a state of weakness rather than suffering. The happy prospect of a better world makes her amends for all she is quitting here. If the destinies would cut the thread of her poor mother's life, I imagine hers would be loosed at once. The thought of rendering the comfortless season of old age unhappy to the parent who afforded every assistance to her helpless infancy must be grievous, and her grateful soul seems to exert all its efforts to continue in a tenement hardly habitable.

I felt unspeakable concern for the loss of Mrs. Grenville. I could never bear to think of what poor Mr. Grenville and the children must feel upon such a separation. Nature, birth, and everything seemed to conspire to make her the first woman of this country, and as, added to that, she was the best too, when can regret and sorrow cease to weep?

There seems always to me a disproportion between persons of great excellence, and the duration of human life. Fifty years is enough for ordinary characters: they may have finished their *petite pièce* by that time, and it is fit they should quit the stage to a new harlequin and a new Soubrette. A short space is enough for those who are to do or to enjoy silly things. The part of wisdom and virtue must always seem too short to those to whom it is performed, and the felicity arising from it to the performer allows not of ennui or satiety.

I am rejoiced to hear Miss Stapleton will show her friendship to her lost friend, not by unavailing tears merely, but by tender care of the children. Miss Stapleton's character makes one rejoice in this; it will take off a great deal of anxiety from Mr. Grenville, and though it cannot cure his sorrow, will soften it. Miss Grenville[a] promises to resemble her mother; may she have a longer life! I wish she would early accustom herself to taking rhubarb if she has any disorder in her stomach; it is the best antidote to her mother's complaint.

However, to speak of things more cheerful, when will your *Leonidas* appear? I believe your Lordship and I shall have many a battle upon the subject: you will come like the Persian monarch, you will appear in all the pomp of learning, with a vast muster of eloquence, and abundance of art, and you will dazzle by the brightness of your arms, and terrify with the number of your troops; all the epic poets but

---

[a] Afterwards the wife of Sir Watkin Williams Wynn, and the grandmother of the present Baronet.

stroke. It was a very sincere satisfaction to us, on every account, to hear that you had opposed so much fortitude

Horace and Ossian, perhaps, on your side; I shall be as a poor Spartan, unassisted, uneloquent, unadorned, but if your poem cannot enter the *straits of the heart,* I shall be invincible.

If your poem touches neither the passions nor the imagination, why —it may be very respectable to be sure, and I shall own [it] to be a very fine funeral oration. I am very angry at what you say of Paoli. Good my Lord, are there not dead heroes and patriots enow? The rarity is to be a living one. I should not have taken the least notice of the man if I had met him in the Elysian Fields. Epaminondas would have stood before him, Timoleon would have overtopped him, Dion would have been more conspicuous; but oh! when he stood in the drawing-room by the D—— of ——, and the Earl of ——, and Lord ——, he looked more than human! I know my patriot is not likely to be made an alderman, as modern patriots are, but I like him the better. I like not the plum nor the sugar-plum patriot. He shall die to please his vanity another time, when Corsica can spare him better. "Il est plus difficile d'être saint que martyre," says a wise man: if my patriot continues pure and holy in a Court, I shall honour him more than if he had died in a pet of virtue.

As Lady Anglesey[a] has drunk up her caudle, I wish your Lordship would come to town. It is a dull town, I must confess, but that fault your Lordship will mend, and render it agreeable to your friends. I am sorry to tell you that a friend of yours is no longer a concealed scribbler[b]. I had better have employed the town crier to have proclaimed me an author; but being whispered, it has circulated with incredible swiftness. I hear Mr. Andrew Stone is very indulgent to my performance, which flatters my vanity. Mr. Melmoth, at Bath, puffs me, but I am most flattered that a brother author says the book would be very well if it had not too much wit. I thought there had been no wit at all in it, and am as pleased as M. Jourdain was when his preceptor told him he spoke prose. If my wit hurts anybody or anything, it is chance medley, no premeditated malice, neither art nor part has my will therein; I don't love wit; it is a poor paltry thing, and fit only for a merry Andrew. I look very innocent when I am attacked about the Essay, and say I don't know what they mean. I shall set about a new edition as soon as your Lordship comes to town,

---

[a] Lord Lyttelton's only daughter Lucy was the wife of Arthur Annesley, Earl of Anglesey, afterwards created Earl of Mountnorris.

[b] Mrs. Montagu alludes to her Essay on the *Genius and Learning of Shakspeare,* first published about this time.

to the cruel misfortune of being deprived of what was so justly dear to you. Thank God! you are in possession of the greatest consolation possible for you to receive, in the great promise and amiable dispositions of your dear children, and by having your care for them so much lessened by the attentive affection of Miss Stapleton's most valuable friendship.

I am in hopes, my dear brother, that the time is not to be long before your removal to London, which will put in my Lord's power and mine the opportunity which we wait for with great impatience, of assuring you by word of mouth of our truly affectionate regard for you and yours.

My Lord is enough recovered of his last fit of the gout to be able to take the air, which he bears without fatigue, and feels perfectly well. I have had a cold, but am now better. The young people are all well, and will be happy to hear of their cousins being within their reach.

My Lord desires to join his affectionate compliments with mine to our agreeable guest, to dear Charlotte, and

for the first thousand is in great part sold, though the booksellers have done me all the prejudice in their power.

I was so provoked at Mr. Black for disappointing you again, I gave him a good lecture by the post. If the fences of your woods are not well kept up they will be ruined, indeed good fences are of great consequence to all ground, but most particularly for woods.

Mr. Black will certainly be of use to your Lordship. My best respects attend Lord and Lady Anglesey, and affectionate wishes the little Lord.

Of all my scrawls this is the worst, but by orders of the doctors I write by the inch of candle, but I cannot write by the inch of paper.

Mr. Montagu desires his best compliments; he was very desirous Mr. Black should attend your Lordship, having found himself good consequences from his care. I am, my Lord, &c., &c.

E. Montagu.

to the rest of the brothers and sisters. I am, my dear brother, your loving sister, HESTER CHATHAM.

MR. WHATELY TO MR. GRENVILLE.

December 27, 1769.

DEAR SIR,—By the time you receive this, I suppose you will be able to guess when you shall be in town; as my going thither depends on the time you fix for your removal, I shall be glad to be apprized of it.

This country is full of reports about Junius: some say he is a Mr. Lloyd[1], Chaplain to Lord Shelburne, and that he is in custody. The discovery, they pretend, was produced by Colonel Burgoyne threatening the printer, if he concealed his name: another story is, that

---

[1] Respecting this person I have no information, nor do I think that he has ever before, or since, been mentioned as the supposed Author of Junius. There were several of the same name who were much connected with the literary and political history of this period.

Philip Lloyd, afterwards Dean of Norwich, had been tutor to the sons of Mr. Grenville, and was probably the means of introducing his brother Charles, who became Mr. Grenville's private and very confidential secretary. He had been Receiver of Gibraltar: he held some appointment in the Treasury, and was one of the Deputy Tellers of the Exchequer. Both these brothers were political writers, as authors of pamphlets and occasional articles in the newspapers. Charles died in January, 1773, and Philip died at the Deanery House in Norwich, May 31, 1790.

Dr. Pierson Lloyd was one of the Masters of Westminster School: he died in 1781, and was the father of Robert Lloyd, the poet satirist, and intimate friend of Wilkes and Churchill: he died in 1764.

In the *Gentleman's Magazine* for 1764, p. 603, I find recorded the death of Robert Lloyd, Esq., Housekeeper and Wardrobe-keeper at Kensington Palace.

Of one Thomas Lloyd, who was supposed to be Secretary to Lord Chancellor Camden, I have spoken in another place.

the printer has disavowed a direct knowledge of the Author, but declared that the direction of the cover which enclosed the last paper was in Mr. Wilkes's hand, though the paper itself was in another[1]; and some say that Wilkes has long been engaged to the Author to father any libel which may be taken notice of, as he supposes the Ministry will not choose to meddle with him any more.

I do not give you any one of these reports as true; I think them all improbable; but each of them is believed by many, and, together, they prove the noise which that paper has made.

In the elections in the City, I apprehend both sides have been disappointed: the Opposition have carried more than the Court expected, but I hear it is not clear that they have a majority now of the Common Council, though I should think they must.

It seems to me, by the papers, that the Ministry have given up the point in dispute with the Irish House of Commons; but I have no better authority for it than

[1] If this were true, it would be a curious corroboration of Mr. Butler's *Reminiscence*[a] respecting Junius's letter to the King, and would account for his assertion, that the *original* of that paper was produced to him by Mr. Wilkes, together with the private letters addressed by Junius to himself. It is very possible that Junius may have submitted this production, as we know he did the Dedication and Preface, to Mr. Wilkes for his perusal and correction, and that the latter, having made some alterations, had it copied for Woodfall, and retained the original in his own possession. This is not, however, very probable, for Wilkes certainly returned to Woodfall the originals of the Dedication and Preface.

If ever Wilkes's papers, which have so strangely disappeared since the publication of Woodfall's edition of the Letters in 1812, should again be discovered, they will, I imagine, throw some new light upon this question.

[a] *Reminiscences of Charles Butler*, 3rd edit., 1822, vol. i. p. 81; and see also *ante*, vol. iii. p. lxxxiv.

the *Chronicle*. I have had no communication with any authentic person since I wrote to you. I saw the other day Mr. Hotham, the member for Wigan. The turn of his conversation implied, that the heads of the Opposition must *concert* their measures before the session. He has himself been always desirous of union, but he knows also, I presume, the sentiments of the Duke of Portland, and he spoke of this as a thing that was obvious, and which he concluded would be.

MR. WHATELY TO MR. GRENVILLE.

January 11, 1770.

DEAR SIR,—The news at the Levée is, that Mr. Yorke will be Chancellor, yet I hear from other hands that it is a doubt whether Lord Camden will be removed. General Keppel tells me he has heard and believes that Lord Granby will go out, and the Duke of Gloucester be Commander-in-Chief; I have seen Colonel Faucett, Lord Granby's secretary, and his language was resignation.

I hear of others disposed to resign if Lord Chatham [Camden?] should seem likely to go on: Sir George Savile said yesterday in the House, that *the House of Commons had betrayed the trust reposed in them by their constituents*. General Conway and Lord North checked him, and imputed the expression to heat: he disavowed the heat, but said, as I understand, that he would examine the assertion coolly, and if on deliberation he kept to the same opinion, he would repeat his expression on Friday; if so, a debate must arise relative to the main question, and a question must be put upon the censure to be inflicted on him, from which I presume you would not willingly be absent, and on which I apprehend the minority must be very strong.

MR. WHATELY TO MR. GRENVILLE.

January 12, 1770.

DEAR SIR,—The words used by Sir George Savile were these:—*I, a Member of Parliament, here in my place, do say to you, Sir, that you, the House of Commons, have betrayed the rights and interests of your constituents*—hard words, Sir, and epithets, instead of aggravating, alleviate a charge founded upon facts; for that reason, mark my words, Sir, for that reason only, *I do not say that you have corruptly, servilely, and profligately betrayed the rights of your constituents, but I do say that you have betrayed the rights of your constituents.* Mr. Burke, who gave me this account, was not sure whether the second epithet was *servilely* or *perfidiously*; he further told me that from many circumstances it was evident Sir George Savile had determined to use these or such expressions, on the first occasion, but had not communicated his intention to his friends: the occasion he took was a little debate begun by Sir William Meredith, who excepted to the King's speech for the general approbation of our conduct, because it included our conduct in the Middlesex election. He was answered by Mr. Jenkinson. Sir George Savile rose next, and said he came with a premeditated answer to that gentleman, having read every word of his speech that morning in the newspaper. He then proceeded to the question, and said the words I have given you. Jenkinson replied without taking the least notice of the words; next General Conway, and after him Mr. Charles Fox, observed upon the impropriety of using such expressions, and imputed them to heat in debate. Sir George Savile rose again and said he was not sensible of any heat when he spoke them; he hoped there was none in his manner; that, however, the House usually allowed a member who had been intemperate time to cool before they condemned him, as the law allowed time to cool before it pronounced killing to be murder, that he meant to avail himself of this indulgence; that he had now had time to cool, and that now coolly and deliberately he repeated, that this House of Commons had betrayed the rights of their constituents.

Burke rose next, his expressions the day before having been animadverted upon by Mr. Fox; he enforced them; he applied them to the present case, and said that the words used by Sir George Savile deserved the highest animadversion, if their authority were entire; that he ought to be sent to the Tower for them, but they had not now authority to vindicate their honour. There it ended; neither Lord North nor Dyson said a syllable.

I told Burke that I had heard from more than one person, that Sir George Savile had pledged himself to repeat the expressions to-day; he answered that he did not recollect it; that from the conversation he was present at between Sir George Savile and Lord Rockingham, he understood otherwise; and that my not knowing it authentically was an evidence that the party did not expect it, for that if any of them had intended to stir anything of importance, I might be sure they would have communicated it to Mr. Grenville.

I give you this detail to set right the more vague account I sent you yesterday, and to prevent your coming down unnecessarily, if you had any thoughts of it, and as I know you wish to avoid every attendance which the occasion does not call for.

If you hear nothing more, I think you may conclude that Sir George Savile does not intend to repeat the words, at least to-day; when Lord Rockingham asked him whether he did intend it, he answered he did not know that it was necessary, when he had told a gentleman that he was a scoundrel in a public coffee-house, to repeat it wherever he met him, but wished to know what others thought of it. If he should at last resolve to repeat the words, and his intention should come to my knowledge, I will acquaint you with it.

MR. THOMAS COLEMAN[1] [TO MR. GRENVILLE?].

Port Egmont, March 4, 1770.

MY DEAR SIR,—Having an opportunity by the *Tamar* sloop to send to England, I very readily embrace it to send you this, from the most detestable place I ever was at in my life, and shall be truly happy if this finds you well and in every respect agreeable to your wishes both in body and mind.

Our voyage was the shortest to this place any ship has ever made, but God knows disagreeable enough; no entertainment but what I'm obliged to make for myself;

---

[1] Mr. Thomas Coleman appears to have been a Lieutenant of Marines, stationed at the British settlement on one of the Falkland Islands. This letter arrived in England early in June with the first tidings, brought by Captain Hunt of the *Tamar*, that the Spaniards had disputed our right to the miserable island in question.

but by keeping my time constantly employed, I find near four months of my time already passed almost insensibly. Thank God, I have had my health perfectly, except one day, in crossing the broiling latitudes, I dropped down on the deck, lost my sight for a while, and with the violence of pain I felt in my head, I was soon deprived of either sense or motion. Bleeding directly quite recovered me, except being very sick for a few hours after.

I wish any occurrence of the voyage would afford you entertainment, but it has been as barren of events worthy notice as these islands are of everything else except sea lions and seals. I assure you I speak truth when I say there is not an inch of Braddock down that is not better than the very best of any of these islands; there is not a stick so big as the pen I am writing with, on any of them.

The soil turf chiefly, and in short is one wild heath wherever you turn your eye. We were particularly unlucky with our stock of fresh provisions. Out of 25 sheep (without eating a bit for the whole voyage) we brought in only three; fowls, ducks, geese, &c., went off likewise, and my own private stock, the most part of it spoiled, the ship being so small it could not be properly stowed away.

People who can eat fishy geese every day of their lives may live tolerably well here; I think I have not sat down one day since I have been here without one at least at table, so that by the time the station is at an end I shall be sufficiently surfeited. There are a great many fowl of different sorts here, but most of them fishy. There are some goats and fishy hogs, but I must do the mutton justice, which I think by much the best I ever tasted; there was a sheep killed for joy at our arrival, and another will be next year, when the next relief comes, there being only two or three here. Very good vegetables of all sorts, but so much trouble and care required to raise it, it is hardly worth the pains.

We have been ordered off the island by the Spaniards, the French having given up their pretensions to their settlements. They have 150 inhabitants at Port Solidade, 14 pieces of cannon mounted, and stores of all kinds, and their ships from Buenos Ayres constantly increasing their strength. Two of their men-of-war came here about ten days ago, and warned us off, which we refusing, the Commodore said he should not act any further at present, but wait for further orders from his Court. Their force, if they choose to oppose us, is greatly superior, we having no more than two miserable little sloops, and those not sufficiently manned, for when any ships come in the marines are landed to defend the settlement. I believe there never was such a command given to two lieutenants of marines anywhere but here. I have a sergeant, drummer, and ten; my brother officer, a corporal and eight; with which we are to defend a block-house that has not a gun in it, or a loop-hole cut, but from top to bottom is filled as full as it can hold with naval stores.

The only things that inhabit the settlement when we are not there, are hogs, goats, &c., who live in turf-houses. There is one grand house here which I think has walls of stone, cemented with clay, of about 7 feet high and about 16 or 18 long. This is the Governor's, and is lined with red baize.

I did what I could, both at Madeira and St. Iago, to get some birds, but could not get one of any kind, except I had taken goldfinches. There is a pretty sort of bird here about the size of a thrush, and pretty near the same colour, except the breast, which is a beautiful bright scarlet. I shall try to get some of them, but am told the moment they quit these islands they generally die; however, that shall not prevent me making an attempt. Here are very uncommon penguins, three different species of them, and are very curious indeed. If I could get them to live they would be very well worth the carriage to England.

Though 't is now summer here, I am now so cold I can hardly hold my pen. I have now been here for these five weeks, have not seen above two or three fine days, hardly ever being able to go out without a great coat. One comfort I have, that all the people chance has thrown me with are very sociable and obliging, which is a very great matter on such an occasion as this. I suppose long before this all is determined relative to petitions, addresses, &c. God send you health and true happiness, and though I never should be so happy to see you again, remain (in as good spirits as I can, so circumstanced as I am) most sincerely, &c., &c.

THOMAS COLEMAN.

MR. CHARLES LLOYD TO MR. GRENVILLE.

Thursday, March 15, 1770.

DEAR SIR,—As I know you do not dislike receiving letters, I flatter myself that an account of the political debate yesterday, in the Lords, will not be less agreeable than any other subject.

Lord Rockingham made a motion, that an account be

produced of the expenditure of the Civil List, from the 5th of January, 1768, to the 5th of January, 1769, the same papers as had been moved for in the Commons, last week.

Lord Chatham supported this motion by a very able recapitulation of the origin of the Civil List Act, its specific appropriation directed in the preambles of the several Acts settling that revenue, and concluded his first speech with some reflection on the ignorance of those who did not know that a Minister was impeachable who diverted the revenue which was so specifically appropriated.

Duke of Grafton took up the words ignorance and novice as meant for him, and said, novice as he was now, he had not always been thought so by Lord Chatham, particularly when he had been recommended by him for the Treasury.

Lord Chatham in reply. It is very true, I did submit the noble Duke's name to the King, for the Treasury. I thought him equal to that department, limited and confined. I never did think of him beyond a young nobleman of expectation. I never did think him equal to the government of a great kingdom.

Duke of Grafton insisted upon it, that Lord Chatham himself had burthened the Civil List with pensions to the amount of 8000*l.*, meaning Lord Northington's, &c.

Lord Chatham denied it, and was observing the consistency of the noble Duke's Administration, which set out with disgracing the man[1] to whom we owed our successes in America, and was wound up with dis-

---

[1] Sir Jeffry Amherst. Upon the subject of America, Lord Chatham had recently made a very remarkable speech in the House of Lords,

mission of a Chancellor for the *vote he gave in that House.*

which has been given by Mr. Jared Sparks, in his edition of the works of Franklin, from a report written at the time by Mr. Johnson, the agent for Connecticut. Lord Mahon has reproduced an extract from it in the Appendix to the fifth volume of his *History of England,* p. 35, in which Lord Chatham exclaims :—" I think the idea of drawing money from them by taxes was ill-judged. Trade is your object with them, and they should be encouraged. But (I wish every sensible American, both here and in that country, heard what I say), if they carry their notions of liberty too far, as I fear they do, if they will not be subject to the laws of this country, especially if they would disengage themselves from the laws of trade and navigation, of which I see too many symptoms, as much of an American as I am, they have not a more determined opposer than they will find in me. They must be subordinate."

These sentiments of Lord Chatham coincide with those of some other leading statesmen who were the chief promoters of the Repeal of the Stamp Act. I subjoin some extracts from a very remarkable letter, I believe not hitherto printed, written by Sir George Savile to Dr. Thomas Moffatt, a physician at Newport, in Rhode Island. It is from a copy certified by the autograph of Mr. George Chalmers; and Mr. Astle, in a note, observes that—" *this letter shows the writer's* [Sir George Savile] *dissatisfaction, and contains many remarkable sentiments. A wild politician with a good character, and with popular talents, may do great injury to a State.*" Sir George Savile says,— " You know I spoke and voted for the Repeal of the Stamp Act. My single vote turned no scale, and is a small matter now to speak of; but I shall be sorry to think I then had done wrong ; I do not think so *yet;* pray attend to that last word ; are they all determined with you not to have a friend in Great Britain, not a single friend ? Let them count upon those they once had here, and coolly consider whether it is policy, gratitude, or just calculation, or by what name shall I call it to you, to put their present talkers in competition with us, for talkers and mere talkers they will prove in the ensuing day of trial. The spirit of party may at times lead any man or set of men, and makes them guilty of personal indiscretion among ourselves ; but I am not to be suspected surely of any private enmity to Mr. Otis, or to any of your violent men ; and therefore I cannot yet believe that any of your sober-minded people can look for anything but mischief and confusion from the violences they have incited your people to commit. God only knows what their real motives be ; and I speak

Lord Marchmont sprung up, and insisted on the above words being taken down; they were taken down,

now only of the effect of their councils, because I know that just so, I, or any other person here that could be hired for the purpose, by the worst enemies of this country and the colonies, would have advised your people to have acted. But for argument sake with you, I will suppose that the Americans have been right in every point and instance; but was there no better way, then (for I speak now from motives of policy only), for them to gain their point over this enemy of theirs, Great Britain? Is there any wisdom in their conduct? Is there any cunning, craft, or probability in any of their devices or designs? As we are so violent and very tyrannical here, may we not also be raised into a passion? Or will not the Americans permit us also to be mad as well as they? Was there never yet a rash or an obstinate Minister of State in Great Britain? And may not a House of Commons and Peers be inflamed also? And may we not then overlook these your pleaded rights and pretensions, but even sacrifice them with a part of their own interest? Suppose we should do it but for a single session of Parliament? With what bands would you tie our arms in that moment of rage? Are you prepared for this, or have you thought of it? On the other hand, has America never known the time and season when their complaints were not only attended to here, but even some hasty expressions of ours, that were indecently enough retorted and thrown daily in our teeth by you, were not only overlooked, but the single grievance of which you complained immediately redressed? Are you determined that it never shall be so again? Or is there such a pleasure in buffeting against the wind and tide of power that you are afraid of fine weather? Yes, you say, you will do it by force this time: there was not difficulty enough the last time to make that simple flavour relish; but I pray you, how long, or have you computed how long it shall be before you have completed this your conquest over us, or that we are subdued, and made to submit to you? You will reap great glory in achieving this, but you will be somewhat longer in doing it, I think, than the Stamp Act was in repealing."

"I argue with you as if your people heard me, and indeed it would be much to the same purpose, for one may as well talk to the wind as to the multitude, when they have gotten a word among them which they do not rightly understand. I do not now speak of any particular set of men, because I think we are all of us very much alike in this respect; and I believe there is not so wild a beast in your wilderness, as a multitude of well-meaning people agitated with a well-sounding but ill-understood phrase; therefore I yet say unto you, that the Americans are my countrymen, fellow-subjects, and brethren, far, very

and ten minutes' confusion ensued, one moving one thing and another another. Lord Temple desired the words

far, from being the special object of my resentment; nor can I yet find in my heart to condemn your country in a lump. You write me that there are sensible and very moderate men among you; I dare say there are; but I conclude and fear that the major part of you are infatuated, and that your sensible and temperate people can neither help nor prevent it; but infatuated you are, in proceeding to your ruin, because so far as I see there is nothing left but to lament it, as it cannot be hindered now, morally speaking, by any means that either are gentle or severe. There will not be wanting many here, I assure you, who will call your punishment a just chastisement, nay, they will rejoice and triumph in it, because they can say the Americans have brought it on themselves. But I think and say, that you are a distempered and delirious people, and therefore deserve much pity and compassion, because you certainly have not known what you were doing. I do not know or think that ever I shall be benefited twenty pounds by all the taxes that will ever be levied in North America, and from the local situation of the chief part of my landed estates, there are but few persons in England that will be more immediately affected by the increase or decay of your trade. But, do you think, because of that consideration, that I shall be at any loss to choose my side, if matters shall be insolently driven up to an extremity by you? And the Americans have supposed that they have fast hold upon us, upon account of their commerce with us, and have piqued themselves upon it, and have boasted that they will go in rags, and be proud of them, rather than purchase the commodities of Great Britain. Lord pity them! Because there was once a clamour raised here, which we turned to their favour and advantage, do not they think or can they not consider what we can do, if we are heated, driven, or worked into a frame of spirit big with resentment and rage against you? But I say again, that you are mad, or else you conclude that we are debilitated and heart-broken with the burden and expenses of the late war. But tell them, because I tell it to you, that the eighty millions which we then spent has scarcely wounded us through the skin; not a single luxury either lopped off, or retrenched here; hardly enough of our fulness and fatness purged down, to fit us for hard labour: we are but breathed, if we should come to be in earnest with you."

"It is melancholy, very melancholy, for me to write in this strain to you, but it had better be twice written than happen once, because it will then be as ridiculous, as it is now foolish and evasive in you to talk to us of your right and your principles. Power shall

might be read. Lord Sandwich moved to adjourn. Lord Mansfield was for conciliating matters[1]. Lord Chatham seconded the motion that the words might be taken down. Lord Rockingham, Lord Temple, Duke of Richmond, Lord Shelburne, and Lord Lyttelton, repeated Lord Chatham's assertion.

Lord Chatham reasserted, and said, he stood as an accused man, insisting on a hearing and on justice[2].

---

then be the right. The trunk may be sorely wounded, but the branches can be destroyed and cut down, and you may then with grief and bitterness of spirit remember these precious moments which you have lost and abused, and may bewail the imprudent, and to say no worse, the very impolitic use which America made of the kind and very indulgent advances of a certain year: then was the time to have secured your interest here, perhaps your being."

"From a reflection of what has followed upon the Repeal of the Stamp Act, and a survey of some occurrences in New England, I am determined that my conduct in Parliament shall show forth that I am for measures of moderation and lenity, founded in vigour, without a mark of passion or resentment."

[1] "I think," says Horace Walpole, "it was in this debate (which was a very heterogeneous one), that Lord Mansfield, being called upon for his opinion on Luttrell's case in the Middlesex election, declared his opinion should go to the grave with him, having never told it but to one of the royal family: and being afterwards asked to which of them, he named the Duke of Cumberland, a conduct and confidence so absurd and weak, that no wonder he was long afterwards taunted both with his reserve, and with his choice of such a bosom friend."—*Memoirs of George III.*, vol. iv. p. 102.

Lord Temple, it has been seen, took part in this debate, and Junius, in allusion to Lord Mansfield, wrote:—"He said in the House of Lords that he believed he should carry his opinion with him to the grave. It was afterwards reported that he had entrusted it, in special confidence, to the ingenious Duke of Cumberland."—*Junius*, vol. ii. p. 179, *note*.

[2] Lord Chatham was at this time extremely warm in his opposition to the Government. Walpole, writing to Mann, says, "he had grown so violent, that even *Lord Temple* could not *moderate* him. Lord Temple also was still a very eager politician, and constantly the object of abuse from the ministerial writers. The following character of him,

The motion for adjourning was withdrawn, and then a question moved by Lord Marchmont, that nothing

under the sobriquet of Lord Gawkee, is from the *Morning Chronicle* of Saturday, June 16, 1770, by a writer under the signature of "Soranus."

"The external form of this nobleman discovers nothing to his advantage. It does not announce any great promise of capacity or talents; and we are not deceived by it. Length, but without shape or proportion; and a countenance in which the most penetrating eye perceives no expression, can excite only the idea of insignificance. His mind, if possible, is as awkward and tame as his exterior. Nature seems to have thrown him into existence in one of her moods of frolic, and to make him the more conspicuous, she has given him rank. No one can view him without a smile, or hear him without laughter. No gravity of face can withstand his air of importance and his frivolity. In the highest assembly of the nation he appears without dignity, and of the most momentous concerns he judges without capacity. But he is not content with being a legislator, he must likewise be a minister. A creature that should have stalked during life, a tall infant in the nursery, has the vanity to imagine that he can govern men. While he himself has occasion for leading-strings, he would direct the most enlightened people in Europe. A few scraps of what he fancies is political wisdom, he has picked up from his noble friend and associate, and these he is perpetually retailing. For though his judgment is not very considerable, he must be allowed to have some memory. Liberty, a word of which he knows not the meaning, is perpetually in his mouth. The Constitution, too, he talks of,—and has he not a right to talk of it? He is a Member of the House of Lords. The enaction of laws requires doubtless the greatest extent of capacity; and for the regulation of the affairs of a great nation some acquaintance with men and some knowledge of the forms of its Government are surely necessary. . . . . . . In the character of this Lord there is one feature which must not be omitted. Violent passions are generally connected with great talents. He is an exception to this rule: with the most contracted understanding, he is subject to the greatest rage or extremity of passion. But his resentment is excited he does not know how, and it subsides in the same unaccountable manner. He should study to conceal himself, but he is fond of being seen. He should bury himself in the gardens of Stowe; but he must perpetually be walking in the purlieus of St. James's. His ambition he should sacrifice to his ease. Civil employments he should leave to those who are able to sustain them. The ox should not affect the ornaments of the horse."

appeared to the House to justify the assertion as a fact. The House divided, 83 to 35. Lord Chatham treated Lord Marchmont with great contempt, and said, if any noble Lord was to ask me whether I thought there was much corruption in both Houses of Parliament, I would laugh in his face, and tell him he knew there was.

Upon the main question the same division as before.

The King gave a pretty sharp answer to the Remonstrance, the same as in the Public Advertiser of this day; he calls the Remonstrance personally disrespectful to himself, injurious to his Parliament, and irreconcileable with the principles of the Constitution.

I am going to hear in the Commons, Motion for an Address to the King to lay the Remonstrance before the House. Yours, &c. &c. C. LLOYD.

MR. WHATELY TO MR. GRENVILLE.

April 10, 1770.

DEAR SIR,—I hear your Bill[1] went through the Lords yesterday, without any opposition but from Lord Egmont, who was inveterate against it, upon the subject of the oath; the jurisdiction of the House of Commons, which he said was extended by this Bill, though originally delegated from the House of Lords, upon the republican idea of a ballot, and other particulars. Lord Temple answered him shortly, dwelt most on the notoriety of the evil, and the analogy of the remedy proposed to the principles of the constitution, observing, that after the vote passed by the Lords the other day, disclaiming all interposition in elections, it was too late to complain of

[1] To regulate the trial of Controverted Elections.

the modification of the jurisdiction proposed by the Commons. His speech was as moderate as the other had been petulant; he was followed by Lord Mansfield, who entered fully, not into the defence, but the applause of the Bill; said it was the most impartial Bill he had ever seen; he believed the wisest; not that he supposed it to be perfect, he had the vanity to think he saw some defects in it himself, but that the operation of the Bill would point them out if they were real, and experience show the remedies; but that he would not suggest the amendments which might risk the fate of the Bill, and was happy to do justice to the Author of it. By all accounts his speech was as decisive in support of the measure, and as obliging to you as possible.

I hear no particular news. The talk of the dispositions of the Bedfords gains ground. Alderman Trecothick's motion for the repeal of the Tea Duty was opposed on the point of order, and lost by 52 against 80.

Lord Charles Spencer has lost his eldest son.

MR. WHATELY TO MR. GRENVILLE.

June 3, 1770.

DEAR SIR,—You see by the papers that the departure of the Princess[1] approaches. It is fixed, I understand, for Friday next. The Duke of Gloucester sets out with her, but leaves her at Brunswick, and proceeds with his own attendants, Colonel Rainsford and Major Heywood, to Berlin and Vienna.

[1] The Princess Dowager of Wales, who after an uninterrupted residence of thirty-four years in England, was about to make a tour in Germany on a visit to her brother the Duke of Saxe Gotha, and her daughters the Queen of Denmark, and the Princess of Brunswick.

Lady Howe[1] also takes the opportunity to go from Brunswick to Hanover. Lord Boston only, stays with Her Royal Highness all the while she is abroad. Lord Holland is ill, at Paris; some say that Lady Holland having informed him of the situation of his son, the news has affected him so much as to make him much out of order. Mr. Charles Fox is gone over to him. Lord Bute is pretty well, and will soon be here. The conduct of Lord North is, I am credibly informed, that of a man who does not expect to be long Minister. His neglect of every person of consequence is principally alluded to in this account of him. The Bedfords seem out of spirits, but I do not know they have any particular reason for it, which they have not had for some time. The Lord Mayor is, I hear, omnipotent in the City; his speech to the King[2] has gained him great credit with the citizens; they will obey his call to anything. I am told he means to use his power with discretion, but I believe he will show it on more occasions than one, not, however, on a refusal to pay the Land Tax.

Lord Suffolk is very happy that orders are given for draining the ponds in the park, near his house. Rosamond's Pond[3] is also to be filled up, and a road to be carried across it to George Street; the rest is to be all lawn.

---

[1] Lady Howe was the daughter of George I. by Lady Darlington, and she was at this time Lady of the Bedchamber to the Princess Dowager of Wales.

[2] The well-known Remonstrance, addressed to the King by Beckford. He died three weeks afterwards from the effects of a violent fever, caused, as was supposed, by political excitement.

[3] Rosamond's Pond was at the South-west corner of St. James's Park, nearly opposite the house now occupied as the Stationary Office.

MR. WHATELY TO MR. GRENVILLE.

June 10, 1770.

DEAR SIR,—I cannot yet find with certainty what has been the transaction at Falkland Island; I only know, that the report first spread, and the account since propagated to contradict that report, are neither of them true. I do not understand that the Spaniards have carried off our people, and you, who I suppose know that a Memorial was transmitted long since from Spain, on the subject of that settlement, and that advices were received during the winter, of two frigates preparing to go thither, will not believe those two frigates accidentally put in for water and refreshments. The best account I can get is, that the commander of the frigates required of the English commanding officer to quit the island; that the latter refused; upon which, as some say, the Spaniard made a formal claim and departed; as others say, he left a requisition to the English to depart in six months.

You will see by the papers, that a Remonstrance was voted unanimously at Guilford, but as it was pressed on at that time by Sir John Mawbey, against the opinion of the gentlemen in general who are named to present it, and who wished to see what other counties were inclined to do before this county stirred, most of those gentlemen have declined to present it.

Lord Rockingham was yesterday at Hayes; I heard it accidentally, for he lost his way, and seeing a friend of mine whom he knew, asked him the road.

The stocks, you see, are got up again, partly because the report about Falkland Island was contradicted, and partly because they never are much or long affected by alarms of a Spanish war. The alarm is accompanied with the hopes of an influx of silver. The silence of the Gazette will, I suppose, restore some credit to the report.

MR. CHARLES LLOYD TO MR. GRENVILLE.

Salt Office, Thursday, June 14, 1770.

DEAR SIR,—I hope you found your sons well at Eton, and every part of your family at Wotton in good health at your return. The jury on Woodfall's trial stayed out last night 'till half-an-hour past nine, and then brought Woodfall in guilty *only* of publishing Junius's Letter of the 19th December last. This verdict is to be entered not guilty, and it is said will be moved to be set aside by the Crown Lawyers. I hear that ten out of the twelve jurymen had determined at five o'clock yesterday to bring Woodfall in not guilty, but there were two who stood out, viz., the King's plasterer and a baker, and the result seems to have been a compromise.

I conjecture that Lord Grosvenor is driving a bargain for the lieutenancy of Chester. I am, &c., &c.

C. LLOYD.

MR. WHATELY TO MR. GRENVILLE.

June 23, 1770.

DEAR SIR,—I am sorry to begin my intelligence with telling you, that the Pynsent cause is determined to-day against Lord Chatham: the three Commissioners were so unanimously and clearly of opinion for Mr. Daw, that probably the decree would not be reversed on an Appeal to the House of Lords.

The late Lord Mayor [Beckford] has died, they apprehend without a will. It is said that he has left fourteen natural children [1].

Mr. Oliver, an eminent West India merchant, will be the Member for the city: he is of a respectable private character: his party is strong with the Bill of Rights men. The Ministry thought of Paterson, but I doubt whether they will push it. Old Trecothick will be the Mayor for the next four months, and, as some imagine, for the next year also. Lord Rockingham, with whom I had a long conversation in the street this morning, is of that opinion. I doubt it: the practice, I believe, is against even such a re-election, and, if I am right, the party will be distressed for another person. The two intended sheriffs, also, would hesitate, especially I think Martin, though Mr. Oliver would supply his place should he only decline, but Lord Rockingham doubts whether Baker would continue without Martin.

A Red Ribbon is to be sent out to Sir John Lindsay, and he is to have the character of Plenipotentiary; to what Sovereign I do not know, but I suppose to the Mogul, on the same errand as was intended for Mr. Monson.

They have hesitated at Philadelphia about continuing the Resolutions against Importation: when the last accounts came away they seemed inclined to come into

---

[1] Horace Walpole relates that Lord Holland's youngest son being ill, and Beckford inquiring after him, Lord Holland said he had sent him to Richmond for the air: Beckford cried out "Oh! Richmond is the worst air in the world; I lost twelve natural children there last year!"

them, but took time to inquire whether the other colonies would agree.

Philip Carteret Webb is dead [1].

MR. CHARLES LLOYD TO MR. GRENVILLE.

Salt Office, Tuesday, July 3, 1770.

Dear Sir,—I hear to-day that Mr. Bradshaw has actually resigned his post of Secretary of the Treasury. Mr. Knox's promotion [2] was quite new to me, though I find it is not so to you, as I understand he says that you approved of his acceptance, and pressed him exceedingly to it. As I am not called upon to say anything in this matter, and wish always to be on the good humoured side, I confine myself to the strict truth, and declare that I know nothing of your opinion upon the subject, having never heard you mention a syllable about it.

If (between ourselves) my opinion is asked of what you did say to him, I own I do not believe it was exactly as it was said to be stated by him. I *conjecture* that you might tell him, if he thought his acceptance of the office fitting for him in every other respect, that you begged him not to decline it from any personal considerations relating to yourself. This, conveyed in the language of good will and good humour, which is natural to you, will be easily metamorphosed, by a partial relator, into what is construed as a request from you to

---

[1] At the age of seventy. He had been Solicitor to the Treasury, and in the performance of his duty had incurred much odium for the prosecution of Wilkes, &c. He is better known as a distinguished antiquary, and the author of many tracts and pamphlets principally on antiquarian subjects.

[2] Knox became Under Secretary of State to Lord Hillsborough.

him that he would take it. Am I a good guesser, or is all this mere chimera? I send you, enclosed, all the Grosvenor letters yet published. The cause is to come on next Thursday. It is much doubted by the lawyers whether there is proof enough to obtain damages. The Duke's council[1] moved for a second special jury, upon the pretence that, since the striking the first jury, terms had been offered for a compromise, but the motion was not complied with. His Royal Highness writes excellent grammar, and the Lady is particularly delicate.

Sir John Lindsay, besides his East India command, has a Red Riband and five pounds per diem, to treat with Mr. Law concerning differences to be adjusted between the French and Great Britain in that part of the world. People impute this to his being Lord Mansfield's nephew, and perhaps they are not much out. Lord Bute is determined not to come over yet, as my *Court Gazette* says. Sir James Pennyman, supported by the Osbaldiston interest, and Lord Rockingham, stands at Scarborough against Cockburn, the Comptroller of the Navy, who, I understand, has little or no chance, though supported by *Lord Granby*, which last you may depend upon as a fact.

You may likewise be assured that a certain journey is the effect of not being able to carry certain points here; that supplications and entreaties were used to the son, and that, on finding them ineffectual, no offer of accommodation, either to the waterside, on the water, or on the other side of the water, would be accepted.

---

[1] So written in the original: but the peculiarity is not uncommon in writers at this time. Junius always substituted *council* for counsel. Lord Temple wrote counsel, but in one instance the word has been altered, so as to leave it doubtful which mode of spelling he intended to adopt.

I set out for Bristol to-morrow, and shall stay as little time as I can with decency, being too nervous to like a place where people are continually coming in the very last stage of illness.

I hope you continue as well as I left you, though I can brag more of your good looks than of your spirits. I saw your brother, Mr. James Grenville, at St. Martin's Church on Sunday. I am, &c., &c.

CHARLES LLOYD.

THE PRINCESS AMELIA TO COUNTESS TEMPLE.

Gunnersbury, July 10, 1770.

I ARRIVED here a [sic] Saturday at five, in perfect health, and hope to hear from you, my dear Lady Temple, that you and Lord Temple were not the worse for all the attentions and civility you showed to me, in the very pleasant, agreeable, and *easy* week, I passed with you at Stowe [1].

I found Lady H. Vernon here in great spirits and happiness, that the affair was so well over for her daughter;

---

[1] Horace Walpole was one of the party at Stowe upon this occasion, and an account of it forms the subject of one of his most entertaining letters to Mr. Montagu. He begins by saying, " The party passed off much better than I expected. A princess at the head of a very small set for five days together did not promise well. However she was very good-humoured and easy, and dispensed with a large quantity of etiquette. Lady Temple is good nature itself, my Lord was very civil, Lord Besborough is made to suit all sorts of people; Lady Mary Coke respects royalty too much not to be very condescending; Lady Ann Howard and Mrs. Middleton filled up the drawing room, or rather made it out, and I was so determined to carry it off as well as I could, and happened to be in such good spirits, and took such care to avoid politics, that we laughed a great deal, and had not one cloud the whole time."

she thinks that the Court has judged her innocent, by not complying with the first sum that was demanded to be paid. She is convinced that the letters are false, and that her daughter will be a single lady, Baroness of England, with 2000*l.* a year. I believe you will agree with me, my dear Lady Temple, that greater geniuses could not have patched up a bad thing (I mean the appearances of it) better than good Lady H. Vernon has done, but I fear it will turn out but a pleasant dream to the family [1].

God bless you, my dear, and believe me most truly sensible of your partiality for me, and having infused it also in *one* in whose acquaintance I am much pleased with : being your very sincere friend, AMELIA.

THE HONOURABLE AUGUSTUS HERVEY TO MR. GRENVILLE.

Chesterfield Street, August 4, 1770.

DEAR SIR,—I proposed myself the honour and pleasure of waiting on you at Wotton next week, and, therefore, declined going into Lincolnshire with my brother to-morrow, and only meet him at Ickworth for a few days ; but I have such frequent flying pains, and am so constantly obliged to have recourse to Dr. Ingram, that I have not yet ventured to quit this dismal, hot, and forlorn town, even for a night, since my return from Lisbon ; though I have not been better on the whole

[1] The princess alludes to the recent affair between the Duke of Cumberland and Lady Grosvenor. Lady Henrietta Vernon was the mother of Lady Grosvenor, and the daughter of Thomas Wentworth, Earl of Strafford. She had married Mr. Vernon of Hilton, in Staffordshire. Lord Grosvenor laid his damages at 100,000*l.*, but the jury only awarded him 10,000*l.*

these four years, yet I am thinking to sail for Lisbon next month, in order to bathe in some particular baths there, and wish I may not be obliged to come back again here sooner than I would choose, could I pursue my own inclinations.

The fire at Portsmouth has been a dreadful stroke, but, I hope and believe, not so very destructive as it was at first represented. I would go down there to be a judge myself, but that I have some time seen and felt that no attention in our profession can avail the public any more than the individual who shows it: I do assure you, my dear Sir, 'tis a ruined service, without being one who despairs in every situation. I see the Navy of England going very fast to its destruction, but I suppose it is to keep pace with the rest of the fate of this unhappy divided country. Our harbour at Chatham fills up fast, and, for want of care, in sending our large ships away from thence as soon as they are launched, and ready to go to other ports, they are destroyed by remaining in that river, where they ground every low water, for which reason they can keep no ballast in them, and are therefore ruined.

I have the particulars of many instances of neglect very alarming to this country, but when ignorance and obstinacy are predominant at that Board, it is of little consequence to represent. Adieu! my dear Sir; I hope you will do me the justice to be assured, that, for the good of this country, without any particular selfish motive, I do sincerely wish to see you, with some of your friends, in that situation which alone can, I think, relieve us. I am sorry to be so insignificant an individual as not to see any prospect of success, in attempting to bring so desirable an event about, but, were it otherwise,

I would sacrifice my present pursuit of health to that object.

Sir Edward Hawke *will not* go out without the peerage, and, however wished, *they* cannot obtain it for him. I hear the arrangement that was to be *there* for the Duke of Grafton is over, Lord North not caring for such an auxiliary; but if Sir Edward should die, as is likely to happen, that Lord Sandwich will go to the Board, Lord Harcourt to the Post-office, and Lord Stormont to Paris, till Lord Townshend is obliged to leave Ireland, and then Lord Harcourt will go there, 'tis said. The Duke of Richmond has been at a great old house[1], not far from Kensington, some days, and 'tis thought the old Lord has been tempting his Grace with the Government of Ireland, if they can get Lord Townshend to come away. Believe me, &c., &c.

A. HERVEY.

MR. CHARLES LLOYD TO MR. GRENVILLE.

Wednesday, August 8, 1770.

DEAR SIR,—I will, with your leave, postpone my visit to Wotton till the winter, having some thoughts of returning to see a college founded by Lady Huntingdon[2] in Wales for Missionaries. She gave me a very obliging reception on the 22nd of last month. I dined with her, stayed the whole day, and heard the tenets and parti-

---

[1] Holland House.

[2] Lady Selina Shirley, wife of Theophilus, ninth Earl of Huntingdon. She was celebrated for her attachment to the Methodists, and employed all her ample resources in founding a sect, and in disseminating the principles of Whitfield and the Calvinistic Methodists. The college mentioned by Lloyd was erected at her expense for the education of young men designed for the ministry. She died in 1791.

culars of her faith very much in extenso. The 24th of this month is kept as the anniversary of her birth-day, and is celebrated by the chief of her clergy in prayers and preaching. The college is situated in a most fertile vale near Brecknock, at a place called Trevecke. There are 20 young men from 17 to 25 years of age. These are instructed by masters in the Latin and Greek tongues for two years, and then are sent out into the country villages 16 miles round to pray and preach both on Sundays, and week days. They perform extempore exercises every day, having a constant auditory composed of about 150 persons, of every kind of trade, who are maintained, lodged, and clothed by Howell Harris at a house about 150 yards distant from the college. The several wages of these artisans is thrown into a common stock (they are employed at any distance sufficient to enable them to return each Sunday), and from that stock they are fed, &c., the sick are taken care of, and those who are past their labour are lodged, and have every kind of proper assistance. These two institutions coincide very happily so as to provide for both temporal and spiritual wants. I was exceedingly pleased both with their preaching and singing. Two of the college have been ordained and sent to America. I am, &c., &c. C. LLOYD.

LORD LYTTELTON TO MR. GRENVILLE.

Hill Street, October 8, 1770.

MY DEAR SIR,—A letter I received from Dr. Ashe, last post, has given me much consolation, in telling me that he sees a daily amendment in all your complaints. As for my own health, I was feverish during my whole journey, and passed two nights without sleep, but am now got pretty well.

I find the Duchess in good health, and supporting her misfortune with that patience and calmness which is natural to her temper, and goes beyond all the lessons of philosophers and divines. Sir Richard has left her the house at Chelsea in her own disposal, besides the 10,000*l.* that were settled upon her, and the house in town for her life[1].

Pitt and my brother will have each about 20,000*l.* in present or in reversion. The interest of 8000*l.* which is part of my brother's share, is given to me for my life. Legacies are left to all the servants, particularly to the Owens, one of whom has 500*l.*, and the other (Rachel) a better portion. The Duchess is residuary legatee. This is the substance of my poor brother's will.

All is yet doubtful about peace or war. I believe I shall not return into Worcester 'till Monday next. About the end of this month I hope to find you at Wotton entirely recovered, which will be the greatest joy to, Dear Sir, yours, &c., &c. LYTTELTON.

To the Countess Temple.

A TRAVELLER wandering through the maze of Stowe,
The fairest garden here on earth below,

[1] Sir Richard Lyttelton died at Chelsea on the 1st instant. He had married Lady Rachel Russell, widow of the first Duke of Bridgewater. Sir Richard's nephew, Thomas Pitt, afterwards Lord Camelford, erected an obelisk to his memory, in the park at Boconnoc, in Cornwall, now the property of Lady Grenville, the only daughter and sole surviving heir of Lord Camelford. The brother mentioned by Lord Lyttelton, was William Henry, who was created Baron Westcote, and subsequently Baron Lyttelton.

Says to his guide:—"'Midst all the domes and shrines,
Where Garden-Venus in her Temple shines,
Where George's statue rears its awful head,
Adorns and seems to rule the neighbouring mead,
I see no Temple to Minerva's name,
No grateful line to celebrate her fame."
"No," says the guide, "the sage Minerva dwells
Within the house, and in each art excels,
For both her wisdom and her skill you find
In worthy Temple's virtuous dame combined."

WILLIAM WYNDHAM GRENVILLE[1].
Ætate suâ 11.
2nd January, 1771.

THE EARL OF SUFFOLK TO EARL TEMPLE.

Duke Street, Westminster, January 22, 1771.

MY DEAR LORD,—Whether I take the liberty of informing your Lordship of a circumstance pleasant, unpleasant, or indifferent to you, I don't presume to guess, but am sure in either case your Lordship will pardon a liberty that proceeds from sentiments of the most perfect respect and esteem.

I am unwilling your Lordship should hear from any authority but my own, that I have kissed the King's hand this morning for the Privy Seal.

I won't trouble you with reflections and considerations which either must have struck your Lordship already, or will obtain but little weight from my representation. But in any situation permit me to assure you that I shall never cease to entertain that respect and esteem for your

---

[1] Afterwards Lord Grenville, He died in 1834.

Lordship, which the tenderest recollection of those who were nearest to you, and dearest to me, can inspire[1].

I am, my dear Lord, your most obedient and most faithful servant,   SUFFOLK.

EARL TEMPLE TO THE EARL OF SUFFOLK.

Stowe, January 24, 1771.

MY DEAR LORD,—Retired as I am and wish to be, it is impossible, however, that any important change in your Lordship's private or public situation, can be indifferent to me. Our private intercourse for some years past, our public warfare in so many glorious days of battle against the common enemy, and your great talents, forbid it. As I am entirely a stranger to every circumstance of this business, but the tenderest recollections of our common loss, your Lordship can only receive my thanks for the obliging manner in which you have communicated to me the step which you have taken, at-

---

[1] I have already referred to Lord Suffolk's letter in the Introductory Notes to the third volume of this Correspondence, and I have there quoted some passages from the writings of Junius, which relate to the subject of his desertion from the Grenville connection so soon after the death of his friend Mr. Grenville, of whom he had been so long a devoted follower. In one of Lord Suffolk's latest letters to Mr. Grenville, he says:—" It will be my constant endeavour to preserve the Constitution of my country, and my pride and my ambition to work with you in that task: conscious of the many advantages it has been my good fortune to receive from the unreserved communications and instructive effects of your friendship, and the example of your integrity, which no man better knows or values more." However calmly Lord Temple replied to the above communication, there can be little doubt but that he received it with the most profound indignation and contempt, and that he fully concurred in the expression of Lord Chatham's opinion: " the part of Wedderburn is deplorable; *of Lord Suffolk, pitiable!*"

tended with my good wishes, that your Lordship may have reason to be better satisfied with your new situation than my experience of the Court, and of the public, can allow me to hope for you.

I have the honour to be, with the greatest respect, your Lordship's most obedient and most humble servant,

TEMPLE.

THE COUNTESS OF CHATHAM TO EARL TEMPLE.

Hayes, Monday, March 4, 1771.

MY DEAR BROTHER,—I was so much in haste when I wrote yesterday to make a return to your letter, and to express the lively joy it gave me, as well as not to have it known how I was employed, that what I said was very short of what I felt, in consequence of the kind warmth of affection with which you answered the painful feelings I had conveyed to you.

I must now repeat the entire comfort and satisfaction which my mind enjoys, from the eager and affecting assurances of that tender regard, which will always be an equal pride and pleasure to me. When you know that what wounded me, so unfortunately for both, passed Saturday, in the moment I was with you alone after dinner, you will disculpate me from having coolly remained days without explanation. I went instantly to the play, with sensations very ill suited to the entertainment, and which were often on the point of conquering me, and of manifesting the situation of my heart.

However, used to trials, I just preserved the power to command myself, and to veil from the eyes of my kind hostess and others the emotions which were within.

Do you remember the answer *you* made, to the mention *I* made of the civility of the persons next to us on Friday night? There was the *word* that shocked me, which spare me, if you please, the repeating, since it was an error either in the speaker or the hearer. If it had been as I supposed and felt, there was no wrong-headedness in being touched as I was; and, being touched, I could not then have taken it up without totally unfitting myself for keeping my engagement to the play. As little did I feel it possible afterwards to do it in any other way than I did.

Now, my dear brother, you have the whole of what a certain delicacy of feeling, on some points, produced in a mind, that considers itself no way debased by any circumstances that have happened.

You should not have had another letter on this subject, but that the kindness of yours required a fuller explanation than what you received yesterday in acknowledgment of it.

I found my Lord, upon my return, with an increase of lameness, and in the night he has had pain in his foot, so that, in my opinion, he is likely to be in for a fit.

If you write me a line in return to this, to tell me that all traces of this unpleasant dream are vanished with you, as they will be with me from this moment, I shall be made still the more happy; but, in that case, let me desire you will cause your letter to be enclosed to Mrs. Sparry, and directed by one of your people, that I may not receive it so as to be questioned on the contents[1]. I am, with all truth and affection, your loving sister,   HESTER CHATHAM.

[1] I can offer no explanation of the subject of this letter, which appears to have been a secret between Lord Temple and his sister, and

THE EARL OF CHATHAM TO EARL TEMPLE.

Hayes, April 17, 1771.

MY DEAR LORD,—I hoped to have had the pleasure of seeing you before now, if severe and obstinate pains in the head had not rendered a journey to London above my force. If there is a western gale in the stores of spring, I trust by that aid to be able to crawl thither by the end of next week. I am sorry in the meantime to give trouble to the Lords on Friday next. I am not enough a Frenchman to solicit my judges. How this antiquated proceeding will be interpreted, I know not; by some, I trust, not disapproved. In the meantime I rest in confidence on the goodness of my cause, and the candour of my judges.

The Public now must beg from my pen a moment's attention. Great is the absurdity of the City, in putting the quarrel on the exercise of the most tenable privilege the House is possessed of: a right to summon before them *Printers printing their Debates during the session.* Incomparable is the wrong-headednesses and folly of the Court, ignorant how to be four-and-twenty hours in good ground: for they have most ingeniously contrived to be guilty of the rankest *tyranny* in every step taken to assert the *right.* A happy state of the country, but a true one.

Now, my dear Lord, to the point; what is to be done, rebus sic stantibus. I am clear that *Dissolution* should be moved *in Parliament*; in the House of Lords, unquestionably: in the House of Commons I think also. In the former, who so fit to move as Lord Temple?

as the reply was to be enclosed to a confidential servant, and to be directed by one of Lord Temple's "people," it was intended to be unknown even to Lord Chatham.

Should you judge otherwise for yourself, I am ready to move it, but prefer your Lordship doing it, in every light.

What do you think of young James [1], the deserved favourite of the House, for the Commons?

Allow a speculator in a great chair to add, that a plan for more *equal representation*, by additional *knights of the shire*, seems highly seasonable; and to shorten the *duration of Parliaments* not less so, if your Lordship should approve: could Lord Lyttelton's caution be brought to taste these ideas, we should take possession of strong ground, let who will decline to follow us. One line of men, I am assured, will zealously support, and a respectable weight of law. Si quid novisti rectius istis candidus imperti. A petition from the City for dissolution would, with peculiar propriety, close the scene [2]. I am ever, my dear Lord, most affectionately yours, CHATHAM.

---

[1] James Grenville, jun., afterwards Lord Glastonbury.

[2] Lord Temple's reply to the above is printed in the *Chatham Correspondence*, and it furnishes two or three pointed illustrations of the Letters of Junius: he says, "I totally agree with you in respect to the City transactions. I lamented with those of the City whom I first saw, that they did not content themselves with standing upon the impregnable ground of the illegal proclamation; however, that, since they were in the scrape, it must be covered and got out of as well as they could. The incredible imbecility and rashness of the idiot [a] Ministry have been very helpful to them; and, upon the whole, the embarrassment and disgrace to the Court put them in a lower and more distressful light than if my Lord Mayor had not interfered at all. . . . . I confess the general state of the Opposition, the implacable division in the City [b], which the demon of discord hath so plentifully scattered, have, without blaming either side particularly, reduced me to a state of despondency for the public, which

---

[a] "What an abandoned, prostituted *Ideot* is your Lord Mayor!"—*Junius to Woodfall*, i. 250.

[b] "If I saw any prospect of uniting the City once more, I wod readily continue to labour in the vineyard."—*Ibid.*, i. 253.

THE PRINCESS AMELIA TO COUNTESS TEMPLE.

Gunnersbury, September 2, 1771.

IF the 16th is agreeable to you, my dear Lady Temple, and to my Lord Temple, I shall be with you before three, which is your dinner-time, and I have got, with your leave, Lord Besborough for to play at whist, the evenings, and I hope that Lord Temple won't dislike to have a virtuoso admire what he is a doing. Our visit will be short, as I must be back here a Wednesday. I hope you have been well, though the weather was wretched when you set out for Lord Lyttelton's. I am, and ever shall be, your sincere friend, my dear Lady Temple, AMELIA.

MR. DAYRELL TO EARL TEMPLE.

[September 27? 1771.]

MY LORD,—Your Lordship's obliging letter found me in Cambridgeshire, but, on my return to town, I communicated your answer to the Friends of Liberty.

Mr. Alderman Bridgen's refusal brought on great confusion, as your Lordship will observe, and, I firmly believe, will lose the present Lord Mayor his re-election. makes me think it almost unmanly to step again into any public transaction [a]. . . . .

" As to the other points, of shortening the duration of Parliament, and increasing the knights of the shire, my general notion of the former your Lordship knows, and for the latter, in general, I should wish it success when matured and ripened." [b]

---

[a] " In the present state of things, If I were to write again, I must be as silly as any of the horned Cattle that run mad thro' the City, or as any of your wise Aldermen. I meant the Cause & the public. both are given up."—*Junius*, i. 255.

[b] " Lord Chatham's project, for instance, of increasing the number of knights of the shire, appears to me admirable, and the moment we have obtained a triennial parliament it ought to be tried."—*Junius to Wilkes*, i. 287.

The Shelburne party will be totally ruined in less than forty-five hours.

The friends of the Lord Mayor, who support Sawbridge, sent to Mr. Townshend to desire he would decline the poll, as he had no chance of succeeding, and, by that means, he would secure the return of Mr. Sawbridge and the present Mayor: he listened awhile to the overture of strengthening Mr. Sawbridge's interest, but wanted terms for himself to succeed another year; *that* we absolutely denied him, upon which he took time to consider of it till six this evening, when he returned a very insolent answer in the negative. The application and answer I have drawn up and sent, by the desire of the Committee, to the papers. It will most effectually do his business with the Livery, and what was only suspicion before, of his dividing the popular interest to serve the Court, will now be conviction to the citizens at large.

Nash is most likely to be Mayor [1], which we do not secretly dislike, as he is more likely to be with us, than any of the Shelburnes can be. If that should be the case, a certain person [Wilkes] whom your Lordship knows, has a trap for *him* which he longs to communicate to your Lordship, with many other important things now in plan, particularly an attack upon the privilege of commitment the House of Lords has lately exercised upon the Printers, and Mr. Bull [2] has agreed to act with him in everything. The attack will begin by a letter against Lord Pomfret; if the Printer is committed, the sheriffs will certainly release him, by first bringing him before the Mayor and some other alderman, to be discharged.

---

[1] Nash was elected by a majority of 220 over Sawbridge, and more than 2000 over Townshend.

[2] Wilkes and Bull were the Sheriffs of London and Middlesex.

This I am commissioned to mention to your Lordship in confidence, and to beg your consideration and good advice upon, when I have the honour of seeing your Lordship at Stowe.

There are several other things I shall be entrusted with to bring to your Lordship, too long to communicate by paper, which Cæsar [Wilkes] wishes to repose in the faithful bosom of his Mentor [Lord Temple], who never deserted him in his greatest difficulties, and in whom *alone* he will confide.

Your Lordship will forgive the scrawling of this letter, being wrote in a very great hurry, and in a noisy place, the Paul's Head Tavern[1].

I beg my dutiful respects to Lady Temple, and I am, my Lord, your Lordship's most obliged and affectionate servant,   E. DAYRELL.

THE EARL OF CHATHAM TO EARL TEMPLE.

Hayes, June 9, 1772.

MANY acknowledgments are due, my dear Lord, for your kind hasty epistle with your foot in the stirrup for Stowe. I have, in consequence of the intimation contained therein, suspended writing to excuse performance of my former notices, and shall wait the pleasure of another letter from you, not without some hope.

Nuthall could not wait on your Lordship, having company to dine with him, and the hour being late when I saw him. I sent him away not a little abashed with his *rough* calculation; and a more absurd and unjust one I never heard of. I gave Mr. Walpole 20,000*l.*, besides 3000*l.* more, upon valuations of stock, utensils of farm,

[1] I have already made some observations on the subject of this letter in the INTRODUCTORY NOTES: see *ante*, vol. iii. p. lxxxii.

&c., and have bills to produce of 9000*l.* more expended on the premises since. The house is insured, though not for its full value.

Tom Nuthall is enough a man of this generation to know how to choose between a purchasing and a selling client.

I hope your Lordship has found the palace of Stowe advancing apace. I wish it would rise, as Milton says of a piece of architecture of his immortal pencil, *like an exhalation*, for I long to behold it once finished [1]. May you find your gardening legs. Mine serve me as yet but very indifferently. I am, my dear Lord, your ever affectionate CHATHAM.

EARL TEMPLE TO MESSRS. COUTTS.

Stowe, June 24, 1772.

SIRS,—Though I have not the smallest doubt of your prudence and honour, yet, as it is impossible to say how far even you may in the end be affected by the general run upon credit, I think it my indispensable duty, as a trustee, and having public money in my hands, to take the India Bonds into my own keeping; the amount, you know, is 15,000*l.* which I must desire you will put into the hands of Mr. Astle, and his receipt shall be your full discharge. I am, Sirs, &c. TEMPLE.

As to my own cash in your hands I think not about it.

[1] Lord Temple having now finished, or rather having now become disgusted with, and tired of his political labours as the Author of Junius, his active mind still required employment, and he seems to have turned his attention entirely to the completion and decoration of his mansion and buildings at Stowe. About this time he commenced the alteration of the whole of the south front, which before his death had assumed the architectural appearance which still remains: and the colonnades on the north front were also added, besides many very considerable improvements in the Gardens.

MR. GLOVER TO EARL TEMPLE.

Bulls Cross, near Enfield, July 12, 1772.

MY DEAREST LORD,—Your clear, concise, and mercantile favour came duly by the post, and was forwarded to me last night; accordingly I draw for half a buck to be received in London the latter end of this week, or beginning of next, because next Tuesday se'nnight I propose to feast an old lady of 85, my mother, who is a lover of venison.

I fully intended to have given your Lordship a narrative of the late tragedies in London by next Tuesday's post, but have reason to believe that my letter of this day will be sufficiently explanatory.

A few days after the flight of Fordyce, finding no bankruptcies ensued, I retired to Weybridge, and spent ten days quietly; but was hurried up on Monday fortnight passed [1].

By ten o'clock I reached Mr. Payne, the Governor of the Bank, who informed me that public credit was in the utmost disorder, Sir Richard Glynn broke, and many

---

[1] The banking-house of Messrs. Neal, Fordyce, and Co., of Threadneedle Street, had stopped payment on Wednesday the 10th of June, and the effects of their failure caused the greatest possible consternation throughout the City. The spirit and energy of the merchants, aided by the timely interposition of the Bank of England, fortunately prevented many of the numerous bankruptcies that were expected to ensue. So fatal a blow, however, was given to trade and public credit, that the stoppage of almost every banker in London was at one time anticipated. It was mentioned as a remarkable instance of rapid conveyance at this period, that the news of Fordyce's failure reached Edinburgh from London in forty-three hours. If this were true, it was a still more wonderful feat than that performed by Sir Robert Carey, who carried the news of Queen Elizabeth's death from Richmond to Edinburgh in about 60 hours; but Fordyce, who was a Scotchman, had not improbably given his friends some earlier intimation of what was about to happen.

other bankers in danger, but that he was going to consult with his brethren on some immediate measures to check the increasing evil. From him I went to Lombard Street, and learned from my own banker, that they were all run upon at that instant, some more, some less, and that several capital ones were expected to follow the example of Sir Richard Glynn, and stop that very day; among others Sir George Colebrooke. This was confirmed by every man I met.

Confiding in the faculties of the Bank, nor less in the magnanimity and liberal spirit of my friend the Governor, from whom I had so lately parted, I assumed a cheerful countenance, and treated the whole affair so lightly, that I raised up many from a dejection which I had never observed before. In fact the Bank of England, to its eternal honour, furnished that very forenoon such immense and quick supplies of money, that every house stood firm; there was indeed a small space of time that Sir George Colebrooke stood still, by reason that the Bank could not issue notes fast enough to meet the run upon him, it was so violent; but another private banker, Martin, stepped into his aid, and threw in cash sufficient to set him afloat, and keep him so, 'till the Bank had made out all the notes adequate to his necessities. Happy was this operation, for the keeping him up prevented the extension of the calamity to Holland, where he had been carrying on a most alarming circulation for many months.

By the evening I had made myself master of the causes whence all the mischief was derived. Sir George himself, having among many projects made a recent purchase in Scotland to the amount of 70,000$l.$, had his circulation of paper to raise money for the payment. A great house of the Alexanders at Edinburgh, in order to pay for an immense plantation at Granada, had their circulation, which had already ruined Sir Richard Glynn; and lastly the great bank of Ayr, otherwise of Douglas, Heron, and Co., had, for the purpose principally of improving agriculture, enlarged their paper credit to such a degree, that there remained to the amount of 300,000*l.* in the possession of London only. When I considered, that, in addition to that sum, all the commercial concerns between our capital and Scotland, and that multitudes of my fellow citizens, such as grocers, woollen-drapers, mercers, upholsterers, cabinet-makers, haberdashers, and silversmiths, besides linendrapers and merchants, would be all grievously involved, and many fatally, in the confusion of Scotland, whose chief currency consisted in the Douglas paper, I clearly saw that the support of that great bank was become the principal object of attention, and indeed the single one remaining, after Sir George Colebrooke had been upheld.

I reported to the Exchange in the evening of this black Monday, and was soon applied to by a Scotch merchant, who said that if a subscription was opened by the merchants of 500*l.* each man to indemnify the Bank against any damage sustained by a further and free discount of the Douglas paper, and that if I would begin such a subscription, he was sure it would be filled in time to answer the purpose. I answered that I would contribute all in my power, that the supporting that bank should be the object of every man's attention on both sides the Tweed, but that the proper method was to call a general meeting of the merchants and traders, to which end I would consult some proper persons that night. I did so, and was assured, that if I would take the lead myself, and keep all the North-Britons entirely out of sight, I might depend on success; that if the plan appeared to be of North-British growth, I should meet with insurmountable difficulties; for as the mischief apparently originated from the Scotch themselves, the minds of men were too much heated with indignation to discern, like me, that the aiding Scotland in the present instance was equally beneficial to England.

Unfortunately my North-British friend put an advertisement that evening into the papers for a general meeting without my knowledge.

Seeing it in the morning papers I got some very considerable English merchants to attend. We consulted privately together, and though the meeting was but thin, we agreed that to separate without doing anything would be prejudicial to public credit. Mr. Long accepted of the chair, and I proposed a subscription of 500*l*. each to indemnify the bank against damage in continuing to discount the Douglas paper. A committee of twelve was chosen, of which but three were Scotch, yet the merchants in general were disgusted at the appointment of those three; however, in three days I got 60,000*l*. subscribed, and would have carried the point against all prejudices, but fortunately did not find it necessary. Four Directors of the Douglas bank were come up to London, and made their application to me for assistance.

In fine, by an unwearied attendance of mine on the Bank, and keeping up their own spirits together with the generous interposition of the Dukes of Queensberry and Buccleuch, and Mr. Douglas, who have given their bonds and judgment for all they are worth, as a security to the Bank of England, our Directors have agreed to circulate the Douglas paper to the amount of 300,000*l*. upon condition that the said paper be reduced to 150,000*l*. in three successive half-yearly periods. The subscription of the merchants became unnecessary for that particular purpose, but while it was going on greatly tended to quiet people's minds, by showing that there were some eminent persons who were not frightened out of their wits.

In the meantime the head of the house of Alexander posted up to London, and gave in such a state of the solidity of his affairs, that with the additional security of Walpole the merchant, and his brother the banker, the Bank of England agreed last Thursday evening to set them afloat likewise, and on Friday when I quitted London for some relief in the country, it was universally believed that this last assistance of the Bank to Alexander would restore Sir Richard Glynn again, with other good mercantile houses which had been forced to stop in this confusion, and finally would put public credit upon a much more solid basis than for these twelve months past. I conclude with Mrs. Glover's and my most cordial compliments to Lady Temple. My dear Lord, your most affectionate, and I fear most tedious,

R. GLOVER.

THE EARL OF CHATHAM TO EARL TEMPLE.

Burton Pynsent, August 30, 1772.

MY DEAR LORD,—I am under a necessity to trouble your Lordship with another epistle on a subject you have declared yourself so tired of, the mortgage on Hayes. The matter is as follows:—Mr. Nuthall acquaints me by yesterday's post, in the words transcribed from his letter, "that if the portion of lands purchased by Mr. Walpole of Cox and Chapman was intended to be comprehended, as well as the trust premises, in the mortgage deed to Lord Temple, I must take upon myself the blame of its being done otherwise; for in the deed laid before Mr. Madocks, by Lord Temple's direction, Cox and Chapman's lands are not comprised." He adds, "It is never too late to confess a fault, when it is known to be so, and this mistake may be easily rectified, by Lord Chatham executing a short deed, conveying to Lord Temple these lands, as a collateral and further security for the mortgage money, and to bear even date with the mortgage deeds to him."

Here is a tedious story of a *mistake* to me quite incomprehensible, had I not often found that lawyers, hurried by variety of business, are the most signal blunderers imaginable. This strange incident vexes me not a little, and, could it not be so easily supplied, my uneasiness would be infinitely greater.

I write this post to Nuthall, directing him to prepare forthwith such a deed as he suggests for my execution, which, as soon as executed, shall be deposited with the rest at Mr. Coutts's.

Your Lordship may imagine that I have not been sparing in my compliments on the Solicitor of the Treasury's accuracy and punctuality. I must not, however, omit, angry as I am, to say the gentleman cries quarter, and throws himself particularly on your Lordship's mercy, as well as mine.

I suppose this tiresome renewal of this tiresome affair will find your Lordship returned from your peregrinations. I hope pleasure has constantly attended your steps, and that health Herculean enables you to pursue, without fatigue, the Herculean labours of magnificence and taste in which you are engaged. All here, thank

God, are well, and our *Hill*[1] knows no complaint but want of rain. Kind loves, and respectful duties, conclude this long epistle, from my dear Lord's most affectionate,
CHATHAM.

EARL TEMPLE TO THE EARL OF CHATHAM.

Stowe, September 8, 1772.

MY DEAR LORD,—Though I never can be tired of any business in which I am engaged in your service, and that I execute it with zeal you and yours have allowed, yet, as these are of different sorts, some may, to a kind well-wisher, be in their nature more agreeable than others.

At my return to this place, on Sunday last, I found your Lordship's letter, together with one of the 4th from that facetious man of business, in so many departments, Mr. Thomas Nuthall, whose fellow is not easily to be met with : witness your marriage-settlement not witnessed, his peremptory and repeated assertions, that your trustee had no power to advance the trust-money on mortgage, even though I quoted the very words to him, and his late unparalleled proceedings, which the better to ascertain, I send you copies of the letters which have already passed, leaving the comparison of his letters to you and me, the dates, the contradictions, and the comments to your Lordship, who cannot fail to see that though he was trusted for all, and only referred to Mr. Madocks as a matter of form, upon his own suggestion, yet he was in utrumque paratus, if you had

[1] Lord Temple had written a poem of sixteen stanzas, called *Stowe; or, the Hill of Hills*, of which the following is a specimen :—

" Tell me no more of Tempe's vale,
Nor boast of Arno's flowery dale ;
Taste must confess, superior still
The charms, which decorate my Hill."

wished otherwise than you did, and I would have been paid with jargon[1]; for my own part, I am in no wise concerned but for the honour of the trust, and to silence whispers which his irregularity had produced.

After many and many disappointments, I am now going on prosperously here. The north side is charming, and the south will be very magnificent, attended with much expense, but, what is worse, with infinite trouble. I hope, however, that the worst is over. For Hagley news I have none to add to what you must have heard from the once young and lovely lips of Madame Hood[2]. It is a charming place, and I think we have got an amiable and very sensible acquisition in our new cousin[3].

To-morrow I enter upon the delights of a race at Newport Pagnel, of which proh pudor! I am a steward.

I hear your young folks have again greatly signalized themselves[4], which cannot but give pleasure to papa and

---

[1] " The reason is most inadequate, and must appear so to every man who is not beat out of his senses by the *jargon of lawyers*," &c.—*Lord Temple on the Seizure of Papers.*

" What in their prerogative *jargon* is called a concealment," &c.— *Junius*, vol. iii. p. 20.

[2] Wife of Captain Hood, afterwards Lord Bridport. She was the sister of Gilbert West the poet. She died in 1786.

[3] The wife of Thomas, afterwards second Lord Lyttelton: he had recently married Mrs. Apphia Peach, the widow of a gentleman who held some high office in the Government of India. She survived her second husband many years, and died at Malvern in the year 1840, at the great age of ninety-six years.

[4] In allusion to a play which had been written and performed by the children at Burton Pynsent. It furnished a curious instance of the erroneous estimate Lord Chatham had thus early formed of the talents of his eldest and second son. Dr. Addington having remarked upon the singular accuracy of emphasis with which the speeches were delivered, Lord Chatham replied, " William is certainly very correct, but Pitt will be *the* orator."

mama, as well as to, my dear Lord, your most affectionate, TEMPLE.

I rely with the fullest security on your Lordship's honour[1], but not at all on Mr. Nuthall's law, when he tells me that the method now taken is full as safe and effectual as if Mr. Walpole had conveyed to the trustee, for, if you had given a general mortgage, or a judgment in the interim, they would take place.

LORD VERE TO COUNTESS TEMPLE.

Hanworth House, July 31, 1773.

DEAR MADAM,—I hope I may assure you H. M. is perfectly well again in health, but the chronique scandaleuse says a little uneasy about a dairy-maid.

Lady Margaret Compton dined here yesterday, and recovered the disagreeable operation of having been robbed, last Saturday night, at the end of Gunnersbury lane: she was coming from town, and told seventy carriages in the way, and many on foot, and yet it is now reported the same man picked up above a hundred pounds. You will have heard Lady Blandford was robbed on Wimbledon Common, as have been also Lady Jane Scott, Lady Schaub, coming from Lady Westmoreland's, and several others, which puts our dowagers into some fears, but not enough to keep them at home; for what signifies keeping their money, if they are kept without quadrille.

We have the felicity of Lady Bridget Lane in our neighbourhood: she has been here, and in great vogue.

The Duke of Gloucester, we saw go to her last Saturday, when we were at Lady Brown's, and he looked very well. The Duke and Duchess of Cumberland are

[1] "Confiding implicitly in your Lordship's honour," &c.—*Junius to Lord Chatham.*

going abroad for three years: a relation of his, and friend of yours, [Princess Amelia] said it was very well, and would be better if it was for thirteen. Lady Margaret was with her a few days ago, says she is perfectly well, and is now at Lord Boston's.

They say here that Lord Bute's daughter having run away and married is true[1]: by what I have long heard of the manner they were permitted to behave in at Brighthelmstone, I can't wonder at it, as poor Lady Bute was got into the country, and, of course, a little happy from that, I concluded it would not be long before some accident or other would bring her back to her usual situation of having something to fret her. They say Lord Carmarthen[2] can't be married 'till September, and Lord Cranbourn[3] they don't know when.

Miss Keck has got a great acquisition by the death of a Tracy; it will be, when all the jointures fall in, 3000*l.* a year.

I am ever, my dear Lady Temple's most affectionate and obedient servant, VERE.

THE HONOURABLE HORACE WALPOLE TO COUNTESS TEMPLE.

December 20, 1773.

I HAD a person with me that prevented my answering your Ladyship's kind letter immediately, which I wished

[1] Lady Augusta Stuart was married about this time to Captain Andrew Corbett of the Horse Guards Blue. She died in 1778.

[2] Afterwards fifth Duke of Leeds: he was married in November following to Lady Amelia D'Arcy, only daughter and heir of Robert, last Earl of Holdernesse, from whom he was divorced in May, 1779.

[3] Afterwards first Marquess of Salisbury: he married in December of this year, Lady Emily Hill, second daughter of the Earl of Hillsborough. This Lady was burnt in the fire which destroyed part of Hatfield House, in November, 1835.

to do, and to thank you for having relieved my mind from the greatest anxiety imaginable. The enormous sum of 800*l*. compared with 300*l*., which I had thought a very great price, made me apprehensive that I should seem to have offered far below the value of the pictures, the plain English of which could only be that I would have defrauded orphans for my own advantage, an idea that would make me shudder. If a lady in the country is so amazingly deceived as to expect to get half the sum of 800*l*., I doubt she will keep them 'till they are of no value at all, which must be the case of miniatures, that must lose their beauty by time, and which makes them so greatly less valuable than enamels.

My behaviour to Miss Stapleton, I hope, has been perfectly respectful, and allow me to repeat, Madam, that my great esteem for her character, and gratitude for having made me the offer of purchasing the pictures, carried me beyond my judgment, and made me desirous of pleasing her by the handsomeness of the offer. I heartily beg her pardon if regard for my own honour has carried me too far in disculpating myself.

The more esteem I had for her, the more shocked I was at seeming to have acted in an unworthy manner; and I own I should still wish that she should show the pictures to some good judge, and see what such a person would say of 800*l*. for them. I shall always be Miss Stapleton's obliged humble servant, if she justifies me, and I shall be, if possible, more than ever Lady Temple's most devoted humble servant, who I am sure will forgive my not being able to bear the thought of being lowered in her esteem.

P.S. I am prevented to-day, but will have the honour of calling on your Ladyship to-morrow.

MR. GEORGE GRENVILLE TO EARL TEMPLE.

Naples, March 26, 1774.

MY DEAR UNCLE,—I am uneasy to find by my sister's letter that you think me in your debt for letters. I can safely assure you that the post must have cheated you of some of mine, as I can answer for having regularly answered every letter which I have been so happy as to receive from you. A few days more will be sufficient to show us everything that can be seen at Naples, for we have not hitherto left one morning unemployed. The antiquities round Naples are in every point of view wonderfully interesting; the remains of ancient architecture are very great, some of them remain in a fine state of preservation; the discouragement, however, of new researches is so great, that it probably will prevent any new discoveries taking place.

The excavations carried on at Pompeii show us one whole Roman street remaining perfect; the houses all perfect, except the roofs, which have fallen in from the burning of the beams. This unfortunate city was destroyed not by the lava, but by a shower of ashes and pumice stones; this makes the digging very easy and preserves the form of every building, every utensil and ornament, in a state of perfection little short of what they originally were: the paintings are very pretty, every other discovery is highly interesting, from the good taste which reigns throughout; it is, however, worth while to observe how little their useful implements differ from those of modern date. The stucco work is now in finer preservation than the reliefs on the hardest marble, some of the friezes are infinitely superior to anything I ever saw; the jealousy, however, of the natives will not suffer any drawings to be taken of them, so that the world must wait till the King orders them to be published. A Temple remains entire with every implement of sacrifice, and every minute part in the highest preservation, and what is extraordinary is, that they have built it entirely of marble, and stuccoed it over afterwards through choice.

The ancients' houses, notwithstanding the rich furniture found in them, are very indifferent; in the course of 50 houses I did not see one room 20 feet long, nor can it be answered that these were houses belonging to people in bad circumstances, for they are fitted up with every profusion of painting and mosaic. Herculaneum does not afford so large a field for observation, for the lava having been in a state of fusion, when it overwhelmed it, the workmen were obliged to dig through the solid substance for about 50 feet, before they came to the roofs of the houses, and even then in striving to detach the vitrified substance, they often destroyed the ornamental parts of architecture, which they were in search of.

The theatre, however, afforded them a profusion of statues in bronze and marble, the latter rather of the second rate, excepting one equestrian statue, which is very near equal to the Marcus Aurelius at the Capitol.

This subject easily leads us to the consideration of the volcano which destroyed these two cities. I have been twice on the summit, the first time about a week ago, and the second time the night before last; a small eruption of lava having taken place, I went thither at eleven at night, and did not leave it till six in the morning, very well repaid for the fatigue of ascending it in the dark, and for the danger of hazarding it. I have given my sister a more particular account of it in a letter of yesterday, and will refer you to that, rather than fill this with a repetition of what I told her. I have passed many days on the coast of Baiæ; the profusion of ancient buildings affords ample amusement, especially with Horace and Virgil in my pocket; the scene, however, is now changed, and the Baiæ amænæ are now deserted, on account of the infectious air which the marshes send forth; most of the antique Temples are under water, I mean overflowed; I have, however, ventured into several of them, and am very well repaid for my trouble; the stucco roofs are entire; most of them have been published: they are not however very interesting, as they only mark the changes of ornament in the square and octagon compartments of a vaulted ceiling. The Temple of Jupiter at Puzzuoli is now entirely demolished, to supply materials for the palace at Caserta, which is beyond dispute the most extensive building (as far as I can judge) upon the worst plan I ever saw. It never will be finished, though the King of Spain, who began it, annually remits about 18,000*l.* for that purpose, but this young King commonly stops the workmen, and employs the money for some other purpose; he is now throwing off a great deal of the authority which the King of Spain assumes over him, and though he is represented as entirely ignorant and neglected, he certainly is no fool, though immoderately fond of field amusements, which engross a great part of his time. He is extremely beloved by all ranks of people, who do not dislike him for some of the boyish follies and excesses into which he sometimes breaks; he seems little attached to the Queen, though that may proceed from his indifference to the whole sex; she is certainly clever, and seems a very amiable woman. Under all these circumstances the gallantries of the court are more private than what they have been; the morals, however, of the people are, if anything, more corrupted; the men are very devils; I am afraid to say that I am told from good authority that 8,000 murders are annually committed in the Kingdom of Naples and Sicily: the punishment is very slight, if the fact be proved, which is seldom the case. With this disadvantage, as well as that of the disease which is supposed to have made its first appearance here, I cannot but be astonished at the infinite population of the city: to give you an idea of it, assure yourself that the calculation affirms the number of beggars and people who pass their nights in the streets to exceed 22,000. The country, however, is much deserted; the disadvantages attending their trade is very great, and the decrease of cultivation ought to alarm them, from the recollection of what they suffered in 1766; this is the more inexcusable as their soil is certainly the richest in the world, for in the parts highly cultivated I have seen three crops on the ground at the same time. I mean corn growing in a vineyard where the vines were supported by the fig-trees; nor have they the excuse of their riches being drawn from them, for Spain actually sends money occasionally to them, and never takes one farthing from them: Sicily pays to them annual subsidies, yet the face of poverty reigns throughout. We can, therefore, ascribe this only to the natural depravity of their spirits, which are only employed in searching for means to add new crimes to their old account.

The women are in general lively and agreeable; the spirit of gallantry governs every action, and the only requisite necessary to recommend is a promise of making a long residence at Naples, a promise which they are as sure of gaining from their admirers, as they are of seeing it afterwards broken. There have been, however, instances of Englishmen having been followed to Rome by the assassin employed to revenge such an affront. The disease to which the natives of this city are supposed to be more particularly exposed, is, I am convinced, much abated, and though dreadful when it takes place, it is less frequent than commonly they were; in some families, however, it adds one to the horrid list of hereditary disorders.

The fondness for conversaziones is much abated, for, excepting the more elderly part of the noblesse, very few men attend them; this makes it very difficult for a foreigner to make many acquaintances amongst the natives; the advantage, however, is very great which the English have, owing to the universal esteem in which Sir William and Lady Hamilton are held, and the universal attention which is paid them. Lord Bulkeley and I have received from both of them every civility that can be imagined, and in the kindest way, for he always tells me that my father sent him here, for no other purpose. I live almost entirely with them, and find my time pass away more agreeably than in any part of Italy. I have taken the liberty of sending you a Vase of the lava of the year 1771; it is intended for a chimney-piece: when the ship sails you shall have proper notice, and I hope that you will conclude from it how much I make it my object to think on the many kindnesses you have always shown me. I cannot conclude this letter without congratulating you and myself on the tribute paid to my dear father's memory; I cannot but exult in the relationship I bear to him, and if the pleasure is not complete, it is because I cannot share it with my family; and this happiness we have above all other Englishmen, that the utility of the Bill is for a moment the least object with us. Adieu, my dear uncle: commend me kindly to Lady Temple's remembrance, and assure yourself of the sincere affection and gratitude of your dutiful and devoted nephew,

GEORGE GRENVILLE.

Lord Bulkeley[1] desires his *best respects* to you; he insists on that expression, 'till you will allow him to use some other; believe me, if I am proud it is of the choice I have made of my friend, for since I have travelled with him I have never found in him one quality which I did not admire. We are on the happiest terms, and mean to continue our intimacy in England, by seeing as much of each other in the country as we can make convenient to ourselves, and by living together when in London: a thing which he requested from me, and which I love him too affectionately to refuse. You will probably have heard before this letter comes of the death of the son of the Prince of Asturias, which gives the King of Naples a very fair chance for the crown of Spain, as they say that the Princess of Asturias is not likely to have any more children.

MR. GEORGE GRENVILLE TO EARL TEMPLE.

Rome, April 16, 1774.

YOUR two letters, my dear uncle, followed me here from Naples, from whence I came in twenty-eight hours in order to see the cupola of St. Peter's illuminated for the Duke of Cumberland: I have seen many shows of

---

[1] Thomas James, seventh Viscount Bulkeley in the peerage of Ireland. He was made a Peer of Great Britain, as Baron Bulkeley, in 1784, and died in 1822.

splendour and magnificence, but never one that struck me like the show of the whole front, colonnade, dome, and even cross of the church, illuminated in an instant with 5000 torches, and after this blaze had been sufficiently shown, on the discharge of a cannon, the whole was as instantaneously changed to a form infinitely more bright, and more surprising; this manœuvre was executed by 1200 men, disposed in different parts of the roof.

His Royal Highness is now gone; he embarked at Cività Vecchia, on board the Pope's fleet for Toulon, after having met with every honour that could be paid. The universal testimony in favour of him and of his Duchess made his residence very agreeable to the English who were at Rome. Having heard that he had inquired particularly after me, I went to Colonel Garth, desiring to know the hour when the Duke would receive me; he named the same night, and the moment I came he took me aside, and began a very interesting conversation, which lasted three hours: he did me the same honour on the two successive nights; during this he gave me leave to speak my sentiments to him on every subject with the utmost freedom. I must, however, reserve the whole till we meet in England, as this passed under the seal of confidence, and ought not to be hazarded to the post. Of one thing be sure, that he has been astonishingly well advised, and whoever judges of his parts by the boyish correspondence between him and Lady Grosvenor, will do him the utmost injustice, and be deceived by him in the end. Some parts of our conversation having been overheard, have been reported in Rome; fortunately for me, it was chiefly what did me the most honour, and reflected very great honour on him: notwithstanding all this, I was explicit with His

Royal Highness on the Scripture text of "Put not your confidence in princes." The particularity, however, has made some noise here.

As to your observations on the jilters and being jilted, I agree perfectly with you. I own that, with the utmost respect for the character of a virtuous woman, experience has taught me not to hold the sex in so very sublime a light as I used before I left England; and, I believe, that with respect to the women abroad, one observation will do (with very few exceptions) for the whole of that *amiable corps*.

As to the *grand question,* as you call it, you will judge of my sentiments upon it, when you hear (under confidence, nay the strictest confidence) that I have refused advances from an heiress with 5000*l.* a year. Upon reflection you will know whom I mean. Without meaning it, I have (it seems) engaged her affections, for which I made my excuse, offered some sober advice, and have made a point of absenting myself as much as possible from the family, so that her only resource now is with Bulkeley, who is daily entertained with this edifying topic. Raillery apart, I am really concerned for the girl, as I have a great regard for her sense, understanding and disposition, and am sorry that anything of this kind should give her uneasiness: but of this, my dear uncle, I beg that not a word may transpire. For many reasons I rejoice in my good fortune, in escaping in England so very early a settlement. I have gained a few lessons, but many more remain, and though experience is a severe mistress, she is at least a sure one. At present, without a serious predilection for any one woman whatsoever, I am happier than I have ever been. I own this looks very much like bachelor's boasting, yet I assure you that no one has a higher opinion of the happiness which may attend a married life, though, at the same time, the lottery is so much against the adventurers, that it would defy even the office-keeper Molesworth's calculations: but, after all, we are so apt to form our opinions of propositions in general from the objects before us, that possibly the living in a family where the happiness of that station of life is, and has been, conspicuous, would make me change my opinion; a thing which does not give me quite so much uneasiness as it used to do, as I have already changed every sentiment and opinion ten times over since I came abroad, and never shall be ashamed of altering it again whenever the propriety of it strikes me [1].

Count Czernichew, the last Russian Ambassador at our Court, is just gone from hence to Naples; he was extremely civil to me, and begged to be remembered to Lady Temple and to you: he is disgraced, and travelling to avoid a disagreeable scene at home; his stay, therefore, at Naples is uncertain. He told me that

[1] Some months later, Mr. George Grenville married Lady Mary Nugent, the only daughter and heir of Robert, Earl Nugent, of Gosfield in Essex. The following letter from Lord Chatham to Lord Nugent was written somewhat in anticipation of that event.

"Hayes, December 21, 1774.

"MY DEAR LORD.—I am all impatience to return your Lordship my very sincere thanks for the honour of your most obliging letter. The kind share you have the goodness to take in an event so full of domestic happiness to us, and the too flattering sentiments with which, my dear Lord, you have accompanied this friendly participation in our joy, is very sensibly felt at Hayes. Your Lordship will allow Lady Chatham and me, leave to express in return (with a little anticipation) our joy on another approaching union, which is fraught with every happiness to all parties, and will, I am assured, make your Lordship as happy a father as I am, and I need not wish you to be more so. May I beg to offer my respects to the young lady I had the honour to be presented to at Hayes.—I am, &c., &c. CHATHAM."

the idea, when he left Russia, was to push everything this campaign by sea, and to endeavour to force the Dardanelles. Some of our English are at Constantinople; amongst others, Lord Winchilsea, and, as I hear, Lord A. Percy[1], who has tried this sea-voyage as his last stage: he told me, however, in the summer at Lausanne, that it was of no consequence whether he was dead or alive, as it was *impossible* that he could have any children. Your ever affectionate nephew,

GEORGE GRENVILLE.

MR. GEORGE GRENVILLE TO EARL TEMPLE.

Rome, May 4, 1774.

DEAR UNCLE,—I yesterday received a letter from my uncle Mr. Henry Grenville, in answer to one I had written to him from Naples: in this he expresses the satisfaction he feels in applying (in consequence of your wishes) for the Stewardship of the Hundreds, for the purpose of vacating at Buckingham in my favour; a resignation, he says, which he was ready to make for an indifferent person, but which it was matter of particular satisfaction to him to have an opportunity of making on the supposition that I was to succeed him: as I have received no intimation of this from you, let me hope that the affair is not yet concluded, and, upon that supposition, suffer me to open my whole heart to you on the subject. In the first place then, let me, on the supposition that the vacancy was intended in my favour, express to you, my dear uncle, the sense I entertain of

---

[1] Afterwards Lord Lovaine and Earl of Beverley. He not only recovered his health, but survived 'till 1830, having married the second daughter of Peter Burrell, and sister of Lord Gwydir, by whom he had a very numerous family.

your kind partiality to me. I ought to thank you, but the topic is so much exhausted, that I want language to express my feelings; judge, then, of my gratitude by your own kindness; suppose me happy in this proof of it, flattered by the distinction, impressed with a sense of the advantageous consequences which I may draw from it; yet suffer me to plead for liberty to decline the seat, if it be your intention to nominate me on the ensuing vacancy.

Do not, my dear uncle, misinterpret this application. I have no pride but to receive favours at your hands; they do me honour, and I glory in acknowledging them, and that I must owe my future situation to them; your candour, therefore, will prevent you judging so meanly of my understanding, or my disposition. The unhappy disagreement with any part of your family, interests me no further than it ought as a relation to the same family; I hope, therefore, you will suppose me not to attempt to decide on it in the reasons which I beg to offer to you; and, indeed, I only mean to allude to it, as far as it may be supposed to concern me.

Supposing the vacancy to be made, no one can doubt your right to apply to Mr. G. for that purpose, nor that of disposing of the seat afterwards to any one to whom your wishes lead you; yet consider, my dear uncle, the relationship I bear to the late Member, the kindness he always showed to me, the regard he always showed to my late father, the little part I ought to take in a dispute between two uncles, and you will probably agree that I should look upon him in no other light than as an uncle whose affection to my father and to me has the same hold upon me that I always acknowledged with gratitude in your instance. I do not mean to carry the comparison through, as it never has been, nor can be in Mr. Grenville's power to show me the same instances of kindness that you have done.

If, then, I am to consider him in this light, put yourself in my situation, and determine for me how to avoid the reproach, which the want of candour in the world will cast upon me, on the supposed imputation of *supplanting* an uncle, who required every attention at my hands. The word, I own, seems a strong one, yet what other will be made use of by the censorious world, who see the nephew in the seat which has been taken from the uncle? This is, I own, strongly stated, but I fear that I shall be exposed to this, or perhaps to still stronger censure, as it never will be supposed that I was not only uninformed, but even unsuspecting of a measure so nearly concerning myself. Shall I not be supposed to have hazarded the widening of a family breach for the vanity of a seat in Parliament? As it never was understood that he held it in trust for me, as it never was my poor father's wish that I should come into Parliament, at least before the general election, will it not, even in this light, be liable to censure? Nominate any other person, and the objection ceases: these reasons can operate only with respect to me, and I own, that in my case, they seem (in my weak judgment) to operate most strongly.

I do not apprehend these reflections from Mr. Grenville: he will, I am sure, think more candidly of me; and, indeed, he says no more on the subject, than what you see in the beginning of my letter, excepting many professions of satisfaction in my being (as he understands) destined to be his successor. It is only from the unkind reflections of those who either cannot or will not know the true state of this business, that I apprehend reproach for supplanting my uncle. I have written to him to inform him, upon my honour, that I neither knew nor suspected your intentions; that I did not mean to enter upon the subject further than concerned myself, but only to prove to him how incapable I was of forming a separate interest from him, that I should write to you, begging your permission to decline these kind intentions in my favour, "for that as my wishes did not lead me to it, *nothing short of your commands* should make me take it; but that from the moment they were signified, I owed too much to your parental care and kindness to dispute them."

Here, then, my dear uncle, the affair stands at present; and now let me entreat you, if it can be made compatible with any plan of yours, to excuse my acceptance of the honour which your goodness has made you call me to. It will always be matter of joy to me to think that your kindness had, at so early a period of my life, destined for me so distinguishing a mark of your favour. It is, however, the offer which does me the real honour, and, should you allow me to decline it, I shall be sensible of one additional claim on my gratitude. At the same time, the moment that your commands are signified, they shall be obeyed [1]. I remain, &c., &c.

GEORGE GRENVILLE.

[1] The result of this appeal to Lord Temple was, that Mr. Henry Grenville did not at this time vacate his seat for the borough of Buckingham, and that Mr. George Grenville did not come into Parliament until the general election in the ensuing autumn, when he was chosen one of the knights of the shire for the county of Buckingham, which he continued to represent until he succeeded to the Peerage, upon the death of his uncle, in September, 1779.

MR. GEORGE GRENVILLE TO EARL TEMPLE.

Vienna, July 9, 1774.

I TAKE the first opportunity of the post to answer my dear uncle's three letters, which I found here on my arrival, after a most tedious journey from Venice, which was prolonged by the overflowing of the Adige, which confined us seven days in a little village in the Tyrol, without a possibility of moving one way or the other.

The civilities which we meet with here are very great. I am peculiarly flattered in the kind partiality which Prince Kaunitz shows me: the society, indeed, of the women falls very short of what I expected; I confine myself, therefore, to very few who are reasonable enough to allow me their acquaintance, without insisting on my purchasing it at the loo-table.

The Emperor is at present at his camp in Bohemia: he reviewed there 27,000 men; his great encampment takes place in Hungary, the beginning of September; he there reviews 56,000 more, and in October another is formed in Poland; so that he will, in the course of this year, have seen more than 100,000 men under the tents. He returns to-morrow, and we are to be presented to him, I believe, next day. No news as yet from the Turkish army; the great effort, however, on the Russian side, is to be made by sea. We met Count Orlow going to take the command; it seems to me, however, as if they had lost much time this campaign. The Turkish Envoy still remains here. I have seen him, but am much disappointed in his appearance: it was hoped that some advances might have been made between the two envoys at this Court for peace between Russia and the Porte. The Prince Gallitzin, however, is so totally devoid of common sense, that he is equally unfit for this or any other negotiation.

Sir Robert Keith has been singularly attentive to all his countrymen here: he has procured for us every agrément which we could wish for, and is himself so much respected, that it facilitates our introduction to the best company: in short, Vienna is the only Court where we can hope for the easy civilities, which render a place so entertaining and useful to a traveller. Adieu, my dear uncle, &c., &c.   GEORGE GRENVILLE.

MR. GLOVER TO EARL TEMPLE.

London, July 11, 1774.

MY DEAREST LORD,—The dispatch I have used in procuring the enclosed answer to your Lordship's case, is but a slight proof of what you are well assured is my attention to all your concerns in mind, body, and estate: I fear the latter will suffer on the present occasion, without affecting the former in the least degree; however, we must try to render a loss of property as small as possible.

I plainly perceive that Mr. Mackintosh is a bankrupt[1], a circumstance from which no rank and condition are exempt by the laws of Scotland.

---

[1] It will have been seen by some letters from Mr. Mackintosh in these volumes, that he had formerly been in very intimate and confidential intercourse with Lord Temple, but these money transactions had no doubt entirely put an end to it. By Lord Temple's reply to Mr. Glover's letter, it appears that he was a considerable loser by the bankruptcy of Mackintosh, for money lent to him, but he adds, "This gentleman was so pure an angel of virtue, with sentiments

The process, in that case, I will describe. A creditor begins it in the Court of Session against the insolvent person, and all the other creditors; by which means the amount of all demands is discovered, or of so much as exceeds the insolvent's effects: upon ascertaining this excess the court grants a sequestration, the effects are converted into money, and distributed among such creditors as have appeared; it will be, therefore, necessary for you to lay in your claim for a proportionable share. Send me up your account of principal and interest. In the mean time, my friend and fellow labourer, M'Konochie, whose knowledge, judgment, and probity, rank in the highest class, will write to Scotland for every circumstance of information relative to Mackintosh, and is most obligingly ready both to advise and act in the affair.

Let me know if your Lordship hath not the collateral security of the brother, in whose behalf you lent so generous an aid in a season of so much danger.

This affair, which I am determined to pursue, to-

of so much refined delicacy, that I am the *less* surprised at what has happened."

Mackintosh lived for many years afterwards in Argyle Square, Edinburgh, where he died at an advanced age in 1810.

After Lord Temple's death, he occasionally corresponded with his successor, and in one of his letters, dated in January, 1784, in reply, as it would seem, to a recommendation that he should apply to Mr. Pitt for some promotion he had solicited, he writes as follows:—

" As to throwing myself upon *your cousin* in any situation, that I will not. He has the regards I owe his father's son, and I dare say he must have seen among his papers a very interesting correspondence, the most dangerous to me I ever hazarded, from which he cannot be ignorant of me, or my devotedness to the name he bears."

In answer to my inquiries, I have been obligingly informed by Mr. William Stanhope Taylor, one of Lord Chatham's grandsons, that no traces of this correspondence have been found in the Chatham Papers, and I have consequently no clue to the nature of it.

gether with the public one of the bank in Ayr, will keep me in town all this month, but about the beginning of August, at least before the middle, Mrs. Glover, who desires her best compliments to Lady Temple and your Lordship, will with me enjoy the supreme felicity of visiting both at Stowe : in the interim, I draw upon you at sight for half a buck, if the season permits, or as soon as it can, and remain, my Lord, &c., &c.

R. GLOVER.

THE COUNTESS TEMPLE TO EARL TEMPLE.

January 12, 1775.

You have left my body behind, but my heart is with you; indeed you cannot think how unhappy I was last night to see you so uneasy : if anything troubles you, I always wish to take my share, for I cannot help fancying what I bear will lighten your load.

If this * * * * *[1] should put you into any distress, there is no scheme you can propose that I will not with cheerfulness come into, even to the living at Eastbury 'till Stowe is finished, which I think we may do at a much less expense, more especially if we come to London but for a little time. This is no grimace, but comes from a heart full of sensibility and anxiety with regard to everything that relates to you; if you are not convinced of this, you do not know your truly affectionate little wife, A. TEMPLE.

[1] A word has been effectually obliterated, evidently by Lord Temple, as the colour of the ink corresponds with that of the following note, on the same paper, and in his handwriting:—"This kind offer was quite unnecessary, as my circumstances are so great."

EARL TEMPLE TO THE BAILIFF AND BURGESSES OF THE
BOROUGH OF BUCKINGHAM.

[About September, 1776.]

GENTLEMEN,—Having been informed of the eloquent oration delivered by the Earl of Verney, in your Town Hall, to his own tenants and others, in consequence of a meeting advertised to be holden here, for the express purpose of considering of an application to Parliament, to enable the parish in the ordinary way to rebuild their parish church, I am not a little surprised to hear that his Lordship was pleased, in so peremptory a manner, to call upon the Corporation, and the friends thereof, to take upon themselves to do what so peculiarly belongs to the possessors of lands in the parish of which his Lordship enjoys so very considerable a share. I trust that neither the one nor the other will be thus dictated to by him. He adduced, it seems, some notable precedents to favour these his commands, the most remarkable of which was his own generosity to the town of Carmarthen [1], where he was a perfect stranger. What were the advantageous terms of that bargain *to his Lordship* I know not, but I doubt not they were good. In this Corporation we neither buy nor are sold, being unused to any unworthy traffic of that kind. His Lordship will, I dare say, be to hear, that the estate of the Corporation is scarce equal to the necessary expenses thereof; that it was a parish meeting advertised by the

---

[1] Lord Verney was formerly M.P. for Carmarthen, and the present representative was elected through his influence. Lord Verney was now one of the members for the county of Buckingham. The borough of Wendover was also at this time *the property* of Lord Verney.
He died in March, 1791, when the title, which was an Irish Earldom, became extinct.

churchwardens, with his privity, for the expressed purpose of an application to Parliament, to enable the parish to rebuild the church; that at this meeting, in their corporate capacity, the Corporation had no special concern; that the revenues of the parish considerably exceed 4000*l.* a year; that the bailiff and burgesses, in order to save his pocket, and that of other great land proprietors, will not take his private hint of selling themselves to Lord North, nor, indeed, to any borough-monger whatever; that they should have rather expected to have heard from so respectable a member of the Opposition, of precedents which testify to the commitment of the Mayor and Corporation of Oxford to Newgate, and of General Smith and Mr. Hollis to the King's Bench, for practices not so corrupt as the proposed application to the King's Minister. Such a hint partakes less of the generous and disinterested sentiments which should animate the representative of an independent County, than of that meaner sort which sometimes recommends Court Members to poor boroughs for a valuable consideration, when the poor are sold, and a profit made on their perjury. On my behalf, who have the honour to rank myself as a sincere friend and servant of this Corporation, I shall only say at present, that I trust you are convinced that I and my family are too sensible of the many obligations you have conferred upon us, to hesitate a moment, when any proper opportunity offers, of manifesting the great respect and affection which we bear towards a set of gentlemen, who have acted with a friendship and generosity scarce to be parallelled, and worthy of better times. It is the honour of a late friend of this Corporation [Mr. Grenville], to have chalked out the most effectual means hitherto proposed, of detecting and punishing corrupt and scandalous violations of the constitution, so justly alarming to every good man. Here it may be pleaded as a merit, and we flatter ourselves that a time may come, when the actors in such foul practices, [the great vulgar as well as the little [1],] will, in consequence thereof, be more fully detected and brought to condign punishment.

The interested proposition of his Lordship being thus negatived, you will be to hear from him, as first proprietor of lands, what he has to offer on a subject where he has taken so extraordinary a lead, and I desire that the contents of this letter may be communicated to the meeting. Whatever plan may be proposed to save the purse of great and considerable landholders, I shall think very unbecoming: ready to facilitate every fair and reasonable mode for the accomplishment of so desirable an end as rebuilding your church [2], and happy at all times in proving to you the sincere regard, gratitude, and affection with which I am, &c., &c.

TEMPLE.

Before estimates had been called for, it might have been proper to have fixed where the church is to be built, and by what means it is to be paid for.

[1] The passage within brackets is partially obliterated in the draft.
[2] Lord Temple, with his accustomed princely generosity, contributed a very large proportion of the sum required for rebuilding the church at Buckingham.

THE PRINCESS AMELIA TO EARL TEMPLE.

April 21, 1777.

I INQUIRED after your health, my good Lord Temple, and was glad to hear that you had not suffered in it by your mind being so agitated [1].

After the loss of a friend, the only way of showing one's affection to their memory, is having a regard for those they had so sincere and warm a friendship for as they had for you.

I shall ever retain in my mind the partiality Lady Temple had for me, and then I hope, my Lord, you will do me the justice to believe how much I regret her; being your sincere friend, AMELIA.

EARL TEMPLE TO THE PRINCESS AMELIA.

April —, 1777.

OVERPOWERED as I am with this fresh instance of Your Royal Highness's condescension and great humanity, I presume only to say that nothing can exceed my devotion and gratitude.

The happiest days of poor Lady Temple's life were those, in her estimation, which she had the honour to pass with Your Royal Highness, and she never returned from Cavendish Square but delighted and charmed. Her attachment was unfeigned and inviolable, founded in a veneration for those great qualities so universally respected, which makes it the pride of my life to be permitted to subscribe myself, Madam, your Royal Highness's, &c., &c. TEMPLE.

[1] The death of Lady Temple had taken place on the 7th instant.

EARL TEMPLE TO MR. GEORGE GRENVILLE.

[September? 1777.]

As I cannot find in my heart to tear myself from my Stowe solitude, even for the sake of the amiable society of Gosfield, it becomes necessary I should at last thus open to you the result of a very distressed mind, on the subject of our plan of living together for better and worse; and first, I must express to you my hearty thanks for the kind readiness with which you offered to sacrifice your new walls and old waters, even all the clay of the beloved Wotton, to the friendly object of endeavouring to render my heavy loss the more supportable; but having now had some experience of that solitude after which my affliction hath sighed, and finding myself still wholly unequal to that society which the gaiety of youth calls for, and necessarily occasions, I would deliver you and myself from the constraints which the great difference of gray hairs and green heads must create, notwithstanding all the sacrifices your good-nature and Lady Mary's would make. Past recollections for ever haunt me. I know not with certainty which way to turn, nor, therefore, what will become even of Stowe or Pall Mall, but I hold that it is wiser, in due time, *retrorsum vela dare*, than to prosecute further an experimental voyage through seas unknown, in which so many able navigators have been shipwrecked; at least I would wish to lay in my claim at present, so far as more to shape things gradually, in a manner to occasion the fewest comments on restoring matters to their ancient footing, not like the Americans going back to 1764, but only to the beginning of the fatal month of April. It might be better had we never been tempted to put to sea at all, but by it you have at least got to the full knowledge of your own crew, a science which will prove useful to your pocket and to your credit, and you have made almost a clear ship: your wines are entire, your plate unmelted, and such of your property as has been removed may be most easily returned, your finances will not have suffered, and all the blame shall lie at the door of my wretchedness. Sound discretion, in general, declares that a joint voyage through life should never be undertaken but in the course of wedlock, so that though the full consummation of our matrimonial contract appears to be in many lights very desirable, yet, as it must be attended with many of the constraints and evils of that state, in an age, too, not very favourable to it, deprived, at the same time, of many of its most precious sweets, even Mr. Cleaver[1] himself would hesitate at such an alliance of Church and State.

I have written this with the less reluctance, since I am clear Lady Mary and you will look upon it as a release. The sevants you still leave at Wotton, and the keeping it as you mean to do, manifest to me where the treasure is, and, in consequence, the sacrifice you have been making. I, like Lord N. [Nugent], must be a wanderer through life, though, in my probably short pilgrimage, I am never likely to stray into happiness. As we have not had the smallest altercation, the town tea-

---

[1] Mr. Cleaver was afterwards tutor to Mr. Grenville's children, particularly to his eldest son, the late Duke of Buckingham and Chandos, by whom he was always mentioned with great affection. He became Bishop of St. Asaph, and was a constant visitor at Stowe, until his death: a suite of apartments which he occupied were called the Bishop's rooms as long as Stowe existed.

tables will be the less able to give in their respectable verdict upon this appearance of change. In all events I shall continue to love you and Lady Mary, and to show myself, my dear nephew's most truly affectionate,

T.

THE EARL OF CHATHAM TO EARL TEMPLE.

Hayes, September 24, 1777.

MY DEAR LORD,—Emerging out of a long silence, where can my newly-restored pen address a few lines so naturally, as to the place where my thoughts have constantly resorted, though my disabled hand could not give expression to them? My dear Lord Temple's health perpetually interests my mind, and, of late, with too much room for anxiety.

" For we were bred upon the selfsame hill,
 Fed the same flock, by fountain, shade, and rill."

I trust the sight of my handwriting will not be unwelcome, and I shall be made happy by the sight of your Lordship's, if it brings good tidings of your health and spirits.

News from America is slow. The delay is at least a sort of protraction of our political existence: for the event, I consider as ruin; be the victory to whichever host it pleases the Almighty to give it, poor England will have fallen upon her own sword.

But I am growing too serious for a letter which I meant to dedicate to true affection and solicitude to learn from the fountain head, an account of a health for which I shall ever form the most sincere and warm wishes [1]. I

---

[1] Lord Temple's reply to this letter has been printed in the *Chatham Correspondence*.

am, with the truest affection, my dear Lord, your invariably devoted, CHATHAM.

THE COUNTESS OF CHATHAM TO EARL TEMPLE.

Hayes, Friday noon, October 17, 1777.

I HAVE spared you the trouble of a letter for some time now, my dear brother; the best news I could send you from hence having been communicated to you by a still more welcome authority than mine. The account of yourself, contained in your kind answer to my Lord, putting me at ease on the subject that had been so anxious to me, your health, left me nothing interesting enough to say, to tempt me to break in upon the leisure that you love.

If I had but a dawn that I could, by anything in my power to offer to your mind, afford any diversion to that strain of depressing thoughts which still, by your last letter, seemed to possess it, it would be matter of very real joy to me.

I will, however, hope that by degrees you will feel the blessings you possess, and, though some are taken away, be able to enjoy, with your own natural cheerfulness, those that are continued to you.

That you should feel for the public, the past, the present, and your wishes for the good and safety of the country, render impossible to be otherwise. I will allow it a just cause of serious and afflicting thoughts, but that, however, call for exertion of spirits, that the power of action may not be lost, when it may be wanted to guard against approaching ruin. Let me lament that my Lord and you, meaning the same great object of public happiness, should think the road to it so different, as the direct opposites of peace and war. You and he, I believe, are equally solicitous at this moment for news, but of a very contrary colour. He, that nothing may have happened to render reconciliation more impossible, and you, that unhappy victory (pardon the expression) should have reduced America into a beaten *enemy*. I, as you will allow a lady ought, wish peace and good-will among all men, and that the event, *somehow or other*, may bring you and my Lord to the same point of opinion, which I should rejoice in, that the latter end may be like the beginning, when both shared in every triumph and in every sorrow [1].

When I sat down to write, I never proposed the saying a syllable on the subject that I have gone on upon, but merely to express why I had not writ before, and to make inquiry after you, so long an interval having

---

[1] Lord Temple, in his reply to Lady Chatham, says:—

"My dear Sister,—However animating your expressions may be of feeling for the public, the past, the present, and the future, it is impossible to look to that dreadful scene without every depression which can sink the mind of a zealous friend to *this* country. I am no party to the war, nor am I to the causes of it, which I think my greatest happiness; but engaged as we are, in, I think, a most just cause, I cannot but wish victory to dear, dear England: reconciliation founded in the independence of America makes me rather choose to treat with a beaten enemy; at the same time, I confess, I see no promising solution any way."

Lord Temple continued in the same desponding opinion with regard to the aspect of public affairs even to the time of his death, which happened at Stowe on the 10th of September, 1779. One of his latest letters was addressed to Almon, on the 24th of August, in that year:—

"Lord Temple is much obliged to Mr. Almon for the interesting intelligence he has sent, is perfectly well in health, and not a little unhappy at the state of the country."

"—————— quantum mutatus ab illo
      Hectore!"

elapsed. You will forgive me, I am sure, for letting my pen follow my thoughts, and if you don't like what I have said, burn my letter, and forget all of it, except the assurance that I am, my dear brother, your most affectionate sister, HESTER CHATHAM.

INDEX.

A.

ABERCROMBIE, General, i. 243. 254.
Addington, Dr., iv. 32. 34. 42. 154. 163.
Address from the Merchants of London to the King, ii. 58.
Ailesbury, Thomas Brudenell, Earl of, i. 316.
Aix, Isle of, i. 208. 219. 350.
Albemarle, William, second Earl of, i. 67. his death, 133.
Albemarle, George, third Earl of, ii. 133. 200. iii. 106. 225. 257. iv. 37. 228.
Allen, Joshua, Viscount, ii. 159.
Allen, Ralph, of Prior Park, ii. 289. death of, 379, 381.
All Souls' College, Fellowship of, iii. 297.
Almon, Mr., the bookseller, ii. 65. 428. 457. iii. p. xxviii. lxiii. lxiv. 46. 51. 248. 292. iv. 368. 469. 472. 475. 479. 575.
Alt, M., Resident from Hesse Cassel, ii. 169.
Amelia, Princess, ii. 42. 242. 245. 315. 316. 333. 362. 406. iii. p. xxxv. 83. iv. 360. 535. 570.
America, North, i. 240. 254—262. 274. 303. 318. 321. 322. 323. 326. ii. 114. iii. 11. 13. 100. 109. 253. 316. 358. iv. 4. 11. 13. 83. 317. 370. 373. 376. 387. 389. 391. 394. 397. 401. 408. 421. 435. 439. 449. 456. 459. 460. 480. 486. 510. 573. 575.
Amherst, Captain William, i. 258.
Amherst, General, afterwards Sir Jeffry, i. 231. 240. 304. 319. 321. 324. 344. ii. 13. iii. 49. iv. 326. 339. 341. 349. 359.
Amyand, Claudius, i. 180.
Ancaster, Duke of, iii. 191. 394.
Ancram, William, Earl of, i. 335.
Anigada, Island of, ii. 9.
Anonymous letter to Calcraft, iii. p. cxv.
Anonymous, *see* Junius.
" Another Letter to Mr. Almon," &c., iii. p. clxxvi. clxxxiii.

VOL. IV.

Anson, Admiral, i. 53. 58. 60. orders to Captain Grenville, 61.
Anti-Sejanus, Letters of, by Scott, iii. 91.
Argyll, Jane, Duchess of, iv. 9. 11.
Ashburnham, Earl of, iii. 217.
Astle, Mr. Thomas, iii. 237.
Aston, Philip, sixth Lord, i. 358.
Aston, Mr. Justice, iii. 48.
Athol, Duke and Duchess of, iii. 6. 7.
Attainder, Bill of, iii. p. lxxv.
Auction duty, iv. 257.
Augusta, Princess, ii. 246. her marriage, 247.
Aylesbury, manor of, i. 102.
Aylesbury, meeting at, ii. 77. iv. 438. 446. 454. 462.
Aylesbury, Wilkes's letter to the Electors of, ii. 456.
Aylesbury men, case of, iii. p. xliii. cciv. ccxii.
Ayloffe, Sir Joseph, iii. 75.
Ayscough, Dr., i. 32.

B.

Baker, Sir William, M.P., ii. 457.
Balfe, Mr., Printer, ii. 157.
Baltimore, Charles, sixth Lord, i. 34.
Banffshire, Sheriff Depute of, ii. 388.
Barbadoes, Island of, ii. 18.
Barclay, David, his account of American opinions on the Mutiny Act, iii. 11.
Barré, Colonel, i. 326. ii. 229. 230. 236. iii. 28. 74. 79. iv. 321.
Barrington, William Wildman, Viscount, i. 34. 67. 188. iii. p. xxxii. xlviii—l. li. cxiii. 74. 220. iv. 164. 298. 300. 360. 407.
Barrington, Captain, i. 298.
Barrington, Dr., Dean of Windsor, ii. 486.
Barrymore, Richard, sixth Earl of, iv. 9.
Bath, William Pulteney, Earl of, i. 17. 50. ii. 264.
Bathurst, Allen, Lord, i. 50.
Bathurst, Henry, afterwards Earl, i. 19.

P P

INDEX

Beardmore, Mr., i. 459. ii. 60. 62. 73. 81. 137. 140. 157. 459. iii. p. cix. 84.
Beauclerc, Lord Harry, i. 358.
Beauclerc, Lord James, Bishop of Hereford, ii. 136. 312.
Beauclerc, Lord Vere, i. 59.
Beaumont, M. Elie de, ii. 437.
Beckford, Alderman, ii. 8. 133. 158. 195. 202. 214. 217. 495. iii. 341. 386. 389. 396. iv. 213. 517. 520.
Bedford, John, Duke of, i. 54. 466. 469. 474. 475. 476. 480. 481. 493. ii. 29. 31. 57. 89. 102. 108. 121. 195. 203. 205. 206. 220. 231. 235. 241. 249. 280. 298. 377. 484. 534. iii. p. xxv. xxxvii—xli. 44. 57. 59. 160. 164. 171. 193. 194. 211. 219. 223. 242. 264. 291. 303. 337. 346. 355. 360. 363. 369. 370. 377. 379. 381. 391. 393. iv. 4. 18. 45. 76. 83. 95. 96. 102. 127. 177. 197. 222. 232. 234. 236. 252. 312. 341. 432. 433. 451.
Bedford, Gertrude, Duchess of, ii. 242. iii. 291. 321. 377. 390. iv. 341.
Bedford, Mr. Grosvenor, ii. 113. 114.
Bedford House, Bloomsbury, i. 157. iii. 168. 172–174.
Bedford, election of the mayor at, iv. 451.
Belleisle, Marshal, i. 247.
Belleisle, siege of, i. 363. 364.
Belvidere, Robert, first Earl of, ii. 276.
Bentley, Richard, iv. 47.
Berenger, James, i. 29.
Berenger, Moses, i. 12.
Bergen-op-Zoom, siege of, i. 64.
Berkeley, Hon. George, i. 3. death of, 52.
Berkeley, Colonel Norbonne, afterwards Lord Botetourt, i. 91. 477.
Berkeley Square, Lord Shelburne's house in, iii. 88.
Bernard, Sir Francis, iv. 307. 333. 352. 459. 470.
Bertie, Lord Robert, iv. 341.
Besborough, William, second Earl of, ii. 198. iii. 217.
Betty, the fruit girl of St. James's Street, iv. 382.
Bindley, James, ii. 466.
Blackstone, Dr., iii. p. cxxix. 30.
Blandford, Lady, i. 26. ii. 52.
Blenac, M. de, the French Admiral, ii. 1.
Bligh, General, i. 253. 272.
Blosset, M. de, ii. 409.
Blount, Mrs. Martha, i. 27.
Bodens, Colonel, iv. 279.
Bolingbroke, Henry St. John, Viscount, i. 27. 117.
Bolingbroke, Clara de Marsilly, Viscountess, i. 7.
Bolton, Charles, fifth Duke of, ii. 199. iii. 70.
Bolton, Henry, sixth Duke of, iii. 394.

Bolton, Mr. Crabb, M.P., ii. 46.
Bolton, Miss Arabella, iii. p. ccxxvi.
Boscawen, Admiral, i. 136. 203. 221. 240. 247. 313.
Boston, riots at, iii. 100. 108. iv. 307. 319. 333. 353. 360. 362. 391.
Botetourt, Lord, ii. 455. iii. p. liv. 224. iv. 189. 223. 327. 341. 349.
Boutdeville, a *sobriquet* for Lord Townshend, iv. 233.
Bowes, John Lord, Lord Chancellor of Ireland, iv. 109.
Braddock, General, i. 243.
Bradford, Earl of, i. 17.
Brand, Mr., ii. 21. iv. 200.
Bradshaw, Mr., iii. p. li. ccxxi. iv. 434. 458. 459. 521.
Breton, Sir William, ii. 208—209.
Bridgen, Alderman, iv. 535.
Bridgewater, Rachel, Duchess of, iv. 528.
Bristol, George William, Earl of, iv. 32. 41. 47. 56. 92. 109. 112. 137. 212. 245. 393. 402. 405, 415. 464.
Broderick, Admiral, his ship, the *Prince George*, burnt, i. 236.
Broglio, Marshal, i. 345. 346. 354. 360.
Brookes, Mr., the "*John Cæsar Wilkes*" of the "North Briton," ii. 137.
Brown, Lady, iv. 322.
Brudenell, Colonel, iv. 384.
Brunswick, Hereditary Prince of, ii. 245. arrives in England, 246. his marriage to the Princess Augusta, 247. 251.
Brunswick, Hereditary Princess of, ii. 486. iii. 393.
Buccleuch, Duke of, iv. 131.
Buckingham and Chandos, Richard, first Duke of, i. p. xix. iii. p. xv.
Buckinghamshire, John Hobart, Earl of, i. 85. ii. 92. 415. iii. 328.
Buckinghamshire, Address from 1762, i. 478. 488.
Buckingham, borough of, iv. 473. 559. 567.
Buckingham Church, proposal to rebuild, iv. 569.
"Budget," the, pamphlet by David Hartley, ii. 428.
Bulkeley, Thomas James, seventh Viscount, iv. 555.
Bull, Mr. Sheriff, iv. 536.
Buller, John, M.P., i. 445.
Bunbury, Sir Charles, ii. 186. 413. iv. 186.
Burgoyne, Colonel, iv. 474. 484. 495. 500.
Burke, Edmund, iii. 86. 347. iv. 99. 119. 173. 194. 235. 250. 314. 381. 391. 392. 438. 440. 445. 448. 464. 503. 504.
Burke, Mr. William, ii. 49. iv. 54. 450.
Burrell, Mr. Peter, M.P., iii. 26.
Burton, Dr., of Winchester, i. 486. 489.

INDEX.

Busby, Dr., iii. p. cxxxix.
Bussy, M. de, i. 289. 362. 363. 370. 380. 381. 383. 386.
Bute, John Stuart, Earl of, i. 148. 360. 452. ii. 2. 6. 22. intended retirement, 32. 48. 101. 106. 118. 119. 132. 133. 144. 197. 201. offers to Mr. Pitt, 202. 203. 204. 206. resigns the privy purse, 208. takes leave of the King, 210. 214. 216. 230. 231. sends strong professions to Mr. Grenville, 242. 377. 484. 493. 497. 500. iii. p. xliv. xlvii. 82. 87. 90. 121. 125. 150. 156. 173. 184. 185. 196. 214. 220. 222. 244. 270. 305. 309. 313. 354. 356. 360. 363. 368. 369. 370. 380. iv. 7. 29. 31. 32. 93. 98. 112. 114. 116. 120. 126. 129. 144. 164. 167. 208. 211. 215. 221. 251. 340. 407. 408. 433. 517. 522.
Butler, Dr., afterwards Bishop of Hereford, ii. 330.
Butler, Mr. Charles, iii. p. lxxxiv. iv. 501.
Byng, Admiral, i. 161. 163. 169. 172. 176. 221. 435.
Byron, Commodore, iii. 1.

C.

C., see Junius.
Cabinet Council, Minute of, iii. 15. 41.
Cabinet dinners, probable origin of, ii. 256.
Cadogan, Charles Sloane, M.P., ii. 327. iii. 360. 371.
Calcraft, Mr., ii. 90. 122. 231. iii. p. xcvi—ci. cx—cxxiv.
Calcraft, Colonel, ii. 128.
Calvert, Mr. Nicholson, iii. 8.
Cambridge University, High Stewardship of, ii. 227. 236.
Camden, Lord, iii. p. xc. cxxx—cxxxiv. ccx. ccxii. 77. 217. 282. 290. 346. 397. iv. 28. 64. 74. 98. 115. 116. 159. 180. 225. 227. 241. 247. 249. 268. 336. 344. 382. 392. 402. 404. 463. 478. 493. 502.
Campbell, Lord, iii. p. xvii.
Campbell, Lord Frederick, ii. 262. iii. 28. 187. 188. iv. 131.
Campbell, Lord William, iv. 165.
Campbell, Lady Harriott, ii. 363.
Campbell, Mr. Hume, i. 153.
Canada, expedition against, i. 54. Civil Government of, ii. 476.
"Candor," another Pamphlet by, ii. 459.
Candor,' Letter to the "Public Advertiser" by, iii. p. clv. clx.
Candor, a Son of, " Principles of the late Changes," &c., by, iii. p. clviii.
Cannon taken at Louisbourg and Cherbourg, i. 264.
Cape Breton and St. John's, islands of, taken, i. 259.

Cardross, David, Lord, afterwards Earl of Buchan, iv. 208.
Carleton, Colonel, i. 326.
Carlisle, Henry, fourth Earl of, i. 50. 267.
Carlisle, Charles Lyttelton, Bishop of, iii. 240.
Carlisle, siege of, in 1745, i. 49.
Carmarthen, Lord, iv. 548.
Carnarvan, James Brydges, Marquess of, ii. 145. 400.
Carteret, Lord, i. 32.
Carysfort, John Proby, first Lord, moves the Address, ii. 5.
Catherine, Empress of Russia, ii. 31.
Catherlough, Lord, iii. 31.
Cavendish, Lord George, iii. 170.
Cavendish, Lord John, iii. 28. 218. 281. 389. iv. 229.
Cavendish, Mr., iv. 469. 482.
Chalmers, Mr. George, iii. 237.
Chamber, Mrs. Anna, i. p. iv. see Temple, Countess.
Chamier, Mr., ii. 416.
Chancery, Court of, Hereditary Registrar of, ii. 329. 332.
Chandos, Henry, second Duke of, iv. 415.
Charleville, Charles, second Lord, ii. 276.
Charlotte, queen of George III., i. 400. ii. 243. 245. iii. 93. 122. 360. iv. 144. 157. 233.
Charter House, election for Governors of the, ii. 280.
Chatham, William Pitt, Earl of, iii. p. xxiii. xlviii. lxxix. cxvii—cxxvi. 304. 305. 313. 315. 330. 346. 379. 385. 393. 396. iv. 1. 7. 9. 23. 26. 28. 31. 33. 34. 38. 42. 46. 64. 66. 108. 113. 116. 118. 124. 131. 154. 157. 159. 163. 167. 180. 185. 199. 208. 212. 236. 250. 273. 310. 344. 390. 393. 398. 402. 413. 426. 428. 429. 431. 509. 513. 515. 519. 573. see Pitt.
Chatham, Hester, Countess of, iii. p. cvii. 228. 279. iv. 280. 310. 398.
Cherbourg, expedition to, i. 250. 253. 256.
Chesterfield, Philip, Earl of, i. 4. iv. 300.
Chetwynd, William, Viscount, iv. 147. 487.
Choiseul, Duke de, i. 363. 364. 367. 369. 462. ii. 410. iii. 301.
Christening at Lord Egremont's, Court ceremonial of the, ii. 50.
Christian the Seventh, see Denmark.
Churchill, Charles, i. 490. ii. 24. 56. 59. 73. 77. 100. 141. 156. 428. 455. death of, 459.
City Address and Remonstrance, iii. p. c—cix. iv. 515.
Civil List, iii. 521. iii. 235. 334. iv. 509.
Clare, Robert Viscount, afterwards Earl Nugent, iv. 182. 199.

P P 2

Clavering, Colonel, i. 306.
Cleaver, Mr., iv. 572.
Clerke, Colonel, i. 213. 225. 229.
Cleveland, Mr., Secretary of the Admiralty, i. 187. ii. 45.
Cleveland Row, Lord Bute's office in, i. 361.
Clive, Robert, Lord, ii. 46. 161. 273. 302. 304. 501. iii. p. cxxxviii. 317. 325. 326. iv. 14. 55. 94. 135. 146. 200. 422.
Coal Trade on the Tyne, ii. 475.
Cobham, Richard Temple, Viscount, i. 19. 25. 76. 80. 427.
Cobham, Anne Halsey, Viscountess, i. 25.
Cockpit, meeting at the, ii. 6.
Cocks, Mr., wounded at Cherbourg, i. 257.
Coke, Lady Jane, i. 358.
Coke, Lady Mary, i. 77. ii. 42.
Colden, Cadwallader, iv. 385.
Coleman, Mr. Thomas, iv. 505.
Colland, General, ii. 273.
Colleton, Mr., M.P., ii. 454.
Coloredo, the Austrian Minister, i. 196.
Commons, House of, Debates, i. 19, 94, 95. ii. 223. 228. 229. 490. iii. p. cxxvii. 5. 8. 21. 23. 26—33. 35. 37. 165. 383. iv. 193. 210. 214. 216. 225. 235. 240. 483. 503.
Compton, Lady Margaret, iv. 547.
"Conduct of the late Administration Examined," &c., iii. p. lxxv. clxxxvii. 365.
Coni, siege of, i. 31.
Constantinople, embassy to, iii. 95.
Contades, M. de, i. 302. 307. 308.
Conveyancing part of Junius's correspondence, iii. p. cci.
Conway, Mrs., i. 135.
Conway, General, i. 67. 200. 208. 216. 225. ii. 162. 166. 176. 187. 224. 230. 233. 234. 248. 258. 296. 320. 335. iii. 26. 88. 115. 235. 257. 310. 341. 345. 386. 396. iv. 26. 31. 37. 41. 76. 83. 89. 94. 109. 119. 138. 157. 160. 193. 197. 228. 240.
Cooper, Mr., afterwards Sir Grey, iv. 157.
Corn, embargo on the exportation of, iii. 338. 340. 383.
Cornbury, Henry Hyde, Viscount, i. 1—7. 9.
Cornwallis, Charles, afterwards Lord, i. 200. ii. 159.
Cotes, Humphrey, ii. 56. 73. 156. 455. 459. iii. 80. 92. 97. 292. 306. 314. iv. 3. 15. 262.
Cotter, Sir James, iv. 473.
Cotton, Rev. Nathaniel, i. 240.
"Counter Address," pamphlet by Horace Walpole, ii. 428.
Court life, description of, iv. 25.
Court-martial on Admirals Lestock, Matthews, &c., i. 36.
Coutts, Messrs., iv. 538.

Covent Garden, fire in, iv. 414.
Coventry, Maria Gunning, Countess of, i. 158. 309.
Cranbourn, Lord, iv. 548.
Creveldt, Battle of, i. 244. 246.
Cumberland, William, Duke of, i. 66. 158. 190. 196. 198. 203. 206. 223. 226. ii. 230. 235. 443. iii. 37. 58. 59. 83. 87. 105. 172. 173. 175. 177. 197. 202. 224. 225. 234.
Cumberland, Henry, Duke of, iv. 226. 522. 555. 556.
Cunningham, Colonel James, ii. 22. 164. iv. 9.
Cust, Sir John, the Speaker, ii. 226. iii. 281.
Cüstrin, bombardment of, i. 263.
Czernichew, Count, iv. 558.

D.

Dalkeith, Lady, ii. 120. 295. iv. 9. 11.
Dartmouth, Earl of, iii. 220.
Dashwood, Sir James, i. 197.
Daun, Marshal, i. 197. 251. 324.
Dayrell, Mr., iii. p. lxxxii. iv. 535.
Deal, smuggling at, ii. 432.
"Defence of the Minority," Chas. Townshend's pamphlet, ii. 426. 428. reply to, 459.
"Defence of the Majority," by Charles Lloyd, ii. 459.
De Grey, Mr., Solicitor-General, ii. 153. 472. iii. 287.
Delaval, Sir Francis Blake, ii. 144—149.
De Lolme, J. L., iii. p. cxxxix—cxliii.
Dempster, Mr., M.P., iii. 27. iv. 190.
Denbigh, Basil Feilding, sixth Earl of, i. 316. ii. 244. iii. 368.
Denton, George, M.P. for Buckingham, i. 20.
Denmark, Christian the seventh, King of, iv. 341. 342. 360. 363. 365. 372.
Denmark, Queen of, iii. 235.
D'Eon, Chevalier, ii. 124. 280. 282. 286. 288. 289. 383. 501. iii. 10. iv. 451. 464.
D'Estrées, Maréchal de, i. 205.
Devonshire, William, third Duke of, i. 146. 182. 437. ii. 22. 443.
Dickenson, John, iv. 336.
Digby, Mr., afterwards Earl Digby, i. 180. ii. 41.
Dingley, Mr., iv. 66.
Dodd, Matthew, coachman to Kitty Fisher, his execution, ii. 193.
Dodington, George Bubb, afterwards Lord Melcombe, i. 18. 153. 190. 427. 448.
Dominique, Island of, i. 376. ii. 11. 25. iii. 234.
Doneraile, Arthur St. Leger, Viscount, i. 66.
Dowdeswell, Mr., M.P., iii. 28. 218. 281. 290. 294. iv. 83. 211. 411. 450. 464.

INDEX. 581

D'Oyly, Mr., iii. 281. iv. 177.
Draper, Colonel, afterwards Sir William, ii. 301. 304. iii. p. xcvi. iv. 367. 471.
Drax, Thomas Erle, ii. 454.
Drumlanrig, Lord, his accidental death, i. 130.
Duff, William, created Baron Braco, i. 257.
Duncan, Dr., afterwards Sir William, i. 94. ii. 193. iii. 189. iv. 158. 407.
Dundas, Sir Laurence, iii. p. cxxxviii. iv. 162.
Dunning, Mr., ii. 62. 65. 73. 81. 137. iii. 47. 48. 287. iv. 2. 248. 303. 470.
Dupplin, Thomas Hay, Viscount, i. 190. 193.
Durell, Admiral, i. 303. 320.
Durham, Trevor, Bishop of, i. 287.
Dutch deputies, i. 297. 300.
Dyson, Mr., i. 399. 403. iii. 73.

E.

Eastbury, in Dorsetshire, iv. 9.
East India Company, affairs of, ii. 181. 184. 433. iii. 255. 312. 316. 317. 323. 324. 326. 334. 389. 396. iv. 6. 10. 18. 19. 122. 135. 194. 201. 213. 225. 240.
East India Company, French establishment of, ii. 372.
East Indies, French expedition to the, iii. 1.
Edgecumbe, George, Lord, iii. 218. 345. 389. iv. 186.
Edwin, Lady Charlotte, ii. 245.
Effingham, Thomas, Earl of, i. 472. ii. 227.
Eglintoun, Earl of, iii. 363. 367. iv. 132.
Egmont, John Perceval, second Earl of, ii. 6. 110. 115. 171. 203. First Lord of the Admiralty, 206. iii. 73. 88. 195. 204. 236. 256. 303. iv. 27. 56. 131. 136. 371.
Egremont, Charles, Earl of, i. 190. 193. 450. ii. 34. 40. 99. 193. iii. p. xl.
Egremont, Lady, i. 383.
Elections, Mr. Grenville's Bill, concerning controverted, iv. 515.
Elliot, Captain, captures the French squadron, i. 340.
Elliot, Mr., afterwards Sir Gilbert, i. 159. 187. ii. 32. 33. 197. 200. 242. 243. iii. 81. 332. 384.
Ellis, Mr. Welbore, i. 153. ii. 21. 23. 68. 116. 208. iii. p. xxii.
" Enquiry into the Conduct of a late Right Honourable Commoner," pamphlet so called, iii. 292. 298. 306. 314. 380.
Epsom, powder mill at, blown up. i. 201.
Erskine, Sir Henry, i. 189.
Estaing, M. d', ii. 423. 436.
Ewer, Dr., Bishop of Llandaff, ii. 534.
Exchequer tellership, ii. 496.
Exeter, Countess of, her will, i. 157.
Exeter, Deanery House at, iv. 21.

F.

Falkland Islands, iv. 505. 518.
Fane, Charles, Viscount, i. 130.
Farnham, Robert, Lord, ii. 274.
Ferdinand, Prince, i. 232. 244. 246. 248. 252. 257. 260. 294. 299. 301. 308. 313. 325. 336. 345. 346. 360. 453.
Fermer, the Russian General, his retreat, i. 266.
Feronce, M. de, ii. 163. 300.
Fielding, Sir John, ii. 141. 286. 369. 385. iii. 169.
Fife, James, second Earl of, ii. 301. 387. iii. 222.
Findlater, James, Earl of, ii. 390.
Fire in Bishopsgate Street, iii. 109.
Fisher, Kitty, i. 297.
Fitzherbert, Mr., M.P., ii. 166. 180. 457. 459. iv. 1. 271.
Fitzroy, Colonel, iv. 68.
Flanders, campaign in, 1744, i. 26.
Fontenoy, battle of, i. 37.
Forbes, Captain, ii. 99. 138.
Forbes, General, i. 243.
Fordyce, Mr., bankruptcy of, iv. 539.
Fortescue, Mrs., i. 15. 98.
Fortescue, Lucy, wife of George Lyttelton, i. 15.
Fouquet, General, i. 345.
Fowke, General, i. 165. 171.
Fox, Charles James, iii. p. xxiv. iv. 504. 517.
Fox, Right Hon. Henry, afterwards Lord Holland, i. 68. 107. 113. 114. 132. 190. 194. 197. 432. 434. 451. 452. 483. see Holland.
Fox, Lady Susan, ii. 447.
Francis, Rev. Dr., ii. 250. 254. his pension, 255. iii. p. xxii.
Francis, Sir Philip, iii. p. xvii—xxiii. xxvi.
Frankland, Mr. Frederick, iii. 192.
Fraser, Simon, iii. 244.
Freeholder, the, a letter so signed, iv. 495.
Free Port Bill, iii. 240.
French finances, disordered state of, ii. 412.
French fleet, Byng's engagement with the, i. 163. 165.
French prisoners, expenses of, ii. 391. 411. 417. 419. 503. iii. 14. 19.
Fuentes, Count de, i. 344.
Fuller, Mr. Rose, M.P., iii. 25.

G.

Gage, General, iii. 13.
Game Laws, iii. p. xxi.
Gascoyne, Mr. Bamber, i. 357.
Gashery, Francis, M.P., i. 443.
Garrick, David, iii. p. lxxi—lxxiv.
Garter, Order of the, Installation at Windsor, i. 473.

"Gazetteer," letters, &c., in the, iv. 70. 133. 435.
General Warrants, debate on, ii. 491.
George III., King, i. 485. his first letter to Mr. Grenville, ii. 161. proposes the dismissal of General Conway, 162. 163. 165. 166. endeavours to strengthen his Government, 191. offers to Lord Hardwicke, 191. praise of Mr. Grenville, 192. advised by the Duke of Bedford to send for Mr. Pitt—announces to Mr. Grenville his intention of calling in Mr. Pitt, 195. his account to Mr. Grenville of Mr. Pitt's terms for taking office, 198. refuses Mr. Pitt's terms, and restores Mr. Grenville to confidence, 201. his assurance of support to Mr. Grenville, 205. arrangement for the disposal of offices, 207. opinion of Lord Halifax and Mr. Pitt, 219. account of Lord Holland's audience, 219. indignation at the abuse in the "North Briton," 222. 223. his resentment against General Conway, 229. 230. opinion respecting riots in the City, 235. behaviour to Lord Shelburne, 239. resists the King of Prussia's demands, 240. 255. 261. 267. 284. 296. 365. 441. 514. iii. p. xxiii. xxxiii. 3. his first illness, 7. 11. 12. 14. 15. 22. 34. 37. 40. ironical observations of Junius upon, 59. 73. 81. 93. 111. 113. 115. 121. 125. 135. 149. 152. 153. 160. 189. 220. his illness consequent upon political perplexities, iii. 357. his opinion relative to the repeal of the Stamp Act, 365. 370. conversation with Lord Mansfield, 374. 385. iv. 29. 31. 55. 88. 102. 107. 144. 184. 212. 214. 224. 225. 268. 273. 293.
Germain, Lady Betty, i. 135. iii. p. lxviii. iv. 192. 491.
Gibraltar, Receivership of, iii. 86.
Gisors, Duke de, i. 205. 247.
Gloucester, Duke of, iii. 114. 141. 147. 151. 234. iv. 225.
Glover, Richard, M.P., ii. 265. iii. 285. iv. 539. 564.
Glynne, Sir John, iii. 296.
Glynn, Mr. Serjeant, ii. 61. 62—65. 71. 73. 81. 137. iii. p. cix. 47. 48. iv. 2. 291.
Good, Dr. Mason, iii. p. xvi.
Gower, John, Earl of, i. 19. ii. 89. 102. iii. p. xvi. 67. 265. 267. 272. 303. 306. 308. 321. iv. 36. 197. 251. 301.
Græme, Major-General, iii. 92. 190. iv. 123. 157. 233.
Grafton, Augustus Henry, third Duke of, ii. 53. 199. iii. p. xxxv. xxxvi. xci. xcvi. cxxvi. ccxix. 81. 88. 90. 106. 199. 223. 243. 283. 303. 308. iv. 1. 15. 23. 27. 34. 37. 38. 45. 66. 87. 89. 100. 119. 163. 173. 197. 199. 226. 228. 236. 241. 249. 253. 268. 273. 275. 276. 293. 301. 309. 314. 316. 337. 350. 382. 402. 417. 458. 461. 474. 478. 493. 509. 526.
Grafton, Duchess of, iv. 299.
Granby, John, Marquess of, i. 184. 325. 357. ii. 69. 107. 133. 200. 208. 494. iii. p. xcvi—xcix. 41. 49. 70. 113. 172. 184. 185. 193. 206. 208. 209. 218. 308. iv. 42. 89. 100. 132. 305. 493. 502.
Granby, Frances, Marchioness of, i. 157.
Grand Council upon the Affairs of Ireland, iv. 171.
Grantham, Henry de Nassau, Lord, i. 383.
Grantham, Thomas, Lord, iii. 217.
Granville, John Carteret, Earl of, i. 50. 160.
Granville, Lady, her death, i. 31.
Gray, Sir James, iv. 108. 208.
Grenada, Island of, ii. 9. 17.
Grenville family, account of, i. p. iii.
Grenville pedigree, i. 79.
Grenville, Right Hon. George, some account of, i. p. viii. his character, by Burke, x. by Wedderburn, xii. by Knox, xiv. by an anonymous writer, xv. his marriage, xvi. his descendants, xvi. his papers and correspondence, xix. 2. 119. 148. 188. 194. 359. 422. 449. 453. ii. 87. 138. 143. 152. 191. 192. 196. 197. 201. 204. 205. 220. 223. 224. 230. 233. 236. 239. 240. 241. 261. 265. 293. 490. 493. 499. 500. 505. iii. p. lx. cxi. 5. 25. 28. 31. 32. 33. 43. 112—222. 174. 178. 183. 191. 211. 221. 222. 232. 353—354. 360. 362. 363. 383. 386. iv. 29. 45. 61. 68. 71. 73. 77. 92. 96. 116. 122. 125. 128. 135. 142. 145. 161. 208. 218. 224. 230. 235. 237. 272. 274. 403. 469. 471. 475. 479. 483.
Grenville, Mrs., Narrative of Events in 1761, i. 409. Narrative of Events from November, 1763, to January, 1764, ii. 242. iii. 315. iv. 487.
Grenville, Hester, afterwards Countess of Chatham, i. p. xviii. 24. 85. see Chatham.
Grenville, George, jun., ii. 496. iv. 550.
Grenville, Lady Mary, iv. 572.
Grenville, Right Hon. James, account of, i. p. xvii. 26. 96. 136. 394. 424. 437. ii. 198. iii. 199. iv. 182.
Grenville, Mr. James, jun., iii. 192.
Grenville, Right Hon. Henry, account of, i. p. xvii. 426. iii. 117. 118. 191. iv. 559.
Grenville, Richard, afterwards Earl Temple, account of, i. p. iii. 18. see Temple.
Grenville, Richard Percy, death of, i. 313.
Grenville, Captain Richard, i. 377.
Grenville, Captain Thomas, account of, i. p. xvii. 20. captures a prize from the

West Indies, 21. 29. 35. 58. his death, 61. his monument at Bath, 99.
Grenville, Mr. Thomas, i. 154. 330. iii. p. xv. lxxxix. iv. 467.
Grenville, William Wyndham, verses by, iv. 528.
Grimaldi, Spanish Minister, i. 462. ii. 131.
Gros. M. de, ii. 418.
Grosvenor, Lady, iv. 522.
Guadaloupe, i. 301. 306. 450. 493. ii. 11. 25.
Guerchy, M. de, ii. 126. 173. 188. dispute about his wine, 259. 334. 360. arrest of his servant, 503.
Guilford, Earl of, ii. 209.
Guthrie, Mr. Andrew, Surgeon of the *Defiance*, his account of Captain Grenville's death, i. 61.

H.

Habeas Corpus Act, i. 235. iii. p. xlii. cciv. ccvi. ccvii.
Hagley, masque of fairies at, iv. 323.
Halifax, George Dunk, Earl of, i. 161. 450. 456. ii. 40. 83. 89. 118. 225. 228. 253. 427. 514. 520. iii. p. xxxv. 132. 150. 157. 166. 172. 192. 221—223. iv. 2.
Hamilton, James, sixth Duke of, i. 186.
Hamilton, Mr., afterwards Sir William, ii. 295. iii. 351.
Hamilton, William Gerard, i. 193. ii. 274. iii. p. lxii. xciii. 255. iv. 23. 26. 31. 36. 41. 52. 62. 86. 90. 97. 99. 108. 115. 129. 136. 159. 167. 174. 303.
Hampshire election, Mr. Legge's papers on the, ii. 517.
Handwriting of the Author of Junius, iii. p. cxc—cci.
Hanoverian troops, debate on the subject of, i. 20.
Harcourt, Duke de, ii. 100. iii. 259.
Harcourt, Earl of, i. 180. iii. 351. 353. 367. 394. 395.
Hardinge, Mr. Justice, iii. p. cxxx.
Hardwicke, Philip, first Earl of, i. 160. 400. ii. 83. 149. 191. 199. 225. 241. 279. iii. p. clxxii.
Hardwicke, Philip, second Earl of, iii. 240. iv. 223. 253.
Hardy, Sir Charles, i. 242. ii. 1.
Harley, Mr. Alderman, ii. 232.
Harris, James, M.P., ii. 151. iv. 483.
Harrison, Mr., iv. 12.
"Harry and Nan," by Junius, iii. p. ccxix.
Hartley, David, ii. 428.
Harvey, General, iv. 305.
Haslang, Count, iii. 361.
Hastenbech, battle of, i. 203.
Havannah, i. 450. 469. 476. 479. 481. 483. 488.
Havre, bombardment of, i. 311. 312.

Hawke, Sir Edward, i. 210. 212. 213. 214, 219. 220. 354. iii. 392. iv. 213. 526.
Hay, Dr., M.P. for Stockbridge, i. 138. 167. 187. ii. 263. 531.
Hayes, the Duke of Cumberland visits Mr. Pitt at, iii. 225. Lord Chatham's repurchase of, iv. 181.
Hayter, Dr. John, Bishop of London, i. 384.
Henley, Lord, Lord Chancellor, ii. 89. 237. 238. *see* Northington.
Hensey, Dr. Florence, trial of, for high treason, i. 239.
Heron, Robert [*i. e.* Pinkerton], his edition of Junius, iii. p. ccxxii.
Hertford, Earl of, ii. 58. 177. 248. 514. iii. 256. 282. 325. iv. 130. 197. 251. 298.
Hervey, John, Lord, i. 16.
Hervey, Lady, iv. 357.
Hervey, Honourable Augustus, i. 350. iii. p. xiv. 39. 42. 87. 174. 176. 382. iv. 24. 29. 32. 70. 130. 133. 175. 271. 340. 356. 383. 393. 405. 415. 496.
Hesse, Landgrave of, i. 206.
Hesse, Mary, Princess of, i. 206.
Hessian troops, i. 187.
Hewitt, Mr. Serjeant, afterwards Lord Lifford, iii. 8. iv. 160. 232.
Hillsborough, Wills Hill, Viscount, afterwards Earl of, i. 34. 190. ii. 116. 206. 246. iii. p. lii—liv. 224. 282. 291. 294. 342. iv. 247. 297. 320. 344. 349. 352. 359. 364. 388. 392. 400. 480.
Hine, Mr., iv. 484. 495.
Hoare, William, painter, i. 51. his brother a sculptor, 99. 103. his portrait of Mr. Pitt, 120. 121.
Hobart, Mr. George, ii. 31.
Hobart, Lady Dorothy, i. 76.
Hodgkinson, R. Banks, i. 66.
Hogarth, Mr., his grief for the attack upon him in the "North Briton," ii. 5. Churchill's Epistle to, quoted, 73. his death, 457.
Hoghton, Mrs. [Nancy Parsons], iv. 275.
Holbourne, Admiral, i. 200. 202.
Holdernesse, Robert, fourth Earl of, i. 148.
Holland, Lord, ii. 199. supports Mr. Grenville, 208. 220. 241. 465. 485. 488. iii. p. xxii. xxiii. 41. 87. 90. 184. 256. iv. 38. 46. 88. 93. 124. 179. 295. 303. 304. 467. 517.
Holmes, Admiral, i. 320. 322.
Holt, Lord Chief Justice, iii. p. ccxii.
Home, Rev. John, ii. 246.
Hood, Commodore Samuel, iv. 164. 306. 332. 361. 373.
Hood, Mrs., iv. 546.
Hopkins, Mr., M.P., ii. 160.
Horne, Mr., iii. p. lxxxv.
Hotham, Colonel, iv. 147.

584 INDEX.

Howe, George Augustus, third Viscount, his death, i. 254.
Howe, Captain, afterwards Viscount and Earl Howe, i. 136. 208. 213. 215. 225. 247. 260. iii. 74. 243. 281.
Howe, Lady, iv. 517.
Hume, David, ii. 246. iii. 91.
Huntingdon, Earl of, iv. 372.
Huntingdon, Selina, Countess of, iv. 526.
Hutchinson, Mr., iv. 110. 137.
Hyde, Thomas Villiers, Lord, Postmaster-General, ii. 116. 206. 285. iii. 353.
Hyde, Charlotte Lady, ii. 317.

I.

Imhoff, General, i. 302. 345. 346.
Indemnity, Bill of, iii. 341. 344. 347. 349. 386. 394. 395. 396.
Informations, ex-officio, debate on the subject of, iii. 8. 9.
Ingersol, Mr., iv. 170.
Ireland, riots in, i. 440. pensions and grants in, ii. 147. 166.
Irwin, Sir John, iii. p. xv. 51. iv. 183. 200. 233. 300. 418.
Isenburgh, Prince, i. 299.

J.

Jamaica, command of, i. 57. free port of, iii. 234.
James the Second's Journal, ii. 456.
Jenkinson, Charles, afterwards Earl of Liverpool, i. 179. 182. his Treatise on the Laws of Nations, 270. appointed Secretary to Lord Bute, 359, 482. ii. 197. 217. 231. 242. iii. 73. 163. 220. 258. 350. 381. 384. 392. 393. 395. iv. 236. 304.
Jesuitical books, iii. p. cxliv.
Johnson, Dr. Samuel, his pension, ii. 68.
Johnstone, Governor, ii. 137. 449.
Junius, Notes relating to the authorship of, iii. p. xiii. Letters from, to Mr. Grenville, xiv. Lord Temple first suggested to be the Author of, xvi. Claims of Sir Philip Francis to the authorship mentioned and disposed of, xvi. et seq. The Stamp Act, xx. The Game Laws, xxi. Lord Holland, xxii—xxvi. Mr. Welbore Ellis, xxii. King George the Third, xxiii. Lord Chatham, xxiii. Character of Lord Temple, xxvii. et seq. Lord Temple's attachment to Wilkes, xxx. The King's dislike to Lord Temple, xxxiii. Letters from Junius to Wilkes, xxxv. The Duke of Grafton, xxxvi. The Bedford party, xxxvii. Lord Temple's animosity towards the Duke of Bedford, xxxviii. Junius and Lord Egremont, xl. Dr. Musgrave, xl. The Duke of Bedford and the Grenvilles, xli. Mr. Pitt and Lord Temple, xlii. Lord Temple and Lord Mansfield, xlii. Habeas Corpus Bill, xlii. Case of the Aylesbury men, xliii. Lord Temple and Lord Bute, xlv. Lord George Sackville at Court, xlv. Lord Temple and the "North Briton," xlvi. Junius, Lord Temple and the War Office, the Secretary of State's Office, xlviii. Lord Temple and Lord Barrington, xlix. Bradshaw and Chamier, li. Lord Temple and Lord Hillsborough, lii. Sir Jeffry Amherst and Lord Botetourt, liii. Lord Talbot and Wilkes, liv. Character of the Bedfords, the Bloomsbury gang, liv. Lord Suffolk, Whately, Wedderburn, Augustus Hervey, &c., lv. Junius and Lord Suffolk, lvi. Lord Temple and Junius, lix. Junius, George Grenville, Chatham, and Wilkes, lxi. Junius and George the Third, lxii. Lord Temple the author or encourager of libellous publications, lxiii. Lord Temple and Almon the bookseller, lxiv. Junius, and Lord and Lady Temple, lxiv. Lady Temple the amanuensis, lxv. Junius nevertheless the sole depositary of his own secret, lxv. The Dukes of Grafton and Bedford, Lord Tavistock's wardrobe, the Princess Dowager, &c., lxvi. Junius and Mr. Henry Sampson Woodfall, lxvii. The author's fear of dicovery, lxvii. Private notes from Junius to Woodfall, chiefly without any date, lxvii. Junius, Swinney, and Lord George Sackville, lxviii. Lord Temple, Lord George Sackville, and Lady Betty Germain, lxix. The assumed names of Junius, Middleton and Fretley, lxix. Junius and Garrick, Lord and Lady Temple, and the Princess Amelia, lxxi. Coffee-houses used by Junius in his correspondence with Woodfall, lxxiv. Junius and the Bill of Attainder, lxxiv. Junius, Lord Temple, and Montesquieu, lxxv. Junius corresponded with only four persons, lxxvi. If Lord Temple were Junius, why he should correspond with Mr. Grenville, lxxvii. The disguised handwriting of Junius, lxxviii. Private letters from Junius to Lord Chatham, lxxix. Junius, Lord Temple, and Lord Mansfield, lxxix. Junius, Wilkes, and Lord Temple, lxxxi. Mr. Dayrell's letter to Lord Temple on the election of Lord Mayor, compared with those of Junius to Wilkes on the same subject, lxxxii. Lord Temple and City politics, lxxxiii. Mr. Charles Butler's reminiscence of Wilkes, Junius, and Lady Temple, lxxxiv. Junius and Mr. Horne, lxxxv. Rank and fortune of Junius, lxxxvi. Junius a man of leisure,

INDEX. 585

the progress of his employment, lxxxvii. The author of the "Grand Council," and the "Letter to an Honourable Brigadier-General," lxxxviii. Mr. Thomas Grenville's anecdote of General Wolfe, Lord Temple, and Mr. Pitt, lxxxix. Lord Temple, Lord Camden, and the Corn Bill: Junius and Scævola, xc. Lord Chatham and Lord Camden, xcii. Lord Temple and William Gerard Hamilton, xciv. Sir William Draper, xcvi. Correspondence between Lord and Lady Chatham and Lord Temple, compared with the Letters of Junius, xcvi. *et seq.* Junius and Lord Granby, xcvii. The City Remonstrance, xcix. Lord Temple, the Letters of Junius, and Locke's Essay on Civil Government, cii. *et seq.* The *second* Remonstrance, in the handwriting of Lady Chatham and Lord Temple, cvii. The right of pressing seamen, cix. Junius's Letter to Lord Mansfield, cx. Mr. Grenville's illness and death, cxi. Junius and Lord Barrington. Lord Mansfield and Woodfall's trial, cxiii. Anonymous Letter to Calcraft attributed to Junius, cxv. The substance of it used by Lord Chatham in the House of Lords, and by Junius in his Preface, &c., cxvii. Junius, Lord Chatham, and Gibraltar, cxix. A Letter to Calcraft communicated by him to Lord Chatham, compared with the Letters of Junius of the same period, cxxi. Lord Lyttelton and Junius, cxxii. Calcraft, Lord Chatham, and Junius: the privilege of Parliament in the matter of the printers, cxxiii. Lord Temple's visit to the Duke of Grafton: Junius and the King's timber, cxxvi. Lord Temple's frequent attendance in the House of Commons, cxxvii. Mr. Grenville, Dr. Blackstone, and Sir Fletcher Norton, cxxix. Mr. Daniel Wray's information about Junius, Lord Temple, and Lord Camden, cxxx. Lord Temple, Lord Camden, and the King's Speech in January, 1770, cxxxiii. Expulsion of Wilkes *predetermined* in the Cabinet, cxxxiv. The Falkland Islands question in the House of Lords, cxxxv. Whether Junius was a member of either House of Parliament, cxxxvi. Junius and De Lolme, cxxxix. Burning of the Jesuitical books, cxliv. Lord Temple in France at that period, cxlv. Similarity of phrases and opinions in the speeches of Lord Chatham and the Letters of Junius, cxlvi–vii. Tracts and Pamphlets written by, or attributed to Lord Temple, cxlix. Extracts from a "Letter to an Honourable Brigadier-General," clii.—from a "Letter on the Seizure of Papers," cliii.—from a "Letter from Albemarle Street to the Cocoa Tree," cliv. Letter from Candor to the "Public Advertiser,"clv. "Letter concerning Libels, Warrants, &c.," in a Letter to Mr. Almon, from the Father of Candor, clvii. "Principles of the late Changes impartially examined by a Son of Candor," clviii. Extracts from the Letter of Candor, clx.—from the "Letter concerning Libels, &c.," clxvi. *et seq.* "Another Letter to Almon in Matter of Libel," clxxvi. *et seq.* A Second Postscript to that Letter, clxxxiii. "Summary of the Law of Libel," by Phileleutherus Anglicanus, clxxxiii. *et seq.* Extracts from the "Conduct of the late Administration examined," &c., clxxxvii. *et seq.* The handwriting of the Author of Junius, cxc. *et seq.* The conveyancing part of the correspondence with Junius, cci. Fragments in the handwriting of Lord Temple compared with the Letters of Junius, cciv. *et seq.* Parallel passages from the writings of Junius and Lord Temple, ccxii. *et seq.* Poem by Junius, entitled "*Harry and Nan*"—the Duke of Grafton and Nancy Parsons, ccxix. Lines by Lord Temple on the return of Wilkes to England, ccxxi. Scriptural allusions in the writings of Junius and Lord Temple, ccxxii. Lord Temple and Mr. Luttrell—libellous papers, ccxxiv. Lord Temple and the Stock Exchange, ccxxvi. Junius well acquainted with every occurrence at Court, iii. 59. George Onslow and Lord Temple, 76. Whately "undertakes to be a courier," 262. Debate in the House of Lords, which "I myself heard," 344. False facts, 380. Lord Chatham and Lord Camden, iv. 64. 116. George Ross, "the Scotch agent and worthy confidant of Lord Mansfield," 145. Grand Council upon the Affairs of Ireland, 171. Pay office accounts, 179. The Duke of Grafton and the Bedfords, 199. "A Word at Parting," 202. Whately's letters and Lord Lyttelton's letter compared with one from Junius to Lord Chatham, 241. Duke of Grafton and the Bedfords, 253. C. to Mr. Grenville, 254. Lord Temple and Junius, 254. Auction duty, 257. Lord Hertford, 275. Nancy Parsons, 276. Whately and Junius, 279. Colonel Bodens, 279. "Conveyancing part of our correspondence," 281. Whately's letter and Junius, 321. Sir Jeffry Amherst and Lord Hillsborough, 326. The Duke of Grafton, 348. C. to Mr. Grenville, 354. Lady Temple and Junius—mode of spelling certain words,

361. Anonymous to Mr. Grenville, 379. Letters of Atticus, 379. Writing paper used by Junius, 382. Newspaper paragraphs written by Lord Temple, 433. Buckinghamshire petition and Junius, 441. Newspaper paragraphs written by Lord Temple, 455. Affair of Hine's patent, 484. Junius's Letter containing the Address to the King. 491. 501. Junius supposed to be Wilkes, 495. 500. Lord Temple's letter to Lord Chatham compared with Junius, 534.

K.

Kearsley, Mr., bookseller, ii. 79. his trial, 430.
Keck, Anthony, M.P., iv. 20.
Keck, Miss, iv. 548.
Keene, Dr., Bishop of Chester, ii. 534.
Keith, Mr., British Minister at St. Petersburgh, i. 421.
Kelly, Dr., iii. p. ccxxvi.
Keppel, Colonel, i. 203.
Keppel, Admiral, iii. 309. iv. 186. 300. 304.
Keppel, Dr., made Dean of Windsor, iii. 91.
Ker, Lady Louisa, i. 335.
Kerry, Lord, i. 77.
Kildare, Earl of, iii. 49.
Kingston, Duchess of, iv. 413.
Kingsborough, Robert, Earl of, i. 77.
" King's Friends," the term first used, ii. 33.
King's Speech, spurious copy of the, i. 186.
Kirch-Denckern, battle of, i. 377.
Knowles, Vice-Admiral, i. 208.
Knox, Mr., iii. 109. 110. iv. 297. 319. 335. 359. 363. 368. 521.
Knyphausen, the Prussian Minister, i. 421. 466.

L.

La Lippe, Count, i. 458.
Landschut, battle of, i. 345.
Land Tax reduced, iv. 211.
Lauffeldt, battle of, i. 66.
Law of Lauriston, Baron, iii. 1.
Le Despencer, Lord, ii. 77. iii. 224.
Lee, Sir George, death of, i. 280.
Lee, Dr., i. 107.
Leeds, Thomas Osborne, Duke of, ii. 107. 203.
Leeward Islands, ii. 15. 25.
Legge, Henry Bilson, i. 69. 120. 188. 193. 425. 433. 437. ii. 460. 517.
Lennox, Lord George, i. 335.
Lennox, Lady Sarah, the King's attachment to, iv. 209.

" Letter from Albemarle Street to the Cocoa Tree," ii. 428. iii. p. cliv.
" Letter to an Honourable Brigadier General," iii. p. clii.
" Letter concerning Libels, Warrants. &c.," ii. 65. 459. iii. p..clvii. clviii. clxvi. 46.
Lichfield, Henry Lee, third Earl of, i. 287. ii. 7.
Lighthouse, grant of, to Mr. Grenville, ii. 512.
Ligonier, Sir John, afterwards Lord, i. 66. 190. 227. 311. iii. 309.
Lincoln, Henry, Earl of, i. 268. ii. 4.
Lincoln, Lady, death of, i. 348.
Lincoln's Inn, fire at, i. 96.
Lindsay, Sir John, iv. 520. 522.
Lisbon, report of the Plague at, i. 226. fire at, ii. 369.
Lloyd, Mr., Chaplain to Lord Shelburne, iv. 500.
Lloyd, Mr. Charles, ii. 459. iii. 86. 251. 282. iv. 54. 106. 170. 500.
Lloyd, Dr. Philip, ii. 213. iii. p. ccxxvi. 247. iv. 500.
Lloyd, Dr. Pierson, iv. 500.
Lloyd, Robert, ii. 56. iv. 500.
Lloyd, Thomas, iii. p. ccxxv.
" Locke's Essay on Civil Government," iii. p. cii.
Logwood cutters, interruption of by Spain, ii. 381. 409.
"London Evening Post" Newspaper, ii. 430.
London, Address from the City of, i. 355. iii. 80.
Lord Mayor's feast, ii. 459.
Lords, House of, debates in, ii. 230. iii. 242. 383. iv. 222. 224. 404. 509. 515.
Lorraine, Prince Charles of, i. 26.
Loudon, Lord, i. 201.
Louis XV. at Compiegne, ii. 83.
Louisa, Princess, iv. 299.
Louisbourg, i. 243. 250. 253. 254. 258. 261.
Lowther, Sir James, i. 384. ii. 295. iii. 255. iv. 92.
Luttrell, Mr., ii. 276. iii. p. ccxxv. iv. 413.
Luxborough, Lord, ii. 48.
Lyttelton, George, afterwards Lord Lyttelton, i. 13. description of by Lord Hervey, 14. 15. 68. 85. 106. 120. 126. 424. 430. ii.. 230. iii. 72. 197. 223. 227. 267. 307. 397. iv. 8. 113. 192. 223. 231. 234. 249. 323. verses by, 324. 423. 429. 496.
Lyttelton, Rev. Charles, afterwards Bishop of Carlisle, i. 78. 418.
Lyttelton, Colonel, afterwards Sir Richard, i. 49. 113. 252. ii. 23. 442. iii. 309. iv. 528.
Lyttelton, Mr. Thomas, afterwards Lord, supposed to be Junius, iii. p. xix. 170.
Lyttelton, William Henry, afterwards Lord

INDEX. 587

Westcote and Lord Lyttelton, i. 78. appointed Governor of South Carolina, 130.
Lyttelton, Apphia, Lady, iv. 546.

M.

Macaulay, Mr., iii. p. xxviii.
Macartney, Mr., afterwards Sir George, ii. 415. iii. 90. iv. 301.
Macclesfield, Earl of, his death, ii. 496.
Mackay, John Ross, iv. 107.
Mackenzie, Mr. Stuart, i. 385. ii. 242. iii. 41. 184. 186. 187. 190. 203. 313. iv. 35.
Mackintosh, Robert, ii. 140. 159. iii. 81. 92. 96. 97. iv. 190. 564.
Mackintosh, Sir James, his Letter on the Authorship of Junius quoted, iv. 173.
Mahon, Viscount, iii. p. lxxxviii.
Malpas, George, Viscount, ii. 274.
Man, Isle of, iii. 6.
Manchester, Robert, Duke of, i. 383.
Manilla Expedition, iii. 1. ransom, 88.
Mansfield, William Murray, Earl of, ii. 199. 205. 226. 235. 238. denounces the conduct of Lord Chief Justice Pratt, 239. 429. 521. iii. p. xl—xliv. cx. cxiii. cxlvii. clxx. clxxx. 117. 153. 161. 169. 172. 208. 218. 223. 337. 373. 382. 390. 397. iv. 2. 18. 19. 93. 106. 118. 126. 138. 144. 148. 150. 162. 174. 185. 215. 221. 232. 239. 247. 251. 268. 283. 294. 315. 513. 516.
Marble Hill, Twickenham, i. 8. 76. iv. 147.
March, James, Earl of, ii. 102. iii. 167. iv. 131.
Marchmont, Hugh, third Earl of, i. 153. iii. p. xxxii. cxlvii. 355. iv. 511. 514. 515.
Markham, Rev. Dr., ii. 474. 485. iv. 166.
Marlborough, George, second Duke of, i. 197. 247. 260.
Marlborough, George, third Duke of, i. 297. ii. 6. iii. 210. 217. 308.
Marlborough, Sarah, Duchess of, her death, i. 31. her legacy to Mr. Pitt, 32.
Marmora, M. de, ii. 309.
Marriott, Dr., ii. 346.
Martin, Samuel, M.P., i. 444. ii. 224. iii. 29. 32.
Martinique, Island of, i. 440. ii. 10. 25.
Masham, Lord, iv. 415.
Massachusetts Bay, Assembly of, iv. 13. 297. 307.
Masserano, Prince, ii. 422. iv. 68.
Mauduit, Mr., iv. 391.
Mawbey, Mr., afterwards Sir John, ii. 81. iv. 518.
Maynard, Charles, Viscount, iii. 333.
Michell, the Prussian Minister, i. 421. 466. ii. 450.

Middlesex, Earl of, i. 65. 426. ii. 285. 287.
"Middlesex Journal," iii. p. ccxxvi.
Militia, Bucks, appointments in the, i. 460. 470. ii. 23. 63.
Militia in Norfolk, ii. 59.
Militia of Wiltshire, i. 316.
Militia Bill, debate in the House of Lords on, i. 160.
Militia, claim of exemption from the, i. 328.
Milles, Jeremiah, Dean of Exeter, iv. 20.
Ministry, project for the formation of a, iv. 8.
Minorca, Island of, i. 159. ii. 449.
"Minority, History of the late," iii. 244. 248. 250.
Mitchell, Mr., afterward Sir Andrew, i. 197. 252. 464. 465.
Mead, Mrs., i. 127.
Medmenham Abbey Club, i. 126.
Mello, M. de, Minister from Portugal, i. 440.
Meredith, Sir William, ii. 261. iii. 26. iv. 213. 503.
Moffatt, Dr. Thomas, iii. 237. iv. 510.
Monckton, Brigadier, i. 319. wounded at Quebec, 326.
Montague, George Brudenell, Duke of, iii. 336.
Montagu, Mrs., iv. 425. 496.
Montesquieu, iii. p. lxxv.
Montcalm, Marquis de, i. 254. his death at Quebec, 326. iv. 410.
Moore, Sir Harry, iv. 471.
Mordaunt, Sir John, i. 200. 212. 214. 215. 224.
Morocco, Ambassador from, i. 157. ii. 278.
Morton, Mr., M.P., ii. 143. 443. 448. iii. 29. 32. 159. 163.
Mountague, Mr. Frederick, M.P., ii. 221.
Mulgrave, Constantine, Lord, iv. 137.
Munchausen, Baron, ii. 203.
Murray, Honourable Alexander, ii. 124.
Murray, Brigadier, i. 319. 322. 344.
Murray, William, afterwards Earl of Mansfield, i. 6. 11. 16. 101. 107. 162. 193. 279. see Mansfield.
Murray, Mrs., ii. 242.
Musgrave, Dr., iii. p. xxvi. xl. iv. 450. 452. 464. 465.
Mutiny Act in America, iii. 11. 13.

N.

Nash, Alderman, iv. 536.
Nassau, Prince of, i. 157. visits Stowe, 165.
Navy, state of the English, iv. 525.
Navy, supply for, i. 56.
Navy Estimates, ii. 174. 175. 290.
Navy Pay Office accounts, iv. 179.
Navy of France, condition of, ii. 172. 441.

588 INDEX.

Newbottle, William, Lord, iv. 210.
Newcastle, Thomas Holles Pelham, Duke of, i. 82. 85. 172. 193. ii. 21. iii. 74. 87. 217. 223. 257. 291. iv. 18. 77. 82. 89. 127. 139. 205. 215.
New Forest, office of Woodward, ii. 400.
Newfoundland, St. John's Fort at, taken, i. 488.
"Newhall's Letters on Junius," iii. p. xvi.
Newspaper, new one proposed by Almon, ii. 457.
Newspaper paragraphs, iii. p. cxxxv. iv. 433. 435. 454. 455.
Neville, Mr. Aldworth, ii. 29. 52. 57. 99. 126. 249.
Newton, Dr., Bishop of Bristol, ii. 51. 534.
New York, Assembly of Deputies at, iii. 100.
Nivernois, M. de, i. 475. 481. ii. 29. iii. 302.
Norfolk militia reviewed by the King, i. 313.
North, Frederick, Lord, ii. 120. 133. iii. 27. 239. 299. iv. 101. 162. 163. 169. 194. 213. 247. 517. 526.
North, Lady Louisa, i. 384.
"North Briton," Lord Temple's admiration of No. 25, i. 457. 471. 486. 489. ii. 4. 72. Wilkes's new edition of, 74. 81. 96. 138. burning of, 175. 223. 232. 330. 429. iii. p. xxxi. xlvi.
Northington, Earl of, ii. 502. iii. p. xxxiv. 53. 57. 59. 177. 209. 223. 249. 252. 256. 263. 282. 290. 293. 346. 356. 397. iv. 28. 32. 33. 88. 104. 108. 154. 226. 382. 384.
Northumberland, Earl, afterwards Duke of, ii. 6. 223. 225. iii. 113. 175. 224. 225. 329. 384. iv. 113. 209.
Northumberland, the ship, taken by the French, i. 28.
Norton, Sir Fletcher, ii. 67. iii. p. cxxviii. 48. 73. 75. 78. 84. 256. 268. 330. 381. 384. 394. iv. 23. 35. 65. 93. 144. 185. 221. 269.
Nova Scotia, description of, iv. 164.
Nugent, Robert, M.P., afterwards Viscount Clare and Earl Nugent, ii. 452. iii. 349. 382. 394.
Nuthall, Mr. Thomas, i. 128. iii. 75. 271. iv. 537. 543. 545.

O.

O'Brien, Mr., ii. 447.
O'Conor, Dr. Charles, iii. p. xiv.
Offices, arrangements for the disposal of, ii. 211. 212. 213. 221.
Olmutz, siege of, i. 245. 249.
Onslow, Right Hon. Arthur, the Speaker, iv. 205.
Onslow, Mr. George, ii. 78. 158. 160. 180. iii. 24. 26. 31. 63. Junius's opinion of, 76. 218.
Onslow, Colonel, iii. 30.
Opera House, iii. p. xxxviii.
Orange, Princess of, i. 280.
Orford, George, third Earl of, i. 313.
Osbaldiston, Dr., Bishop of London, i. 419.
Oswald, James, i. 70. ii. 200. iii. 81. iv. 214.
Owen, Sir William, M.P., ii. 119.
Oxford, Edward, Earl of, ii. 206.
Oxford, election for the chancellorship of 1759, i. 286.
Oxfordshire election petition, i. 132.

P.

Palmerston, Lord, iii. 32. 310.
Panmure, William, Earl of, iv. 190.
Paoli, General Pascal, iv. 296.
Parsons, Nancy, iii. p. ccxix. iv. 276. 299. 348.
Paulet, Lord Harry, afterwards Duke of Bolton, ii. 159.
Paymastership accounts, iv. 179.
Peace, preliminaries of, in 1748, i. 73. 74.
"Peace, a Letter on the Prospect of," i. 334. conditions of, 369. 372. 373. 376. 379. 380. 381. 382. 385. 474. 476. 480. 483. Mr. Pitt's disapproval of the, ii. 4. treaty of, signed, 29.
Pearce, Dr. Zachary, Bishop of Rochester, ii. 474.
Pelham, Right Hon. Henry, i. 36. 74. 79. 106. 429.
Pelham, Mr. Thomas, iii. 218.
Pelham, Lady Catherine, i. 172.
Pension List in 1763, ii. 272.
Percy, Lord Algernon, iv. 559.
Petersburg, embassy to, ii. 415. 417.
Petersham, Lady Caroline, i. 157.
Peter III., Emperor of Russia, i. 420.
Petition from Buckinghamshire, iv. 441. 448.
Petition from Yorkshire, iv. 465. 493.
Petre, Lord, ii. 160.
Phelps, Richard, iii. 62.
Phileleutherus Anglicanus, "Summary of the Law of Libel" by, iii. p. clxxxiii.
Phillips, Mr., an attorney, ii. 57. 73. iv. 16.
Phillips, Sir John, i. 184. ii. 6. 8. 117. 206. iii. p. clxviii.
"Pinkerton's Walpoliana," iii. p. xiv.
Pitt, William, afterwards Earl of Chatham, i. 4. 8. 12. 32. 50. 52. 65. 73. 99. 101. 103. 105. 110. 112. 117. 120. 131. 137. 149. 186. 190. 196. 392. 415. 418. 424. 436. ii. 93. 104. 105. 107. 164. 195. 196. 199. 201. 202. 223. 224. 226. 376. 386. 443. 487. 530. iii. 39. 53. 58. 65. 72. 96. 173. 191. 198. 200. 201. 202. 225. 226. 231.

INDEX. 589

252. 262. 267. 271. 272. 274. 279. 282. 291. 376. 377. *see* Chatham.
Pitt, Right Hon. William, jun., birth of, i. 301.
Pitt, John, i. 66. 99. 114.
Pitt, John, afterwards Earl of Chatham; his birth, i. 173.
Pitt, Thomas, afterwards Lord Camelford, ii. 198. 232. 320. iii. 79. 241. 341.
Pitt, Mrs. Anne, i. 11. iv. 199.
Pitt, Hester, afterwards Countess Stanhope, i. 168.
Plate, proposed tax on, i. 156.
Police arrangements, ii. 367.
"Political Apology," a pamphlet, iii. 104.
Pollington, John, Lord, ii. 150.
Pomfret, George, second Earl, ii. 295.
Pompadour, Madame de, i. 205. 368. ii. 303.
Pompeii, excavations at, iv. 550.
Pondicherry taken, i. 376.
Pope, Alexander, i. 7. his death, and account of his will, 27.
Port Egmont, settlement at, iv. 505.
Portsmouth, John, second Earl of, i. 292.
Portsmouth Dockyard, fire at, iv. 525.
Portugal, King of, i. 442. iv. 489. 495.
Postage arrangements, ii. 289. 381.
Post Office, Secret Office at the, iii. 311.
Potter, Thomas, i. 102. 104. political speculations, 137. 186. 193. 439.
Poulet, John, second Earl, i. 297.
Powis, Henry, Earl of, i. 77.
Powis, Earl, iv. 11. 404.
Pownall, Governor, i. 305. iv. 312. 320.
Praslin, Duc de, ii. 411.
Pratt, Sir Charles, afterwards Lord Camden, i. 296. ii. 137. 199. iii. 210. 226. *see* Camden.
Press Warrants, iii. p. cix.
Pretender, the Young, i. 366.
Prideaux, Brigadier, i. 322.
Privilege of Parliament, iii. p. cxxii.
Privy Council Extraordinary, i. 374.
Privy Purse, the King's disposal of, ii. 209. 210.
Prowse, Thomas, M.P., i. 397. 398. 402.
Prussia, Frederick, King of, i. 172. 217. 229. 252. 260. 263. 324. 327. 345. 356. 380. 421. 463. 464. ii. 240. 241. 533.
Prussia, Prince Henry of, i. 235. 302. 324. 354.
Pynsent, Sir Robert, iv. 137.

Q.

Quebec, capitulation of, i. 325. officers killed at, 326. 343. revenue of, ii. 375.
Queensberry, Duke of, i. 130.
Queensberry, Catherine Hyde, Duchess of, i. 130. ii. 424.
Quiberon Bay, i. 351.

R.

Ranby, the surgeon, ii. 443.
Ravensworth, Lord, his charge of Jacobitism against Murray, &c., i. 101.
Regency Bill, iii. 15. 17. 18. 19. 21—23. 26—33. 35. 125. 152—159. 223. 224.
Resolutions of the Ministers submitted to the King, iii. 184. 186.
Rhè, Island of, i. 207. 210.
Rich, Sir Robert, iii. 193.
Richelieu, Maréchal, i. 205. 230.
Richmond, Charles, third Duke of, i. 158. ii. 83. 176. 233. iii. 235. 281. 282. 396. iv. 37.
Richmond Park, iii. 14.
Rigby, Mr., M.P., ii. 21. iii. p. xxv. 265. 321. 346. 370. 384. 386. 388. 389. 391. 392. iv. 6. 42. 44. 57. 61. 95. 104. 119. 122. 196. 198. 218. 229. 233. 238. 246. 293. 339.
Rio Janeiro, Lord Clive's opinion of, ii. 446.
Riot Act, iv. 419.
Robinson, Dr., afterwards Archbishop of Armagh, ii. 479. iii. 113.
Robinson, Sir Thomas, afterwards Lord Grantham, i. 120. 430.
Rochelle, i. 208.
Rochfort, Earl of, ii. 378.
Rochford, Earl of, iii. 236. 240.
Rochfort, expedition to, i. 209. return of the Fleet from, 212. 213. 216. 217. 218. 219. 225. 229.
Rockingham, Marquess of, ii. 198. 252. iii. 86. 205. 206. 209. 218. 220. 237. 271. 282. 290. 314. 357. 365. iv. 12. 28. 36. 37. 40. 44. 53. 54. 63. 66. 87. 88. 98. 102. 107. 112. 119. 127. 161. 218. 228. 304.
Rodney, Captain, afterwards Sir George Brydges, i. 207. 215. 218. 221. 234. 310. ii. 9. 20. 170.
Rodondo, iii. p. xxxiv.
Rosbach, battle of, i. 229.
Ross, George, iv. 145.
Rouen, Parliament of, remonstrance against new taxes, ii. 100.
Roxburgh, John, Duke of, iii. 241. iv. 131.
Royal Family, meaning and extent of the, iii. 148. 149.
Rushout, Sir John, ii. 287.
Russia, treaty with, iii. 90.
Rutland, Duke of, ii. 7. iv. 481.
Ryde, Mrs., ii. 22.
Ryder, Sir Dudley, i. 162.

S.

Sackville, Lord George, i. 247. 325. 327. 357. ii. 21. 487. iii. p. xlv. lxviii. 26. 271. iv. 71. 79. 124. 173. 391. 491.

590 INDEX.

Sackville, Lady George, iv. 9.
St. Albans, George, third Duke of, i. 153. ii. 329. 332.
St. Lucia, Island of, i. 493. ii. 15. 25.
St. Malo, expedition to, i. 237. 248. 266. 272.
St. Mawes, ii. 452.
St. Peter's at Rome, illumination of, iv. 555.
St. Vincent, Island of, ii. 16. 25. 28.
Sandwich, John, Earl of, i. 153. ii. 115. 133. Secretary of State, 206. 227. 228. 229. 236. 240. 241. iii. p. cxix. 198. 223. iv. 513.
Sandys, Samuel, Lord, i. 50.
Sandys, Edwin, M.P., i. 184.
Saunders, Admiral Sir Charles, i. 303. 320. iii. 310. 390.
Savile, Sir George, i. 394. iii. 27. 237. iv. 502. 503. 504. 510.
Sawbridge, Alderman, iv. 536.
Saxby, Mr., of the Post Office, iii. 311.
Say and Sele, Richard, Lord, iii. 145.
Scævola, iii. p. xc. xciv.
Scriptural phrases used by Junius, iii. p. ccxxii.
Scriptural phrases used by Lord Temple, iii. p. ccxxiv.
Secret service money, account of, iii. 144. 311.
Secretary of State's Office, iii. p. xlviii.
Seilern, Count de, ii. 240. 241.
"Seizure of Papers," ii. 53.137. iii. p. cliii. clxxiv. 242.
Selwyn, George, iv. 372.
Sewell, Mr., afterwards Sir Thomas, ii. 472. iv. 132.
Shebbeare, Dr., list of his works, and memorial in favour of, ii. 271.
Shelburne, John, Earl of, i. 356.
Shelburne, William, Earl of, ii. 35. 37. 41. 116. resigns office, 203. 204. 226. 230. 236. 244. iii. 223. 271. 279. 309. 315. 397. iv. 28. 32. 199. 244. 249. 296. 300. 309. 360. 371. 382. 389.
Shuvalow, Count, iii. 60.
Silhouette, M. de, i. 342.
Silk Bill, disturbances on account of, iii. 164. 224.
Smith, Commodore, i. 50.
Soor, battle of, i. 40.
Soubize, Prince de, i. 205. 253.
Spain, Ferdinand, the sixth King of, i. 325.
Spain, Queen of, her death, i. 261.
Spanish Main, commerce with the, ii. 48.
Speed, Colonel, i. 63. death of, 68.
Speed, Miss Harriett. i. 25. 68.
Spencer, Lord Charles, ii. 5. 21. 163.
Stamp Act. ii. 373. iii. p. xx. 100. 109. 237. 248. 250. 357. 359. 365. 367. 370. 371. 373.
Stanhope, Philip, second Earl of, i. 160.
Stanhope, Sir William, ii. 160.

Stanley, Mr. Hans, i. 113. 362. 366. 367. 375.385. ii. 42. 219. 221. 400. iii. 90. 99. 104. 284. 320. 394. iv. 132.
Stapleton, Miss, i. 135. iv. 549.
"State of the Nation," a pamphlet by Mr. Knox, iv. 368. 394.
Stawell, Lady, ii. 460. 517.
Stephenson, Sir William, ii. 459.
Stewart, Archibald, his trial, i. 71.
Stock Exchange, iii. p. ccxxxvi.
Stormont, Viscount, iii. 373.
Stowe and Wotton estates, settlement of, i. 428.
Stowe, account of the Princess Amelia's visit to, ii. 406.
Stowe, Mr. Hervey's praise of, iii. 89.
"Stowe, Hill of," poem by Lord Temple, iv. 545.
Strachey, Mr., ii. 46.
Strange, James, Lord, ii. 104. 135. 206. iii. 362. 366.
Strangways, Lady Susan, iv. 209.
Strathmore, John, Earl of, iv. 191.
Stuart, Mr., ii. 457.
Stuart, Lady Anne, ii. 385.
Stuart, Lady Augusta, iv. 548.
Stuart, Lady Jane, ii. 244.
Sturt, Mr., M.P., ii. 454.
Styles, Dr., iii. 237.
Suffolk, Earl of, iii. p. lv—lviii. 355. 397 iv. 4. 48. 283. 529.
Suffolk, Henrietta Hobart, Countess of i. 3. 52. 76. iv. 147.
Sullivan, Laurence, ii. 46.
Swinney, Dr., iii. p. lxviii.

T.

Talbot, William, second Lord, i. 471. 474. 486. ii. 56. 165. iv. 188. 343. 416.
Tavistock, Lord, iii. 303. 308. 379.
Taylor, Mr., Architect, iv. 311.
Taylor, John, "Junius Identified," iii. p. xv. xvii.
Tea duty, iv. 516.
Temple family, pedigree of, iii. 297.
Temple, Hester, Countess, i. p. iii. her death mentioned, 98.
Temple, Mr. John, iv. 396. 460.
Temple, Richard Grenville Earl, description of, by Wraxall, i. p. vii. account of his death, i. p. vii. verses upon his cane, i. p. vii. his correspondence and papers, i. p. xviii. his gift of £1000 per annum to Mr. Pitt, 149. 161. 174. made First Lord of the Admiralty, 187. succeeds the Duke of Marlborough as Lord Lieutenant of Bucks, 278. resigns the Privy Seal, 330. resumes office, 332. Knight of the Garter, 339. his *advice in writing* relative to the Spanish war, 386. his resignation, 394. gift of £5000

INDEX. 591

to James Grenville's sons, 408. dines at Guildhall, 415. 423. 437. 473. forbid the Court, ii. 52. 53. 55. 59. 75. 100. 138. 157. 159. proposed to the King by Mr. Pitt to be First Lord of the Treasury, 198. 201. 230. 235. 428. 496. iii. p. xvi. xxvii—xxxvi. lix. lxi. lxxxix. cxxiv. cxxx. cxlix. cciv. ccx. ccxii. ccxxvi. 37. 43. 65. 92. 97. 170. 174. 176. 177. 179. 183. 191. 200. 223. sent for by the Duke of Cumberland to assist in forming a Ministry, 225. 226. presents a sum of £1000 to George Grenville, 227. 242. 244. 263. 264. 266. 272. 274. 279. 292. 360. 362. 365. 368. 376. 380. 383. 388. iv. 29. 36. 45. 53. 61. 68. 73. 77. 86. 92. 116. 122. 128. 132. 135. 142. 175. 178. 188. 224. 230. 235. 237. 279. 281. 325. 363. 398. 403. 406. 433. 454. 459. 490. 512. 515. 545. 573. 575.

Temple, Anna Chamber, Countess, her account of Lord Albemarle's death, i. 133. 237. ii. 189. verses addressed to, by Horace Walpole, 253. her poems, 256. edition printed at Strawberry Hill, 257. 315. iii. p. xxxv. lxv. lxvi. lxxxiv. cxii. 285. iv. 8. 323. 414. verses addressed to, 528. 570.

Terrick, Dr., Bishop of London, ii. 313.
Thetford, borough of, ii. 480.
Thicknesse, Philip, iii. p. ccxxvi.
Thomond, Lord, ii. 212. iii. 216.
Thomson, James, i. 69.
Thurlow, Mr., afterwards Lord, iii. 237.
Thynne, Mr. Henry, iv. 484.
Ticonderago, i. 254. 322.
Tiddy Doll, Lord Temple's *sobriquet*, iii. p. xxxviii.
Tobago, Island of, ii. 18.
Todd, Mr. Anthony, Secretary of the Post Office, iii. 311.
Torgau, battle of, i. 356.
Townshend, George, afterwards Viscount, i. 187. 311. 319. 322. ii. 277. iii. p. xxxviii. 65. 118. 207. 209. iv. 92. 130. 131. 160. 169. 171. 173. 232.
Townshend, Admiral, ii. 170.
Townshend, Mr. Charles, i. 190. 439. ii. 22. 36. 63. 103. 157. 198. 204. 224. 448. 465. opinion of Mr. Pitt and Lord Temple, 462. attack on Mr. Grenville, 485. 501. iii. 65. 87. 90. 101. 106. 118. 120. 188. 205. 207. 209. 211. 225. 235. 258. 281. 288. 332. 389. iv. 28. 41. 43. 92. 104. 130. 158. 160. 213. 214. 220. 222.
Townshend, ("Spanish") Charles, ii. 73.
Townshend, Colonel Roger, death of, at Ticonderago, i. 323.
Townshend, Thomas, i. 157. ii. 303. iii. 218. iv. 236.
Trecothick, Alderman, iv. 516. 520.
Trevecke, college at, iv. 527.

Trevor, Lord, iv. 205. 409.
Troops in Ireland and Scotland, i. 56.
Turk's Island, ii. 418. 422. 436. 438.
Turner, Sir John, i. 449.
Tyrawly, James O'Hara, Lord, i. 165. 422. iii. 247. iv. 341.

V.

Vane, Mr. Frederick, M.P., ii. 262.
Vere, Lord, ii. 8. 21. iv. 490.
Verney, Ralph, Earl, ii. 49. 160. iii. p. cxxxviii. iv. 137. 567.
Vernon, Lady Henrietta, iv. 524.
Vienna, society of, iv. 563.
Villiers, Lord, ii. 55. iii. 217.
Vindex, letter so signed, iii. p. xxxv.
Virginia, resolutions of the Assembly of, iii. 78. government of. iv. 345.
Viry, Comte de, i. 250. 261. 386. 462. 475. ii. 288.
Viri, Madame de, iv. 413.

W.

Waldegrave, General, afterwards second Earl of, i. 238. 295. ii. 42.
Wales, George, Prince of, i. 96. 329.
Wales, Princess Dowager of, her opinion of the King's temper, ii. 242. 246. excluded from the Regency Bill, iii. 148. 149. 162. 194. 224. iv. 406. 516.
Wallace, Mr., iv. 179. 187.
Waller, Edmund, i. 30. 32.
"Wallet," the, a pamphlet so called, ii. 404.
Walpole, Horace, afterwards Earl of Orford, i. 195.
Walpole, Horace, ii. 42. 113. 178. verses addressed to Lady Temple, 189. 232—234. anecdote of Princess Amelia and Lord Northumberland, 245. opinion of Lady Temple's poems, 252. 256. 320. 335. 428. 458. iii. p. xxviii. iv. 100. 103. 132. 153. 154. 548.
Walpole, Maria, afterwards Lady Waldegrave, i. 295.
Walpole, Mr. Thomas, iii. 102.
Walsh, John, M.P., ii. 46. 73. 159. iv. 263.
Warburton, William, afterwards Bishop of Gloucester, i. 27. 118. ii. 154. 314. iii. p. clxii. 3. 45.
Warkworth, Lord, ii. 149. 168. 385. 516.
War Office, iii. p. xlviii.
Warrants, General, debate on, iii. 5. trial respecting, 51. 117.
Wauchope, Mr., M.P., ii. 155.
Weavers, petition of, iii. 164. 224.
Webb, Philip Carteret, ii. 67. 72. 79. 137. 140. iv. 521.
Wedderburn, Mr., afterwards Lord Loughborough and Earl of Rosslyn, iii.

592 INDEX.

p. lviii. 246. 251. 257. 287. 314. 394. iv. 35. 64. 66. 99. 116. 120. 134. 146. 160. 193. 247. 263. 293. 303. 311. 391. 404. 423. 464.
Welderen, Madame de, ii. 245.
West, Gilbert, i. 15. 27.
West, Captain, afterwards Admiral, i. 27. 168.
West, Mrs. Admiral, i. 158.
West India Islands, description of, by Admiral Rodney, ii. 10.
Westmoreland, John Fane, Earl of, i. 287.
Weston, Mr. Edward, i. 360. ii. 45. 79. iv. 468. 476.
Weymouth, Earl of, ii. 102. iii. 49. 124. 163. 191. 213. 242. 308. 392. iv. 58. 251. 268. 274. 301. 312. 339. 341. 382.
Whately, Mr. Thomas, ii. 133. iii. p. lix. 251. 271. iv. 33. 39. 60. 64. 71. 79. 113. 128. 134. 148. 160. 233. 241. 266. 278.
Whittlebury Forest, iii. p. cxxvi.
Wildman's Tavern in Albemarle Street, ii. 47.
Wilkes, John, i. 102. Berwick election, 125. 176. 328. 477. 486.
Wilkes, John, ii. 54–56. 63. 66. 70. 73. satirical character of, George III., 74. list of books printed by, 81. at Paris, 83. verses to, by Lord Temple, 130. 135. account of his property, 138. 151. 152. daily account of him reported to the Secretary of State, 155. 165. duel with Martin, 180. 188. 220. 223. 224. 228. at Paris, 249. anecdotes of Chevalier D'Eon, 253. sends Lord Temple a pamphlet entitled the " Anti-Financier," 254. expelled the House of Commons, 258. 267. 277. 330. 455. 484. 490. iii. p. xxx. xxxv. lxxx. lxxxi. cxxiii. clxviii. clxxiii. ccxxi. 95. 232. 241. iv. 1. 15. 188. 262. 264. 267. 271. 273. 279. 284. 291. 371. 383. 393. 409. 480. 482. 495. 537.
Wilkes, Miss, i. 477. ii. 75. 81. 83. 99. iii. p. lxxxi. iv. 17.
Willes, Mr., iv. 248.
Williams, Sir Charles Hanbury, i. 147. 280. ii. 92.
Williams's trial, ii. 429.
Willoughby de Broke, Lord, i. 384.
Wilmot, Sir John Eardley, iii. 46. iv. 110. 115.
Wilmot, Dr., afterwards Sir Edward, i. 435.

Wilson, Dr. Thomas, Dean of Carlisle, ii. 385.
Winchester, French prisoners at, i. 316.
Winchilsea, Daniel Finch, Earl of, i. 50. 191. iii. 217. iv. 559.
Window Tax Bill, iii. 242.
Windsor Park, Rangership of, iii. 257.
Wine, importation of, duty free, ii. 393.
Wintringham, Sir Clifton, iii. 189.
Wodehouse, Sir Armine, iii. 79. 85.
Wolfe, General, i. 242. 310. 311. 319. 322. 324. 325. his death, 326. iii. p. lxxxix.
"Woman, Essay on," i. 490. ii. 154.
Wood, Robert, Under Secretary of State, ii. 137. 262. iii. 94.
Woodfall, Mr. Henry Sampson, ii. 159. iii. p. xxxv. lxvi.
Woodfall's trial for publishing Junius's Letter to the King, iv. 519.
Woodfall's edition of Junius, iii. p. xvi.
Woronzow, Count, Russian Ambassador, ii. 240.
"Word at Parting, to the Duke of Bedford," iv. 200. ascribed to Lord Temple and Junius, 203. 240.
Worsley, Mr., M.P., ii. 300. 496.
Wotton, Mr. Grenville's seat at, i. 171.
Wray, Mr. Daniel, iii. p. cxxx.
Wrottesley, Sir Richard, ii. 486.
Wyndham, Miss Elizabeth, afterwards Mrs. George Grenville, i. 26.

Y.

Yarmouth, Amelia Sophia de Walmoden Countess of, i. 291. 349. 435. 436.
Yates, Mr. Justice, iii. 48. iv. 291.
Yonge, Sir William, i. 73. 74.
York, Edward, Duke of, ii. 328. 384. 511. 517. iii. 113. 141. 147. 151. 222. 234. 369. 370. 371. 373. iv. 168. 176. 214. 224. 226. 227.
Yorke, Mr. Charles, i. 97. 113. 184. 296. ii. 71. 149. his resignation, 218. 226. 229. 239. 262. 461. 495. 526. iii. 9. 73. 78. 84. 115. 219. 290. 332. iv. 37. 301.
Yorke, Sir Joseph, i. 250. ii. 219. 221.
Younge, Sir George, iii. 310.

Z.

Zorndorff, battle of, i. 263. 265.